THE LIFE

OF

SAINT FRANCIS OF ASSISI;

AND A

SKETCH OF THE FRANCISCAN ORDER,

BY A

RELIGIOUS OF THE ORDER OF POOR CLARES.

WITH

EMENDATIONS AND ADDITIONS,

BY

VERY REV. PAMFILO DA MAGLIANO, O.S.F.

PUBLISHED WITH THE APPROBATION OF

The Most Reverend John McCloskey, D.D.

NEW YORK:
P. O'SHEA, 27 BARCLAY STREET.
1867.

THIS

AMERICAN EDITION

OF

ST. FRANCIS AND THE FRANCISCANS,

IS DEVOUTLY DEDICATED

TO THE

LATELY CANONIZED FRANCISCAN SAINTS:

NICHOLAS PICKIUS, JEROME WERDTEN, JULIAN DAMOS, NICASIUS STESIUS, THEODORIC EINDEM, ANTHONY VEERTEN, GODFREY VERUELLANUS, FRANCIS BRUXELLENSIAN, ANTHONY ORNANIENSIAN, (Priests;) and PETER ASCANIUS, (Lay-Brother;) with CORNELIUS BATAUADUR, (Tertiary,) Martyrs of Gorcum; LEONARD DA PORTO-MAURIZIO, Apostolic Missionary; and MARY FRANCES OF THE FIVE WOUNDS, Virgin of the Third Order.

June 29, 1867, the Centenarian of St. Peter and St. Paul.

PREFACE TO THE AMERICAN EDITION.

THE author of ST. FRANCIS AND THE FRANCISCANS declares, in the beginning of the second part, that the work was intended principally for the English public, in England and Ireland; and therefore the account of the Order given there, relates, in a great measure, to these two countries. In this American Edition we have thought it proper to make some improvements in what relates to the Franciscan Order in America. We have, however, revised and supplied whatever else we deemed more important. The authorities which we have consulted for this purpose are, Torquemada, *Monarquia Indiano;* P. Da Civezza, *Storia delle Missioni Francescane*, and *Cronaca delle Missioni Francescane;* P. Sigismondo da Venezia, *Biografia Serafica;* P. D'Osimo, *Colombo e P. Giovanni Perez*, and *Storia de' Martiri Giapponesi;* Darras, *History of the Church;* Da Latera, *Manuale de' Frati Minori;* Henrion, *History of the Missions; Annales Minorum;* Andres, *Storia di ogni Letteratura;* Hennepin, Shea, De Courcey, and others.

ADVERTISEMENT TO LONDON EDITION.

To avoid interrupting the text with frequent footnotes, it is thought better to give in one place the names of the authorities used in preparing this volume. The same opportunity is taken to thank several clergymen, whose kindness in lending books of reference will be ever gratefully remembered.

For the Life of St. Francis, the Histoire de St. François d'Assise, by M. Chevin de Malin; the Chronicles of the Order in French and English, the latter a translation from the Spanish of John Parent; the Fioretti; and the Antwerp edition (1613) of the Historia Seraphica, by F. Henrico Sedulio, have been principally used. For the History of the Order, Heylot's History of Religious Orders; the Certamen Seraphicum, by F. Angeli a S. Francisco; the Collectanea Anglo-Minoritica, by A. P. (Father Antony Parkinson); the Ecclesiastical History of Ireland, by Rev. M. J. Brennan, O. S. F; Ware's Works, by Harris; the Monasticon Hibernicum; Archdall; Challoner's Missionary Priests; Shea's Catholic Missions; with some other works of less note, and private manuscripts, belonging to religious houses of the Order.

NEWRY,
Feast of the Stigmata of St. Francis,
1861.

CONTENTS.

CHAPTER VII.

CHAPTER VIII.

CHAPTER IX.

CHAPTER X.

CHAPTER XI.

CHAPTER XII.

CHAPTER XXVI.

PAGE

CHAPTER XXVII.

CHAPTER XXVIII.

CHAPTER XXIX.

CHAPTER XXX.

CHAPTER XXXI.

CHAPTER XXXII.

PART II.

THE FRANCISCAN ORDER.

CHAPTER I.

CHAPTER II.

CHAPTER III.

CHAPTER IV.

CHAPTER V.

CHAPTER XI.

CHAPTER XII.

CHAPTER XIII.

CHAPTER XIV.

CHAPTER XV.

THE LIFE

OF

SAINT FRANCIS OF ASSISI.

CHAPTER I.

The birth and early days of the Saint.—His gaiety of disposition.—Joins an expedition against Perugia.—Is taken prisoner.

"The Providence, that governeth the world,
In depth of counsel by created ken
Unfathomable, to the end that she,
Who with loud cries was 'spoused in precious blood,
Might keep her footing towards her well-beloved,
Safe in herself and constant unto him,
Hath two ordain'd, who should on either hand
In chief escort her: one, seraphic all
In fervency; for wisdom upon earth,
The other, splendor of cherubic light.
I but of one will tell: he tells of both,
Who one commendeth, which of them soe'er
Be taken: for their deeds were to one end."

DANTE, PARADISE, Canto xi.

THE Seraphic Saint was born A. D. 1182. His father, Peter Bernardone Moriconi, was an Assisian merchant of considerable wealth; his mother, Pica, a lady of noble birth. Ottavio, bishop of Assisi, in a work which he published in 1701, says, that when he was preaching the Lent at Lucca, in 1689, a canon resided there named Moriconi, who showed him an old memorial in which were these words: "There were at Lucca two brothers, merchants, named Moriconi. The one remained in his own country; the other, named Bernardo, established himself at Assisi, where he was called Bernardone. He married, and had a son called Peter, who, being already wealthy, took as his wife a lady called Pica, of a noble family. St. Francis, out of humility, called himself son of Peter Bernardone, not choosing to take his family name, which was Moriconi." The Bishop adds, that the family was still extant in his time at Lucca, and ranked amongst the nobility of that city.

It is often to be observed in the lives of the Saints who have been called to perform some great work for the Church of God, that extraordinary presages of their future eminence have preceded or accompanied their entrance into the world. As might be expected, in the case of one whose life was so singularly to resemble that of his Divine Lord, such harbingers of celestial favors bore a remarkable likeness to the circumstances attending the Saviour's nativity.

For some time previous to the birth of Francis, a poor man was constantly heard in the streets of Assisi crying out, "*Pax et bonum; Pax et bonum;*" nor did he discontinue his prophetic utterance until the Saint had entered on his apostolic mission. Pica suffered severely for many days before the birth of her child; nor did he enter the world to which he was to give so bright an example of poverty and mortification, till his mother, in obedience to the commands of a pilgrim stranger, was laid on a bed of straw in a poor stable. That very night some holy and simple souls heard the angels singing canticles of joy in a way-side chapel, which from this circumstance obtained the name of our Lady of the Angels, and afterwards became a place of peculiar veneration to the Franciscan Order. The stable has also received its share of honor, and is now the Chapel of "San Francesco il Piccolo." Over the door is a very ancient inscription which runs thus:

> "Hoc Oratorium fuit Bovis et Asini stabulum,
> In quo natus est Franciscus, mundi speculum."*

At his baptism a stranger presented himself as sponsor, and was accepted for that office; an old tradition at Assisi records that he disappeared immediately after the ceremony, leaving the impression of his knees on a marble step of the altar, still shown in the cathedral church. The font in which Francis was baptised may also be seen there; it bears the following inscription: "Questo è il Fonte, dove fù battezzato il Serafico Padre San Francesco."

Immediately after the baptismal ceremonies another mysterious visitant appeared; he requested to see the child, and to have it placed in his arms. After caressing it with great affection, he marked its right shoulder with a well-formed cross, and then, returning it to the nurse, charged her to have a special care of the child, as the devils, whose great enemy it would one day be, would leave no means untried to deprive it of life. This statement was afterwards singularly confirmed by an evil spirit whom the saint himself drove from the body of one possessed, and who declared that the powers of darkness had used many stratagems to destroy him, foreseeing how successfully he would one day counterwork their wiles.

Bernardone was absent from home on commercial affairs when his child was born. On his return he found the little one already baptised. Pica had given him the name of John, perhaps because her pious, affectionate heart inclined her to a peculiar devotion to the

* "This chapel was the stable of the ox and the ass, wherein was born Francis, the mirror of the world.

beloved disciple. His father, not less characteristically, surnamed him Francis, in memory of his successful voyage, and probably with a joyful anticipation that he would one day be a merchant-prince of the country (France) from which he had just returned. It has been said that he was the first who bore this name; but there are good reasons for doubting this assertion, as well as another conjecture which has been hazarded, that it was given to him at a later period, from his having learned the French language with unusual facility.

The care of the Saint's education was confided to the clergy of the parish of St. George, and all they taught him he learned with great rapidity. His humility led him in after life to represent himself as uneducated; but this was far from being the case. French was then the principal medium for the communication of polite literature, and in this language, as we have just said, he was remarkably proficient, while his knowledge of Latin was by no means inconsiderable.

It would be no slight error to suppose that a Saint must, if not himself uneducated, at least undervalue the culture of the intellectual powers. True sanctity by no means involves the absence of mental superiority or acquirement. In truth, these two departments of excellence have an obvious relation with each other. From the infused wisdom which illuminated the great St. Thomas as with a full-orbed sun of science, to the enlarged perceptions of truth and beauty which are the portion of the simplest and poorest in proportion to their personal sanctity, the Eternal manifests Himself as the source at once of light and of love, gives knowledge together with the power of obedience, and illuminates the understanding while He inflames the heart and will.

That Francis was endowed with intellect of no common order we can scarcely doubt: his writings are the offspring of a highly poetical and cultivated taste; his life is in itself a magnificent poem; and it may be that this poem in action will one day be manifested as far more sublime than any which the most gifted intellect has composed.

The early manhood of Francis, however, full as it was of intellectual promise, gave little indication of the heroic virtue he was one day to practise, and of the true greatness to which he would attain. The jarrings of party strife, insignificant in their origin, though often disastrous in their result then constantly engaged the young nobles of the Italian states. In the intervals of peace, their time was spent in banquets and convivial meetings; and they banded together in companies called *Corti*, to give themselves with less interruption to these festive scenes. Francis, light of heart, with his affectionate turn and joyous imagination, with unlimited means also, which he lavished profusely wherever it could add to the enjoyment of the hour, was naturally attracted to these gay revellers, and beloved by them in turn, so that he became their chief leader in his native town. Still, with all his love of amusement and dissipation, his early religious impressions remained; and he never uttered, or allowed another to utter in his presence, a coarse word or an unseemly jest.

It may be supposed that Francis was but little assistance to his father in his commercial affairs, yet Bernardone did not complain; probably he was proud of his son, and of the popularity he enjoyed. Though he at times rebuked him as living more like a prince than a merchant, yet when he heard the gay songs and joyous shouts of the youth and his companions as they paraded the streets of Assisi, it might be the father's pride outweighed the trader's economy, and Bernardone admired, as much as Pica loved, the noble youth.

When Francis had attained his twenty-fourth year, a war broke out between the inhabitants of his native town and those of Perugia; the light-hearted, fearless youth threw himself into the conflict, and was taken prisoner in a skirmish: but even this misfortune did not lessen his natural cheerfulness. His dejected companions could not understand this, and reproached him with his levity; but his reply silenced them, they knew not why. "For you I am truly sorry," he said, "but for myself, I am thankful to say I feel nothing but joy. Now indeed I am prisoner; but you will one day see me honored by the whole world." Among the prisoners was one whose quarrelsome temper made him an object of dislike to the rest; Francis begged them to look with pity on the companion of their misfortunes, and bear with his defects; but as they still kept aloof, he paid him all the more attention, and at length succeeded by his charity in softening his manners and restoring peace.

CHAPTER II.

Francis returns to Assisi.—Enlists against the Emperor.—An Interior voice calls him.—He has a vision of Jesus crucified.—Receives a divine command.—Sells goods from his father's stores.—Becomes an object of contempt in Assisi.—Endures persecution from his father.—Is cited before the magistrates, then before the Bishop.—Renounces all worldly possessions.

After a year's captivity we find Francis once more at Assisi. Heavy illness, however, withheld him for a time from his former companions and their gay revels. He was reduced to extreme weakness, and his recovery was slow. At length, being able to drag himself along with the aid of a staff, he once more wandered forth into the country. But his former gaiety had fled; he was no longer the light-hearted, joyous youth who had cared only for the dance and the song. He wanted something more; but what that something was he could not tell. He had not yet learned to say, *Deus meus et omnia!* The work was begun, or rather its foundation had been laid, in suffering and humiliation. The world, which had once seemed so bright; the beautiful country, which had so peculiarly harmonized with his poetic soul, looked other than it had looked before. The change in himself surprised him; but as yet his heart was unchanged. What he felt was merely the result of that depression which sickness brings, especially to those of naturally ardent temperaments, and with the return of physical strength it passed away.

Once more, then, the young warrior-merchant was buckling on his sword and spurs; there was war between Walter, Count of Brienne, in Champagne, and the Emperor of Germany. This knight had been surnamed the Gentle Count, and was in truth a very model of a chevalier "*sans peur et sans reproche.*" The cause for which he fought, and his personal reputation, were both attractive to Francis, who, hearing that a young knight, poor in worldly goods, but richly endowed with courage and devotion, was preparing to join the Count in Naples, immediately proposed to accompany him thither, at the same time aiding him with all the temporal means at his command.

Some lives of the Saint assign to this period his meeting one day an officer of noble family, but meanly apparelled, on whom he immediately bestowed his own rich suit. Whether this was the soldier whose fortunes he was about to follow under the banner of the Count de Brienne, or another as poor, does not clearly appear; but it is certain that, consequent on this act of generosity, his more immediate intercourse with the spiritual world commenced. That night, in a dream, he beheld a sumptuous palace, containing piles of armor, each marked with the sign of the cross. It was made known to him that these were for his soldiers. Thinking only of earthly warfare, he entertained bright visions of military honors and future greatness; and joyously departed on his expedition, saying to his friends, as he bade them farewell, "Of a surety, I shall become a great prince." Prophetic words, though in a sense far other than he intended.

Spoleto was his first halting-place. And here, in the silence of a sleepless night, he became aware that God was speaking to him, not indeed in audible tones, but by that interior voice, which is as distinct and clear to those whom it addresses, as any articulate sound. He was asked what was the object of his life, and what his desires; he frankly replied, they were bent on earthly honor and renown. "And which of the two can serve you most," replied that loving voice; "the Master or the servant?" "And why," it continued, "will you forsake the Master for the servant, and the Lord for the slave?" Then Francis, recognizing the Divine voice, replied, with all the generous eagerness of his heart, "What would you have me to do, O Lord?" "Return into the city," said the voice, "and there it shall be told thee what thou shalt do, and how thou must understand this vision."

Heedless of the contempt and scorn that he might expect on his return, Francis set out the next morning for Assisi. And now in truth began the gallant fight, not under the banners of Walter de Brienne, but under the standard of the Crucified; a fight that was waged amid blood and tears, and had its trophies in the seals of his seraphic martyrdom.

His unlooked-for return was probably attributed to illness, as he seems not to have forfeited his position in society by a step which would else have involved him in the charge, if not of cowardice, at least of wayward caprice. But he had not yet advanced far enough on the road to perfection to merit the honor of suffering contempt. Again his gay companions flock around him; again they claim the "Flower of Assisi" as the leader of their revels; and Francis, still unenlightened regarding his future, passively assents to all they ask. One day, after an unusually splendid entertainment, they paraded the streets, singing according to their custom. Francis walked apart, carrying a wand as lord of the feast, when, ravished into a most sweet ecstacy, even in the midst of their noisy mirth, he lost all consciousness of exterior things. His companions after a time observed that he was not joining in their song; and rallied him on his abstraction, which they attributed to some human love. "I am indeed thinking of a bride," he answered, "but it is one so noble, so rich, and so beautiful, as the whole world has never seen."

From this moment his communications with the spiritual world became daily more frequent and more marvellous. He freed himself gradually from commerce, and his time was spent in constant prayer. It was while thus occupied, and wholly absorbed in God, that he was favored with a vision of Jesus Crucified. Our divine Lord appeared to him hanging on the cross, and the soul of Francis was moved to an intensity of love and tenderness such as he had never before experienced. This vision left so deep an impression on his affections, that even to the close of life he could not recall it without melting into tears. All that was naturally good in him became now more and more spiritualized. His love for the poor, and his lavish generosity increased every day; he would keep nothing; he would have nothing. Even needful food and clothing were given without a thought to those in whom he saw his Master's image.

The frequent absence of his father gave him opportunities of practising his charities unmolested. His mother, gentle and devout, to whom doubtless he owed many natural graces, was no hindrance to his pious almsgiving. One day she beheld an extraordinary supply of bread placed upon the table; on inquiring the reason, Francis replied, "It is for the poor who are ever in my heart. I cannot bear to hear their complaints; they pierce my very heart." Pica was satisfied; nor did she complain when her son left her alone at table, to carry the food of which he stinted himself to the sick poor who lived near their abode.

Many of the country churches were but scantily provided with things needful for celebrating the Holy Sacrifice. To furnish what was suitable, and as far as possible, what was costly, now became one of the chief objects of his pious zeal. He purposely sought out the poorer churches; and priests, whose means did not permit them to do all their hearts desired, were sure of his ready and munificent aid. Indeed, charity to the poor and afflicted, and a peculiar tenderness for all who were in trouble, with an especial devotion to whatever concerned the Sacramental Presence of Jesus, were henceforward to form the lifelong yearnings of the Saint.

But all this time there was a secret attraction drawing him to yet higher things. He longed to carry out his ideas of perfection to the full; nor could he see the way to do so, as long as he remained at home. He was not content with giving to the poor; he would be poor himself. Desiring, however, the special blessing of God on his resolution, he determined on a pilgrimage to Rome. There, prostrate before the tomb of the Apostles, he poured out his soul in prayer, to obtain the protection and blessing of those illustrious Poor Ones. Then, rising to make an offering at their shrine, he observed how niggard were the alms given there. "Why," he exclaimed, "are such miserable offerings made to the Prince of the Apostles?" And as he spoke he placed a large piece of money on the altar. Leaving the church, he joined the throng of beggars, who then, as now, surrounded the porticoes. Giving to one of them his rich garments, he took the poor man's rags; and clothing himself in them, began to practise the poverty he was so soon to preach, and spent the remainder of the day asking alms in French.

It may be remarked in passing, that this ardent desire to see the tomb of St. Peter honoured by rich offerings, and adorned as befitted relics so venerable, was accomplished by one of his spiritual children. Sixtus the Fifth was a religious of his order, and we are mainly indebted to him for having rendered the basilica of St. Peter the magnificent shrine it is to-day.

Again we find our saint at Assisi, and now enduring those terrible assaults of the demon, which must in their measure be borne by all who, renouncing a life of worldly pleasure, begin to give themselves to God. His was no easy strife or painless victory. His natural character was ardent, generous, and affectionate; he had enjoyed the world, and no domestic calamity, no pressing poverty, no blight of fickle fortune, had cast a shadow over his early life or dimmed the brightness of his joyous career. Beloved as he had been by all, his warm heart clung fondly to others, and led him to seek for, and live in, the sunshine of human love. He was rich, and the rich have "many friends;" he had, as we have seen, his own bright dreams of future greatness, and of the fair fame of knightly valor. What heroic courage, then, must he not have possessed; what grace must he not have received, when at so early an age he could turn from all this, and against every solicitation or allurement, do battle with the powers of darkness, as an humble follower of a crucified God? Prayer was now the consolation and support of the young champion. Again he wandered into the fields, occupied in deep and solemn thought; and the bright sunshine and flower-starred meadows of his native land were no longer to him a source of depression; though tempted and tried within and without, his heart was full of peace; he had begun to be in earnest in the right path, and an earnest soul is ever happy.

One day, as he returned from his usual thoughtful walk, he entered the old church of St Damian, and poured out his soul to God. Prostrate before a crucifix, he implored with tears and sighs for light to know, and grace to do His holy will. Thrice he uttered these words: "O great God of Glory, and Thou, my Saviour Jesus Christ, I beseech Thee to enlighten me, and to dispel the darkness of my spirit, to give me pure faith, steadfast hope, and perfect charity. Grant, O my God, that I may know Thee so perfectly that I may never act but in accordance with Thy light, and in conformity to Thy holy will."

His prayer was immediately answered. The Divine voice, not now speaking in the depths of his heart, where it had spoken before, but in clear and audible accents, thrice uttered these words: "Francis, go and rebuild My house, which is falling into ruin."

The command had probably a two-fold meaning; and Francis, unaccustomed to such immediate intercourse with the Unseen, naturally understood it in a literal sense. He little anticipated the great work to which he was then called. As he left the church, he placed a sum of money in the hands of the priest, saying, "I pray you, master, buy some oil with this money, wherewith to keep a lamp burning before the crucifix." Then returning home to take some pieces of stuff from among his father's stores, and setting out for the neighboring city of Foligno, he disposed of them there, at the same time selling his own horse. The money he received for this, his last transaction in commerce, he immediately brought to Peter, the poor priest of St. Damian's. Prostrating himself at his feet, and kissing his hands with tears and devotion, he offered him the money he had brought for the repairs of the church; and begged earnestly to be allowed to remain with him. The priest consented to receive him under his roof; but fearing the anger of Bernardone, he refused the money. Francis then cast it on one of the window-sills of the church, valuing it only as a means of fulfilling the command of God.

Meanwhile, Peter Bernardone, who had been on a journey, found on his return that his son had quitted the paternal mansion, and, what was worse, had converted some of his precious merchandise into money.

Bernardone was probably not more avaricious than his neighbors. He was simply what the world calls a sensible man, and objected to making investments where there was no prospect of a speedy return. In the excitement of passion on discovering his loss, he never considered his son's right to a share of the goods as partner in his business. Stormy scenes followed. The indignation of Bernardone knew no bounds, and accompanied by a party of friends, he proceeded to St. Damian's, vowing condign vengeance on his son, but above all eager to recover the value of his merchandise. Francis, unused to such conflicts, deemed it most prudent to avoid an interview with his father; and when the angry party approached the house he hid himself in the priest's room. Here he would have been discovered, but for a miraculous interposition of Providence, which is related by Wadding as well authenticated. When his father entered in search of him, he hid behind the door, he would soon have been seen there, had not an opening been made miraculously in the wall, in which he was concealed until Bernardone left the house.

Immediately after this occurrence Francis fled to a cave, known only to a servant, who supplied him with the necessaries of life. Here he passed his time in fervent prayer, preparing himself thus for the severe conflicts which he foresaw he must soon encounter, and receiving an abundance of heavenly lights and supernatural graces, by which he was consoled and fortified. Having passed a month in this place, he began to consider that, however great his internal weakness, he should place his confidence in God, and go on his way with courage. He therefore returned once more to Assisi. Reproaches, revilings, insults and mockery were his portion. Indeed, his wan countenance and disordered garb might have justified the general supposition that the once gay and gallant Flower of Assisi had lost his mind.

Francis rejoiced exceedingly at the treatment he received. To be called a fool, nay, more, to be thought such, was now his highest ambition. There was a brighter sunshine in his breast than ever before, even in those bright days when he ruled the joyous convivial bands in his native town. Meanwhile, Bernardone was informed of his son's return, of the current opinion regarding him, and of his newly adopted mode of life. Indignation, which sought to relieve itself by acts of violence, fired his breast. Forgetting even the respect due to himself, he fell on his son, beat him severely, and with unmeasured reproaches, dragged him to his house, and locked him up safely in a dark hole under the staircase. Poverty and humiliation were as little fashionable in the thirteenth century as in our own, and we can scarcely be surprised at the indignation of a father who considered his family thus disgraced. In vain did Bernardone endeavor to move his son; angry threats and gentle words were alike unheeded, and Francis remained a prisoner till his father's absence on a journey enabled the gentle Pica to release her child. And now the generous confessor was called to endure a harder struggle, to gain a more glorious victory. The music of a mother's voice, the softening tenderness of a mother's fondest caress, the winning smile, the meek heart-broken entreaty, were not spared, and the affectionate heart of Francis needed all the grace he had received to bear up against the strong influence of maternal love.

When Bernardone returned he found his son had been released, and had taken shelter once more at St. Damian's. Venting his indignation on his wife in no measured terms, he again sought out Francis, who this time presented himself boldly before his father. He cared not, he said, for stripes or imprisonment; sufferings were now his joy for the love of Jesus Christ.

Finding the case hopeless, Bernardone consoled

himself by recovering the money of which he considered he had been defrauded, and which he found in the window where Francis had thrown it. Still, his avarice was not satisfied; he imagined there must be more in reserve, and cited his son before the magistrates. When Francis received the summons, he exclaimed, "Thanks be to God, I have entered into the full liberty of His servants; I have nothing to do with magistrates." They seem to have admired the courage and resolution of the young man, and referred the matter to the ecclesiastical authorities, saying to Bernardone, "Since he has entered the service of God, he is no longer under our authority."

Vido Secundi was at this time bishop of Assisi; he was a prelate of holy life and great wisdom, and Francis was well pleased that the matter should be left to his decision. Whether the Saint had previously had any spiritual communication with him is doubtful; at all events, the bishop was one who could appreciate an heroic zeal for the divine service. He sent for Francis, who exclaimed, "I will go willingly to the Lord Bishop, who is the father and master of souls." The holy prelate received him kindly, and said to him, "Your father is greatly incensed against you. If you desire to serve God, return him the money which you have; perhaps it has been unjustly obtained. God does not desire that you should use in His service what might serve to calm your father's anger. My son, have confidence in God; act openly, and fear nothing. He will be your protector, and will supply you with all that is needed for the good of His Church." Francis immediately arose, and, burning with a heavenly inspiration, he exclaimed, "My lord, I will give him all that is his, even my very clothes." Then casting off his garments, and retaining only his hair shirt, he laid them at his father's feet, crying out, "Peter Bernardone, until now I have called you my father; henceforth I can truly say, Our Father who art in heaven! for He is my wealth, and in Him do I place all my hope."

The spectators and the venerable bishop were moved to tears. Covering him with his own mantle, the saintly prelate pressed him to his heart, and assured him of his continual love and protection. An old garment, which had been worn by a laborer in the bishop's service, was brought, and Francis clothed himself in it with joy, first making a large cross on it with some mortar that was at hand. It was in the year 1206, and in the twenty-fifth year of his age, that he thus proclaimed himself the lover, and commenced as the apostle, of poverty.

O brave, O noble Francis! Hast thou courage to despise all, to be stripped of all? Wilt thou no longer have friends or country, kindred or estate? Hast thou forgotten all earthly love, and wilt thou sever all earthly ties? Where are the tears of Pica and her gentle words? where the yearnings of thine own loving heart, and thy bright dreams of worldly honor and military renown? Are all forsaken, all despised? Art thou willing to become the scorn of all, to be despoiled of all the world esteems? Well may it count thee for a fool, and esteem thy life madness! Thou carest not; the Crucified has turned on thee one burning glance of love; thou hast seen Him forsaken by all, and dying naked on Calvary; and thou wilt follow Him, brave Francis! Truly thy reward is sure, though not the hope of reward, but the ardent fire of love, stimulates thee on. Noble Saint, noble because of thy poverty, noble because of thine ignominies! Alvernia and the stigmata await thee, and thy heart's deep longing shall be satisfied; for as thou hast been like to Jesus in His birth, so shalt thou be like to Jesus in His life and in His sufferings.

CHAPTER III.

Francis devotes himself to lepers.—Service to lepers a devotion of the middle ages.—He effects many miraculous cures.—Repairs three churches, as symbolical of his three orders.—Practises poverty.—His reply to his brother Angelo.

Having freed himself from all earthly ties, Francis was now able to follow, without reserve, those divine impulses which were leading him gently, but surely, to the attainment of the most exalted sanctity. He was now, in the words of Bourdaloue, "an evangelical poor one, and a disinterested poor one;" it yet only remained for him to attain the perfect consummation of all his desires, and become "a crucified poor one."

With a joyous heart, he hastened into the woods and other solitary places near Assisi, that he might enjoy more intimate and undisturbed converse with his Beloved. One day, while engaged in singing the praises of God in French, he was met by a band of robbers, who inquired who he was. "I am the herald of the great King," he replied. They beat him severely, and then, casting him into a ditch filled with snow, said in bitter mockery: "Rest there, then, great herald of God." When they had passed on, Francis arose, in no way disconcerted, and, overjoyed to have suffered something for Christ, went on his way singing louder than before. Passing a monastery, he begged an alms from the monks, and spent some days there, discharging the meanest offices in the kitchen. From thence he went to Gubbio, where he was recognized by a former friend, who bestowed on him some alms and a hermit's habit, a short tunic, leathern girdle, shoes and a staff. But true love is never satisfied without action; it must work as well as suffer. Francis, therefore, amid the interior joy of his heart, looked around him for some tangible representation of his Beloved, that his love might satisfy itself by active employment for Him.

Service to those afflicted with leprosy was one of the peculiar devotions of the middle ages. To this he now devoted himself, notwithstanding the extreme natural repugnance which he felt to the very sight of such poor sufferers. His Divine Master had indeed specially called him to his service, saying to him, "Francis, if thou wouldst know My will, thou must learn to hate all which thou hast hitherto loved and desired according to the flesh. Be not terrified, however, at the new path which lies before thee; for the things which have pleased thee hitherto shall become bitter, and the things which have displeased thee, shall henceforth become sweet to thee."

This holy employment he may be said to have inaugurated, at least in the heroic degree to which he carried it. Many other servants of God have become eminent on the same difficult path to perfection. St. Elizabeth of Hungary, St. Louis of France, the Blessed Mary of Oignies, St. Catherine of Sienna, and St. Edward the Confessor, will be remembered as bright examples amongst the saintly souls attracted to the service of the leper. The Church, that tender mother, ever watchful over the feeble and afflicted, had taken these poor stricken ones under her special protection. They were not unlovingly separated from their fellows, even when placed by stern necessity where others would be secure from infection. Husband and wife were never parted; the holy tie of marriage remained inviolate. Nor was this all; the dire infliction was softened by all which the tenderness of supernatural charity could devise. The leper, it is true, was required to live apart; yet this very separation was sanctified by holy rites and a special religious ceremony. Each portion of the dress he wore, everything he had in use, received a blessing; then, with tender word of exhortation and comfort, he was led to his lonely dwelling by God's priest. Even here he was not forgotten or untended, for there were self-devoted souls who gave themselves exclusively to this work of mercy; whose joy it was to dress his wounds and wash his sores, pouring, as best they might, the balm of peace upon his troubled heart.

Foremost amongst these ministers of love were afterwards the children of our Saint, the members of the great Franciscan order. Hence, in ancient litanies, we find these invocations:

"Sancte Francisce, leprosorum mundator,
Sancte Francisce, infirmorum consolator,
Ora pro nobis."

(St. Francis, cleanser of lepers,
St. Francis, consoler of the sick,
Pray for us.)

St. Bonaventure dwells with peculiar pleasure on this devotion of the Saint, and relates a most touching incident regarding it. Riding one day through an open plain near Assisi, Francis perceived a leper in the distance. He felt more strongly than ever his natural repugnance to approach him; but mastering it by a violent effort, he dismounted, and bestowed on him an alms, at the same time tenderly kissing his hands. That instant the leper had disappeared, and Francis could not see any object resembling a human being in the vast expanse of plain. Filled with joy, he remounted his horse and continued his journey, not doubting the miraculous nature of the apparition, knowing that He who had not disdained to be counted as a leper upon earth, might still be pleased to assume that form for the instruction or encouragement of His servants. From this time his natural repugnance entirely vanished; and it was his joy and constant occupation to perform the most painful and revolting offices for these poor outcasts.

Once, when on foot upon the road near Assisi, a leper approached him, whose face was almost eaten away by this terrific disease. The poor creature attempted to kiss the feet of the saint; but Francis raised him from the ground and tenderly embraced him, and his kiss instantly healed the loathsome sores. Well might St. Bonaventure exclaim, "I know not which most to admire, a kiss of such humility and love, or a miracle of such stupendous power."

In the early days of the Order, postulants were usually sent to the lazar houses for a first trial of their vocation. If, overcoming themselves, they entered with devotion on this labor of love, Francis would embrace them tenderly, exclaiming, "O my brethren, let us love and cherish the leper; he is indeed our Christian brother;" but if the postulant showed any repugnance, he was dismissed. Indeed, it was the intention of the Saint that such as had no talent for study or preaching should employ themselves thus, or in the service of their brethren. Brother James the Simple was distinguished among all his brethren for his zeal in this service. He was called the procurator and physician of the leper. Francis had charged him specially with the care of one of these poor sufferers. It was a painful task, and one peculiarly revolting to human nature, as the leper was diseased even more loathsomely than the rest. The good brother, however, was nothing discouraged, and his care almost restored the leper. Thinking that a little exercise would do him good, brother James brought him to St. Mary's of the Angels. Francis was there when they arrived, and reproved his disciple severely for his indiscreet charity. "You ought not," said he, "to bring the Christian brothers here, it is neither well for them nor for you. I wish you to serve them well in the hospital, but I do not wish you to bring them abroad; there are many persons who cannot bear even to see them." The poor leper was much distressed to hear his kind benefactor reproved thus. Francis instantly perceived that he had given him pain, and, throwing himself at his feet, asked his pardon. Then, as a self-imposed penance for his fault, he took his refection outside the convent door, eating out of the same dish with the leper; after their meal he embraced the poor man tenderly, and sent him home consoled and satisfied.

There is another instance among the many that could be cited, which is too touching to omit. In one of these hospitals was a poor man whose disease appeared to have extended itself even to his very soul. The friars who served him received only blows and angry words, and were compelled to listen to his ceaseless blasphemies against God and His blessed Mother. They strove in vain to console him, but were at last obliged to leave him to his unhappy fate. Francis heard of his sufferings and his sin, and hastened to him. "May God give you His peace, my brother," said he; "have patience; sickness is sent from God for the cure of the soul, and when we suffer with resignation, it is a great grace." "What can I expect from God?" exclaimed the leper; "He has deprived me of happiness and of every blessing! How can I bear such constant suffering with patience? God has forgotten me, and the friars take no pains to please me." Seeing that words were useless, the Saint retired to pray. On his return he found the sick man calmer, and asked what he could do for him. "I should like you to wash me all over," replied the leper; "I cannot myself bear this infectious taint." Francis at once prepared warm water and sweet herbs, and began his task. Wherever he placed his hand the leprosy vanished; and soon the poor creature was perfectly restored. The cure extended itself even to his soul. No longer a murmurer against the hand of providence, he shed tears of joy and of the deepest contrition. After a short time passed in rigorous penance, he died; and, appearing to Francis, who was praying in the woods, he cried out in sweet and joyous accents, "Do you know me? Behold the leper whom our Saviour cured through your merits. I am going now to eternal glory to return thanks to God on your behalf, for many souls will be saved through you." Then he ascended to heaven, leaving the Saint full of consolation.

Had it not been for the voice from the crucifix, which still rung in the ears of Francis, he would have been well content to spend his life in the lazar houses of Gubbio. But, holy as his employment was, a more important duty awaited him; he was to rebuild the house of God. He commenced by obeying the injunction simply in its material sense, his humility leading him to suppose that this was all God required of him.

Regardless, therefore, of paternal anger and his own sensitive feelings, he returned to Assisi, and traversing the streets, asked alms for the repair of its churches, crying aloud, "He who gives me one stone shall have a reward; he who gives me two shall have two; he who gives me three shall have three." Many thought him mad, and passed him by with contempt or silent pity;

others were moved to tears by his fervor and relf-renunciation. And so the work went on.

It was towards the close of the year 1206, that Francis completed the repairs of the Church of St. Damian; he worked daily at it himself, carrying the materials on his shoulders like a common laborer. At first, he accepted the hospitality of the good priest, who used to have a comfortable meal prepared for him after his day's toil, but this was not the poverty he had chosen. "Wilt thou find a priest everywhere to show thee all this kindness?" he said to himself, "this is not the poor life which thou hast chosen; rather thou must go from door to door with a dish, and take whatever may be bestowed on thee in charity. Thus must thou live for the love of Him who was born poor, who lived in poverty, who was nailed to the cross, without covering, and, after His death, was laid in the tomb of another." The next day, accordingly, he began his quest, and seated himself in the street to take his meal. At first he shrank at the very sight of the coarse and revolting mess before him. But one strong effort of his resolute will, and the same divine grace which had enabled him to conquer his abhorrence of the leper, enabled him now to carry out this practice of absolute poverty. He returned to the priest, saying cheerfully, "You need take no further trouble about my food, father, for I have found a good housekeeper and a very skilful cook, who will prepare excellent dishes for me in future."

Our Saint at this time foretold the foundation of the order of Poor Clares. "Help me," he said to the workmen who were assisting him in repairing St. Damian's, "for one day there will be a convent of poor nuns in this place of a most holy life, who throughout the whole Church shall glorify our Father in heaven."

Peter Bernardone, as may be imagined, was not too

well pleased with the conduct of his son. Finding, however, that blows and reproaches had no power to turn him from his purpose, he gave vent to his indignation by cursing him whenever he crossed his path. The affectionate heart of Francis felt this keenly. At length he sought out a poor old beggar, and said to him, "Thou shalt be my father. Come with me; we will share our alms between us. Then, when my father Bernardone curses me, I will say to thee, Bless me, father! and thou shalt bless me." The next time he met his father he said to him joyfully, "See, God has given me another father, who blesses me as often as you curse me." His brother Angelo also reviled him. One bitterly cold day during the same winter, Francis was praying in the church, the keen, frosty air pierced through his poor hermit's coat, and, unused as yet to such hardship, he shivered again and again. Angelo entered with a party of his gay companions, all well defended against the cold. Turning to one of them, he said, "Go and ask yonder fellow to sell you some of his sweat." The Saint replied, "I do not sell my sweat to men, for I can sell it at a higher price to God."

In the spring of the following year, Francis began the repair of an old church dedicated to St. Peter, situated a little way without the city. He next turned his attention to the small chapel of the Porziuncola,* called St. Mary's of the Angels, of which we shall hereafter have much to relate. These three churches have been taken to symbolize his three Orders, St. Peter's representing the body of apostolic men who were to evangelize nations and edify the Church by their lives and sufferings; our Lady of the Angels, those holy women who should triumph over the weakness of their sex in

* So named because built near a small plot of ground belonging to the Benedictines of Subiaco.

the austere rule left them by their sainted patriarch; while St. Damian's may represent the third Order, open to both sexes and all classes among Catholic Christians, from the prince of the Church and the crowned head,* to the poor mendicant, the penniless widow and the toiling artizan.

CHAPTER IV.

Francis espouses Poverty.—Renounces money, and goes barefoot.—Giotto, Dante, Bossuet.—Disciples come to Francis.—With two others, he goes to reside at Rivo Torto.—Some notice of the twelve first members of the Order.

THE Order of Friars Minor was founded in the year 1208. Francis was one day hearing mass in his beloved chapel of our Lady of the Angels, when he heard these words read in the gospel of the day: "Do not possess gold, nor silver, nor money in your purse, nor scrip for your journey, nor two coats, nor shoes, nor a staff." Immediately he cast away his purse, though probably it contained neither gold nor silver; his shoes and staff were also discarded, as contrary to the evangelical poverty he was about to espouse. He substituted for his hermit's habit one of coarse gray serge, which he bound round his waist with a cord, and exclaiming, "This is what I seek for, this is what I desire with all my heart," he went forth, everywhere preaching penance to his fellow men.

This mystical espousal with holy poverty has been a theme for the eloquence of the orator, the pen of the poet, and the pencil of the artist. As you enter the

* St. Louis, King of France, and Saint Charles Borromeo, were tertiaries of the Order of St. Francis. The great Ximenes was a Franciscan of the strict observance, as also his successor, the present apostolic Archbishop of Toledo.

lower church of the Friars Minor at Assisi, a magnificent fresco is the first object which attracts your attention. The connoisseur in art will quickly recognize the exquisite freshness which characterizes the coloring of Giotto. There you behold the first great lover of poverty, the incarnate God, who, though rich with all the riches of the celestial mansions, for our sakes became poor. His face and form are radiant with the immortal beauty of His risen humanity. He presents the hand of a young maiden to Francis, who places on her finger the mystical ring, the pledge of an eternal alliance. Beautiful indeed is this fair bride, and glowing with the freshness of an immortal youth. A calm smile is on her slightly parted lips, and the light of an unearthly beauty in her gentle eye. She is crowned with flowers, but her garments are coarse and torn. Her naked feet bleed, for she is treading a hard and thorny path. Angry words are uttered by the crowd around her; but she goes on her way calm and unmoved amid their insults, while the angelic choirs offer her their joyous congratulations. Here angels are seen chasing away greedy misers, who are hugging their bags of gold, while in another compartment they present to the Eternal Father the "houses and lands" forsaken for love of Him, by those who have taken holy poverty for their spouse.

Nor is the sublime word-painting of Dante less expressive. Singing, in his own lofty strains, the beauties of the spouse of Francis, her sorrows and her wrongs, he says:

"A dame to whom none openeth pleasure's gate
More than to death, was 'gainst his father's will,
His stripling choice, and he did make her his,
Before the spiritual court, by nuptial bonds,
And in his father's sight, from day to day,
Then loved her more devoutly. She, bereav'd
Of her first husband, slighted and obscure,

Thousand and hundred years and more, remain'd
Without a single suitor till he came,
Nor aught availed that with Amyclas,* she
Was found unmoved at murmur of his voice,
Who shook the world, nor aught her constant boldness,
Whereby with Christ she mounted on the cross."—
PARADISO, Canto xi. CARY'S Translation.

Bossuet too pours forth, with all the eloquence of his gifted intellect his panegyric of Francis and of poverty. "A thousand times blessed art thou, O poor Francis, the most ardent, the most enthusiastic, and if I may so say, the most infatuated lover of poverty that has ever appeared in the Church." And again, "Now has poverty become noble, because she has wedded royalty; she whom the king's son has espoused becomes ennobled by her espousals, however mean her former condition. Let men complain, let them murmur as they will, the poor are become the friends of God; for He has said, '*Blessed are the poor in spirit, for theirs is the kingdom of Heaven.*'"

We have said that the Order of Friars Minor was founded in the year 1208. Bernard da Quintavalle, a rich and respectable citizen of Assisi, was the first follower of our Saint. The history of his conversion is remarkable. He was probably a friend of Bernardone's, and held much the same position in his native town; but he had a less avaricious disposition, and a more thoughtful mind. He heard of the strange doings of Francis. Who indeed had not? They were the town and table talk of Assisi, the nine days' wonder of its respectable inhabitants. And while the general opinion was that the young man had shown symptoms of insanity, while some laughed, and others grieved over his disgrace, Bernard formed his own opinion, and was anxious to put it to the test. After all, he thought, this

* An allusion to Lucan's Pharsalia, lib. v. 531.

strange conduct might have some mystery in it worth unravelling. But three or four years had passed since this young man had been the pride of his native town, admired and applauded by all, with wealth enough and power of enjoyment to gladden his life. Why had he forsaken all this? why thrown it all from him? His thoughtful mind saw a method in this madness that told of some deep motive power, and he could not rest until he had fathomed it.

The mystery was soon made clear. He invited Francis to his house, and that night they occupied the same apartment. Bernard feigned sleep, and the Saint, thinking himself unobserved, arose, as was his wont, to pray. The chained eagle was unloosed, the caged dove was freed, the pent up torrent had burst its bonds, the soul that pined for its Beloved could cast itself into His embraces. With one bound the spirit of Francis sprang up to Him in whose bosom was his rest, his joy, his all; and, while burning tears streamed from his eyes, and yet more burning sighs issued from his heart, he kept repeating the words which were but the faint expression of his desires; for what earthly words can express heavenly love? "*Deus meus et omnia*" (my God and my all). Bernard now understood why Francis had left father and mother, had despised houses and lands; it was because that which he had forsaken was *nothing*, and that which he had found was *All*.

So the night passed, and morning found the Saint still absorbed in prayer. Bernard had prayed also, and had received the wonderful grace of vocation to a life of poverty, and it may be his courage in corresponding with it has hardly had its due meed of praise. He was called to follow one who as yet had no home, no religious rule, no order, no subjects, certainly no reputation but that of one beside himself. Francis was but the poor despised beggar of Assisi, and the courage of those who first resolved to follow Him was, therefore, not unlike theirs who followed Jesus of Nazareth in His life of humiliation and contempt.

A few days afterwards, Bernard came to Francis and addressed him thus: "If a servant has received a treasure from his master of which he has no need, what should he do with it?" "He should restore it to his master," replied the Saint. "Well then," said Bernard, "I will return to the Lord the earthly goods which he has bestowed on me." "What you propose," said Francis, "is a serious matter; we must consult God about it. Let us go to the church and hear holy Mass, and after we have prayed, the Divine Spirit will teach us what we ought to do." Before they went, another disciple presented himself; this was Peter of Catania, canon of the church of St. Rufinus, the cathedral of Assisi. Francis, with the calm and holy wisdom of true sanctity, was unwilling either to repress the ardor of his two disciples, or to lead them on to a vocation in which they might be unable to persevere. He therefore went with them to the church of St. Nicolas, where they heard Mass, and remained in prayer until the hour of terce. He then, according to a custom not unusual in those times, requested the priest to open the holy Gospels thrice, and to read the words upon which he should first cast his eyes. It was done in simple faith, and simple faith ever obtains what it desires. On the first opening of the book, they read, "If thou wilt be perfect, go, sell what thou hast, and give to the poor." The second time they read, "Take nothing for the way." The third time, "If any man will come after Me, let him deny himself, and take up his Cross, and follow Me." "This," exclaimed

Francis, "is the rule which we must follow; this is the counsel of God; let us go and put it in practice."

Bernard had large possessions; but, unlike the rich young man in the Gospel, he immediately sold them, and assembling the poor of Assisi in the square of St. George, distributed to the widow and orphan all his worldly goods.

These events took place on the morning of the 16th of April, 1208. The same day, Francis and his disciples took up their abode in a poor hut at a place called *Rivo Torto.* It was near Assisi, and so named from a small rivulet which wound its devious course through the plain. But the little stream may become a mighty river, bearing in its bosom a thousand sources of fertility for many lands. Thus was it with the streamlet of grace springing up in the souls of these voluntary poor ones, from whose heroic yet simple act came results so great and so splendid. In this little hut, three poor men who had forsaken the world, and were despised by it in turn, laid the foundation of an Order that was to extend far and wide, hold sway over the counsels of kings, influence the destiny of nations, make its voice heard and reverenced alike in the camp and the senate, in the cottage and on the throne; and number in its blessed ranks canonized saints, holy confessors, teachers and evangelizers, pontiffs guiding, and martyrs suffering for the mystical Body of Christ.*

* There is now at Rivotorto a convent, with a church belonging to the fathers conventual of Assisi. St. Francis lived about three years in this hut with his twelve companions. The site remained as he left it until the year 1586, when the foundations of a large church were laid, which enclosed the place where he had dwelt; this was not finished, however, until 1640. In the month of May, 1646, F. M. Michael Angelo Catalonia laid the foundation of a spacious convent, which was soon completed, and remains to the present day. Here is preserved a very ancient *Pietà*, or picture of our Blessed Lady, with the body of her Divine Son in her arms, as taken down from the Cross, to which St. Francis had a special devotion.

After seven days, another disciple came to ask a share in the poverty of Francis. Brother Egidius was also a native of Assisi, and a man of wealth and position; but divine love had touched his heart, and he, too, desired the lowly life of a poor mendicant friar. On the feast of St. George he went to hear Mass at the church dedicated to that saint, and then set out in search of Francis and his companions. Not knowing which road to take, he prayed that he might be led to choose the one which would bring him to the hut, saying: "O Lord and heavenly Father, I beseech Thee by Thy mercy, if I am to persevere in this holy vocation, to guide my steps to the dwelling of Thy servants." Instinctively he followed one of the three roads which lay before him, and soon met Francis coming out of a neighboring wood, where he had been engaged in prayer. Throwing himself at his feet, he begged most earnestly to be permitted to join his holy company. Francis replied: "My dear brother, you ask God to take you for his servant and His knight. This is not a small grace; it is as if the Emperor should come to Assisi in search of a favorite. Each one would say in his heart, God grant that he may choose me! See, then, how God hath chosen thee." Then raising him from the ground, he led him to Bernard and Peter, saying: "Here is a good brother whom God has sent us." With joyous hearts these simple ones sat down to their morning repast, while the angels hovered over them uttering canticles of praise that one more saintly soul was called from earth and earthly things to consecrate his whole being to Him who loves man with such unutterable but unrequited love. When their poor meal was ended, Francis took his new disciple to Assisi, that he might get materials for his habit. On their way they met a poor woman, who asked an alms.

The Saint, turning to Egidius, said: "My brother, let us give the cloak you wear to this poor woman for the love of God." The gift was willingly bestowed, and immediately it was caught up to heaven.

But these devoted men could not remain long inactive; zeal for the salvation of souls was to be a characteristic of their Order, and it was early manifested. Bernard and Peter went out to preach in the Romagna; Francis and Egidius into the Marches of Ancona. After a time they returned to Rivotorto, and a new disciple named Sabbatin presented himself. But little is known of him, save that his life was saintly, his end blessed; his mortal remains await the morning of the resurrection in the Church of Ara Cœli in Rome. The fifth disciple of our Saint was Morique, a religious of the Order of Crociferi, so called from the cross they wore on their habit. His vocation was remarkable. Being seriously ill at the hospital of St. Saviour's in Assisi, he sent to Francis to beg his prayers. He had heard of the Saint from many, and although the physicians had pronounced his case hopeless, he doubted not that the holy friar could obtain his recovery. Mixing a little bread with the oil of the lamp that burned before the altar of our Lady of the Angels, Francis sent it to him by two of his companions, saying: "Carry this to our dear brother Morique. The power of Jesus Christ shall not only restore him to perfect health, but shall also dispose him to be His servant in our company." Morique took the remedy, and was cured instantaneously; for, as the old Chronicles quaintly remark, "it was not confected by any worldly apothecary, but of the unction of the Holy Ghost." He lived for many years after in remarkable vigor and health, although he practiced the greatest austerities, neither eating bread nor drinking wine, but contenting himself with herbs and pulse. As for his habit, it was rather that of a beggar than of a Friar Minor.

We must now turn to a sad history. John of Capella (who is not to be confounded with the simple-hearted and saintly brother John, who followed Francis from the plough) began well but ended miserably. In spite of repeated warnings from his holy master, he allowed attachment to temporal things and a spirit of relaxation to overpower him. At length he was stricken with a dreadful leprosy, but not having patience to endure the affliction, he ended his life, Judas-like, by suicide. His place was afterwards filled by brother William, an Englishman, of most holy life, at whose tomb so many miracles were wrought that the concourse of suppliants at the gate interfered with the recollected spirit of the convent. Brother Elias was therefore obliged to visit his sepulchre, and command him by holy obedience to work no more.

Philip the Long was the seventh disciple. He was the first confessor and visitor of the religious of St. Clare. Of him it is said that an angel purged his lips, touching them with a burning coal, as did the seraph to the prophet Isaias; "which" says the chronicler, "was not a little necessary to him that was to administer the word of God unto religious women." Of John of St. Constantine, Barbarus, and Bernard of Viridant, we have no specific account; but concerning the priest Silvester, the eleventh in order of vocation, some interesting details are given. Francis had purchased from him some of the materials with which he rebuilt the Church of St. Damian, and had paid him what he considered a sufficient sum. The priest seemed satisfied at the time; but shortly after, seeing Bernard distributing his worldly goods in the public square, he accosted Francis, and claimed an additional payment. The saint took a handful of money from the bag, saying, "Sir priest, have your full payment now?" "I have all I require," replied Sylvester, who retired overjoyed at his success. But ere a few days had elapsed, his conscience smote him, and he said to himself, "Is it not a miserable thing that I, an old man, should so eagerly seek after earthly things, while this young man despises them for the love of God?" That night he had a wonderful dream. He beheld an enormous dragon, which encircled in its coils not only the town of Assisi, but the whole surrounding country. Then Francis appeared, and out of his mouth proceeded a fair and large cross of gold, the top whereof touched the heavens, while the arms stretched even to the ends of the earth, and at sight of it the dragon fled. At first the priest was not inclined to pay much attention to his dream. But as it was repeated for three successive nights, he went to Francis and related it to him, begging at the same time to be admitted into his society. His request was granted, and the remainder of his life was spent in a scarcely interrupted prayer.

The twelfth disciple of our Saint was an officer in the army called Angelo Tancredi. His vocation did not occur for some time later; but we will anticipate it, that the account of the twelve first disciples may not be disconnected.

Francis and his companions were journeying to Rome, and as they passed through Rieti he beheld a young knight hitherto unknown to him. Addressing him by his name, Francis thus accosted him: "Angelo, you have worn your military equipments long enough, it is time you should have a cowl instead of a belt, the Cross of Christ instead of a sword, and mud and dust instead of spurs. Follow me therefore, and I will make you a soldier of Jesus Christ." The young officer instantly obeyed, and left all to follow Francis, in whom he beheld the likeness of his Lord. Thus the number of twelve disciples was completed; another striking coincidence between the life of the servant and that of the Master.

Such were the "living stones" of that magnificent building, which was to rise even to heaven, and to support the Church of God in its time of greatest need. Prayer, manual labor, and begging alms for necessary food, formed the employment of these first diciples of the Saint. Hard words, and even rough blows, were often their only gain after a day's questing in the city where once they had been respected and esteemed, for poverty was little loved or courted in the native city of its great apostle.

Meanwhile Francis was not without prophetic intimations of the future greatness of his order. One day, after he had been long absorbed in prayer, he called his children to him, to send them forth to preach. They were then few in number, for he had but just received his seventh disciple, Philip the Long. "Take courage, my brethren," he cried, "rejoice in the Lord; let not our small number dishearten you, nor my simplicity and yours alarm you, for God has shown me clearly that by His blessing He will spread through the entire world this family of which He is the Father. I would fain keep silence on what I have seen, but charity compels me to make it known to you. I have seen a great multitude coming to us, to receive the same habit, and to lead the same life. I have seen the roads thronged with men, who address us. The French come, the Spaniards hasten, the English and the Germans run towards us; all nations are moved, and my ears are filled with the sounds of footsteps hurrying hither and thither to fulfil the commands of holy obedience. Consider, my brethren, what is our vocation. It is not merely for our own salvation, that the mercy of God has called us, but for the salvation of many other souls. It is that we may go forth and exhort all men, rather by our example than our words, to do penance and keep the divine commands. We seem, indeed, mad and contemptible; but fear not, take courage, and be assured that our Saviour, who has conquered the world, will speak efficaciously through you. Let us beware lest, after having renounced all, we lose the kingdom of heaven through some slight imperfection. If we meet with some who revile and despise us, we shall also find simple and holy souls who will hear us with joy. Let us, then, have courage; be patient in tribulation, fervent in prayer, laborious in work, and the kingdom of heaven, which is eternal, shall be our reward."

After this holy exhortation St. Francis gave his benediction severally to his little band, saying to each: "Cast your burdens upon the Lord, and He will sustain you." Then forming a cross, which pointed to the four quarters of the globe, he took one side for himself with a companion, and sent the other six in like manner on their apostolic mission.

CHAPTER V.

At the prayer of the Saint, his disciples return to their mission.—The Novitiate at Rivotorto.—Trials and fervor of the Novices.—Francis proposes a rule for them.—Solicits the approbation of the Holy See. —Innocent the Third.—The Cardinal Paoli.—Cardinal Ugolini.—The Pope's dream.—The Parable of Francis.—He obtains all he desires. —Promises obedience to the Sovereign Pontiff—Receives the vows of his children.—They return home.—A miracle occurs by the way. —New disciples crowd around him.—He obtains the chapel of St. Mary of the Angels.—The Benedictines the first patrons of the Order.

This dispersion of the brethren was not of long continuance; it was but a first essay of that life of poverty, contempt and suffering, to which they desired solemnly to consecrate themselves. The prayers of the Saint brought his children together once more, and each gave an account of his mission, its trials, and its success. When asked from whence they came, their reply always was, "We are poor penitents from Assisi." They never passed by a church without entering it; prostrate on the ground they said the prayer which Francis had taught them, and which is still used by the religious of his Order, "We adore Thee, O Lord Jesus Christ, here, and in all Thy churches which are in all the earth; and we bless Thee, because by Thy holy cross Thou hast redeemed the world."

The greater number of the twelve first disciples of Francis were men of rank and wealth; unaccustomed to the slightest privations or sufferings, and leaving a position in society where they knew only how to command. It must have required no common grace to enable them to turn at once from their wonted ease to the bare floor and rude hut of Rivotorto. No quiet noviciate was theirs, in which to be inured gradually to such hardness of life; where thoughtful, loving care would lead them on, step by step, and mould them daily to something of heroic perfection. But their courage, or rather their measure of grace, was equal to the trial; none, except the one unhappy apostate, even faltered. He who had come, "not to be ministered unto, but to minister," nerved them by His example and strengthened them by His Spirit. They were true children of their saintly father, who had already exclaimed, "There is nothing, O my God, that I am not ready, with my whole heart to give up for Thee; nothing too hard or painful for me to endure with joy; nothing which according to my powers of body or soul, I am not ready to undertake for the glory of my Lord Jesus; and I desire as far as I possibly can, to urge and lead on others to love God with all their hearts and above all things."

As the number of the Saint's disciples increased, it became necessary that he should give them some definite rule of life; he therefore prepared constitutions for their government, in twenty-three chapters.

The fourth Council of Lateran had not yet issued its decree, requiring all religious orders to solicit the approbation of the Holy See, but saints do not wait for injunctions where there is a question of doing what is most perfect. Francis assembled his disciples and said, "I see, my brethren, that it is the Lord's good pleasure to extend our association. Let us go then to our mother, the holy Roman Church, and make known to the Sovereign Pontiff what God has been pleased to design by our ministry, in order that we may carry on our labors according to his will and under his direction."

Bossuet, Bishop of Meaux, in an address to his clergy, speaks thus: "Paul, after he had been rapt to the third heaven, came to Peter, to teach all future ages, that no man, be he ever so holy or so learned, should live without seeing Peter." This has ever been the guiding principle of all the true sons of holy Church; and in times like our own we may do well to ponder over the deep reverence and tender affection shown by the Saints to the successor of St. Peter and representative of their God. In proportion to the sublimity of their revelations and the greatness of their sanctity, has been the depth of their child-like submission to all spiritual superiors, from those immediately over them to the supreme head of the Church on earth. The first sin was a disobedience of the human will, too proud to submit even to a direct command, and the same spirit still manifests itself, from lesser resistances to lawful authority to the open rebellion of heresy or schism.

Pride, that caused the fall of angels, has often since then hurled down to the same dark abyss souls who, but for its rebellious sway, might have filled their vacant thrones. "Who is like God?" was the war-cry of the archangel, and what is opposition to authority but the answer of Lucifer, *Similis ero Altissimo*, "I will be like the Most High!" It is not then wonderful that the Saints were obedient in proportion to their other tokens of sanctity, and that they dared not believe a vision, however apparently clear, or act on a revelation, however sublime, until assured by their superiors that it was from God. In the higher paths of supernatural gifts there may be delusions and snares; in simple obedience there can be none, for the voice of Eternal truth has said, "*He that heareth you, heareth Me; and he that despiseth you, despiseth Me; and he that despiseth Me, despiseth Him that sent Me.*"

Bernard da Quintavalle, the eldest born of the spiritual family of St. Francis, was appointed their leader and guide on their journey; the humility of the Saint making him decline the direction of the little band. On their way they passed through Rieta; and here Angelo de Tancredi received his vocation, as was related before.

Poor, friendless and unknown, as they were, no wonder they should have had fears and misgivings by the way. But the faith of the holy Patriarch was not easily shaken; and a vision with which he was favored, and which he related to his disciples, revived their faith and courage. Their happiness was not a little increased when, on their arrival at Rome, they found there the venerable bishop of Assisi, the first friend and patron of the Seraphic Order. This good prelate was much disconcerted at their arrival; he feared they intended to leave his diocese, where they had already done so much by their exhortations and good example; but as soon as the real object of their visit was made known to him, he assisted them by every means in his power. The Cardinal, John of St. Paul, bishop of Sabina, was then in Rome; he was specially devoted to the service of the poor, and was one who could understand and appreciate the fervor of the Saint. As a personal friend, the Bishop of Assisi requested him to use his influence in favor of Francis, and he willingly complied.

Innocent the Third was at this time engaged in affairs of great moment. One day, as he paced to and fro on a terrace of the Lateran Palace, he was accosted by a poor man, of whom he knew nothing, who asked permission to establish a new religious order. We can scarcely wonder that the apparent visionary was repulsed, and that the careworn Pontiff forgot, amid his many and pressing anxieties, the momentary interruption.

That night, however, he beheld in a dream a palm which sprang up at his feet; at first it seemed but a little shoot; presently it grew up into a stately tree. In the morning he was given to understand that this tree symbolized the poor man whom he had dismissed the day before. He sent immediately for Francis, and received him surrounded by his cardinals. The Saint fully explained his intentions and desires; and Innocent thanked God that there was now a son of holy Church who, manifesting by his example wherein true poverty consisted, would thus expose the errors of the false "poor men" of Lyons, at that time drawing souls into peril of heresy by their professed contempt for worldly things. The cardinals, however, were not all of this mind. Some feared, not unreasonably, that the poverty proposed was excessive; and that few, if any, could be found who would persevere long in such a life. Again, the very important question arose, How were these men to live? Every other religious order was more or less self-supporting, had its own funds, or means of maintenance; whereas it was a special requirement, nay, the essential rule and foundation, of this new institute, that its members should possess nothing, but should depend for their daily bread on the alms of the faithful.

There was one, however, of the consistory, well prepared to defend this absolute poverty, the holy cardinal, John of St. Paul. He arose, answered the objections, point by point, and concluded with these words: "If we refuse the petition of this poor man, on the pretext that his rule is hard and too difficult, let us beware lest we reject the Gospel itself; for the rule which he desires to have approved is in conformity with it; and to say that evangelical perfection contains anything unreasonable or impossible, is to blaspheme against Jesus Christ, the author of the Gospel." Innocent was struck with this reasoning, and said to Francis: "My son, pray that Jesus Christ may make his will known to us, that we may further your pious desires." The Saint retired to pray, but soon returned, and thus addressed the Pontiff: "Holy Father, a poor but very beautiful maiden once dwelt in a desert. A great king saw her, and was so charmed with her beauty that he espoused her. He remained with her some years, and they had several children, who had the features of their father and the beauty of their mother. Then he returned to his court. The mother brought up her children with great care. One day she said to them: 'My children, you are born of a great king; go to him, and he will provide you with all that you need.' The children came to the king, and when he beheld their beauty, he said, 'Whose children are you?' and they answered, 'We are the children of that poor maiden who dwelt in the desert.' Then the king embraced them with great joy, and said: 'Fear nothing, you are my children. If strangers are fed every day at my table, shall I not much rather take care of my own offspring?' This king, most holy father, is our Lord Jesus Christ. This beautiful young maiden is Poverty, who, being rejected and despised by all, lives in this world as in a desert. The King of kings loved her so much that when He came down from heaven to earth, He espoused her in the manger. And she bore Him many children in the desert of this world; apostles, anchorets, cenobites, and many more who have embraced voluntary poverty. That good mother sent them to the King of heaven, their Father, bearing the stamp of His royal poverty, as well as of His humility and obedience. The great King received them with kindness, and promised to provide for them, saying, 'I make my sun to rise upon the just and the unjust; I provide what is necessary for every creature; shall I not much rather take care of My own children?' If the King of heaven has promised that those who follow Him shall reign eternally with Him, how much more certain may we be that He will provide them with those things which He pours forth so liberally on the good and on the evil?" "Of a truth," exclaimed Innocent, "this is the man who, by his works and by his doctrine, shall sustain the Church of Jesus Christ." Then he declared how, on the preceding night, he had beheld him in a dream upholding the falling Basilica of the Lateran.

There were now no further difficulties in obtaining the sanction of his Rule. Innocent gave it a verbal approbation which was all the Saint asked at the time. Francis made him a promise of obedience, and his children made the same to himself. The holy Pontiff assured him of his protection, conferred on him the order of deacon, admitted his companions to minor orders, and constituted the Saint superior-general of all the religious of the order of Friars Minor present and to come. It was at this time also that Francis made the acquaintance of Cardinal Ugolini, afterwards so powerful a protector of the Order.

Thus encouraged and fortified, the little band set out on their homeward journey. Once, after a long and fatiguing day's march, they rested a little by the way-side, famished with hunger. They had no food, and there was no habitation within sight where they might beg for their necessities. Presently a man appeared, who presented them with some bread, and immediately vanished. Thus were the words of Francis verified; and the great King who feeds the raven, proved Himself not unmindful of His own children. In the Dominican annals we read that, under a like trial of faith, angelic youths of wonderful grace and beauty entered the refectory, and served the friars with religious ceremony, retiring as they came. In the Franciscan Order, when such miraculous supplies have been vouchsafed, it is by the toilsome way-side or in the desert waste. With such discerning love and adaptation do the miracles of God's providence towards each institute harmonize with their design and character. The Order of poverty and love is fed by a poor man on the way-side; the Order of light and wisdom receives its refection within the calm silence of its cloistered walls.

The Friars remained for a time at Orta, but this place was soon abandoned; the people were too kind to them to make it a desirable abode for those who sought poverty and contempt; while the singular beauty and convenience of the locality made Francis fear lest his young soldiers should be enervated by its attractions. Once more we find them in their poor little hut at Rivotorto. Here there could be no danger of the temptations from which they had just retreated. The place was surrounded by an unwholesome marsh; and the dwelling itself so contracted that each brother had to write his name on the wall, to mark the spot he was to occupy at prayer. Often their only sustenance was herbs and roots, which they moistened with tears of love and penance. The Saint now devoted himself to train and instruct his disciples. Their book was a large wooden cross, fixed in the centre of their poor hut, round which they knelt in prayer.

Sometimes they went to preach in the surrounding villages. On one occasion, Francis went on a Saturday evening to Assisi, where he was to preach next morning in the cathedral. He passed the night in a small shed, in a garden belonging to one of the canons. About midnight, the brethren who slept or watched at Rivotorto were startled by a light of unearthly brilliancy, which filled the hut, and at the same time, they beheld a fiery chariot supporting a golden globe, which passed three times round the room. When the Saint returned on the following day, they conversed together on the miraculous event, which seemed to them to symbolize the spiritual greatness of their holy father. Francis then told them many things regarding their own interior, as also relating to the future extension and greatness of the Order. All this tended to confirm their trust and confidence in him, and they resolved more earnestly than ever to yield themselves implicitly to his guidance.

New disciples now began to crowd around the Saint, and the little hut of Rivotorto could no longer shelter the increasing family of Franciscans. They were too poor to build a convent, and so their only resource was to beg; it was no little joy to them thus to found their first conventual establishment. The good bishop and canons of Assisi were both appealed to, but neither had it in their power to bestow sufficient alms, or to give a church suitable for them. Francis then applied to the Benedictine fathers of Subiaco, and they immediately and generously bestowed on him and his children the little chapel of St. Mary of the Angels,* with the house adjoining it. This was, on all accounts, a most welcome gift. It will be remembered that this church was one of the three which the Saint had repaired soon after his conversion, and it was one which he especially loved. A good priest, named Peter Mazancoli, had taken charge of it since that time; Francis now hastened to inform him who were its new proprietors, and to invite him to join the little band. Mazancoli warmly embraced and congratulated him, saying, "This place is surely beloved by the Blessed Virgin, for choirs of angels are often heard singing in it." That night, as Francis prayed long and fervently before the altar, recommending his little family to the care of our Blessed Lady, our Divine Lord appeared to him, accompanied by His Mother and a host of angels. The Saint

* It is said that the Chapel of Porziuncola was built by four hermits who came from Palestine in 352, during the pontificate of Pope Liberius. They were sent by him to the valley of Spoleto, where they settled, and built a rude oratory of stones and mud, dedicating it to the Mother of God. In process of time, it came into the possession of the Benedictine fathers, who had a large monastery near Assisi. It was almost in ruins when they obtained it, but they rebuilt it, making it like the church which their venerable father, St Benedict, had erected on Mount Subiaco, in honor of the Queen of Angels, and giving it the name of Porziuncola. It remained just as St. Francis had repaired it, until the pontificate of St. Pius the Fifth. On the Feast of the Annunciation, 1560, the first stone was laid of a new church, which is one of the largest and most magnificent in Italy. It was materially injured by an earthquake in 1832, but the nave and choir have been rebuilt. Happily the cupola, under which is the original chapel, escaped injury, as also a magnificent fresco, representing the vision of St Francis, which had only been completed by Overbeck a few years previously, and which is very justly considered his masterpiece.

exclaimed in ecstatic joy, "O most holy Lord, King of heaven, Redeemer of the world, sweet love; and Thou, O Queen of Angels, by what excess of goodness do you come down from heaven into this poor chapel?" Immediately he heard this reply, "I am come with My Mother to settle you and yours in this place, which is dear to Me." Well might Francis exclaim, "This is a holy place, fit rather for the habitation of angels than of men; it will be an eternal monument to us of the goodness of God." Next morning he assembled his religious there, and told them what had passed. He said, moreover, that the Benedictine fathers had given them their new habitation on condition that it was from henceforth to be considered the principal house of the Order, however much it might afterwards extend. In token of gratitude to his benefactors, and also to show that he received their gift only as an alms, Francis sent each year to the Benedictine Abbot a basket of small fish which abound in the Chiasco, a river which flows by the place.

CHAPTER VI.

Francis invites postulants to join his Order.—A short account of several of his early disciples.—Brother Leo, his friend and confessor.—Brother Rufinus.—Massco di Marignano.—Brother Juniper.—Brother Simeon.—Brother Christopher.—He desires his disciple, who is familiar with his guardian angel, to ascertain his state before God.—Brother William, the Englishman.—Brother Peregrinus of Falcron.—Brother Philip the Long, first confessor to the Poor Clares.—Brother Giles, or Egidius.

THE Franciscan Order may now be considered as fairly established; it was approved by the holy See, its disciples were increasing, and, poor as it was, they had a house where they could receive postulants. Full of joy, Francis went through the surrounding country, crying out, "O ye who desire the precious pearl of the Gospel, come join us in our trafficking for heaven; sell your goods, give them to the poor; come, and be free with me from all earthly cares; come, we will do penance together; come, we will serve and praise our God in poverty and simplicity." His invitation was accepted, crowds flocked around him to listen to his earnest burning words, and amid those crowds many blessed ones heard and answered the interior call. Many "forgot their own people and their father's house," and soon the Friars Minor had no need to seek for postulants.

Most touching details are recorded of some of these saintly souls; and as a life of St. Francis would be very imperfect without an account of his children, we must notice a few of them here.

First of all comes Brother Leo, "The Little Sheep of God," *(La Pecorella di Dio,)* as Francis used playfully to call him. He was the confessor and most intimate friend of the Saint, who confided to him his greatest secrets, and even those divine favors which he so sedulously concealed from all beside. What is related of their intercourse is full of that exquisite simplicity which has always characterized the most saintly souls of the Order.

One bitterly cold winter's day, as Francis and his companion walked along the road from Perugia to Saint Mary of the Angels, the Saint exclaimed, "God grant, Brother Leo, that the Friars Minor may give an example of great sanctity to all the world! Nevertheless, mark well that therein is not perfect joy." Then going on a little further, he added, "O Brother Leo, though the Friars Minor should give sight to the blind—should cast out devils—should restore hearing to the deaf, and speech to the dumb, or even bring back to life those who had been four days buried, this is not perfect joy." A third time he cried: "O Brother Leo, if the Friar Minor knew all tongues and all knowledge—if he had the gift of prophecy and of discerning spirits—this is not perfect joy." Then, going a little further: "O Brother Leo, dear little sheep of God, if the Friar Minor should speak with the tongues of Angels—should know the courses of the stars, the virtue of plants, the secrets of earth, and understand the nature of birds, of fishes, of men, and all animals, of trees, of stones, and of the waters—even here is not perfect joy." Then once more he cried, "O Brother Leo, though the Friar Minor should by his preaching convert all infidels to the faith of Christ, even here is not perfect joy." Thus he spoke as they journeyed on, mile after mile, the external cold chilling their weary limbs, and the internal fire consuming their loving hearts. At last Brother Leo cried out, "Dear Father, where then in the name of God, is perfect joy?" and the Saint answered thus, "When we come to Saint Mary of the Angels, pinched with cold, famished with hunger, and covered with dirt; and, when we knock at the door, if the porter shall say, 'Who are you?' and we answer, 'We are two of your brethren;' and he replies, 'You lie; you are two idle vagabonds who roam about, getting the alms of those who really need it;' and if he leaves us all night at the door in the frost and snow, and if we suffer this treatment with patience, without murmuring or vexation, and even think charitably and kindly of the porter, and that he has just taken us for what we are, and that it is by the permission of God that he uses us in this manner; then, believe me, we have found perfect joy! And if, when we continue knocking at the gate, the porter comes out and beats us, saying, 'Away with you, villains, go to the hospital; we have nothing for you to eat here;' if we endure all this with patience, and forgive him with all our hearts, then, believe me, we have found perfect joy! If at last, in this extremity, hunger, cold, and darkness compel us to entreat once more with tears that we may be let into the convent, the porter should be enraged against us, and coming out with a great knotted stick, should take us by the hood, throw us down in the snow, and beat us until we are all over wounds and bruises, and if we should bear all this with joy, thinking that thus we share in the sufferings of our blessed Lord Jesus Christ, then believe indeed, O Leo! that we have found ecstatic joy; for of all the gifts of the Holy Spirit which Jesus Christ has given, or will yet give to His servants, the greatest of all is to overcome themselves and to suffer for the love of God. In other gifts we cannot glory, for they are not our own; but with the Apostle we may glory in the cross of Jesus Christ."

Another conversation of these simple ones is also on record, and it might make an angel smile. When they were travelling together on one occasion, the hour of matins arrived, but they had no breviary. Francis said, "Dear brother, we have no books, but nevertheless we must sing the praises of God. I will say, 'O Brother Francis, thou hast committed so much sin on earth, that thou deservest to be cast into hell;' and thou, Brother Leo, shalt answer thus, 'It is true indeed, that thou dost deserve to be cast into the very depth of hell!'" With the simplicity of a dove, brother Leo answered, "Willingly, father; let us begin." Then the Saint exclaimed, "O Brother Francis, thou hast committed so many sins, and done such evil on earth that thou deservest to be cast into hell." Leo answered, "God will do so much good by thee that thou shalt be received into Paradise." Then Francis answered, "Say not thus, Brother Leo; but when I say, 'O Brother Francis, thou hast committed so much evil against God that thou deservest to be accursed of Him,' thou shalt reply, 'It is true; thou art worthy of a place among the accursed.'" And again the simple-hearted friar replied, "Willingly, father;" but again his answer was not according to the desire of his master, for when Francis had uttered his self-accusing versicle, Leo replied, "O Brother Francis, God will show thee such favor, thou shalt be blessed even amongst the blessed." Then the Saint with gentle anger exclaimed, "Why answerest thou not as I have taught thee? I command thee by holy obedience to repeat the words I say." Once more he began his new matins: "O Brother Francis," he cried, with many tears, "O miserable Brother Francis, after so many crimes committed against the Father of mercies and the God of all consolation, thinkest thou that He will show thee mercy?" Brother Leo was desired to say, "It is too true, thou art unworthy of mercy;" but instead of these words he cried out, "God will show thee mercy and overwhelm thee with His favors." Francis could bear these praises no longer. "Why," he exclaimed, "have you acted thus against obedience, and refused to answer as I have taught you?" "My very dear father," replied Leo, "God knows I have always intended to say the words you desired me." "This time, at least, answer as I tell you," replied Francis; and again he repeated his self-accusing words. But Leo broke forth again in his master's praise, and cried out, "Thou shalt receive from God the richest mercy; thou shalt receive from God the richest mercy; thou shalt be eternally exalted and glorified by Him; for he who humbleth himself shall be exalted. I cannot say otherwise, for it is God who speaks through my mouth."

Those who loved each other so tenderly in life were not separated in death; the *Pecorella di Dio* lies at the feet of his saintly and canonized master, close to the altar where the Immaculate Lamb, whom he so much resembled in the innocence of his life, is daily offered for the faithful.

Brother Rufinus next claims our attention. Of his eminent sanctity we cannot doubt, since Francis himself declared during his life-time that he was one of the three holiest souls then on earth: "I may safely call him Saint even now, since it hath been revealed to me that he is already canonized in heaven." The old chroniclers tell us that "he was as a shining rainebow, with a beautiful variety of faire colours, and as a vermillion rose for his fervent charity, and as a white lily for his purity, yielding a most pleasing savour to the Churche of God."

Rufinus was a native of Assisi, of a noble family, and nearly related to St. Clare; he was converted by the preaching of St. Francis. Soon after his entrance into the order the Saint desired him to go and preach at Assisi. His disciple was unwilling to comply with this injunction, for he was so constantly rapt in prayer that even necessary speaking had become painful to him. But with all his tenderness, Francis knew how to enforce obedience. He therefore repeated his command, and as a penance for the reluctance which Rufinus had shown, desired him to go without his hood. The humble brother at once fell on his knees, craved the pardon and blessing of his master, and went cheerfully to do his bidding. When he appeared in the pulpit, the good people of Assisi were not a little amazed at his appearing hoodless, and he met with more scorn than attention. They decided at once that the austerities of the friars had affected their reason.

Meanwhile the tender heart of Francis was giving him a heavier penance than he had inflicted on his disciple. "What are you doing, miserable son of Peter Bernardone?" he mentally ejaculated; "how can you treat a gentleman and a knight in this manner?" Then throwing off his own hood, he hastened to the church where Rufinus was preaching. At first the people were inclined to treat him as they had done the friar; but when he had uttered a few burning words on the Passion of Christ, their laughter was changed to tears and they were now as ready to kneel at the feet of the brethren, and call them Saints, as they had been a short time previously to account them insane.

When Brother Rufinus was dying, Leo (or as we can scarcely choose but call him, the Pecorella) was also, it was supposed, about to receive the eternal recompense of his saintly life. Both at the same moment had a vision, in which they beheld the soul of Brother Bernard ascending to heaven in exceeding glory. They saw a light of wonderful brightness streaming from his eyes; this, they were told, was a recompense for his charity in judging others. If he saw a poor man in rags, he would say to himself, "This poor man observes poverty far better than I who have vowed to do so." If he saw a rich man sumptuously apparelled, he would exclaim, "This good man tries to conceal his penitential spirit; no doubt, under his costly garments he wears hair cloth, and mortifies himself far more than I do." Thus he judged well of all, and went about thanking God for the wonderful sanctity which he supposed was the possession of every one but himself. And so Brother Bernard went to heaven. But the angels were looking for some one to accompany him. The "Little Sheep of God" thought that it might be for him they were seeking, and that he should then go to the eternal pastures. But Rufinus cried out, "Good Brother, it is for me the angels are waiting, and even now our holy Father Francis calls me." In a short time his words were verified; five days after he had seen this vision he also went to his celestial country. This holy Brother, with the assistance of Leo and Brother Angelus of Rieti, wrote the first account of the life and miracles of Saint Francis.

Masseo de Marignano was also of noble birth, and in addition to the high gift of contemplation with which he was favored, he was singularly attractive in his discourse and manner; so that Francis often called him to the guest-room for the edification and entertainment of strangers. Masseo did not over much relish this employment, but he was too perfect a religious to show the least sign of repugnance. One day Francis called him and said, "Brother Masseo, your companions have received the gift of contemplation; you have that of fluent discourse. It is therefore right that they should give themselves to prayer without interruption, and that you should be employed in those active offices which suit you better. I give you, therefore, the charge of the gate and the kitchen, and any time you have to spare after these duties are fulfilled you can employ in asking alms. Above all, take care that secular persons do not interrupt the quiet of the religious, satisfy them with some pious discourse, that no one else may be obliged to appear. Go and do all this, and you will have the merit of holy obedience." Masseo simply bowed his head, and immediately occupied himself in the manner prescribed. But the brethren, who tenderly loved each other, could not bear to see him thus overwhelmed with such distracting duties, and entirely withdrawn from the retirement he so much loved; they therefore came to Francis and asked him to divide these labors amongst them. The Saint called Masseo once more, and told him their request. The holy brother, more than content with whatever obedience ordained, answered simply, "My father, I considered all your commands as the will of God for me." Then Francis, who could no longer contain his joy at beholding so much virtue in his children, broke forth into a heavenly discourse on the merit of obedience and the grace of charity, and with his blessing distributed the offices of the convent in equal measure to each.

Hearing one day a discourse on humility, which was made by Brother Leo, Masseo could no longer contain his desire to possess this virtue in its utmost perfection; so with tears and prayers, with fasts and discipline, he strove to obtain it of God. At length he heard the voice of his Beloved addressing him thus, "Masseo, what wilt thou give Me, if I give thee this grace which thou so earnestly askest?" "Lord," he answered, "I will give Thee all I have; I will give Thee my very eyes." Then the voice spoke once more, and said, "I will give thee without price all that thou hast asked."* From this moment to his dying hour, the life of Masseo was one unceasing prayer. At times he was so overwhelmed with Divine love that he could utter no word; but the brethren heard him moaning

* In the annals of the Poor Clares, we read of a case not unlike that of Brother Masseo. Sister Elizabeth Van den Broncke, who had the same blessed desire for the grace of humility, made it the object of her prayers, the intention of all her mortification for nine years, during which time she was employed in the meanest and most laborious occupations of her community, and in harassing and distracting duties in the care of the kitchen and domestic arrangements. Her petition was heard, and she was frequently seen, even while engaged in her work, rapt in ecstacy, or so absorbed in God as to be unconscious of all around. Her guardian angel and other blessed spirits were her familiar companions and constant helpers; so that afterwards, when any Sister was overwhelmed with work, her Sisters would say, "May Elizabeth's companions come and assist you."

out his love in accents like the plaining of a dove.* At midnight he would arise and pray till the day had dawned, and the religious, who often watched him unperceived, could hear that he asked only for the forgiveness of his sins, and that he might ever fulfil perfectly the holy will of God. Then, when mass was over, he would return again to prayer, and ask for love, burning love, and then would come those plaining tones, for words failed him to express his desire. It is douhtful whether his body lies in the great church of Assisi, or in the Marches of Ancona. His soul at least drinks to its fill of those torrents of love whose droppings caused him, even here, such unutterable joy.

What shall we say of Brother Juniper; of a simplicity so unparalleled, that no wonder if many esteemed it more akin to folly? Such a history as his is rarely met with for attainments in sanctity.

Well might St. Francis exclaim: "Would to God I had a forest of such Junipers!" And well might St. Clare, whose sweet, simple spirit could appreciate his innocence, ask to have him near her as she lay dying, and call him "the pastime of Jesus." His one desire seemed to be, to meet with occasions of contempt and humiliation; and if he could not find, he took care to make them. Perhaps it was this desire, so incomprehensible to the world, that brought on him its greatest scorn, and made him so often to be esteemed a fool. Some, indeed, knew and revered his sanctity; but they were few in number. Once he was sent to a house of the Order in Rome, whither his character had already preceded him. Curiosity, or a better motive, led crowds to await his coming, but it was an unwelcome honor,

* "Quand' egli orava faceva un giubilo, conforme a quello d'una columba."—*Fioretti*, cap. xxxi.

and Juniper bethought him how to avoid it. Two boys were engaged in a merry game of see-saw on a low wall hard by. One of those he speedily dislodged; and, taking his place, kept up the amusement with his companion till the impatient crowd dispersed, subscribing to the general opinion that brother Juniper was more fool than Saint.

But it was not only in the world that he met with contempt. Even among his brethren his simplicity was often a subject of ridicule, and his superiors were obliged to reprehend him severely for the mischances it occasioned, though they would afterwards declare in private their admiration of his humility and charity. One Christmas day, the sacristan, wearied with his arduous duties, left his post for a time, and confided the altar to the care of Brother Juniper. It was decked in its richest ornaments, for Francis would have no poverty exercised there. Juniper was supremely happy at receiving such a charge, and was soon absorbed in prayer. Presently an old woman came in, and begged an alms for the love of God. The good friar had nothing to give, but he could not bear to refuse anything to the poor; they were Christs to him, and he believed, in its simplest and most literal sense, that what was asked by them or given to them, was asked by or given to his beloved Lord. Some rich fringe adorned the hangings of the altar; Juniper speedily cut it off, and satisfied the mendicant. Meanwhile the sacristan returned. He had doubts as to the perfect safety of his charge, and an anxious glance around soon convinced him they were well founded. He carried his complaint to the superior, but got only the unsatisfactory reply that he might have had more discretion than to trust brother Juniper with such a charge. However, the poor friar was ordered to do public penance for his fault; and, saith the Chronicle, "the General (Brother John Parent) did so chapter and check him publicklie in the refectory, and with such vehemence that he got the rheume and pose withal!" This was the hardest penance of all to the tender-hearted friar, who could not bear to see his superior suffer; so he at once set out on the quest, and brought home some medicine, which he hoped would cure him. His mission of charity was not accomplished until late at night. The Father Guardian had retired to his cell, but Juniper ceased not to importune him to take what he had procured. Although he was again severely reproved, his request was at length complied with, and the Father was immediately cured.

One more anecdote of his most interesting life, ere we turn to others of the saintly band. He was once in a monastery where all the brethren were required to go out for the day on an important and fatiguing mission, and they left Juniper at home in charge of the house. This was now no act of indiscretion. He had been put under strict obedience neither to give away the habit he wore, nor the common property of the religious, nor even to allow his garments to be taken from him, as he had once desired a poor man to do when perplexed between the obedience to *give* nothing and his extraordinary charity. Presently he remembered that his brothers would require some refection on their return home. Cogitating next on the length of time it took to prepare food every day for so large a community, he determined to obviate that inconvenience, at least for a fortnight, and then, he said, we shall have so much more time for prayer. Accordingly he sallied forth with a large sack on his shoulders, and succeeded so well in his quest, that in a few hours he retured home with a load which only his good will could have enabled him to carry. A large fire was soon made, and an immense cauldron procured, into which he poured the contents of his wallet. Fowls with their feathers on, eggs in their shells, cheese with its rind, vegetables with their tops—all were employed in the preparation of this marvellous dinner. When the friars returned Brother Juniper was at his task, and as he had found the heat almost intolerable, he had hung a large piece of board from his neck by a string to serve him as a screen. Alas, for his anticipations of the pleasure he should give his superiors and brethren! Again he was publicly penanced for his fault, and for the great waste of food occasioned by his extraordinary method of cookery. But he so humbly acknowledged himself in the wrong, and so heartily accused himself of being the greatest sinner and most useless person in his Order, that his superior could only exclaim to his companions, "Would to God there were as much waste of food every day, if we received as much edification thereby!" Can we wonder that Brother Juniper had singular power over evil spirits, or that his prayer seemed rather an ecstasy than a petition? The Church of Ara Cœli at Rome possesses the mortal remains of this great servant of God.

Brother Simeon next claims our attention. He had received no instruction in human science, scarcely the elements of the most ordinary education, yet he spoke of divine things and of the love of God so sublimely, that his words seemed rather angelical than human. He received such extraordinary consolations in prayer, that he would hide himself when he felt the first approach of these celestial favors, lest his exterior should betray the joy with which his soul overflowed. Sometimes he would be found so rapt in prayer, as to be unconscious of all that passed around him. Even what would naturally cause pain, such as the application of burning coals to his bare feet, failed to recall him to the world of sense. He is buried in the convent of Spoleto, and many miracles wrought through his intercession have attested how pleasing to God had been his life.

Brother Christopher was born in Romagna, and had been some time a priest when he received his vocation to a life of poverty. He was especially devoted to the service of lepers, and showed a remarkable tenderness towards all who were in any affliction. Towards himself he exercised an austerity almost boundless; his fasts were continual, and yet, notwithstanding all, he reached the age of one hundred years. His appearance and manner were peculiarly attractive, and, like many of his Order, he was remarkable for his cheerfulness. He was greatly favored by visions, and a most familiar intercourse with the world of spirits. Still, neither this, nor his possession of the gift of contemplation and tears, satisfied his delicate conscience, and he wept unceasingly, lest his sins, which he imagined so great, should be still unpardoned. One of his spiritual children, called Brother Peter, a religious who had forsaken much that the world values, and who was remarkable for his simplicity, was especially favored by apparitions of his guardian angel. Christopher begged him to inquire of this blessed spirit how he stood in the sight of God, and soon he obtained the joyful assurance that his sins were indeed forgiven. The night before his death he called the religious to him, and made them a long discourse on heavenly things. At six o'clock, on the vigil of All-Saints, he went to reign with them eternally. His happy departure was made known miraculously to many, particularly to two religious women of the Order, who beheld him ascend to heaven in exceeding glory. He died at Cahors, in the year of grace, 1272. Even a brief relation of the miracles said to have been worked through his intercession would require no small space.

Of Brother William, the Englishman, who took the place of the unhappy apostate, John of Capella, and whose miracles were so inconvenient to the religious, from the crowds who thronged to his tomb, we have already spoken.

Besides Brother Peregrinus of Falcron, who was indeed a pilgrim on earth, and sighed unceasingly for his celestial home, there was Brother Philip the Long, first visitor and confessor of the poor Clares, of whose life we have also recorded a miraculous circumstance. Many others were there, whose histories would fill a volume, and whose lives were as saintly as their end was blessed.

With a few words of Brother Egidius, or Giles, one of the first disciples of Francis, we must turn from this part of our subject, not without regret, so beautiful are the old Chronicles in which their lives are narrated.

Like many of his saintly companions, Brother Giles lived in continual prayer, and he was favored more than many in his communications with heaven. Still, his life was by no means as unemployed as those who are not familiar with such histories might suppose. Though he never preached publicly in a church, yet he would go hither and thither, as obedience prescribed, on missions of mercy, and many would gather round him to hear his exhortations. On these occasions he always refused to eat any food which had not been given either in alms, or (what he much preferred) as a payment for some laborious occupation. Once, when a cardinal had prevailed on him to be his guest, he complained not a little that Egidius adhered so resolutely to this determination, but the holy friar simply answered, "*Labores manuum tuarum quia manducabis, beatus es, et bene tibi erit.*" Indeed, he was in this, as in all else, a perfect model of religious poverty. His example proves that no gifts, however sublime, no incapacity of mind or body, however great, should exempt a religious from that spirit of labor which, under one form or other, ranks among their characteristic virtues. Once, when he could in no other way obtain an alms, he went to the kitchen of his host, and after employing himself for some time as an assistant to the cook, received payment in some broken victuals, which he carried to the cardinal's table, at which he was obliged to dine. Nor was his obedience less admirable. While walking one day with a companion, he received an order from his General to go to Assisi. At once, he turned in the direction prescribed, nor could his companion, who urged him to return first to the convent which had been his temporary home, obtain from him any other answer than this: "Brother, I am commanded to go to Assisi, not to the convent." And when a religious complained to him that he was sent from prayer to beg alms, and was thus obliged to leave the greater good for the lesser, Giles replied, "Brother, believe me, you know not yet what prayer is, for the most true and the most perfect is to do the will of your Superior.

Like his holy father St. Francis, and many religious of the Order, he was especially devoted to the Feast of the Nativity of our Divine Lord. Once, after he had kept the Lent of St. Martin in great austerity, and had been favored with many apparitions, and even with the spiritual presence of Francis (who had at this time been dead several years,) our Divine Lord himself appeared to His faithful servant on Christmas Eve, and for many hours he was lost in ecstacy, and this continued with little intermission until the Epiphany. Obedience obliged him to declare that during this time he had been caught like the Apostle Paul to Paradise, and had seen and heard what he dared not utter. After this vision, he was so frequently absorbed in God that he scarcely ever left his cell. The brethren who came to converse with him, either for their consolation or instruction, were obliged carefully to avoid speaking of the blessedness of heaven, or uttering the word Paradise in his hearing. If they did so he would at once lose all consciousness of exterior things. When he went abroad, which was now indeed but seldom, the people, who knew of this wonderful grace, through devotion or curiosity, would flock around him, and when some little child could be persuaded to approach him and whisper softly, "Paradise, Brother Giles! Paradise!" they would obtain all they desired. He would at once become insensible to all around, and his body would seem as though it would fly up whither his pure and burning heart had already gone.

Gregory the Ninth was at this time at Perugia. He was naturally anxious to see the friar of whom every one spoke and to witness his wonderful raptures. Brother Giles was therefore desired to appear before his Holiness. But as he entered the palace, he felt that interior sweetness and excess of spiritual joy which usually preceded his ecstacies, so he at once retired. His companion, however, went to the audience, and informed the Holy Father why the humble friar had sought to defer the interview. Gregory, who greatly desired to see him in one of these raptures, sent a message to him to come without delay. Giles obeyed; but he had no sooner with great humility kissed the foot of the Sovereign Pontiff, than he fell into a rapture, and remained immovable, his eyes raised towards heaven. "Verily," exclaimed the Pope, "if thou die before me, I will seek no other miracle to canonize thee."* Once, when Gregory came to his cell, he could not enjoy the converse he desired; the poor friar was unconscious even of his presence. At another time, when the Pope had asked him to dine at his palace, Giles fell into so long an ecstacy, that supper time had come, and he had not yet returned to himself. The cardinals, who much desired to hear him speak on spiritual things, advised the Pontiff to put him under obedience to return to them in spirit as well as in body. No sooner did the command issue from his lips, than Giles, who before had appeared like a corpse, and had proved insensible alike to fire, cold, and pain, returned at once to his usual state, and falling at the feet of the Pope, asked pardon for his faults.

The joyous manner and extreme affectionateness of this saintly friar, made persons eagerly seek to be in his company; but he loved solitude, for there he could give free vent to the love that consumed him. Sometimes he was seen embracing the trees and kissing the flowers; for so greatly did he love God, that even inanimate things, as being the work of His hands, were inexpressibly dear to him. He was often seen raised from the ground while assisting at Holy Mass, particularly on the Feast of the Nativity. If any one spoke to him of the Church, he could scarcely contain the fervor of his love and devotion, and would exclaim, "O holy Mother, O Roman Church! ignorant and miserable as we are, we do not know thee; nor can we understand or value as we ought, the zeal and charity

* This has been made the subject of a striking picture by Murillo.

whereby thou laborest to save us. Thou teachest us the way of salvation, thou dost direct us in the right and secure path, wherein he that walketh cannot stray; and he that seeketh and followeth another shall only find therein eternal damnation."

St. Bonaventura especially loved this holy friar. Once, as they conversed together, Brother Egidius said, "Father, God has bestowed many graces on you who are learned, but what shall we do to save ourselves, who are but poor ignorant ereatures?" "If," replied St. Bonaventura, "God had bestowed on us nothing but the gift of divine love, it would suffice, because love is more pleasing to Him than anything else we can offer." "Tell me, then," continued Giles, "if an ignorant person can love God as well as a learned man." "A simple poor old woman may love God as much, or more, than a doctor of theology," was the reply. No sooner was it uttered than the friar ran into the garden, and standing at the gate, cried aloud, "Poor ignorant people, love God and Jesus Christ, and you shall be greater than Brother Bonaventura."

A friar of another Order, who had some hesitation of mind regarding the most pure virginity of the Mother of God, went to consult him on the subject. Egidius knew his difficulty before he had time to explain it, and greeted him with these words, "Brother preacher, she is a virgin before childbirth, a virgin in childbirth, and a virgin after childbirth." Even as he spoke, he struck the ground three times with his staff, and three pure lilies sprang up at his feet to attest the truth of his assertion.

As the saintly king Louis of France was on his pilgrimage to the shrine of St. Francis, he stopped at Perugia, desiring to see this wonderful brother. They met, and spent some time on their knees, embracing each other with the tenderest affection. Then the king rose and pursued his journey, but no word had been spoken by either. The companions of Brother Egidius reproached him with want of courtesy to his distinguished guest. But he told them to have no such apprehension; since God had revealed to each what passed in the heart of the other, and they had thus communicated far more intimately than if their thoughts had been expressed.

Brother Giles died at Perugia. When it was known that his end was near, the inhabitants, who greatly feared to lose the mortal remains of so great a Saint, set a guard round the convent, as they knew he wished to be buried at St. Mary of the Angels. When the dying brother heard it he exclaimed, "Tell the Perugians that the bells shall never ring for my canonization, nor for any miracle of mine ; and I give them the sign of the prophet Jonas." His words were verified to the letter. When they sought where and how to entomb him, they found a marble sarcophagus, on which was sculptured the history of Jonas,* and in this they laid his body.

He went home on the eve of the Festival of St. George, 1260. There was no death struggle, no agony; but lying back on his straw pallet, he simply closed his eyes to the light of earth, to open them, we may not doubt, in the radiance of His face who is the light of the Jerusalem above. Fifty-two years before, and on the same day, he had received the holy habit of his Order from its saintly founder.

* A very frequent subject of representation on the tombs of the early Christians, and often repeated in the Roman Catacombs, as typical of death and resurrection, in the sense referred to by our Lord, *St. Matt.*, xii. 39, 40.

CHAPTER VII.

Francis founds the Second Order.—The vocation of St. Clare.—Her holy childhood.—She attends the preaching of Francis during the Lent of 1212.—Palm Sunday at Assisi.—Clare leaves her father's house forever.—Is followed by her younger sister Agnes.—The anger of the Count de Scefi.—Miracles confirm her vocation.—Her character as Abbess.

A RELIGIOUS order of men without its counterpart among the weaker sex, could scarcely (if at least we speak of the more ancient establishments) be considered as a thing complete. The work of creation was perfected when male and female were endowed with existence to the image and likeness of God; and if the first Eve brought ruin on him whose helpmate and solace she would have been, the second Eve has more than compensated for that transgression, and once more raised her sex to the dignity which it had all but forfeited.

The Friars Minor were now an established Order, with their special mission and character. It only remained that their form of life should be embraced by some courageous and heroic woman, to inaugurate among her sex a share in their sufferings and their merits. The noble lady, Clara de Scefi, was the instrument chosen by Divine Providence for this blessed work.

In the neighborhood of Assisi may still be seen the ruins of the old castle of Sasso Rosso. Here dwelt the chevalier Favorino de Scefi, the father of St. Clare. Her mother's name was Ortolana. She too was of noble birth, her father being a scion of the illustrious house of the Fiumi. The lady Ortolana was long childless; but, after a pilgrimage to the Holy Land, where she poured out her tears and prayers at the

Crib and the Sepulchre of our Lord, her desire of becoming a happy mother was granted. Soon after her return, the little Clare was born, and so named in consequence of a supernatural voice which the mother had heard while engaged in prayer: "Fear not, for thou shalt bring forth a light, which shall illuminate the whole world."

It is said that the little one was born with a smile on her infant lips—a presage of that singular sweetness of character which was one of her most attractive virtues.

We know but little of her childhood, but that little was full of promise of her future sanctity. Her spirit of mortification manifested itself at a very early age. She denied herself even the innocent pleasures of amusements of childhood; if this can be called a self-denial, when her pleasures and recreations were of another kind. For the poor, whom she tenderly loved, she would deprive herself even of necessaries, while all dainty meats and delicacies were concealed to be bestowed on them. She soon learned to mortify herself by disciplines, and by hair-cloth worn under the rich attire in which her parents required her to appear. Her prayer was continual; and as the use of beads was then unknown, she counted her Paters and Aves on little stones. At the age of fifteen her parents urged upon her the thought of marriage. As she was singularly beautiful, and the heiress of their ancient house, many nobles came forward to ask her hand. But Clare had already dedicated her heart to a celestial Spouse, and only waited for some clear indication of the will of Heaven that she might give herself irrevocably to these blessed nuptials, while her parents, thinking it was affection for them which made her unwilling to leave her home, ceased to urge the matter further.

Francis preached the Lent of 1212 in the church of St. George of Assisi, and Clare, with her kinswoman Bona Guelfuccio, attended constantly at his instructions. It was now revealed to her that he was the guide for whom she had so long sought—the one who should lead her in the much-desired path of perfection. It was also made known to the holy patriarch that Clare should be his coadjutor in the glorious work that lay before him. Their first interview is thus touchingly described in an old English translation of the Chronicles of the Order: "Then was she inflamed with divine love and moved by his holy actions, which she admired, as seeming unto her more than human. And therefore she began very exquisitely to dispose herselfe to the effecting of the words of the holy servante of God; who having very lovingly entertained her began to preach unto her the contempt of the world, and that all the beauty of thinges present is but vanity, filled with false and deceitful hopes. Then he persuaded unto her pure ears the honourable and amiable espousel of Jesus Christ, and counsayled her to conserve that most precious pearle of virginal purity for that most glorious Spouse, who out of love He bore to the world, being God, became Man, and would be borne of a virgin."

Clare had but one object in view, to give herself wholly to her Beloved; therefore, when Francis proposed that there should be no delay, the pure and innocent victim of Divine love neither hesitated nor doubted in her obedience. The Feast of Palms was kept in the old city of Assisi that year on the 18th of March. Clare, accompanied by her mother and her sister Agnes, attended its solemn and heart-stirring ceremonies. All had gone up to receive the palms from the hands of their venerable bishop. But the Lady Clare remained in her place, unconscious and absorbed in prayer. The prelate, either from respect to her devotion, or urged by a divine inspiration, left his place at the altar, and proceeding towards her, presented her with the symbol of victory. For the last time she took her place in the mournful triumphs of the day, mingling with the procession of dames and knights, all arrayed like herself in their richest costumes and brightest jewels. But there was a joy in her sorrow, even like the joy which the exiled feel when they think of the day when they may hope once more to see their fatherland. The hour of release from earthly ties and earthly fears was near; soon, very soon, she would be a maiden "dedicate to Christ;" one of those thrice blessed souls whose nightly dream and daily thought is still

"Of Him who is the sun to that pale flower,
The virgin's heart."

Her friend and kinswoman Bona was again her confidante. Francis had advised her on the following night to leave her home forever, and, lest her design should be frustrated, to conceal her intention. When all had retired to rest that night, the Saint and her companion fled in noiseless haste. Nor was a miracle wanting to confirm their faith and courage. Unable to open the great gate of the castle, they sought egress by a small postern door, usually left open. To their dismay, this was barricaded with large stones; but Divine Providence gave them a supernatural strength, and they were able to remove these impediments to their flight, though they scarcely knew how the labor was accomplished. The little chapel of St. Mary of the Angels was their destination. There they were welcomed by Francis and his brethren, who came out to meet them with songs of thanksgiving. After a moving exhortation to the young bride of Jesus Crucified, he clothed her with the poor habit and cord of his Order, and, cutting off her long hair, placed the consecrated veil upon her head. The magnificent dress and ornaments which she wore at the ceremony were given to the poor. At the altar of Mary Immaculate, and in the hands of her saintly father in Christ, she pronounced the three solemn vows of religion. And, says the old Chronicle, "it was, indeed, convenient that this new order of flourishing virginity should begin in the angelicall pallace of that most emminent Lady, who had bin alone a mother and a virgin, and consequently more worthy than all others. In the very same place had the noble chevalrie of the poore of Jesus Christ, the Frere Minors, had their beginning under the valourous captaine St. Francis; to the end it might evidently appeare that the mother of God in this her habitation did engender both of these religious, and equally cover with her mantle her first and second Order of Franciscans."

When morning came, a cry of grief and indignation resounded through the old castle of Sasso Rosso. Its brightest ornament, its fairest flower, the heiress of its wealth and hopes had fled—and whither? To follow the steps of a wandering friar, who had already received little else than scorn as the meed of his heroic sanctity. In our day, an independent line of action is rather a matter of commendation than of reproach, and women appear in positions which, in a former age, would have been considered quite incompatible with the retirement that should characterize their sex. Hence it is difficult to estimate the courage and self-devotedness which enabled one so young, so delicately nurtured, to brave the world's opinion and contempt, and to enter on a path untried and most painful to nature. But a father's anger and a mother's tears were alike foreseen and accepted as a part of that chalice of suffering which the spouse must share with her celestial Bridegroom.

As soon as Clare had made her solemn profession and received the holy habit of her Order, Francis led her to the convent of the Benedictine Dames of St. Paul, and again this grand old Order sheltered and protected the poor ones of Jesus Christ. Her retreat was soon discovered, and the Count de Scefi, with all the characteristic passionateness of an Italian noble, sought and demanded his child. But Clare calmly uncovered her head, shorn of its natural ornament, and declared her intention never to re-assume her former position in her father's house. Her quiet determination of manner was not without its effect, and for a time she was left unmolested. In a few days Francis removed his young disciple to another Benedictine monastery, that of St. Angelo, which was nearer to Assisi.

But the vocations in the family of Scefi were not yet complete. Agnes, the younger sister of our Saint, her companion, her friend, her treasure, was also fain to be the disciple of Francis and of poverty; and scarcely had Clare been a fortnight absent from the paternal mansion, when the little Agnes followed, and asked if she might not also be the spouse of the Immaculate Lamb. Clare received her sister with open arms. Since their short separation she had not ceased to pray that the favor granted to herself might be extended to the companion of her childhood. "Sweet sister!" she exclaimed, "I will give eternal praise to God, who has heard and answered my most earnest desire."

This joyous meeting was soon followed by a storm. Scarcely had Agnes arrived ere her indignant father demanded that his child should be restored to him;

and truly it seemed hard that this mendicant brother, whom some called Saint and some fanatic, could find no other subjects than the children of a wealthy noble, to embrace his strange rule of poverty and humiliation. Beautiful indeed it was, and heart-thrilling, to hear him preach in the Lenten time of the contempt of riches and worldly vanities, and of the poverty and sufferings of the God-man. It was grand and soul-stirring to behold the devotedness of his companions, and the prompt gladness with which they forsook home and earthly joys. All this was well. But it was quite another matter to see the nearest and dearest fly from the domestic hearth, and leave a vacant place there, never again to be filled. Count Favorino de Scefi reasoned as most parents reason under like circumstances; and felt as most parents feel when a similar case occurs in their domestic circle. His piety, and that of his noble lady, suffered indeed a severe trial, and one which few can bear with calmness. The gentle Ortolana wept heart-broken for her beloved child, little imagining that in a few short years she would herself receive the same vocation, and correspond to it as faithfully.

As is usual in such cases, the friends of the Count de Scefi were not slow in urging him to take an active part in recovering his daughters. They determined that Agnes at least should return home; and so, accompanied by a party of his nearest kinsmen, Favorino set out for the Monastery of St. Angelo. At first they used persuasions and entreaties; but finding that Agnes was as resolute as her sister, they determined on measures more effective. Clare was but eighteen, Agnes four years younger; still they calmly and courageously bore up through these stormy scenes. At length these valiant knights seized the little Agnes, and was determined that nothing but main force should be the means of her leaving the monastery, they dragged her from it. Heedless of her cries and sufferings, they succeeded in bringing her some distance. But here a difficulty occurred which they had not anticipated. The body of the holy maiden suddenly became so ponderous that their united efforts were unable to raise it from the ground; and so these twelve strong-armed men were foiled in their attack on a poor weak child. The prayers of her sister Clare had obtained this grace. It was followed by another miracle. The indignation of her uncle, the Count Monaldo, was only increased by the difficulty that had occurred. He raised his hand to strike a blow on the head of Agnes, which must have proved fatal; suddenly his arm was struck by an invisible power, and fell nerveless by his side. Nor was its use restored until some days after, when he obtained this favor through the intercession of her whom it had been raised to harm. Meanwhile Clare, who had followed at a distance, drew near, and begged they would at least leave her the body of her sister; for the rough treatment she had received had left her apparently lifeless. The knights withdrew, baffled and disappointed, and Clare with her young charge returned to the monastery. Francis now gave the holy habit to this young disciple of poverty, and desired her to retain her sweet name of Agnes, in memory of the Immaculate Lamb for whose love she had already sufferred so much.

Francis then placed the sisters at St. Damian's. It will be remembered that he had already predicted the establishment of a society of holy women in that place. Many were now found desirous to imitate the heroic example of those first female disciples of poverty, and before the close of the year Clare found herself abbess of a considerable community. In this office, which she accepted with the greatest reluctance, and only in obedience to the command of Francis, her character shone forth with singular beauty. Perhaps few superiors have ever governed with such wise and gentle love, and such deep humility. She made her office a pretext for humiliations. No employment was too lowly for this young maiden, who had been reared in all the luxury and refinement of a noble family. Once, when washing the feet of a lay-Sister who had just returned from a weary day's questing, the foot which she held in her hand was accidentally withdrawn, and as accidentally she received in this way a violent blow in the face. Neither disconcerted nor displeased, Clare calmly and tenderly pressed her lips to the foot which had been unwittingly the cause of her pain, and continued her pious occupation.

Her austerities have seldom been equalled, and they were as frequent as they were painful to flesh and blood. She always wore hair cloth of the roughest kind. Her cilice is still preserved, a most precious relic, by the Poor Clares at Assisi. It is so rough and so full of sharp-pointed bristles, that it cannot be handled without pain; yet this was worn for years, not only without complaint but with joy, by a female delicately nurtured and constantly suffering in health. During Lent and from the Feast of All-Saints till Christmas, she fasted on bread and water, and even this she denied herself on Mondays, Wednesdays, and Fridays of Lent. Her prayer was ceaseless, and her vigils many and protracted. Scarcely could her children bear to recall her to the world of sense, so joyous and beautiful was the light that shone on her angelic countenance as she conversed with God.

But with all her austerity towards herself, Clare was

full of tenderness towards her spiritual children, especially those whose souls or bodies needed her maternal care. In the cold winter nights she would glide softly from cell to cell, to see that they had all the protection from the severity of the season which their austere rule allowed, and if any, not yet inured to its hardness, were suffering from hunger or cold, she would not rest till they were comforted and refreshed. She had, moreover, a special power of soothing the tempted and sorrowful. With a winning, gentle love, peculiarly her own, she would draw from them an avowal of their griefs; then, if all else failed, she would even fall at their feet and implore them to weep no more, and thus "put away the force of their grief with her motherly cherishings." Nor were her Sisters unthankful for such love. Few superiors were so tenderly cherished, so deeply loved by their children as the young abbess of St. Damian's. The same sweet spirit still lingers, dove-like, in the cloistered homes of the Poor Clares, and there are successors of that dear Saint who preside with as heavenly a grace, and as thoughtful a charity, over the children of Francis and Clare.

CHAPTER VIII.

Death of the Count de Scefi.—Agnes founds a convent at Florence.—The poverty of the Poor Clares.—Their holy rule is drawn up by the Cardinal Protector and St. Francis.—Bread and oil miraculously multiplied by the prayers of St. Clare.—She works many miracles by the Sign of the Cross.—Blesses bread by order of the Pope.—Delivers her monastery and the town of Assisi, twice from the armies of the impious Frederic.—She receives a spiritual favor on the Feast of the Nativity and on Maunday-Thursday.—Her death.—Agnes' visit.—Poor Clares who lived in the same century.

THE Count de Scefi lived ten years after his daughter's consecration to God. Before his death his proud spirit had been subdued, and he no longer murmured at her choice or grieved that he had no heir to his vast possessions. The prayers of Francis had obtained his conversion. Ortolana was now free from earthly ties: she had long been a penitent of the third Order of St. Francis, but in her widowhood she sought and obtained a higher grace. Having distributed her goods to the poor, she joined her saintly child at St. Damian's, leaving the little Beatrice, her only remaining daughter, to the care of her uncle Monaldo. At eighteen, Beatrice also followed her mother and sisters. The sanctity of Ortolana was so great that Francis frequently sent sick persons to her for healing. Beatrice, a few years after her profession, was the foundress of several communities. Both went to their eternal reward some time before the death of St. Clare.

The gentle, affectionate Agnes, was soon separated from the sister whom she so tenderly loved. It must have been a severe trial to both; but perhaps the separation was as necessary for their own perfection as for the extension of the Order, since there is danger even in the most sanctified human affection. Three years after the foundation of the Order at Assisi, Francis sent Agnes to Florence. There she founded the Convent of Monticelli, and thence, thirty years later, she was summoned to attend the death-bed of her sister. A letter is still extant, touchingly beautiful in its simplicity and child-like affection, written by Agnes to Clare after their separation. It will tell us how necessary this parting was, and how much the holy sufferings which it caused must have glorified God.

"AGNES, THE POOR SERVANT OF JESUS, TO THE MOST BELOVED CLARE, HER VENERABLE MOTHER AND MISTRESS IN CHRIST JESUS, AND HER COMMUNITY:

"It is the condition of created things never to remain in one estate, thus it often happens that at the moment of our greatest happiness we are suddenly plunged into a sea of misery. Know, then, my mother, that my heart is full of grief and deep sadness. What do I not suffer by being separated from you—you with whom I had hoped to have lived and died? I see the beginning of my sorrow, but I do not see its termination. It is one of those troubles which ever increases, and to which one can see no end; it is a dark shadow ever darkening, a weary oppression which cannot be cast away. I had thought that those who were united in heaven by the same faith and the same conversation, would have on earth the same manner of life, and the same death—that the same tomb would enclose those of the same blood and the same nature; but I was deceived. I am forsaken, and my soul is overwhelmed with sorrow.

"O my sweet Sisters, pity me, weep with me, and pray God that you may never suffer so terrible a trial. Believe me, that there is no sorrow like this sorrow; a sorrow which wrings my heart, a languor which wearies me continually, a fire which consumes me without ceasing. Afflictions pressed me on every side. Oh! of your charity help me by your holy prayers, that God may give me strength to support them. O my Mother, what shall I do? What shall I say, I who never hope to see you or my Sisters again? Oh, that I could express to you all that I feel! Oh, that I could open my long grief to you in this letter! My heart is continually consumed with the fire of affliction. I sigh and weep, and seek for a consolation which I can never find. I am burthened with sorrow upon sorrow, and I sink under the sad thought that I shall never see you more. No one here can understand my grief.

"But I have one consolation, and you will rejoice in it with me; it is in the perfect harmony which reigns in our community. I was received with great joy and satisfaction, and all have promised me obedience with the utmost respect and devotion. All recommend themselves to God and to you. Think of us often, and regard them, as well as myself, as daughters and sisters who will be always ready to follow your advice and obey your commands. Our Holy Father the Pope has been pleased to acquiesce in my desire concerning the matter you know of. Beg Brother Elias, from me, to visit and console us oftener. Farewell."

The matter alluded to regarded her practice of poverty, in which Agnes was as earnest and fervent as her saintly sister could desire. So deeply were both attached to this virtue, that it was hard to content their wishes. The Cardinal Ugolini drew up the first rule for the Poor Clares; but this did not satisfy their abbess, and on the return of Francis from his mission to the East, she complained to him of its mitigations. The holy patriarch represented her wishes to the Cardinal, who was his friend and the protector of his Order. The prelate was moved even to tears, that a poverty which seemed to the Papal wisdom almost too great for men, should be thus earnestly desired by weak and helpless women.

The result of their conference was a fresh Rule, which gave Clare all she desired. It was thus it declared what the poverty of her children must be:

"Let the religious appropriate nothing to themselves; let them serve God in this world as pilgrims and strangers in all poverty and humility, asking alms with confidence. Nor shall they be ashamed to do this, for our Lord Jesus Christ made Himself poor for us in this world. It is the sublimity of this most exalted poverty, O my sweet Sisters, which makes us heirs of the celestial kingdom."

In the early days of the Order, the Poor Clares subsisted entirely on alms; but as the fervor of the faithful or their interest in the new institute cooled, it was found necessary that some of its houses should be no longer quite dependent on charity—the vow of enclosure, which was taken later, and their withdrawal from the government of the friars, making it desirable that they should have a provision for their absolute necessities, which they could no longer beg or obtain through the questing brothers.

But though the poverty of the Poor Clares, in some

houses of the Order, differs in its literal exactions from that so ardently desired by their sainted foundress, its spirit is still the same, and is preserved and practiced in proportion to the fervor of the superiors and religious of its several convents. The essence and true spirit of poverty consists not so much in having nothing (for even the poorest must possess some trifle of their own) as in holding what we have dependently on the will of another, so that we can no longer call it ours.

A vow of poverty may be made, and sacredly kept, by those whose fare is neither poor nor common; but the child of St. Clare, who would carry out the spirit of her Order in its essential characteristic, must have no other than the poorest and commonest food, the plainest and coarsest clothing—a trial by no means light to those whose previous station has made luxuries almost necessary. When this spirit of poverty is carried into the minutest details of conventual life—when the merest trifle possessed by the religious may at any moment be given to another; when the time, the occupations, the whole exterior life, is in a spirit of poverty, no longer considered or used as their own; when the permission of a superior is necessary to receive or give in the smallest matter, and this permission not granted, as in other Orders, in a general way, but required in each instance—then surely the Poor Clare who is faithful to her observances, who treasures her poverty in memory of the homeless cradle and tomb of Jesus Christ, can scarcely be far from that perfection of utter self-renunciation which is the special end of her sublime vocation.

Nor was this practice of poverty without its trials, even in the lifetime of the saintly Clare. Once, when a severe famine raged in the Italian States, the procuratrix came to inform the abbess of St. Damian's that only one loaf remained for the use of the religious. She was desired to divide it into two portions; to send half to the friars, who dwelt in the extern house, and with the remainder to give the religious their next meal in the refectory. "But, mother," exclaimed the Sister, "this would require a miracle, since we need sufficient for fifty portions." Clare, who with all her gentleness knew well the merit of obedience, and how to enforce it when necessary, calmly replied, "My child, do simply what I command you." Sister Cecilia obeyed, and this morsel of bread was miraculously multiplied into an abundant supply for the whole community. At another time, when their little store of oil was exhausted, the Saint, having washed the vessel in which it had been kept, desired it to be placed in the turn, so that the friar who quested for them might beg a little for their use. But great was his astonishment, when he came, to find it filled with the purest oil, and as he exclaimed at the carelessness of the nuns in giving him this unnecessary trouble, the miracle was thus manifested.

The paternal heart of Gregory the Ninth, and the peculiar tenderness he bore towards the Franciscan Order, had made him unwilling to grant all that Clare desired regarding her practice of poverty. Once he visited her, and endeavored to dissuade her from her great strictness on this point, adding that if she feared an infringement of her vow he would absolve her from it. With the sweetness of manner and inflexible firmness of character which always marked the conduct of this Saint, she replied, "Holy Father, I shall be very joyful if your Holiness will please to absolve me from my sins, but I dare take no absolution from performing the counsels of God."

The sanctity of Clare, and the gift of wisdom and

clear judgment with which she was singularly endowed, led many to visit her and seek her counsel. Francis himself, as we shall see later, was desirous to be guided by her in important matters, and Popes and Cardinals did not disdain to ask the advice of this gentle maiden. A miracle of special interest is related as having occurred during one of these visits. The Holy Father, (whether Innocent or his predecessor, Gregory, is doubtful,*) visited the convent of the Poor Clares. After a spiritual conference, our Saint desired that some refreshment should be brought to him. Kneeling humbly, she begged that he would bless the bread which she placed before him. The Pope, either to try her humility or her obedience, desired that she would herself give the benediction. But the Saint exclaimed: "Holy Father, pardon; for I should deserve reprehension were I to give a benediction in your presence." Then the Pope replied, "In order that no presumption may be imputed to you, and that you may merit thereby, I command you in holy obedience to bless this bread, making thereon the sign of the Cross." The Saint obeyed in all simplicity, and her obedience and humility were rewarded by a miracle, for the sign of the Cross remained clearly impressed on each portion of the bread, part of which was eaten with devotion, and part preserved as a precious relic.

Nor was this the only instance in which Clare effected miracles by the holy sign. Many are the favors related as having been vouchsafed to her spiritual children, and even to strangers, who flocked from all parts of the country for the cure of their diseases. The gentle touch of her saintly hand, and the sign of the Cross made by it, never failed of effect. But all was done silently, and with as little observation as possible.

* See "St. Clare, St. Colette, and the Poor Clares," p. 2.

While much of her marvellous graces became known during her lifetime, far more remained to be told by her children, and others whom she had assisted, when the process for her canonization demanded a rigorous and searching inquiry into the truth of these marvels. Her life was a hidden one, as the life of a cloistered nun must ever be. The world obtains glimpses now and then of the deep things, the rich graces, the supernatural gifts, bestowed so abundantly on those privileged souls; but glimpses they are at best. The day of manifestation yet tarries; then their hidden mortifications, their heroic sanctity, will shine forth, and all flesh shall glorify their Father who is in heaven. Twice only does Clare appear before her age in a way likely to attract its observation, or to impress it manifestly with her sanctity. Of these two events we must now speak briefly.

The impious Frederic had already made Europe ring with the report of his cruel deeds, and insolent resistance to the Holy See. Not satisfied with the ravages committed by his own troops, he called the Moors to his assistance; and himself, nominally a Christian, dyed his soul yet deeper in crime by urging their barbarism to wreak itself especially on the Papal States. His most sacred oaths to Honorius, his coronation by the hands of the Pope in Rome, were alike forgotten; and when Gregory the Ninth reluctantly placed him under the Church's censure, his proud spirit sought to revenge itself by unheard-of outrages. The valley of Spoleto was already filled with these savage troops, and the Moors, thirsting for Christian blood, were encamped beneath the walls of Assisi. The terrified nuns ran trembling to the cell of their Mother, on whom years of ceaseless austerity and the heavy cares of her office had now done their work: she had long lain on a bed of painful sickness. But her holy zeal for the Divine honor thus insulted, and her maternal love, aroused the courage of her heart. In spite of the remonstrances of her children, who trembled for her precious life, she caused herself to be carried to the church, and there, prostrate before the Blessed Sacrament, she poured forth her prayer. In a few moments she arose, and with a supernatural strength proceeded to the battlements of the convent—but not alone. In her hand she held the Remonstrance, and bore in it the Sacramental Presence of her God. When the savage army beheld the light and glory which streamed forth from it, they ceased their wild shouts and yells of execration, and fell back trembling and dismayed.

It is related in the Chronicles of the Order, that while St Clare lay prostrate before the tabernacle, and implored our divine Lord to protect the spouses whom she had cherished for Him, a sweet clear voice, as of a young child was heard to utter these words, "I will ever protect you." Then gathering fresh courage, she continued: "My Lord, if such be Your holy will, protect also this city of Assisi, which maintains us for Your love." The voice again answered, "This city will suffer much, but My power will protect it." Then turning to the Sisters, she exclaimed, "My beloved ones, have faith in Christ, for I am assured that no harm shall happen to us."

Later again, Clare was the protectress of her native city. As if unsatisfied with the cruelties of the Moors, Frederic determined that further vengeance should be executed by one of his own generals. Vitalis d'Aversa, a man as irreligious and unscrupulous as himself, was the instrument chosen for this purpose. He laid siege to Assisi, and determined to complete the work which the Saracen army had begun. But the prayers of Saints were still left to the devoted city. Clare assembled her religious. "My sisters," she exclaimed, "the inhabitants of this city provide daily for our necessities. It would indeed be impiety if we did not aid them to the utmost of our power in this extremity." Then, with ashes on their heads, the troop of consecrated virgins prostrated themselves before God, and asked His mercy for their fellow-citizens. Their prayer was heard. That night the Assisians attacked their besiegers, and the army of Vitalis was completely routed. Shortly after, he perished miserably. Again the weak had conquered the strong, and the spiritual arms of fasting and prayer had inflicted death-wounds on the pride of earthly greatness. The cloistered nun had vanquished the crested warrior; and if the results of the prayers of religious persons are not always so manifest, should we therefore doubt their value and efficacy? How much is hidden which will one day be revealed!—how much despised which will one day be exalted! Men ask for visible signs of the utility of a cloistered life—for some tangible result of hours of prayer and contemplation. Incidents, such as that which we have just recorded, are not often manifested to the world, but it were scarcely wise to conclude that they are therefore less frequent.

But we must hasten from the brief sketch of the child, to continue the history of the father. The long life of prayer was nearly ended, and increasing favors presaged the dawn of eternal light. Once, as Clare lay on her sick bed on the Feast of the Nativity, which, as a true disciple of Francis, she especially loved, she wept that she could not join in the matins of her Sisters, or gather them around the crib of the Infant Jesus. "Ah, my Lord," she exclaimed, "look upon my loneliness." Scarcely had she uttered the words ere her Spouse had answered the desire of her heart; and she heard the chanting of the friars and the notes of their deep-toned organ, even as if she had been assisting at the midnight office at St. Mary of the Angels. Nor did her consolation end here. She was given to see in a vision the stable of Bethlehem, and to behold the Infant Jesus wrapped in swathing-bands, and lying on His bed of straw. Once, also, she was favored with a long ecstacy while meditating on the Passion of our Lord. She had a special devotion to the mystery of His agony in the garden, and on Maunday-Thursday, on this occasion, she seemed wholly absorbed in thought of His bitter sufferings, and retired to her cell to hide her deep emotion. Seated on the side of her straw pallet, she still continued her prayer, but soon became unconscious of all around. This rapture lasted till the evening of Holy Saturday, when one of the religious who was most familiar with her, endeavored to recall her to consciousness by reminding her of the command of Francis, that she should never pass a day without taking some nourishment. But when the Saint became aware how long her ecstacy had lasted, she charged the Sister never to speak of it, and exclaimed, "Blessed be God, my child, for this sleep which I have so long desired, and which His mercy hath granted to me."

The hours of Sext and None were especially dear to her. At the one, she loved to meditate on the nailing to the Cross; at the other, on the death of her beloved Spouse. Personal and severe assaults were often waged against her by the evil spirit to interrupt her devotions, still she remained unmoved. Nor was her devotion towards the most Holy Sacrament less striking than the other supernatural features of her life. During her last seventeen days on earth it was her only nourishment, and her devotion in approaching it during the whole of her earthly pilgrimage moved the Sisters even to tears. When no longer able to leave her bed, she would be propped up in it, and employ every moment in spinning thread. From this were made corporals of the purest white for the neighboring churches, many of which had been pillaged by the armies of Frederic.

In 1251, Raynald, Cardinal Bishop of Ostia, who was now Protector of the Order, came to visit Clare. Finding that the Saint was near her end, he administered to her the holy Viaticum, and then returned to inform the Pope, who was at Perugia. The Holy Father, for her special consolation, wrote a letter with his own hand, confirming to her Order its precious heritage of poverty, which he said was the first privilege that had ever before been asked of the Holy See. It concluded with these remarkable words: "May those who love you and your Order, and above all the religious of St. Damian's, possess the holy peace of God, and at the day of judgment receive the recompense of eternal beatitude." As soon as Innocent was told that the Saint whom he so much revered was dying, he hastened to Assisi. Entering her poor cell with several Cardinals and some of the Friars Minor, he gave her his hand to kiss. But she entreated permission to kiss his foot, and a stool was placed so that it might be within her reach as she lay on her poor bed. Then she asked for a plenary indulgence, which was willingly given, though the Pope could not help exclaiming, "Would to God, my daughter, that I needed this pardon as little." When all had retired, Clare turned to the Sisters around her, and said, "Thank God, my children, for the great blessings He has bestowed on me this day. Heaven and earth would not suffice to acknowledge them. I have received my Lord and my God, and I have seen His vicar." A little while after, she sent for a relaxed nun, for, alas! even in the life-time of Clare there were some less fervent and less saintly than their Sisters; some whom sloth, worldliness, or an unmortified passion, held in chains aloof from a perfect union with their Spouse. The very tenderness of the Saint, and her ardent love for her children, made her at times seem almost severe in enforcing the observance of all the duties of their holy state. Long and anxiously, therefore, did she speak to this poor erring child; with what result we are not told, but the words of such a Mother could scarcely fail of their effect.

Her children, lost in desolation, crowded round her dying bed. Her tender, gentle heart yearned over them; she knew all they must suffer. With a thoughtful, self-forgetting love she gave them her last benediction, the very words of which are still treasured in the rule of their Order; for not only her own immediate disciples were thus enriched, but all, "present and to come," who should follow her rule. Thrice happy children of St. Clare! Ye have not seen her form, not heard her gentle voice, but her rich blessing is ever around you; her motherly care, by her own especial promise, broods over you. More tenderly does she love you now, as she drinks in love from its very Fountain than when on earth she yearned, and prayed, and labored, to bring down upon you every grace of your holy state.

Agnes had been summoned from her convent at Florence to attend the death-bed of her sister. Her affections were as fresh and warm as when they had parted, thirty years before; and she bent over her sister's pallet, imploring her, with tears, not to leave her. But

Clare consoled her, saying, "My tenderly-loved sister, do not grieve; I do assure you that our Lord will soon come for you, and that before your death you shall receive from Him a wonderful grace." Her words were verified. Before three months had passed away, the bodies of the saintly sisters were laid together in the same spot on earth, and their souls forever united in Paradise.

Brother Leo, and Brothers Juniper and Reginald, watched by the dying Saint. The "Little Sheep of God" could not contain his tears, and strove to console himself by kissing the hard pallet on which she lay. Brother Juniper, at her desire, spoke to her of heavenly things, and inflamed with his burning words the hearts of all who heard him. It was the evening of the 10th of August, and Mary would have her beloved child home to sing her Assumption in heaven. Suddenly, the Saint turned towards Agnes, and exclaimed, "My child, do you not see the King of Glory?" Even as she spoke, several of the religious beheld a most glorious procession entering into that lowly cell. There were virgins clad in white, each wearing a golden crown; but there was one more radiantly beautiful than all the rest. She bore on her head a queenly crown, adorned with pearls and jewels of the rarest beauty. From her countenance shone forth a light so dazzlingly bright that the darkness of night was turned into a radiance above that of the summer's noon. The Queen of Virgins, at whose altar Clare had been espoused to Jesus, was come to take her to the eternal nuptials.

Bending over the straw pallet, she tenderly embraced her dying child, and threw a royal mantle over her habit of coarse serge. Before the morning dawned, Clare had passed into unending glory.

The obsequies of the Saint resembled a triumphal procession. The nobles of the surrounding countries and the inhabitants of Assisi vied with each other in doing honor to the mortal remains of her who, a few years before, had spurned all the advantages of rank and beauty, and fled almost alone from her father's mansion. The Pope, who also attended with his court, was with difficulty persuaded not to pronounce her Saint before her burial. Cardinal Raynald ventured to interpose, when the Holy Father wished to have the office of canonized virgins chaunted instead of a requiem. On his representation that it would be more for her honor to allow the usual process of canonization to be carried through, the Pontiff acquiesced, though not without reluctance. A year later this Cardinal, who had meanwhile succeeded Innocent on the Papal throne, confirmed her sanctity by the Church's solemn approval. A splendid church was erected at St. George's in 1260. There her relics were enshrined, and thither her children followed her from their former home at St. Damian's.

The Order extended rapidly, even during the life of its first abbess. Singularly enough, it would seem as though the rich and noble were especially attracted to its poverty. Isabella of France, sister of St. Louis, eagerly sought to extend it within her brother's dominions, and to this end founded the celebrated monastery of Longchamps. Constant illness prevented her from embracing its mode of life, though in that house the great austerities of the Order were mitigated. She had, however, the happiness of dying in the habit of the Poor Clares. Saint Elizabeth of Hungary, with a goodly number of crowned heads and noble princesses belong rather to the third Order, which shall be noticed later. But one royal lady, Agnes of Bohemia, claims a word in passing. She was the foundress of the monastery of Prague, where she lived, and died in the odor of sanctity. She had refused the hand of Frederic the Second, and with difficulty appeased her father's indignation and the tyrant's wrath. But when told of her fixed determination against his suit, he exclaimed, "Had she rejected me for any other man, I would be revenged; but since she chooses God for her spouse, I cannot complain." St. Clare frequently corresponded with this princess, and sent her many little tokens of her affection and esteem.

Then there was the Blessed Salome, a Polish princess of remarkable beauty. She was espoused in childhood to Coloman, King of Galatia, a prince worthy of his bride. Together they made a vow of perpetual chastity. And when her royal husband died, fighting bravely for his faith and country against the Tartars (1225), his virgin widow consecrated herself to God in the convent of Poor Clares, which she had founded at Zavichost, having first distributed all her worldly goods to the poor and to monasteries. She had long been favored with great supernatural graces. In her dying hours the songs of angels were heard in her cell, and she beheld the Mother of God, who came to take her to her Beloved. Even as her soul passed away, the abbess and the Sisters, who had surrounded her bed, saw it ascend to heaven in the form of a brilliant star.

The story of the Poor Clares martyred by the Moors at Ptolemais, must not be omitted. Dreading, more than death or any tortures, the least tarnish on their vow of chastity, their noble abbess, Eusebia, assembled her children around her, and calmly proposed to them that each should follow her example of self-disfigurement. As she spoke, she drew a sharp knife from the folds of her mantle, and inflicted several deep gashes on her own face. Each of her religious followed their heroic Mother; each for herself frightfully mutilated her features; and when, a few moments after, the Moorish soldiery burst their way into the convent, they found an assemblage of ghastly bleeding nuns, whom they immediately despatched by the sword. Truly did these wash their robes, and make them white in the Blood of the Lamb, that they might be without fault before the Throne of God.

In the same century (1232) lived Blessed Cunegonde, princess of Hungary. Like Salome, she and her husband consented in a mutual vow of chastity. The daughter of holy parents, the niece of a saint (Elizabeth of Hungary), she proved herself not unworthy of her descent. After her husband's death, she entered the monastery of Poor Clares at Sandeck, which she had founded. Here, for thirteen years, she continued the austerities she had so long practiced in the world, while the miracles which tracked her heavenward path gave every day fresh proofs of her favor with God. As she lay dying, angelic voices were heard to sing, "*Regnum mundi et omnem ornatum sœculi contempsi propter amorem Domini mei Jesu Christi.*" After her death, the miracles worked through her intercession were so numerous that a mere list of them would carry us too far. Her sister Helena, also beatified by the Holy See, followed her example. Boleslas the Pious, her kingly consort, entered eagerly into all her views, and did his utmost for the extension of the Seraphic Order in his kingdom. He died in 1279. Two of their daughters had formed alliances suitable to their rank; the third, named Anne, retired to the monastery of Sandeck, where she lived a most holy life. Helena, died in the monastery of Gnesne, which her husband had founded. She was especially devoted to the passion of our Divine Lord, and favored with many revelations regarding it. In one of these the day and hour of her death was announced to her. Would there were space in this little volume to speak of even a few of the Poor Clares, who, during this age, edified the Church by their heavenly lives! We cannot entirely pass over the Blessed Margaret, a lady of the noble family of Colonna, yet more distinguished for her sanctity than for her noble birth. After she had received the last sacraments, she still continued kneeling. Then the heavens were opened to her expiring gaze, and as she sang "*In manus tuas, Domine, commendo spiritum meum,*" her Spouse appeared and took her to continue, with the angels, her song of triumph.

The Blessed Eustochia da Calafato, after a life of extreme mental and bodily suffering, of special devotion to Mary, and to Jesus in the most Holy Sacrament, died, exclaiming, *Deus, Deus meus, ad te de luce vigilo;* and even as she spoke her face shone with a splendor of heavenly glory. The light of an earthly morning dawned at this moment for her Sisters; but she was gone to behold for ever the light of unclouded day.

"Ava mater humilis
Ancilla crucifixi,
Clara virgo nobilis
Discipula Francisci,
Ad cœlestem gloriam
Fac nos proficisci. Amen."

SAINT CLARE'S BENEDICTION TO HER CHILDREN PRESENT AND TO COME.

In the name of the Father, and of the Son, and of the Holy Ghost. Amen.

My dearly beloved Sisters, may our Lord give you His holy benediction, and look on you with the eye of His mercy, and give you His peace; and to all who after you shall enter and persevere in this convent or any other of the Order, I, Clare, servant of Jesus Christ, and little plant of our holy father St. Francis, and your unworthy Sister and Mother, do beseech our Lord Jesus Christ, that by the intercession of His most holy Mother, of the holy Archangel St. Michael, and all the heavenly host, of our holy father St. Francis, and of all the Saints, that He will give you His benediction, and confirm in heaven what in His name I give you on earth. May He multiply in you all holy graces, and bring you to the glory of the saints in the heavenly kingdom; and I give you my blessing during my life, and after my death, in all that I am able, and more than I am able, with all the blessings wherewith the Father of Mercies doth or shall bless His spiritual children in heaven or on earth, and all the blessings with which a spiritual mother doth bless her children. Amen.

CHAPTER IX.

Francis consults St. Clare and Brother Sylvester regarding his vocation.—Both receive the same answer from God.—He goes forth to preach.—Restores sight to a blind girl at Bevagna.—Goes to Rome to ask permission to evangelize the East.—Obliged to return to St. Mary of the Angels.—A miracle occurs on his homeward voyage.—The vocation of Brother Pacificus, the "prince of Poets."—The illness of the Saint.—His public penance.—A rich postulant.—How Francis tries the vocation of his novices.—Brother Rufinus sees the throne prepared for him amid the highest Seraphim.—He tests his holy father's humility.—His vision confirmed by a revelation made to the Blessed M. M. Alacoque.

Immediately after the establishment of the second Order, St. Francis began to have some misgivings as to his own vocation. From his great attraction to prayer, he earnestly desired a contemplative life; but love and zeal for souls made him hesitate, lest even in what seemed holiest he should be doing his own will, not that of his Divine Master. Ever distrustful of himself, and of his own lights and graces, he sought guidance and instruction from others.

The holy priest Sylvester lived now in the mountains of Assisi, wholly engaged in prayer. The

Saint wished to have his decision, and that of the young abbess of St. Damian's. He therefore sent Brothers Masseo and Philip to both his spiritual children, charging them to pray for him, that he might know the will of God through them. He added an injunction to St. Clare, to ask the prayers of that one among her religious whom she considered the simplest and most pure-hearted. The friars soon returned from their mission. Francis received them with great respect and affection; then, kneeling with his arms crossed, and his head uncovered, he said, "Tell me now what my Lord Jesus commands me to do." "My very dear father, and Brother," replied Masseo, "both Sylvester and Clare have received the same answer from our Lord Jesus Christ: 'Go and preach, for He has not called you for your own salvation alone, but for the salvation of others, and for them He will put His word into your mouth.'" As if inflamed by the Divine Spirit, Francis arose, and exclaiming, "Let us then go forth in the name of the Lord," he went with burning zeal to execute the heavenly commission. The holy will of God was now made plain for himself and his Order; however simple and unlearned the Friar Minor might be, he had an assurance that the Spirit of God would give him power of speech. Miracles confirmed the preaching of the Saint, as he journeyed on to Rome. At Bevagna he restored a blind girl to sight, and converted many who asked a share in his poverty.

A strong desire to visit the East had long burned in the heart of Francis. He yearned for the martyr's crown, which he there hoped to find, and longed also to water with his tears the earthly home of Jesus of Nazareth. The noble spirit of the reigning pontiff, Innocent the Third, sympathized with such desires, and he readily gave his permission and blessing to the enterprise. Ere his departure the Saint had received two new disciples—one a Roman, named Zacharias, and Brother William the Englishman, who filled the place of the unhappy John of Capella. Now also Francis made the acquaintance of the noble lady, Jacoba de Settesoli, the only woman except St. Clare whom he ever admitted to his friendship. Touched to the heart by his preaching, she sought and obtained an interview with the Saint; and then committing to her sons the care of her large estates, employed herself only in prayer, in penance, and in aiding the establishment of the Order. The Benedictines were again the friends of the Friars Minor. From them the Lady Jacoba obtained the hospital of St. Blasius; and there was established the first house of the Order in Rome.

On his return to Assisi, Francis assembled the brethren at St. Mary of the Angels, and appointing Peter of Catania superior in his room, he set out with one companion for the Levant. At Ascoli crowds thronged round him to hear his preaching; fifteen disciples offered themselves, and were sent to different houses of the Order. Having reached the sea coast, he embarked in a vessel bound for Syria, but stress of weather soon compelled them to anchor off Sclavonia. Seeing that his design was to be frustrated for a time, Francis endeavored to obtain passage on a ship bound for Ancona, but as he had no money the sailors refused to take him on board. However, he and his companions managed to conceal themselves in the vessel, and they were not discovered until it had put out some way to sea. Provisions were already provided for them by a miracle. As the ship was about to weigh anchor, a stranger came on board and gave a supply of food to one of the passengers, desiring him to keep it for two religious who were secreted in the vessel. This was miraculously multipled, and saved both crew and passengers from starvation, as contrary winds detained them so long on their voyage, that but for these provisions all must have perished. Seeing the power which the Saint possessed with God, the sailors returned thanks that they had on board the poor man to whom they had so roughly refused a passsge.

As Francis journeyed homewards, he still obeyed the divine command of preaching. His fame had now extended far and wide. A distinguished poet at the court of the German Emperor had travelled a long distance to hear the lowly friar. Passing through the little town of San Severino, he entered the church of a monastery. Francis was there, and was at that moment preaching on the mystery of the Cross. The poet-courtier listened to him for some time, without knowing that it was the Saint of whom he was in search. But as the title of fervid eloquence rose to yet greater sublimity, and touched his heart, he looked up earnestly at the preacher. Then he beheld two shining swords in the form of a cross behind him, and at the same time he received a divine intimation of his vocation. At the conclusion of the sermon he presented himself to Francis, and was received with joy. Frederic, his former master, had crowned him "Prince of poets;" the Saint now gave him the name of Brother Pacificus, predicting the calm and holy life he would hereafter lead. St. Bonaventura speaks of him with great affection. He says that he was permitted to see a cross, in the form of the Greek letter *Tav*, (T) on the forehead of Francis, which flashed in many colors, reflecting a heavenly brilliancy on his face. Brother Pacificus became eventually the first provincial minister of Tuscany. Francis would often make him use his poetical and musical talents for his recreation. He admired also the promptness with which the courtly poet had become the mortified religious, for Pacificus seemed rather calmly to forget what had been, than with violent effort to force himself to his new mode of life.

The Saint now visited Tuscany, where he had already founded several convents. At Florence, the Ubaldini family gave him a monastery which had been built for religious of the Order of St. Basil. Here he placed several friars, and then, towards the end of the year, returned to St. Mary of the Angels. He was there attacked with quartan ague, which reduced him to extreme weakness. The good Bishop of Assisi came to visit him, and obliged him to return to his palace, where he tended him with the most anxious care. The brethren here visited him from time to time, and brought to him the new postulants who thronged in crowds for admission to his Order. But the Saint could not bear the relaxation from his austerities to which the prelate obliged him. He could not avoid knowing that he was esteemed a Saint, and his humility became alarmed while it also exaggerated the little indulgences he had unwillingly accepted. As soon as he had in some degree recovered, he went with a number of his disciples to the principal square of Assisi. A crowd soon gathered, and Francis led them to the cathedral. Here he took off his habit, and made one of the friars tie a cord round his neck. Then he commanded them to drag him to the place where criminals were executed. When this strange procession had arrived at the spot, he cried aloud, "Let no one honor me as if I were a spiritual man; for I am carnal, sensual, and greedy; one who ought to be despised by all." Indeed, humility, or the ardent desire to possess this virtue, was what the Saint especially required from his disciples. Nor could they complain of his exactions in this matter, since he was himself the first to give the example of it.

Henry Satalis, Archbishop of Milan, had established the Order there. One of the first postulants was a young man of wealth and talent. Being told that he must distribute all his goods to the poor, if he desired to become a Friar Minor, he immediately did so, only reserving what was necessary for his journey to Assisi. Here he was obliged to present himself to Francis in person, as the permission to receive novices was not then extended to others. He arrived in due time, surrounded by a considerable retinue, and was introduced to the Saint as a young man of distinction and talent. Francis smiled, and replied that he could hardly think one who came surrounded by such pomp would prove a fit disciple for a life of poverty. He then assembled the brethren to consult them on the subject. The poor young postulant burst into tears, but the holy patriarch who knew his vocation was sincere, and only wished to test it, continued: "My brethren, if he will serve in the kitchen, shall we accept him?" all consented readily and the Saint tenderly pressed to his heart the young disciple, who was overjoyed to be received on any conditions. He was then sent to act as cook at the hospital of St. Blasius at Rome; but his sanctity became so conspicuous that ere long Francis made him superior of the friars in that house.

Such were the vocations of the days of St. Francis and St. Clare, when no entreaties or submissions were considered too great to obtain the blessedness of a share in their poverty and sufferings. Superiors then could mould to heroic sanctity the willing subjects who present themselves, who, seeking only their own perfection, required neither persuasion nor compliances to sustain them through their noviciate. Indeed he who presented himself at St. Mary of the Angels, with a weak will or a half-formed resolution, soon learned his mistake; yet when there was a real vocation, whatever exterior disqualification might exist, or however unlikely the subject at first appeared, Francis was not the person to repel or discourage. His methods of testing the vocation of his postulants were sometimes not a little amusing. One day he took several to the garden of the monastery, and with a grave countenance desired they would assist him in planting cabbages. He began the work himself and placed them in the holes he had prepared, with the roots upwards and the leaves in the ground. One of his assistants followed his example without any comment, the other assured him that he was planting them the wrong way. "Ah, Brother," replied Francis, "I perceive you are very wise and very learned, and therefore you are unfit for our Order." And so he dismissed him.

The Saint, however, was by no means one to despise the gifts of learning or wisdom. He was desirous that those who entered his Order, possessed of any talent, should continue to use it for the good of religion. But he knew also that one degree of humility was preferable to the greatest wisdom ever bestowed on human intellect. Fallen spirits may boast of knowledge, but only Saints possess the treasure of a meek and humble heart.

It was once revealed to Brother Rufinus how the humility of Francis would be rewarded. Being wrapt in prayer, he beheld the choir of Seraphim resplendent with light and beauty.* Amid their thrones was one

* This revelation was remarkably confirmed by another made to the B. Mary Margaret Alocoque. In her Life, vol. ii., p. 15, it is said that

vacant throne more radiant than any other, and adorned with the most precious jewels. In holy simplicity he asked for whom this glorious throne was reserved. Immediately he heard these words, "This seat was once occupied by one of the highest Seraphim; but he is cast into hell, and it is now reserved for the humble Francis." After this vision Brother Rufinus was extremely anxious to know wherein consisted the great humility of the Saint. He therefore addressed him thus: "My beloved Father, I pray you to tell me exactly what you think of yourself, and to what degree of sanctity you suppose yourself to have attained." The Saint replied, "Of a truth, I believe myself the greatest sinner in the world; and I think no one serves God so little." But Rufinus answered, "I do not see how you can say this in truth, since you must know that there are many who have committed grievous crimes of which you are entirely innocent." St. Francis answered, "If God had favored any other person with the same graces which He has given me, I am certain that, however vile and wicked they may now be, they would have loved and served Him far better than I do, and would more gratefully acknowledge His gifts; and were Almighty God to leave me to myself even for a moment, I should fall into greater sins than have ever been committed. On this account, then, I believe and acknowledge myself to be the greatest sinner who has ever existed."

Francis was shown to her on his festival, "shining with an inexplicable light, and, as it seemed, placed in more eminent glory than the other saints." God made known to her that this favor was granted to him on account of his conformity with the poverty and sufferings of our Divine Lord. She was further told that he had a special power with the Sacred Heart to obtain graces from it, and that he constantly offered himself to appease the justice of God and to obtain mercy for sinners. He was given to her as her special patron.

CHAPTER X.

His sickness returns.—His letters to the faithful.—His canticle of the Sun.—It causes a reconciliation between the Bishop of Assisi and the governor.—Paraphrase on the Lord's Prayer.—His letter to the Priests of his Order.—Thanksgiving on the confirmation of his Rule. The Gloria Patri.

THE recovery of the Saint from his sicknes was but partial. In the spring of the next year (1213) he was again attacked by it, and obliged to discontinue his evangelical labors. But his was a zeal which could not rest; when he could no longer speak he was fain to write—to move, if possible, the hearts of the faithful to more fervor, and lead sinners to repentance.

The subjoined letter, which he wrote at this time is a touching proof of his fervent charity. It is addressed "to all Christians, whether religious or secular, men or women, throughout the world." "Oh! how happy," writes the Saint, "are they who love God and practice what Jesus Christ has taught in the holy Gospel! Thou shalt love the Lord thy God with thy whole heart, and with thy whole soul; and thy neighbor as thyself. Let us then love and adore God with great purity of heart and mind, for this is what he expects from us above all things, saying that the true adorers should adore Him in spirit and in truth, and that He will receive no other adoration. I salute you in Jesus Christ."

This letter was widely spread and eagerly copied. The affection with which it was received led him to write a longer one. It is addressed thus: "To all Christian priests, religious and laics, as well women as men in the whole earth—Brother Francis, their most humble servant, respectfully presents his services, and wishes them the true peace which comes from heaven, and perfect charity in our Lord."

As it is far too long for insertion here, we can but give a summary of its contents. Indeed, it is but a sermon in which he writes what he had so often preached. Declaring first the Christian doctrine, and urging meditation on the passion and death of Christ, he then exhorts to the praise of God and keeping the commandments. He desires all to be constant in prayer, in fasting, and alms-deeds; to frequent churches, and to have the deepest reverence for all priests. He speaks of the love of God and of our neighbor; and then having most touchingly described the death-bed and feelings of a man who has lived only for this world, he concludes thus: "I, Brother Francis, the lowest of your servants, desiring to kiss your feet, beseech you by the charity of God that you will receive with humility and charity these words and all others which may come to you from our Lord Jesus Christ. And let all those who receive and understand them endeavor to make them known to others. If they persevere in these things to the end, may they be blessed by the Father and the Son and the Holy Spirit. Amen."

We need scarcely say that the prayer of Francis was continual. There was also a joyousness and trustfulness about it singularly touching. When we consider the constant bodily sufferings which he endured almost from the moment of his conversion, and their wonderful and mysterious increase at the close of his life, we may almost marvel whence this peculiar gladness came. His tears and bitter grief that his Beloved was not the Beloved of all, that Jesus should have suffered so much and be loved so little, might have given a shade of holy sadness to almost any other Saint. Perhaps his great spirit of thanksgiving brought him this grace of joy.

So averse was he to anything like melancholy or depression, that he specially and continually exhorted his disciples to serve God with cheerfulness. With all the austerity of their lives, and their sympathy, so far beyond our conception, with the sufferings of Jesus, still they were the brightest and the gladdest of men. So true it is, that the sorrow which is for God, and in God, has within its dark mantle a hidden treasure of celestial comfort, given with especial abundance to those who seek no earthly consolation. Yet towards the close of his mortal life, his eyes were almost blinded with constant weeping. The physician who attended him urged him to restrain his tears. "Ah, brother physician," replied the Saint, "we must not for the sake of our corporal sight, which we have in common with flies, seek to lessen our devotion in prayer, or that which may increase the fervor of our spirit."

In pronouncing the holy name of Jesus, he seemed to have ever a sensible refreshment and sweetness. Dear was that name indeed to him. His desire that the deepest reverence should be shown to holy things, was also very great. He even would charge his disciples to pick up any shred of paper they saw on the ground, lest it should contain some holy name, or anything regarding religion. And his "canticle of the sun" was an effusion of the same joyous reverential spirit. He divided it into eight stanzas, or little songs, to correspond with the eight beatitudes:

"Most high Omnipotent and gracious Lord! To Thee be praise, glory, honor, and all benediction. To Thee may all be referred. No man is worthy to name Thee.

"Praise be to Thee, O Lord! for all Thy creatures, and especially for our brother the sun, who illuminates the day, and by his beauty and splendor shadows forth unto us Thine.

"Be Thou likewise praised, O my Lord! by our sisters the

moon and stars, which Thou hast created in the heavens, beautiful, and radiating light.

"Be Thou praised, O my Lord! by our brothers the winds, the soft airs, the clouds, and by all the seasons.

"Be thou praised, O my Lord! by our sister, the water, which is precious and pure, most useful and lowly.

"Be Thou praised, O my Lord! by our brother, the fire, which gives us light in the darkness, and is beautiful, subtle, strong, and invincible.

"Be Thou praised, O my Lord! for our mother, the earth, which nourishes and upholds us, and brings forth many fruits, and many variegated flowers and herbs."

When Francis had composed this canticle, he sent for Brother Pacificus, who, it may be remembered, had chosen to be poet and musician to a saint rather than to an emperor. When the friar had come he desired him to set the words to music, and to teach it to some of the brethren, that it might be sung after their sermons. From this time it gave the Saint especial pleasure to hear it sung; and he would tell the brethren that they were the musicians of God, and must sing for the people, from whom they should ask no other payment than that they repent of their sins. "For," he would also say, "what are the servants of God but His representatives, to awaken true and spiritual joy in human hearts; and, above all, we Friars Minor, who are given to the world for its salvation?" A glorious mission, truly; and still, as was the whole life of Francis, resembling His who came to comfort the weary and the sorrowful. Happy religious! who, if you obey your seraphic father, reflect the very joy of God to the human race. Well might the unknown herald of the appearance of this glorious Saint cry ever till his mission began, "*Pax et bonum, Pax et bonum.*"

Once, while St. Francis lay ill at St. Mary of the Angels, he was told that a serious dissension had arisen between the Bishop of Assisi and the governor of the town. The bishop had excommunicated the governor, who, in his turn, forbade the townspeople to have any dealings with the bishop. The Chronicles of the Order do not mention the cause of this disagreement, or with whom the blame rested. Many had endeavored to make peace, but to no purpose. The Saint, in consequence of his illness, was unable to visit them in person. He therefore called several of the brethren, and desired them to go to the governor, and say that Brother Francis begged him to go, with as many of his retinue as he could take with him, to the bishop's palace. Other friars were sent to the bishop, who assembled a number of his clergy in a large apartment, to receive the governor. When all were assembled, two religious began to sing the Canticle of the Sun, first declaring that they had been sent by Brother Francis, who, in consequence of his infirmities, could not come himself. He had, however, added this verse to it:

"Let my Lord be praised by those who for His love pardon each other, and bear troubles and afflictions in patience. Blessed are they who live in peace, for the Most High shall crown them in heaven."

But a few words of the canticle were sung, when the governor began to shed tears of contrition and devotion. At its close, he turned to the people, and protested his desire to be reconciled to the bishop, whom, as his superior, he ought to have obeyed. Then, turning to the prelate, he added, "My Lord, behold me ready, for the love of God and His servant the holy Father Francis, to do whatever you shall enjoin me." The bishop, no less affected, asked his pardon for any wrong he might have done; and so, to the joy of all, the reconciliation was effected.

One more verse was added to this canticle by the Saint. When told that he was dying, his joy gave itself vent in those words: "Blessed be my Lord for our sister death, whom none living can escape. Alas! for such as die in mortal sin! Blessed are they who in the hour of death are found living in conformity to Thy will; for on them the second death shall have no power. Let all creatures bless the Lord my God, and ever serve Him with all humility."

The Saint's short paraphrase of the Lord's Prayer may prove not less interesting:

"Our Father, most blessed, and most holy; our Creator, our Redeemer, our Consoler; who art in heaven, in Thy angels and Thy saints, enlightening them according to Thy will. For Thou, O Lord! art as a light, inflaming them with divine love; for Thou, O Lord! dost abide in them by love, and dost fill them with Thy beatitude; for Thou, O Lord! art the highest and only Good, from whom all good things proceed, without whom nothing is good.

"Hallowed be Thy name—enlighten us with Thy wisdom, that we may know the immensity of Thy goodness, the greatness of Thy promises, the sublimity of Thy majesty, and the depth of Thy judgments.

"Thy kingdom come—so reign in us by Thy grace, that we may reign with Thee in Thy kingdom; where Thou art manifested openly, where Thy presence gives perfect joy, and Thou art the everlasting fruition.

"Thy will be done on earth as in heaven—that we may love Thee with our whole hearts, think ever of Thee, seek Thee with all our powers; that with our whole minds we may seek to do all for Thy glory, and seek Thy honor in all things; employing for Thee, and for none other, all the powers of our bodies, souls, and spirits; loving our neighbor as ourselves, and ever striving to draw all men to Thy holy love; rejoicing in the good of others as if it were our own; compassionating their miseries, and doing no evil to any one.

"Give us this day our daily bread—that is, thy beloved Son

our Lord Jesus Christ, that we may tenderly commemorate His love, and all He has done, and said, and suffered for us.

"And forgive us our trespasses—by the multitude of Thy mercies, and the passion and merits of Thy beloved Son our Lord Jesus Christ, and by the merits and intercession of the Blessed Virgin Mary and all Thy Saints.

"As we forgive those who trespass against us—and what we lack of grace to fulfil this command, do Thou, O Lord! supply; and may we show our love to Thee by the fervor of our prayers for our enemies, never returning evil for evil, and seeking the welfare of all in Thee.

"And lead us not into temptation—hidden or manifest, unexpected or importunate.

"But deliver us from evil—past, present or future."

In his prayer for poverty, the Saint pours out his whole soul to obtain the grace which was dearer to him than the wealth of earth's richest monarchs. "O Lord Jesu," he cries, "show me the ways of Thy most beloved poverty." Then he pleads the poverty of Jesus most poor, "*pauperrime Jesu*," as he loved to call his Lord; and exclaims, "Oh! who would not love the Lady Poverty above all besides?" Then, with a burning prayer that he and his may never have any possession on this earth, the Saint concludes this outpouring of sublime charity.

Poverty and humility, Bethlehem and Calvary, these were his thoughts, these the objects of his tenderest love. In another place he exclaims, "Happy is he who is as humble before his inferiors as when in the presence of his superiors. Happy is he who never esteems himself more when he is overwhelmed with praises, than when he appears vile and contemptible. Happy is he who receives a reproof with gentleness, who acknowledges his fault humbly, and does penance for it; who is lowly enough to receive a reprimand without excusing himself, and to bear the disgrace of faults of which he has not been guilty. Happy is he who has never desired the dignity to which he has attained, and wishes always to be beneath the feet of all."

One prayer, which the Saint especially taught his disciples, is still said by the religious of his Order each morning as they enter the choir. "We praise Thee, O Christ, and we bless Thee, and we worship Thee here, and in all Thy churches, because by Thy holy Cross Thou hast redeemed the world."

Of his letters, two are addressed to priests, and speak principally of the reverence due to the Most Holy Sacrament. One is addressed to the friars of his own Order who were priests, the other to secular priests. We give an extract to show the spirit with which he strove to animate those who were dedicated to the ministry of the altar. "My brethren," he writes, "if the Blessed Virgin Mary is worthy of so much honor for having carried our Divine Lord in her womb; if the blessed John Baptist trembled, and dared not to touch the head of Jesus Christ; if the sepulchre in which he lay for a time is to be singularly venerated—in what degree ought he to be holy, just, and worthy, who receives Him who is the desire of angels, who administers to others the Most High and Holy God! Behold how great is your dignity, O my brothers, who are priests! and 'be ye holy even as He is holy.' You have been more honored than other men; therefore should you in this mystery honor God more than others. O marvellous greatness; O stupendous condescension; O sublime humility; that the Son of God, yea, God Himself, should so humble Himself as for our salvation to conceal Himself under the appearance of bread."

In the thanksgiving which Francis composed after the confirmation of his Rule, his spirit of joyous thankfulness pours itself out without measure. It begins thus: "Father most high and holy, most sovereign, and most mighty, just Lord and King of heaven and earth we thank Thee for the infinite love wherewith Thou lovest Thyself: and because by Thy will, and with Thy only Son and the Holy Ghost, Thou hast created all things, and hast formed us to Thine own image, placing us in Paradise, whence by our fault we have fallen." Then he returns thanks at some length for the redemption of mankind, and invokes the Blessed Virgin and all the holy angels, saints, prophets, and apostles, to join with him in rendering praise and thanks to God.

The Saint was often wrapt in ecstacy while reciting the divine office, and finished with the angels what he had begun with men. Once, as he and Brother Leo were saying vespers together, his spiritual joy became so great, that at the *Magnificat* between each verse he broke out into a *Gloria Patri.* Perhaps, since the first utterance of that canticle of the Mother of God, it was never recited with more fervent, jubilant love. To one who applied to him for advice under great spiritual desolation and interior trials, he advised the saying of a *Gloria Patri* daily. It proved effectual. What was refused to prayer was granted to praise; the spirit of darkness fled before the spirit of joy and thanksgiving, and the soul was freed from all its depression and gloom.

CHAPTER XI.

The Saint again seeks a martyr's crown.—The Bishop of Terni.—Miracles.—Mount Alvernia.—Imola.—A miraculous escape.—Organo.—Hospitality to the friars rewarded.—The convent of Compostella.—Cotolai.

The desire of martyrdom was always present to the mind of Francis. No sooner had he recovered from his sickness than he made another effort to obtain this crown. And as the Moorish province of Morocco promised fairly for his desires, he hastened thither, accompanied by Bernard da Quintavalle and several of his friars. As he passed through Northern Italy, and over the Alps, he preached everywhere. At Terni, the bishop was present while Francis spoke to the people. When the sermon was concluded, the prelate ascended the pulpit himself and addressed them thus: "My brethren, the man whom you have heard preach to-day is poor and illiterate; see and admire how the Almighty uses the most feeble and vile instruments for the most glorious ends." Francis, who rejoiced as much at humiliation as most persons would at praise, fell on his knees and cried out, "My lord, no one has done me so much honor as you have to-day. People fancy that I am a Saint, and give me the praise which they ought to attribute to God. But you, my lord, have discerned between the sinner and the gifts bestowed by the Divine mercy."

Miracles of the most unexpected character everywhere attended his steps. In the same city he restored to life a young man who had been killed by a wall falling on him. At Narni, he pointed out the place in the river where the corpse of a drowned man had sunk, and restored it to life when brought to land. Here, also, at the request of the bishop of the diocese, he gave sight to a blind woman, by the sign of the Cross; and restored the use of his limbs to a man who for five months had been paralyzed. At Orti, he caused a child who had been completely crippled, to become straight, and at San Gemini delivered from the power of a demon a poor woman who had been long possessed. At Foligno, Trevi, and Sienna, he established convents of his Order. So universal was the impression of his sanctity, and so great the fame of his miracles, that in the archives of a town in Tuscany a deed was found conveying to him a house, in these words, "We grant to a man named Francis, whom all men account to be a Saint," etc.

The number of his disciples daily increased. A young gentleman, having heard him preach at Monte Casali, came to ask admission to his Order. He had been brought up to a life of wealth and luxury; Francis knew this, and hesitated to receive him, as such antecedents were by no means the most desirable for forming a Friar Minor. "You have been brought up delicately," replied Francis; "our life will be very severe for you." The young man bravely replied, "My father, what one man has done another can do, and I hope, with the help of God's grace, to be able to endure, at least patiently, what others bear with joy." We need scarcely say that, after such a reply, the postulant did not require to press his suit further.

It was probably at this time that the Saint obtained the grant of Mount Alvernia, where he afterwards founded a convent—a spot for ever memorable and dear to the Franciscan heart, as that where Francis received the last and most mysterious impress of supernatural grace which perfected his resemblance to his Lord. After leaving Monte Casali, he crossed the

Apennines, intending to proceed through the valley of Marecchia to Monte Feltro or St. Leo. On his way he heard that a great festival was about to be held at the former place, as one of the young nobles of that country was to receive the honor of knighthood. This was good news for Francis, who hoped amid such an assembly to enlist some souls under the banner of the Cross. The Saint was not deceived in his expectation. A goodly company of knights and nobles followed the young aspirant to fame; and all went to hear solemn Mass at the Castle of Monte Feltro. When the ceremony concluded, Francis seated himself on a low wall and began to preach. A large audience soon surrounded him. His text was a singular one:

"Tanto è il ben ch' aspetto,
Che d' ogni pena m' è diletto."

(The boundless prize I hope to gain.
Turns into joy my every pain.)

It was but saying, in other words, what St. Paul had said long before, that the sufferings of this life are not worthy to be compared with the joys that are in store for God's faithful servants. As usual, his hearers hung eagerly on his words, and he enkindled in their hearts some sparks of the fire of love which burned so brightly in his own. The noble Count Orlando da Chiusi was one of his audience. He was a rich and powerful knight, the lord of Chiusi Nuova and of all Casentino. He had often heard of the sanctity and miracles of Francis; and when his discourse was ended he approached him, and begged to confer with him on the state of his soul. Full of courteous charity—that saintly courteousness which is so signally the stamp of souls that are filled with divine love—Francis replied, "My lord count, I am overjoyed to hear you speak thus; but I pray you, first entertain your friends who have invited you to this feast, and then we will converse together as long as you please." The Count went to the feast, Francis to prayer. When the guests had dispersed, Orlando again sought his new friend. Their conference was long, and of the deepest interest to both. Before they parted, the nobleman, who desired above all things to have some of those holy friars near him, told the Saint that he would give him the mountain of Alvernia, where, if he pleased, he could establish a convent. The offer was willingly accepted, and two of the Friars Minor went to take possession of their new field of labor. Orlando received them with the greatest joy, and sent them up the mountain, escorted by a band of soldiers to protect them, both against the wild animals, and the banditti who made this desolate place their favorite haunt. The soldiers assisted the religious in clearing the ground; and when Francis returned from Spain, whither we must now follow him, he came himself to visit his noble benefactor.

Leaving Monte Feltro, Francis and his companions continued their journey towards Spain. At Bologna he visited a convent of his Order, where he remained a short time. On his arrival at Imola, he went to the bishop to ask his permission to preach. On this occasion his request was refused somewhat roughly. "I preach myself," replied the prelate, "and that is sufficient." Francis, with his usual humility and courtesy, bowed humbly and retired. An hour after, to the extreme surprise and annoyance of the bishop, he returned to the charge. More indignant that at his first intrusion, his lordship angrily inquired why he troubled him again. "My lord," answered the Saint, "if a father drives his son out of one door, what can he do but come in at another?" The bishop could not resist a smile. It was all Francis wanted; but ere he had left the palace they had warmly embraced each other; and the bishop had given him ample faculties, both for himself and for every member of his Order.

Once, as they journeyed on until late at night, they were overtaken by darkness at a most perilous point of the road. It lay between a river and a deep morass. The friars were extremely alarmed, but the Saint's confidence in God was unshaken. A heavenly light suddenly shone on their path, and guided them till they reached the nearest town. Here a convent was soon after established, which was called that of the Holy Fire.

Francis was received in Spain with the greatest joy. Alphonsus the Ninth was at this time king of Castile —a prince of unusual piety and sound judgment. His consort was an English princess; and their daughter Blanche must ever be revered as the mother and preceptress of the sainted Louis of France. Nor was he the only prince in the peninsula who had a welcome for the Saint. Alphonsus the Second and his wife Uracca were equally anxious that the Friars Minor should be established in their kingdom, and gave them every encouragement to make foundations in Portugal.

Francis, still dreaming of the martyr's crown, desired to reach Morocco as speedily as possible, but the pious Alphonsus would by no means allow him to depart thus easily. Two houses of the Order were, at his solicitation, established; one was that of St. Michael at Burgos, the other at Lagrono. These foundations were made about the year 1214, so that the Franciscan friars were the first of the mendicant orders established in Spain. As they passed through the province of St. James, they wished to go from the town of Nonis to Organo; but a river which lay between, and the want of a boat, proved a formidable barrier to their progress. Francis betook himself to prayer. Presently a young man approached, who was about to cross the river with several horses laden with bread. Seeing the difficulty in which the Saint and his companions were placed, he at once offered to convey them across; and added to his charity by bringing them to his father's house at Organo, where they were most kindly received, and entertained with great hospitality during their stay. On his departure Francis prayed for a special benediction on the good young man. Shortly after, this pious youth made a pilgrimage to Rome, and prayed at the shrine of the Apostles that he might be taken to a better world while enriched with so many indulgences. His desire was granted, and he died on his homeward journey. But while the office for his soul's repose was being said at Organo, a number of Friars Minor suddenly appeared and joined the chant with wonderful sweetness and gravity. When Mass was ended, the parents of the deceased invited them home, and pressed them to take some refreshment. A crowd followed them, for there was something of marvellous grace and sweetness in their deportment. But the food which was placed before them did not decrease, although they appeared to partake of it; and they departed as unaccountably as they had appeared. It might have been a vision, or that the guardian angels of those friars had assumed their forms. However, this incident served greatly to increase the devotion of the people to the Order.

Another very similar occurrence took place at the same time, and was as well authenticated and as generally known. It chanced that when the friars were travelling between Barcelona and Gerona, one of their number, faint with long abstinence, entered a vineyard as they passed, and took a few grapes. The man who had charge of it was very angry, and seized on the poor friar's mantle, which he insisted on retaining as payment for the fruit. Poor as it was, of course it was much above the value. Francis in vain entreated him to restore the cloak; at length all agreed to refer the matter to the owner of the vineyard. He not only returned the cloak to Francis, but invited the friars to stay with him; and, on further acquaintance, begged they would consider his house their home, whenever they visited San Salomi. The Saint accepted his offer, and said, "Henceforth I shall consider you as one of our brethren." After some time, the good man died, having always most faithfully kept his promise of hospitality to the friars. A large concourse of people assembled at his obsequies. Many priests also were present, but there were no rough habits or white cords to be seen. The people began to exclaim that the friars were not treating their friend as he deserved, but in a few moments, they were silenced and amazed. A choir of friars entered the church, chanting the psalms with a most sweet melody, but as soon as the function was over, they disappeared even as they had come.

At Compostella Francis very much desired to found a house, but he had no funds for this purpose. The Benedictines possessed a great deal of land in that neighborhood, and the Saint betook himself to their abbot to inquire if they would grant him a portion. The abbot very naturally inquired what he could give for it. Francis replied, that if there was any fish in the neighborhood his friars would send him a basket every year. It would seem as if a Benedictine could not refuse anything to a Franciscan; so the good abbot smiled, and gave him all he asked. But there was another difficulty not so easily removed: a convent had to be built, and money was wanted for this also. Francis was lodging with a poor charcoal dealer, named Cotolai. One morning the Saint addressed him thus, "My friend, it is the will of God that you should build us a convent; I pray you, begin the work without further delay." The poor man looked utterly aghast at this announcement, he was willing enough to to undertake the work, but he was almost as poor as the friars themselves. "Nay," exclaimed Francis, who saw his anxiety, "do not fear, dig near yonder well, and you will find a treasure that will suffice for the work." The words of the holy man were verified; the treasure was found, and the convent built by this means. An authentication of this miracle exists in the archives of the abbey of St. Martin at Compostella, together with the agreement between the Benedictine abbot and St. Francis. There are also inscriptions regarding it over the entrance to the convent church, and on the tombs of Cotolai and his wife, who are buried there.

CHAPTER XII.

Francis is desired to return to Italy.—Perpignan.—St. Mary of the Angels.—He objects to a new building, as being too large and commodious.—Sets out for Alvernia.—Assaulted by demons on the way.—Receives with joy the advice of a poor man.—Cautions his friars not to depend too much on the charity of the rich.—Addresses them in the evening on Mount Alvernia.

It was revealed to the Saint at Compostella, while praying at the shrine of St. James, that his return to Italy would be more pleasing to God. He therefore sacrificed his desire of preaching to the Moors, and set out on his way homeward. Convents of the Order had now been established all over the peninsula, and there was promise of an abundant harvest of saintly souls. On his way back to Italy he established a house at Perpignan, and then passed rapidly through Languedoc. The province had been desolated by the Albigensian heresy, but was now enjoying a temporary relief—the consequence of the brilliant and miraculous victory which the brave Count de Montfort had just obtained. This field of labor was soon to be occupied by another Order, perhaps better fitted to cope with its difficulties; since eloquence of speech and intellectual attainments seemed almost as requisite as sanctity to influence and win its heretical and warlike neighbors.

Once more, then, we find Francis at St. Mary of the Angels. His first anxiety was to know if all had gone on well in his absence; his second, to hear of the friars whom he had sent to Mount Alvernia. Peter of Catania, it will be remembered, had been appointed vicar-general of the Order. This good brother, with more zeal than discretion, had erected a large and (for those times) almost magnificent convent. Francis was much displeased when he saw it; and by no means satisfied with his excuse that it was designed for the accommodation of the numerous strangers who resorted thither. "Brother Peter," exclaimed the Saint, "this house is to be the model for all others of the Order. Poverty is our rule, and those who visit, as well as those who dwell here, must learn to bear its inconveniences. Besides, the brethren in other places may take example from it, and their visitors will everywhere expect to be as commodiously provided for." At first he gave directions to have the whole building taken down. However, when the absolute necessity for so large a convent was represented to him, he consented to let it remain, only desiring that for the future all their buildings should be as simple, and even as small, as was consistent with prudence.

The brethren who had been sent to Mount Alvernia had heard that their beloved father had returned from Spain. Eager to tell him of the success of their foundation, and to be pressed once more to his tender, affectionate heart, they hastened to Assisi; he received them with joy, and when he heard of the solitude and magnificent beauty which surrounded Alvernia, his soul yearned towards it, and he determined to visit it himself. He chose three friars to be the companions of his journey—Brother Leo, from whom he was rarely separated, and Brothers Masseo and Angelo. As usual, he appointed one to be their guardian and superior on the way; this office he now gave to Masseo. He preached wherever they rested or could obtain a congregation, and many miracles were granted to confirm his words. The first night was passed in a convent of their Order, the second they spent in a deserted church. The brethren slept; but Francis, as usual, watched and prayed. Here he sustained one of the severest personal conflicts with the evil one which ever befell him. Taunted by temptations and bitter words, bruised and wearied with blows, he still prayed on, only desiring for the love of God to endure even more. Those who are familiar with the lives of the Saints will not be surprised to hear that Francis frequently incurred such assaults. Our wrestling is not against flesh and blood, but against principalities and powers, and the spirits of wickedness in the high places. How can it surprise us that Satan should assume even a visible form to injure or molest those whom he fears as antagonists to his power? Or what more likely than that such assaults should be severe in proportion as the sanctity of the sufferers is heroic and sublime?

When morning came, the brethren found their saintly father so utterly prostrate from the effects of that night's mysterious suffering, that he was unable to continue his journey. Marks of violence were also visible upon him, and he was obliged to reveal the cause; but as he was extremely anxious to reach Alvernia, they sought for some means to convey him up the mountain. A neighboring peasant to whom they applied, offered him the use of his ass; but when he heard it was for the great friar from Assisi, he declared that he would himself conduct him. And so they journeyed on. After they had gone a short distance, St. Francis and the countryman began to converse familiarly. At last the latter exclaimed, "Well, good brother, they say great things of you, and that you are a great Saint. Now, take my advice, and try to be as good as they say you are, lest you deceive those who put such confidence in you." Francis, who above all things loved simplicity, was overjoyed at this speech. Dismounting from the ass, he kissed the poor man's feet, and thanked him again and again for his advice. How true it is that humility is the surest road to sanctity and to the attainment of every grace! Scarcely an hour had elapsed ere Francis, who had so lately dismounted to kiss the feet of his present guide, alighted once more to pray and work a miracle. The steep ascent under a burning sun, and a sudden gust of the hot mountain wind, had so overcome the good peasant, that he cried out, "Alas! if I do not get water, I shall die of thirst." None was to be found at hand; but at the prayer of the Saint a spring of the purest, freshest water suddenly gushed forth, of which the poor man drank, and revived. No water had been seen in that part of the mountain before, nor was it ever seen there again.

Francis stayed a short time on his way at the castle of Count Orlando. The young nobleman was rejoiced to see him, and in the evening came himself to the mountain. Again he confirmed his gift, and assured the Saint that he and his family would ever protect and specially venerate his Order, and would provide in every way for their support. Then the good Count departed, enriched by the blessing of Francis and the prayers of his friars.

It was evening, with the clear and glorious hues of an Italian sunset. A thin golden veil alone seemed spread between the saintly pilgrims of Alvernia and their royal home above; and as the light became less gorgeous and the moon arose, the huge fantastic rocks, the giant oaks and beech-trees threw dreamy shadows on the mountain side. Far away, the Tiber and Arno murmured their evening hymn, while the brethren, gathering round their saintly father, listened eagerly to his every word.

Francis spoke long and earnestly to his children. He warned them not to avail themselves too readily of the extreme kindness of the Count Orlando, lest it should lead them to infringe their vow of poverty. He told them that if they acted up to their profession they would never suffer actual want; for God had promised to provide for them.

The mountain, the scene of so much that is deeply interesting in the life of our Saint, is situated on the confines of Tuscany. It is one of the range of Appennines, and lies not far from Camaldoli and Vallombrosa. It seems, of all others, a spot dedicated to the supernatural. Its masses of riven rock, shaken (as is piously believed) into wild commotion, when the cry of the Divine Victim on Calvary had pronounced that all was "consummated," appeared to designate it as the scene where the same Lord, from His throne of glory, should bestow on his "crucified poor one" the stigmata of a mystical resemblance to Himself. Added to this circumstance of heart-subduing awe, the yawning chasms and grottoes of Alvernia—its giant trees of primæval growth; its beautiful patches of green pasture embosomed in forest tracts; its steep and almost inaccessible ascent—combined to produce a wild grandeur of effect, which demanded for its expression the pencil of a Salvator, the pen of a Dante. To the poetic soul of Francis they were especially attractive; but our Saint, much as he loved this grand and solemn mountain-home, might not linger here. The culminating point of his life was not yet reached; he had much to do, much to suffer, ere, in this very spot, he should "bear in his body the stigmata of the Lord Jesus."

CHAPTER XIII.

His prediction at Fabriano.—A new monastery under the patronage of our Lady.—The Curate of La Città.—Thirty new postulants.—Francis at the Lateran Council.—His Rule is publicly confirmed and its former approbation declared.—Returns to Assisi.—First general chapter at St Mary of the Angels.—The Provincial Ministers empowered to receive postulants.—Dispersion of the Brethren.—Meeting of Dominic and Francis.—Letter addressed to both Orders by B. Humbert and St. Bonaventura.

Rome, immortal Rome, was now the destination of the Saint; thither he journeyed, still preaching as he went. Monte Casale, Fabriano, Ancona, Ascoli, and many other places, were evangelized on the way. At Fabriano he warned some workmen, who would not attend to his preaching, that the labor on which they were engaged would not succeed. In a few days his words were verified, for the whole building fell. At a place near this town, called the Rocky Valley, there was a deserted church and convent which had been inhabited by Benedictines. It was dedicated to the Mother of God; and Francis, from special devotion to the glorious Patroness of his Order, asked and obtained possession of it. One day, in going to it, he lost his way; but seeing a laborer ploughing in a field, he asked him to be his guide. The man did not like to leave his employment; but Francis assured him he would lose nothing by his charity. When he returned, he found his field already ploughed. At La Città, the curate was extremely kind to him. The Saint especially loved this good man, and told him he would one day be a Friar Minor, as he must be indeed his brother. After the death of the Saint, the curate, Raniero, entered the Order. At Osimo, thirty young men of rank joined his Institute; and at the same time he obtained, by earnest prayer, a vocation for a gentleman of wealth and distinction, who had entertained him and his companions with special kindness. This postulant was so peculiarly attractive in his manner, and so distinguished for his saintly courtesy, that the first affection which the Saint felt for him constantly increased. After a time, by the direction of Francis, he was made guest-master of his monastery, as being likely to edify strangers by his hospitable and religious demeanor.

On the 11th of November, in the year of grace 1215, the fourth Lateran Council assembled in Rome. The project which had been conceived by the capacious mind of Innocent, immediately after his elevation to the Pontifical throne, was to be fulfilled. For two years and a half previous to this time, exhortations had been addressed on the subject to the whole Christian world, and those whose presence was most required at the Council had been specially invited to attend it. Constantinople and Jerusalem were represented by their patriarchs; the Maronites by the venerable Jonas; Alexandria by its deacon, for the patriarch was unable to leave his flock, then cruelly oppressed by the Saracens. The religious houses were represented by their superiors, while the bishops of the principal sees in Christendom swelled the anointed crowd. Besides these were sixty-nine primates and metropolitans, among whom the celebrated Rodriguez of Toledo was conspicuous. This prelate pronounced a discourse on the prerogatives of the Holy See. It was first given in Latin; but was again repeated with so much facility in French, German, and Spanish, that his audience scarcely knew which most to admire—his wonderful gift of languages, or the capacity of intellect and depth of learning displayed. Another prelate, noticeable in a different manner was also present. As Cardinal Archbishop of Liege, he appeared first in his scarlet hat and mantle; as duke, he next arrayed himself in green; and lastly, as bishop, he wore his pontificals. The Council opened its session on the Feast of St. Martin. The crowd was so overwhelming that several persons were seriously injured, and the Archbishop of Amalfi was suffocated in the vestibule. Innocent addressed his numerous audience, taking for his text these words of our Divine Lord: "With desire have I desired to eat this pasch with you before I suffer." His words were prophetic. Scarcely nine months had elapsed, and the Pontiff slept with his predecessors—called in the prime of life, and almost suddenly, to his eternal reward.

The extinction of heresies, then fearfully rife; the reformation of morals, the better regulation of ecclesiastical discipline, and the recovery of the Holy Land by the union of Christian princes, were the great objects which Innocent had in view. One only of these immediately concerns our subject. It will be remembered that Francis had asked, and obtained, a verbal approbation for his Rule in 1210. Until the present time this had seemed sufficient; but the ranks of the Friars Minor already contained some thousands, and heresy was rife. It therefore became necessary that the true poor should be distinguished from the false. Besides, this very Council had forbidden the foundation of any new religious Orders; that is, it had required that persons who were permitted by the Holy See to establish a new Institute should found its constitutions on some ancient Rule already sanctioned. As the Pope had already given his approbation to the Franciscan Rule, it could not come under this restriction; still it was needful that the approbation should be publicly renewed. This favor was granted to the Saint. Innocent declared before all the fathers of this great Council his former approbation, and solemnly confirmed it.

St. Dominic was now in Rome. He had come to solicit permission for the establishment of his Order. As, however, the regulations of the Council were stringent, he could not obtain permission to frame a new Rule. He therefore formed his on the Augustinian, adding what was necessary for the distinctive end of his Institute. It was confirmed in the following year by a bull of Honorius the Third.

In the beginning of December, Francis left Rome and returned to Assisi. He then sent letters to all the convents of his Order, convoking a general chapter, to be held at St. Mary of the Angels during the ensuing year. The Feast of Pentecost fell on the 30th of May, in the year of our Redemption, 1216. On this day, the first general chapter of the Friars Minor began its session. Many important regulations were now made, superiors appointed for different houses, and certain brethren selected for evangelizing distant countries. Hitherto Francis had reserved to himself the power of admitting postulants; now he extended this privilege fully to the provincial ministers. At the termination of the chapter, the brethren were allotted their various fields of labor. John de Strachia was sent into Lombardy; Benedict of Arezzo into the Marches of Ancona; Daniel the Tuscan into Calabria; Augustine of Assisi into the Terra di Lavoro; Elias of Cortona into Tuscany; Bernard da Quintavalle, with Brothers Zacharias and Walter, went to evangelize Spain; John Bovella, a Florentine, with thirty companions, set out for Provence; John de Penna, and sixty brethren, for Germany; while Francis chose for himself Paris and the Netherlands.

Before the brethren departed on their various missions, he assembled them together and addressed them thus: "In the name of the Lord, go forth with modesty and humility. As ye journey, walk two and two, keeping strict silence until the hour of Terce, and let your thoughts be occupied with God. Let no idle or useless word be heard among you. Even while travelling, let your deportment be as recollected as if you were in a hermitage or in your cell; for wherever you may be, or whithersoever we may be going, we should always carry our cells along with us. Our brother the body is our cell, our soul the hermit who dwells therein, and its occupation should be ever to think of God, and to worship Him. If a religious soul cannot rest peacefully in the cell of his body, exterior cells will avail it little. So conduct yourselves before the world that all who shall see or hear you may have their devotion increased, and praise the Eternal Father, to whom all glory belongs. Preach peace to all men; but seek rather to have it in your hearts than on your lips. Give no occasion of anger or scandal to any; but strive, on the contrary, to lead all men to a spirit of union and charity. Our vocation is to heal the wounded, to console the afflicted, and to recall the wanderers. Many who now seem to you to belong to the devil will one day be the disciples of Jesus Christ."

After the brethren had dispersed, Francis set out for Rome, accompanied by Brother Masseo. He was anxious again to visit the shrine of the Apostles, which he so especially venerated, and to implore their blessing on the labors of his children. His piety was signally rewarded. Even as he prayed at their tomb, they appeared to him surrounded by ineffable glory, and assured him that his poverty was approved and accepted by God.

It was probably about this time that St. Francis and St. Dominic first met. Some authors place their interview during the session of the Lateran Council, but the best authorities are against this opinion, and it would seem more likely that St. Dominic's stay at Rome on that occasion was very brief. His natural energy of character would urge him to return at once to prepare the Rule for his new Institute, and as nothing could be done till that was completed, he would not be likely to delay its execution. However this may be, the facts regardiug their meeting are related alike by all. One night, while Dominic was engaged in prayer, he saw in a vision our Divine Lord, who appeared in great anger with the world. His blessed Mother presented two men to Him, to appease His wrath. In one of these, the Saint recognized himself; the other was a stranger, but he considered him attentively. The next morning, on entering a church, he saw the person who had been shown to him the previous night.

Hastening to him, he embraced him warmly, and cried out, "You are my companion; let us go together, and no one shall be able to prevail against us." Truly, a striking and momentous scene! Here were two poor men uniting themselves and their Orders in an eternal friendship, and dividing the world between them to conquer it for God. We cannot wonder that, in consequence, a special friendship should exist between the children of Francis and Dominic, and that they should celebrate the festivals, each of the other, as days of peculiar devotion. Many regulations have been made by the general chapters of both Orders for the preservation and increase of this mutual charity. A beautiful letter, addressed to the brethren of both institutes by Blessed Humbert, Master-General of the Friars Preachers, and St. Bonaventura, General of the Friars Minor, cannot be read without interest; it is addressed thus:

"TO OUR WELL-BELOVED BRETHREN IN JESUS CHRIST THE FRIARS MINOR AND THE FRIARS PREACHERS WHO ARE DISPERSED THROUGHOUT THE WORLD.

"The Saviour of mankind, who loves all men, and desires not the death of any of His children, has at different periods of the world's history made use of various means to repair the ruin in which our race is involved; and in these latter days we believe that He has raised up our two Orders for this purpose. We firmly believe that it is He who has called, and enriched by His gifts, this vast number of devoted men, who seek by their words and their example to save the world. They are like two immense flames, which, not for our honor but for the glory of God, enlighten with heavenly brightness those who are sitting in the valley of the shadow of death; they are like two cherubim filled with knowledge, each reading the inmost soul, the thoughts and desires of the other: they are like the two breasts of the Spouse, nourishing and bringing up children."

This letter is too long for inserting fully, but too beautiful to be altogether omitted. It concludes thus:

"How strong and fervent should be the love which unites us, since that which existed between the blessed Francis and the blessed Dominic, our ancient fathers, was so unbounded. They regarded each other as angels of God; they entertained each other as if they had received Christ Himself. Each rejoiced at the advancement of the other, aiding him in all things, and carefully avoiding the least scandal. May we never be surprised by the evil one, but always found on the watch, eager to guard and defend this most precious charity, which our holy fathers have left us a legacy. Let us for this end implore the divine assistance, and take care that all our actions are regulated by heavenly love. And let one Order never seek to exalt its saints or its privileges above the other."

Two centuries later, Sixtus the Fourth, himself a Franciscan, exclaims, "These two Orders, like two rivers of Paradise, have watered the universal church by their prayers, their virtue and their merits, each day rendering it more fertile. They are like two seraphs, who, elevated above all earthly things by the wings of sublime contemplation and burning love—by their ceaseless chanting of the Divine praises, by declaring the immense blessings which God has conferred upon the human race—are continually bringing into the storehouse of Holy Church, the sheaves of an abundant harvest of perishing souls, purchased by the most precious Blood of Jesus Christ."

CHAPTER XIV.

The Saint at Florence.—Cardinal Ugolini.—A mysterious dream.—He preaches before the Pope.—Seeks a Protector for his Order.—Cardinal Ugolini confirmed in this office.—His attachment to the Saint and to the Order.

Cardinal Ugolini, the friend and special protector of the Order, was now at Florence, and thither Francis bent his steps in order to confer with him before entering on his mission in France. With some difficulty the Cardinal succeeded in dissuading him from this project. He represented to him that, while the society was yet in its infant days, the presence of its founder and his constant superintendence of his own work, were essential to its prosperity. He overruled the objections of the Saint, that younger members of his community might not see these reasons, and might be tempted to think of their superior, as leading a comparatively easy life in his native land, while they were exposed to the trials of foreign or difficult missions. "And why," asked the Cardinal, "send them to a distance from you? Surely there can be no necessity for it." The reply of Francis was almost prophetic: "My lord," he exclaimed, "you think that God has destined the Friars Minor only for our own country; but I assure you that He has chosen them for the salvation of the whole world. Their mission will be among the infidel and the heretic, and they will thus bring many souls to God."

Brother Pacificus and Albert of Pisa, were therefore sent to France as his substitutes, and he returned to St. Mary's. About this time the Saint had a singular dream, which he at once perceived was not without a spiritual signification. He saw a hen vainly striving to shelter her chickens under her wings, and threatened by a hawk that hovered over them. Presently another bird appeared, whose wings were much larger and more powerful, and afforded protection to the trembling brood. On awakening, he prayed to be enlightened as to the signification of this dream, and was told that it was a warning to him to provide a protector for his Order who would have more power to defend it from dangers than himself. Francis immediately returned to Rome. Cardinal Ugolini was there, and he consulted him how he should act in this matter. By his advice he asked permission to preach before the Pope. His request was granted, and he carefully prepared a sermon for the occasion, which by the desire of the Cardinal he learned by heart. But when the moment came in which it should have been delivered, he could not remember a single word of what he had intended to say. He was, therefore, obliged to explain his difficulty to the Holy Father, and after a few moments' prayer, he spoke with his usual eloquence and irresistible force. Cardinal Ugolini was now empowered by the Holy See to act with full authority as Cardinal Protector of the Franciscan Order. Hitherto, as the personal friend of the Saint, he had done much for him and his; but the voice of Peter had not confirmed his authority until now. The friendship between these holy men was singularly beautiful, and in the way in which Francis clung to this good prelate, there was something of holy simplicity and childlike trust, such as we seldom see but in the most saintly souls. It is remarkable, too, how the natural disposition still shows itself, even when so purified by grace as scarcely to breathe on earth. The clinging, affectionate disposition of Francis sought some one to lean on, while he himself is the support of thousands: and with all his miracles, his ecstasies, and supernatural knowledge, his own "wings" were too small to cover his brood, and he must seek the fostering care of another. As if to teach us that the least are necessary to the greatest and that none may rely entirely on their own powers, natural or above nature—as if to show us that in our land of exile and temptation, even Saints must learn humility by dependance on others, and charity from the ready tribute of others' sympathy.

The Cardinal returned the feeling with which Francis regarded him, and tenderly cherished these children of his adoption. He assisted at their general chapters, regulated the constitutions of the three Orders, and when he visited St. Mary of the Angels, it was his delight to lay aside the exterior signs of his dignity, to wear their poor habit, and with bare feet to join in all their mortifications and exercises of piety. Later still, when called to wear the triple crown, as Francis had so frequently and joyfully predicted, it was his happiness, we had almost said his privilege, to enroll among the number of the Saints his dear personal friend, the founder of the Order he had so carefully cherished.

CHAPTER XV.

The Second general chapter.—A Mass ordered to be celebrated every Saturday in honor of Mary Immaculate.—Letter of Honorius the Third.—The devils also hold a chapter.—Francis wishes his children not to receive episcopal dignities.

In the month of May, 1219, the Friars Minor assembled in crowds from all parts of the continent to assist at the second general chapter of the Order. The number then collected together was so large that, had we not the authority of St. Bonaventura for the statement, it would seem scarcely credible. Five thousand, he says, were present. If we calculate those who must have remained at home, either through infirmity or in charge of their several convents, the increase of the Order is little short of miraculous. Even the large building which had been recently erected for the friars by the good people of Assisi could not accommodate such multitudes. They were, therefore, obliged to encamp, as best they might, in the plain near the city;

and from this circumstance their assemblage was called the Chapter of Mats. The deliberation opened on Whit Sunday, 1219. Cardinal Ugolini officiated pontifically and preached; then he went through the ranks of these devoted soldiers of the Cross, exhorting them to fidelity and perseverance. This chapter was a cheering and most joyous one for Francis. As he passed through the camp he saw his children, sheltered only by rude huts of matting and reeds, utterly destitute of every earthly comfort, and even of necessary food. Here were true Friars Minor, souls worthy of their glorious vocation. Nor was their confidence in God unrewarded. Their temporal wants were supplied with eagerness by the inhabitants of the surrounding country. Each day they brought an abundant provision; so that, immense as was the concourse of friars, none lacked his daily bread, and more they neither asked nor desired. Some engaged in prayer, some in spiritual conferences; everywhere the most perfect harmony and love existed. As the Cardinal passed through the camp, and saw the friars thus employed in groups of sixty or a hundred, he could no longer contain his joy. "O brother," he cried out to his friend, "O brother, truly this is the camp of God!" Nor was the Saint less moved. Assembling all his brethren together, he poured forth his whole soul to them in a fervent address. "My children," he exclaimed, "we have promised great things, but we are promised still greater. Let us keep our own promises, and sigh for the fulfillment of the promises of God. There is a brief pleasure which ends in an eternal suffering, and there is a light suffering which brings an eternal joy. Many are called but few are chosen, and each one shall receive what he has merited." Then he exhorted them ever to reverence and love their holy mother the Church; never to forget the strict obligation of their vow of poverty; but to cast all their care upon God, who would sustain them.*

At this chapter three statutes of great importance were made. First that on every Saturday a Mass should be celebrated in honor of our Lady Immaculate —thus placing the Order, from its very commencement, under her special protection, and honoring her by that most dear title which they were afterwards so signally to defend. Secondly, that a special commemoration of the holy Apostles, Peter and Paul, should be made in the prayers, "*Protege nos Domine*," and "*Exaudi nos Deus*." This commemoration was practiced by the Church at large, some years afterward, when Aymon, fifth general of the Franciscan Order, revised the Roman Breviary, by the command of Innocent the Fourth. The third regulation regarded the monastic buildings of the Order, which it was strictly enjoined should be erected in accordance with their rule of absolute poverty.

It was probably about this time that the question was raised regarding their acceptance of ecclesiastical benefices. Cardinal Ugolini had his own views on the subject, and was naturally anxious that the friars of the two new Orders should give the Church the advantage

* Wadding asserts that St. Dominic was present at this chapter, as do also the Bollandists and Fleury; but Father Echard and the Dominican authorities deny the correctness of the assertion. The Franciscan writers maintain that on this occasion St. Dominic expressed surprise that Francis should carry his rule of poverty so far as to make no provision for the wants of so vast an assemblage; but when he saw their needs so wonderfully supplied, he determined that his own Order should carry out the same spirit, and made regulations to this effect at the first general chapter, held at Bologna in the following year. It is also said that he asked his beloved Brother Francis for his cord, which he thenceforth always wore under his habit. This statement is confirmed by Bernard de Besse, secretary to St. Bonaventura, who had received it from Brother Leo, the most intimate friend of Francis. Still the Dominican writers find a discrepancy between these statements and their chronological accounts of the movements of their saintly founder.

of their sanctity and disinterestedness in its highest offices. But when the subject was proposed to Dominic and Francis, both shrank back, fearful lest even spiritual works of mercy for others, while raising their brethren above the level of poor friars, should endanger their humility, or diminish their fervor. Each wished the other to speak first, in reply to the Cardinal. At length St. Dominic yielded. It was honor enough, he said, for his children to defend the faith against heretics. Nor was the reply of our Saint less characteristic. "My children are called Friars Minor," he exclaimed, "and I will not have them belie their name. If you would see the Order prosper, never raise them to ecclesiastical dignities." However much edified by such humility, Ugolini did not allow it to influence him when raised to the Papal throne; for he then placed many religious of both Orders in the highest offices of the Church.

But this general chapter, as far as regarded external arrangements, occupied itself chiefly among the missions of the Order. They were now about to be greatly extended, and it was necessary that the friars should have authentic testimonials of their Catholicity, that the faithful might recognize their authority, and more readily receive their instructions. Honorius the Third had succeeded Innocent as Pope; and he willingly complied with the request of Francis to give an apostolic letter, which the friars might always carry with them when about to engage in new missions:

"HONORIUS, BISHOP, AND SERVANT OF THE SERVANTS OF GOD, TO THE ARCHBISHOPS, BISHOPS, ABBOTS, DEACONS, ARCHDEACONS, AND ALL ECCLESIASTICAL SUPERIORS:

"As our beloved sons, Brother Francis and his companions have renounced the vanities of the world, and embraced a form of life which the Roman Church has approved, and, following the example of the apostles, desire to preach the word of God throughout the world; We beseech and exhort you in our Lord, and command you by these apostolic letters, to receive as Catholic, and faithful, the brethren of this Order, who, bearing these, shall present themselves to you. Show yourselves favorable to them, and treat them with all kindness, for the honor of God and from regard to us. Given, the third of the ides of June, in the third year of our pontificate."

Thus fortified, the brethren departed on their various missions. Before their dispersion, Cardinal Ugolini addressed them, and at the close of his sermon he could not help expressing his unqualified admiration of their heroic sanctity. This alarmed Francis. He trembled for their humility, and when the prelate had ended his discourse, he begged permission to speak. Then, pouring out his soul with prophetic knowledge of the future, he declared how relaxations would creep into his Order, and that soon its original fervor would be cooled. He concluded by reproaching those who had just been so highly commended, and accusing them of corresponding so imperfectly with the designs of God in their regard. The Cardinal was greatly astonished, and privately inquired from the Saint why he acted thus. But he was soon satisfied, and could not but admire the prudence and sanctity of his friend. "I feared, my lord," exclaimed Francis, "lest your praise should excite a feeling of vain-glory in the minds of those who as yet are not deeply grounded in humility." In truth, though many of those present had been in the Order almost since its foundation, a large number had but newly joined its ranks. During the chapter as many as five hundred postulants had offered themselves, and had been accepted, and new members were every day crowding in.

The Saint had other reasons also for his fears. It

had been revealed to him that, while he and his friars were deliberating on their plans for the advancement of the kingdom of God, Satan and his spirits of darkness had held their conclave, and proposed their schemes to frustrate the designs of the Saint. The plan which they devised was, indeed, worthy of diabolical subtlety. Knowing that while Francis lived they could do but little, they forecast the schemes which they might be able to execute after his death. "Then," said they, "we will induce young men of noble birth and effeminate habits to enter the Order, and through them bring in relaxations. We will make use likewise of those who are filled with intellectual pride, who may cause the ancients to be despised. Thus the reputation of the Order for sanctity will in time be tarnished, and its power against us be materially decreased." With this knowledge before him, Francis had cause to fear for the future. No wonder that he should cautiously seek to check in his children every approach to pride, and to guard every avenue by which this most subtle temptation might find entrance.

After the Saint had been thus warned of the designs of our ancient enemy, he spent two days in prayer and tears that the dreaded danger might be averted, or that at least his beloved children might not yield to their deceitful foe. Even amongst these his earliest disciples, all were not alike fervent; and, though he had strictly to forbid the excessive austerities of some of his friars, and had found it necessary to take from them an immense number of most painful instruments of penance which they had hitherto used, there were others who were far from being all he could desire. Already brother Elias and several of his companions had endeavored to procure some relaxation of the strictness of his discipline, and applied to the Cardinal

Protector for his coöperation in their design. But the whole affair had been revealed to Francis, and before they had time to act on their deliberations he informed them of what they intended. When the holy prelate began to speak to him on the subject he at once rose up, and leading him to where the friars were assembled in chapter, he cried out, " My brethren, my brethren, God has called me to follow Him by the way humility and simplicity, and in the folly of the Cross. For His glory, for my confusion, and to set your consciences at rest, I will tell you what He has said to me : " Francis, I desire that you may be in the world a new little foolish one, who shall preach by your actions and your words the folly of the Cross. Do thou and thine follow Me only, and not any other manner of life.' Speak not then to me of any other rule," continued the Saint, "be it of St. Augustine or St. Bernard, or whom you will; for I will follow and obey none other than that to which God hath called me. And they who swerve from it shall feel the divine vengeance, and be covered with confusion."

So decided an answer silenced all objections for the time; but, alas! for the time only, as we shall see later. There were those in the Order at that day, as unhappily there are even in the most fervent communities, whose tendency was downwards. They would be covered with the mantle of Francis, and sheltered by his name; but they would not live in his spirit. Love of ease, a lingering attraction to the Egypt they had left, an anxiety to appear well before the world, to make their poverty respectable to the intellect and less painful to the flesh, an evasion of the spirit of a Rule of which they were bound to keep the letter—such was the evil leaven at work, doing service to the powers of darkness. We cannot marvel at the Saint's fears lest, when his vigilant eye was withdrawn, they should relax in the strife which *must* be waged when a soul is earnest after perfection. Again Francis warned; again he urged the greatest caution in the admission of subjects to their society, assuring them that no greater evil could befall them than to receive those who, though in many other respects estimable, were not earnest in their desire to become saints.

CHAPTER XVI.

Dispersion of the brethren.—Benedict is sent to Greece, John Parent to Spain, Angelo of Pisa to England.—St. Francis sets out on his mission to the East.—Elias made Superior in his absence.—Brother Fly.—Asks a child to choose who shall go with him to Morocco.—The Crusaders.—Francis warns them of defeat.—Enters the Moorish Camp.—Offers to prove his mission by entering a burning pile.—The Order established in Palestine.—Letter of de Vitry.—The Benedictines of the Black Mountains.

The brethren now dispersed on their various missions. Each was provided with a copy of the Apostolic Letter given him by the Holy Father for their protection. Besides, Francis had already given them letters from himself, which we have noticed above. These letters were written to the superiors of his Order, to priests and other religious; one was, moreover, addressed to magistrates and all secular authorities. The most enlightened and holy friars were appointed as superiors to the various missions. Benedict of Arezzo and his companions were sent into Greece, where the province of Romania was soon formed; Brother Giles and his friars set out for Morocco. Those who had been already in France and the Low Countries, returned to their convents. Brother John Parent, with a hundred friars, was sent into Spain; the blessed Christopher had Gascony given him as a field of labor; and

Angelo of Pisa, was made provincial of England. The form in which this last obedience was given is still preserved; it ran thus: "I, Brother Francis of Assisi, minister-general, command you, Brother Angelo of Pisa, in virtue of holy obedience, to take the office of provincial in England."

The Saint, with twelve companions, set forth on the Eastern mission, which he had so long desired, and Brother Elias was appointed superior during his absence. As they passed through Ancona a postulant presented himself, who seemed very anxious to join their Order. As he was rich, Francis desired him to distribute his goods to the poor and then come to him. The young man soon returned; but it was discovered that his parents, not the poor, had been the objects of his charity. When Francis heard of it, he called him, and said, "Ah, Brother Fly! as you have given all your goods to your relations, you should give yourself to them also; go then, for you are not fit to live in poverty like our poor friars." And so the young man departed, perhaps sorrowful, yet unwilling to make the entire renunciation demanded of him. He had received the call, but had not obeyed it. Human love, that most terrible obstacle to all heroic sacrifice, had interfered, or, perhaps, worldly prudence, scarcely less dangerous. The Order was a new one, and might end in failure; his vocation was not sealed by profession—he might be rejected. It was prudent to make some provision for the future, in case of unforeseen accidents. At least it was not well to risk both worlds. So he made sure of one; but we are not told that he secured the other.

When the brethren arrived at the sea-coast, their number had greatly increased. All who could, were anxious to see their beloved father once more before he embarked on his perilous mission, and when the time of the inevitable separation came, all were alike eager to accompany him. This, however, could not be. The captain of a vessel bound to Damietta offered to take twelve of the friars with him; and now a most loving contest arose, who should be of the favored number. Francis could not decide; his great loving heart had an equal, or almost equal, affection for all his children. What then could be done? Presently the Saint saw a little child near him, and said, "My brethren, we will ask this little child how we shall arrange our journey; you know God often reveals His will through the simple and ignorant." It was a suggestion such as might have been expected from a mind so noble, yet so childlike. Then, turning to the little one, he said, "Tell me, my child, is it the will of God that all those friars should go with me to Egypt?" The child at once replied, "It is not the will of God." "Tell me, then," continued Francis, "who shall go?" The boy, without hesitation, named eleven of the religious, and pointed to each as he named him. All were then perfectly satisfied. They only desired to do the will of God; and whether that were martyrdom in Syria, or the martyrdom of more hidden life-long penance in Italy, mattered but little to them.

A tender and affectionate parting followed. Francis gave to each his blessing and the kiss of peace, and in a few days he and his companions had landed on the island of Cyprus, where they remained a short time. Then, sending the friars to preach in different places, he took Brother Illuminatus as his companion, and journeyed on to the camp of the crusaders.

It will be remembered that one of the great objects of Innocent in convoking the Council of Lateran, was to organize a movement for the rescue of the holy places from the hands of the Saracens. The assembled prelates warmly seconded his views, and on their return to their homes, preached the new crusade with ardor. The Pope himself proclaimed it in the Tuscan States, where he died a martyr to his zeal. His successor was no less earnest in the cause. Almost his first act, on ascending the Papal throne, was to issue letters to the princes and prelates of Europe, urging them to carry out promptly what had been so well designed. His wishes were obeyed with a zeal beyond all anticipation; and early in the month of June, 1217, an immense army was ready for the glorious conflict. The Holy Land itself had been hitherto the scene of the crusades. Now, however, it was resolved to try a different mode of warfare—to attack the enemy in his stronghold, instead of attempting to wrest from him his usurped possessions. The Christian army therefore laid siege to Damietta, and for a short time all went on prosperously; but, towards the end of July, the Sultan of Damascus came with a numerous host, and beseiged the crusaders in their intrenchments. On the last day of that month, being reinforced by a large body of soldiers, under the command of Meledin, the Sultan of Egypt, they attacked the Christians, and a fierce battle ensued. It lasted till night, and the Saracen army were on the point of gaining the victory, when the Grand Master of the Temple and his knights roused all their valor, and by one brave rally gained the day.

The Cross might have triumphed finally, and the crescent been forever hidden, had not a more formidable foe than any earthly warrior engaged in the lists. Such a victory promised too much for the triumph of good to permit the powers of darkness to let it pass quietly. Nor were they without resource; a spirit of discord was suddenly raised among the crusaders; bitter recriminations and harsh words passed between the cavalry and foot soldiers, each charging the other with cowardice, until at last, in the very face of their foe, they demanded to justify their quarrel by force of arms. Things were in this state when Francis reached the camp; he knew by divine revelation, all that was passing, and the disastrous results to which it would lead. Uncertain how to act, he asked the advice of Brother Illuminatus. "Our Lord," he said, "has made known to me that if the Christians now engage in battle they will be overcome. If I declare this to them they will mock me as a fool; if I do not speak, my conscience will reproach me." "My brother," replied the friar, "the judgment of men can be but of little consequence to you; besides, you know it is not the first time you have been counted a fool. Act as your conscience dictates, and fear God rather than man." The Saint acted on this advice, but his warnings were unheeded; they to whom his words were addressed turned them into jest, and treated him as a fanatic. The crusaders again demanded that John de Brienne, the King of Jerusalem, should lead them to battle, that each might prove his valor to his adversary.

On a burning day in August, the Christian army left their lines, and offered battle to the enemy. The infidels feigned a retreat, but only to draw the crusaders into a vast plain, where the scorching sand, fatigue and thirst would have proved a sufficient foe, and hopelessly thinned their ranks. Suddenly the Saracens turned and charged their wearied pursuers. The shock was unexpected and they were ill prepared to meet it. The valor of John de Brienne and of the knights of the religious Orders, alone saved them from total destruction. As it was, a shameful defeat, and the loss of six thousand men, taught them, by a disastrous lesson, how pure an intention is required in whatever is done expressly for God.

But, however much good might be effected in the Christian camp, this was not the end which Francis had proposed to himself in his eastern mission. After passing some hours in prayer, he arose, and chanting those words of the holy Psalmist, "Though I should walk in the midst of the shadow of death, I will fear no evils, for Thou art with me," he set forth to seek martyrdom. He was warned that the Sultan had offered a reward of a golden bezant for the head of any Christian; this, however, was only an encouragement to him to pursue his journey. He had not gone far before he met two sheep. Tenderly alive to all that told in word or symbol of the passion of Christ, or the simplicity of the Christian soul, he exclaimed to his companion, "Brother, let us have confidence in God. His word is fulfilled in us; 'Behold I send you forth as sheep in the midst of wolves.'" In a short time his words were verified. A band of Saracens rushed on them, and having bound them with cords, and beaten them cruelly, led them before the Sultan. This was precisely what Francis desired; and when he was asked who had sent him, and why he had come thither, he boldly replied, "We are not sent by men, but by the Most High God. He has sent me to show you and your people the way of salvation, and to preach to you the gospel of truth." Then, as if the very spirit of God had given him utterance, he declared to them the eternal truths, and spoke of a God in three persons, and of Jesus Christ the Saviour of the world. His courage and earnestness touched the heart of the Sultan, and he began to treat him rather as a friend than as a prisoner. At length he entreated the Saint to remain with him. "I will remain with you," replied Francis, "if you and your people will be converted for the love of Jesus Christ. If you have any hesitation in quitting the law of Mahomet for the law of Christ, command a great fire to be lighted, and I will enter it with your priests, that you may thus prove which faith you ought to follow." The Sultan replied, with some hesitation, that he did not think any of his priests would submit to the test, and the speedy exit of one of his principal imauns, when the matter was proposed, corroborated his supposition. But the Saint was not to be diverted so easily from his purpose; he therefore replied, "Well, if you will promise to embrace the Christian faith, kindle a fire and I will enter it alone. If I am burnt, it will be for my sins; but if I escape, you will then acknowledge that Jesus Christ is the true God and the Saviour of the world."

Meledin dared not accept his offer. Like Pilate, "he feared the people." He was now anxious to get the Saint away; he feared the influence of his eloquent and burning words, and dreaded lest some of his people might be led to embrace the faith so boldly proclaimed, and thus join the ranks of the enemy. After offering many rich presents, which were steadily refused, he sent him back to the Christian camp under the protection of an honorable escort. It is said that the Sultan was baptized on his death-bed; and that he then caused large sums of money to be distributed among the Christians who were in hospital and in prison. This statement is much disputed; and as it would require some space to give the arguments on both sides, we leave the subject without further inquiry. All authorities, however, (including Matthew of Paris,) agree that a Sultan was baptized about that time.

But the zeal of Francis was by no means unrewarded. Though his converts among the infidels were few, his success was greater in the camp of the crusaders, and his Order was established in several places. We find the Bishop of Acre, James de Vitry, thus writing to his friends in Lorraine: "Master Reynor, prior of St. Michael's, has entered the order of Friars Minor. This Order is spreading itself rapidly through the world, because it is a perfect imitation of the form of life which was led by the Apostles and primitive Christians. The superior of these friars is called Brother Francis, a man so amiable that he is revered by all, even by the infidels." He also added that three of the most exemplary of his clergy had joined the new institute, and that he had with great difficulty dissuaded others from following their example. It is said that Francis visited the holy places in Palestine on this occasion, but no particulars are given on the subject.

His visit to Antioch is better authenticated. There was, on a neighboring mountain, a very ancient monastery of Benedictines. The abbot, who had died a short time before, had predicted that a very holy religious would visit the monastery, and desired that he should be received with all possible respect. In consequence of this prediction the Saint was warmly welcomed; and it is said that the religious of this convent, as well as those of several other houses, received the Franciscan rule. We shall see later that Palestine was especially the scene of the sufferings and labors of the Friars Minor, and if Francis himself had not the consolation of finding there a martyr's crown, the prize has been granted, almost down to our own times, to not a few of his devoted children.

CHAPTER XVII.

Francis at Bologna.—Crowds flock round him.—A testimonial of his sanctity and eloquence still on record.—Bernard da Quintavalle founder of this mission.—Nicolas of Pepulis.—State of the Church at this period.—The necessity for authorized preachers.—How it was that the friars effected so much by their missions.

ONCE more we find our Saint in his native land, still everywhere preaching peace; and penance, as the surest way to attain it. Passing rapidly through Padua, Bergamo, Brescia, Cremona, and Mantua, he reached Bologna where he remained some time. Here he was received with incredible enthusiasm; the citizens and students flocked in crowds to welcome him, and his entry into the city resembled a triumphal procession.

This mission had been founded by Bernard da Quintavalle, whom Francis sent thither soon after he had received him into the Order. At first Bernard was treated with the utmost contumely. It was not likely that in proud and learned Bologna subjects would be found for an Order based on poverty and humiliations. The men of intellect passed him with silent contempt; the poorer classes with rude and open mockery. The good friar was in no way disconcerted; he had come to their city in obedience, and in obedience he remained. But there was one heart touched by God—one voice that joined not in the general clamor. One, at least, cared to inquire what motive these strange men had in their conduct. This was Nicholas of Pepulis, a doctor of civil law in the university. When he had conversed with Bernard, and read the rule, he was struck by the standard of heroic sanctity manifested to him, and offered him a house where he might establish a convent of the Order. The tide had turned, and soon the friar's mode of life was applauded by the fickle populace, who had before contemned it. Bernard had not flinched from suffering and contempt; but he shrank from applause and prosperity. Returning to Francis, he told him what had passed, and begged he would send some of the brethren there to continue the work. The hospitable lawyer, however, was to have his reward. When our Saint arrived at Bologna, his eloquent words touched the heart of Nicholas yet more deeply, and he received the grace to give himself to God in the Order of Friars Minor. His example was followed by many others, the principal of whom were Bonizio, Pellerino, Fulleroni, and Niger of Modena.

A curious testimonial of the signal effect produced by the preaching of Francis is still on record. It is preserved in the archives of the church of Spalatro, and mentioned in the history of the bishops of Bologna, written by Sigonius. It runs thus:

"I, Thomas, citizen of Spalatro, and archdeacon of the cathedral of the same town, was studying in Bologna during the year 1220. On the Feast of the Assumption of the Mother of God, I saw St. Francis preaching in the square before the little palace, where the whole town had assembled to hear him. He divided his sermon thus: angels, men, demons. He spoke of these intelligences so well, and with such procision, that many learned men who heard him, marvelled how one so simple-minded could make such a discourse. He did not proceed in the usual manner, but spoke rather like a popular orator. He dwelt on the necessity of extinguishing all animosities, aud on the duty of promoting peace and union. His habit was worn and soiled: his personal appearance mean; his face wan and pale. But God gave such unction to his words, that many nobles who had hitherto lived in enmity were reconciled. So ardent was the love and veneration which was felt for the Saint, that the people surrounded him in crowds, and thought themselves happy if they could but touch his habit."

The spiritual wants of the age in which Francis lived

were peculiar. The old strife between the world and the Church, between the love of the visible and the hope of the invisible, which began in Paradise and caused the fall, still existed, and in this day, as in ours, had its own especial forms of evil. Let us for a moment consider the state of society in that eventful century. The Church, ever infallible in doctrine, since it was founded on the rock by the Eternal Truth, professed the same faith as when Peter was crucified, and fifteen of his successors were swept away by the sword. But the children of that infallible, unchanging mother are but human, and she has to suffer, as her Divine Lord has already suffered, from the sins of those who belonged to her. In the days of Francis, an Emperor, who ought to have been the Church's bulwark, had all but apostatized. He had drawn on himself the terrible sentence of excommunication, often threatened, and at last reluctantly decreed. Far from humbling himself for violated oaths and treaties, he added perjury to perjury; and, having himself warred against Christ in the person of His Vicar, called to his aid the barbarian and the infidel. The multitude, who love to bask in the sunshine of the great, and choose temporal gains before eternal, eagerly followed in what seemed the most prosperous cause. Heresy, too, offered itself to the acceptance of those whose attachment to the ancient faith had been tried by the disorders of the times. While the powerful laid an eager hand on the good things of earth, something also must be thrown to their poorer followers. They were therefore bribed to acquiescence in the spoliations of religion by promises of liberty, which meant a free indulgence of their unbridled passions, and lawless and excited fanatics easily led them to deeds of blood, masked under pretence of religious zeal.

The Church was suffering within and without; her needs were great, her wounds grievous. The capacious mind of Innocent saw both the evils and their remedy; and it was on this account that he so gladly accepted the services of the Mendicant Friars. The people wanted both example and instruction, and these, to be efficacious, must come from a source above the suspicion of interested motives. They wanted teachers who should speak to them the voice of truth in familiar accents; or they would hear and follow those who spoke the voice of error. It was a work which the parochial clergy, however good and zealous, could not adequately accomplish. Hence, in proportion to their earnest desire for the welfare of their people, was the welcome they gave to these new auxiliaries. The friar had no ties of place or kindred; wherever his work was, there was his home. They who followed his counsels, were dearer to him than any to whom he had been bound by human ties. No interested motives could be imputed to one who carried out in his own life the poverty, the penance, the humility which he preached, and that to a far greater degree than he required it in his hearers. He was filled with the peace which he proclaimed, and stood foremost among the "men of good will" to whom he proclaimed it. Like Him whose blessed example he followed so closely, he became poor to win the poor, and simple to sanctify the unlearned. Armed with such recommendations, the poor friar had access where others dared not penetrate. He found himself welcome alike in cottage and camp, by the wayside and in the baronial hall; and his coarse habit appeared with as simple a grace among the hauberks of plumed warriors and the ermine and coifs of grave senators, as when its wearer turned to console and instruct the poor and ignorant peasant.

Moreover, the age needed teaching, and all successful teaching must be adapted, both in kind and in mode, to the receiver. The voice of the Friar Minor was the "cheap library" of the age; his instructions formed a kind of household literature. The monks, so strangely calumniated as despisers of learning, had preserved the treasures of knowledge, the sacred Scriptures, and the most valuable works of antiquity, in the safety of their libraries; and if these valuable possessions were injured or destroyed, it was not by their anxious guardians, but by barbarous fanatics, who thought to display their zeal for God by consigning to destruction the works which taught of His wisdom or His will. But there was more needed than mere knowledge or ability to teach. Men have been known to speak the voice of truth even while living the lives of reprobates: such teaching may convince—it can seldom convert. But here were men who not only asserted truth, but lived it. Their lives were sermons, their penances, their poverty, their rigid fasts, their long vigils, their fervent prayers, gave unction to the words they uttered, and brought down torrents of grace on their zealous efforts. Self had been and was daily disciplined and controlled, until it seemed scarcely to exist: all that was done was the will of God, because it was done in obedience to the will of superiors, who held to them His place. Hence, the poor Franciscan Friar could soon count his hearers by thousands, and his converts by hundreds; and his work prospered as much beyond the calculation, as its motive was beyond the eye of man.

CHAPTER XVIII.

John de Strachia.—His disobedience and unhappy end.—Brother Elias.—His worldliness.—He appears more strict than Francis.—He censures the Saint.—His concealed efforts to relax the Order.—An Angel's visit.

We must now return to Francis and Bologna. John de Strachia had been made provincial there, and, contrary to the express command of our Saint, had built a large and magnificent convent for his religious; and, moreover, had opened a school in which more regard was paid to secular learning than to religious instruction. When Francis saw how matters were, he refused to enter the convent. After a time, however, he was prevailed on to do so, and to permit it to remain as it was. On returning from a visit to his friend, Cardinal Ugolini, he found with surprise and indignation the school still open, which he had strictly ordered to be closed. Such open disobedience required that a public example should be made of the offender. Francis therefore deposed him from the office of which he had shown himself so unworthy, and publicly anathematized him. But even this chastisement failed to arouse the unhappy friar, who, in the sequel, gave a painful warning to his companions how far self-delusion may be carried. In a short time after, this miserable man died in the agonies of despair.

Nor was John de Strachia the only disciple of the Saint who gave him pain. It will be remembered that he had placed the government of the Order in the hands of Brother Elias when he set out on his eastern mission. During his absence rumors had reached him that all was not going on well at home. But Francis was slow to believe evil of any of his children; and

8

though some authors say that a special messenger was sent to warn him of what was taking place, he hoped for the best till compelled to believe the worst. Leaving Bologna, the Saint journeyed towards Assisi. In the valley of Spoleto he was met and welcomed by crowds of his spiritual children. Elias was among the number, and Francis had ocular proof that the complaints made of him were not unfounded. At the first glance he saw a disregard, not to say contempt, for poverty in the dress of this unhappy friar. He wore a new habit made of fine cloth, with wide sleeves and a cowl much larger than was permitted by the strict regulations made regarding the habit; in fact, he had contrived to make the dress of a poor friar look as worldly and as fashionable as he could. Francis at first pretended not to notice all this; after a little he asked Elias to lend him his habit. The unhappy brother did not refuse. Then the Saint put it on over his own, arranged the folds so as to hang gracefully, threw the cowl over his head, and walked about with a courtly air, saying to the friars, " God save you, good people." Then, with a sudden vehemence of indignant zeal, he took off the habit and flung it from him, exclaiming, "That is how the bastard children of our Order will strut." And in a long and earnest address he most affectionately besought his brethren to persevere in the path of perfection, and never to forsake the humility and poverty which were the very foundation-stones of their holy Order.

The history of Elias is an instructive one, and not without its parallel in religious communities. He was strongly attached to his holy superior, though he caused him such perpetual anxiety. His Order, too, he loved, after a certain fashion, even while endeavoring to destroy it by introducing relaxations that suited his self-love and worldly spirit. It will be remembered that at the Chapter of Mats, he, with the unhappy John de Strachia and others, had done their best to bend the holy will of Francis to their views. Since then, Elias had so far recovered the confidence of his superior as to be appointed general during his absence. He had thus full opportunity to carry out his designs; and as is usual with those who wish to introduce relaxations, he began with an appearance of zeal—a strange but not uncommon form of self-delusion. He was going to undermine, as far as in him lay, the very foundations of his Order. Tepidity was the exception, not the rule, among the Friars Minor in the days of Francis; and Brother Elias would not be remarked as less fervent than his companions, yet he could not bear the self-denials required by his Rule. He could not rise to the perfection of his order: he must then lower its requirements to suit his own standard. No sooner had Francis left Italy than the work began; Elias had his friends in the society, and a restless demon, jealous of the great prosperity of the Order, ready to urge him on. Francis was not strict enough for him, he said, and his Rule not sufficiently austere. Thus, as a first step towards reformation in the Order, he began by criticising the conduct of his superior, and endeavoring to lessen his reputation for sanctity. Then, after murmuring these complaints for a time among the brethren, he altogether forbade the use of flesh meat.

This prohibition requires a word of explanation. Austerity was not the special end of the Franciscan Order. It was used, indeed, as a means to the end, and as a most important means. The Saint himself seldom took any other food but bread and water, and perhaps no body of religious ever practiced greater corporal macerations than the Friars Minor. But to practice the most rigid poverty, and to labor for the salvation of their neighbor by word and work, was the great end which the Saint proposed; and whatever tended to promote this end was deemed of the first importance. One half of the year, at least, they were obliged by rule to fast and to abstain from the use of flesh meat; at other times they were permitted to take whatever food was given them—as Francis considered this more in accordance with the spirit of poverty which he so earnestly desired to see practiced. This new regulation, made by Brother Elias, was therefore in direct opposition to the intentions of Francis. It was only used as a cloak to cover a mnltitude of evils. Discipline was relaxed in every way, and poverty disregarded in the dress, the food and the buildings of the Friars. It is curious, and may be not a little instructive, to observe how, in the lives of tepid religious, there is mostly a restless eagerness about some trivial or imaginary point in which they suppose all perfection to consist. Blinded, or blinding themselves, they forget that obedience; for the utter renunciation of their own will and judgment is the essential perfection of a religious life.

The presence and authority of Francis was an effectual check to those threatened relaxations. Trailing habits and wide sleeves disappeared, and poverty was again strictly practiced. Elias and his companions were silenced, but not convinced. Even the fate of the unhappy John de Strachia failed to arouse them to a sense of their danger. But the tares and the wheat must grow together until the harvest; and the Saint, who saw all in God, and strove to do all for God, bore those evils with a calmness and patience even like Him who sends the rain alike on the wicked and the good.

Francis, however, considered it more prudent not to alter the regulation which had been made forbidding the use of meat. He knew human nature well, and thought that the weak-minded might be scandalized. But it was not long before a miraculous event occurred which ought forever to have cured his unworthy children of a disposition to question his authority.

A few days after the return of Francis, a young man attired as a pilgrim, came to the door of the convent at St. Mary of the Angels. He addressed Brother Masseo, who was porter, and said, "I wish to speak to Brother Francis, but I know he is praying in the wood. Will you, therefore, call Brother Elias to me? I hear he is a wise and learned man, and I wish to consult him regarding a doubt which presses on me." Brother Masseo did as he was requested, but Elias, whose manners were not always the most courteous, answered him rudely, and refused to interrupt his employment. The good friar was greatly perplexed how to answer the stranger; he did not wish to offend him, and he feared to expôse the faults of a superior. But before he had time to speak, the stranger addressed him: "Brother Elias does not choose to come," he said; "I beg you will go to Brother Francis, and ask him to desire him to come to me." Masseo went to the Saint. He was absorbed in prayer, and without changing his position or interrupting his occupation, he said; "Go, tell Brother Elias that I order him to go and speak to the young man." Elias dared not disobey, but he went with no good grace, and roughly asked the stranger what he wanted. The young man replied, "I wish to know whether those who follow the evangelical counsels may not also follow the example of Jesus Christ, and eat whatever is presented to them, and whether any one has a right to ordain the contrary." "I know all you would say, but I will not answer you," exclaimed Elias, in extreme irritation, and at the same time shutting the door violently in the young man's face. "Well," replied the stranger, "I do not know what answer you would give to my question, but I do know that you ought to give some reply."

Elias returned to his cell, and in a few moments began to reflect on what had passed. Then, thinking that he had not acted even with common courtesy, he went in search of the young man, but he had disappeared, no one knew how. When Francis returned, he called for Elias and reproved him severely; for it had been revealed to him that their visitor was an angel. "Your conduct is far from what it should be," he said; "You send away with contempt angels who are sent by God to visit and instruct us. I greatly fear that your pride will make you unworthy to be a Friar Minor, and that you will die out of the Order." Again the unworthy Friar was silenced, not convinced. Francis saw it was time to assert his authority; he therefore appointed Peter of Catania general in the place of Elias, and Brother Gratian was sent to Bologna to take the office vacant since the death of its unhappy provincial.

CHAPTER XIX.

The first martyrs of the Order.—Brother Berrardi and his companions.—Death of Brother Vital.—Queen Uracca.—The Princess Sanchia.—Seville.—Morocco.—Don Pedro.—The Friars are sent out of Morocco, but contrive to return again.—Given into the care of a Christian Prince.—They save his army from perishing of drought.—Imprisoned again, and left for twenty days without food.—Their cruel martyrdom.—They appear to the Spanish Princess.—The joy of Francis that he now has five true Friars.—Other Martyrs of the Order.

When the religious were dispersed, after the general Chapter in 1219, six of the brethren were sent into

Spain. Five of these are commemorated as the first martyrs of the Order. Their names were, Brother Berrardi, who was well acquainted with the Arabian language; Brothers Otho and Peter, who were priests; and Adjuto and Accursio, who were lay brothers. Brother Vital was appointed superior. Before their departure the Saint gave them an exhortation, the substance of which has been preserved in the Chronicles of the Order. "My children," he said, "I have some things to say to you, which I hope may assist you in fulfilling the holy will of God, and securing the salvation of your souls. First, I beseech of you to keep peace amongst yourselves, and to live as brothers, not so much in habit and religious profession as in spirit and in heart. Take special care to keep free from envy, which causes the damnation of many. Be joyful and patient in all your afflictions. Be humble before God and men: so will you be victorious againt your enemies, visible and invisible. Take your Rule and your Breviary with you, and say the Divine Office with all possible devotion. Obey your superior in all things, without murmuring or hesitation. And let meditation on the passion of Christ be your food and refreshment, your support and consolation. Believe me, my children, I am much grieved to part with you. Nothing should ever have separated us but the glory of God and the salvation of souls, for which I now send you forth; and I am not a little comforted by your prompt obedience and your readiness to go wherever you may be sent."

Then he embraced them, and gave them his benediction with many tears; and so they went forth on their mission, even as men should do who evangelize and pine for a martyr's crown, having neither money nor scrip, nor staff. When they reached Arragon, Brother Vital was taken dangerously ill. Finding he was not likely to recover speedily, he would not allow them to delay, but appointed Brother Berrardi superior, and commanded them in obedience to continue their journey. They were all deeply grieved to leave their companion thus alone and suffering; but the words of their saintly father still rang in their ears, and their love of obedience triumphed over their holy affection. Having received the benediction of the dying brother, they continued their journey. Brother Vital lingered on in extreme pain and weakness until he heard that his brethren had gained the crown of martyrdom. He soon followed them, and died full of joy that they should have obtained a favor of which he considered himself unworthy.

At Coimbra the friars were received most kindly by Queen Uracca, the wife of Alphonsus the Second. After having entertained them with all hospitality, she earnestly begged them to pray that the day of her death might be revealed to them. At first they declined, saying they were unworthy to ask or obtain such favors. At length they were compelled to yield to her entreaties: and they brought her the joyful news that in a short time they would die for the faith, and that her decease would occur immediately after their martyrdom. At Alenquer they were lodged in a convent of their own Order, and not less courteously entertained by the Princess Sanchia, sister to the King of Portugal, who resided in that city. By her advice they put on secular clothing, and waited for their hair to grow, as their religious habit and tonsure would have attracted attention, and might have frustrated their design. Thus prepared they went on board a vessel bound for Seville; for although this city was in the possession of the Moors, some Christian merchants continued to trade there. One of these received the friars into his house, and they then resumed their religious dress. After spending eight days in prayer and fasting, they informed their host why they had come to the place, and said they would now begin to preach to the people. But they found every obstacle thrown in their way. The merchant was exceedingly alarmed, and did his best to dissuade them from their purpose, assuring them they could do no good to the infidels, and would only bring persecution on the Christians, who were allowed to trade there. Such worldly reasoning was not likely to influence the fervid children of Francis. Fearless of all consequences, they did but the more eagerly covet the danger of which they were warned.

Their first attempt was in the mosque. Even while the Moors were there engaged in their devotions, the soldiers of the Cross attacked them with the sword of God, preaching to them of Jesus crucified. At first, in consequence of their peculiar and mean dress, they only excited contempt, and were driven out with blows and rude words. This treatment increased the zeal of the religious, and they repaired to another and larger mosque, where they again addressed the people, but they were again repulsed. At last they determined to enter the palace, and seek an interview with the Moorish king. With some difficulty they obtained an audience. A strange scene followed. The chief was enraged at their boldness, and ordered them to be scourged and then beheaded. One of his sons, more humane than his father, interposed in their behalf, and the sentence was mitigated to imprisonment. But they soon began to preach to the people from the tower in which they were confined. To prevent this exercise of zeal they were placed in a dark and deep dungeon; but even here they would not be silent, and continued their efforts in behalf of their fellow-prisoners. The

Moorish chief then commanded that they should be brought before him, and endeavored to shake their faith by promises of wealth and honor if they would but acknowledge Mahomet. They thanked him courteously, and replied, "Would to God, noble prince, that you would show mercy to yourself; you need it more than we do. Treat us as you will; you can at the utmost only deprive us of life, and that is a matter of little moment to those who hope for eternal joys."

The king was perplexed what to do with these strange men, who seemed to care nothing for earthly wealth or honors, and to court death and suffering with a heroism he could not but admire; their dauntless bearing, too, contrasting so strangely with their mean appearance. After a consultation with his officers, they came to the conclusion that the wisest course was to send them quietly out of the country. Accordingly they were placed on board a vessel bound for Morocco. Here they were received kindly by Don Pedro, brother of Alphonsus the Second, who had left his native land in consequence of some dissensions between his relations. The personal appearance of the friars was anything but attractive. Suffering and imprisonment had done its work on them; and their wan, meagre faces told how much they had endured for Christ. The Prince earnestly impressed on them the necessity for caution—reminding them of all they had endured at Seville, and begged they would not again expose themselves to danger. But love is strong as death, and they who for love of Jesus crucified had already cast away all that the world most prizes, were not likely to make nice calculations about their personal safety. The next morning found them at their Master's work. Brother Berrardi understood Arabic perfectly; and hearing that the king was to pass through the streets in a public procession, he mounted on a high hill and began to preach as he approached. Public opinion decided at once that the friar was deranged, and he and his companions were ordered to leave the country. Don Pedro, glad to be freed from guests who were likely to prove so troublesome, gave them an escort to Ceuta, where they were to embark.

But the friars were not to be so easily turned from their purpose. They escaped from their guides, and returned to Morocco, where they again began to preach. This was too much for the royal equanimity. They were arrested, confined in a dungeon, and denied every kind of sustenance. Soon after, a severe sickness broke out among the Moors, caused by violent heats and unusual drought. One of the nobles, who was favorably inclined to the Christians, advised the king to release his captives if they were still alive. Twenty days had passed, and they had not eaten a morsel of food or tasted as much as a mouthful of water. But, to the amazement of all, they were found as well and as cheerful as when they had entered the prison. This miracle procured their release. They were given into the care of Don Pedro, who surrounded them by a guard of Christians in order to hinder any fresh inconveniences from their zeal in preaching. Having to take the command of a military expedition against some tribes who had revolted in the interior of Africa, he took the friars with him. While traversing the desert they were three days without water, and all must have perished had not a miraculous fountain sprung up in answer to the prayers of Brother Berrardi. On their return to Morocco they again preached publicly, and the fame of their miracles brought them many hearers. Again they were imprisoned, and one of the royal officers was desired to put them to the torture. But Abozaida had experienced the effects of their prayers while on the late campaign, and he contented himself with placing them in strict custody. He hoped that after a time their resolution would be shaken; but he found himself mistaken, and was obliged to obey the commands of his royal master.

The jailor was a renegade Christian, and a man of most inhuman disposition. The execution of the barbarous sentence was confided to him, and he did not fail to increase the martyrs' merit by the severity of their torments. After a most barbarous scourging, they were tied hand and foot, and dragged almost naked over a floor strewn with flints and broken glass; while, to complete their torture, boiling vinegar was poured into their open wounds. They were then thrown back into their dungeon, where they still continued the hymns of joy which they had not ceased to utter during this inhuman butchery. At night, the keepers who watched them saw their prison filled with a most glorious light, and the friars raised so high above the ground, that they feared they were about to escape from them by a miracle. Next morning they were brought before the king, and the usual scene on such occasions was enacted. Honors, wealth, pleasures, were offered, if they would renounce Christ and confess Mahomet. At length the prince, weary of their constancy, clove their heads with his own sword, and sent them to enjoy that eternal blessedness for which they had so long pined. Their martyrdom was accomplished on the 16th of January, 1220. Their bodies were torn to pieces by the infidels; but the Christians managed to collect the scattered relics. These were eventually translated to Portugal, and solemnly deposited in the church of the canons regular of Sta. Cruz, at Coimbra. At the moment of their happy release, they appeared to the Princess Sanchia, each holding a scimitar in his hand. They saluted her lovingly and exclaimed: "God preserve thee, thou servant of Jesus Christ, forasmuch as thou hast encouraged us and sent us on to this glorious victory. Know that it hath pleased the Divine Majesty that we should appear to thee with those tokens of our triumph; and henceforth we will be thy advocates in heaven."

When their relics arrived at Sta. Cruz, the good Queen Uracca knew that the close of her earthly pilgrimage must be near; since they had foretold she should follow them. Full of joy and confidence, she began to pray that her Lord would not delay long in calling her to Himself. That night her confessor, Peter Nuguez, who was also a canon of Sta. Cruz, had a wonderful vision. He beheld in the church a company of religious, who sang the Divine Office, and who were all surrounded by a light of supernatural brightness. One of them told him that they were Friars Minor, and that St. Francis and their martyred companions were among them, all singing matins for the repose of the Queen's soul, of whose decease he would be presently informed. And it was even so; for the vision had scarcely faded from his sight, ere a messenger came to tell him that Uracca was gone to her eternal reward.

The joy of Francis, when he heard of the martyrdom of his children was unbounded. "Now," he exclaimed, "I can say that I have at least five true friars." Then turning towards Spain, he saluted the convent of Alenquer, from whence they had set out for Morocco, "Holy house, blessed country!" he cried; thou hast produced and offered to thy King five beautiful and purple flowers of a most celestial sweetness. O holy house! mayest thou always be inhabited by Saints."

The king of Morocco and his subjects suffered a severe chastisement for their murder of those holy men. During the space of five years the land was desolated by dearth and pestilence, and the Sultan was unable to raise the hand with which he smote the martyrs. At length he repented so far as to acknowledge that he had done an injustice, and thenceforth he and his people tolerated the Christian faith.

The following year, Daniel, minister of the province of Calabria, with six companions, obtained leave from Brother Elias to preach to the Moors. The Friars who accompanied him were Samuel, Leo, (not the Pecorella,) Donule, Ugolini, Nicholas, and Angelus. After many delays and difficulties they arrived at Ceuta, and began their mission by preaching to the Christian merchants, mostly Italians, who were allowed to live outside the town. At length they determined to enter the city at any risk. On Saturday, the 2nd of October, 1221, they confessed and received the Holy Communion. In the evening, in imitation of the charity of our Divine Lord, they washed each other's feet; and on the following day they entered Ceuta, having ashes on their heads, and crying with a loud voice, "Jesus Christ is the only true God, and there is no salvation but in Him." At first they were treated as madmen, and thrown into prison, heavily ironed. During this time they wrote a letter which they addressed to some religious,* who had lately arrived in Africa. It was to inform them of their imprisonment, and of the joy they felt in being allowed to suffer for Christ.

After a few days they were brought into the presence

* M. Chevin de Malin says this letter was addressed to the Christian merchants in the neighborhood of Ceuta. This is surely a mistake, as the Chronicles of the Order say it was addressed to "Brother Hugo and other religious who had lately arrived in Africa." Probably it was sent to them through these merchants.

of their judges. Each was questioned separately, and urged by every inducement which a Moorish imagination could devise, to renounce the faith. Still they cried out, "Jesus Christ is the only true God, and there is no salvation but in Him." They were condemned to be beheaded, and returned to their prison full of joy. Then casting themselves at the feet of their superior, they exclaimed, "Thanks be to God, and to you, father, for having led us to a martyr's crown. Bless us before we die! The contest will soon be ended, and we shall enter on eternal peace." Daniel embraced them with the tenderest affection, and said, "Let us rejoice in the Lord; this is indeed a feast-day for us. The angels throng round us; the heavens are opened to receive us; this very day we shall obtain the crown of martyrdom." They were then led to execution, rejoicing as though on their way to some festive celebration. In a few brief moments their souls were with God. Their remains were inhumanly mangled, but some relics were secured by the Christians, and these were afterwards conveyed safely to Spain. Leo the Tenth permitted their feast to be celebrated on the day of their martyrdom, October the 10th, 1221.

Many others also gained glorious crowns in the Moorish provinces; but we can only notice one more of these happy friars. Brother Electus had entered the Order while very young. His constitution was extremely delicate, and Francis himself dispensed him from the observance of their rigorous fasts. But his sanctity and the fervor of his spirit overcame the weakness of the flesh, and in a short time he became one of the most austere religious in his Order. No maceration, no fasts, seemed too severe for him. At length he obtained permission to go with some others to preach to the Moors. Soon after their arrival they were seized, and all led to execution. Having arrived at the place of martyrdom, Brother Electus took the Rule of his holy patriarch into his hands, and turning to one of his companions, said, "Brother, I confess my faults before God and you, in whatsoever I may have offended against this Rule." He then bared his head to receive the stroke of the executioner, and sealed with his blood his love of God and his devotion to his Order.

CHAPTER XX.

St Antony of Padua.—His mother's tomb.—Enters amongst the Regular Canons of St. Austin.—Receives a vocation to the Franciscan Order.—Attends a general chapter.—His residence at Bologna.—Is given an obedience to preach.—His talents are discovered.—Miracles.—His love of peace.—Beholds the Infant Jesus.—His devotion to our Lady.—His death.—St. Bonaventura's opinion of his sanctity.

In the Abbey of St. Vincent, near Lisbon, there is a chapel dedicated to St. Antony of Padua, in which may be seen a tomb bearing this inscription:

"Hic jacet mater Sancti Antonii."

The mother of St. Antony! yes, it was honor enough, and more than enough, for the noble Donna Teresa, to have given to the world one of its most brilliant lights —to the Franciscan Order one of its chief ornaments.

Born at Lisbon, in the year of our redemption 1195, Antony, or Fernandez, as he was then called, was descended from the illustrious house of Bouillon, which had already attained a world-wide reputation, as well for chivalry and knightly valor as for Christian courtesy. At the age of fifteen, the Saint made choice of a religious life, and entered the monastery of the canons of St. Augustine. Here he applied himself especially to the study of the sacred Scriptures and of the Fathers, as he wished to prepare in a particular manner for preaching to heretics. Soon after he had entered this convent, the bodies of the holy martyrs of Morocco were conveyed thither; and this circumstance attracted him to their Order, and made him ardently desire a crown like theirs. Friars from the Franciscan monastery of St. Antony were accustomed to beg alms from the Augustinians; and the humility thus manifested became another attraction for the young religious, who was soon to be so eminent among these poor friars. It was plain, indeed, that he was one of those blessed souls who cannot rest at any point short of the highest perfection of their state. For such souls Providence opens, through the greatest apparent obstacles, the paths which will lead them to the attainment of their desire.

In the year 1220 he entered the Order of Friars Minor. He was then preparing for the priesthood, and had been seven years in the Augustinian convent. These good religious were naturally unwilling to part with one who already gave indications of no common sanctity. But, to their eternal honor, be it said, they put no obstacles in his way, and even permitted him to change his habit in their own cloister, whither two Franciscan friars came to conduct him to his new home. It was on this occasion that Fernandez assumed the name of Antony. After a short time he obtained permission from his superiors to visit Africa, hoping there to obtain the martyr's crown he so much yearned for. Such, however, was not the will of God. A severe illness obliged him to return home, and exchange the martyrdom of an apostle to the heathen for the longer and scarcely less painful one of perseverance in a religious life. To Antony it mattered little, he only desired the will and the glory of his God. The vessel in which he embarked for Portugal was driven by contrary winds to a port in Sicily. Here, however, there was a convent of his Order, where he remained some time. From thence he proceeded to attend the general chapter at St. Mary of the Angels, in company with Philip, a Castilian lay brother.

While here, by an especial Providence, he was overlooked by all. The Fathers were dispersing to their various missions with the brethren appointed for each; but none had claimed the two strangers. After a little consideration they presented themselves to Brother Gratian, begging that he would receive them among his novices, and instruct them in their holy Rule. Their request was granted. Philip was sent to Castello, and afterwards to Tuscany, where he died in the odor of sanctity. Antony accompanied Brother Gratian to Bologna. Here he requested permission to live in a little cell hewn out of a rock, and separate from the rest of the Brethren. He lived for some time in this manner, constantly engaged in prayer, and practicing the greatest austerities. But the designs of God towards him were not frustrated by his humility. The words spoken by Him who took upon Himself the form of a slave to subdue the pride of worms, still have their fulfilment: "He that humbleth himself shall be exalted." For a time no one suspected that Antony was other than he seemed to be; his great gifts, natural and supernatural, were alike hidden. To clean the kitchen and cook the poor fare of the friars, was the highest office assigned to him; and in this employment he seemed at home and content. After some months had passed in this manner, the provincial brought him to Forli with several others who were to receive Holy Orders. There they found a large assemblage of friars, both Franciscan and Dominican, and many secular priests. One day, when all were assembled for their mid-day refection, Brother Gratian requested one of the friars preachers to give them a spiritual exhortation; but he humbly declined. Others were asked, and likewise excused themselves. At length the provincial, as if suddenly inspired with the idea, desired Brother Antony to speak. The young friar endeavored to excuse himself on the ground of his incapacity. At length obedience prevailed over humility, or rather humility was perfected, as it ever has been, in obedience.

At first the young friar spoke with hesitation and timidity. But as he proceeded and warmed with his subject, he astonished the brethren by the depth of his learning and the brilliancy of his eloquence. When Francis was informed of the unusual talent which had been found in his young disciple, he desired that he should continue to preach, and also apply himself to the study of theology as a science. To give no excuse for a refusal, and to satisfy the humility of Antony, he sent him a written obedience in these words: "To my dear Brother Antony, health in Jesus Christ, from Brother Francis. It is my wish that you should teach theology to the brethren, but in such sort that the spirit of prayer required by our Rule be not lessened either in you or in them."

The better to fulfill this obedience, Antony set out for Versailles, to study there for a time before he began to instruct others. He was accompanied by Adam de Marisco, an English friar, who afterwards became celebrated as a doctor of divinity. They placed themselves under the instruction of a religious named Thomas. He was abbot of the monastery of St. Andrew, and had a great reputation for learning. But in a short time the young Saint surpassed his teacher, and was obliged to yield to the earnest entreaties of his religious, and to give them the benefit of his instructions.

St. Francis had been asked whether he wished those who entered his Order to continue their studies. "I should wish it," he replied, "provided that, according to the example of Jesus Christ, who prayed more than He read, these brothers do not neglect the duty of prayer; and that they study not so much to know how they ought to speak, as to practice what they have learned, and to teach others how to practice it. I wish my friars to be true disciples of the Gospel, so that as they advance in the knowledge of the truth, they may also grow in simplicity; thus, according to the words of our Divine Master, joining the simplicity of the dove to the wisdom of the serpent." On another occasion he thus severely reproved those who sought merely human science. "In the day of trouble these men will find their hands empty. I desire, therefore, that my disciples should seek rather to be confirmed in virtue, that they may enjoy the presence of their Saviour in the day of evil. For the time will come when books shall be thrown from the windows, and into corners as useless. I desire that my brethren should not be too anxious to know and to read; but rather built up in holy humility, in simplicity, in prayer and in poverty, our Mistress and our Lady. This is the only sure way for their salvation and for the edification of their neighbor; for they are called to imitate and follow Jesus Christ."

Scarcely had Antony commenced his career of sanctity and learning, ere another gem was added to the crown of Francis, and another noble intellect bowed itself to his lowly rule.

The university of Paris resounded with the praises

and fame of Alexander of Hales. He held there the rank of professor—a position at once exalted and important; and he taught with ever increasing success and reputation. But the time came when human applause seemed to him but an empty sound in a dream, and he pined for a meed of praise which should not pass away with the breath that bestowed it. It is said that he had a most special devotion to the Mother of God, and had bound himself solemnly never to withhold what was asked in her honor. Perhaps it was to reward this filial confidence that he received a vocation to an Order of which she is the special patroness, and in which her dearest privileges have been so warmly and so successfully defended. He had been asked to join other religious Orders, but he still wavered in his choice. One day, however, his vocation was providentially decided. A Friar Minor met him, and accosted him thus: "Reverend Master, you have for a long time done service to the world by your great learning. Our Order has no one equally capable of instructing it; I therefore pray you, for the love of God and the Blessed Virgin Mary, to take the habit of the Friars Minor." The name of Mary had been pronounced, and it was enough. Alexander doubted no longer, but at once replied, "Go, my brother, and I will soon follow and do all that you desire." In a few short days the extraordinary vocation of the great professor was the wonder of Paris; and the talents and distinction of the doctor of theology were hidden under the garb of a novice among the mendicant friars.

The world saw the exterior act without sympathy, as without comprehension of its meaning. But who may tell how many and how painful were the interior and renewed acts of the will required to mortify, and so to perfect that soul? While men pitied and wondered, Alexander struggled and suffered. At length, when his trials seemed to have reached a point beyond which he could bear no more, a heavenly vision was sent to console and strengthen him. He saw in a dream the holy founder of the Order whose habit he wore. The Saint toiled up a steep mountain, endeavoring to carry a cross which threatened at every moment to crush him. Alexander wished to help him to bear his burden; but Francis would not permit it. "Away, unhappy man," he cried, "how can you ask to bear this cross, when you are unable to carry one of stuff?" The vision strengthened him; his fears were rebuked, and his courage nerved to persevere.

Nor was he altogether singular in the course he had taken. John of St. Giles, also an Englishman, joined the Dominican Order about the same time. Descending from the pulpit, where he was preaching, he assumed its white habit; and then, in the face of his astonished audience, he returned and resumed the discourse so strangely interrupted. Thus the mendicant Orders, in all their poverty, carried away the palms of martyrdom, of sanctity, and of science, and showed the world how humility and true greatness might exhibit their noblest examples in the one soul.

After Alexander of Hales had been favored with the vision already spoken of, he gave himself more earnestly to the work of preaching. Even while thus occupied he prepared his "Summa,"* which has been justly called the foundation-stone of the magnificent

* "This book," says Alexander the Fourth, "is a river flowing from Paradise, a treasure of science and wisdom, full of irrefragable sentences which crush falsehood by the weight of truth; it is invaluable to those who wish to advance in the knowledge of the Divine laws. It is the work of God, and the author was inspired by the Holy Ghost." —*Extract from a brief of this Pope's in which he required all Friars Minor under obedience to make themselves masters of the Summa.* [Gerson also praises this work most highly in his Ep. de Laud. Bonaventuræ.]

structure erected by his disciple, the great St. Thomas. The chief glory, indeed, of this doctor was reflected from his children; and what the Church owes of theological science and mystic love to St. Thomas and St. Bonaventura, may have had its source in the instructions of the holy friar. So highly was he esteemed in his own age, that the university of Paris offered to present a laurel crown to whoever he considered most worthy of the honor. His choice fell on John of Rochelle, another illustrious member of the Seraphic Order.

The Order began now to be distinguished for its preachers; and of these St. Antony was not the least successful. Preaching, indeed, seemed to be the work to which he was peculiarly called. He has unconsciously described himself in declaring what a true preacher ought to be. In one of his sermons he speaks thus:

"A true preacher is a son of Zachary, that is to say, of the memory of the Lord; for he should always preserve in his mind a recollection of the passion of Christ. In the night of sorrow, it is for Him he must long, and in the morning of prosperity and joy, with Him he must awake. Then the Word of God will descend upon him, the word of peace and life, the word of grace and truth. O Word, which bruises not the heart, but rather inebriates it! O Word, full of tenderness which pours forth the blessedness of hope into suffering souls! O Word, which refreshes the thirsty soul."

In another place he compares the cloud seen by Elias to the effect produced by a holy preacher:

"Elias represents the preacher, who ascends to the height of Carmel, that is to say, to the perfection of a holy life, where he acquires the science of cutting off, by a mystical circumcision, all vanities and superfluities. As a sign of his humility, and in remembrance of his miseries, he prostrates himself on the earth, and hides his face between his knees, to show how deep is his affliction. Elias said to his servant, 'Go and look towards the seacoast.' This servant represents the body of the preacher, which ought to be purity itself, and which ought ceaselessly to look towards the world overwhelmed in sin, that he may assist it by his words. He must look seven times, that is, he must meditate constantly on seven articles of faith, on the Incarnation, on the sacrament of Baptism, on the Passion, on the Resurrection, on the mission of the Holy Ghost, and on the last Judgment, when the wicked shall be condemned to eternal flames. But the seventh time, the preacher will see a little cloud arise from the depths of the sea: from the inmost soul of the sinner arises a movement of compunction and repentance. This little sign of the grace of God in the heart of man will ascend; it will become a great cloud, and will hide with its shadow the love of earthly things. Then the soft winds of penance will uproot the last fibres of sin, and at last the great rain of an abundant satisfaction will refresh and fertilize the earth. Behold the work of a good preacher. Alas for him whose preaching is eloquent, but whose works are evil."

Preaching in all ages must have its distinctive characteristic, and to be effective, must correspond with the needs of the day. The thirteenth century was a time of frequent domestic wars, as sanguinary as they were violent, and they who lived lives of peace needed also to preach it to others. The cruelty of the tyrant Ezzelino was then at its height. We may derive some conception of the woes it inflicted from the common saying, that he must have been born a demon, so far did his wickedness surpass that of even the worst of his cotemporaries. Every effort had been made to check his career of impiety, but in vain. After heading the Ghibelin faction for some time, he made himself master of Padua, Verona, and the neighboring towns. By his command twelve thousand persons perished by fire and sword in the amphitheatre at Verona. Anathemas and excommunications were fulminated against him, and were laughed to scorn. Yet this monster of impiety trembled, and for the moment seemed struck with remorse at the voice of a poor friar. Antony determined at all risks to have a personal interview with Ezzelino, and presented himself before him unexpectedly. "Cruel monster!" he exclaimed; "enemy of God! when will thy rage be satisfied, and when wilt thou cease to shed the blood of the faithful and the innocent? Know that for these things the judgments of God will assuredly visit thee, and thine end will be terrible." The guards who surrounded the tyrant expected every moment the signal to fall upon the unprotected friar, and to make him pay for his boldness with his life. But to their astonishment, they beheld the tyrant descend from his throne, and casting himself at the feet of the Saint, implore pardon of God for his crimes, promising at the same time faithfully to perform penance and to amend his life. But his repentance was of brief duration. Perhaps it did but hinder the commission of some few mortal sins—a matter of small moment to the world, but not so to the Saint. John of Vincenza, another blessed apostle of peace, had also striven to touch this obstinate heart, and the "Festival of Peace" which he caused to be celebrated, had the effect of procuring a brief cessation of his violence. Friar Minor and Friar Preacher had each done their work, and each have reaped their reward. Ezzelino, on his part, did the work of the cruel master whom he served, and his reward was a death as miserable as Antony had predicted.

On one occasion it was announced that Antony was to preach in the neighborhood of Padua. When the day was known, so eager were all to see and hear the Saint, that during the whole preceding night, every road leading to the city was thronged by crowds of people, who vied with each other in their eagerness to reach the place appointed for his discourse. Men, women and children, the highest ranks mingled with the poorest, swelled this great procession; all were dressed in penitential garb, and each carried a lighted torch. When morning dawned, more than thirty thousand people had assembled, and were waiting the presence of the friar. He soon appeared, attended by the bishop of Padua and his clergy, and then a deep murmur of joy and anxious expectation thrilled through the vast multitude. A breathless stillness followed, as each strove to catch the impassioned words which fell from the lips of the preacher, and each drank in with thirsty soul the sweetness of heavenly grace. "O my brothers," he cried, "peace be with you, peace be with you. Peace! it is justice. Peace! it is perfect liberty. Peace! it is unchanging rest." But after a time his burning words could no longer be heard. Sighs and sounds of weeping and heartfelt ejaculations for mercy arose on every side. Then with the impassioned ardor of the south, the multitudes threw themselves upon the preacher, kissing his hands and his feet, and rent his very garments in order to possess a relic of one who they felt was inspired by God. Armed men were often obliged to accompany him to his convent door, or he would have been almost crushed by the eager devotion of the multitudes who constantly flocked around him.

But his preaching was not their only attraction. The promise of Christ to His Apostles and to their successors, that they should do "greater things" than Himself, has been in all ages fulfilled; and perhaps in none more than in St. Antony. His miracles were frequent, and many of them were of so extraordinary a character, that if they had not been well authenticated they would be scarcely credible. Once, while he was guardian of the convent of Limoges in Aquitaine, he was preaching the passion in the cathedral on the night of Maunday-Thursday. His religious were at the same time singing matins in their choir. When it was time to read the lesson which would have come to his turn, he suddenly appeared, and having sung it, again vanished, although during this interval he was not perceived to be absent from the pulpit, or to have discontinued his discourse. At another time, when preaching at Montpelier, he remembered that he was lector, and that he had not appointed any one to sing the *Alleluia* for him. He stooped for a moment in the pulpit as if to rest, and was seen in his convent performing this duty, though it did not appear to those in the church that he had left it even for a moment. On several occasions he appeared miraculously in Portugal to assist his father; once when a large sum of money was demanded of him unjustly, and once when a corpse was laid at his door that he might be accused of the murder. In the latter instance, he not only benefitted his father, but also the murdered man. After a few moments' prayer, he restored him to life, made him publicly declare the accused was innocent of the murder, and then, after absolving him from a sentence of excommunication under which he lay, saved him from eternal death, as in a few moments he expired in peace.

Many instances are related of Antony's gift of prophecy. On one occasion he foretold of a child as yet unborn that he should be a Friar Minor and a martyr. His prediction was fulfilled. When grown to a sufficient age, the boy entered the Order, and while yet quite a youth he was martyred by the Moors in a manner too horrible to relate, bearing his torments with unflinching constancy.

When in the south of France, St. Antony constantly

met a man whom he never failed to salute with singular respect. The honor was unwelcome, and as the man was notoriously profligate, it caused much astonishment. One day he accosted the Saint in great indignation, and informed him that nothing but respect for his religious habit provented him from avenging what he considered an insult, as it drew on him the attention and ridicule of the townspeople. The Saint gently replied: "My brother, God has granted you a grace which for my sins He has denied to me. You will die a martyr, a favor for which I have long prayed in vain. I therefore beg, when you have received your crown, that you will remember me, a poor sinner." In a short time the prophecy was fulfilled. The notary travelled to the Holy Land. He was accused of being a Christian, and boldly avowing his faith, he suffered for it with constancy and courage.

Being at Rome when a jubilee was published by Gregory the Ninth, Antony was desired by the Holy Father to preach. An immense multitude of people from all nations and of all tongues had assembled. The miracle of Pentecost was renewed in his favor; each, to his amazement, heard the Saint preaching in his own language. Two of his miracles have frequently been made the subject for the skill of the painter; and one, at least, is common among our religious prints. When preaching a funeral sermon on the death of an usurer, he took these words for his text: "Where thy treasure is, there also is thy heart." The sermon being ended, he desired the relations of the deceased to repair to the spot where his treasures were stored up. On their entrance they found the heart of the miser still showing signs of life, and lying upon his heaps of gold. He also converted a heretic by a remarkable miracle in proof of the Real Presence of our

Lord in the Blessed Sacrament. At the conclusion of a long argument, this man declared that he could not answer the reasons which Antony adduced for his faith; but averred it was the Saint's skill in argument that had gained him the advantage. St. Antony then offered to perform any miracle he wished as a testimony of the truth of his doctrine. It was, therefore, agreed that a mule should be shut up for three days and kept without food. On the third day Antony was to come to the house of the heretic with the Most Holy Sacrament, and if the hungry animal knelt to adore it, before she touched the corn which her master was to offer her, he promised to embrace the faith. When the day arrived, thousands flocked to be present on the occasion. The mule was let out of the stable; her master held the oats near her; but Antony at the same moment desired her to adore the Blessed Sacrament. At once the poor animal approached and humbly knelt down, seeming as if almost conscious of the Presence before her. Many of the heretics who were present were at once converted, and the faith of the Catholics not a little strengthened.

St. Antony is usually represented with the Infant Jesus in his arms. His devotion to this mystery and his singularly child-like simplicity were often rewarded by visions and other celestial favors. While preaching in the south of France, a gentleman of some distinction wished to have him for his guest. The Saint complied with his desire, and as usual, spent much of the night in prayer. One night, a light of unusual splendor was seen pouring through the chinks of the door in the room occupied by St. Antony. It attracted the attention of his host, who watched him unperceived; and saw that he was caressed by, and caressing, his Infant Saviour. The gentleman continued for some time to gaze in astonishment on this glorious vision. It then disappeared, and the Divine Child told the friar that it had been seen by another. The humility of Antony made him fearful lest this favor should be known, and he exacted a solemn promise from his host not to mention the occurrence to any one during his life.

Perhaps it was this child-like tenderness of the Saint that made him so tenderly beloved by, and so gentle towards his penitents. Once, when a poor man came to him for confession, his excessive grief prevented his uttering a word. "My child," exclaimed the Saint, "go and write your confession." The penitent did as he was desired, and returning with the paper in his hand, no trace of what had been written could be found on it. This favor, he was assured by Antony, was granted in consequence of the depth of his contrition, which had obtained for him the perfect remission of his sins.

It would require a volume to relate all the miracles wrought by the Saint, both during his lifetime and after his death. We cannot pass them over without regret, for some are of peculiar interest. Like his seraphic father, his love of nature made him frequently use the objects which surrounded him as illustrations in his discourses. Once, when some heretics refused to hear him, he called the fish to a margin of a lake, and spoke to them of God their Creator—they, meanwhile, showing signs of joy and satisfaction, so as to confound the unbelievers, many of whom were converted by this miracle. Once, also, when he had written a letter to his provincial, it was carried to him by his guardian angel, and an answer returned in the same manner. But what need to speak further of his miracles, since most of us every day experience his power with God? He is our household friend, our constant advocate and helper. Pray for us then, most dear and gentle Saint, that like you we may die with the name of Jesus on our lips and the love of Mary in our hearts, and that with you we may see and praise Jesus and Mary for all eternity.

Shortly before his death, Antony did two important services to his Order. One was to obtain the dismissal of Brother Elias from the office of superior, which he was so unworthy to fulfil, and from which he was expelled by Pope Gregory in consequence of the representation of the Saint. The other was the compilation of several volumes of sermons. The last Lent of his life was spent at Padua, where he was greatly beloved. He preached constantly; and so great was the eagerness to hear him, that the merchants closed their shops and suspended their business whenever it was known that he would address the people. Finding his end approaching, he visited one or two other cities, but soon returned to Padua. He retired to a convent of his Order near the town. Having received the last sacraments he recited the Penitential Psalms with the religious, and then began the Hymn, "*O gloriosa Domina.*" At this moment our Blessed Lady appeared to him; he had always been specially devoted to her, and often had received favors through her intercession. Shortly after, he turned to a friar who stood near him, and said, "I see my Lord Jesus," and after passing half an hour in an ecstasy of prayer, he passed calmly to his eternal reward, still seeming as if he only slept. His poor worn body looked so beautiful and fresh after his death as to astonish all who beheld it. At the moment of his decease he appeared to the Abbot of Versailles; and telling him he was going home, touched his throat gently and caressingly, and so cured him of a disease from which he had long suffered. At first the good religious thought his friend was going to Portugal; but soon he found that it was of his home in Paradise he had spoken. He was canonized by Pope Gregory: and singularly enough, his companion in the apostolate of peace, the blessed John of Vicenza, was one of the commissioners appointed to authenticate his miracles. On the day of his canonization the bells in the city of Lisbon rang without the touch of human hands; as on the day of his death the little children of Padua had proclaimed it unbidden, crying out, "Saint Antony is dead; the blessed father has gone from us."

St. Antony died on the 13th of June, 1231. He was but thirty-six when called to receive his crown. Some years later, when St. Bonaventura was General of the Order, he ordered his tomb to be opened. The body was reduced to ashes; but the tongue of the Saint, which had so often preached peace, remained as fresh and of as bright a color as if still in life. The great doctor took it reverently into his hands, and kissing it tenderly, exclaimed, "O blessed tongue, which has always praised God, and made others praise Him, how precious art thou in His sight." Then by his desire the relic was placed in a golden case. A magnificent church has been erected in honor of St. Antony at Padua. It was commenced and designed in 1259, by the celebrated architect Nicolas of Pisa. The richly carved stalls are the work of Lorenzo Canotio, and the grand altar and bas-reliefs in bronze, of Donatello Fiorentino. The chapel where the remains of the Saint repose is adorned with exquisite bas-reliefs in marble, in which the most eminent artists have represented various striking incidents in his life. There is a tradition in the city, that during the pontificate of Nicolas the Fourth, some workers in Mosaic placed St. Francis and St. Antony in the same group with the Apostles. Pope Boniface the Eighth thought this arrangement unsuitable, and desired that the image of St. Antony should be removed, and that of St. Gregory substituted. But at the first attempt to do this an invisible power resisted the blows of the workman, and the intention was consequently abandoned, as manifestly against the designs of Providence.

CHAPTER XXI.

Foundation of the Third Order.—The Merchant Luchesio, the first Tertiary.—His wife, Bona Donna, is converted by a miracle.—The Tertiaries increase rapidly.—Letter from Pierre de Vencis to the Emperor Frederic.—The influence of the Tertiaries felt in the German court.

We have already spoken of the marvellous effects produced by the preaching of the friars. Tyrants trembled, and relaxed, if they did not altogether discontinue, their oppressions; while of the vast crowds that hung on the footsteps of the religious, not a few received and obeyed the call to leave all for God. But this call was not given to the majority; and many who would, perhaps, have heard it gladly, were already bound by home and domestic ties. How were their needs to be met? Compunction had been excited in them, and heavenly love enkindled. Was it to die away with no result beyond the fervor of a passing moment? Was it to find vent among the various forms of heresy which then, as now, with counterfeit zeal deceived the ignorant but fervent soul? Francis saw the need, and was not long in meeting it. He knew that the interest or excitement awakened in the breasts of his hearers would quickly pass, without the aid of some abiding power to sustain and consolidate it; and so he founded his Third Order of Franciscans, which has ever since continued to do such service in sanctifying souls.

It was while preaching at Florence in the year 1221, that he carried out this admirable design. A merchant named Luchesio, and his wife, Bona Donna, were its first members. This gentleman had been an intimate friend of the Saint in his early days. Unlike him, however, in disposition, Luchesio was as avaricious as Francis had been prodigal. But grace had touched his heart; and now the rich merchant only sought how he could best distribute the wealth he had before so carefully hoarded. He would gladly have sold all that he possessed, and followed the poor friars in their humble life. As this could not be, he asked to be taught how to sanctify his soul in the world, and make what seemed to hinder his perfection a means of attaining it. His wife at first opposed his design, and blamed his excessive charities. One day she bitterly and angrily reproached him with having given away even the food necessary for themselves, there being not a morsel of bread left in the house. Her husband, who was as patient as he was charitable, replied gently, that He who had multiplied five loves and two fishes to feed thousands, could also supply their needs. A miracle was granted to reward and confirm his faith. On going by his desire to the place where their household stores were usually kept, she found a larger supply of bread than had been taken to feed the poor. Bona Donna complained no more after this; and when Francis arrived, she threw herself at his feet and begged his instructions as earnestly as her good husband.

The Saint yielded to their desire. They were clothed

in a simple grey habit, and wore the Franciscan cord. Shortly after the Rule was given them. It was simple, as such a rule should be; and it was expressly declared that its observance did not oblige under pain of sin. Four things were mentioned as indispensable requirements from those who wished to be admitted into it. (1.) The restoration of all goods unjustly acquired. (2.) A free and entire reconciliation with any with whom they had been at variance. (3.) An observance of the commandments of God, the precepts of the Church, and the Rule. (4.) The consent of the husband in the case of any married woman's reception. The Rule was adapted to the wants of the times. Its end was the sanctification of those who lived under it; and what would best conduce to this was considered most essential. Of the four regulations, which were indispensable, the two first show us the state of the age, its peculiar evils, and its requirements. And the last that the humble friar, whose life was spent, either in rapt communion with heaven, or in laborious works of mercy for his fellow-man, was by no means a dreamy visionary. There was plain, practical, common sense not merely in these requirements, but in every line of the Rule subsequently sanctioned by the solemn bull of Gregory the Ninth. And if our age is disposed to consider Francis a little strict in forbidding any of his tertiaries to be seen at theatrical representations, or to mingle in the dance or the gay revel, we cannot but admire his prudence in ordaining that those who enter this Order should regulate their worldly affairs and make their wills; a precaution not a little necessary in a turbulent age, when life was rendered insecure by the prevalence of treachery and domestic strife. Indeed, a glance over the Rule impresses one with the spirit of prudence which pervades every part. The soul's sanctification was assured by its requirements of a life of constant prayer, of fasting and humility. Temporal prosperity was promoted, and the very life of its subjects protected, by the regulations for preserving peace. Litigation was prevented by the tertiaries having properly disposed by will of their temporal goods. Peace was maintained by their being forbidden all suits or oaths, unless required by the Church, or by the well-being of the government under which they lived. The brethren were also forbidden to bear arms, unless in defence of their faith or country. In a shorter space of time than could have been supposed possible, this new militia of Jesus Christ had spread over the whole continent of Europe. Thousands had enrolled themselves in its ranks, and faithfully adhered to its observances. Among these multitudes were to be found men and women of all classes of intellect, of all grades of rank, and of almost every path in life.

The Third Order of St. Dominic was also established about the same time, or perhaps rather later; but it was not confirmed till 1227. The object of each of these great Saints was much the same; it was, therefore, natural that they should choose similar means to procure their end. But it scarcely becomes the followers of either to be eager in claiming the first institution of any particular practice. In this case, however, the question can hardly be settled definitively. The Franciscan annalists plainly state the Third Order of their Saint as established in 1221. The Dominican authorities, in some instances, while they acknowledge that the existence of their Third Order was not generally known till about the same time, maintain it as possible that St. Dominic may have instituted his before he established his regular orders. Be this as it may, so important was the influence of these tertiaries, and so rapid their increase, that the political world began to look in amazement and fear on the work which had been accomplished by two poor friars. Pierre de Veneis, chancellor to the impious Frederic, writes thus to his master: "The Friars Minor and the Friars Preachers have risen up against us in anger. They publicly reprove our life and our conduct. To weaken our power still more, and draw the people from us, they have erected two new confraternities, in which they enroll both men and women. Crowds are flocking into them, and it is hard to find any one whose name is not inscribed in one or other society." Well might the worldly politician exclaim in indignant amazement, to see the power of royalty, the force of arms, and the snares of heresy and of proffered bribes, falling powerless before these new and strange associations. Cæsar was trembling before the power of Peter, and the Church was succeeding in a work which the world had in vain attempted. Statesmen were getting the lesson, which they cared not to learn, that Saints, with all their unworldliness, were the best legislators; since their laws promoted most effectually the prosperity of nations, the administration of justice, and the peace of empires.

Luchesio, before he entered the Third Order of St. Francis, had ranged himself under the banner of the Guelphs; but, with thousands of his fellows, he learned that the cause of the Church is the cause of God. Henceforth he no longer dared to side with the enemies of his country and his faith. The German chancellor, on his own principles, had, indeed, cause for apprehension; but if, on that and other occasions, triumph was denied to the Church in her visible Head and in her children, it was because her Divine Founder has willed that, for her sanctification and His greater glory, she should seem all but prostrated by the storms that howl around her—all but destroyed by the evil ones who plot her downfall. But the time of retribution is not less sure because it is delayed; and the Church, widowed and exiled, shall one day rest in the glories of her home above, avenged of her enemies and consoled for her sorrows and wrongs.

CHAPTER XXII.

The celebrated Indulgence of the Porziuncola—Given by our Divine Lord Himself.—Confirmed by Honorius the Third.—Miracles attest its authenticity.—St. Frances of Rome.—St. Bridget.—The crowds who assembled to obtain it.

Two events in the life of our Saint have a supernatural character eminent even above the rest. The one is, the impression upon his mortal body of the sacred Stigmata, the crowning token of his conformity with his Divine Lord. The other the grant of the celebrated Indulgence of the Porziuncola, commonly known in Italy as "*Del Perdono.*"

In the month of October, 1221, Francis was keeping his usual nightly vigil in his poor cell. He prayed with burning tears for the conversion of sinners, and for mercy for those who had no mercy on themselves. After he had continued his supplication for some time, an angel appeared to him and desired him to repair quickly to the church, where he would behold our Lord Jesus Christ, His blessed mother, and a multitude of heavenly spirits. With a joyous and hopeful heart the Saint obeyed the summons and prostrated himself before the altar. Then he heard the voice of our Divine Lord, who addressed him thus: "Francis, you and your brethren have a great zeal for the salvation of souls; you have been placed as a light to the world, and as a support to the Church. Ask, then, whatever you will for the benefit and consolation of mankind, and for My glory." The Saint humbly replied, "My Lord Jesus Christ, though I am but a miserable sinner, I beseech You to grant that all who visit this church may receive a plenary indulgence for all their sins, after they have confessed to a priest. And I beseech the blessed Virgin, Your mother, and the advocate of the human race, to intercede for me, that I may obtain this grace." Then our Lady, never invoked in vain, inclined towards her Divine Son to ask the favor. Our Blessed Lord replied: "Francis, you ask great things; but you shall receive still greater. I grant what you demand: but go to My vicar, to whom I have given the power to bind and loose on earth, and ask him to ratify what I now declare." The vision then disappeared, and the Saint remained in prayer, full of confidence and holy joy. Next morning he assembled his disciples, and informed them of what had happened during the night. They meanwhile had seen from their cells the miraculous light which filled the chureh, but had feared to approach it.

Pope Honorius was then at Perugia, and thither Francis repaired in obedience to the divine command, taking Brother Masseo as his companion. Having been admitted to an audience, he addressed the Sovereign Pontiff with all the simplicity of his character. "Holy Father, some years since I repaired a small church in your dominions. I beseech your Holiness to grant that those who visit it may obtain a free indulgence without making any offering." This was a new and a startling request, and the Pope hesitated to grant it. "For how many years do you desire this favor?" he inquired. "Holy Father," answered the Saint, "I ask not years but souls." "In what way would you have souls ?" was the rejoinder. "I wish," continued Francis, "if it be the pleasure of your Holiness, that those who visit the church of St. Mary of the Angels, being contrite and having confessed their sins to a priest, and received absolution, may obtain the grace of an indulgence for all the punishment due to them both in this world and in the next." The Pope replied, "Francis, you ask a great favor, and one which is contrary to the usual custom. Until this time, the giving of alms has been considered a necessary condition for the gaining of an indulgence, not as a means of purchasing it, but as a charitable disposition, which might better fit the soul to receive, and Almighty God to grant, this great favor."—"Holy Father," replied the Saint, "I do not ask this favor in my own name, but in the name of Jesus Christ, who has sent me." Honorius remained for a few moments as if absorbed in thought, perhaps in prayer, asking for light how to act in this important matter. Then, as if under the influence of inspiration, he uttered these words three times: "It is my will to grant what you desire." However, some of the cardinals who were present interfered, and begged he would limit this favor. He therefore added, "I grant this indulgence in perpetuity, but only on one day during the year." At these words Francis humbly bowed his head, and craving the Papal benediction, prepared to depart. "Simple man," cried Honorius, "where are you going, and what proof have you for what has been granted to you?" "Holy Father," he replied, "your word is sufficient for me; if this indulgence is the work of God, He will make it manifest. Jesus Christ will be the notary, His blessed mother the parchment, and the angels the witnesses."

Two years passed away, and Francis and his religious still continued their life of prayer and zeal for the salvation of souls. One night, in the month of January, 1223, while the stars shone bright and clear in the frosty sky, and the snow laid thickly on the ground, Francis prayed in his lonely cell. Dark shadows of temptation passed across his blessed soul; for the demon who can assume a marvellous compassionateness when it suits his evil purpose, whispered to him of rest from this weary strife and of the fruitlessness of these cold vigils. Many a dreary, depressing thought, many a keenly-edged temptation assailed him. Francis might spare himself, the demon urged—at his age sleep was absolutely necessary. He would shorten his life by his austerities, and so lessen his power of usefulness. But the Saint, though he suffered from this conflict, was proof against Satan's wiles. He answered not; but rising quickly, hastened into a neighboring wood, and threw himself almost naked into a bush filled with long and sharp thorns. Though shivering with cold and pain, he rolled himself in it, till blood gushed copiously from every limb. "It is better," he cried, "to suffer with my Jesus than to follow the counsels of His enemy." Scarcely had he uttered the words when he was surrounded by a light of unearthly brightness, and beheld the thorny bush covered with red and white roses. Angels then appeared to him, and said: "Francis, hasten to the church, where you will find Jesus and His blessed mother." When the Saint arose he found himself clothed with a garment of the purest white. Gathering twelve roses of each color, he proceeded to the church, and, as he went, found "the way all tapestried with angelic spirits." Prostrating himself before the heavenly vision, he humbly cried, "Most Holy Father, Lord of heaven and earth, Saviour of mankind, condescend in Your great mercy to fix the day for the indulgence which you have granted me in this holy place." Our Divine Lord then told him that it should be from the vespers of the day on which St. Peter was delivered from prison, until the vespers of the next day. Then the Saint inquired how this should be made known, and he was told to present himself again before the Vicar of Christ, and to take, in honor of the Blessed Trinity, three roses of each color, as a testimony of the truth of his assertion. Francis did as was desired, and the angelic choir touched their golden harps, and sung as angels only can sing, a *Te Deum* of grateful praise. Some friars had seen from their cells what had passed, and had heard the *Te Deum Laudamus*, entoned by voices that were not of earth. Doubtless, they also joined their thanksgivings for this favor—alas! too little appreciated by those for whom it was obtained.

Once more Francis sought the Vicar of Christ, that he might confirm the indulgence which Christ Himself had given. Accompanied by Bernard da Quintavalle, Peter of Catania, and Angelus di Rieti, Francis journeyed to Rome. Presenting himself to the Holy Father with his companions, he related all that had happened, producing the roses which he had brought as a testimony to the truth of his statement. The Pope had no hesitation in believing the revelation, authenticated as it was by the miraculous roses borne to him in the depth of winter in the hands of the Saint. Francis was desired to return the next day. Meanwhile, Honorius had consulted with his cardinals, who were then assembled, and in their presence he solemnly confirmed the indulgence. He then desired that the bishops of Assisi, Perugia, Todi, Spoleto, Foligno, Nocera, and Gubbio should proclaim it at St. Mary of the Angels on the first of October. On the appointed day all the prelates had assembled. By their desire, Francis ascended a platform which had been prepared, and addressed the people. It was indeed most fitting that he who had obtained the indulgence should be the first to announce it. As he spoke, so heavenly was his discourse that it seemed to the people as if it was an angel who addressed them, and not a man. An authentic document, still extant, declares that while preaching, he held a paper in his hand, wherein was written: "I wish you all to go to Paradise. I announce to you an indulgence which I have received from God Himself, and which is confirmed by the mouth of the Sovereign Pontiff. All who are here to-day may obtain a plenary indulgence, if their hearts are truly contrite. And all those who come on the same day in any other year will receive the same grace, if they have the same good dispositions. I wished to have obtained this favor for eight days, but I was not able to do so." When Francis had concluded his address the bishops each spoke in turn. They had all agreed to limit the indulgence to ten years, but when each attempted to pronounce the words, he found himself unable to do so, and was compelled to say instead, "in perpetuity." Thus was another unequivocal testimony given to the truth of the revelation, and consequently to the value of the indulgence.

Other miracles too numerous to relate occurred at the time, as well as later. One, however, is too interesting to be omitted. The religious had retired for their short rest on that eventful night; but they were soon awakened by a murmur of joy and devotion which broke from the crowds who watched in the church. On entering it to ascertain the cause, they saw a white dove which hovered over the altar, and then flew five times round the church. A holy religious named Corrado of Offiedo, was praying near the altar. When questioned as to the cause of this unexpected outburst of devotion, he declared that he had just seen the Blessed Virgin, who had entered the church, holding her Divine Son in her arms. Encircled by a light of ineffable splendor, she had blessed the kneeling crowds, and the dove which they had all beheld had appeared at the same moment. The people had not seen the vision, but they had felt it, and this occasioned their expression of joy and reverence.

A place so hallowed must have been specially treasured by those to whom it belonged. Francis himself gave strict directions both as to the care of this church, and the reverence with which the brethren should behave while praying in it. He ordained that none should be permitted to live in the convent attached to it, who were not distinguished among their brethren for more than ordinary sanctity. Even for its lay brothers he required those to be chosen who were remarkable for their humility. It had been revealed to him by God, says the Chronicle, that "this church was loved by the Blessed Virgin Mary with a particular devotion above all the other churches of the world." A magnificent church now encloses the little chapel of the Porziuncola. Here on each anniversary of its great feast, from fifteen to twenty thousand pilgrims are assembled.* In the evening, while some refresh

* Some of our readers may be familiar with the very beautiful life of St. Frances of Rome. Those who are not, may feel interest in an account of her pilgrimage to gain this indulgence. In the year 1426, St. Francesca, accompanied by two friends, left Rome early in the morning, on the 2nd of August. They determined to travel on foot, and without provisions or money. They had nearly reached the end of their journey; and though exhausted by thirst and weariness, pressed on, as the towers of St. Mary of the Angels rose in sight. But when they almost feared their strength would bear them no further, a stranger appears. He is old and venerable, clothed in the Franciscan habit. He speaks of Jesus and of Mary, and their hearts burn within them, for they have heard words of such eloquent, such entrancing love as never before fell upon their ears. Francesca recognizes the Saint. Her angel, whom she always beheld, appeared

themselves under the balmy sweetness of an Italian sky, others are singing pious canticles within the sanctuary itself. Thirty confessors, or more, are employed in healing the wounds of these numerous souls, and cheering the weary pilgrims on their way to the eternal Sabbath. For many previous days crowds have encamped in the surrounding fields, or quartered themselves within the cloisters of the convent itself. The good friars are ready to give hospitality to all, as far as possible. The very stairs of their usually silent home are now crowded with pious visitors, glad to find any unoccupied spot on which to snatch a few hours repose. In the ages when faith was stronger, because love was more fervent, pilgrims might be counted, not by thousands, but by hundreds of thousands. Bernabio of Sienna, the companion and friend of St. Bernardine, declares that when he visited Assisi in order to gain the indulgence, he found there no less than two hundred thousand pilgrims. "When I saw such a multitude," he says, "I doubted whether there were any persons left to inhabit the rest of Italy."

In 1309, the blessed John of Alvernia, was once engaged in hearing confessions, when a penitent presented himself who was more than a hundred years of age. He wore the habit of the Tertiary Franciscans, and had travelled in it from a village near Perugia. Being asked why he had undertaken so great a journey at his advanced age, he replied, "My reverend father, if I could not have walked, I would have had myself led or even dragged here, sooner than lose the blessings of this great day." On being further questioned by his

more brilliantly beautiful than ever. Rays of light dart from him, and envelope in a dazzling halo the monk that addressed them. St. Francis blessed the holy pilgrims; then, touching a wild pear tree which grew by the wayside, he brought to the ground a fruit of such size and sweetness, that it refreshed and strengthened the exhausted pilgrims.

confessor, who was not a little edified at his fervor and zeal, he declared that St. Francis had stayed at his father's house, when on his way to Rome to obtain the confirmation of this indulgence; and that, from the day it was first proclaimed, he had never once failed to visit St. Mary of the Angels on the second of August.

A remarkable testimony to the authenticity of this great grace has been given by no less an authority than St. Bridget. In her Revelations, she says, that while praying in the chapel of our Lady of Angels to gain the indulgence, she asked our Divine Lord, with reverent love, whether it was indeed true that He had Himself granted it. She was then told that Francis was singularly beloved by God, and that in the friends of God there was no deceit or duplicity; that he had asked for some new manifestation of the love of God, which might enkindle anew the cold hearts of men, and that this wonderful favor had been given in answer to his holy desire. The Church of our Lady of Angels is now one of the most beautiful and spacious in Italy. It is in possession of the fathers of the strict observance. During the pontificate of St. Pius the Fifth, Filippo Geri of Pistoja, Bishop of Assisi, laid the first stone of the present magnificent building, March 25th, 1569. The litile chapel of Portiuncula, where St. Francis obtained the grant of this great indulgence, is safely preserved beneath the great dome. This church is composed of three naves, the vast proportions of which, when viewed from the entrance, present a most imposing appearance. The grotto or little cell is still shown where the Saint was praying when summoned by the angel to the church; and the thorny bush, in which he gave himself so severe a penance, is also carefully preserved. The hour at which the indulgence begins is announced by the great clock of the Sagro Convento.* Then all the Franciscans, Observants, Capuchins, Conventuals, and Tertiaries, who have assembled here, defile in long and solemn procession to the Porziuncola. The Bishop of Assisi follows, with all his clergy; and the procession is closed by the magistrates and other secular persons of distinction. When the doors are unclosed, the crowds who have thronged round the church even for days, rush in with overwhelming eagerness. On all sides are heard cries for mercy and for the pardon (*il perdono*). Each one invokes, in his own fashion, the Sweet Queen of Angels, under whose patronage the church is dedicated, and who, they doubt not, will intercede effectually to obtain for them the favor, the first grant of which she obtained for the seraphic Francis.

CHAPTER XXIII.

Francis is warned by a vision to re-write his Rule.—He retires for this purpose to Mount Columba.—He returns to St. Mary's.—Confides the Rule to Elias.—It is lost or destroyed by him.—The Saint again writes it.—Opposition silenced by a miracle.—The Rule confirmed by Honorius the Third.—Poverty strictly enjoined.—Also fraternal charity.—The Saint declares he was inspired to write it.—Confirmation of his statement by Pope Nicholas the Third and St. Bridget.

ONE night while Francis was engaged in prayer, he had a remarkable vision, and one by which he was much perplexed. It seemed to him that he was busily engaged in gathering up little morsels of bread in order to satisfy the wants of the many hungry brethren

* This great bell-tower contains two bells; one is called the bell of preaching, and is rung to announce the indulgence—it bears this inscription:

A. D. MCCXXXIX. F. Helias fecit fieri
Bartholomæus Pisanus me fecit cum Loteringo filio ejus.
Ora pro nobis B. Francisce
Ave Maria gratia plena. Alleluia.

who stood around him. As he was thus employed, and fearing lest the smallest morsels should escape, he heard a voice which said: "Francis, gather all these crumbs, and make a host of them, and give it to those who wish to eat it." He did as he was desired, and observed, to his surprise, that all those who received this host without devotion, or who afterwards seemed to care little for it, were afflicted with leprosy. In the morning he told the brethren what had happened, and asked their opinion regarding it; but none were able to suggest any solution of the mystery. During the day, while he was engaged in prayer, he heard a voice from heaven which said, "Francis, the crumbs you saw represent the Gospel; the host is your Rule, and the leprosy is sin." After hearing these words, he was made to understand that his Rule was indeed composed of the precepts of the Gospel, and that he ought to condense it and arrange it anew. The better to obey this intimation of the Divine will, he departed at once for the convent of Mount Columba, near Rieti, taking Brothers Leo and Bonzio as his companions. When he had arrived there, he made himself a cell in the cavity of a rock, where he remained fasting on bread and water for forty days. During this time he arranged the Rule which he had already given to his friars. Of this Rule it will not be necessary to speak in detail. But there are several circumstances regarding it which demand special notice.

As may be supposed, its most stringent regulation concerned the practice of poverty. "The brethren," he says, "shall not possess anything of their own, whether of houses or lands; but they shall consider themselves as strangers and pilgrims in the world, and serve God in poverty and humility. Let them ask alms with confidence, and let them not be ashamed to do so; for Jesus Christ made Himself poor for our sakes. Consider, O my beloved brothers, how excellent is this sublime poverty, which has made you inheritors of the kingdom of heaven; which has made you poor in the goods of earth, but rich in virtue." Then, with that thoughtful love so specially his characteristic, he desires that the brethren shall manifest the tenderest affection towards each other. "Wherever the brethren may be, or may meet each other, let them show mutual anxiety to serve each other in all things. Let them, with all confidence, discover to each other their spiritual necessities; for if a mother loves and nourishes her child according to the flesh, with how much deeper affection should each one love and cherish his brother according to the spirit? And if any one shall fall into sickness, the other must serve him even as they would desire to be served themselves." Nor was he less anxious regarding their submission to the authority of the Church. He desired that all who entered the Order, possessed of talent for teaching and instructing others, should cultivate and use this gift; but he also expressly enjoined that none should attempt, on any pretence, to preach in any diocese without the sanction of its bishop. He concludes the Rule with these remarkable words: "Be always subject to the Holy Roman Church, and prostrate at her feet—always immovable in the Catholic faith; practicing poverty and humility, and observing the holy Gospel of our Lord Jesus Christ, as we have solemnly promised."

This Rule was solemnly confirmed by Honorius the Third, on the 29th of November, 1223. It has always been understood in the Order that Francis composed it by Divine revelation. He has himself specially said, "I have put nothing of my own in it, but have written what God has revealed to me." And, again: "My brethren, and very dear children, we have received a signal favor in obtaining this holy Rule. In it is the book of Life, the hope of salvation, the pledge of Glory, the marrow of the Gospel, the way of the Cross, a state of perfection, the key of Paradise, the seal of an eternal alliance. None of you are ignorant how necessary the religious state is for us, how skilful the enemy who fights against us, in planning and executing his malicious designs; and that he lays all manner of snares for our destruction. There are many whose salvation he would greatly have endanged, had not their entrance into religion afforded them protection. Each one should therefore study well his Rule, both to solace him in his sufferings, and to remind him of the vow which he has made to keep it. Yon should make it frequently the subject of your thoughts, and keep it constantly before your eyes, that you may observe it to the letter, and not part from it even in death."

Exterior testimonies to the truth of our Saint's assertion were not wanting. Pope Nicholas the Third, in one of his canonical decisions, says* that it bears on the face of it the evidence of the Blessed Trinity; that it is descended from the Father of Lights; that it was taught to the apostles by the doctrine and example of His Son; and that the Holy Ghost had inspired it to the blessed Francis and his companions.

St. Bridget also, while she was at Jerusalem, was favored with a revelation on this subject. She says that our Divine Lord spoke thus to her: "The Rule of Francis was not composed by the human intellect: it was I who made it, and it does not contain a single word which My Spirit did not inspire him with, and thus he gave it to others." Happy, may we exclaim,

* In Sexto de Verb.

are the children of such a father, and happy the followers of such a Rule!

When the Saint had ended his forty days of prayer and fasting, he returned with his companions to St. Mary of the Angels, bringing with him the Rule he had composed. It will be remembered that, after his return from Palestine, he had deposed brother Elias, and placed the good and holy Peter of Catania in his office. But after the lapse of a year, Elias was reinstated as Vicar-General, since Peter declared he was unable to bear so heavy a charge. Elias was at the Porziuncola when Francis arrived there, and hastened to meet him with his usual affection and respect. Francis placed the Rule in his hands, and desired him to read it. Some days afterwards, when the Saint inquired for it, Elias said he had lost it. The truth was, he dreaded its rigor; and some authors say that the loss was caused more by wilfulness than negligence. Be this as it may, Elias and his party were always anxious for relaxation, and not always very scrupulous as to the means of obtaining their object.

Francis returned to Rieti, and once more wrote the same Rule. While he was thus engaged, Elias communicated with several of the provincial ministers of the Order who coincided with his views. They proceeded to Mount Columba, and approached the cell where the Saint was, though from former experience, not without apprehension as to the result. Their intention was revealed to the Saint; and, as they approached the rock, he came forth and addressed them, inquiring what they wanted. With a trembling voice, Elias replied, that the provincial ministers who accompanied him had heard of a new Rule being in preparation, which they feared would be more severe than they could bear; and that he had been requested in his office as Vicar-General to ask for some mitigation. Francis raised his eyes to heaven, and exclaimed: "O my God, did I not say that they would not believe me? As for me, I will keep this Rule until my dying hour, with all those who are true lovers of poverty; but how can I compel those who make resistance to it?" Then a glorious light appeared, which dazzled those who beheld it, and a voice was heard to utter these words: "Poor, foolish man, why shouldst thou be troubled as if this work were thine? It is I who have dictated this Rule and no part of it is yours. I require it to be observed to the very letter, without gloss or comment, and I know what the frailty of man can endure, and what support I can and will give him. Let those who cannot observe the Rule leave the Order; and if it be necessary I will, even from these stones, raise up others to fill their places." When the Divine voice had ceased, Francis knelt down on the rock and addressed Elias and his companions, who stood trembling below. "You know now," he exclaimed, "that you have opposed the will of God, and thought only of human prudence. If you have not heard the voice which has just issued from the cloud, I will take care that you shall hear it." These words were enough. The friars hurried away, full of fear and confusion, and for a time Francis heard no more of relaxation.

In the month of October, 1223, the Saint again visited Rome; his object now being to obtain a bull for the confirmation of his Rule. This favor was granted on the 29th of November. Wadding, in his annals, declares that in 1619 he saw this bull at the great convent of Assisi, and also a copy of the Rule in the Saint's handwriting. The bull concludes in these words: "Let no man dare to infringe our ordinance, or in any way to contravene it. Should any presume to do so, let him know that he will incur the anger of Almighty God, and of his Blessed Apostles, St. Peter and St. Paul." In the course of the previous year, the same Pope had granted to the Order the signal privilege of permission to say the Divine Office in choir during the time of interdict, provided it were said in a low voice and with closed doors. And in 1224 the friars were granted the use of portable altars for the celebration of the Holy Sacrifice. This was opposed by some French prelates, but it only served for the confirmation of the privilege.

During his stay at Rome many cardinals and noble families earnestly solicited the honor of having the Saint for their guest; but he constantly refused all such invitations, lest they should interfere with prayer and poverty. Still he would not refuse, when asked to allow one or two of his friars to remain with their devout hosts; and hence, few noble or distinguished families in Rome were without a Franciscan guest. Once when asked to dine with the holy Cardinal Ugolini, personal affection and respect to his dignity alike prevented his declining. But when all were seated at table, Francis drew from his sleeve a morsel of bread which he had begged, and refused any other refreshment. Many of the noble guests who had assembled to meet him asked a share in his meal, and ate with devotion the bread given them by the poor friar.

CHAPTER XXIV.

How the Saint kept Christmas at Grecio.—He obtains leave from the Holy See to have a representation of the Nativity.—The first Crib.—St. Francis has a vision of the Infant Jesus at Mass.—He reproves his friars for a departure from their strict poverty on festivals.

Christmas was approaching; the cold was severe, and the roads leading from the Eternal City were in many places dangerously flooded. It mattered not to Francis, for he had determined to spend the feast of the Nativity at Grecio, and there to have the first of those representations of the stable at Bethlehem, which are now so familiar and so dear to us. Few persons are aware that the Church is indebted to St. Francis of Assisi for this most beautiful devotion. Such, however, is the case; and he also obtained from the Holy See a special sanction for its establishment. Having explained his plan to Honorius, that Pontiff warmly encouraged him, and promised an indulgence to all who should assist at his crib. Thus fortified with an authority which none could dispute, Francis set out for Grecio, regarding neither his infirmities, which were very great, nor the severity of the season. He had written to his friend John Velita to prepare everything for the representation, and on his arrival he found all had been completed according to his wishes.

A large and rough stable had been built on the mountain near Grecio, and wooden figures, no doubt rudely carved, of the Holy Child, His Blessed Mother, and St. Joseph, were placed in it. The floor was covered with straw, and as midnight approached, the shepherds crowded in, bringing with them an ox and an ass which they tied up in this simple *presepio*. A great number of friars had also assembled, and the people of the surrounding country came in troops to see the new and strange spectacle. At mignight Mass was sung at an altar prepared for the purpose. Francis officiated as deacon; and after reading the Gospel, preached on the love of the little Babe of Bethlehem with such abundance of tears and joy, that the sermon was turned into a prayer of contemplated love and burning ejaculations. His devotion was shared by the people, who also wept and prayed. The shepherds had brought a great number of torches, so that the whole mountain seemed illuminated. They had also their musical instruments, and sung, in their own fashion, canticles of praise to the new-born King. During the ceremony the Saint was seen caressing an infant of celestial beauty, who appeared to the astonishment of all beholders. The straw on which this apparition had been manifested, was preserved with great devotion, and effected many miraculous cures. Many also who came to see the place afterwards, felt a fire of love kindled in their hearts, for which they could not account. Subsequently, a chapel was erected on the spot, but we may question if ever so much love and devotion were witnessed there again.

Burning with love, and still uttering the name of the Little Babe of Bethlehem, the only name from that day which he seemed able to use when speaking of the Divine Infant, Francis journeyed to a neighboring convent of his Order. Christmas was of all feasts the one he specially loved, and he wished his religious to enjoy it as he did. They did not, however, in their rejoicing, always carry their practice of poverty as far as he wished. A considerable number of the guardians and friars from the neighboring convent had assembled at Grecio. After the midnight Mass, they went to the Convent of Friars Minor which had been established there. The refectory was prepared with more than usual care. Napkins and glasses, no ordinary pitch of luxury in those days, were laid for the guests. When all were assembled, Francis went to the door of the convent, and finding there a poor pilgrim who was asking alms, he begged the loan of his staff and cloak. Thus attired, he presented himself to the brethren, and begged an alms. The superior at once recognized him, and said, smiling, "Brother pilgrim, there are many religious who need all that has been given them; they have received it in alms, but they will share what they have with you." Then the Saint seated himself on the ground, and receiving some scraps of bread and other fragments of the meal on a plate, he took his refection. When dinner was ended, he gave a long and beautiful exhortation to his religious, telling them how they should in future keep this feast—warning them solemnly never at any time to seek for luxuries or delicacies in their meals, but above all, to avoid it on the day on which the Saviour of mankind was born in poverty and suffering. St. Bonaventura relates a similar incident as having occurred on Easter Day, when after begging alms in the refectory, the Saint preached on poverty, and on the way in which he wished his children to keep the feasts of our Lord and of His Saints, and if this warning was necessary in the days of Francis, when his Order was in its first and most ardent fervor, may we not fear lest the luxurious spirit of our age should creep even into our cloisters, and mar the perfection of the sacrifice we have vowed?

CHAPTER XXV.

The power which the Saint possessed over animals.—He is followed by a lamb at Rome, and at St. Mary of the Angels.—His sermon to the birds.—Receives doves from a young man who afterwards enters the Order.—When preaching at Alviano he desires some swallows to be silent.—Makes a treaty with a wolf at Gubbio.—Converts a robber on Mount Alvernia.

Saint Francis retained his love of nature to the last moment of his life; he loved to pray alone in the forest, or on the mountain side. Frequently he was found in ecstacy in the woods near the convent which might be his temporary home. And when it was possible for him to choose a site for a new foundation, he always selected it in or near a wood, and at some little, but not inconvenient distance from a town. Nor was it merely the inanimate works of creation which so much attracted him. The providential love of God extends itself alike to the crushed worm and the fading lily; and the Saints, who burn with the same hallowed fire, love also, in their measure, all created things. But as other gifts, intellectual or supernatural, so the love of nature, and with it a power of attracting and controlling the animal creation, has been vouchsafed in different degrees to the servants of God. Our Saint was singularly favored in this respect. The most timid animals flew to him as their protector and friend; the most savage obeyed and even appeared to reverence him. Perhaps it was that his union with his Lord had become so intimate that even the inanimate creation saw in him the image of Jesus; perhaps his surpassing sanctity had all but worn away the marks of our shame and punishment, and that the fire of his love shone out so brightly and was so filled with that of the Creator, as in its measure to attract all things to itself.

But of all animals those which our Saint most loved were lambs. They spoke to him of Jesus, of His meekness, of His silent sufferings. So, as he passed through the fields where they were pastured, he would call them to him, and caress them tenderly. Once he met a troop of horses and cattle, in the midst of which was a poor little lamb, that seemed unable to keep up with them, as they were roughly driven along. "Ah," exclaimed the Saint, "thus was our sweet Saviour in the midst of the Jews and the Pharisees!" Then, touched with pity, he determined to purchase the poor animal and to free it from its misery. He had nothing but his cloak to offer in exchange, and was greatly perplexed how to effect a bargain, when a merchant came by. On being informed of what was passing. he at once purchased the lamb, and presented it to Francis. The Saint took his new companion with him to a neighboring town, and confided it to the care of the Poor Clares who had a convent there. The nuns tenderly guarded the little lamb, and each year sent him a tunic woven from its wool.

When in Rome, during the year 1222, the Saint was usually accompanied by a lamb which had attached itself to him. On leaving that city, he gave it to Jacoba di Settesoli. This noble lady received the gift most willingly; the more so that the little creature seemed to have learned devotion from its holy master, and showed it in its own fashion. When Jacoba repaired to the church, the lamb always followed her; and, during the Holy Sacrifice, it remained perfectly quiet, giving all signs of exterior respect. It took care also to awaken her in the morning; and if Jacoba slept longer than usual, the lamb showed its dissatisfaction, bleating and pushing with its head, till she obeyed the summons to rise.

At St. Mary of the Angels he was also followed by a lamb, which had been given to him by a friend. St. Francis confided it to the care of the friars, but first gave it an instruction how it ought to behave. He desired it to be careful to praise God, and to be wary not to offend or be offended by the religious. "Which charge," says the Chronicle, "she to her utmost observed with as much care as if she had understood it all, and had discretion to obey her master." When the religious went to chant their office in the choir, the lamb followed them, and would then kneel down with great reverence, though none had taught her; and though she could not sing with the brethren, she omitted not to praise God after her own fashion, bleating and leaping before the altar of Mary and of the spotless Lamb; and when the Sacred Host was raised at the adorable sacrifice, she would kneel, seeming to adore, at least by her attitude, inviting the devout to be still more reverent, and giving an example to those who treated so awful a mystery with carelessness or neglect.

It was a frequent practice of the Saint to call the birds to him, and preach to them when they obeyed his summons. One of these sermons is still on record, and is too beautiful in its simplicity to be omitted. Passing near Bevagna with some of his friars, he saw a great number of birds flocking together on a tree. "Wait for me," he cried out to his companions, "while I go and preach to my brothers the birds." The little creatures seemed to have understood his words, for they approached him with every sign of joy, waiting as if to hear what he would say. "My little brothers," he said, "you ought always to love and praise your Creator for His goodness to you. He has given you feathers and wings with which you may fly wherever you please.

He made you first of all His creatures, and preserved you in the ark with Noe. He has given you the spacious and beautiful region of the air for your dwelling. He nourishes you, so that you have no need to sow or reap, or take the least trouble to procure your food. He has given you the trees for your nests, and He watches over your young ones. Therefore, for all these reasons you ought constantly to praise God." The little birds, who showed every sign of attention, now expressed their thanks also in their own fashion. Then the Saint, admiring them for a few moments, gave them his benediction, after which they flew away.

But of all the feathered tribe, the dove was his favorite. One day he met a young lad who was carrying doves to sell in a neighboring town. The Saint exclaimed: "Good young man, have pity on these innocent birds, which, in Scripture, are compared to chaste and faithful souls. I implore of you to give them to me, and not into the hands of those who might kill them." His request was granted, and he took the doves and placed them in his bosom; saying, as he carressed them again and again, "Chaste and innocent little doves, why did you let yourselves be ensnared? I will prepare a nest for you where you will be in safety and where you may increase and multiply." He then took them to the convent at Bavacciano, where they became so familiar with the friars that they would come and eat out of their hands. Nor was the young man without his reward. He had parted with his doves, perhaps at some loss or inconvenience to himself; but he gained in return the grace of a vocation. Entering the Order of Friars Minor, he lived in it for some time, giving great edification by the sanctity and innocence of his life; then in much peace he went to receive the reward of his labors and his charity.

The lark was also a favorite with our Saint. Its joyous song, its cheerful spirit, its soaring flight, and its sober hue, not unlike that which he had chosen for his Order, all were symbolical to him. He loved to draw the attention of his religious to these birds, and thus to teach them holy lessons in a familiar way.

One day, as a lark, after receiving its food, soared up singing into the blue sky, he exclaimed, "See, what a lesson this little creature teaches us! Thus should we give thanks to God, our heavenly Father; thus despise all earthly things, and eat only for His glory; and so continually raise ourselves to heaven, where our conversation should be.

A nest of larks had established themselves quite close to the convent of Mount Columba. The mother bird came every day to receive food from the hands of Francis; and when her young ones were fledged, she brought them with her. Francis soon perceived that one of the brood, which was stronger than the rest, acted the part of domestic tyrant, and would peck the others when they attempted to feed with him. The gentle-hearted Saint could not bear this, so, addressing the bird as if it had understanding, he said, "Cruel and insatiable creature! you will die a wretched death, and the most greedy animals will refuse to touch your flesh." Next day the bird was found drowned in a vessel of water which had been left for them to drink from; and when the body was thrown away no animal would touch it.

When preaching in the town of Alviano, he was much disturbed by the noise made by a number of swallows. "My sisters," cried the simple-hearted Saint, "my sisters, you have talked long enough; listen now, while I preach the word of God." The birds ceased at once, and remained silent, and without moving, until the sermon was ended.

An anecdote related by St. Bonaventura, shows how well-known these miracles were. A student at Paris was one day much annoyed by the twittering of one of these birds. Turning to his companions, he said: "These are the same kind of birds that disturbed the blessed Father Francis while preaching." Then he addressed the swallow thus: "In the name of Francis, the servant of God, I command you to be silent and to come to me." The bird obeyed; but the young man in his surprise let it escape. However, he had not to complain again of such interruptions.

But it was not only the more timid and gentle animals who were thus obedient to our Saint. The fiercest and the most untamed obeyed his call; and it would seem as if in his case was literally fulfilled the promised grace, that the little child shall lead the lion and the bear, and play with the asp and the poisonous serpent. On his way from Grecio to Cotanello, a flock of savage wolves once surrounded him. To the astonishment of his peasant guide, they caressed him in their own fashion, and showed every sign of pleasure at his presence. The marvel was soon noised abroad; and the inhabitants of the surrounding hamlets came to the Saint, and implored him to deliver them from the attacks of these animals, as well as from the frequent hailstorms which had for some time seriously injured their crops. Francis replied, that if they had no pity on their souls, he would have none on their bodies; for if they did not repent and confess their sins, these evils would only increase. His words alarmed them. Many had long lived in sin; but on their sincere and hearty repentance, they were delivered from the temporal punishment under which they had so long suffered.

An amusing story is related in the Chronicles, of a compact which he made with a wolf, whose ferocity rendered him the terror of the people of Gubbio. A party of the inhabitants, armed to the teeth, had determined to go in search of their enemy, and to destroy him before he did further mischief. The Saint was told of their intention; and, notwithstanding their earnest remonstrances, he declared that he would face this formidable enemy alone and unarmed. Francis departed on his expedition, accompanied by the prayers and apprehensions of the good townspeople. He soon encountered the object of his search, and commanded him in the name of God to do no more violence. The wolf, hitherto so savage, became gentle as a lamb, and laid itself at the feet of the Saint, who thus addressed it: "My brother wolf, you roam about in all directions, committing all kinds of devastation, and destroying God's creatures. Your are a homicide, and every one dreads you; but, brother wolf, I wish to make peace with you. It is hunger which has led you to do so much injury to others, so there is some excuse for you. Promise me to do no more harm if you are supplied with food." The wolf bowed its head immediately in token of assent. "Give me a pledge that you will keep your promise," continued Francis, stretching out his hand. The animal placed his shaggy paw in the Saint's hand; and then, at his command, quietly followed him to the village. There the Saint addressed the people, who crowded round him, and whose welfare he had far more at heart than the taming of a wolf. "God has permitted you to be tried," he said, "on account of your sins; but the flames of hell will be found far more terrible to the damned than the ferocity of a wolf, who could only destroy the body. My little brothers, turn to God and do penance for your sins, and he will deliver you from wolves in this world, and from hell in the next. My brother wolf here has promised me that if you will provide him with food, he will do you no more injury." The people gave consent with joy. The wolf testified his acquiescence as he had done before; and for two years he came daily to the village to receive his food. When he died, the good people of Gubbio were not a little grieved; for they thus lost a memorial of the sanctity of Francis and the edification of a miracle of no common order.

But it would be impossible to relate all the anecdotes treasured in the Chronicles, which declare the power of the Saint over the unreasoning orders of creation. The lake of Rieti and its neighborhood could tell many a tale of his marvellous gifts. Now he releases the hare snared by the hunter, and it refuses to leave his side: now he takes the fish from the net, where it had lain some hours, and places it gently in the water; and it moves not from the spot while its deliverer remains near, and shows in its own way that his presence gives it pleasure. This sympathy with all creation resulted from his natural goodness of heart, regenerated and illuminated by supernatural grace. Therefore it is that he places in safety the worm on the roadside, and thinks of Him who was counted a "worm" for man's salvation. Therefore does he bring honey to the bees lest they should perish in the cold of winter, and bids the friars to have always a little plot in their gardens full of the sweetest flowers, to invite the hearts of those who behold them to praise their Creator.

Gentlest and dearest of Saints, when shall we be

like thee in thy love and tenderness? God was indeed thy Father in Heaven, and all He had created was dear to thee in the measure of thy love to him. The wolf, the bee, the singing bird, spoke to thee of thy God; and in the fulnesss of thy great soul, all creatures were brethren to thee, because they were the creatures of thy Lord.

Such legends may appear to some too simple or too childish. We might expect to meet with more dignity in a Saint, and in one so especially and mysteriously favored by God. Yet is not simplicity the truest dignity? Let us remember, too, that far greater and higher powers were continually exercised by the Saint, even that wonderful power of soul over soul, the spell by which the saintly subdue the sinful. We have heard how Francis tamed a wolf; let us now see how he subdued a robber, to whom, from his lawless and savage life, that very name was given.

In the wildest part of the wild uncultivated mountain of Alvernia, this Lupo had established his abode. His crimes had compelled him to fly from his own country; and here he dwelt, the terror of all who were within reach of his lawless deeds. Lupo was indignant beyond measure when he found that the friars had invaded his domain, and presumed to establish themselves on a mountain which he considered exclusively his own. He came to them several times, and informed them, in no very gentle terms, that they had better seek a home elsewhere, threatening the direst vengeance if his commands were not obeyed. Francis was informed of the danger in which his religious were placed, and determined to be on the spot in order to receive the robber when he again appeared. He had not long to wait. Lupo soon returned to see whether the friars had dared to brave his anger. The Saint went out to meet him, spoke a few gentle words, such as had perhaps never been addressed to him since he lay in his mother's arms; and in a few moments the fierce and lawless robber threw himself at the feet of Francis, and declared he would never leave him. They embraced each other tenderly, and charity added one more to the jewels of her celestial crown. Lupo was received into the Order, and known thenceforth as Fra Agnello; and this man, once so violent and unrestrained, became one of the gentlest and most loving, where all were gentle and full of love.

CHAPTER XXVI.

Mount Alvernia.—The Saint weeps for the sufferings of his God.—His fast of forty days.—Our Divine Lord promises four great favors to his Order.—An angel also promises him great graces.—Brother Leo sees him raised above the trees in ecstasy.—Hears him converse with God.—A falcon awakes the Saint every night for matins.—An angel warns him to prepare for what God will do to him.—He receives the sacred Stigmata.

As the earthly life of Francis drew to a close, his love and thirst for sufferings continually increased. He had sought a martyr's crown, and had not obtained it. Still he pined for pain, for anguish, that might make him like his Lord. He would fain have borne in his body the acutest torments under which martyrs had ever triumphed. His desire was heard, but not as he had dreamed or asked; and he was to bear, not the tokens of an ordinary martyrdom, but the very wounds of the King of Martyrs. Well may we pause and fear ere we speak of so awful a mystery. The grant of the indulgence of the Portiuncula was no ordinary grace. What then shall we say of the impression of the sacred Stigmata of the Passion, and of the awful nearness to the Creator vouchsafed to those who are privileged to bear them? Certainly the favor which we are about to relate as granted to our Saint, was one of the greatest ever bestowed on man. Though this mystic union with the sufferings of our Incarnate God has since been granted to others, St. Francis was, it is believed, the first who ever received this grace;"* and some circumstances connected with his Stigmata distinguish them from those of other saints.

It would seem, from the attraction which he had for Alvernia, from his first visit to it, as if he had some foreshadowing of the favor he was to receive there. He loved to wander alone and unnoticed amid its gloomy grandeurs. It had been revealed to him that its vast chasms and deeply-riven gulfs had been caused by the earthquake which attended the crucifixion of our Lord. Thus all around him spoke of the love and sufferings of his Jesus. Wandering hither and thither on that lonely mountain, he would utter his love in plaintive cries; and call on all creatures, and even on the inanimate creation, to join him in his holy grief. Then he would converse with his Beloved, as though he beheld Him, and cry: "Alas, my Jesus! You are crucified and I am not. You are innocence itself, and You suffer for me, the guilty one. Is all this needed to expiate the greatness of my crimes? See, O my soul, what thou hast cost thy Saviour. Can my heart ever find love enough to repay this love? Sing no more, little birds; but sigh and pour out your grief in strains of sadness. O noble trees, bow your lofty heads, and bend your branches into crosses, in honor of the Cross of Jesus. And you, ye rocks, oh! break, melt into tears." Then seeing the little rivulets which, after

* Unless indeed the words of the great Apostle, "*I bear the wounds of the Lord Jesus in my body*—Gal. vi. 17—imply that he had received this grace.

great storms, rolled down the mountain side, he would exclaim: "Oh, my brothers, the rocks, weep, weep, weep!" And the echoes from the neighboring heights would repeat his cry, "Weep, weep," until it seemed as if nature itself were bent on satisfying his blessed desire.

A young nobleman who was crossing the mountain, found him one day utterly lost in sorrow. He addressed him, inquired the cause of his grief, and sought to comfort him. But his sorrow was not of earth, and earth had no consolation for it. The Saint could only cry out, amidst his tears and sighs: "Ah, if you would comfort me, let us weep together over the most bitter and most loving Passion of our Saviour."

At other times he would seek his disciples, and try to excite their love for God. "Consider," he would say, "what dignity God has given you; your bodies He has formed like that of His beloved Son, your souls to His own likeness. Every creature under heaven serves the Creator, and knows and obeys Him better than you do. It was not the devils who crucified the Saviour; but you by their instigation have done this wicked deed: and still you crucify Him, when you take pleasure in vice and in sin. If you had knowledge of, and penetration into all things, you could not glorify yourself in this; for a devil has more knowledge both of earth and heaven than you, however much you may know. If you possessed the most perfect beauty, the greatest riches, still you could not glory in these things; for none of them could procure your salvation, and might rather hinder it. There is nothing, then, in which we can glory, but in the Cross of our Lord Jesus Christ, in bearing it every day, and in suffering with Him."

As the life of the Saint drew towards its close these

outpourings of Divine love became more and more violent. It would seem as if he was unable to repress them, and cared not to do so; perhaps it was often counted folly, and men dared to pity him. But what can we say who have never felt these unearthly fires, who can only stand and gaze from afar in reverent awe, in humble sympathy? Francis suffered because he loved. His Love was crucified; and the untold anguish of that crucifixion was ever before him! He had seen it all in mystic vision, he had felt it all in his heart's deepest core. But the love of our Saint was not merely a love of words and of tears, if such could indeed be called love; it was a love which produced an incessant thirst for suffering, and a constant practice of every kind of mortification. Our Divine Lord's lonely fast in the wilderness seems to have had a special attraction for him, and he loved in his measure to follow it. One Lent was spent in a little island in the lake of Perugia. On Shrove Tuesday he repaired thither. A friend of his, who lived on the side of the lake, conveyed him across and gave him two small loaves for his nourishment. The Saint charged him not to make known his abode, and to return for him on Holy Thursday. On the day appointed he came for Francis. One loaf was found untouched, and of the other but a small portion had been used. Enough, says the Chronicle, to save the Saint from vain-glory, lest it should be said he had spent forty days without food.

The Feast of St. Michael the Archangel was now approaching. Francis always kept a Lent before it, which he began the day after the Assumption. But this memorable year (1224) he determined it should be spent in even greater solitude than before. Brother Leo was his companion and his confidant. Calling him one day by his familiar name, he said, "Dear little sheep of

God, go and open the holy Gospels three times on the altar, in honor of the Blessed Trinity." The Pecorella obeyed, and each time he opened the Passion of Christ. It was enough. The Saint, like his Divine Master, "steadfastly set his face to go to Jerusalem," and hastened to the spot where the mysterious sacrifice was to be consummated. From this moment his ecstacies became longer and more marvellous. Brother Leo sees him again and again, not only unconscious of his presence and of all around, but raised above the highest trees, his body following the flight of his blessed soul. When not raised beyond his reach, the saintly brother would hold his feet, and bathing them with his tears, would cry for mercy, and pray that the merits of his master might gain for him some grace. At other times when Francis was beyond his sight he would lie prostrate on the earth, and pray on the spot from which he had ascended. After one of these ecstacies our Divine Lord appeared to him, sitting on a stone which the Saint had used as a table. Conversing familiarly with Francis as with His friend, He promises four graces to his Order: 1. That all who sincerely loved it should obtain the grace of a happy death. 2. That they who persecuted it should be severely punished by God. 3. That no religious who lived in sin should long persevere in it. 4. That the Order should exist until the day of judgment. When the vision disappeared, the Saint called his companion, desired him to wash the stone four times, with water, with wine, with oil, and with balm, and then declared to him the favor he had received.

Once, also, when he was thinking anxiously of the future, an angel appeared to him, declaring he was sent from God to console him, and to assure him of the favors which should be granted to his Order. "I assure you, on the behalf of God," said the angel, "that your Order shall continue until the day of judgment. There is no sinner, however great, who shall not find mercy with God, if he sincerely befriends it; nor shall any one live long who attempts to injure it. If unworthy persons enter it, they shall not be able to persevere, but will soon be expelled therefrom. Be not, therefore, grieved if you should see religious in your Order who do not observe the Rule as they ought. They will not have power to injure it; for it will always contain a great number who will live a perfect and evangelical life, and keep the Rule in all its purity. These, after their death, will pass to eternal life without entering Purgatory. There will also be others, less perfect, who must pass through Purgatory before they enter Paradise, but God will commit the time of their purification to you. As for those who in no way observe the Rule, take no care, saith the Lord, for he will take no care for them.

All chroniclers agree that this vision was granted to the Saint on Mount Alvernia, though all do not state the exact period. Francis, however, was not to taste an unmixed cup of joy. Fierce and terrible were the attacks made on him by the evil spirits, whose wrath was now more than ever excited against him. Once, while at prayer, he was suddenly thrown by an invisible force on a hard rock at some distance from where he had knelt. But the demon was powerless to destroy; he could not even seriously harm, for the Saint was miraculously preserved from the injuries he must otherwise have suffered. Then an angel appeared to him, and consoled him with celestial strains of such surpassing sweetness, that he afterwards declared, if it had continued long, he must have died from the excess of rapture it occasioned. His friends, the birds, came also in flocks to welcome him, and sang round him with every demonstration of joy.

By his desire a cell had been prepared for him in one of the wildest parts of the mountain. It was on the northern declivity, and a frightful chasm had to be passed over to reach it. A tree thrown across served as a bridge. None but Brother Leo was allowed to approach, and he was desired to come thither every day, and bring a small quantity of bread and water for the Saint's refection. At midnight he was also permitted to come and say matins with his beloved father; but Francis strictly enjoined him not to pass the bridge until he had announced his approach, by saying in a loud voice, "*Domine, labia mea aperies.*" If he heard the Saint answer, he might come into his cell, but he was desired if there was no reply to go back to the convent. Often the good friar received no answer when he spoke, for Francis was wholly absorbed in prayer. Once, when he could not make himself heard he ventured to look through the chinks of the door, to see how the Saint was occupied. A glorious light filled the poor cell, and he heard voices which made question and answer. He saw Francis prostrate on the earth, and heard him say often, "Who art Thou, O my God, and my dearest Lord? and who am I, but a vile worm and an unprofitable servant?" Then a most brilliant light, which seemed to descend from heaven, rested on the head of the Saint, and Leo heard a voice which appeared to come from it, but he knew not what words were spoken.

Full of fear at what he had beheld, and dreading the displeasure of his master if he was discovered, he was about to retire when he was called by Francis, who inquired who had thus interrupted him. Trembling before him whom he now more than ever revered, he asked pardon for his fault, with many tears; and then kneeling humbly, the Saint—knowing that God had permitted him, for his simplicity and purity, to see so much—forgave him, and told him all that had passed. When uttering the words which Leo had heard, two great lights had illuminated the soul of the Saint. The one gave him a knowledge of the infinite power, wisdom, and goodness of God; the other revealed to him his own vileness and misery. His Divine Lord had asked of him three gifts; but the Saint could only plead his poverty. What had he but his cord and his tunic—and even these he could not call his own. Then he was desired to place his hand in his bosom, and draw forth whatever he should find there. Three times the command was repeated and obeyed, and each time Francis found a golden ball, which he humbly presented to his Lord. These three offerings he was made to understand, signified the three virtues of holy obedience, entire poverty, and most pure chastity, which God, by His grace, had enabled him so perfectly to observe that he was obliged to declare he had nothing to reproach himself thereupon. Having told these things to his disciple, the Saint dismissed him with his forgiveness, but added a solemn injunction never again to approach him unbidden. Still Leo was often a witness to his ecstacies, for the Saint frequently wandered far into the woods, and there remained absorbed in prayer, unconscious of all human sights and sounds, and raised so high above the earth as to be invisible at some distance. Once, as the Pecorella watched him from afar, he saw a scroll descend from heaven, and rest on the head of the Saint. On it were written these words in letters of gold, "Here abideth the grace of God." When he had read it he saw it return again to heaven.

A falcon had built her nest near the Saint's lonely

cell. In the day time she would come to him to be fed and remain fearlessly near him. As if to reward him for his kindness, she called him every night when the hour of matins had arrived, crying and flapping her wings until he arose. Sometimes, however, when he had been suffering more than usual, or had seemed during the day weak and weary, she would take care to prolong a little the short time he allowed himself for rest.

On the eve of the festival of the Holy Cross, an angel appeared to St. Francis as he prayed. "I am come from God," said the blessed spirit, "to desire that you prepare yourself in patience and humility for all that God will give and do to you." The Saint humbly replied, "I only desire that the holy will of God should be accomplished in me, and am ready for whatever it may please Him to send." The hour of sacrifice was rapidly approaching; soon all was consummated. The Saint remained in prayer until morning dawned. Who may tell what passed between him and his God during the silent vigil? As the sun's rays gilded the bleak mountain, he turned towards the east and cried with the whole fervor of his soul, "O my Lord Jesus Christ, I ask of you to grant me two graces before I die; first, that you will make me feel in body and soul, as far as is possible for me, the pains that You, my sweet Lord, endured in the hour of Your cruel passion; secondly, that I may feel in my heart as much as possible of that excess of love by which You were induced to suffer for us poor sinners, such unheard-of torments." His prayer ended, he began to meditate on the passion which our Divine Lord had borne for our love, until his very life seemed to consume itself away in intense desire.

He knew that his petition was heard, that his request would be granted; and now the awful moment had arrived. A seraphic form suddenly descended from the sky, and with rapid flight approached the Saint. As he paused Francis perceived that he had six wings of marvellous beauty and unearthly splendor. Two were extended over the head, two spread out for flight, and two covered the rest of the body. Soon the Saint perceived in the form of the seraph the figure of our crucified Lord. A sight so new and so inexplicable filled him with joy, with grief, and with amazement. Joy at the presence of his beloved Lord, who gazed upon him with inexpressible tenderness; sorrow, at beholding Him thus crucified, and bearing the token of His agony. While he was musing in deep anxiety what this vision might mean, and marvelling how the appearance of suffering should coincide with the glory and bliss of a seraphic being, the purpose of this vision was revealed to him. It was to teach him that not by the martyrdom of his flesh, but by the burning all-consuming love of his spirit, he should be made like unto his Lord. After a short space that glorious vision passed from his sight; but not until he had received in his body the Stigmata of the Lord Jesus and in his soul an intensity of love, as far beyond our comprehension as is the favor which accompanied it. After his death he revealed to one of his disciples that deep and mysterious things had been then made known to him by our Divine Lord. "Knowest thou," said Christ, "what I have done to thee? I have given thee My Stigmata, which are the marks of My passion: that thou mayest be My standard-bearer, and that as I, on the day of My death, descended to Limbus, to release by My wounds the souls who suffered there, and to conduct them to paradise; so, when thou hast left the earth, each year on the anniversary of thy death, I will permit thee to descend to purgatory, and by virtue of thy Stigmata to bring from thence the souls of the three Orders of the Friars, the Sisters and the Tertiaries; and even those who have had great devotion to thee, thou shalt be permitted to assist, and to introduce them thyself into paradise."

At the moment of the apparition, the mountain had appeared as if enveloped in flames. The shepherds who had been watching their flocks in the plains below, were witnesses of this prodigy, and spoke of it to the friars, assuring them the light had been visible for more than an hour, and had caused them exceeding fear, as they were unable to account for so extraordinary an appearance. Some muleteers, who had put up at a hostelry near the mountain, had risen in haste, supposing it was already day; but as they journeyed on, the supernatural light faded away, and the sunrise was perceived soon after. The mystery was soon known to all. Francis descended from the mountain. It was the month of September, summer had now ripened into the rich golden autumn, but a more fruitful autumn still had come to his seraphic soul, and the sheaves were ripening for the harvest. The "tears" on the mountain side trickled slowly down; the summer bee flew heavily, laden with the spoils of that glorious clime; but Francis heeded them not. Henceforward his life was one rapture of love. They brought him hither and thither as they would; they nursed and cherished him, for his frail body daily gave signs of speedy dissolution; but as he journeyed from place to place, he was often perfectly unconscious where he went and what passed around him; as if that seraph had taken his heart altogether to paradise, and had left his body only to display for a time the triumphs of the Cross.

CHAPTER XXVII.

By the advice of Brother Illuminatus, the Saint makes known to his children the favor he had received, but conceals it from others.—He returns to St. Mary of the Angels.—Works miracles and preaches.—Is brought to Assisi to be near St. Clare.—His illness increases.—He is removed to several places near Assisi.—An angel consoles him with celestial music.—He blesses a burning iron, and feels no pain when it is applied.—Works two miracles for his kind physician.—St. Bonaventura's life of the Saint.

The humility of the Saint made him desire that this stupendous favor should be concealed, as far as possible, from all. But as usual he would be guided by obedience, the surest test of true humility. Calling the friars together, he proposed his doubt to them in general terms, asking their counsel. Brother Illuminatus, a holy religious truly enlightened by God, replied at once to his question: "Know, Brother Francis," he exclaimed, "that it is not for thyself alone, but for others also, that God reveals His secrets to thee; and therefore thou shouldst fear lest He be displeased with thee if thou conceal the favor He has imparted." It was this same brother who had so well advised Francis, when he was perplexed how to act in the camp of the crusaders. The Saint followed his advice, and declared to his religious all that had passed; reserving only the words which had been spoken to him, and which were not revealed until after his death. From all others, however, he concealed, as far as was possible, the favor he had received. He wore a kind of slippers made for him by St. Clare, and so contrived that the raised sole permitted him to walk notwithstanding the points of the nails which projected from the soles of his feet. These slippers are still preserved as a most precious relic, at Assisi, and were shown there to Father Luke Wadding, the great annalist of the Order. Nails were also formed in the hands of the Saint, and in both the hands and feet the points and heads were seen distinctly and separate from the flesh. His hands from this time were always covered. The wound in his side was open, and bled frequently and profusely. These wounds caused him the most intense and constant pain, so that he was obliged to allow them to be dressed, but the Pecorella was the only one permitted to perform this office for him. He was allowed to touch and dress these mysterious wounds every day, except from Thursday evening until Saturday; when the Saint would not accept any alleviation to his pain, in memory of the bitter passion of his Lord. Sometimes when Brother Leo removed the bandage from his side, the intense pain would cause his seraphic father to lay his hand on him for a moment. When this occurred, the holy friar declared that it was with difficulty he could keep himself from falling to the ground; so intense and overpowering was the Divine love and sweetness enkindled in his soul by the touch of those holy hands.

The Lent of St. Michael the Archangel being ended, St. Francis prepared by Divine revelation to return to St. Mary of the Angels. Brother Leo was his companion. Brothers Masseo and Angelo he left in charge of the convent of Alvernia; blessing them in the name of Jesus crucified, and permitting them to see and touch his blessed wounds.

His homeward progress was extremely slow, his weakness was so great, and the pain of the Stigmata so severe, that he could scarcely walk; still, he was eager for work. He longed once more to suffer in the hospitals and lazar-houses, and to tend the lepers, his dear Christian brothers. His weakness he regarded as want of fervor, and he would say to his companions, "Ah, my children! let us begin to serve God now, for hitherto we have done nothing." Miracles still testified his power with God. At Arezzo he cured a child of dropsy by one touch; at Mount Casale, and at Castello, he delivered persons who were possessed. A nobleman at Monte-Acutio begged him for some little token of remembrance; the Saint declared he had nothing to give but his habit. This he left with his friend in exchange for a new one. It was the habit in which he had received the sacred Stigmata; and we may imagine with what veneration the relic was received and treasured. When his weakness permitted, he still preached, often visiting five or six towns during the day for this purpose, and riding on an ass when unable to walk. Everywhere he had the same text, for the one thought absorbed his whole being: "Jesus, my love, is crucified." It was at this time he composed that marvellous effusion of Divine love, the hymn,

"In foco l'amor mi mise."

As St. Bernard has said of the "Song of songs," "it is love which sings in this canticle; and if any would understand it they must love. It will be in vain for those who do not love, to hear this song of love; its burning words cannot be understood by a cold heart; its language will seem strange and unintelligible to those who do not love, and will fall on their ears as an empty sound." Some authors say that Francis now composed his Canticle of the Sun, and that the disagreement and subsequent reconciliation between the Bishop of Assisi and the Governor occurred at this period.

It was now plain to all that the Saint's earthly course was nearly run. At last he yielded to the pressing entreaties of Cardinal Ugolini, and of Brother Elias, who, with all his faults, loved his seraphic father tenderly. They brought him to a poor house close to St. Damian's that he might be near his beloved children, St. Clare and her holy sisters. They prepared him such alleviations and remedies as were considered needful for him ; but no earthly love or help could now avail. Many touching anecdotes are related of the forty days he spent there. Brothers Leo, Masseo, Ruffinus, and Angelus of Rieti, were his companions. He began to suffer most severe pain in his eyes. Constant weeping had almost deprived him of sight ; but he would not restrain his tears, lest it should lessen his devotion. He now got no rest, day or night, and was obliged to pray earnestly for patience to support his sufferings ; but celestial voices consoled him, and he was told that his pains were a richer treasure than all the wealth of the world, since they would obtain for him a kingdom, whose joys were unimagined by mortal heart.

The long years of suffering which St. Clare endured before the close of her mortal pilgrimage had already begun. When this revelation was made to him, Francis sent for her, that she might also be consoled by it. After a long conference they parted, to meet no more on earth. That very day the holy patriarch was suddenly wrapt in ecstasy while partaking of his mid-day refection ; and during the blessed visitation of grace, a revelation was made to him of the certainty of his eternal salvation.

He was next removed to St. Mary of the Angels, where he remained during the summer. While here he recovered a little, and frequently wandered into the woods unseen. Once when he had retired thither, he wished to speak with Brother Bernard, his "eldest born." Calling him thrice, he said, "Brother Bernard, come and talk to this poor blind man." But Bernard was speaking to another, and so absorbed in prayer that he was unconscious of external sounds. Francis returned to the friar who had guided him into the wood; perplexed that the spiritual child he so tenderly loved should seem so indifferent to him. But a voice spoke to him from heaven, and declared to him that the Creator must not be forsaken for the creature; and that this apparent neglect had been permitted by God for his instruction. The Saint at once concluded he had been guilty of a grievous fault; and could not rest until he had atoned for it by penance. Assisted by his guide, he at length found Brother Bernard, who had returned from his rapture, and was still in the wood. Throwing himself at his feet, he asked pardon: then, lying on the ground, commanded the poor brother in virtue of obedience to trample on him three times, and to place his foot on his mouth. Bernard resisted as long as he dared; but obedience prevailed, and with tears he obeyed the command.

In the autumn (1225) St. Francis was brought, first to Rieti, then to San Fabiano, a village near it, as it was hoped the air of the vineyards would help to restore him. While he was residing at the last-named place, Pope Gregory and his court came to Rieti. Many cardinals and prelates visited the Saint; and so great was the concourse of people who flocked to him, that the vineyards of the parish priest were seriously injured. He complained of this to the Saint, who promised he should not be a loser. His words were verified—the poor priest obtained considerably more than the usual quantity of wine even from the few vines which remained uninjured. A convent and church were subsequently erected on the spot in memory of the miracle, and consecrated by the same Pontiff.

While remaining here, the Saint suffered for a time

from a depression which he knew was occasioned by his constant bodily infirmities. His old love for poetry and music never left him : and he now requested one of the friars to cheer him by playing on an instrument. It was represented to him that this recreation, however innocent in itself, might give scandal to others; and with his usual humility he acquiesced in the opinion of his spiritual children. That night, as he lay on his poor bed, his body unable to rest from pain, but his soul soaring up to his Beloved, and the more united to Him by his sufferings, an angel gave him the consolation denied to him by men. Familiar as the angels were to him, no form was then visible to his corporeal sight; but he heard a melody so unearthly, of such surpassing sweetness, that he thought his soul had gone to paradise. Consolations of this heavenly kind were often granted to him; he tried to conceal them, but in vain—the joy and peace they brought appeared on his countenance, and visibly heightened its already seraphic expression.

His next resting place was the convent of Mount Columba. There was a very skilful physician in this place, and it was hoped his care might tend to restore the Saint. He advised the application of a burning iron to relieve the pain in the eyes. When the operation was to be performed the friars left the room; for they could not endure to see the father they so tenderly loved suffering so severely. Even the Saint appeared to shrink from the painful infliction; and he who had so courageously offered to enter a furnace in Egypt to prove his faith, dreaded the touch of the burning iron. Was it for his humiliation, or for our consolation, that for a moment natural weakness seemed to mingle with such supernatural graces as were his? But a miracle quickly followed. Just as the iron was about to be applied, he made the sign of the cross on the instrument, and addressing with saintly simplicity his "brother the fire," he begged that He who had created it would temper its power. When, a few moments after, it was applied, the Saint felt no pain, and even requested that the operation should be rapeated, if necessary.

Several other miracles are related regarding his intercourse with this good physician. His name is not mentioned by any of the chroniclers of the Order; but we are told that he was a person of great learning and piety; and that he would accept no remuneration from the friars for his attendance and remedies, except their prayers. St. Francis loved to have him near him; and once he desired the friars to take their honorable brother, the physician, to dine with them. They expostulated, even in the presence of the good doctor, and declared that they had nothing to give him but their usual fare—poor hospitality for a person of his rank and circumstances. But the Saint told them to be obedient and to have faith, and so they went to the refectory. As they were sitting down, a messenger arrived, bringing a present of some very rare dishes of meat, dressed ready for use, which had been sent by a charitable lady who lived near the convent. But the good doctor was to see a greater miracle. He had just built a new house, and expended a large sum of money on it, when, to his dismay, he found that a principal wall had given way, and was cracked from top to bottom. He at once applied to the friars, and begged for something belonging to the Saint to place in the wall. After many entreaties they gave him some of his hair. The physician took it home carefully, and placed it in an opening of the wall. Next morning the fissure was so completely closed that he could not even discover where it had been, nor find any of the hair he had left there.

An interval of convalescence, and the partial restoration of his sight, enabled the Saint again to preach. For this purpose he visited Tuscany, still working miracles wherever he went. It was probably during this apostolic tour that he saved the life of an infant, who was to be one of the most illustrious members of the Seraphic Order. Saint Bonaventura was born at Bagnara, a small town belonging to the Ecclesiastical States. His parents, John Fidenza and his wife Ritella, were of noble birth. This Saint was born in 1221, and baptized by the name of John. But a mortal illness threatened his life while yet an infant. Ritella, trembling for her little one, had recourse to the prayers of Francis to avert the threatened calamity, making at the same time a vow that if the infant's life were spared she would dedicate him to God in the Order of Friars Minor. To the surprise of the physicians, the child recovered; and the Saint's expression of joy, "*O buona ventura!*" gave him the name by which he was known thenceforward and afterwards canonized.

CHAPTER XXVIII.

St. Francis returns to Assisi, and the Bishop insists on having him as his guest.—The people place guards round the palace, lest they should be deprived of the body of the Saint after his death.—He blesses his chiidren.—Writes to St. Clare.—Desires to be carried to St. Mary of the Angels, that he may die in the house which Mary loves.—His joy when told his Sister Death is near.—He blesses the town of Assisi.—Writes to the Lady Jacoba de Settesoli.—She arrives as he is writing, having been warned by an angel to do so —Blesses his children again, and especially Brother Bernard.—His death.—His wounds seen now by all.—An incredulous officer examines them.

THE time of our Saint's departure to his heavenly home was drawing near. The silver cord was breaking the golden fillet shrinking back, and in his inmost soul he heard the voice of his Beloved: "*Surge amica mea, et veni.*" The Bishop of Assisi insisted on taking him to his palace, where he remained till the spring of 1226. In the month of April he was removed to Sienna; but he still grew weaker, and brought up blood in such quantities that his remaining strength could only have been preserved by a miracle. Here he was visited by the Dominican Fathers, who loved him almost as if he had been their own, and grieved to see him in such suffering.

One morning, after a night of unusual weakness, caused by loss of blood, the Saint called his infirmarian, Brother Benedict, who, during his illness, said Mass in his room. "Priest of God," he said, "write the benediction which I now give to my brethren, as well to those who are now in the Order, as to all who shall enter it even till the end of the world. May they all love each other, as I have loved them, and do love them. May they always cherish and love poverty, my lady and mistress. May they be always submissive and devoted to their prelates. And may the Father, and the Son, and the Holy Ghost, bless and protect them. Amen." Then he dictated a long and touching letter to the absent brethren.

Brother Elias now heard that St. Francis was sinking fast. He hastened to him, and then brought him to the convent of Celles, near Cortona. But in a few days the Saint desired to be taken back to Assisi. The bishop again insisted on having him in his palace, and Francis complied with his desire. The people, who heard he was dying, fearful lest his precious remains should be taken from them, placed guards around the house. Their precaution was unavailing; he was not to die here, but at his beloved Porziuncola. A good physician from Arezzo, John del Buono, now came to see him, and remained with him constantly. When Francis was told that his end was near, his face shone with a radiance of unearthly joy. He called Brother Leo and Brother Angelo to sing his Canticle of the Sun, and added the verse to his Sister Death. Then he said he would bless his children before he died. His sight had entirely failed; so, when they knelt before him he asked on whose head he had placed his right hand, for he had crossed them over each other, even as Jacob in blessing the children of Joseph. Being told that it was Brother Elias, he said, "It is well"—and blessed him abundantly; for through him, he said, the Order had much increased. And in truth the poor friar dearly loved his holy master, and was perhaps led astray more through the influence of others than by any real malice of heart.

Nor did Francis forget those who could not at that moment minister to him as their hearts desired, his poor children at St. Damian's. He dictated a letter to St. Clare and her sisters, exhorting them to perseverance in their holy state, fervor in the practice of virtue, and patience in their sufferings. Wadding, who relates the circumstances, says it is well authenticated ; though this letter, with several others written to the same community, has unfortunately been lost. He says that the Saint felt an especial tenderness towards those religious, not only because they were the children of his own Rule, but as foreseeing how much they would edify the Church and promote the Divine glory by their sanctity ; and the same writer adds, notwithstanding their austerities and the severity of their Rule, no religious excel them in harmony, content, and peace of mind ; for their joy is the joy of the heart, which no man can take from them.

Bodily weakness, extreme as it was, no way lessened the mental vigor of the Saint, which, to the last, was almost supernatural. When the day of his release drew near, he begged to be carried to his dear St. Mary of the Angels, that he might die there among his brethren and in the place which Mary loved. As they bore him along on a litter, he desired them to stop when they were outside the town. He then said, " Turn my face towards the town." Then raising himself on his poor couch, he solemnly blessed it and all who dwelt therein : " Be thou blessed of the Lord," he exclaimed, " O city faithful to God ! for many souls wlll be saved in thee and by thee. Many of the servants of the Most High dwell within thy walls, and many of thy citizens are chosen to eternal life."* Then, foreseeing the sufferings impending over the town, and the scenes of cruelty so soon to be enacted by Frederic and the Moorish troops, he wept bitterly.

Immediately after his arrival at St. Mary's he dictated a letter to the Lady Jacoba de Settesoli. When it was partly written, he exclaimed that there was no need to send it, as she had left Rome and would soon be at the convent bringing all he desired. In a very short time his words were verified. This was probably on Sunday, the 28th of September. The noble lady arrived the same day, with her sons and a large retinue, declaring that she had been warned during the night by an angel to set out at once for Assisi, and to bring what the Saint had asked for in his letter. By the de-

* The benediction of St. Francis is inscribed on the principal gate of Assisi. It runs thus :

BENEDICTIO S. FRANCISCI.
BENEDICTA TU, CIVITAS, A DOMINO,
QUIA PER TE MULTÆ ANIMÆ SALVABUNTUR,
ET IN TE MULTI SERVI ALTISSIMI HABITABUNT,
ET DE TE MULTI ELIGENTUR AD REGNUM ÆTERNUM.
PAX ✠ TIBI.

sire of Francis, she was admitted into the convent—a privilege not allowed to any other of her sex; but he said her house had always been opened to his friars, and she should therefore be allowed to enter theirs.

The day before his death, (Friday, Oct. 3d,) he called the brethren together again, that he might bless them once more before he died. Then he desired that they would bring him some bread. When it was given to him, he made the sign of the cross upon it, and divided it among them. Each took his portion, and ate it with tears. Brother Elias wept bitterly, as if he already foresaw the evil he would do, and the weakness to which he would yield when the grace of his blessed father's presence was withdrawn. The Saint then inquired for Brother Bernard, his beloved "eldest born." Bernard knelt beside him, with Brother Giles, and the Saint crossed his hands, so that the right hand might rest on the head of Brother Bernard. Then he blessed him, saying, "The first religious and companion whom God gave me was Brother Bernard da Quintavalle. As he was the first who began, so has he been the most fervent to continue, in observing the rule of the Gospel and the evangelical counsels. On this account, as well as for the many graces which God has given him, I am compelled to love him more than any religious in the Order. Be thou, therefore, blessed of our Lord Jesus Christ. Be the superior of all your brethren. Receive or reject from the Order whom you will, and be free to live wherever and however you desire. In the name of the Father, and of the Son, and of the Holy Ghost."

The poor brother was so completely overcome, that he was obliged to hurry away to hide his grief. When he had left the room, Francis turned to the brethren, and charged them to love and cherish his beloved son as they would have loved and cherished himself. He declared to them what great graces God had bestowed on him; and that on this account he wished whoever might be appointed minister-general after his death, should leave Bernard free to go wherever the Divine Spirit might inspire him. He also declared again, that he gave him a special power of admitting or rejecting novices, as having been himself the first to enter the Order. Then he dictated his last testament. It was but a summary of the Rule he had already given—an earnest and last exhortation to observe it without gloss or comment, and to practice the poverty it enjoined to the very letter. He entreats them even more and more deeply to reverence all holy houses and places, especially to honor the Adorable Mystery of the altar, and all churches and priests on this account. He desires them, if they should see papers lying on the ground, to take them up, lest holy names should be profaned, and begs them always to use the salutation, "May our Lord give you His peace;" since it was revealed to him that our Lord desired they should do so. He concludes thus: "May whoever observes these things be filled in heaven with the blessings of the Eternal Father; and on earth, with the blessings of His beloved Son, and the Holy Spirit the Paraclete. May he be assisted by all the heavenly powers, and by all the saints; and I, Brother Francis, your poor little servant in our Lord, give to you, as far as I am able, this blessing."

Then he gave special directions about his beloved Porziuncola, charging the ministers generally to see that all who lived there should be distinguished for their sanctity—above all, for their humility and love of silence.

It was now the morning of the fourth of October, and

the Saint knew it was the last day he should spend on earth. His mental vigor seemed almost to increase with his decaying strength. He desired to be taken from his poor bed, and laid almost naked on the bare floor. Then one of the brethren, who, says the Chronicle, was inspired by God for the consolation of His Saint, brought him an old tunic, and the other parts of the dress worn by the friars, and said: "Here, we will lend you these things: take them as an alms and wear them in obedience." With a joy commensurate with his love of his "lady poverty," the dying Saint accepted this last alms. It was indeed fitting that he should die thus. His life began in a stable; his career of evangelical poverty, with a renunciation of his very clothing; and now he dies in the borrowed garments of another as poor as himself; so perfectly was he conformed, both in life and in death, to Him who had not where to lay His head. Crossing his arms and laying his hand on the wound in his side, he bade farewell to his children, and cried: "I leave you in the fear of the Lord: take care never to depart from it. The time of trial is coming: happy are they who shall persevere in the good which they have begun. I go to God, for whom my soul pines, and I recommend you all to His grace."

They asked him where he wished to be buried, and he replied at once, on the "Infernal Hill, where criminals are executed." Then he desired them to call Brother Leo and Brother Angelo, that they might sing his Canticle of the Sun and praise his Sister, Death. After this he bade them bring the Holy Gospels, and read to him the Passion of Christ. Then with a broken voice, he began the psalm, "*Voce mea ad Dominum clamavi;*" and as he uttered the last words; "*Me expectant justi, donec retribuas mihi,*" he went to dwell with the just, and to receive his eternal recompense.

The Saint was in his forty-fifth year when he died; it was on the evening of Saturday, the fourth of October, At the very moment of his departure, one of the brethren saw his soul ascending to heaven in the form of a luminous star. The saintly brother Austin, superior of the province of Naples, was in his agony, and had been speechless for some hours, when suddenly he raised himself on his pallet, and cried out, "Wait for me, my father: wait for me!" The brethren who stood around him inquired anxiously to whom he spoke. "What," he exclaimed, "do you not see our Father Francis going up to heaven?" These were his last words, for at that moment his soul also fled to join that of his blessed father. It is also related that a holy man, whether of the Order or not is uncertain, had a vision on the same day, on which he saw Francis going up to heaven, with several of his religious, whose release from Purgatory had been obtained through his merits. The night of his death, the Saint appeared to the Bishop of Assisi, who, through devotion, had gone to visit the Church of St. Michael at Mount Gargano. The holy prelate related the circumstance to his attendants, and soon the intelligence of the Saint's death left no room for doubt.

The wounds which he had so carefully concealed during his lifetime, were now visible to all. The friars, assisted by the Lady Jacoba, had laid out the body; and having clothed it in a new tunic which she had brought from Rome, they placed it on rich tapestry, leaving the side exposed, that all might see its marvellous wound.

As soon as the intelligence of the Saint's death had spread, the people flocked in crowds to honor his remains, and to kiss and touch the sacred Stigmata. An officer named Jerome had serious doubts of the truth of this supernatural favor; and being a person of influence, he requested and obtained permission to examine the body more minutely than others. So satisfied was he with the result, that he became a most zealous advocate of the truth of this miracle, and even testified to it on oath on the holy Gospels.

CHAPTER XXIX.

The funeral of the Saint.—The procession stops at St. Damien's on its way to St. George's.—The canonization of St. Francis by Pope Gregory IX.

The night was passed with songs of joy. With all their grief, the brethren could not weep; and all who approached the body of the Saint were so filled with spiritual sweetness, that it seemed as if the multitudes who watched with the friars had assembled to keep one of the Church's brightest festivals. The frail tabernacle of that seraphic soul, hitherto so worn, and embrowned by toil and constant austerities, now became fresh and fair, even as theirs who have washed their raiment in the Blood of the Lamb. The limbs were pliable as those of a young child; the miraculous nails in the hands and feet could be moved, and were found to be separate from the flesh which they pierced, having all the appearance of iron nails with large black heads. The next morning, Sunday, a triumphal procession bore the body of the Saint to its temporary resting-place in the old Church of St. George. At day-break the clergy and magistrates of Assisi, with an immense concourse of people, had assembled at St. Mary's. The Friars Minor from the neighboring convents had collected during the night. The people carried branches of olive, a fitting honor for one whose salutation was always a *Pax vobiscum.* The friars carried lighted tapers. The holy remains, placed on a bier covered with the richest tapestry, was borne by two friars and two of the magistrates, while the clergy closed the procession. Shouts and songs of triumph, with the clangor of trumpets, resounded as it passed along.

St. Francis had promised his beloved children at St. Damian's that they should see him again. During his long illness they had suffered deeply. His forty days' residence near them had but made them more conscious of the value of the treasure they were to lose. And now his promise was to be fulfilled, though it was not his living face they were to see. The *cortège* paused at St. Damian's, and the body was carried into the church, that St. Clare and her children might venerate the remains of their blessed father. But those eyes which had once shone so brightly, telling of the tenderness of one of the tenderest of human hearts, were now closed in death; and those lips which had so often poured forth the instruction and consolation which only a Saint so loving could give, were sealed until the resurrection morn. The poor Sisters wept bitterly; they could scarcely rejoice as did the friars; they were women, and sorrow sinks deeply into a woman's heart. To Clare the trial must have been almost overwhelming. Henceforward she must bear alone the heavy burden of her office: there would be none to sympathise with her, to comfort, to encourage her under the weight of care inseparable from it. What could her children do, as much afflicted as herself? they who were her care could scarcely lessen it. Many of them, it is true, lived lives of surpassing sanctity; but she must now be their only guide, and tremble lest she were not doing her utmost to increase the graces already so abundantly given. There were also the less fervent—the relaxed—and she must now weep in secret in her long nights of suffering for those who turned to their own loss the favors bestowed on them. "Alas, alas," she cried, as she bent over the sacred body, and kissed again and again, those holy wounds; "alas, alas!—O my father, what shall we do, and to whose care have you left us? Ah, who will now assist us in our tribulation, and who support us in our temptations? Sweet Jesus, Son of Mary! why have you forgotten us? O merciful Jesus! this grief is more terrible than death. O Francis! our father, our master, why did you not send us home before you?—and now you will leave us and we shall see you no more."

But the procession might not delay longer. Clare had vainly endeavored to remove one of the nails from the wounded hand of her seraphic father. As she could not succeed, she was fain to content herself with dipping a linen cloth in the blood which flowed from it. She then took the measure of the body in order to have a niche made of the same size. The crowds who surrounded the bier were deeply moved at the grief of the poor religious, and tenderly sympathised in their sorrow. But the procession moved on, and they were left alone. Had the young and gentle abbess known that her exile must last for nearly thirty years longer, her very heart might have died within her. But we may not doubt that when the natural grief of her deeply affectionate heart had calmed into the resignation of true sanctity, this trial, deep as it was, but added to her joys. Her bodily sufferings constantly increased; the cares of her office weighed more heavily upon her. But the spouse of Jesus can never suffer alone; her Beloved is still in the tabernacle on earth, and at the right hand of God in heaven; and the more she is deprived of earthly consolation, the closer is she united to Him even by her very sufferings.

The after-life of the saintly abbess was one of silence, of pain, and of prayer. The *Agony in the Garden*, where Jesus was left alone, was her constant meditation. He had borne her burden in anticipation, and it weighed less heavily on her as she thought of His. But the canonization of the Saint, which took place in the following year, must have given no little joy to his children at St. Damain's. Honorius III. died soon after Francis, and it therefore remained for his beloved friend, Cardinal Ugolini, now raised to the pontificate under the title of Gregory IX., thus to honor him whose Order he had so long protected.

Political troubles which disturbed the Roman States immediately after this Pope's election, obliged him to retire to Spoleto, and from thence to Rieti. After a time, he removed to Assisi, where doubtless, it was no small solace to him to pour forth his prayers, and seek consolation for his anxieties at the tomb of Francis.

He had already appointed his nephew, Cardinal Rainaldi, protector of the Order, and he now instituted a commission of inquiry, to make the necessary examination into the merits and miracles of the Saint, in order to his canonization. The process of inquiry having been conducted with the customary exactness, the holy father appointed the 16th of July as the day on which he would proclaim to the whole Church the sanctity of his friend.

On the evening previous to the ceremony the Pope came with his cardinals and retinue from Perugia, where he was then residing. An immense concourse of nobles and other persons of rank had assembled from all parts of Italy for the occasion. The sun rose gloriously on the day appointed, as though it would contribute its share in honoring the festival of him who had called it brother. A throne was prepared for the Pope in the little church of St. George. He ascended it to pronounce the eulogium of his friend; and as he proceeded with his address, it seemed to his enraptured audience as if he had caught the seraphic fire of him of whom he spoke. "Behold," he cried, "a new ambassador has sprung, even from the side of Christ, bearing on his blessed body the burning impress of the Cross. Francis, this noble prince, bears the royal standard, and assembles the nations from all parts of the earth. He has organized a threefold army to fight against the powers of the dragon, and disperse his infernal hordes." Then he declared that, brilliant as were the miracles of Francis, so that there could be no doubt that he reigned in the Church triumphant, still the Church militant had not yet proclaimed him a Saint; but that, as his miracles had been examined and proved by most rigorous investigation, he had resolved, with the advice of his brethren, to proclaim him amongst the number of the Saints—"Having confidence that through the mercy of God, we, and the flock committed to our care will be assisted by his prayers, and that we shall have him for our protector in heaven who was our friend on earth."

The allocution ended, Cardinal Octavian read aloud the miracles which had been examined and approved. Most of those on whom they had been wrought were present; and he was constantly interrupted by their ejaculations of assent and thanksgiving. Cardinal Rainerio Capoccio spoke next, and declared all that he knew of the Saint; but his affectionate remembrances were too much both for himself and his audience, and they wept together over the memory of their beloved patron. Then the Sovereign Pontiff rose, and, amid the solemn silence of that vast assembly, spoke with his arms extended: "In honor of the Most High God, the Father, the Son, and the Holy Spirit; of the glorious Virgin Mary; of the blessed apostles St. Peter and St. Paul; and for the glory of the Roman Church; we have resolved, with the advice of our brethren and other prelates, to inscribe in the catalogue of the Saints the Blessed Father Francis, whom God has glorified in heaven, and whom we venerate on earth. His feast shall be celebrated on the day of his death."

Then the cardinals and Friars Minor intoned the *Te Deum*. The people replied with joyous shouts, and the soldiers stationed outside the church proclaimed the happy event with the sound of trumpets. The Holy Father then prostrated himself before the tomb of St. Francis, and made a rich offering in his honor. The cardinals and nobles followed his example. The Pope then offered the Holy Sacrifice, during which the friars stood round the altar, bearing lighted tapers and branches of olive.

CHAPTER XXX.

The "Infernal Hill" is blessed by the Pope, and named the Hill of Paradise.—The Basilica of Assisi, and Sagro Convento erected here. —Translation of the relics of the Saint.—Description of the Church and Convent.—Giotto, Cimabue, Cavallini, Giottino, Solimene, Frà Mino, Frà Philippo.

It will be remembered that the dying Saint had asked to be buried on the *Infernal Hill.* His request was not forgotten; but it was granted in a different way from that intended by his humility. After the canonization, Brother Elias considered how he could best fulfil the Saint's desire. He assembled the people of Assisi, and proposed the matter to them. But they cried with one voice: "Take any of our palaces; take the most honorable places in the city, if you will, we will gladly yield them. But do not place* our greatest treasure in so impure a spot." Elias expostulated. He wished to fulfil the dying injunction of his master, and suggested a method by which they could comply both with the last wish of the Saint, and their own ardent desire to honor his remains. In consequence the Infernal Hill was declared a fief of the Holy See; and Elias, after some correspondence with the most eminent architects of the age, selected a plan for the erection of the present stately church and convent, the greatest ornament of Assisi, and one of the noblest structures of its kind in the Italian states. Jacopo, of Germany, was the architect whose plans he had approved. He came to Assisi, and brought with him a child whom he was training in his noble science. This youth was known later as Frà Philippo of Campello, and was distinguished for his artistic skill.

The work was commenced on the 15th of May, 1228. Workmen were sent from all the neighboring towns: and many who had benefited by the miracles and the teaching of Francis offered themselves for the undertaking, asking only their daily bread as payment for their labor. The friars themselves joined in the work with incredible zeal, and so fervently did they labor, that in a month's time a sufficient space was levelled and prepared for the foundation of the building. The day after the canonization of the Saint, Gregory visited and inspected the work. Then, surrounded by his court, and an immense concourse of

* The act of donation is preserved in the archives of the town of Assisi. It is dated March 30, 1228, and signed by Simone Puzzarelli, magistrate.

people, he blessed the eminence, changing its name to the *Hill of Paradise;* at the same time laying the foundation-stone of that church which was to be an eternal monument of the sanctity of St. Francis and the piety of his native country. In the beginning of May, 1230, the greater part of the convent and the lower church were completed. Brother Elias therefore decided on removing the body of the Saint to the sepulchre prepared for it. Having obtained the approbation of the Holy Father, he convoked the general chapter for the Feast of Pentecost. Thousands flocked unbidden from all parts of Italy to witness the translation of the holy relics.

Political troubles deprived the Pope of the happiness of assisting at this ceremony: but his absence did not lessen his deep interest in it. He was represented by three legates, who brought, in his name, a large sum of money for the completion of the building, with other most valuable offerings; among these were richly embroidered vestments, sacred vessels of silver and gold, and a large golden cross enamelled with precious stones, containing a portion of the true Cross. The vigil of Pentecost, May 25th, was the day appointed for the ceremony. The bull of Gregory is full of touching affection for his beloved friend! "In the midst of the afflictions which overwhelm us, we find a source of consolation and thanksgiving in the glory which God has shed over the blessed Francis, our father and yours; and yet, perhaps, even more ours than yours. Among other marvellous miracles of which he has been the instrument, we have authentic proofs that a dead man was lately restored to life in Germany through his intercession. Therefore, we desire to the utmost to publish more and more the praises of this great Saint; having confidence that, as he loved us so tenderly while in the world, where he lived as if not of it, he will love us still more now that he is united to Jesus Christ, who is Love itself; and will intercede for us continually. We hope also that you, whom he has brought forth in Jesus Christ, and whom he has left heirs of the riches of his extreme poverty—you whom we so tenderly love, and the welfare of whose Order we so ardently desire, will also pray earnestly for us, and obtain from God the grace that our tribulations may promote our eternal welfare."*

The sacred remains were borne in solemn procession to the Hill of Paradise. The bier was placed on a chariot drawn by oxen, covered with crimson tapestry, with birds and flowers embrodered in gold; as if the Saint must even in death be honored by the creatures whom he had made his friends. This was a gift of the German emperor. The Papal legates and Brother Elias attended the chariot; the bishops and vicars-apostolic surrounded them. The friars came in procession in two long files; and the nobles and magistrates, followed by the soldiers and an immense multitude of people, closed the long triumph. As they passed slowly along, they sung psalms and hymns composed by the Pope himself. They told of the sadness of his care-burdened heart, and of his love and confidence in his sainted friend—

" *O Francis, our father! visit our dwellings, our gates, and our tombs, and awaken from the sleep of death the unhappy children of Eve.*

" *Saint Francis, master! come, O father! come and succor this people, who groan beneath their burden.*"

Well might the holy Pontiff sigh out his sorrow to his friend, bearing, as he did, in an evil day, alone and

* Bull dated St. John Lateran, 17th June, 1230.

almost unsolaced, the burden of his triple crown; his sainted friends, Dominic and Francis, gone to their rest; himself, at an age beyond the common term of life, with the solicitude upon him of all the churches.

An extraordinary event occurred at the translation of the relics, which for a long time threw a cloud of mystery over the last resting place of the Saint. The Assisians trembled for their treasure, and just as the *cortège* had arrived at its destination, a strange and unaccountable movement was felt in the crowd. How it had arisen, no one knew. But an impression was made on the people, and they imagined the body of the Saint would be taken from them, unless they secured it themselves. In a few moments they threw themselves upon the chariot, and heedless of the entreaties of the friars, or the authority of the prelates and magistrates, they brought the body into the church, closed the doors, and placed it in the tomb prepared for it, which they built up at once.

When the account of this irreverent proceeding was conveyed to the Pope, he could scarcely restrain his indignation. He wrote to the Bishops of Perugia and Spoleto, complaining of the conduct of the Assisians; nor were they pardoned until they had made humble submission for what they had done. In consequence of this lawless proceeding, a doubt always remained regarding the exact spot where the relics had been deposited. But under the pontificate of Pius VII. the mystery was cleared. The friar de Bonis, Minister-General of the Conventuals, obtained permission to search for the sacred body. The work was undertaken in secret, and prolonged for fifty-two nights. At length an iron grating was discovered; beneath it lay a skeleton in a stone coffin, which emitted an odor of exceeding sweetness. The Holy Father, when informed of the result, appointed the Bishops of Assisi, Nocera, Spoleto, Perugia, and Foligno, to make the usual examination. Afterwards a commission of cardinals and theologians was appointed for the same purpose, and the result of their lengthened investigation proving satisfactory, a brief was published, September 5, 1820, authenticating the discovery of the relics.

The Sagro Convento, with its magnificent church, was completed in 1243. Early in April of that year, Innocent IV. came to Assisi, and on the 25th of May he performed the solemn ceremony of its consecration. The crosses, where it was anointed with the holy chrism, are still visible in its ancient walls. From this day the church obtained the title of a Papal chapel, and the monastery was called, *par excellence*, the Sagro Convento.

A brief description of this magnificent structure can scarcely fail to interest our readers. The designs of Jacopo of Germany, whom Brother Elias employed for the work, show him to have been penetrated with religious feeling, as well as imbued with a knowledge of his craft—so magnificent is it, and so complete; so pervaded by deep symbolism and the spirit of poetry; so full of strength and grace—and this at a time when Italy had scarcely developed its own architecture, and was resting on the cold, unregenerate forms of Grecian art. Still, the light of a new school was dawning: a society had been formed for the restoration of ancient churches and the erection of new ones, whose symbolism should develop the perfection of Christian sacred art. Jacopo was a member of this association, as was also the German Arnolf, architect of the Santa Maria del Fiore, the pride of the Florentine republic. Thus Germany furnished the architects, the minds of thoughtful design, while in painting and embellishment, the poetic Italian took the palm.

The symbolism of the great church of Assisi is as thoughtful as it is beautiful. The poetry of its fresco paintings evidences that a spiritual mind is the true basis of all that is most perfect in the creation of genius. The Church is double. The lower portion, solemn and tearful, speaks to us of the earthly life of the Saint —of his mysterious sufferings, his soul's anguish and temptations, yet gleams with the promises of beauty to come. The upper church is full of joy, and tells of the triumphs of the Saint, his celestial bliss, and his spiritual glories throughout the Church universal. The most imposing view of the entire edifice is that from the bridge of San. Vittorino. So massive and extensive is thc *coup d'œil* presented as we gaze on that grand pile, that it seems rather a fortress than a church or convent.

Traversing the long mediæval corridors, we reach the entrance of the lower church. Its dim light, and the rich tones of its magnificent organ, invites us to tears and compunction. The little side chapels, so exquisite in taste, are the work and design of a Franciscan friar, Frà Philippo, mentioned before. The paintings are the memorials of the eminent artists who vied with each other in paying the homage of their genius at the shrine of the seraphic friar of Assisi. How little did he dream that his lonely wanderings, his bitter sufferings, midnight vigils, and burning raptures would become a theme for the poet's pen, the painter's pencil, and would not merely develop genius but inspire it with its sublimest conceptions! To use the words of a great modern writer: "The sanctuary of Assisi became a centre of inspiration and of pilgrimage. Here all the artists of any renown prostrated themselves, one after the other, and have traced on its walls the pious homage of their pencil. Far from the multitude, withdrawn from the tumultuous highway of the vulgar, they came to ask for peace, and that holy solitude which is the inspiring angel of all human genius. Bending over their palettes, they labored on, day after day; then, when they saw the night descending, they calmly crossed their arms, and laid themselves to rest in the sculptured tomb. They gravely closed their thoughtful eyes, and slept in God, thinking that the eternal glory of Francis of Assisi would shed its lustre on their works."

Giunta Pisano, the friend of Brother Elias, was the first who pictured the Saint. Nor was it only strangers who honored his memory. From among his own children artists arose, who, in all their poverty, and pursuing a life considered by so many as contemptible and useless, not only encouraged and supported the first intellects of the age, but themselves added to its treasure of beauty. Frà Mino da Turrita, a true disciple of Francis and of poverty, has pictured the story of his master's life* in the frescoes on the left side of the lower church. On the right he delineates the life of Him who first ennobled poverty by assuming it.

In 1250, Cimabue came to Assisi. He executed some frescoes in the upper church, and delineated the four great doctors, St. Ambrose, St. Augustin, St. Gregory, and St. Jerome. But

> "Credette Cimabue nella pittura
> Tener lo campo?—*Dante Purgat.* xi.

His glory and his joy was to have made of the shepherd boy of Vespigniano the most glorious of artists. Giotto, indeed, was destined to be the Franciscan

* It is said that Bartholomew of Pisa took the idea of his *Book of Conformities* from these fresco paintings. In this work he particularly notices the many remarkable parallels between the life of St. Francis and that of our Divine Lord,

painter, *par excellence*, and the true regenerator of art. The pride of poets and of princes, it might be a matter of surprise that his genius should expend itself on the life of a mendicant friar; but the poor shepherd boy could estimate, perhaps, better than many, the sublimity of poverty, and the poetic beauty of a life which soared above all that was less grand and glorious than the Eternal beauty.

In the upper church, beneath the frescoes of his master Cimabue, Giotta has pictured the principal scenes of the life of Francis. In the lower, over the tomb of the Saint, he has allegorized the great virtues of Humility, Obedience, Poverty, and Chastity; and in the background is seen the apothesis of the Saint, wherein he appears seated on a golden throne, radiant with light, and clothed in a rich vestment as deacon, while around him choirs of angels sing his triumph.

But it was not only at Assisi that the great artist loved to picture the glorious Saint: at Verona, Ravenna, Rimini, and Florence, the life of Francis was still his favorite theme. Even in the decorations of the sacristy, in the chapel of the Holy Cross, his attraction displays itself. The designs of the stained glass windows in the basilica are supposed to have come from his pencil; and Francis possessed a master-piece of his in the Louvre, representing the Saint receiving the Stigmata. It would be impossible to enumerate here the artists who employed their talents in the church and convent of Assisi. Simon Memmi, one of the glories of the school of Sienna, represented in the chapel of St. Martin various scenes from the life of that Saint. In the great refectory he executed a Madonna. Margaritone and the saintly Cavallini followed; and a century later, Puccio Capanna painted much in the lower church. In the chapter-room is a crucifix, surrounded by angels and saints weeping, while at each side St. Francis and St. Clare are prostrate in adoration of their suffering God. This is the work of Giottino, an artist singularly happy in the harmony of his colors and the depth of his expression. Unfortunately, the action of a constant moisture has all but effaced the labor of years. Taddeo Gaddi, Buonamico Buffalmacco, and Stefano of Florence, have also contributed their share to the glories of the sanctuary; while Aluigi of Assisi painted with marvellous grace four prophets and four sybils in the chapels of St. Louis of France, and Louis of Toulouse.

Nor was the art of sculpture without its kindred offerings. The Florentine sculptor, Fuccio, has left his memorial in the *Tomb of Hecuba of Lusignan;* and the exquisitely carved stalls of the choir in the upper church are the work of Domenichino of San Severino. The tabernacle of the lower church is also a masterpiece of its kind, and was executed by Giulio Dante, of Perugia. Even in the Sagro Convento itself there are works of art of surpassing interest. Its grand and solemn cloisters are adorned with scenes from the life of the Seraphic Father by the pencil of Adone Doni of Assisi. In the great refectory he has painted a *Crucifixion,* in the background of which we see the towns of Jerusalem and Assisi, while in the foreground, St. Francis and St. Clare are kneeling in adoration. In this place also, perhaps the most spacious and beautiful apartment of its kind, we find the *Last Supper,* by Solimene, which is considered the most perfect of his works. The walls are adorned with portraits of the Popes, and in the cloister there are portraits of the great men of the Order. At the end of the Chapel of the Crucifix are two gates, which open into a double cloister. This is the Campo Santo of the Franciscan basilica; and here the mortal remains of the friars wait the resurrection morning. The name of each is inscribed on the stone slab which shuts in his niche of repose.

CHAPTER XXXI.

The Churches of Assisi.—San Rufino.—St. Damian's.—St. Clare's.—The Poor Clares remove to St. Clare's.—Translation of the Relics of St. Clare.—Re-finding of the body in 1850.—Devotion of the Bishop of Assisi to the Order.

Assisi is not so much a town that incloses a sanctuary, as a sanctuary inclosing a multitude of shrines. St. Damian's, St. Clare's, the Minerva, the Cathedral of San Rufino, with its grand tower and its curious gateway; the new church built on the site of the Saint's paternal house—all are sanctuaries, amid which we would fain linger a while to muse over old memories, and pour forth earnest prayer. But a volume would scarcely describe the glories of Assisi. A brief word on each is all that is here possible.

The Cathedral of St. Rufinus still preserves the font in which Francis was baptized—perhaps its greatest treasure, after the relics of its martyr-saint. The new church dedicated to St. Francis was erected by the piety of Marcello Crescenzi, a bishop whose memory is still revered by the people of Assisi. He laid the foundation stone in 1612. The design was executed, and the erection superintended, by a Franciscan friar, Frà Rufino da Cerchiara. The exterior is elegant and symmetrical, and the interior decorated by artists of no common skill. Near this church is the little chapel of St. Francisco Piccolo.

The Church of St. Damian is a little way outside the Porta Nuova. It is now in the hands of the Friars

Minor of the strict observance. This church is more remarkable for the relics it possesses, and its memories of the first abbess of the Poor Clares, than for any architectural beauty. The body of the blessed Sabine of Campello reposes here, and also the incorrupt remains of blessed Antonio of Stroncone. Here, too, is the crucifix from which St. Francis received the command, in literal obedience to which he restored this church and two others. The choir used by the Poor Clares remains as they left it, and the altar is still shown where St. Clare was allowed to keep the Blessed Sacrament, by a special permission of the Holy See.* The dormitory where she breathed her last earthly sigh, and where she was consoled and visited by the Mother of God, is still there in all its poverty. The refectory in which she miraculously multiplied the bread, and in obedience to the command of Gregory, blessed the repast which he was about to share with her religious, is now used by the friars.

But the Church of St. Clare is that which, after the basilica of St. Francis, presents the greatest object of interest to the pious traveller. This edifice was erected on the site of the old hospice of St. George. Frà Philippo was the architect, and the building was erected by the desire and at the expense of the Sovereign Pontiff. This spacious and beautiful edifice was completed in 1260; and on the thirtieth of October,† in the same year, the body of St. Clare was

* The Poor Clares have a particular privilege allowed to them of keeping the Blessed Sacrament in the choir, and of exposing it whenever the Reverend Mother Abbess judges convenient, by drawing up of the door of the tabernacle where it stands. This favor was granted on account of the great devotion their foundress, St. Clare, had to the Adorable Sacrament, and the miracles attending her devotion.—*See Life of Lady Warner*, p. 253.

† The anniversary of the translation was at first celebrated on the day on which it occurred; it is now, however, kept on the second October, so as not to interfere with the first vespers of St. Francis.

translated to it, seven years after the first interment of the holy abbess. The bishops of the surrounding states were specially invited, by Pope Alexander, to attend; the original letter of invitation is still preserved in the church. The body of the Saint was found incorrupt, and in entire preservation. It was conveyed in triumphal procession to its new and more fitting shrine, and deposited under the high altar in a stone coffin, at a great depth below the surface. The church was consecrated in 1265. The religious had already removed to the adjoining convent from their old home at St. Damian's, now far too small for their constantly increasing numbers. In 1602, the bodies of St. Agnes, the blessed Amata, and Benedicta, the abbess who succeeded St. Clare, were also removed.

In the month of August, 1850, permission was obtained from the Holy See to institute a search for the body of the Saint, as her religious had long desired to possess this treasure where they could better venerate it. The work commenced on the twenty-third of the month. First, the religious assembled at the grate of their choir, and there joined in earnest prayer with the grand vicar, chancellor, and other priests of the diocese, who had assembled to unite their suffrages for the success of the undertaking. The bishop of Assisi was unable to attend. On the thirtieth, the tomb, after more than five hundred years' concealment, was discovered. News was brought to the religious while they were in choir; and hardly could they finish their office, so eager were they to express their joy in a *Te Deum* of thanksgiving. While it was sung, the bells of the monastery rang out a joyous chime, summoning the clergy to join their voices in praise. On the twenty-third of September, the holy relics were solemnly authenticated. The archbishop of Spoleto celebrated a Mass of the Holy Ghost; after which the assembled prelates, superiors of religious houses, the civil and military authorities, and the principal inhabitants of Assisi, descended into the vault to view the coffin. The anxious work of opening it had still to be accomplished. For obvious reasons but a few could be present.* A curtain was drawn across the vault to exclude the air. The Bishops of Spoleto and Perugia stood by the coffin; the iron bands were sawn asunder, the lid raised, and a perfect skeleton discovered. The necessary witnesses then went down to view the holy remains, and all that the Church's wisdom and prudence require having been complied with, the veneration of the body of the Saint began. It was a touching sight. The bishops having paid their devotions, the Bishop of Assisi left the church, but returned in a few moments leading in the community of religious, with their novices and lay-sisters. A special dispensation of their vow of enclosure had been obtained for the occasion. The poor nuns tried in vain to restrain their tears of ardent love and devotion to their sainted mother. Her spirit still lingers in the monasteries of her Order—a spirit of peculiar sweetness and tenderest affection. As one by one they approached the coffin and kissed the dear remains, their tears and sobs broke forth in reverent joy. Prelates and priests and people caught the infection, and after vain efforts at self-mastery, "lifted up their voices and wept." When the Poor Clares had retired, the people were permitted to satisfy their devotion. The relics were then enclosed in a crystal case, sealed by seven bishops, and exposed to public veneration on the high altar.

* This account is given from a private letter written by an English priest who was present on the occasion, and by a special favor allowed to attend the bishops in the vault during the opening of the coffin.

A *Triduum* had been performed during the time occupied in the exhumation of the relics: another was now celebrated in thanksgiving for the success of the pious undertaking. On both occasions the celebrated orator, D. Dominic Zanelli, who had come from Rome, through his own devotion for the purpose, proclaimed the virtues and praises of the Saint. On the evening of the 28th, the whole city was brilliantly illuminated; and on the next day, the Feast of St. Michael, the relics were carried in triumphal procession through the town. The enthusiasm of the people had daily increased, and the laity and nobles from the surrounding country vied with the ecclesiastics in honoring their virgin Saint. The procession visited six monasteries of religious women who had asked this favor, and at length reached the church of the Sagro Convento. Strange and mysterious visit! more than five centuries before, they had borne the mortal remains of Francis to his weeping, desolate child; now, after the lapse of so many ages, the relics of the child are borne in triumphal procession to the tomb of her seraphic father.

But the religious of St. Clare's were not to be deprived of their treasure. The business of the day being ended, the precious remains were again confided to them, and the proceedings terminated by a solemn benediction, given in their chapel by the Archbishop of Spoleto. The remains are so perfect that they have obtained permissson to dress them in a habit similar to their own. The face remains uncovered, and in the crossed hands is placed a lily, emblem of her spotless purity.

A feast in memory of the re-finding of the body in 1850, is kept on the twenty-third of September. Numerous miracles which have occurred since then, and which have mostly been the result of an application of relics from the body of the sainted virgin, have testified her continued power with God. Several of these have occurred at Assisi. Their authentications can be seen at the palace of its saintly Bishop, Mgr. Landi Vittorj,* a prelate singularly devoted to the Order.

CHAPTER XXXII.

The three bulls of Gregory IX. confirm the faithful in their veneration of the Stigmata of St. Francis —Other testimonials on the same subject.—The Church on Alvernia.—The Mount blessed under the name of the Seraphic Mountain.—Anecdotes.

Before we invite the attention of our readers to a very brief sketch of the history of the Seraphic Order, a few words may be necessary regarding the authenticity of the great miracle of Mount Alvernia. Wonderful and supernatural beyond all previous conception as it may appear, we can have no doubt as to the fact itself, since the Church comfirms it by a yearly festival,† in which the great event is commemorated, not merely by the three Franciscan Orders, but by the faithful at large. Yet the numerous testimonies to this great miracle may enliven our faith in the merits and intercession of a Saint so highly favored by God and honored by man.

During the two years previous to the death of St. Francis, his wounds had been seen and examined by many persons. In 1226, Brother Elias wrote a circular

* Relics of the Saint have been sent to several towns in France and Belgium where there are convents of the Order. They were received with as much joy and honor by the inhabitants as by the religious. [See the *Life of St. Clare*, by l'Abbé F. Demore. Paris, 1856.] The religious at Assisi could never have borne the expenses of this exhumation, but for the very practical charity of their Bishop, and his zealous coöperation.

† September 17th.

letter to the brethren of his Order, in which he speaks of this mysterious gift as a circumstance known to all.

The first doubt regarding the Stigmata was raised, as is usual in such cases, by persons who had never seen the Saint, and who lived in a country so distant from Assisi as to have little opportunities of communication with its inhabitants. An account of their false zeal in disputing the miracle was soon reported to Gregory IX. He had been himself an eye-witness of the life and miracles of the Saint, and was justly indignant that any should presume to cast a doubt on the favors merited by such sanctity. Three important bulls were published in consequence. One is addressed to the faithful in general, and is simply a declaration of the truth of the disputed point. The second is addressed to the Bishop of Olmutz, in Bohemia, who had been misled in the matter, and had published some letters forbidding any representations (then already common in 1237) of St. Francis receiving the sacred Stigmata. The third bull was to the priors and provincials of the Order of Friars Preachers, one of whom had failed in the charity always shown by the more perfect members of that Order to their Franciscan brethren. These bulls are given at length in M. de Malin's life of St. Francis. They breathe so deep a love for the Saint, and so affectionate and paternal a care for his Order, that we cannot but regret the limited space which forbids their insertion.

In 1255 and 1259, Alexander IV. also gave confirmation to the miracle of Alvernia. The testimony of St. Antony, the cotemporary and disciple of the Saint, and the burning eloquence of St. Bonaventura when treating of the subject, might also be adduced.

But Alvernia is itself one of the most glorious proofs of the truth of the favor granted on the once desolate mountain. Protected by the Church, and honored by emperors, it stands an eternal monument of the sanctity of the great Seraph of Assisi. In 1255, Alexander IV. addressed a bull to the Friars Minor, in which he says: "Who can be anxious for his eternal welfare, and not love this place, where the King of kings, by an excess of goodness, has, in these last ages, honored His knight with a royal impress, in order that he might reanimate those timid soldiers who were flying before their enemy?"

The following year, William, Bishop of Arezzo, in whose diocese Alvernia is situated, promulgated this bull, and added a grant of large indulgences to all who should visit the mountain.

In 1260, St. Bonaventura, then superior of the entire Order, visited this place on his return from the general chapter of Narbonne. He was accompanied by a thousand friars. During their stay, the bishops of Arezzo, Florence, Perugia, Assisi, and several others, assembled to consecrate the church, which was then dedicated under the title of St. Mary of the Angels and of St. Francis. After the ceremony, they descended the mountain in solemn procession; then, passing round its base, blessed it, under the name of "Seraphic Mountain."

In 1312, the Emperor Henry VII. passed some days here, enjoying the pious conversation of the blessed John of Fermo, and declared, by a public act, that he took the mountain under his special protection. "Where is the good Christian," cries the Cardinal Napoleo, who visited the convent as legate of the Holy See, "where is the good Christian who would not desire to visit this spot, consecrated by so many marvels? Neither the difficulty of the way, nor the rigor of the season, should be a hindrance to visiting Alvernia, not merely without complaint of the inconveniences, but, in spite of them, flying to it with seraphic ardor."

The convent is built on the summit of the mountain. It is a large and massive building, reminding one of the baronial castles of the middle ages. Multitudes of pilgrims are constantly flocking thither, and are entertained with the most liberal hospitality. The hospice for the upper classes is served by the priests of the Order; that for females is lower down on the mountain, while the hospice for peasants is attended by lay brothers. These buildings were constructed after the plans, and under the direction, of Brother Gregory of Rasina. The great church is double, and was begun by the piety of Tarlat, Count of Chiusi, in 1348. In the next century it was completed by the Senate of Florence. The small church of the Stigmata is at a little distance, and a gallery connects the two buildings. The vault of the chapel is azure, with golden stars. The spot where St. Francis knelt when he received the marks of the passion of Jesus, is enclosed in it, and covered with an iron grating. Five golden lamps, offered in 1609 by Cardinal Monaldi, hang from the roof, and on either side are twenty-four stalls of carved oak. This church was built by Simon, Count of Batifolio, and was consecrated, in 1310, by the Archbishop of Ravenna and the Bishop of Arezzo. It is dedicated to the Holy Cross, the Holy Angels, and St Francis.

Every evening after compline, and every night after matins, the religious visit it in procession. Many legends are related in connection with this pious practice. Once when a heavy fall of snow made the way impassable, and hindered the friars from performing their usual devotions, animals of various kinds were seen wending their way to it in procession along the mountain path; and on this account the gallery was constructed, so that the religious might not be outdone in their devotion to their Seraphic Father by God's inferior creatures which he had loved so well. At one time, also, our Lady was seen blessing the friars as they passed along. Almost every part of the mountain is redolent of some pious tradition, replete with the memory of a Saint, who had communed there with heaven in ecstatic prayer.

The great church is adorned with some exquisite enamelled work by Andrea Della Robbia. The powerful organ, of peculiar sweetness, was constructed by a Franciscan Friar, Eusebio of Mignano. He was guardian of Alvernia in 1586.

SANCTE FRANCISCE PROPERA
VENI PATER ACCELERA
AD POPULUM QUI PREMITUR
ET TERITUR SUB ONERE
PALEA LUTO LATERE
ET SEPULTO EGYPTO
SUB SABULO NOS LIBERA
CARNIS EXTINCTO VITIO.

NOTE.

In the life of the great painter, Raphael, published in the "Lives of Distinguished Men," the influence of the Franciscan Order on the artists of that age is specially noticed. An intensity of expression on sacred subjects, indicating a deep religious feeling, is remarked as a characteristic of the Umbrian school. The impulse, it is said, was derived from Assisi, and its source lay in the doctrines of St. Francis. Religion was exhibited under its suffering rather than its triumphant aspect; and this imparted a touching earnestness to some of the noblest works of art, which failed not to enhance alike their beauty and their interest. When the orthodoxy of Perugino was questioned, the religious tone of his pictures was appealed to, and accepted as a sufficient evidence of his faith. Raphael imbibed from his master his peculiar realization of things saintly; and afterwards, in his second manner, combined with it all the perfection of art which he learned in the Florentine schools.

PART II.

THE FRANCISCAN ORDER.

CHAPTER I.

The Three Orders of St. Francis, and their various denominations and vicissitudes.—The First Mission to Italy, the Second to Europe, and the Third to the World.

THE holy patriarch St. Francis established three Orders—the First Order, or *Order of Friars Minor* (1208); the Second Order, or *Order of Poor Ladies*, or of *St. Clare* (1212); and the Third Order, or *Order of Penitents* (1221), for men and women living in the world. The First Order remained one body, with one head, for three hundred and nine years, and from the very lifetime of the holy patriarch, there were a great many who followed him in the observance of the Rule, to the letter; yet there were some, who, after the example of Friar Elias, introduced relaxations and obtained privileges and dispensations. Hence the distinction of *Observantines* and *Conventuals*. Those who were zealous for the strict observance of the Rule, began, also, to be distinguished by peculiar names—as *Cesarini*, so called from Friar *Cesario*, of Spira (1236); *Clareni*, from the convent founded (1300) by Friar Angelo de Cingoli, near the river Clareno; also *Celestini*, because they were taken under his special protection by Pope Celestine V.; *Coletani*, those who accepted the reform of St. Coletta (1406); *Amadei*, those who followed the reform (1460) of Friar Amadeo Revez; and *Discalced*, those who were reformed by Friar John de Puebla (1488).

There were also some other denominations; but the most important, most extended, and most numerous, was that of the *Observantines*, distinguished amongst whom were the venerable Brother Paul Trinci (1406), St. Bernardine, St. John Capistrano, St. Didacus, St. Peter Regalado, St. James of Marca, and many other holy and celebrated men.

Pope Leo X., wishing to establish a better uniformity in the Order, convoked in Rome, in 1517, the representatives of all the denominations of Franciscans to celebrate the General Chapter, which, from this circumstance, is called the most general. He desired, especially, to reduce to the observance, those who had deviated from the Rule as it had been given by St. Francis, particularly in regard to the poverty therein inculcated; but they being unwilling to yield to the desire of the Pope, he, in consequence, by the bull "*Ite et vos*," divided the Order into two—decreeing that the former should henceforth be distinguished by the name of *Observantines*, and the latter by that of *Conventuals*, all other designations being abolished.

He also decreed that the minister-general of the Observantines should be recognized as the legitimate successor of St. Francis, and the representative-general of the whole Order of the Friars Minor, and assigned to him the ancient seals of the Order. Leo also gave to the Conventuals a master-general, whose election required the approval of the minister-general, but who was not otherwise subject to his jurisdiction; and even the necessity of this approval was afterwards dispensed with; but the right of precedence, and the title of minister-general of the whole Order of the

Friars Minor, remained with the General of the Observantines.

Besides the Observantines and Conventuals, there are also the *Capuchins*, which third body of Franciscans originated in 1525, under the pontificate of Clement VII. Friar Matthew da Bassi, a priest of the Observantines, obtained permission to adopt a peculiar manner of dress and life, and having found many followers, his reform increased to such an extent that Paul V. recognized them as a distinct body (1619), and gave them power to elect their own General.

Thus the First Order of St. Francis, at present, consists of the three distinct bodies of the *Observantines* (under which name are included the Regular Observantines and the Strict Observantines, as the Reformed, the Recollects, and the Discalced or Alcantarines), the *Conventuals* and the *Capuchins*. They are all Friars Minor, or Franciscans. The designations Reformed, Recollects, and the Discalced or Alcantarines, are assumed by those belonging to the Observantines, without any division from the same, and they are all comprised under the names of Observance, either Regular or Stricter. The designations *Gray Friars*, common in English, and *Cordeliers*, in French, signified Franciscans.

The color of the habit not having been determined in the Rule given by St. Francis, a variety existed in this respect. The gray and brown were, and still are, the prevalent colors of the Franciscans of the Observance ; the black is that of the Conventuals, and the brown is also the principal color of the Capuchins. The only characteristic apparel which really distinguishes the Franciscans from religious of other Orders, is the *chord ;* and the poet Dante designated them by the name of *Cordeglieri.*

The Second Order of St. Francis—called also the *Order of St. Clare*—experienced modifications not dissimilar to those of the First Order. Those who adhered to the observance of the Rule, in its integrity, were called *Poor Clares*, and those who followed the Rule as modified by Urban IV. were called *Urbanists*. The Bernardines, from St. Bernardine; the Coletanes, from St. Colette; and the Capuchines, from the Capuchins—are all Poor Clares; and the Conceptionists, and the Sisters of the Annunciation, belong also to the Second Order of St. Francis.

All these, though having different constitutions, profess the Rule given by St. Francis to his first spiritual daughter, St. Clare; and as she became the mother of all the sisters of the Second Order, they can all be called *Clarisses*.

The Third Order of St. Francis was instituted for men and women, single or married, living in the world; and such it still continues to be. In course of time, several ladies of this Third Order began to form communities, and to take the three religious vows, and they were approved by Urban VI. The same approbation was afterwards extended to similar communities of men of the Third Order, by Nicholas IV. Thus the Third Order began to be two-fold—regular and secular. Leo X. adapted the Rule to communities of the Third Order, as well of men as of women, (1521) living in convents, and thus they became distinguished from tertiaries living in the world. The Brothers and the Sisters of the Third Order were to be subject to the General of the Friars Minor; and, at present, the secular members are subject to either of the three Generals of the First Order. Although by their Rule, the communities of the Third Order ought to have been under the jurisdiction of the friars of the First Order, yet several convents were exempted, and became subject to the diocesan ordinaries; and there are even some communities of the regular Third Order, that have been permitted a General of their own, in Rome.

The first mission of the disciples of St. Francis, after he had received the approbation of his Order from Innocent III., was to Italy. While the fourth Lateran Council was in session, (1215) at Rome, St. Francis went thither to treat, in that Council, of affairs concerning his institute; and on that occasion the Pope announced to the assembled Fathers the approval of the Order.

While at Rome, St. Francis convoked the first General Chapter, to be celebrated at Assisi. In the following year, on the appointed day of Pentecost, the chapter was held, the principal object of which was to send his disciples to the various parts of Europe.

The celebrated Chapter of Mats, where over five thousand friars were assembled, was held in 1218, at St. Mary of the Angels; and in that chapter was decreed the mission to all parts of the world. Honorius III. gave them the following commendatory letter:

"HONORIUS, BISHOP AND SERVANT OF THE SERVANTS OF GOD: TO THE ARCHBISHOPS, BISHOPS, ABBOTS, DEACONS, ARCHDEACONS, AND ALL ECCLESIASTICAL SUPERIORS:

"As our beloved sons, Brother Francis and his companions, have renounced the vanities of the world and embraced a form of life which the Roman Church has approved; and, following the example of the Apostles, desire to preach the Word of God throughout the world; we beseech and exhort you, in the Lord, and command you, by these Apostolic letters, to receive, as Catholic, and faithful, the Brethren of this Order, who, bearing these, shall present themselves to you. Show yourselves favorable to them, and treat them with all kindness, for the honor of God, and from regard to us.

"Given the third of the Ides of June, in the third year of our Pontificate."

In addition to this letter, the holy patriarch gave the friars the following:

"TO ALL POWERS AND GOVERNORS, JUDGES AND RECTORS, AND ALL OTHERS, IN THE WHOLE WORLD, TO WHOM THESE LETTERS SHALL COME; YOUR BROTHER IN THE LORD GOD, FRANCIS, LITTLE AND HUMBLE, WISHING TO YOU ALL HEALTH AND PEACE:

"Reflect, and consider that the day of death approaches. I therefore humbly and earnestly beseech you that you let not the cares and solicitudes of this world, cause you to forget the Lord, or to turn from His commandments; for those who forget Him, and decline from His commandments, are accursed, and will be forgotten by Him; and when the hour of death comes, all which they think they possess shall be taken from them; and inasmuch as they were wiser and more powerful in this world, so much the greater torment shall they suffer in hell. Therefore I strongly counsel you, my lords, that, laying aside all care and solicitude, you devoutly receive the most holy Body and most sacred Blood of my Lord, Jesus Christ, in His Holy Sacrament; and that you cause God to be honored by the people committed to you, sending an officer each evening, or in some other manner warning them all to give praise and thanksgiving to God. And if you fail to do this, know that you will have to give an account to your Lord God, Jesus Christ, on the day of judgment. Let those who retain and observe this writing know that they are blessed by the Lord God."

St. Francis and his three Orders, with all their varieties, realized the two visions of Innocent III. in one of which he saw a poor man sustaining the Lateran Church, and in the other, a prophetical palm growing at his feet, and extending far and wide its branches.

The influence of St. Francis and the Franciscans, on the world, is acknowledged by the modern infidel Renan, in these words: "The great Umbrian movement of the thirteenth century, which is, among all attempts at religious foundation, that which most resembles the Galilean movement, was made entirely in the name of poverty. Francis d'Assisi—that man of all the world who, by his exquisite goodness and his sympathy, delicate, refined, and tender, with universal life, has most resembled Jesus—was poor."—*Life of Christ*, chap. xi.

CHAPTER II.

The Spanish province founded by St. Francis.—Bernard and John Parent sent there afterwards.—Incident regarding the foundation at Toledo.—Sicily.—Palermo.—The friars in Paris.—Their extreme poverty and sufferings.—Brother Pacificus.—St. Louis protects the friars, and builds a magnificent church for them.—De Thou.—Flanders.—Anecdote of a boy friar.—Hungary.—Great difficulties of this mission.—Cesarius—Brother Giordano.—Final success.—Kindness of several bishops.—Mayence, Worms, Spiers, etc.—The Archbishop of Salzburg.—St. Elizabeth of Hungary.—The Order in Sweden and Norway.—Laurence Octave.

Nearly all the principal provinces of the Order were founded during the life of St. Francis, and many at his special desire. We are now to present a brief sketch of those of which particulars have not hitherto been given.

It may be remembered that St. Francis himself founded the Spanish mission. We cannot then wonder that it yielded such a harvest of saintly souls. Brother Bernard was his companion on this journey, at least until they entered the province of Navarre. Here they met a poor traveller, who was suffering from severe illness. The tender heart of Francis was touched; the poor man was friendless and alone; so he left his beloved Bernard to nurse and comfort the invalid.

The monastery at Burgos was, probably, the first house of the Order in Spain. This was established in 1214. Other foundations followed rapidly during the same year. At Logrono, Medrain, an officer in the royal army, generously presented the Saint with his own house and gardens, where a convent was at once established. Many other monasteries were also begun during the nine months of St, Francis' detention in the peninsula from sickness. As he returned to Italy he was joined again by Bernard, whose care had completely restored the poor sick man.

After the general chapter of 1216, this brother was sent to complete the work which St. Francis had begun, and the Spanish provinces was soon one of the largest, as it eventually became one of the most fruitful in saints. In 1219, after the second general chapter of the Order, John Parent was sent, with a hundred friars, to assist in this important field of labor.

The brethren who were sent to Toledo, lived for some time in great poverty. One day, as they were going out on their usual quest, they met a party of young nobles leading a bull to the circus, where they expected to enjoy the pastime so popular in their country. One of them, turning to the friars exclaimed merrily, "If you have the courage to take this bull, I will give it to you." "And I," added another, "will grant you the ground where we stand to build a convent." The friars took the furious animal by the horns, and in a moment he became gentle as a lamb, and allowed them to lead him about as they would; they then claimed the promise made by the young knights; and thus, in 1217, was founded the convent of Toledo.

Brothers Zachary and Walter had been sent into Portugal. Here they established the convent dedicated to St. Antony, at Coimbra, and subsequently a much larger one at Lisbon. John Parent arrived at Saragossa in 1219, and was so well received by both priests and people, that he was soon able to effect a foundation of some magnitude.

The first convent in Sicily was built at St. Leo, near Messina. It was erected by the piety of three noble ladies—Violanta di Pelizzo, Eleonora di Procida and Beatrice di Belfiore. It was here that St. Antony remained a short time on his way to Italy. The convent at Palermo was built by the order of Gregory IX.

The French mission had been assigned to Brother Pacificus. The former poet-courtier and his companions arrived at Paris in the winter of 1216. Their life, at first, was by no means a pleasant one to flesh and blood; yet in this very life their greatest joy consisted. Without a shelter to cover them, even at night, from the inclemency of the season; without any means of procuring food, except from the charity humbly asked, and scantily doled out to them; they passed their time in prayer and suffering, sowing the seeds of the abundant harvest which was afterwards reaped with joy in this very city. At midnight they assembled in any church where it was customary to recite the divine office, and, after assisting at it, they remained in prayer before the altar till morning; then, if no one offered them hospitality, they went out to beg from door to door for their daily bread. When the small quantity sufficient to support them in their austere life had been obtained, they went to the hospitals, and passed the remainder of the day in consoling and ministering to the poor sufferers, but especially to the lepers. Their saintly life aud unobtrusive piety soon attracted the attention and the hearts of the good people of Paris. After a time of suffering and privation they obtained all they asked—a shelter and a sufficiency for their daily bread. The Benedictines were, as usual, the first and warmest friends of the

Order. They gave the friars a house, where the famous monastery of the Strict Observance now stands, and, in addition to this charitable gift, purchased some land adjoining it for their use. Various additions to this property were purchased later from the abbot and community of St. German-des-Près.

In 1234, a magnificent church dedicated to St. Mary Magdalene, was erected here by the piety of St. Louis. This was, unfortunately, destroyed by fire in 1580; but in the following year it was replaced by another scarcely less magnificent. The Franciscans were indebted for this munificent gift to the family of De Thou—both father and son having an equal and very practical attachment to the Order. The younger De Thou, John Augustus, famous as a statesman and writer, notwithstanding the pressing cares of public business and the absorbing pursuit of literature, his laborious and only recreation, found time to think of the mendicant friars; he superintended the completion of their great church, and was chosen in 1600, as the temporal father and protector of the Order.

Angelo of Pisa was the first guardian of the convent in Paris; nor was it long ere his zeal and energy made itself felt on the fortunes of the Order. Through his influence and exertions a school was founded there, which soon bid fair to rival the university, and in which some of the most eminent men of that and of succeeding generations were trained.

Friars were now sent to found houses in different parts of the kingdom, while Pacificus, having accomplished his mission, proceeded to preach in the Low Countries. Here, under the protection and assistance of Joanna, Countess of Flanders, many convents were established. Those of St. Trond, Valenciennes, Arras, Ghent, Bruges, and Oudenarde, were among the first.

At Thorouth, a town in Flanders, a child of five old, having seen the habit of the friars, entreated his parents to get him one; at length they yielded to his tears, and from this moment he would wear no other clothing. With a coarse serge dress, a cord round his waist, and bare feet, he began to preach to his little companions, telling them of the pains of hell and the joys of heaven. Once, when he heard his father swearing, in a state of intoxication, he cried out, with tears, "O my father does not our curé tell us, that those who do such things shall not enter into the kingdom of God?" Once, also, when he saw his mother dressed in scarlet, he warned her of the danger of vanity, and told her to fear lest the color she wore should draw her into the pains of hell; and from that day she never appeared in any but the plainest dress.

The boy-friar, for such we may call him, died at the age of seven. After he had confessed, he earnestly entreated permission to receive the Holy Communion, which was denied to him on account of his tender years. Finding his entreaties useless, he raised his little hands to heaven, and exclaimed, "My Lord Jesus Christ, Thou knowest that all I desire on earth is to receive Thee; I have asked to have Thee; I have done what I could, and now I hope that thou wilt not deprive me of the blessedness of possessing Thee." Then he consoled and exhorted those who stood weeping around him; and so his young soul passed calmly to Him for whose presence he so ardently thirsted.

Nor was the mission of the blessed Christopher in Gascony less successful. Here the convent of Mirepoix was soon established, and followed by many others.

The friars who were sent to the Hungarian provinces had not fared so well. But St. Francis was anxious that another attempt should be made; and, in the chapter of 1221, he proposed the matter to Elias, who was then minister-general. There were peculiar difficulties connected with this enterprise. In one part of the country the friars had been taken for heretics; their poor appearance, their singular dress, their strange language, combined to make an unfavorable impression. Sometimes they were literally hunted out of the towns; and sometimes the shepherds let loose their dogs on the unfortunate brothers. Africa and some parts of Spain promised at least a martyr's crown; no small compensation for a failure in converts or foundations. But here was no hope of that kind to encourage; while the prospect of the painful imputation of heresy tended to depress them.

Severe illness prevented St. Francis from addressing the brethren himself; but Brother Elias spoke for him, "My brethren," said he, "the Brother desires me to speak to you. There is a country called Germany, many of whose inhabitants are Christians, and very devout. We see them passing through our own country on pilgrimages in the heat of summer, carrying long staves, and wearing high leathern hose; and as they go, they sing the praises of God and of His Saints. I have already sent some of the brethren thither; but they have returned, having received much ill-treatment. On this account, I would not oblige any one to go thither. But if any one is sufficiently animated with zeal for the glory of God and the salvation of souls to undertake this journey, I promise him the same, and even a greater merit of obedience, than if he went beyond the sea."

About ninety friars offered themselves at once for the mission; and Cesarius a priest from Spiers, who had joined the Order through the preaching of Elias, was appointed superior and provincial-minister of Germany. He was allowed to choose his companions from the number who had offered themselves. Having selected twenty-seven, twelve of whom were priests, and fifteen lay brothers, he approached a young friar, named Giordano, who had not expressed any wish to accompany the party. "Giordano," he said, "you also will come with us." "I!" exclaimed the startled brother; "I am not one of yours. If I rose, it was not that I wished to join you, but that I desired to bid farewell to my brothers, all of whom, I am sure, will be martyred." Germany was indeed, of all places, the special dread and horror of the poor friar; and it had been his daily prayer that he might never be sent to that country. He was firmly convinced that he had neither the grace to brave the slow martyrdom which would there befall him, nor to confute the heretics whom he must encounter on his way. Cesarius, however, continued to urge, and he as steadily to refuse. At length Brother Elias heard of the dispute; and coming to Giordano, commanded him under obedience to say positively either that he would or would not go. Unwilling to consent he still did not like to give this kind of positive and express refusal. On the one hand, he feared his own weakness in the trials he expected from the dreaded Germans; on the other, he trembled lest he should lose a martyr's crown, or do what was less pleasing to God, by remaining in Italy. At last he betook himself to a friar who had already been on this mission, and had suffered much there. The good brother advised him to go to Elias and state his perplexity, begging him as his superior, to decide for him. Brother Elias at once gave him the obedience to join Cesarius. From this moment the young brother's fears all vanished, and he became eventually one of the most courageous and effective missioners in the new province.

Cesarius divided his friars into little bands of two and three, and thus arranged, they departed by different routes; all agreeing, however, to meet at Trent before the feast of St. Michael. Here they were most hospitably received and entertained by the bishop. All had assembled at the time appointed, and on the feast, Cesarius, who was distinguished for his eloquence, preached with unusual effect in the cathedral. Brother Barnabas meanwhile addressed the crowds who had assembled outside. So great was the multitude, that the numbers who could not obtain admittance were immense.

It was here Brother Pelegrinus received his vocation. Having sold all his goods, he asked and obtained the habit of the Order, of which he soon became a distinguished member. The mission succeeded so well at Trent, that Cesarius left several friars to found a convent there. Meanwhile the good bishop had gone to Botzen, whither the rest of the band followed him. They remained here some days, and then continued their progress. At Brixen, also, the bishop received them with great kindness. But their difficulties had by no means ended; as they passed over the mountains of the Tyrol, hunger and fatigue almost overcame even the most fervent. Wild roots and herbs often formed their only food; and even these they scrupled using on the morning of a fast-day, though on the previous day they had been almost without food of any kind.

At Augsburg, however, they met with a very kind reception from the bishop, whose nephew charitably bestowed on them his own house. Here a convent was soon established. On the feast of St. Gall, October

16, 1221, Cesarius held there the first general chapter of the German province. About thirty friars assembled, and these were soon dispersed to various parts of the country. Monasteries were quickly founded; those of Mayence, Worms, Spiers, and Cologne were among the first. The timid Giordano had become a perfect hero of zeal and missionary courage, and effected wonders for the extension of the Order, under the fostering care of the Archbishop of Salzburg, to whom he was sent with two companions. Cesarius travelled from mission to mission, inspiriting his disciples, and attracting crowds by his eloquence. While preaching at Wurtzburg, a young man of distinction, named Hartmod, begged to be admitted into the Order. This friar having been received on the feast of St. Andrew, took the name of that apostle. In course of time he was received to holy orders, eventually became a distinguished preacher, and was the first guardian of the province of Saxony.

An amusing anecdote is told by Wadding regarding the German mission, which accounts in some measure for the great trials the brethren had to endure in its commencement. Those who were sent thither, at first did not understand the language; and even when their mother-tongue was understood they were not skilled in questing *(et fratres mendicare nescirent:)* so it is no wonder they were often houseless and hungry. Soon, however, they learned the affirmative, "*Ja.*" On several occasions it served them very well; as the people who crowded round them to gaze on their new and strange costume and appearance, sometimes asked if they would receive food or alms. "*Ja,*" in such cases, always answered admirably. But sometimes the first question put to them was, if they were heretics; and as they always answered with the never-failing "*Ja,*" their treatment was severe in proportion to the fervor and Catholicity of their questioners.

But there were some even in this country to whom the name of Francis was familiar, and who revered him as a Saint. The sweet and gentle St. Elizabeth of Hungary, that very model of saintly conjugal affection and of womanly patience under the most cruel wrongs, was now developing into that sanctity of which she had given such promise even from her very cradle. No sooner had she heard of the self-devotion, poverty, and burning love to Jesus Crucified, which inflamed the heart of the seraph of Assisi, than she yearned towards his Order with all the warmth of her enthusiastic nature. The fame of her sanctity had also reached the ears of Francis, who could well admire and appreciate a Saint so peculiarly pure and child-like. Once, as he conversed of her to Cardinal Ugolini (afterwards her stay, and almost her only protector, in the overwhelming trials of her early widowhood), the good prelate suggested that St. Francis should send to the young princess his cloak, as a token of affection and esteem. The Saint complied; and Elizabeth received it as a treasure of priceless value. A strange present truly, the worn and threadbare mantle of a mendicant friar, for a lady surrounded with all that earth could give of wealth and enjoyment. Rarer still, the simplicity which gave, and the faith which accepted and valued the gift.

In the year 1222, the Order extended itself northward, and in the scarcely christianized provinces of Sweden and Norway found a home and subjects for its rule. Laurence Octave, a man of illustrious birth and great piety, was one of the first to enter it. In 1245, he was elected Archbishop of Upsal, but steadily refused to accept the dignity, until compelled by the command of Innocent IV.: to the last, however, he lived, as Friar Minor. In the interregnum which followed the death of Eric the Bald, he governed the kingdom; fulfilling, with the most scrupulous integrity, all the arduous duties which such a charge involved. When dying, he desired to be carried to the convent of Friars Minor, that he might yield his last breath among the brethren so dear to him. Soon after, he calmly expired, having given to the world another incontestable proof that sanctity and the poor life of a Franciscan were neither obstacles to the development of intellect, nor incompatible with the well government of a kingdom.

CHAPTER III.

The Holy Land and the Franciscans.—Late Martyrs of Damascus.—Principal Holy Places in charge of the Franciscans.—Present state of the Missions in Syria and Palestine.—The other Franciscan Missions in the Levant and in Africa.

The holy patriarch, in dividing the world among his brethren, after the example of the Apostles, took Syria and Egypt for himself and twelve of his companions, in the hope of shedding his blood where the Son of God had shed his own for the redemption of the world. Although God did not permit him to receive then the crown of martyrdom, still he seemed to have led him to the Holy Land, and to have said to him what He had before said to the patriarch Abraham: "Arise and walk through the land in the length and in the breadth thereof, for I will give it to thee." Indeed, God disposed that the children of St. Francis should take possession and charge of the Holy Places, where the mysteries of our redemption were accomplished. The Franciscans have been the guardians of the Holy Places, all through Palestine and Syria, for the space of over five hundred years. If they have succeeded in keeping them so long, in the midst of the greatest enemies to Christianity, they did so only at the cost of thousands of lives. The late massacres committed by the Druses and Mussulmans are too well known ; yet if such be the efforts of a weak power, now that the Christians are so strong, what must have been the persecutions and cruelties committed against the Christians in the palmy days of Islamism ? Within the last six centuries, therefore, no less than seven thousand five hundred Franciscans fell victims for the sake of the Holy Places, either by the sword of the infidel, or the oriental plague.

In the late massacre, eight Franciscans—six priests and two lay brothers—were martyred by the Druses and Mussulmans, in Damascus, and their college burned. A great privilege is theirs, to have in charge the Holy Places ; but a dear privilege, too, for which they freely gave up their lives. The time seemed to have come at last, when they might possess in peace the enviable privilege, under the shelter and protection of the Christian nations ; but it appears God still wants victims of propitiation slain where the Son of Man was cruelly sacrificed.

It will be interesting to mention at least a few of the holy places in charge of the Franciscans : 1. In Nazareth — the Sanctuary of the Annunciation, the very spot where stood the house of the Blessed Virgin, and where " the Word was made flesh." 2. In Bethlehem—the cave where our Saviour was born and adored by the wise men. 3. In Cana — the place where Christ wrought his first miracle, by changing water into wine. 4. In Bethania — the sepulchre where Lazarus lay buried for four days, and where Christ performed the miracle of his resurrection. 5. In Galilee, on Mount Thabor—the sanctuary of the

Transfiguration. 6. In Tiberias—the church raised over the place where Christ constituted St. Peter Prince of the Apostles. 7. On the Mount of Olives—the Garden of Gethsemani, where Christ sweated drops of blood. 8. In Jerusalem—the "Chapel of Flagellation," where Christ was scourged; the "Chapel of the Crucifixion," where He expired on the Cross; the "Stone of Anointment" on which His sacred body was laid to be embalmed, by Joseph of Arimathea; and, greatest of all, the "Holy Sepulchre."

The Franciscans also have the chapel which, by tradition, is said to be built on the place where Christ appeared to Mary Magdalen, after His resurrection, and the spot on the Mount of Olives whence our Saviour ascended into heaven. We may also mention the chapel built where St. Paul was cast on the ground, and heard the voice crying out to him, "Saul! Saul! why persecutest thou Me?"—and where the eight Franciscans were slaughtered in the last massacre; the Church of the House of SS. Anne and Joachim, in Sephoris; and the Sanctuary of the Visitation, where the Blessed Virgin sang, for the first time, the canticle *Magnificat.*

The present number of Franciscans who have charge of these and other holy places in Syria and Palestine, is two hundred and seventy; and their occupation is not only to guard the Holy Places, but likewise to be the missionaries and pastors of the Catholic population of the Latin Rite, and to lodge, gratuitously, all kinds of pilgrims who visit the Holy Land. Thus St. Francis was privileged not only to bear himself the Stigmata of our Saviour, but he also secured for his children the very spots where Jesus accomplished our redemption, by his life, death and resurrection.

We might here speak of the other missions of the

Franciscans in the Levant and in Africa, but we should be trespassing on the limits within which we must keep in this work, should we dwell for any length in the recital of the operations of the Friars Minor in those countries, from the beginning of the world to the present day. Let it suffice to say, that in our own time the Franciscans have flourishing missions in Constantinople and the Archipelago, in Macedonia, in Albania, in Herzegovina, in Bosnia, in Servia, in Vallachia, in Russia, in the High and Low Egypt, in Central Africa, in Tripoly of Barbaria, and in Morocco.

CHAPTER IV.

The Order in England.—Angelus of Pisa.—The Friars graciously received by Henry III.—Names of the Brethren who came on the first mission to England.—The first convent founded at Canterbury.—Kindness of the Benedictines.—A large convent and church built in London.—Benefactors of the Order.—The consorts of Edward I. and III. munificently aid the Friars.—The library built and supplied with books by Whittington, Lord Mayor of London.—Royal and distinguished personages buried by their special desire in the convent they had assisted to found.—The house suppressed in 1539.—Now called Christ's Church, or the Blue Coat Hospital.—Desecration of the tombs, and injustice suffered by the Friars.—Oxford.—Northampton and Cambridge.—Munificence of Henry III. to the Friars at Oxford.—Suppression.—Tomb of Brother Angelus.—Cambridge.—Munificence of Edward I.—Coventry.—The Black Prince a great patron of this convent.—The "Ludus Coventriæ," or famous mystery plays.—Suppression of this monastery.—Form of surrender which the Friars were compelled to sign.

IN England the Order was founded early. The words in which St. Francis gave the obedience to Angelus of Pisa have already been cited; we must now track the steps he took in compliance with his seraphic father's will.

After a short delay at Paris, the brethren crossed the Channel and landed at Dover—the good monks of Teschamp in Normandy having defrayed the expenses of their passage—they were graciously received by the king, Henry III., and during their stay at Canterbury were indebted to their old friends, the Benedictines, for a temporary home. It is probable that they arrived in England in the autumn of 1219, or perhaps as late as the spring of the following year. The Superior, Brother Angelus, or Agnellus, was in deacon's orders when he arrived in England, but shortly after was raised to the priesthood—an honor which his humility had long made him decline.

Brother Richard Ingeworth was already a priest, and some years older than his superior. He was subsequently appointed provincial minister of Ireland, when John Parent had succeeded Brother Elias as minister-general of the Order. Ingeworth died in Syria, where he obtained permission to evangelize. Brother Richard of Devonshire was in minor orders; but long pilgrimages and austerities had so worn him out, that he was incapable of much active exertion. Brother William Essebey, or Eton, was also an Englishman, and is mentioned as a religious of rare virtue. Once, when asked by the Provincial of France, (then Brother Gregory) whether he would go into England, he replied at once, "Father, I know not whether I will or no." The provincial expressed some surprise at his uncertainty regarding a matter about which he would naturally be anxious. But the friar replied, that he knew not what he willed, since his will was not his own, but his superior's, who would determine it as he pleased. We cannot be surprised that one who aimed at such exalted perfection should labor more effectually than many for the increase of his Order, or should attract numbers to it. There were also five lay brothers—Henry de Cervise, Laurence di Belvaco, William of Florence, Melioratus, and James Ultramontanus; of these, little is recorded beyond their names. Brother Laurence returned to Italy after a few years, and was with St. Francis when he died. It is said that the Saint esteemed him much for his sanctity. Brother Henry was for some time guardian* of the convent of Friars Minor in London. It is probable that a second detachment of missioners followed quickly after the arrival of those above named. Brother Albert of Pisa is said, by some authors, to have accompanied Angelus; while others give reasons for supposing him to have come later. Brothers Peter and Thomas, both Spaniards, respectively the first guardians of Northampton and Cambridge, as also Henry of Pisa, joined the English friars about the same time.

The first English convent of the Order was founded at Canterbury. The Benedictine monks of that city entertained friars for some days, and then they were received for a time into a house called the Poor Priest's Hospital; here there was a school, and the brethren employed themselves in teaching the boys who attended it. During the ember days of the following September, Agnellus, or Angelus, was made priest, and Richard of Devonshire subdeacon. Stephen Langton was at that time archbishop. When the archdeacon was calling them forward during the ceremony, he exclaimed in a loud voice, "*Accedunt fratres de Ordine Apostolorum,*" from which circumstance the friars were long known as the Brothers of the Order of the Apos-

* The fervor of many gentlemen of noble birth who entered the Order in its early days, led them to solicit, and sometimes by their entreaties to obtain, that they might be received as lay brothers. But their talents and sanctity could not always be concealed; and they were often compelled by obedience to take office as superiors. After a time, however, it was found expedient to forbid that any lay brother should be allowed to become a superior. This was enacted by Brother Haymo, of Feversham, fifth general of the Order, in a general chapter held in the presence of Innocent IV. Probably the occasional elevation of those who were really fitted to hold office, was a temptation to such as were not to aspire beyond their station.

tles: an appellation, says the chronicler,* by no means inappropriate, since their rule, for the greater part, is the same as Christ himself delivered to His apostles both by word and example.

A convent being now established in Canterbury, Angelus was anxious to extend the Order; he, therefore, sent four friars to London—Ingeworth, Richard of Devonshire, Henry de Cervise and Melioratus—the two former being desired to proceed to Oxford as soon as they had established a foundation in London.

The house at Canterbury, with a small plot of ground attached to it, was the gift of one Alexander, provost or master of the Poor Priest's Hospital. The precise time at which the building was completed is not known; but Wood says that the first establishment of the Friars Minor in England was held for them by the corporation of Canterbury—their vow of poverty not allowing them to possess it in their own name. Archbishop Langton, the archdeacon before mentioned, who was also his brother, Henry Lord Sandwich, and a certain noble lady, styled by Eccleston, Domina Inclusa de Baggynton, were the first patrons and great benefactors of the Order. In 1270, a worthy alderman of Canterbury, named John Diggs, gave a considerable portion of land to the friars; here a large convent was soon established by his zeal and charity. This was situated on an island called Bennewith, so named because bounded on each side by the double channel of the River Stour. Many persons of distinction were buried here. The church was dedicated to St. Francis.

* Father Anthony Parkinson *Collectanea, Anglo-Minoritica.* This most accurate and careful author has compiled his history from various sources, evidently with unusual exactness. His authorities are given in foot notes to every page, and are principally Francis A. Sta. Clara, in *Hist. Univ. Annales Minorum* Wood, *Athen. Oxon.*, Weever, Baker, Fuller, Wharton, etc.

The friars sent to London were not less successful in their undertaking. A house was hired for them in Cornhill by John Trevors, and "fitted conveniently with cells." But in a short time their piety and devotion gave such general edification, that a large convent was erected. The principal patron was one Irwin, or Ewin, who afterwards became a lay brother in the Order he had so munificently befriended. The site purchased for the new building was in the market-place of St. Nicholas, in Farringdon Ward Within. The foundations were laid in 1220, probably about Christmas-tide, and the whole completed five years later, when Brother Henry de Crevise was appointed guardian. His prudence in this important undertaking is much commended. Many noble and wealthy gentlemen were attracted to the Order, and renounced fame and fortune for its rough habit and cord. Gilbert de Wyke, John Zatmestre, Walter de Burgo, and Matthew Gayton, are amongst the number whose names have been transmitted to posterity. Nor were the wealthy citizens deficient in their alms-giving; for Leland tells us the names of those whose charity erected the different parts of the monastery. The church was principally built at the the cost of the Lord Mayor, William Walleys: the chapter-house by William Porter, alderman; the dormitory by George Bokesley; the refectory by Bartholomew de Castello; the infimary by Peter de Haliland, and the library by Roger Bond, Herald King of Arms.

In 1306, a still larger building was erected by the piety of Margaret, second wife of Edward I. This princess gave two thousand marks towards the expense, leaving one hundred more by her will. The work was not completed until 1337. Elizabeth, the queen mother of Edward III., and Philippa, his wife, also contributed largely. The Earl of Richmond, the Countess of Pembroke, the Lady Margaret Segrave, Countess of Norfolk, and others too numerous to mention, gave their munificent aid. William Taylor, shoemaker to King Henry III., is also honorably mentioned as having borne the expense of the arrangements necessary to provide the friars with their "water-course and conduit-head."

But the building of the library, and supplying it with books, was the greatest undertaking, and for this charity the Franciscans were indebted to Richard Wittington, Lord Mayor of London in 1429. The cost of the building is not mentioned, but it must have been considerable. It was one hundred and twenty-nine feet long by thirty-one broad, wainscotted all about, "having in it twenty-eight desks and eight double settles of wainscot." Four hundred pounds were given by the Lord Mayor for books; and for the "writing out of Brother Doctor de Lyra's works in two volumes, to be chained there, one hundred marks."

The church was dedicated to St. Francis, the chapels to our Lady, the Holy Apostles, and All-Saints.

Many nobles, and even those of royal blood, were, at their own special desire, laid to rest in the church they had assisted to found; near the friars, whose prayers for their benefactors would, they knew, be fervent and sincere.

The complete list of these occupies several pages in Stowe's Survey of London. Of queens we have Margaret, foundress of the church, whose monument was placed in the choir. Isabel, wife to Edward II., and his daughter, "Joan of the Tower, wife to David Bruce," are also mentioned, with many nobles and their wives; among whom we find the Lady Segrave, Duchess of Norfolk, the Countess of Devonshire, the Earl of March, Lord Say, and Eleanor his wife, with many an old

English name, the most familiar of which still preserve the faith of their fathers ; as Walter Blunt, Alice Blunt, Baron Clinton, John Gisors, Thomas Beaumond, etc. At the end of the long catalogue Stowe remarks, that "all these, and five times as many more, have been buried here, all of whose monuments have been defaced."

This house was, of course, suppressed, or, as Burnet politely expresses it, "surrendered." In 1539, the guardian, Brother Thomas Chapman, and twenty-five friars, were driven from their only home; the buildings, goods, and ornaments taken for the king's use. It is probable that the friars lived entirely on alms, as there is no mention of any rents which they received or funds which they possessed. The buildings, etc., were valued at a yearly rent of £32 19s., and it is stated that they were very spacious. The church was used for a time as a storehouse for goods taken from the French. Henry, who had no scruple of appropriating the property of others to his own use, would, of course, have none as to its ultimate destination. But, as several other churches in the neighborhood had also been shut up, it was thought advisable that one, at least, should be left open. The church of St. Francis was at first proposed, as being the one of least value. But though its poverty might be a recommendation to the royal giver, it was not so with those for whom it was destined. Henry was therefore obliged to add to it the endowments of St. Bartholomew's Hospital, in Smithfield. This arrangement, while it satisfied those whom the king was obliged to remunerate for their subservience to his wishes, was an economical one besides. Two neighboring churches were pulled down,*

*It might have been supposed that the graves of the dead, and their monuments, would at least be respected, especially when so many whose remains were interred here had been of royal blood or

and four parishes thrown into one; St. Nicolas', St. Evin's, St. Pulchers', and St. Bartholomew's; while the king transformed the church of St. Francis into Christ Church, which was henceforward known as the munificent foundation of Henry VIII. But we shall find other equally peculiar arrangements in the course of the Franciscan history in England.

In 1552, the "Grey Friars' house," or convent attached to this church, was opened to receive orphan children. On Christmas Day they all appeared in "one livery of russet cotton;" and at Easter they were in blue. On both occasions, it is to be presumed, they exhibited those wonderful yellow stockings which they have since preserved through every vicissitude in dress around them. And thus was established the famous Blue Coat Hospital.

The friars who were sent to Oxford did not accomplish their journey without adventures. When about six miles from that city they lost their way, and wandered into a marsh which lay between the Isis and the Cherwell. After some time they came to a grange, or farm-house, belonging to the Benedictine monks of Abingdon. Here they begged a night's lodging, and were admitted by the porter, under the impression that these strange men were strolling minstrels. The foreign accent and peculiar dress of the friars had given rise to this conjecture. However, when the mistake was discovered, the monks drove them out* with hard

noble descent. But as little regard was paid to their memory as to the injustice done to the expelled friars. Money was the object; and all that could bring it in, even to the most trifling amount was sacrificed. The beautiful marble and alabaster tombs, and even the iron railings which protected the graves, were all pulled down and sold for fifty pounds to Sir Martin Bowes, Lord Mayor of London, 1545.

*These monks were probably lay-brothers. Granges, or farm-houses, were generally attached to every large monastery. The religious in those ages employed a great deal of time in tilling, draining, and cultivating land; and when the ground they possessed was extensive, many of these granges would be scattered over it. They words, and even with blows; and the two Franciscans found themselves again exposed to the dangers of cold and darkness. But there was one young brother more charitable or more pious than his companions. When all had retired to rest, he rose softly, and, calling the porter, opened the gates, and brought in the half-famished friars. Then, having given them some refreshment, he showed them a loft in a stable, where they might pass the night, at least in comparative shelter. The monk retired to his cell, and soon fell asleep; but, as he slept, he beheld in a dream a marvellous vision. The Day of Judgment was represented before him and he saw his companions brought before our Divine Lord, and accused of cruelty and uncharitableness, by one who was clothed in the same manner as the friars they had treated so roughly. Then the Judge demanded, in anger, to whose Order they belonged. They replied, to St. Benedict's; but the Saint also stood by, and sternly denied that they were his children, declaring they were the overthrowers of his institute, and its greatest enemies. Sentence was passed on them, and then the young monk was asked to whose Order he belonged. Fearing to meet the doom of his companions, which in his dream, he saw already executed, he cried out that he belonged to the same Order as that poor man (pointing to St. Francis) who had spoken first. The Saint ran to him and embraced him, declaring that from this moment he would consider him as his son. The young man awoke, and so vivid was the impression made by his dream, that he

were usually taken care of by lay brothers, who in some cases might be without sufficient education, or not long enough under religious training to enable them to distinguish between impostors and real objects of charity. Or, living separate from their superiors, they may have become relaxed, and have really been guilty of a desire for worldly amusements, and then of revenging themselves on those who disappointed them.

doubted not it was a supernatural warning. Hastening to the cells of his companions, he found them in a most deplorable state, having all the appearance of persons who were dying of suffocation. When he had restored them to consciousness, he went in search of the two friars; but they were not to be found, having pursued their journey at daybreak. This circumstance was soon noised abroad; and, in consequence, great devotion and charity were shown towards the Franciscans. The Abbot of Abingdon, having satisfied himself of the authenticity of the occurrence, afterwards joined the Friars Minor at Oxford, with several of his religious.

Brother Ingeworth and Brother William having now arrived safely at Oxford, were not long in finding a temporary settlement. One Richard Mercer, or Le Muliner, a rich townsman, "let them a house in the parish of St. Ebba, between the church and the water-gate." And here the first convent of the Order in Oxford was established.* The two friars then proceeded to Northampton, where they were kindly received. Brother Peter the Spaniard, who had lately arrived in England, with several companions, was the first guardian of this house. Cambridge was next visited, and Thomas the Spaniard appointed superior there.

Brother Angelus was now on a visitation of his various foundations, and had arrived in Oxford, where Ingeworth and William came to meet him. Finding the Order there in so prosperous a state, he appointed Brother William Eton, or Essebey, guardian of the convent, and "humbly prayed the famous Doctor

* It has been said that they were at first entertained by the Dominicans; but F. Antony Parkinson doubts this statement. If the Friars Preachers came to England the same year (1219), they might have arrived in Oxford a little before the Friars Minor. Certainly they did not come earlier; but Wood says the Franciscans preceded the Dominicans some time, and dates the arrival of the latter in 1221.

Robert Grostete to undertake the charitable office of teaching the friars therein." Angelus was no great scholar himself; and it seems he left his friars pretty much to themselves as regarded their progress in learning. Returning, however, to the convent after a short absence, he bethought him that he would enter the schools and see how his subjects were employed. To his utter amazement and horror he found them engaged in a disputation, the question being: "*Utrum esset Deus?*" The provincial could only exclaim: "*Heu mihi, heu mihi! fratres simplices cœlos penetrant, et literati disputant utrum sit Deus!*" "Alas, alas! simple friars penetrate the heavens, and the learned dispute whether there is a God!" The good friars, however, had engaged in the argument only to exercise their dialectic skill, and at once acquiesced in the wish of their superior that no more such disputations would take place, even for the laudable purpose of self-improvement. Angelus, satisfied with their prompt obedience, interfered no more in their studies; but, having collected some alms for the purpose, "he procured from Rome for their use, the best corrected edition of the Decretals and other similar works; begging they would apply themselves wholly to these, and lay aside all sophistry and sceptical disputations."

The friars profited so well by the instructions they received, that they were soon able to teach; and several eminent divines having joined their Order, their importance and authority in the university rapidly increased. Brother William Eton was the first who taught publicly in their schools. He was succeeded by Brother Adam de Marisco, and others no less eminent for learning and piety. Indeed, Fuller says, that "for skill in school divinity they beat all other Orders quite out of distance."

It was not long before the increase of the Order, and the numbers who attended their schools, made it necessary that the friars should enlarge their convent. Henry III. resided at this time at Oxford; and by his favor, and the munificence of their numerous patrons, they were soon able to accomplish their object. Master Thomas Walonges, Doctor Richard de Mepham, and a good widow, named Agnes Gray, gave them the ground for building; the king himself assisting, not only with the most liberal alms, but (it is said) working, with many of the nobles, among the common laborers. The church was dedicated to St. Francis, and many noble and illustrious persons were buried here. This house also was suppressed in 1539; the guardian at that time being Brother Edward Baskerville, a doctor in divinity. Their buildings, with some land adjacent, and an island which had been given to them by Henry III., were let to William Freer and John Pye, aldermen of Oxford. These, says Wood, paid their rent to the king. It does dot seem to have occurred either to that monarch or those of his subjects who assisted in his suppressions, that any compensation was needed by the friars for the property of which they were defrauded. The place was sold by Henry in 1545, to Richard Andrews and John Howes, and by them to one Richard Gunter and his wife Joan. By these last the work of destruction was thoroughly completed, the trees cut down, and the sacred images and monuments of the dead sold "for any use that could make the sale of them bring in a penny."

The tomb of Brother Angelus had long been a place of devotion; and many miracles are said to have been wrought through his intercession. It was, of course, desecrated in the general ruin. The celebrated friar Roger Bacon, was also buried here: of him we shall have more to say among the great men of the Order. Duns Scotus, and one of the Franciscan Popes, Alexander V., were educated in this college, with many other famous men of their age.

Wood gives a well-authenticated list of seventy-five Franciscan friars, who were at different times professors in the University of Oxford. Matthew of Paris says, that "England was suddenly filled with these men; not only in the large towns and cities, but in the very hamlets and villages." Nor is the statement exaggerated; for we find that as early as 1255, when St. Bonaventura held a general chapter at Narbonne, the English province is reckoned as having seven guardianships, namely: London, York, Cambridge, Bristol, Oxford, Newark, and Dorchester. In 1399, these guardianships contained sixty convents, many others being founded shortly after; besides several in France and Ireland under the English provincial.

The convent of Cambridge was founded by Edward I., and was situated in the place where Sidney Hall now stands. Wood gives a list of seventy-three friars who publicly taught divinity in that university. The first house occupied by the Franciscans was soon found too small for the rapid increase of novices and pupils; but so munificent was the royal foundation, that Ascham says: "The house of the Franciscans is not only the grace and ornament of the university, but also has in it, great conveniences of holding the assemblies, and doing all the business of that learned body; so that convocations are commonly held here, scholastic exercises performed, and the vesperiæ and inauguration of graduates and doctors solemnized in this church." Burnet says this convent was surrendered by the guardian and twenty-three friars; but, as he gives no date, it is probable that in this case, as in many others, the surrender was simply a violent expulsion.*

The precise time at which the Franciscan convent in Coventry was founded is not known, but it must have been about the year 1234. Probably King Henry III., the great patron of the Order, assisted the friars in forming this establishment, as he founded and assisted in the erection of so many others. Dugdale says that in the accounts of Ralph Fitz-Nicholas, sheriff of Warwickshire in 1234, mention is made of wooden shingles allowed by the king to cover the oratory of the friars, which shingles were delivered out of the woods at Kenilworth for that purpose. The ground was given them by the Earl of Chester, out of his manor of Cheylesmore. In a charter executed by the Black Prince, he styles himself their patron, and gives them permission to take all the stone they require for building from his quarries at Cheylesmore, and likewise liberty to have a postern from their convent into the park for the use of the sick and infirm. He specially enjoins, however, that none other should pass that way, and requires the key of this door to be kept by the warden or his substitute. This concession shows a thoughtful kindness, which tallies well with the character of the heroic young prince. The noble family of Hastings also became great benefactors to the friars. Dugdale gives a list of the names and a description of the escutcheons on the windows of a chapel in this

* At the Dissolution the buildings were demolished; a few walls only being left to mark the site which had been occupied by this spacious convent. The ground was given by Henry VIII. to Trinity College; and was subsequently purchased from them by the executors of Lady Frances Sydney. What remained of the very extensive buildings erected by the Friars Minor was now used for Sidney College. It was built by Simmons, who also erected Emmanuel Chapel on the site of the Dominican convent; and ingeniously contrived, says Cole, to convert the chapel of the Dominican friars into a refectory, and the refectory of the Franciscans into a chapel.

church, called the Hastings chapel. The patrons of the religious must indeed have been most liberal, as their church and convent became one of the largest and most beautiful possessed by the Order in England.

As the Franciscans were themselves generally highly educated, and in many instances occupied the first positions in the universities as professors, they would naturally do all in their power for the instruction of the people of the town where their houses were so generously supported. At a time when the use of books was almost confined to the upper classes, if not to the clerical, or "clerkly" body, and when oral teaching, or vivid representation on wall, and tablet, and "storied window," formed the only exterior sources of intellectual light, it became necessary that knowledge should be imparted in a popular form, suited to the wants of the age. Thus arose the famous mystery plays of Coventry, the "Ludus Coventriæ," as they are styled in the Cottonian MS., which contains the complete collection. True, the representations were rude in the extreme, the rhyme, if rhyme it may be called, sounds barbarous to modern ears. Still, if an action be good in itself, we are surely to value it by its motive and its results. The friars were in fact the servants of the people; and if their churches were beautiful, and their convents spacious, this was not for themselves, but for the use of those whom, for the love of Christ, they served. The sick in body or soul they ministered to and consoled, not only at the cost of their personal ease, but often, as we shall see, at the risk of life, and hazarding torments, the barbarity of which we can scarcely bear to hear of. Even the recreations of the people were also provided for with a paternal love, combining what interested and amused with what instructed and edified. The principal stories from the Old Testament, and the yet more touching incidents of the New, were in this way represented to the people. There were theatres for the different scenes "high and large;" those were drawn on immense wagons to places outside the town, which might be most suitable for the purpose. Surely, setting apart all romance about the "middle ages," when we duly consider the effect that must have been produced by these pastimes, their tendency to promote all the best, because holiest, feelings of our nature, their unpretending instructiveness, their softening and elevating influence, scenes such as these were as much more Christian and christianizing than our penny theatre or gin palace, as the mediæval works of piety were more beneficial than our penny novel.

The week of Corpus Christi was a time at which these mystery plays were specially exhibited. It was the great holiday time of the good people of Coventry; what they hoped to see was talked of many a week previously; what they had seen was a pleasant fireside or wayside gossip for many a week to come. True, it was all of God and of heaven; all of the Saints and the King of Saints; of what He did and said, taught and suffered. But, then, this was all one with the life of the friars, who thus taught them the sublimest mysteries while they knew not that they came to learn. To say these representations were bad because in process of time they were abused, not by the religious who had instituted them, but by those who found in them a source of selfish gain, is simply to say that nothing good may be used because it is capable of a perversion to evil. But the mystery plays and the Coventry friars are amongst the things that *were*, and both friars and pastimes were driven from that quaint old town.

CHAPTER V.

Distinguished men of the Order.—Adam de Marisco and John of Kent appointed to the Holy See to examine the miracles of St. Richard.—English friars requested to teach in foreign universities.—Brother Nicholas made Bishop of Assisi.—Brother Haymo of Feversham.—Religious and ecclesiastics seek admttance in amongst the friars.—The Abbott of Reading.—Remarkable vocation of Ralph, Bishop of Hereford.—He resigns his see to enter the Order.—His vision.—Friar Bacon---Bungey.—A Franciscan friar mainly instrumental in founding Baliol College.—The first proctor always chosen from that Order.—Pembroke Hall, at Cambridge founded at the solicitation of a Friar Minor.—Miracles worked at the tomb of Brother Angelus.

The Franciscan colleges in the English universities furnished some of the most learned and celebrated men of the thirteenth and fourteenth centuries. The names of many are doubtless familiar to our readers. We have already mentioned the vocation of Alexander of Hales, and the circumstances connected with his entrance into the Seraphic Order. Adam de Marisco next claims our notice, as having embraced the life of a Friar Minor about the same time. He had been for several years parish priest of Weirmouth, in the diocese of Durham; "but," says the Chronicle, "being divinely inspired with a holy hatred of this world, he, of his own free choice, changed the manner of his life and his habit." Brother Angelus received him into the Order. He became as distinguished for his learning as for his piety; and the same author says, "the famous and discerning Dr. Grostete loved him above all his beloved Franciscans." The fame of his learning reached even to Italy, so that St. Francis sent for him, that he might study with St. Antony of Padua under the famous Abbot of St. Andrew's. On his return to Oxford, he taught in the schools there with great success, and soon after received the degree of Doctor of Divinity. He was nominated to the bishopric of Ely, but for some reason which does not appear, another priest was consecrated to that see. Marisco was at this time residing at Rome; and was appointed by the Pope as his legate, in conjunction with Brother John of Kent, to examine the miracles of St. Richard, Bishop of Chichester, who died in 1253. The friars returned to England to execute this command, and here they both died about the year 1258.

Indeed so great was the reputation of the English friars, both for learning and sanctity, that they were frequently requested to undertake offices of trust and importance in foreign countries. Brother John and Brother Simon (*Anglici ambo*) were successively provincials of Saxony, and in 1247 Innocent IV. appointed Brother John apostolic legate and collector of alms for the holy wars. Two English Friars, Philip Vallensis and Adam of York, were sent to teach philosophy at Lyons, at the request of Brother Elias. In 1243, Nicholas, a lay brother, having shown an unusual aptitude for learning, was desired to apply himself to the study of divinity, in which he made such progress that his fame reached to Italy. Innocent IV., who then filled the Papal throne, sent for him in consequence, and, having employed him for some time as his confessor, subsequently raised him to the episcopate as Bishop of Assisi. At a general chapter held in 1242, and presided over by Brother Haymo* of Feversham, General of the Order, the interpretation of the Rule of St. Francis, made by the four great doctors of the Order, was approved, and received as its true and genuine sense. The relaxations introduced by Brother Elias had caused much confusion and dispute among

* He was commanded to revise the Breviary and Missal by Innocent IV. The chronicler of the Order in England adds, that this revision was again confirmed and approved by Nicholas III.

the friars, each party being anxious to bring the Rule to bear on their own opinion regarding its observance. Haymo, appointed general at this critical moment, desired four of the leading men of the Order to decide on the disputed questions. Of these four, three were Englishmen—Alexander of Hales, Richard Middleton and Geoffrey Fountain—the fourth being an Italian, Brother John of Rupella. The reputation of the English friars was thus extended far and wide. In their own country, so highly were they respected, that numbers not only of the nobility, but also of the superiors of other religious orders, and even several bishops considered themselves privileged in being allowed to exchange their rank and dignities for the cord of St. Francis and his rule of poverty.

These remarkable vocations are well authenticated, and the particulars of them in many cases especially interesting. We have mentioned the circumstances which induced Robert de Hendred, the Abbot of Abingdon, to resign his office and exchange his Order for that of the mendicant friars. The Franciscan annals say that he died about the year 1234, in great repute for sanctity. Another abbot followed his example. In 1235, John of Reading, superior of the monastery of Canons Regular at Osney, left all the advantages of that station to clothe himself with the poor habit of St. Francis.

But the vocation of Ralph Maydston, Bishop of Hereford, is still more remarkable. Educated at first in the university of Oxford, he went to Paris while still young, to complete his studies; on his return to England he was made priest, and through the favor of Henry III., who had a high opinion of his talents and virtue, promoted to the see of Hereford. Having governed his diocese for six years with great prudence and edification, he joined the Order of Friars Minor, having first obtained leave from Gregory IX. to resign his bishopric. His vocation is attributed to a remarkable vision, related by St. Antoninus, the archbishop of Florence, as well authenticated. While in prayer, the good bishop was called away in spirit to the heavenly Jerusalem. There he beheld the mansions of the blessed, and saw the saints on their glorious thrones. Bnt he looked in vain for a Friar Minor, and as he was greatly attached to the Order, he was grieved and perplexed that none were present where he hoped so many would be. Then appeared to him a lady of exceeding beauty, whom he knew to be the Mother of God. She inquired why he was so distressed. When he told the cause, she replied, "Come with me, and I will show you where these friars dwell." Then he beheld them hidden under the very mantle of the Judge and protected by Him. "Look where they are," continued his holy patroness, "and save thy soul with them." We may well believe that after such a vision the bishop was not likely to delay following his vocation. We may also reasonably suppose that some such intimation of the Divine will must indeed have been made to him, or he would not so promptly have resigned his important charge.

The celebrated Friar Bacon entered the Order about the year 1234. Probably that great friend and patron of the Franciscans, Grostete, bishop of Lincoln, had some influence in his choice. His profession, it is most likely, was made while a fellow of Merton College, before his first visit to the university of Paris. Bacon was descended from an old English family resident at Ilchester, Somersetshire. "He added," says the Chronicle, "to his great endowments of nature, an indefatigable study and a continual exercise of his wit and memory, whereby he soon became an excellent poet and an eloquent orator; after which hopeful beginnings he applied himself to his philosophy in Merton College, at Oxford, where the eyes of all were upon him as a prodigy of parts." Bacon studied for some time under St. Edmund, afterwards Archbishop of Canterbury; a man of such saintly life, and so famous for his miracles, which he wrought principally by the devout use of holy water, that even Fox calls him a saint. He was canonized by Innocent IV.

At Paris, Bacon applied himself to the study of divinity, and also to Greek, Hebrew and the oriental languages. But his unusual skill in mathematics, and his acquaintance with natural science, procured for him his fame as one whose knowledge surpassed the usual limits granted to mortal men. His intellect was in advance of the age: inconveniently so for himself, as we shall presently see. His skill in constructing mathematical and other instruments, and a marvellous story having gone abroad that he had made a brazen head which could speak, gave him the reputation of dealing in the black art. The whole university ran to his lectures; the ignorant and the learned were alike amazed; and while the latter could readily believe that his experiments were wrought by lawful and natural means, the former were not slow to attribute the marvels they beheld to a magical power, and rather to accuse the friar of sorcery, than themselves of ignorance.

The brazen head seems to have been the great source of popular mystification. Probably, if such a thing existed, by some simple mechanical contrivance it was made to utter sounds which were easily imagined to be like those of the human voice. But whatever may have been the true state of the case, the affair was reported to Brother Jerome de Æsculo, then general of the Order, and Bacon was desired to remain in some convent not named until the matter was cleared up. The friar, however, was not idle; he knew the justice of his cause, and that it only needed to be explained to those who could understand an explanation. Therefore he prudently determined to send Brother John of London to Rome, with all his books, writings and mathematical instruments, that the entire case might be laid before the Holy Father. Brother John was well fitted for his task. He had been educated by Bacon from the time he was a mere youth, and had entered the Order by his advice. So well had he profited by the instruction he received, and his constant intercourse with the great professor, that no one so thoroughly understood those arts which his master professed; he was also warmly attached to him, so the cause was in good hands. The Pope, Innocent IV., was perfectly satisfied; and "was convinced," says the Chronicle, "by a careful examination of these books and instruments, and by the explanations of Brother John, that the poor friar's only fault was being wiser and more knowing than others of his time."

Friar Bacon was also celebrated as a preacher. The English historian, Speed, gives an amusing account of a sermon which he is said to have delivered in the presence of King Henry III. It illustrates the simplicity of manners of those times. The king, it seems, had allowed himself to be too much influenced in his choice of ministers by a French prelate whom he had made Bishop of Winchester. His barons were indignant at the constant promotion of foreigners to offices of trust and importance. Henry had been expostulated with by many of his nobles, but in vain. However the pleasant wit of a friar proved more effectual. A parliament was summoned at Oxford, but the members of both houses refused to appear until their grievance was redressed. Bacon preached before the king; and assured him that *Petræ et Rupes* were most dangerous things at sea, and therefore to be avoided, even on land. The king smiled at the conceit; the obnoxious prelate, who was called Petrus de Rupibus, was dismissed, and peace restored.*

Whatever the fame of Bacon may have been as a preacher, he certainly was most voluminous as a writer.† The subjects he treated were as various as his works were numerous; many are still preserved, but a mere list of them would fill several pages of this volume. Friar Bacon died at Oxford in 1292, on the feast of St. Barnabas, and was buried there in the Franciscan convent.

Another Franciscan friar, named Bungey, shared in the magical fame of Bacon; but, as his learning was not so great, nor his experiments of so startling a

* A learned Dominican divine informs us that the authority of Speed is not altogether to be relied on in this matter, and has most kindly given us the version of Matthew of Paris, under the year 1233. He says, the rebuke was given to the king in a private conversation by *Robert* Bacon, of the Order of Preachers, who at that time was preaching before the Court; and the witticism about *Petræ et Rupes* emanated from a clerk of the Court, Roger Bacon, who was present at the interview. It is supposed that Robert was an uncle of Roger Bacon.

† The titles of some of his works may interest our readers: "Of Multiplying Glasses," one book; of "Distinct Perspective," three books; "Of the Causes of Human Ignorance," one book; "Advantages of Science," eleven books; a "Hebrew Grammar;" a "Greek Grammar;" "Of the Value of Music;" "Of the Sight and Looking Glasses,;" "Rules of the Quadrant;" "Making Colors by Art;" "Against Necromancy;" "Of Divination, Astronomy, Geometry, Chemistry," etc. Nor was divinity forgotten: "Of Divinity Studies," five books, and "On the Sentences," four books. Fuller and others who follow him, say that Bacon was ordered to Rome by Clement IV., and there imprisoned until his death. But Wood, and the English annalist of the Franciscan Order, Father Antony Parkinson, disprove both this statement and the dates on which it is made to rest; besides remarking it as unlikely that Bacon would have appealed to Rome, and sent a friar thither to defend his cause, if he had been summoned thither himself. It is also shown that he and his disciple, Brother John, were specially favored by the Holy See.

kind, he was either less noticed or less envied than his famous cotemporary. Bungey was for some time provincial of the English Franciscans, and also taught in their schools at Cambridge: he died at an advanced age, in the convent of Northampton.

In or about the year 1266, we find two Franciscan friars employed in the founding of colleges at Oxford and Cambridge. Wood, in his *Athenæ Oxonienses*, gives an account of both foundations. He says that John de Baliol, knight and father to the king of Scots, gave, during his lifetime, certain stipends for the support of poor scholars at Oxford, intending further to build and endow a college. Baliol died in 1269, a little before Whitsuntide. When on his death-bed, he earnestly requested his lady Dervorguilla and his executors to carry out his design; there was, however, much difficulty in accomplishing this, the lands from which the rents were derived not having good security; but on the persuasion of Brother Richard Slickbury, the lady Dervorguilla determined to acccomplish this laudable undertaking, At the request of Brother Richard she hired a house in the parish of St. Mary Magdalene, and here for some time students were maintained. Brother Hugh de Hertlepool, also a Friar Minor, and Dr. William Menyl, an Oxford scholar, were made proctors. After a few years, the Lady Dervorguilla purchased land on which she built and endowed a college. Walter de Foderingay was appointed principal, and the students removed from their first residence, thence called old Baliol Hall, and settled in their new establishment. John de Baliol, son of their foundress, and Oliver, Bishop of Lincoln, assisted in the completion of the work. In 1284 the statutes were drawn up and delivered to Brother Hugh Hertlepool. From this time the annals say, the first proctor of the college was usually a Franciscan, in memory of the efforts made by the Order for its establishment. The statutes obliged the scholars to have three masses said every year for the repose of the soul of John Baliol, knight, and his ancestors and all the faithful. Likewise at grace before meat, they were every day to pray "for the soul of her said husband, and for the proctors above named." Wood adds, that Pembroke Hall, in Cambridge, and another hall at Paris, for poor students, were founded by the solicitations of a Friar Minor, whose name he does not give, but who (he says) was confessor to the Countess of Pembroke.*

Queen's College also, according to a Protestant historian, may claim to be a Franciscan foundation. It was founded by Margaret of Anjou, wife of Henry VI., in 1488. She appointed Andrew Ducket, a Franciscan friar, president. The troubles of Henry's reign proved a temporary hindrance to the completion of this work; but this friar, who is said to have been a person of great capacity for learning and aptitude for business,

* This lady was a great benefactress to the Order. She was the daughther of Guy de Chastillon, a French nobleman, and married, while quite young, to the Earl of Pembroke. The Lady Mary de St. Paul was a maid, a wife, and a widow in the same day—her noble husband being killed in a tournament which was held at their marriage feast. She then came to England, and devoted herself to works of charity, living in the strictest seclusion. The Lady Mary was nearly related to Edward III. With his permission she founded a monastery for Poor Clares, called Denney Abbey, eight miles from Cambridge, of which Elizabeth Throgmorton was the first abbess. The religious for the new foundation were brought from Waterbeach, where a monastery of Poor Clares had flourished for some time. Her next care was the foundation of Pembroke Hall, which was at first called St. Mary de Valence. It seems more than probable that the Franciscan fathers had induced her to do this, as she specially charges the Fellows of her college with the care of the nuns; indeed her attachment to the Order must have been very great, as she died with the Poor Clares, after having disposed of her large property in charitable bequests, and was buried between the choir of the nuns and that of seculars. The intention of her foundation is expressed in a charter which runs thus: "We, Mary of St. Paul, etc., for the benefit of the soul of the Lord Adamarus de Valentia, late Earl of Pembroke, our husband," etc.

effectually persuaded the consort of Edward IV. to continue it; he also obtained large sums of money from many of the nobility for its endowment, as may be seen in the records of the college. It was dedicated to St. Margaret and St. Bernard, the second patron being added in consequence of Ducket's having been principal of St. Bernard's Hall, which now, with many other valuable endowments, was by his charitable efforts added to the new foundation.

The year in which Hertlepool died is not recorded in the annals, but a remarkable incident which happened during his guardianship is related at some length. Brother Angelus of Pisa had been buried at Oxford. The body was laid in a poor wooden coffin, as was usual, and suitable to the poverty of his Order. Great devotion, however, had been shown to his remains, and many miracles worked through his intercession; in consequence the friars were desirous to give him "a more decent and honorable sepulchre." When the coffin was opened, it was found full of a sweet oil, emitting a most fragrant perfume. The skeleton was entire, and was removed with careful reverence to a stone coffin. This circumstance still further increased the devotion of the people, and in consequence such crowds flocked to the Franciscan Church that Brother Hertlepool presented two-and-twenty friars to the Bishop of Lincoln, the diocesan of Oxford, praying him to give them faculties for hearing the confessions of the pilgrims. The provincial, however, could only obtain this permission for eight of his friars; the secular clergy having already begun to object to the great privileges granted to the Mendicant Orders, although the well-known controversy on this subject did not arise till some years later.

CHAPTER VI.

The Friars employed on important missions.—Brother Haymo sent by the Pope to Constantinople.—Treats with the Emperor and Greek Patriarch.—Other Friars sent to England as Papal legates.—Appointed to collect alms for the holy wars.—The Franciscans refuse a valuable present from Henry III.—Sandford, Archbishop of Dublin, employed as Lord Lieutenant.—Gainsborough negotiates important affairs with the French King.—A navigator and a physician.—Kilwarby.—Peckham.—Duns Scotus.—The Immaculate Conception.

It cannot be denied that, in England at least, the Franciscan friars took the palm, as regards capacity for teaching, from the professors of all other orders. The most distinguised prelates of the age were raised to the episcopate from their ranks, and the friars were employed in the most important missions, as well secular as religious. Lest this statement should be attributed to the partiality of their annalists, we will briefly refer to a few of these circumstances, and to the history of one or two of their most distinguished prelates.

A curious proof of their love of literature, and their eagerness in availing themselves of every means to promote scientific and literary research, is given in the complaint made against them by the Archbishop of Armagh. This prelate declares them to have been so industrious in procuring books and manuscripts, that they bought up all within their reach; so that there was scarcely a book to be had of arts, of divinity, or of the common law. The account of their library, at Oxford seems almost to justify the complaint; for there alone they are said to have had soon after their establishment, a library of several thousand volumes, including many valuable Greek and Hebrew works.

Such men would naturally be selected by the Holy

See for important and difficult missions. Accordingly, in 1233, we find Brother Haymo deputed by Gregory IX. to negotiate with the patriarch of Constantinople. He was accompanied by Brother Rodolphus, an English friar, and two other persons whose names are not mentioned. In the Papal bull they are styled "*Viros virtutis religione conspicuos, morum honestate præclaros, et scripturarum sacrarum scientia præditos.*" The legates were cordially received by the emperor and the patriarch. By the latter they were invited to attend a synod, in which they argued before the assembled fathers on the Procession of the Holy Ghost. They were so far successful in their undertaking as to procure the signatures of those present to an orthodox profession of faith, with which they returned to Rome.

When alms were collecting in England for the holy wars, the Franciscan friars were usually employed to beg for them,* as being above all suspicion of self-interest. A remarkable proof of their integrity occurred about this time, which still further increased the confidence of the people in these good religious. Their great patron, Henry III., had sent them as present a large quantity of grey woolen cloth. It was suitable for their habits, and would have been a most acceptable gift; but the friars hearing that it had been unjustly taken from some merchants, returned it at once to the king, humbly but firmly declining to accept the gift.

In 1246, Brother John Anglicus was sent to England as apostolic legate, with full authority over all prelates, and power to interdict, suspend, and excommunicate.

* They were also employed for the same purpose in Ireland. In 1292, Nicolas Cusack, a Franciscan friar, who had been raised to the See of Kildare by the Pope, was appointed in conjunction with Thomas St. Leger, Bishop of Meath, to collect tithes for the holy wars, and the sheriffs were ordered to aid them in making this collection.

This religious was for some time provincial of the Order in England. In 1258, Brother John Kent was also sent to England, and empowered to act as Papal legate by Alexander IV. In 1272, we find Franciscan friars employed by Gregory IX. in an embassy to Constantinople. The religious deputed to conduct this negotiation were headed by Brother Jerome de Æsculo, who during his absence was chosen minister-general of the Order, and subsequently elected Pope under the title of Nicholas IV. A few years later John de Sandford,* an English friar, was advanced to the archbishopric of Dublin; "and employed," says the historian, "in important and weighty affairs; being made *prorex* for the king." The following year (1285) Brother Stephen Fulborn was made Bishop of Waterford, and in 1286, Archbishop of Tuam. Brother Hervey de Saham, professor of canon law, and guardian of the Friars Minor at Oxford, was now chosen for two successive years to be chancellor of that university.

Collier says, that through the interposition of the Franciscans during this reign (Edward I.) the Jews were preserved from a general massacre with which they had been threatened. About the same time also the king accepted the mediation of the minister-general of the Franciscans, and of the master-general of the Dominicans, sent to him by the Pope to negotiate a peace with the French king. By their prudence and unanimity in conducting the affair, it was soon happily concluded. In the course of the following year, Brother Hugh and Brother William Gainsborough, afterwards

* A learned and eminently prudent man, says Ware, and a great favorite with the king. He succeeded in the See, though not immediately, Fulk de Sandford; and received a salary of £500 as Lord Justice of Ireland. The Archbishop died in England on his return from an important embassy to the German Emperor. He is buried in St. Patrick's Church in Dublin, his body being conveyed thither at the request of the canons of that cathedral.

Bishop of Worcester, were employed by Edward to negotiate the restitution of some lands in Aquitaine, in which negotiation they honorably acquitted themselves.

Gainsborough was indeed one of the most distinguished men of his day. The fame of his learning and eloquence had reached the Papal court; and thither he was summoned by Boniface VIII. who employed him as reader of the Sacred Palace. Here "his name became daily more and more famous for the clearness of his explications, the subtility of his disputations, and the eloquence and fervor of his preaching."

He remained in this office until raised to the episcopate. On his return to England he was again employed by the king in state affairs of the greatest importance; particularly in negotiating a marriage between the eldest son of the English monarch, and the princess Isabella of France.

It may surprise some of our readers to hear of a friar skilled in the art of navigation, sailing to the "most northerly islands, taking an exact dimension of all those parts with his astrolabe, and being the first man that left to posterity an accurate description of them." All this, however, and much more is related of Brother Nicolas of Lynn. This friar entered the Order while young, and studied for some time at Oxford, where he became an eminent mathematician. His anxiety to test his calculations and to make useful discoveries, induced him to apply for permission to make this voyage. He is mentioned by Mercator as having discovered a remarkable and dangerous current or whirlpool in the northern seas.* Brother Nicolas wrote an account of his voyage in a work entitled, *Inventio Fortunata*, which he dedicated to Edward III.

* Perhaps the Maelstrom.

Another friar was no less famous as a physician. He lived in the reign of Henry II., and died regretted, we might almost say, by the nation, so extensive were his charities and so wonderful his cures. These, indeed, were so numerous that it is said his sanctity must have had even a greater share in them than his human skill. Brother William Holmes has left some writings on medical subjects, which were much valued in his own age. He applied himself to the study of medicine, with a hope that the natural gifts he had received might, through the relief of his fellow-men's temporal sufferings, lead them to seek the far more important cure of their spiritual diseases. Nor was he disappointed. His advice and attendance were given gratis. The fame of his almost miraculous cures was noised abroad, and many who would have been won in no other way, listened to the holy exhortations of the friar, who ministered to their distressing maladies with such disinterested care.

But a volume would scarcely contain even a brief mention of bishops, professors, divines, preachers of peace—of men famed for science, and yet more for sanctity, who flourished in the Seraphic Order while England was Catholic England still. Later, when the first attempts were made to sever it from the Communion of Saints, and the branch was torn from its parent stem, we shall see that the Order which had graced the Church by its men of literary fame, and its preachers of saintly life, became the Order of martyrs, and enriched with its blood the land which it had long watered with its tears and prayers.

Two celebrated archbishops of the Order, and its great doctor, Duns Scotus, at least claim a word.

Archbishop Kilwarby* was a native of England. Af-

* Parker, Godwyn, Collier and others say that Kilwarby was a

ter having received the first elements of education, he was sent to Paris to prosecute his studies. On his return, he entered the Franciscan Order. He resided for some time at Oxford, and there applied himself to divinity, which he taught publicly. He was then made Provincial, and was subsequently raised to the see of Canterbury, being consecrated February 26, 1272. While in this high position, he built a second convent for the Friars Minor in London. Six years after his elevation to the archiepiscopate, he was summoned to Rome by Nicolas III., and made Cardinal Bishop of Ostia and Porto. He died shortly after at Viterbo. Kilwarby was distinguished both for his learning and the sanctity of his life, and was particularly attached to the study of the Sacred Scriptures. He has left many commentaries on the Epistles, and also wrote commentaries on, and summaries of, the works of St. Augustine.

But an archbishop still more distinguished next claims our attention. Peckham succeeded Kilwarby in the see of Canterbury, and few men could have been better fitted for this important charge. If in his zeal he seemed at times to overstep the bounds of prudence, or to enforce strictness on points where discipline had been relaxed, it was only that he required from others, in a degree, what he himself practiced to perfection. So great was his love for the charge committed to him, that he was willing to run all risks of personal incon-

Franciscan, and it seems scarcely possible that there could be a mistake about one who is said to have been Provincial. It is, however, only fair to state that the Dominican Order also claim the Archbishop and refer to documents in the State Paper office in support of their assertion which certainly can scarcely be questioned. Perhaps Kilwarby was a tertiary of both orders ; this seems not to have been a very uncommon occurrence in those times. Be it as it may, we cannot pretend to decide the question, or even to offer an opinion. We only give the authorities which appear of equal weight on both sides.

venience or even suffering, to obtain the perfection of those whom he governed. Peckham was born in Suffolk, of a family in poor circumstances. He received his first education from the Cluniac monks of the Abbey of Lewes. These good religious, perceiving their pupil gifted with unusual aptitude, sent him to prosecute his studies at the university of Oxford, where they supported him until he entered the Order of Friars Minor. After his profession he was sent by his superiors to Paris, where he studied under St. Bonaventura. While here, he enjoyed the friendship and protection of Margaret, widow of St. Louis. Returning to Oxford, he was made Doctor of Divinity, and, shortly after, provincial minister of the English Franciscans, an office for which his sanctity, prudence, and learning had fully qualified him.

The austerity of his life was extreme. He never tasted flesh, and even abstained during a considerable part of the year from fish and eggs, always fasting, except on a few of the great festivals. His prayer and watching were continual, and amid the great cares attendant on his exalted station, he still continued the same severe rule of life. It is truly said that he hungered in the midst of plenty ; for he kept a hospitable table and open house for his clergy, or for strangers whom business or devotion might bring to his palace. While superior of the Friars Minor in England, he made all his visitations on foot, and when summoned to attend a general chapter of his Order in Italy, steadily refused to use a horse or carriage on the journey, so great was his love of poverty and mortification. He is said to have worked many miracles, both during life and after death. Of his numerous works, two deserve a word in passing ; his Concordance of the Sacred Scriptures, and his Collection of the Statutes of Synods and Provincial Constitutions, the first work of the kind ever compiled.

But it was in his most difficult and trying position as ruler of the first episcopal see in England, that his character showed itself to most advantage. His determination at any cost to preserve and enforce strict discipline, was sure to draw on him the indignation of those less fervent than himself. He had to defend the Church from her enemies both within and without; hence, we can scarcely wonder that his path was a thorny one. Amid constant apprehensions of being driven from the kingdom, he pursued his episcopal career with unflinching determination. Once, when a knight (Sir Osburn Gyfford) had violently entered a monastery at Wilton, and carried off two of the religious by force of arms, Peckham pronounced sentence of excommunication against him; nor could he be prevailed on to remit it, until the knight had atoned for his offence by severe penance. Sir Osburn submitted, and underwent the discipline prescribed. He was forbidden to wear his sword, or the knightly apparel he had so foully disgraced, and was compelled to make a three years' pilgrimage to the Holy Land; to fast for some months, and, more humiliating still, to appear in Wilton parish church three successive Sundays; and there, stripped to the waist, to be beaten with rods. This discipline was also repeated in the parish church of Shaftsbury, and in the market place.

Nor was the archbishop less energetic in enforcing discpline among his clergy. In 1281, he called a provincial synod at Lambeth. The instructions which he then gave, and his zeal in enforcing their observance, have seldom been equalled. He enjoins his clergy to preach on the points of faith and practice which he lays before them; and that none may plead ignorance, he gives them a written and peculiarly clear and simple explanation of the mysteries of faith, the ten commandments, the seven sacraments, the seven works of mercy, etc. This synod ended, the archbishop visited the greater part of England and Wales, consecrating churches, enforcing the observance of ecclesiastical discipline, examining carefully into all causes or occasions of scandal which might exist among the clergy or in religious brothers, and promptly applying the necessary remedies. In 1282, he founded a collegiate church at Wingham in Kent, and about the same time wrote a pressing letter to the king, who had attempted many things to the prejudice of the Church, particularly by endeavoring to deprive the abbey of Westminster and other monasteries of several of their ancient privileges and immunities. The archbishop also insisted that priests, of whatever rank, should not possess a plurality of benefices; refusing on this account, to confirm two of the king's chaplains to the sees of Winchester and Lichfield. They appealed to Rome; but the archbishop carried his point. Nor was he less exact with the lower clergy. All who possessed pluralities were obliged to resign them, and to content themselves with a single benefice. One priest, being unhappily found guilty of a grievous crime, was condemned to a severe penance of fasting and pilgrimage for three years.

A synod had also been held by him at Reading, soon after his return to England. On this occasion, at the request of the chancellor of the university of Oxford, Peckham made some particular decrees for the maintenance of good order and regular discipline among the students, and also for the protection of their rights and privileges.

The archbishop was made protector of his Order in

England by the Holy See; and in this office he defended his brethren with prudence and zeal, when occasion arose. He assisted, by every means in his power, in building convents, and increasing the number and influence of the religious. The Franciscans were not without their enemies, and such a protector was not a little necessary at this particular juncture. Many religious from other orders had asked and obtained the habit of the Friars Minor, and, as we have already seen, even abbots and prelates considered themselves privileged in being allowed to exchange their mitres and croziers for the cord of St. Francis. Some of the most eminent and learned men of the day, and even persons of noble birth, were flocking into its ranks, and it was natural that this should excite a little opposition if not envy. Public complaints were made, even sermons preached against the friars. The secular clergy complained of their privileges of hearing confessions and preaching in so many places; but all murmurs were soon silenced by their energetic defender. The archbishop published the bull of Alexander IV. given in 1257, by which full power was granted to the English friars of his Order to preach in public, and to hear the confessions of lay persons of either sex. He further declared that all who dared to oppose them in the exercise of these privileges should be severely reprimanded. He desired the chancellor of the university to silence such as had preached against them, and to make known to all, that in receiving persons into their Order, though already professed in others, they only acted in accordance with the permission of the Holy See.

The holy archbishop died in 1292. His body was buried in his cathedral of Canterbury; his heart, it is said, was sent to his Fraciscan brethren, to be enshrined in their church in London.

Another remarkable member of the Order now claims our attention. The birthplace of Duns Scotus has caused nearly as much dispute as that of Homer. It is, however, certain that he studied in England, and was a distinguished member of the university of Oxford. The Franciscan chronicler, Father Antony Parkinson, gives strong reasons for the belief that the great doctor was born in the hamlet of Hemildon, or Emildon, in Northumberland, and at a village called Dunston. He says that all who wrote before this dispute were unanimous in declaring him to be English, and quotes Leland, Camden, and Harpsfield, to prove his point. In the records of Merton College, Scotus is called Duns, and in a MS. catalogue of the fellows of that college, under King Edward II., he is thus mentioned: "Joannes Duns, alias Scotus, a man of great and subtile wit, was declared the Subtile Doctor by the Pope." In a still more ancient catalogue he is registered thus: "*Joannes Scotus, hic Doctor Subtilis, vulgariter tamen Duns, Ordinis Minorum.*" A statute of Merton College is also cited, requiring that none but an Englishman should be admitted as a fellow of the college. The dispute probably arose from an inscription on the tomb of Scotus, of comparatively modern date, which begins thus: "*Scotia me genuit,*" etc., but, as Fuller quaintly observes, it was a natural enough mistake for a foreigner to write him a Scotchman who was born in Northumberland.

The early boyhood of the "subtile doctor" gave little promise of his future greatness. He was dull and apparently averse to learning. But either from fear of his companions' jests, or, more probably, from a better motive, he applied himself to prayer, to obtain a greater quickness of perception. From childhood he was especially devoted to that more than royal Lady whose champion he was destined to become. To her he applied in the sorrows and trials of his boyhood—and who, with a true and honest heart, ever appealed to her in vain? Our Blessed Lady appeared to him in a dream, and promised to obtain for him those intellectual gifts he so ardently desired. When Mary gives, she gives as a queen, and her devout client had soon reason to rejoice at her beneficence. The stupid boy became rapidly the youth full of intellectual vigor, with unusual quickness of perception and powers of application. So great was the change, and so amazing his progress in his studies, that the chroniclers declare such a vast fund of knowledge, such universal learning could not have been attained without a miracle.

Shortly after his admission to Merton College, he was unanimously elected fellow, inasmuch as the fame of his intellectual attainments was noised everywhere abroad. After a time, he returned to his native county, and was soon after professed at the convent of the Friars Minor in Newcastle. Returning once more to Oxford, he pursued his studies under the great Franciscan, Dr. William Ware. The assiduous learner then began to teach. His lectures were attended by such crowds that the very professors are said to have left their chairs, and hung in rapt attention on the eloquence and learning of the young friar. Scotus was now sent by his superiors to Paris; and here his famous defence of the Immaculate Conception of our Blessed Lady obtained for him his highest praise as a theologian, and his greatest honor as a religious.

The controversy on the doctrine arose shortly before his birth. The yearly festival in honor of our Lady's conception had been instituted long before. In the

West it was observed on the eighth, and in the East on the ninth of December.* In the most ancient of the eastern liturgies (that ascribed to St. James) the Blessed Virgin is commemorated as "our most holy immaculate, and most glorious Lady, Mother of God, and ever Virgin Mary." In the tenth century the Feast of the Conception was kept as a solemn festival in Spain.

But it was in these islands that Mary's dearest privilege received special honor. Soon after William the Conqueror had established himself on the English throne, he heard that the Danes, who considered the island as their chartered field of pillage and plunder, were fitting out a new and formidable fleet to attack the new invaders, who, they pretended, had usurped their more ancient privilege. Anxious to ascertain the truth of the report and the strength of the foe, William despatched a prudent and religious man, Helsinus, Abbot of Ramsey, to the Danish coast. The voyage thither was performed in safety; but as the vessel returned, a sudden tempest threatened its immediate destruction. Helsinus and his companions betook themselves to prayer, and called earnestly upon the Mother of Mercy. Suddenly a venerable man in pontifical garments appeared to them. Standing on the waves close to the ship, which was now almost engulfed, he addressed the Abbot, asking if he did indeed desire to escape the threatened danger. Helsinus having replied, he continued: "Know, then, that I am

* It was observed as a holiday, says Alban Butler, before the emperor, Emanuel Comnenus, enforced its observance about the year 1150. George, Bishop of Nicomedia, in the reign of Heraclius, calls it a feast of ancient date. And Jos. Assemani demonstrates, from the marble calendar of Naples, engraved in the ninth age, that this feast was then kept in that city, and that the Church of Naples was the first in the West which adopted it in imitation of the Orientals. Pope Sixtus IV., in 1483, commanded it to be kept as a holiday.

sent by our Lady, Mary the Mother of God, whom thou hast so piously invoked; and if thou wilt attend to my words, thou shalt be saved from the great peril of the deep, thou and thy companions." The Abbot promised obedience, and the heavenly messenger continued: "Promise, then, to God and to me, that thou wilt solemnly celebrate each year the Feast of the Conception of the Mother of God, and that thou wilt preach the celebration of this festival." Helsinus promised, and inquired on what day the festival should be kept. The eighth of December was named, and he was told that the office of the Nativity should be used. The vision then disappeared; the tempest was appeased; and on the return of the Abbot and his companions to England the festival was established.

These events are said to have occurred in 1070. In 1328, the feast was made one of solemn observance by the Archbishop of Canterbury; and was so kept in England until the change of Religion. St. Anselm had been the great promoter of the devotion in England; and when exiled thence, he became the means of introducing it into France. The festival was already celebrated at Lyons in the days of St. Bernard, who, with his usual energy, wrote at once to the canons of that church, reproving them severely for having acted in this matter without the express permission of the Holy See. The mystery itself then began to be questioned, and the argument was carried on warmly on both sides. The authority of St. Thomas was at that time paramount, and he was supposed to hold back from the essential point of the doctrine. The question presented itself how Mary could have been redeemed if she had never been under sin. St. Bonaventura was the first to open the way for clearing up the difficulties so finally and triumphantly removed by Scotus. The Seraphic Doctor declared that our Lady was preserved from original sin, and this by a new "kind of sanctification," which redeemed and exempted her from it. Scotus went further. He showed that Mary was indeed redeemed, and that in the most glorious and perfect manner. Her redemption was the master-piece of Calvary, the costliest and purest jewel purchased by the most precious blood. Until the day of the Franciscan professor, the most devout client of Mary, with St. Bernard, and the most profound theologians, with St. Thomas, had hesitated to declare that at the moment of her conception she was immaculate. This was partly because the distinction between the active and passive conception had not been carefully drawn; and for want of clear definitions men have argued against the very doctrine they firmly believed. Partly, too, because, as has been remarked with regard to St. Thomas, they raised the point how Mary could have been redeemed if she had never been under original sin.

The discussion was rife in the university of Paris. Even the great Albertus wavered; and it was determined that a public disputation should take place. Duns Scotus was desired to appear as Mary's champion. The interest of the question, and the fame of his eloquence, drew thousands to hear the cause. The Papal legates presided, and all the great men of the university attended the debate. Scotus betook himself to prayer; above all, invoking her whose special privilege he was to defend. On his way to the hall he passed a statue of our Lady. Kneeling before it, he prayed fervently; and as he rose, exclaimed: "*Dignare me laudare te, virgo sacrata; da mihi virtutem contra hostes tuos.*"* Even as he spoke, our Blessed Lady in-

* This versicle is said at the *Angelus* by the members of the Fran-

clined her head towards her faithful client; and the young friar, full of joy and confidence, proceeded to address the assembly. His eloquence, and the astuteness of his intellect, or rather the supernatural lights with which he was favored, soon convinced and silenced every objection. He showed that the exemption of Mary from sin by her redemption from even its original stain, far from being derogatory to the mediatorial office of her Divine Son, was rather His most glorious victory over the enemy. He proved that her perfect redemption was the one dearest purchase of the most precious blood, inasmuch as redemption from even the passing taint of sin is a higher exercise of Omnipotent power and Divine clemency than salvation from a guilt already incurred. Thus he presented Mary to them as the one perfect type of the redeemed, and the mode of her redemption as that which was congruous to the mother of God, and to her alone. He declared that in her redemption from original, and in her preservation from actual sin, her Divine Son had exerted the efficacy of His atonement in the highest degree, and that in the celestial courts she would appear the brightest and most perfect jewel of His redeeming grace. So that the exaltation of Mary, and the confession of faith in her exemption from all taint of sin, was the highest honor we could pay to the merit of the mediatorial office of her Divine Son. This line of argument had never been used before. It had been almost suggested by St. Thomas, and more clearly seen by St. Bonaventura, who, in his office of general, introduced the feast of the Immaculate Conception into the whole

ciscan Order, in memory of this event. Any of our readers who may wish to see a detailed account of the opinions of the Fathers, &c., on the doctrine of the Immaculate Conception, with particulars regarding its definition, and a most interesting dissertation on the question itself, are referred to a little work, published in 1855, by the Right Rev. Dr. Ullathorne, entitled "The Immaculate Conception."

Franciscan Order. But it remained for Scotus to complete the work. Few objectors now remained and these were almost confined to the members of the Dominican Order, most of whom still adhered to the implied opinion of their great doctor. The universities and the religious orders were loud in their praises of Scotus, and rejoiced that what Catholic instinct had so long felt to be true, was now received by theologians as a more than probable doctrine. How much greater would have been their pious gratulation, could they have seen the day when the voice of Peter, speaking from Peter's chair, proclaimed the immaculate conception of Mary as an article of faith! Then, indeed, was the Son more than ever honored in the mother whom He had exalted above all creatures by the dignity of her Divine maternity; whom He had redeemed as the very first fruits of His most Precious Blood, with a redemption which distinguishes her among the redeemed, as not merely delivered from the punishment of sin, but exempted from its lightest taint.

The cap, with the title of *Doctor Subtilis*, was now bestowed on Scotus; and, at the same time, the university paid the highest compliment to his eloquence, and declared their adhesion to the doctrine he had advanced, by requiring all who would enter their learned body to testify on oath their belief in the immaculate conception. Nearly two hundred years later, in 1497, this statute was renewed by eighty-two doctors, with all the graduates of the theological faculty of Paris. Toulouse followed their example. In Rome, the feast was established soon after the triumph of Scotus. The universities and theological schools of Bologna, Naples, Cologne, Mayence, Vienna, Louvain, Salamanca, Toledo, Seville, Valentia, Coimbra, Evora, Mexico, Lima, and even Oxford and Cambridge, followed the example of the Parisian professors, and bound their members by oath to teach and defend the immaculate conception. It will be remembered that St. Francis himself had been forward in this matter, and had required the priests of his Order to celebrate Mass on Saturdays in honor of Mary Immaculate. In a general chapter, held in 1621, the friars declared that they had, from the very foundation of their Order, honored this mystery, and bound themselves by oath to teach it in public and in private, and to promote devotion to it.

Scotus was little more than five-and-twenty when he obtained his fame as Mary's champion. He died at Cologne at the early age of thirty-four, on the eighth of November, 1308. It is said that he was the founder of its university, which, however, was not permanently established until some years later. Many interesting anecdotes are related in the Chronicles of the Order, which show that Scotus was as much to be honored for his sancity as for his learning and intellectual gifts. With all the applause lavished on him, he was still the humble, obedient religious. He was walking with some companions when he received the direction of his superiors to go to Cologne, there to defend Mary's immaculate conception, as he had already done in Paris. Immediately on reading the letter containing the obedience, he set out in the direction indicated to him. His companions entreated him to return to the convent, if only for a few hours, and, as they knew personal convenience would be no consideration to him, they pleaded the duties of politeness, and the pain his sudden departure would give to his many friends and admirers. But Scotus was immovable. Obedience was dearer to him than fame or friends, and with a kind farewell to those who were around him, he at once pursued his journey. "Pardon me," he said, "if

I seem wanting in courtesy, but my obedience is to go to Cologne, not to return to the convent."

But though the young friar thus escaped the applause and distinction by which a public departure from Paris would have been accompanied, he could not prevent an almost triumphal entry into Cologne. The news of his approach had preceded him, and his arrival was anxiously watched for. Nobles and magistrates, the clergy and townspeople, all vied in doing him honor, and accompanied him to the convent of his Order. In this place he began to deliver lectures which were attended by crowds, and here his memory is still revered. His character is thus beautifully summed up by an old writer: "From his very youth no man was more disengaged from the world, or more truly poor in spirit—none more scrupulously obedient, none more chaste, none more humble, none more forward in the practice of watching, fasting, and all other penitential austerities, none more fervent and assiduous in prayer, none more zealous for, or ready to contribute to, the salvation of his neighbor. All his writings breathe humility and a submissive disposition; his lowly sentiments of himself appear in his manner of treating of the highest mysteries of the Christian faith, and when he opposes the opinions of others, he still forbears all pungent expressions or censures."

Scotus, like many of the saints of his Order, was peculiarly devoted to the mystery of the Nativity. One Christmas night, as he meditated on the love of his God in becoming man, the Divine Infant appeared to him, and even permitted the young friar to embrace Him, and take Him in his arms. Other circumstances of a supernatural character, and scarcely less wonderful, are related of him. Once, when he preached to an immense audience, and could not be heard by those at a distance, the pulpit in which he stood was miraculously raised from the ground, so that all could see and hear him. "This prodigy," says the Chronicle, "caused great admiration, so that the people listened to him as though he had been an angel sent down from heaven." He was also favored with an eminent spirit of prayer, and frequently passed an entire day in rapture, so absorbed in God as to be unconscious of all that passed around. The disputations of Scotus gave rise to two great parties, who long divided the theological world. Even of his own disciples, some joined the ranks of the Thomists, as those were called who followed the scolastic definition of the great St. Thomas of Aquin. It was an age of speculative disputations and subtle distinctions. But whether we admire the Realists, who held for the opinion distinguished as *a parte rei*, or the Nominalists, who contended for that *a parte mentis*, we must acknowledge that the great glory of Scotus was in removing the obstacles which had hitherto prevented an intellectual acceptance of the doctrine of the immaculate conception. . Far higher honor this, than that of being the founder of a new school, or the originator of scholastic distinctions, which, however acute or ingenious, might pass with current opinions, and could scarcely survive the praises of a century.

CHAPTER VII.

Brother Elias.—His character.—Enters the service of Frederic.—His unhappy end.—St. Bonaventura.—His conduct as superior.—Holds a General Chapter, makes important regulations regarding the vow of poverty.—His fame as a theologian.—The Angelus.—He is made Cardinal, presides at the Council of Lyons.—Resigns his office as superior of his Order.—His illness brought on by over-exertion at the council.—Death.—Magnificent funeral.—His relics disturbed by heretics.—His writings, and their influence on the Church.

Our readers will remember that, in the General Chapter held by St. Francis in 1220, Brother Elias was deprived of his authority in the Order, and this because the more fervent had complained of the relaxations he endeavored to introduce. Peter of Catania was then made vicar-general, but at the end of a year, he resigned his office, declaring himself unable to bear so heavy a responsibility, and Elias was again restored. After the death of St. Francis, a General Chapter was convoked at Rome 1227,) under the protection of Gregory IX., and here the authority of Elias was confirmed by a majority. His undoubted talent for government, and the zeal he had shown in forwarding the temporal interests of his Order, influenced many. Others preferred his relaxations to the primitive fervor of their holy Rule. But a large number of the religious foresaw the consequence of investing with authority a man who had shown himself so unworthy of it, and these earnestly desired the election of John Parent. In the General Chapter of 1230, Elias was again deposed, and the friar above mentioned elected to fill his place. The influence of St. Antony of Padua and Adam de Marisco had effected this important change, and certainly the charges made against Elias were sufficiently serious to warrant their most energetic interference. These points principally regarded his relaxations of the rule of poverty. Personally, he failed in its observance, by requiring the attendance of two servants, the use of a horse, and many other dispensations for his comfort and convenience. These he grounded, indeed, on the pretext of ill-health, but it was obvious to all who were not influenced by his example, that his requirements far exceeded his needs, supposing them to be as great as he represented. In the government of the Order he was charged with allowing the use and possession of money to an extent completely contrary to the spirit and even the letter of his Rule. In 1236, however, he was once more appointed superior, but after a short time finally deposed. His energetic, restless temper now sought exercise in a new and more congenial sphere. He entered the service of the Emperor Frederic, and shared in his opposition to the Holy See, thus incurring a sentence of excommunication from Innocent IV. In 1253, he was seized with a fatal illness, and one of the friars who came to visit him compassionated his unhappy condition, and hastened to throw himself at the feet of the Sovereign Pontiff to obtain pardon and release from the excommunication. His charity was rewarded; Elias was forgiven, and, it is said by some authors, was permitted to die in the habit of his Order.

St. Francis had foreseen the miserable career of his unhappy child, and had by his prayers averted a still more terrible fate. Once, when the Saint and brother Elias were residing for a time in the same convent, it was revealed to the former that his disciple would die out of the Order, and that his crimes had merited eternal damnation. From this moment St. Francis could never bear to be with him, even for a moment, and fled from him whenever he approached. Elias was alarmed, and by tears and entreaties obtained a knowledge of this fearful secret. His terror may be imagined, but he took the surest way of averting the threatened judgment by appealing to the paternal affection of St. Francis, refusing to quit his presence until he had promised to intercede with God for his salvation. The Saint complied, and his prayer was heard and accepted. It is but fair to say that Elias has had his advocates and defenders as well as his accusers. M. de Malin warmly espouses his cause, and declares that the more ancient writers of the Order have not uttered a word to his disadvantage. There is no doubt that he was sincerely devoted to St. Francis; that he was anxious for the increase and advancement of the Order, and that the Franciscans are mainly indebted to his energy and zeal for the erection of their magnificent church in Assisi. But it is equally undeniable that Elias was excommunicated by the Holy See, and that St. Antony, Adam de Marisco, and the saintly Bernard de Quintavalle, were unanimous in their opposition to his government, and loud in their condemnation of his conduct.

In 1256, St. Bonaventura was elected minister-general, and ruled the Order with a prudence and zeal which bade fair to remove any occasions of scandal to which former administrations might have given rise. This Saint received the habit of the Friars Minor from Brother Haymo, in the 22d year of his age, 1243. He was sent to study in Paris under the direction of Alexander of Hales, who was so touched by the singular purity and innocence of his young pupil, that he often declared Bonaventura seemed as if he had not sinned in Adam. His life was as remarkable for its austerity as for its cheerfulness. The two virtues indeed are seldom separated. Like his seraphic father, he loved to linger near the image of Jesus crucified, and pour forth at His feet tears of compassion and sighs of burning love. Once, when a great master of theology came to visit him, he inquired where he had learned so much heavenly science. St. Bonaventura pointed to his crucifix, and exclaimed, "This is the fountain of all my knowledge; for I desire no other book, save Jesus crucified." And so indeed it was. While the great St. Thomas was soaring amid the cherubim, and flooding the world with the celestial light and ineffable brightness which illumined his soul in his enraptured contemplations, St. Bonaventura, his friend and companion in sanctity, had sprung aloft among the burning seraphim and drank in their torrents of unutterable love, to diffuse them again in the cold hearts of his fellow-men. The one enlightened the intellect, the other inflamed the heart; the one extended the kingdom of God by the love of theology, the other by the theology of love.

When appointed superior of his Order, St. Bonaventura applied himself at once to the work of reform. The evils which Brother Elias and his supporters had introduced, or failed to check, had taken deep root; for it is easier to relax than to invigorate what has partly decayed. His first exercise of authority was to assemble a General Chapter at Narbonne. Then he collected the constitutions of all the preceding chapters of the Order, and made such new regulations as seemed best suited to check the impending danger. Anxiety to celebrate the merits of St. Francis had induced an almost pardonable emulation among the friars in erecting magnificent churches in his honor. But this in time degenerated, and led to many serious breaches of their most sacred vow of poverty. Its strict observance would have honored the Saint far more truly. Money was as much the root of all evil in the thirteenth century as in our own day, and without money these splended structures could not be completed or adorned. The friars spent time in begging alms, which should have been given to prayer or to preaching. Then, the very possession of money, and the power to spend it, brought a train of temporal cares and distractions, which certainly did not tend to their sanctification. And the inability to obtain what was necessary to finish splendid churches, unwisely begun before they had counted the cost, added anxieties as painful as they were unmeritorious. St. Bonaventura at once laid an axe to the root of this great evil. He strictly forbade all unnecessary ornaments. Any new churches which were to be erected were to have but one dome, and no towers, unless by special permission. Nor were windows of stained glass allowed except in the sanctuary. The sacred vessels alone might be of gold; all other ornaments were to be of less costly material. An earnest and affectionate letter to the provincial ministers accompained these regulations. It explained their necessity, and enforced their observance. "Why," exclaims the Saint, "why is the ancient splendor of the Order obscured? and why in the purity of our consciences sullied? It is by reason of all this officious business, which requires the use of money; and this money is kept and handled with pleasure. Importunate demands make the friars dreaded, as if they were bandits; and their magnificent buildings only trouble the peace of the religious, burden their consciences, and make men judge us severely. And although all are not guilty, all are equally condemned."

It was indeed true that all were not guilty. The very fact of St. Bonaventura's election was in itself a proof what vitality still existed in the Order. A restoration was needed rather than a reformation; and soon it was so thoroughly effected that the Saint had no further occasion to complain of relaxations.

But it was not only in the government of his Order that our Saint distinguished himself. As a theologian, he ranks with the great St. Thomas, though of a different school; as a Saint, he equals him in the supereminent science of divine love. Together they pleaded the cause of the mendicant friars, which was attacked by William de St. Amour in the well-known dispute for the professors' chairs of the universities. And when the dispute was silenced by Alexander IV., and the friars permitted to enjoy the privileges their learning so well merited, the two Saints received the doctor's cap together, while St Bonaventura prevailed in humility, and persuaded his friend to receive the honor first.

It may not be generally known that we owe to St. Bonaventura the devotion of the *Angelus ;* one, indeed most congenial to so devout a client of Mary, to a soul so full of burning love to a God incarnate. What increase of his accidental glory must he not have merited, by instituting a devotion which sends up daily to heaven such fervent aspirations from countless hearts!

"*Ave Maria!*" It is morning; and we are awakened by the sound. The first dawn of light has gleamed, and our day of anxious care, of busy labor has begun. But the sound of the *Angelus* bell falls cheerily on our hearts ; and we spring up to adore the Incarnate God, to offer our all to Him who has given His all to us. We think of Bethlehem and Nazareth, and remember Him who was called the carpenter, and bore a life of weariness and labor to lighten ours. "The Word was made flesh," and the burden of our humanity becomes easier as we bend the knee in adoration of His.

"*Ave Maria!*" It is mid-day, and the battle of life is thick around us. Heaven seems far away, like the beautiful mountains, which in the clear morning looked so near, but now are shrouded with the mists of earth, But the *Ave Maria* has made our hearts lighter. It is an echo from home; the "*Angelus Domini nuntiavit Mariæ*" falls sweetly on the ear, and tells us that bright celestial spirits are keeping watch and ward for us, for love of their triumphant queen.

"*Ave Maria!*" Once more we hear the call to prayer. It is evening. A day is gone, and we are weary, and we long for the day that will have no evening, for the morning that will have no night. It is Paschal time, and our thoughts are of the bright appearances of our risen Lord, as we cry, "Abide with us, Lord, for it is towards evening," or, with Mary, "Behold the handmaid of the Lord, be it done unto me according to Thy word." It is our "*Nunc dimittis.*" The shades of sorrow, of age, of faded hopes and dreams, are closing around us; it matters not. With a calm, or even joyous "*Ecce ancilla Domini,*" we go to rest. Happy they who hear it the last of earthly sounds. "*Ave Maria!*" An angel first breathed it on earth, and it is oftenest uttered by those whose lives are most like to angels. "*Ave Maria!*" May we be worthy one day to sing it with those blessed spirits in the Paradise of God!

In 1265, St Bonaventura was nominated to the archiepiscopal see of York. This dignity, however, he steadfastly declined, though he was obliged to throw himself at the feet of the Sovereign Pontiff, Clement IV., and with tears and the most earnest entreaties implore his release. Gregory X., however, was not so easily moved by his humility. This Pontiff, a man of most saintly life and exalted virtue, determined that the Church should not be deprived of the services of this great doctor. He therefore nominated him Cardinal Bishop of Albano. As he knew that the Saint would raise every objection to the acceptance of this dignity, he anticipated his refusal by requiring him to accept the two-fold charge without alleging any pretext against it; and ordering him at once to set out for Rome. There was now no escape. The Saint was compelled to submit to what was probably the most painful obedience of his life. Two nuncios were sent to meet him. St. Bonaventura had arrived at San Michele, a few miles from Florence, where there was a convent of his Order. He was engaged in washing the dishes when the Papal envoys arrived: but he quietly continued his occupation, requesting them to walk for a while in the garden until he could entertain them. Probably the lavatory process was performed *al fresco;* for it is said the Cardinal's hat was hung on a tree until the Saint could "take it decently in his hands."

At Florence, Gregory himself met the bishop elect, and there ordained him with his own hands. The Council of Lyons was then about to commence. Thither St. Bonaventura was desired to repair that he might take a leading part in its deliberations. The Greek schismatics had already made proposals for a reunion, and Gregory zealously pursued what Clement had begun. The Greek patriarch Joseph made a violent opposition; but the Emperor obliged him to silence. The fourteenth general council was about to be held. The Greeks were invited to assist at it, and all were hopeful of a successful issue. St. Thomas Aquinas died on his journey thither; and St. Bonaventura was consequently overwhelmed with care and anxiety, a portion of which at least might have been otherwise shared with his saintly friend.

The Pope and St. Bonaventura arrived together at Lyons in November. The council did not open until the following May; but the intervening time was but too shrot for the necessary preparations. The Saint who sat at the Pope's right hand, was the first to address the assembly. Between the second and third sessions, he held his last general chapter of their Order, and resigned his office of superior. The few intervals of leisure were employed in preaching, and in establishing the confraternity of the Gonfalone.

The Greek deputies, at once charmed with the sweetness of the Saint, and convinced by his reasoning, agreed to all that was proposed. The Pope sung Mass in thanksgiving on the Feast of St. Peter and St. Paul. When the Gospel was sung, first in Latin and then in Greek, St. Bonaventura preached on the unity of the Faith: then the Creed was sung in Latin and in Greek, the words, "Who proceedeth from the Father and the Son" being thrice solemnly repeated. The anxieties and labors attendant on these public duties told on the already enfeebled frame of the Saint. He assisted at the fourth session of the council, but the following day it became manifest that his illness would terminate fatally. He himself seemed aware of it from the first, and calmly prepared for his approaching end. The Holy Father administered to him the last rites of the Church. The image of his crucified Lord, from which he had drawn so much love and wisdom during his earthly pilgrimage, was now his stay and consolation at its close. Calmly gazing on it with an expression of exceeding joy, he passed with a smile to the eternal embraces of his Beloved, July 14, 1274.

The funeral obsequies were attended by the Pope and his whole court. An historian of that age describes them as at once the most solemn and affecting ceremony of the kind ever witnessed, not excepting even the requiem of sovereign princes. Peter of Tarentaise, a Dominican friar, afterwards Pope under the title of Innocent IV., preached on the occasion. He did credit to himself, to his Order, and to the saint whom he eulogized. The tears of the orator and the lamentations of the assembled clergy testified their deep and sincere grief. The Church had indeed lost one of her brightest ornaments, while the personal bereavement was felt by not a few; the gentle and affectionate character of the Saint having endeared him to all who came within the range of his influence. St. Bonaventura was canonized by Sixtus IV. in 1482. Sixtus V. enrollod his name among the doctors of the Church. His relics were translated several times. In 1494, Charles VIII. founded a Franciscan monastery at Lyons, where they reposed in a rich chapel until 1562, when the Calvinists gratified their cupidity by plundering the shrine, and their sacrilegious hate by burning his relics and casting the ashes into the river Saone. The guardian of the convent, with several others, was stabbed to death; and the valuable library and manuscripts all destroyed. Some small portion of the saint's body which had been previously removed happily escaped the sacrilege.

Devotion to the mystery of the Adorable Eucharist was the life-long attraction of the Saint. His prayers of preparation for, and thanksgiving after Communion, are of unequalled beauty. The *Transfige, dulcissime Domine,* he composed for his own use. Often, particularly in his younger days, his deep humility made him fear to approach the holy Table to which his burning love attracted him daily more and more. Once, several days had passed in this conflict. Humility and love held equal balance; yet the young friar could not but weep; for how could he live without his Life? While he was hearing Mass in this state of perplexed love and sorrow, He for whom he so ardently pined, Himself rewarded the humility and love of His servant; and the Saint received by the ministry of an angel the Creator of the Heavenly Host. From this moment he no longer feared to approach frequently to the Adorable Sacrament; and in communion his soul was flooded with such ineffable joy, that it seemed as though a mortal frame could hardly support such raptures of love.

CHAPTER VIII.

St. Bernardine.—His early life.—Labors in the hospitals.—Preaching.—Influence on the order.—Death.—St. John Capistran.—His novitiate.—Penances.—His active exertions for the Church's welfare.—Hunniades.—St. Peter of Alcantara.—St. Teresa.

Two great Saints, born towards the close of the fourteenth century, exercised a considerable influence alike on the Order and on the age in which they lived. St. Bernardine was born at Massa, near Sienna, in 1380. He was of noble family; but his parents dying while he was still a child, the care of his education devolved on an aunt, who well fulfilled the trust imposed on her. From his very infancy she taught him to love the poor, and to practice the most tender devotion towards the immaculate mother of God. Even from childhood, Bernardine was a very model of piety. To serve at Mass, to spend hours at prayer in the churches, to give alms to the poor, were the chief, the only pleasures of the gentle boy; while by an exceeding natural sweetness and affability, he won the hearts of all who approached him. His love of mortification showed itself early. When only eleven, he began to fast every Saturday in honor of the Blessed Virgin, and to practice many other self-denials. Once, when a poor man came to beg an alms, and was sent away without any relief, Bernardine exclaimed, "For the love of God, let us give all we have to this poor man, or I will eat nothing to-day. I would far rather be without food than see the poor in want." After a time his uncle placed him at school; here he made rapid progress in every department of learning.

In the year 1400, an awful pestilence ravaged the Italian States. Bernardine was now at Sienna, and had for some time attended the hospitals there with great devotion. Several young men, attracted by his gentle and unobtrusive piety, joined him in this service of love. When the plague was at its height, and the terror stricken inhabitants dared not render the commonest services even to the nearest and dearest, Bernardine came forward and begged that the hospital might be placed under his charge. Young as he was, he proved himself fully adequate to the important duty. His companions imitated his heroic example, and in a few months multitudes of lives had been saved by their unwearied zeal, and a degree of order established in the hospital to which it had hitherto been a stranger. Bernardine persevered in his charitable occupation until the pestilence had passed away; then he sank under the fatigues he had so long endured, and for months was prostrate on a bed of sickness. He now gave as much edification by his patient resignation as formerly by his zealous charity. On his recovery he devoted himself to an old and saintly relative, who was blind and bed-ridden. After the death of this lady, Bernardine retired to a small house near the city, where he remained in solitude, asking in earnest prayer to know the will of God regarding his future life.

His decision was soon made: his heart had long yearned towards the Order of poverty and love, and he now entered the novitiate at a solitary convent called Colombiere, where the Fathers were of the Strict Observance. The year of his probation was and ever increasing fervor, and on the eighth of September, 1404, he made his solemn profession—he had chosen this day from a special devotion to our Blessed Lady. He was born on the feast of her Nativity, and now wished to place his birth in religion under her peculiar patronage. This was indeed a day especially chosen for all the principal actions of his life; on it he took the religious habit, made his vows, said his first Mass, preached his first sermon, and he died in the month dedicated specially to Mary's honor. His devotion to the Mother of God was indeed great; yet not greater than might have been expected in one whose love to Jesus burned with an ardor so far beyond our experience or conception. To preach the love of Jesus and the love of peace was the life-long employment of this gentle saint. So dear to him was the very sound of the holy name, that its utterance ravished him into transports of divine love; it was the music of his life, and he went about everywhere breathing its celestial melody into the hearts of his fellow-men. What marvel, then, that his converts should be numbered by thousands—that the sinner should be converted, the just strengthened and consoled? A celebrated preacher of that age, being asked why the sermons of the Friar Bernardine effected so much more good than his own, replied with a touching humility, Brother Bernardine is a furnace of love; and how can that which is only warm kindle a flame in the souls of others? But it was not merely his eloquence and the impassioned tide of fervor which he poured out on his hearers, that produced such wonderful fruit. He himself, in his instructions to other preachers, unconsciously told the secret of his success. Once when he was asked how to preach with profit, he declared they only could do so who practiced first themselves that which they preached to others, and sought only, with a most pure intention, the glory of Him for whom they labored. When first desired by his superiors to apply himself to preaching as his special mission, his natural weakness, increased by the excessive austerity of his life, and also a constant hoarseness, threatened to prove serious impediments to the usefulness of his labors. The obstacle was removed through the intercession of the Immaculate Mother of God, to whom he had recourse in his difficulty. His cure was so complete as to appear miraculous, and was, doubtless, no small encouragement to him in his painful labors.

St. Bernardine refused two bishoprics, not only offered to him, but pressed on his acceptance by different pontiffs. Preaching was his work, and this, he alleged, he could not continue as he desired, if burdened with episcopal cares. His devotion to the Holy Name of Jesus once threatened to bring him into serious trouble. He had caused this sacred name to be emblazoned on boards in letters of gold; often at the close of his sermons he would show them to his hearers, inviting them to some little practices of devotion in honor of that name at which every knee must bow. This practice was too holy not to meet with opposition. Heresy has always strangely shrunk from honoring the name of Jesus. Complaints were made; his burning love and the tenderness of his expressions were misconstrued by cold hearts, who censured what they could not understand. At length the Holy See took cognizance of the matter, and Bernardine was summoned to Rome. Martin V. then filled the chair of Peter; a brief examination into the life and doctrines of the Saint more than satisfied him, and Bernardine was dismissed with the Papal benediction, and leave to preach when and where he would.

The factions of the Guelphs and Ghibellines gave him abundant employment. Wherever there was discord he hastened, like a true Friar Minor, to preach peace. At Perugia he had once succeeded so far in quieting the turbulent spirits, that a general amnesty was proclaimed. One young nobleman, however, refused to join in it, and stood apart, muttering revenge. The Saint warned him that a sudden death would be the punishment of his impenitence. But he heeded not, and soon after the awful fate befell him, and he died without the sacraments.

The efforts of the Saint to preach peace accelerated his death. His last public sermon was on this subject, and was delivered at Massa, his native town. A malignant fever had settled on him, but the peace which was in his heart would give his tongue no rest; he spoke of it to all as he passed to the little town of Aquila, in the Abruzzi. There his illness increased so much that he became unable to leave his bed. After receiving the last rites of the Church he became speechless, but made earnest signs to be laid on the floor. His brethren complied with his request. Then his soul passed into the eternal enjoyment of that peace which passeth the understanding of even the most saintly while in our land of strife and exile.

St. Bernardine exercised the office of vicar-general of the Observants for five years, but resigned it to continue his favorite occupation of preaching; still, his influence was felt, and his saintly life served both as a stimulus to his brethren, and a means of drawing attention to the more fervent friars. Bernardine was succeeded by Brother Albert Sartianensis, who appointed St. John Capistran visitor of the provinces of France, England, etc. The Observants were early established, in Great Britain, and, as we shall see, obtained much assistance from its kings and nobles.

Pope Eugenius IV. especially favored this part of the Order, and, in 1445, bestowed on them the Convent of Ara Cœli.

Nor was the influence of St. John Capistran on his Order less remarkable, or less beneficial, than that of his saintly contemporary, though their careers were strikingly different. St. John did not enter the Order until the thirtieth year, and his antecedents by no means promised his after sanctity. His father was a gentleman of fortune, an officer in the Neapolitan service. St. John was born at Capistran in 1385, and when advanced to a sufficient age, chose the legal profession. His practice was in Perugia, where his fortune and abilities procured him every distinction he could desire. Soon after his marriage he was imprisoned, and most cruelly and unjustly treated, while endeavoring to make peace between the Perugians and Ladislaus, king of Naples. His wife died during his imprisonment, and St. John resolved at once to enter the Order of St. Francis. Impatient to effect his purpose, he sent to implore the habit from the fathers, but they refused it until he could enter their novitiate. His fervor brooked no delays, and he was fain to satisfy it by cutting his hair in the form of a tonsure, and contriving something that looked like a religious habit. Soon after, he sold his estate and thus purchased his ransom; his remaining property he bestowed on the poor. In 1415 he was received into the Franciscan Convent Del Monte at Perugia. His superiors treated him severely, either because they thought his vocation doubtful, or as knowing his sanctity could bear humiliations which to others would have been insurmountable; but the Saint had counted his cost, and was prepared for all. Twice he was expelled from the convent, without any reason being assigned for this proceeding, and could only obtain admission again by complying with the most humiliating conditions. Once he was ordered to ride through Perugia on an ass, with a paper cap placed on his head, on which many sins were written, as though he had been guilty of them. The Saint seemed scarcely to be conscious that it was a humiliation, and calmly obeyed the directions given him, while the Perugians must doubtless have thought that suffering and domestic calamity had unsettled the intellects of the once famous lawyer.*

But the talents of the Saint were by no means thrown aside as useless; they were to be employed now for their noblest end and in the most exalted manner. Hitherto he had pleaded with man for man; now he pleads with man for God. The full tide of his eloquence, the acuteness of his intellect, and his extraordinary talents, cultivated by all the learning of the age, were consecrated to the service of his Order. His fervor was not satisfied either with the austerities of his Rule, or the penances imposed on him by his superiors. With their permission he practiced mortifications which, even among his fervent brethren, seemed excessive. When preparing to receive the religious habit, he spent three days in prayer, without taking food of any kind; and, after his profession, he subsisted on one meal a day, except when on long and

* The Franciscan Order seems to have been a favorite with members of the legal profession. St. Ivo, the patron of lawyers, was a distinguished advocate, and equally renowned for his talents and his sanctity. Once, after harvest, a gentleman had in vain endeavored to persuade him to keep some corn for his own use. Shortly after, his friend met him, and exclaimed. "I have gained a fifth by keeping my corn." The Saint replied, "And I have gained a hundredfold by giving mine away." The history of St. Fidelis, another lawyer, is less known. After practicing his profession for several years with great reputation, he received the Franciscan habit among the Capuchins at Fribourg. On entering his novitiate, he was given the name of Fidelis, and truly did he merit the appellation. His saintly life was crowned by a martyr's crown. . The Calvinists did him this favor, and he died beneath their swords, with his arms extended in the form of a cross, and imploring mercy for his enemies. The Calvinist minister who urged the soldiers to execute him was soon after converted.

fatiguing journeys, when he took a very small collation at night. For six-and-thirty years he never tasted flesh meat, and three or four hours' rest taken on the ground was the only repose he allowed himself, however exhausted by his evangelical labors. His sermons touched his hearers so deeply, that often, when he preached on the vanities of earth and the joys of heaven, they would run eagerly to their houses, and bringing back all their superfluous ornaments, their perfumes, cards, and dice, burn them before him, in their zeal to begin a new and more perfect life. Knights, nobles, ladies of rank, simple peasants, all were alike moved by this "son of thunder." Like St. Bernardine, he was especially devoted to the holy name of Jesus, and to His Immaculate Mother. But his natural gifts and previous legal career superadded powers of eloquence that struck terror whenever he spoke of the more awful mysteries of the faith. The one Saint, charmed by his sweetness, had won the hearts of men by the tenderness of seraphic love. The other, a very Boanerges, overwhelmed the soul with the terrors of judgment and hell, until his alarmed hearers fled in very panic of fear to Him whose love alone could save them. After a sermon on the "Last Judgment," which he preached in Bohemia, one hundred and twenty young men forsook the world, lest they should perish with it, and of these, sixty demanded the habit of the Friars Minor. The missionary labors of the Saint commenced in the Italian States, but ere long, his zeal and the needs of the Church led him further. Bavaria, Austria, Bohemia, Hungary and Poland were successively evangelized by him, while in Germany, by the express command of Nicholas V., he preached a crusade against the Mahometan power.

The Christian world was at this period in a state of

more than usual disturbance ; and everywhere we find St. John the great instrument in the hand of God for promoting the Church's welfare. In 1437, when the Council of Basle was removed to Ferrara, he was employed by the Holy See to withdraw those who had unhappily fallen into the schism which then took place. In 1439, we find him acting as one of the theologians at the Council of Florence, the great object of which was to reconcile the Greeks. Shortly after, Eugenius IV., sent him into the March of Ancona, to repress the Fraticelli, who had again appeared to disturb Christian peace and unity. At the request of the Emperor, Frederic III., St. John was sent as apostolic legate to Germany. In all these missions he was eminently successful. It is said that in Moravia alone he converted four thousand Hussites.

Calixtus III. was even more anxious than his predecessor for the crusade against the infidels. His zeal, indeed, was not a little necessary ; for Mahomet II., flushed with the capture of Constantinople, was besieging Belgrade, not doubting that he would soon be master of Christendom. Strange, that a mendicant friar should have been called in by the brave Hunniades as his best auxiliary in humbling the Turkish power. This great general was the very model of a Christian hero. Appointed guardian of the young king Ladislaus during his long minority, he had well and faithfully fulfilled his important charge ; and now that danger menaced the Church and the State he was prepared to meet the emergency. Assembling a fleet of a hundred and sixty vessels, he met the Turks, who had sailed up the Danube, with a much more powerful force. A sanguinary engagement ensued. The infidels were routed, and Hunniades and his brave troops entered Belgrade. St. John, who had brought forty thousand crusaders to the rescue, appeared everywhere in the foremost ranks, encouraging the soldiers to fight bravely for their faith, and holding in his hands a cross which had been blessed for the occasion by the Pope.

The Turks at last roused their courage, ashamed to see themselves conquered by a force so inferior to their own. They entered the town and repulsed the Christians. Even the valor of Hunniades would hardly have saved it from destruction, had not St. John himself rallied the soldiers to a second victory. He threw himself before the Crusaders, and braving all personal danger, cried out: "Victory, Jesus! victory!" thus animating the warriors to aspire to a martyr's crown. Ere a few hours had passed Mahomet was finally overcome, his best officers slain, himself wounded, and, on the 6th of August, he raised the siege, leaving behind him all his artillery and baggage.

The noble-hearted Hunniades soon after received the eternal recompense of his warfare for God. The fatigues of the campaign brought on a malady which proved fatal. St. John never left him during his last sickness. When the dying warrior was told to prepare for the holy Viaticum, he rose from his bed, and declared he would go to the church to receive his Lord, thinking it too great an honor that the King of kings should be brought to him. Shortly after this heroic act of faith and devotion he departed calmly to the land of unending peace. His death was considered a universal calamity, and he was mourned for throughout Christendom. The Pope himself wept bitterly, and Mahomet declared there was now no one left in the world whom it would be either an honor or a pleasure to conquer.

St. John did not long survive his warrior friend.

Scarcely had he pronounced his funeral oration, ere he too was seized with fever, which soon took him home. Princes, nobles, and peasants flocked to the convent where he lay dying, to receive his last blessing and hear his last words. On the 23d of October, 1456, he passed peacefully to the abode of the blessed. His shrine was desecrated by the Lutherans, but the relics were afterwards discovered. St. John was canonized by Alexander VIII., in 1690.

In the year 1454, Henry VI. used every argument and entreaty to induce this saint to visit England. The better to insure his purpose, the Marquis of Baden was desired personally to solicit the favor. A very beautiful letter is still extant which St. John wrote on this occasion to the English king. Henry had offered to build some convents for the friars of the Strict Observance, and St. John writes in reply: "Moreover, concerning the building of new monasteries to the honor of God, and to the memory of St. Bernardine, I add no more to your pious disposition, but that (as I have said) faith without good works availeth nothing; wherefore, if you are pleased to build the said monasteries, I would have you know that you build (not for me or others, but) for yourself so many everlasting palaces in heaven." A present of some relics of St. Bernardine, which the king had requested, accompanied this letter, in concluding which St. John expresses the most lively regret that the obedience he had received to go to Hungary, and the great spiritual necessities of that country, made it impossible for him to visit England.

In 1430, St. John Capistran made an effort to unite the Conventuals and the Observants, which met with only a temporary success. In 1434, the Observants were put in possession of the holy places in Palestine;

and shortly after, they had so increased, that separate vicar-generals were appointed for the cismontanes and the ultramontanes. The former were placed under the direction of the Saint. In 1506, the cismontanes had twenty-five provinces, exclusive of the Holy Land, and about seven hundred convents. The ultramontanes reckoned twenty provinces and three guardianships, with about six hundred convents. These, however, were greatly increased, when Leo X. united all the reforms into one. In 1517, this Pope made most important and excellent regulations for the government of the Order. He required the Conventuals to submit to the Observants, as the latter kept most strictly to the letter of their Rule. Each was allowed to elect their own superior, and to hold their own general chapter; but he required those elected by the Conventuals to be confirmed by the minister-general of the Observants; or, as they were now called, the Friars Minor of the Regular Observance. It was also decreed that, on all public occasions, the Observants should take the first place, and these arrangements, being confirmed by a bull, proved of the greatest advantage to the Order. In time, it is true, some other reforms arose; but they were rather distinguished by the names of the Saints whose influence had promoted them, than by any real difference in character from the Observants.

Of these reforms the most remarkable was that of St. Peter of Alcantara. This Saint was born in the city from which he is named, and of parents whose extraction was noble. His father had been for some years governor of Alcantara. At the age of sixteen, St. Peter entered the Franciscan Convent of Mangarez; and from the time of his entrance to the last moment of his life his austerities were unabated. For a time he was permitted to live alone in a rude hut, which he had built for himself; but he could not even thus conceal the mortifications he practiced, nor the marvellous graces bestowed on him. In 1519, though but in his twentieth year, he was employed to found a new monastery at Badajos; and when his three years of superiority were ended, he was required to prepare for Sacred Orders. Afterwards he was employed in preaching, and his fame spread rapidly in all directions. The Portuguese king, John III., desiring to see one so famous for his eloquence and his miracles, requested that the Saint would visit him. The result was the vocation of his royal sister, the Princess Mary; who made the vows of a religious, though, by the advice of St. Peter, she still continued to live at court. This princess was a munificent pratroness of the Poor Clares. She founded for them a convent at Lisbon, where the strictest observance was maintained, and where many noble ladies consecrated themselves to God.

While still young, the Saint was elected provincial; and in 1540 he endeavored to introduce a more austere Rule among the Spanish Franciscans, but his plans were not approved by his brethren; few, indeed, had a vocation for austerities so great. His time of superiority having expired, the Saint retired to Portugal with Father John of Aquila. Here they joined Father Martin of St. Mary, who was living a most austere life in a mountain near the mouth of the Tagus. They were visited by the general of the Order, F. John Calrus; who was so charmed with their simple and humble life, that he gave them permission to receive novices, his companion being the first to join them. This, however, did not serve to extend the reform. Father Martin died shortly after, and St. Peter was recalled by his superiors. Still, the desire to see a convent established where his own strict Rule would be carried out, was ever uppermost in his mind.

With this view he applied to Pope Julius III., and obtained the permission he desired. But, though the Strict Observance of the Alcantarines (called in Italy the Riformati, and in France the Recollets) was thus established, it never extended greatly; and probably St. Peter did more service to his Order by his personal sanctity, and to religion by the assistance he gave to St. Teresa, than by his efforts in founding convents. His introduction to that great Saint was so purely providential and unexpected, that it is supposed her trials and her sanctity were revealed to him by God. Those who are familiar with her history, and aware of the opposition she had to encounter, particularly in endeavoring to carry out the poverty of her Rule, can in some degree value the support she received from St. Peter, whom she calls the father and author of this reform.*

Of the first subjects who presented themselves for this undertaking he provided four; and, during the latter part of his life, his chief wish appeared to be that he might see her foundations well established before he died. Nor did his care end even with his life. After he had passed to the eternal enjoyment of the Master whom he had so faithfully served, he still remembered and aided his child, who yet remained in exile. At the moment of his death he appeared to

* St. Teresa herself writes thus of St. Clare, "As I was going to receive the Blessed Sacrament on St. Clare's day, that virgin appeared to me in wonderful beauty, and bade me vigorously pursue the work I had begun; for she would aid me. Hereupon I became greatly devoted to her; and what she said proved exactly true, for a monastery of nuns of her Order that was near helped to keep us; and what is more, she brought this my desire punctually to be accomplished, that the same poverty which is observed in the monastery of this blessed Saint is now observed in this of ours. And further, our Lord provides in such manner for us (perhaps upon the prayers of this blessed Saint), that, without so much as our asking, all necessaries are abundantly sent to us."

her, surrounded by indescribable brightness, to console and help her amid her many trials. Shortly after this apparition, she had another vision of the Saint, seated on a glorious throne. On this occasion, he told her that he would especially assist all who humbly and devoutly invoked him. Once again, when she had all but yielded to the persuasions and oppositions of those who could neither share nor appreciate her ardent desire of perfection, St. Peter visited her. His countenance was now sad and stern, and he warned her not to let human respect influence her conduct, whatever she might suffer by her firm resistance. Indeed, so constant were his visits, and so opportune the aid thus afforded, that St. Teresa often declared the Franciscan friar had assisted her more by his apparitions after death than by his visits during life.

CHAPTER IX.

The Order in England.—Henry VIII. a warm patron of the Observants.—Queen Catherine a Tertiary Franciscan.—Persecution begins.—The Franciscans openly oppose the Divorce.—Martyrdom of Friar Forrest—Queen Catherine's confessor.—Letters.—Friar Peto.

The early years of the reign of King Henry VIII. found the Franciscan province in England as flourishing as its most ardent well-wishers could desire. The strict reform of the Observants had been generally embraced throughout the country; or rather, the friars in England had hitherto maintained so strict a poverty as to need little reform. When, therefore, the Order was divided into Conventuals and Observants, they naturally took their place in the latter division. Henry showed special partiality to the Order, and even wrote to the Pope on behalf of the Observants. He gave a grant of a thousand crowns yearly towards the maintenance of the friars in Palestine, the original of which grant Wadding had in his possession. He gives a copy of it in his annals. It begins thus: "*Innatum studium quo erga vestram familiam ab ineunte ætate sumus affecti, ob evangelicæ vitæ imitationem*," etc. Queen Catherine was a Tertiary Franciscan; and when the court was at Greenwich, she was accustomed to rise at midnight to recite the Divine Office in the church, while the friars sang it in their choir.

Of Henry's fall, and its unhappy consequences, we need only speak so far as may illustrate the history of the Order and its sufferings in England at that eventful period. It is a well-established fact that he never thought of proclaiming himself head of the Church, or founding a new religion, until he saw that the successor of Peter would neither be bribed nor intimidated into sanctioning his lawless passion. Probably, when he took the first downward step, he little foresaw where his course would end. It was not until the universities and divines had refused to give a favorable opinion regarding the king's divorce that he turned to the German reformers. The French king had been won by four hundred thousand crowns, and the "lily of diamonds," worth, at least, fifty thousand, to exact an approbation from the theological faculty at Paris; but, to their eternal credit, they were firm, and Francis had no other resource but to oblige his royal friend with a spurious decree, which Henry published as the real decision of that university. Luther and Melancthon were more accommodating, and would have allowed him the patriarchal privilege of a second wife; but Cromwell came to the rescue when all resources seemed to have failed, and his advice proved at once the ruin of the king's conscience and the destruction of religious houses. With many expressions of humility and diffidence in his own judgment, he suggested the course to be pursued. The approbation of the Holy See, he said, was the only thing still wanting—but was this necessary? True, it might be useful to check the resentment of the German emperor; but if it could not be obtained, why should the king's pleasure depend on the will of another. Many of the German princes had thrown off their allegiance to the Papal authority; why, then, should not the English king? The law could establish a Church of its own, and mould it to the will of the sovereign. Let the Parliament declare Henry the head of the Church, and all difficulties would be soon disposed of. The law could frame its articles of faith and sanction its canons, and, obviously, the founder of a new religion could regulate its morals as well as its belief.

This counsel was but too acceptable to a monarch resolved to gratify his evil passions at all hazards, temporal or eternal. The crafty statesman was advanced to the Privy Council, and already anticipated the spoils of the richly endowed charities of Catholic England. The statutes of *præmunire* had already been passed, and power given to the sovereign to modify or suspend their operation at his discretion. Wolsey had, it is true, obtained a patent under the great seal, authorizing him to exercise the legatine authority; he was, however, accused of violating the law, and the clergy were condemned for admitting his jurisdiction. The attorney-general was required to file a bill in the King's Bench against the whole ecclesiastical body. Convocations met and offered to compound the matter by a present of one hundred thousand pounds. To their surprise, the offer was refused, unless they would acknowledge the king "to be the protector and only supreme head of the Church and clergy of England." After several days passed in warm debate, the clause "*as far as the law of Christ will allow*," was inserted. This clause obviously invalidated the acknowledgment required, since those who rejected the royal supremacy could maintain that it was not allowed by the law of Christ; however, it answered the king's purpose for the time, and so was graciously accepted.

The dismissal of Catharine from the Court, and the public acknowledgment of Anne Boleyn as queen, soon followed, while the death of Archbishop Warham, whose attachment to the faith could not have been easily shaken, opened the way for the advancement of Cranmer, whose conscience was not troubled with many scruples, when they would interfere with his temporal adavncement. He was, indeed, a fitting person to carry out the king's projects of divorce and of ecclesiastical change. Accordingly, we find him, after a series of miserable subterfuges, of which a respectable heathen might have been ashamed, pronouncing judgment on the divorce, and declaring it not only allowable, but right and lawful. Henry had now only two subjects of anxiety—one was to secure the succession, the other to establish his ecclesiastical supremacy. The first, indeed, depended on the second. If he remained in communion with the Catholic Church, the succession was at once invalidated, and the lady who now shared his throne was the usurper of the honors and the rights of his lawful queen. All persons, lay or ecclesiastic, were now required to take the oath of succession. The next step was a parliamentary acknowledgment of the king's supremacy in matters ecclesiastical, and, as a necessary consequence, his right to receive the first fruits of all benefices and spiritual dignities.

The storm now began in earnest. Cranmer made the opportune discovery that the Pope was Antichrist, and his very name was required to be erased from every book in the kingdom, as though some spell lurked in its four simple letters. Bishops and priests were bidden to inculcate the new doctrine at the peril of their lives, and some appearance of submission was thus obtained among the secular clergy; but there was still a large body of religious men, whom neither fear nor favor could sway for a moment. Of these, the foremost and the bravest were the Carthusians, the Bridgetins, and the Franciscans of the Observance. The strict poverty which these religious observed saved them from one great source of temptation, and perhaps the courage which they received in the day of trial was a reward for their lives of constant extreme austerity and self-sacrifice. Accordingly, the priors of the three Chartreuses, or Charterhouses, of London, Axeholm, and Belleval, with Reynolds, a monk of Sion, and Haile, a secular priest, were executed in the atrocious manner then common in cases of treason, because they would not take an oath which as yet had not been sanctioned by the Parliament. Three monks from the London Charterhouse soon followed. These executions, as well as all the rest, were carried out with a barbarity too horrible to relate, the quivering victim often dying with the name of Jesus on his lips, while the executioner was tearing out his heart.

Father Forrest was one of the first who suffered from the royal displeasure. His position as provincial would mark him out as a special object for the royal vengeance; but his office of confessor to the ill-fated Catharine was doubtless the cause of his early execution. He was imprisoned on pretence of having opposed Latimer; but the real cause was the zeal which he and his Order had manifested in opposing the divorce. Forrest had entered the Order while young; he completed his studies at Oxford, and either there, or at Paris, was made doctor of divinity; soon after he was appointed the queen's confessor, probably from the regard which Henry either entertained or professed for the Franciscans. This duty brought with it a long train of sorrows, which ended in the glories of a martyr's crown. He was accused of denying the king's supremacy in spiritual matters, or, as an old rhyme has it,

Forrest the fryar,
That obstinate lyar,
That willfully will be dead;
  Incontinently
The gospel doth deny,
  The king to be supreme head—

Though neither rhyme nor reason informed the poor friar in what part of the Gospel the keys of the kingdom of heaven had been given to a temporal prince. But in that reign the Gospel and the royal will were synonymous terms, and certainly to deny that, was "willfully to be dead," were the unbeliever priest or layman. Forrest was one of the earliest to suffer. The king supposed that he could have influenced his royal penitent, and induced her to enter a convent and renounce her rightful claims; that he did not do so was reason enough for a summary vengeance. Father Forrest was imprisoned in 1533. About this time he had written a book, "Of the Authority of the Church and the Pope," which opens with this sentence: "Let no man assume to himself this honor, unless he be called, as Aaron." Such plain speaking by no means improved his temporal prospects, and he was condemned to die for his "willfulness." For some reason, which does not appear, his execution was delayed several years. During his imprisonment he found means to correspond with and console his royal mistress, to whom he appears to have been most sincerely attached. The queen herself writes to her suffering confessor in so pious and touching a strain that we cannot altogether omit a notice of these letters, which are extant.

Catherine was the first to write. The news of Forrest's imprisonment had deeply affected her; indeed, Sanders says that it was one of her most cruel sufferings. We cannot but admire the resignation, nay, the heroic love of the cross, which every line of her letter breathes:

My Reverend Father,—You, who have been accustomed to give advice to others under hard circumstances, cannot be at a loss of what is most proper to be suggested to yourself, now you are to be put to the trial for Christ's cause. If you will bear those few and short torments to which you are condemned, you will (as you know very well) receive an everlasting reward; which, whosoever will choose to lose for any tribulation of this life, seems to be wholly void of all sense and reason. But, O you, my happy Father, to whom God has granted the blessing of knowing this above many mortals, and of finishing your life and the course of your labor by these chains, by these torments, and by this most cruel death for Christ! and, O me, your wretched daughter, who, in this sad time of my distress and solitude, am to be deprived of such a monitor and a father, so beloved in the bowels of Jesus Christ! And truly, if I may freely confess my most earnest desires in this matter to you, to whom I have always (as I ought) laid open all the secrets of my heart and conscience, I acknowledge to you that my most ardent wishes are to die with you or before you, and that also with the greatest torments imaginable, provided it were pleasing to the Divine will, to whom I always submit all my desires most willingly, as also my life itself; so far am I from any enjoyment of this unhappy world, after those are gone whom the world was not worthy of. Go before me, therefore, my reverend Father, happily and courageously, and be importune with Christ in your prayers, that by this, though difficult way, I may soon without fear follow you. And in the meantime, I desire this as your last blessing in this life, that I may be a partaker of your holy labor, of your torments, and of your conflicts, and after your sufferings and your crown, I shall expect more plentiful favors from heaven by your intercession. And I think it superfluous to animate you to that immortal reward, preferable to all other goods, though purchased with the most excessive pains; you, who by your birth are entitled to a generous mind—you, who from your very youth have (which is the main) been trained up in the holy religion and professions of a Franciscan. Yet, since to suffer for God's sake is the greatest happiness bestowed upon man in this life, I will implore His Divine Majesty with continual prayers, tears, and penitential labors, that you may happily finish your course, and may obtain a never-fading crown of eternal life. Farewell, my reverend Father, and be always mindful of me with God, both on earth and in heaven.

Your sorrowful daughter, CATHERINE.

We now subjoin the reply of the generous confessor:

MOST SERENE PRINCESS, MY SOVEREIGN QUEEN, AND MY DAUGHTER IN JESUS CHRIST,—Your Majesty's servant delivered to me your most gracious letter, which was not only a great joy and consolation to me, but also a fresh encouragement to patience and constancy in this my affliction and continued expectation of death. For, though I plainly see that not only all perishing goods, but likewise all the miseries and evils of this world, are to be despised for the future glory which will be revealed in us, if we fight a good fight; yet I find my soul, which (as it is usual with human nature on the like occasions) was somewhat heavy and pensive on the near view of death, and not without some fear and solicitude on the consideration of its own unworthiness and frailty, is now enlivened by those most pious expressions of your great charity, and wonderfully animated in the contempt of all torments, and inspirited with a fresh fervor in the hopes and contemplation of future joys. My Sovereign Lady and well-beloved Daughter, may Jesus Christ reward your goodness with eternal glory and bliss for this consolation; and I do most earnestly beseech you to recommend my approaching sufferings, conflict, and agony to the Divine mercy, and to assist me therein by your continual prayers. And for the rest, I do most humbly entreat you not to doubt of my constancy, nor to be troubled for the grievousness of the torments appointed for me; for it does not become my gray hairs to be disturbed in God's cause with such childish bugbears; it does not become a man to fly from death basely, after he has lived sixty-four years. Much less does it become a religious man not to love God, and with his utmost endeavors aspire to heavenly things, after he has been for four-and-forty years in the habit of St. Francis, learning and teaching the contempt of all that is earthly. I will be mindful of you (my Sovereign Lady and Daughter in Christ) both in this life and in the next; and will never cease from praying to the God of Mercy to give you, according to the greatness of your sorrows, all grace and comfort. In the meantime, vouchsafe to pray most earnestly for me, your devoted servant and beadsman, especially at the hour when you shall understand I am to be laboring under those dreadful torments prepared for me. I presume to make you a poor present of my beads, having, as it is given out, but three days longer to live on earth.

The immediate execution of the friar was expected, when these letters were written; but, as we have said, it was delayed for a time, and Catherine was spared the account of the barbarities which accompanied it. Of this, we now proceed to give some account. A strange old Welsh legend had declared that the celebrated crucifix at Darvel Gatharen would one day burn a forest. Whether to prove the tradition true, or by a singular coincidence, this venerable relic was used as part of the funeral pile of the martyred friar. On the morning of the 22d of May, 1538, Forrest was drawn on a hurdle to Smithfield, the place appointed for his execution. Here he was suspended by iron chains from a high gallows, beneatn which a fire was slowly kindled, that his torments might be the more protracted. It would seem as if Divine Providence would have his merits increased; for a strong breeze arose which drove the flames from his body, and, even when they did reach him, checked their fury; so that his tortures were increased as much as his enemies could have desired. When he arrived at the place of execution, he cried out, with the heroic fervor of the Church's early martyrs: "O Lord God! neither fire, nor gallows, nor any other torment whatsoever, shall part me from Thee." Hugh Latimer, who was present on this occasion, used all his efforts to shake the martyr's constancy. But he courageously declared, that if an angel should come down from heaven to teach him any other doctrine than that which he had been taught from his childhood, he would not hearken to him; that if they cut him to pieces, joint by joint, and limb from limb, still he would not swerve from the faith of his fathers.

The storm of persecution now fell thick and fast, and the noblest and best of England's children were not spared. More* and Fisher had already bowed their heads beneath the fatal axe, rather than frame their religious belief by that of their sovereign and his

* Sir Thomas More's son-in-law, Roper, gives the following account of his condemnation: "Mr. Rich, pretending freely to talk with him, among other things of a set course, said this unto him: 'Admit there were, sir, an act of parliament that the realm should take me for king, would not you, Mr. More, take me for king?' 'Yes, sir,' quoth Sir Thomas More, 'that I would.' 'I put the case further,' quoth Mr. Rich, 'that there were an act of parliament that all the realm should take me for pope, would not you then, Master More, take me for pope?' 'For answer, sir,' quoth Sir Thomas More, 'to your first case, the parliament may well, Master Rich, meddle with the state of temporal princes; but to make answer to your other case, I will put you this case. Suppose the parliament should make a law that God should not be God? would you then, Master Rich, say that God were not God!' 'No, sir,' quoth he, 'that I would not, sith no parliament may make any such law.' 'No more,' quoth Sir Thomas More, 'could the parliament make the king supreme head of the Church.' Upon whose only report was Sir Thomas indicted of high treason on the statute to deny the king to be supreme head of the Church, into which indictment were put these heinous words—maliciously, traitorously, and diabolically."

advisers. Soon after the martyrdom of Forrest, thirty-two Franciscans died in various prisons in consequence of the severe usage they received. They are commemorated in the Franciscan martyrology on the last day of July. In 1539, the convent and church at Oxford were seized and confiscated to the crown. Dr. London was the chief instrument in this act of injustice and sacrilege. A few of the expelled friars received for a time a miserable pittance from the proceeds of the sale of their property; others were compelled to leave the country, and starve or beg in foreign lands. Henry was afraid to execute too great a number, lest public indignation should be aroused at such outrages on men who were revered by all but their interested accusers.

Friar Peto was one of the earliest who suffered from the royal vengeance. He was an Observantine friar, and guardian of the convent at Greenwich. Perhaps the Franciscan Order never gave a more glorious example of its contempt of all earthly fame and favors than was now given in the determined opposition of the friars to their royal patron, and their firm adherence to his persecuted queen. Peto's first offence was given in a sermon which he preached at Greenwich before the king. The subject was, "Elias reproving Achab;" and the moral plainly pointed at the king's present position as equally sinful and scandalous. The friar, indeed, used very plain language, and told the king that whatever opinions he might extort from the learned, or obtain by bribes or threats from his preachers, they only sought to procure his favor at the expense of his conscience and their own. At first, Henry appeared to take the sermon in good part; but he desired Dr. Curwin to preach on the following Sunday, and to endeavor to remove the unfavorable impression made by Peto's plain speaking.

The Doctor fulfilled the royal command *con amore*—styled Peto a "dog," and expressed his own full and unqualified approval of whatever had been, or might be done, or believed by the king, now supreme head of the Church. Meanwhile Peto had been summoned to Canterbury on the affairs of his Order. Another friar named Elstow was therefore deputed to reply to Curwin. This religious proved even more energetic in his denunciations. Both were therefore called to appear before the Privy Council, which was now empowered to decide questions theological as well as civil. Their mode of proceeding had at least the merit of simplicity. To argue and explain would have been undignified and a waste of time. The king was supreme head of the Church; therefore his authority was infallible in all matters of faith. It was true that Henry had not discovered his ecclesiastical authority till the successor of St. Peter had refused him permission to repudiate his lawful wife; but the Privy Council were not obliged to show how, or when, the king had become infallible. Might was right, and their theology resolved itself into that of the axe and cord. Death or submission was therefore the simple alternative.

The friars Elstow and Peto were brought before the Council. The Earl of Essex presided, and addressing them in angry tones, declared that they deserved to be tied in a sack and thrown into the Thames. "My lord," replied Elstow, "keep your threats for those that fear them. You may alarm your court epicures with such words as these; men that have lost their courage in their palates, and softened their minds with pomp and pleasure. Such persons are tied to the world by their lusts and senses, and will yield to a word. But for us, we thank God, who gives us courage in our trials, and who think it an honor to suffer for our consciences.

And as for your Thames, the road to heaven is as sure by water as by land, and therefore it matters little to us what way we go."

Fear of public opinion, or the boldness of the friars, saved them for a time from the executioner. A sentence of banishment from the kingdom was passed, and they were driven into exile with two hundred of their brethren. Many of these escaped death through the influence of Sir Thomas Wriothesley, who was still in favor, and who warmly defended the friars, as far as was possible. Hundreds, however, died in prison from their sufferings; while many, like Father Forrest, obtained more speedily a martyr's crown.

CHAPTER X.

Other Franciscan martyrs in England.—Father Brockbey.—Cort.—Belchiam.—Libraries destroyed.—Friar John.—Father Buckley is allowed to hang until he is dead.—Father Gennings.—His conversion.—Restores the English province.—Father John Baptist—Father Heath.—His conversion—zeal—martyrdom.—Conversion of his father, who becomes a lay brother.—Sees his son's sufferings and triumph in a vision.—Father Bell.—His letters before his martyrdom.—Scotland.

Father Antony Brockbey was another who suffered for his boldness in opposing the king's pseudo-marriage. This religious had been educated at St. Mary Magdalene's College in Oxford, where he was made professor of divinity. His knowledge of Greek and Hebrew was considerable, and he was celebrated as a preacher. After a sermon delivered in St. Lawrence's church in London, Brockbey was thrown into prison, and there so severely racked that he was unable to raise his hand to feed himself. A pious matron came daily to his prison to perform this office for him, regardless of the dangers to which she thus exposed herself. At the end of six weeks, the friar obtained a martyr's crown—being strangled in prison with his own cord.* He is commemorated in the Franciscan martyrology on the 19th of July. On the 27th of the same month, Brother Thomas Cort followed his friend. He died from the combined effects of starvation and of disease produced by the loathsomeness of his dungeon. This holy friar was of noble birth, and had renounced wealth and fame for Christ. At the moment of his death, the prison was filled with a glorious light, which so alarmed and surprised his jailers, that the matter was reported to the king. In consequence of this, or from respect to his family, he was buried honorably.

The martyrdom of Brother Thomas Belchiam occurred in the same year, 1537. He was literally starved to death; so that, says the Chronicle, "there remained nothing of him but skin and bone." The vigor of his soul, however, did but increase with the decay of his body. His last words were: "In Thee, O Lord! have I hoped: let me never be confounded." It is said that a work of great learning which he wrote was presented to Henry, and that the monarch wept bitterly during the perusal of it. The result, however, showed how little real impression it had made on that sin-hardened heart.

The universities were, of course, visited by the same sweeping scourge that desolated the homes of religion. The schools of the friars established there, were distin-

* The cord of St. Francis. This is worn both by the Franciscans and Poor Clares over their religious habit, and by the Tertiaries under their secular attire. It is simply a long cord of a hempen or woollen material, which passes round the waist, and hangs down at the side. It has five large knots on the part pendant, in memory of the Five Wounds of our Divine Lord, and of the mysterious Stigmata of St. Francis. It was frequently used as a means of executing the friars both in England and Ireland; and surely they must have esteemed it no common grace thus to end their religious career.

guished for the learning, no less than the piety of their members, and for the literary treasures collected in their libraries. Leighton and Dr. London, however, being sent to purge out "Popery," from those ancient seats of learning, determined that neither book nor manuscript should be spared, that might tend to its continuance or ultimate revival. Whatever escaped their zeal, received its *coup de grace* from the advisers of the weak-minded Edward; and if London could boast that he had "bound Duns Scotus in Bocardo," Edward might congratulate himself over the "*Funus, seu exequiæ Scoti et Scotistarum*," in which not only the works of that learned doctor, but countless volumes of the most venerable antiquity, priceless to the man of letters as to the theologian, were committed to the flames.

On the accession of Mary, the Franciscans removed to Greenwich, and another house was built for them in London. As they were restored before any of the other Orders, it is probable the queen had a particular regard for them. She could not well forget what they had suffered in defending the cause of her royal mother. The Franciscans might now have retaliated on those who caused them so much suffering; but their holy faith taught them a different lesson, and one which they did not fail to practice. Alphonsus, confessor of Philip, and a Friar Minor, was the first to speak against the severities exercised in this reign. It is true, the so-called reformers had brought these on themselves, and seemed to justify them by plotting against their lawful sovereign. Indeed, a candid historian of the reigns of Henry, Mary, and Elizabeth, cannot but remark the difference between the punishments inflicted under their respective governments. The reformers were the first to urge persecution, and to practice it, not against Catholics only, but even against those who, holding in the main their own opinions, still claimed liberty to differ from them in details. On the other hand, the priests and Catholic ecclesiastics were ever forward to recommend mercy, and to condemn any persecutions to which a false zeal might urge the temporal power.

One of the first acts of Elizabeth was to suppress the convent at Greenwich and to expel the friars, though in their church she had received holy baptism.

A certain Friar John, whom the Earl of Derby took under his protection, and who lived at this period, also deserves notice. So great was the fame of his miracles, and his reputation for sanctity, that Elizabeth was prevailed on by the Earl to give him special letters of protection, and to allow him to wear his habit publicly. He lived in a retired part of Lancashire, and died in a good old age. Here, when confined to bed with his last sickness, the people still flocked to him to cure their diseases, and even cattle were brought to him from distant counties. But Friar John was an exception, and the only one, to the universal rule of persecution.

In 1598, we find Brother John Buckley among the white-robed army of martyrs, and to him was granted the unusual favor of being allowed to hang until he was dead. This friar was a native of Wales, and entered the Order while still young. After an imprisonment at Wisbeach Castle, he went abroad, and remained a short time at the convent of Ara Cœli in Rome. But a burning thirst for martyrdom, and an earnest zeal for the salvation of his countrymen, gave him no rest. With the permission of his superiors he set out for England. Before his departure, he threw himself at the feet of Clement VIII., to crave his benediction. It is said that the Holy Father embraced him with peculiar tenderness, and exclaimed, "Go, you are a true child of St. Francis, and pray to God for me and for the holy Church." Buckley was imprisoned soon after his return to England. After four or five years' patient suffering, during which he continued to labor, as far as he could, for the salvation of souls, he was executed. His only crime was that he had received Holy Orders; and this from the very same source whence the ministers of the Established Church, who were foremost in condemning him, professed to derive their own authority.

The English Franciscans were now entirely dispersed, their convents suppressed, and the province broken up. The friars who had escaped imprisonment, or missed the grace of martyrdom, were scattered here and there on the Continent. Never did destruction seem more complete; but, as we shall presently see, never was restoration more triumphant. Who would have supposed that a restorer of the fallen, a confirmer of the wavering, should arise from the very ranks of those who had been foremost to oppose the Catholic faith? Yet, so it was. The saintly Father Gennings, by whose prayers and exertions this great work was accomplished, was a convert. Born in Staffordshire, and descended from an ancient family of great respectability, the young man's early career gave no promise of its glorious end. His eldest brother had renounced the heresy in which he had been educated, at the early age of sixteen. His martyrdom, which occurred soon after he was made priest, was the first circumstance which aroused his thoughtless brother. The parents of these young men appear to have died before their conversion; as we find Edmund Gennings leading a life of thoughtless dissipation in London, at the very time of his brother's execution, and apparently subject to no control but that of his own inclinations. The martyr, before his happy end, had made every effort which fraternal love could suggest, for the conversion of his brother; but it appeared as if his efforts were to fail. Doubtless, his prayers in his last agony, and perhaps his first supplications in Paradise, were for the same intention; since the conversion of the dissipated youth was little short of miraculous.

A few evenings after his brother's death, he returned from a party of pleasure, and, weary even of amusement, shut himself up alone; perhaps thoughts of his early home, of household kindness, and gentle words, came before him. He frequently thought of his martyred brother, and a strong feeling of curiosity arose in his mind to know something of that Faith, which could thus brave death and torments, and prefer a life of ignominy and suffering to one of respectability and ease. He remembered, also, that his brother had once been as bitterly opposed to the Catholic Faith as himself. The result of his lonely musing was a conviction that the life he was leading was sinful, and he resolved to inquire what Catholics believed. The inquiry soon led to conversion, and to a most zealous amendment of life. In 1607, Gennings was ordained priest at Douay College, that "blessed school of faith and martyrdom." Four years later, he entered the Franciscan Order, and soon after received the seal of the English province from Father Stanney, with full powers to effect its restoration. In 1616 he had six subjects prepared for this undertaking; they were assembled at Gravelines, but soon removed to Douay, where he established the convent of Bonaventura. In 1625, a General Chapter of the Order declared that the English province should be restored as soon as there were a sufficient number of subjects. In 1629, Father Gennings was made provincial, and, in 1630, the first chapter was held in Brussels.

It now only remains for us to notice briefly a few of the martyrs of the restored province. One of the first of this happy number was Father John Baptist. Thomas Bullaker, his father, was of an old Catholic family, and practiced physic with great reputation at Chichester. He sent his son, while still young, to pursue his education at the English college of Valladolid, and here he received his vocation. By the advice of the saintly Father Baker, who was his confessor, he entered the convent of Recollects of the Immaculate Conception, at Abroyo. After being admitted to Holy Orders, he expressed an earnest desire for the foreign mission; but, by the advice of his superiors, chose England in preference. He was imprisoned a few days after his arrival, and confined for a long time in Exeter jail, then one of the worst in the kingdom. Here he passed the winter of 1630. Though afterwards released by the interposition of powerful friends, he never recovered the severities of his incarceration. After a short time, spent in the secret exercise of his priestly functions for the benefit of his persecuted brethren, he was again arrested. Acknowledging at once that he was a priest, he was condemned to immediate execution. At his trial he uttered a remarkable prediction, which was printed in the *Certamen Seraphicum* several years before its fulfillment. In answer to one of the questions put to him, he said: "I assure you, that in the very next parliament which shall sit, that very religion (the Presbyterian,) which you now pretend to establish, will be overthrown." He was executed with the usual barbarities on the 12th of October, 1642.

The next year Father Henry Heath and Father Francis Bell also suffered. The history of their sufferings, and of the conversion of Father Heath, is too interesting to be entirely omitted. Like many converts, this saintly Father might be said to have read himself into the Church. Educated a Protestant he never doubted the grounds of his extraordinary belief, till his office of librarian of St. Benedict's College, Cambridge, and his love of reading, opened to him a wider range of thought and perception. The works of Bellarmin, and Whitaker's reply, fell into his hands, and he was at once struck with the unfair quotations of the latter, while he found that those of the former were in every instance correct. This led to further inquiry, which ended in conviction. He communicated his doubts and discoveries to four of his college friends. The result was, that, after a short time, they all embraced the faith. Three of them joined the Order of St. Francis, and the fourth became a distinguished member of the Society of Jesus. Father Heath was received into the Church by one of the few priests who still, in disguise, ministered to the faithful in London. He at once proceeded to Douay, to prepare for Holy Orders, but the poverty and fervor of the Franciscans there attracted him so strongly, that he begged to be received among them. After a year's novitiate, he was professed under the name of Father Paul, of St. Magdalen. Here his life was seraphic, and his austerities very great. He fasted four or five days each week on bread and a little weak beer ; his rest was but for a few hours, during which he always lay on the ground. He passed the hours from matins until prime in prayer; his disciplines and other mortifications were proportioned to his fervor.

Esteemed and loved by his brethren, he was for many years their superior and instructor in divinity; we cannot then wonder that his earnest entreaties to visit his native land were long denied. But a martyr's crown shone out brightly before him; it was his constant thought by day, and his dream in his brief rest at night. In 1641 several priests were executed in England, one of them an intimate friend of Father Paul's. He now urged his superiors once more for leave to suffer and die for the faith to which he had proved himself so fervent a convert. Again he was refused. Not discouraged, he determined specially to invoke our Blessed Lady, to whom he was tenderly devoted, and he obtained, in the most unexpected manner, what he asked. It was not the first favor, little short of miraculous, which he had received from the Queen of Heaven.

His mother had been long dead; but he had left his father in England, an old man, well nigh heart-broken at conduct which seemed to him so undutiful in a son whom he had always tenderly loved, and who had ever shown himself full of reverent affection to his parent. Father Heath could only pray and bear in silence the pain he knew he was inflicting on one of the kindest of hearts, from which he suffered himself full as much as his poor father. After many years, suddenly and most unexpectedly, the good old man received the gift of faith, and braved the dangers and fatigues of a journey by sea and land, that his own and only son might receive him into the Church. Nor was this all; he was so edified by, and attracted to, the Order of poverty, that he renounced all the property not already forfeited by his conversion, and entered the Franciscan Order as a lay brother. But a further trial awaited both father and son. Father Paul had obtained permission to visit England, and he who had obeyed the call of God in his conversion and vocation, even at the cost of a father's love, would not now be stayed in his onward course to martyrdom. He was arrested almost immediately after his arrival in England, whither he had journeyed like a true Friar Minor, barefoot and penniless. On his way to execution he reconciled to the Church a malefactor who suffered with him. He received his crown on the 17th of April, 1643. At the same moment his venerable father beheld in a vision the sufferings and triumph of his son, and related the circumstances to the brethren. A few days later the revelation was verified by accounts from England. We do not know how long the old lay brother survived his martyred son, but the joy of their eternal reunion could not have been much delayed.

The parents of Father Francis Bell were Catholics; his mother is said to have been a person of unusual piety, who educated him with the tenderest care. While preparing for Holy Orders on the continent, he was attracted to the Friars Minor, and made his profession at Segovia, on the 8th of April, 1619. Soon after, he joined the religious at Douay, who were taking measures for the restoration of the English province. Here he remained two years, and then removed to Gravelines, where he was for some time confessor to the Poor Clares. At length he was sent on the English Mission, where he labored for nine years, suffering the greatest hardships from the concealments he was obliged to use. On the 6th of November, 1643, he was arrested at Stevenridge in Hertfordshire. Some papers were found in his bag, which the schoolmaster of the place was summoned to decipher. This learned personage pronounced them to be witchcraft; an opinion in which several members of the House of Commons, to whom they were afterwards consigned, fully agreed. The witchcraft, however, was simply the form of blessing, the cord of St. Francis, and the lessons of the Office of the Most Holy Sacrament. Father Bell saved all the trouble of further inquiry by declaring at once that he was a priest. For this crime he was brought to London, dressed in rags, to excite the contempt of the populace as he passed along. The design fully succeeded, and the father was as well pleased as his persecutors; in truth, it was the most joyous journey he had ever made. The execution of Father Heath had left the office of Superior at Douay vacant. Father Bell had been scarcely twenty-four hours in Newgate when he received an obedience from his superiors to become guardian of that convent. His reply to the provincial and to the commissary-general are models for every religious. To his provincial he writes as follows:

REVEREND FATHER,—I received your command with all humility and readiness at the very time I was putting it into execution; for I took possession of Father Paul's place in Newgate about twenty-four hours before yours came to my knowledge. As to what remains, I beg your prayers that I may persevere to the end, and I beg of all Christians, with St. Andrew, that they would not hinder my sufferings.

Your poor Brother, F. BELL.

To the commissary-general he writes thus:

MOST REVEREND FATHER, Obedience and Reverence,—I received the command of your most reverend paternity with humility, and am disposed, with all possible readiness, to put it in execution as soon as this present impediment which stands in the way shall be removed. Now, the impediment is this: On the 6th of November, O. S., I was apprehended on my way to

London, by the Parliamentary soldiers, and being examined and found to be a Catholic, I was put under the custody of four soldiers night and day; and after I had been stripped of all things, sword, money, clothes, and even my very shirt, and clad in an old tattered coat of some poor soldier, I was brought before the Parliament at London, where, being again examined, I was found out, by certain arguments, to be a Friar Minor, which I did not deny; and being, withal, suspected to be a priest according to the order of the Roman Church, I was for this reason committed to the prison of Newgate. I am to be tried on the 5th of December; what will then be done with me my Lord Jesus Christ knows, with whom I am ready to go to the cross and to death, if His mercy will vouchsafe to extend itself so far as to be willing to accept the sacrifice of such and so great a sinner; but if I am still necessary to His people, the will of our Lord be done. I have begged death for Christ. This I will continue to beg, for my sinful life has been a long time hateful to me. Pardon me, I know what is for my profit; to die is my gain. I humbly beg your prayers, and those of my brethren, that if (as I wish) it may be my lot to die, I may depart with obedience in the grace of Jesus Christ, and with St. Andrew, I beseech all Christian people not to be a hindrance to my death. If I shall not be condemned to die, I will labor by all lawful means to procure my liberty, that I may be able to obey, as it is my duty, the command I have received.

God preserve your reverence, etc..

Newgate, November 22, 1643.

How beautiful the obedience of the martyr, who, if he is not condemned to die, will leave no means untried to fulfil the commands of his superior! Like St. Martin, he is willing to linger on earth if he is necessary for the work of God; like the martyr, St. Ignatius, he "knows what is expedient for him," and thirsts for the sufferings which will make him a true disciple of his crucified Lord. He was martyred on the 11th of December, and though many powerful friends would have pleaded in his behalf, he implored them not to deprive him of his crown.

In 1646, Father Martin, of St. Felix, who had been professed by Father Bell, followed in the same glorious path. His martyrdom was indeed most painful. The rope was cut so soon that he perfectly recovered in a few moments, and was therefore compelled to ascend the ladder a second time. Even after this, he again became conscious while his heart was being cut out; but that was no uncommon occurrence in those barbarous times.

The martyrdoms of Father Joachim of St. Anne, and Father Mahoney, an Irish priest, occurred later. Father Levison, of St. Clare, died of actual want and misery while in prison. But time would fail were we to name all the English children of St. Francis who suffered for their faith. The last in England was, we believe, Father Paul of St. Francis. He was noted for his zeal in bringing back those who, through fear or temptation, had strayed from the fold of Christ. Father Paul died in Hurst Castle, after an imprisonment of thirty years, October 15th, 1729.

SCOTLAND.—According to the ancient annals, the province of Scotland was founded during the lifetime of St. Francis, the first friar going there in 1224. In the year 1400 it numbered fourteen convents. In its early years, this province gave a bright example of all those virtues which shone in the first disciples of St. Francis, and it bore those blessed fruits which the nascent seraphic family everywhere produced. These were the golden days of this province; but through the neglect of holy discipline—receiving an annual income, and possessing lands—it gradually fell away from the spirit of St. Francis, and its good name was nearly obliterated, when in the fifteenth century its pristine virtue was restored.

King James I. besought the friars of Cologne to send some of their number to Scotland to restore the ancient discipline ; and John Maubertus, vicar-general of the ultramontane Observantines, sent Cornelius à Ziriczea, with six companions, who were so well received by the king and people, that in a few years they numbered nine convents of the Regular Observance, which number constituted the province in 1517, when arose the heretical fury which drove out the friars and demolished their convents.

The citizens of Edinburgh built a spacious convent, surrounded by a beautiful garden, for the friars, in 1447; which, however, Cornelius hesitated to receive, on account of its grandeur, until ordered by Pope Pius II. to accept it. In this convent there were sometimes eighty friars, of whom sixty were priests, most of them of noble families; for the fame of Cornelius and his companions spreading, many sons of Scotch noblemen flocked thither, from the schools of Paris and Cologne, where they had graduated with honors, and taking the habit of St. Francis, in this convent, the study of philosophy and theology continued to flourish there, until 1559, when it was closed by the heretics.

Conspicuous among the young friars of this province was Robert Creythins, son of the Count of Muchobusium. Though he had obtained the honors of doctorate, he was no less remarkable for his humanity than for his learning. At the instance of his father, the Count, the Archbishop of St. Andrew and Primate of Scotland erected a convent for the friars in the city of St. Andrew, in 1458. This convent was a novitiate, and contained forty friars. It was also ruined by the heretics.

Jerome Lindsey, *utriusque juris Doctor*, son of the Count of Grawfort, was one of the first to join Cornelius Ziriczea, after his arrival in Scotland, and he was remarkable for his humility, spirit of prayer, and mortification. Through his influence, the Count of Oliphant built a convent for the friars in the city of St. John, in the year 1460. It accommodated twenty friars.

The Bishop of Aberdeen, among other educational and religious establishments which he founded and endowed, erected in the city of Aberdeen, in the year 1470, a convent for the friars of St. Francis, which numbered forty inmates. It suffered the usual fate of all religious houses at the hands of the reformers.

The Archbishop of Glasgow (one of the principal cities of Scotland), founded a convent for the Franciscans in that city, in the year 1472, of which he was a great patron during his lifetime. It had thirty friars.

The citizens of Arear, a town in the west of Scotland, hearing of the good fame of the Franciscans, besought them to take up their abode in their town; and they erected for them a convent which contained thirty friars. This convent became celebrated throughout Scotland, on account of the many miracles which were wrought there at a shrine of the Blessed Virgin Mary.

John, Viscount of Innesensium, founded a convent for the Franciscans at Elgin, a town in the north of Scotland, in 1479. It had thirty friars. It also was profaned by the heretics.

James IV. founded a convent for the friars, near Stirling, in 1494, which contained forty inmates. Whenever he was at Stirling he attended the public offices in this convent; and each year, he passed Holy Week there, joining in the patriarchal observances of the friars.

In the reign of James V., in 1513, the Scotch nobles founded a convent for the friars at Jedvardiac, on the borders of England. It was burned, together with the town, during the war between England and Scotland.

In Scotland, also, the friars suffered severely. Knox proceeded against them with his characteristic violence. Among the many exiled and persecuted religious who lived in this reign, Stephen Fox and Thomas Bouchier claim a passing notice. The latter, it is said, was descended from the earls of Bath. After his expulsion, he resided principally at Rome, and was penitentiary of the Church of St. John Lateran, where he was buried. Fox fled to Antwerp; but even there persecution followed him, and he was driven to Normandy with the religious of a monastery of Poor Clares, also victims to the zeal of the foreign reformers. They afterwards found a home at Lisbon, where they were most cordially received and generously supported by King Philip II.

CHAPTER XI.

The Order in Ireland.—Youghal Convent.—Kilkenny famous for its schools.—Clynn, the annalist.—Dublin.—Multifarnham.—Timoleague.—Injustice of a protestant bishop.—Donegal.—The Lady Nuala.—Father Bernard Grey.—His sanctity.—Miracles.—Drogheda.—Dundalk.

The Order in Ireland was not less fruitful either in saints or martyrs; its foundations were no less munificent, its churches in many places even more stately, than in the English province. But they who would know what the Franciscan Order did and suffered in Ireland, must search the archives of its ancient convents on the continent, where its records have been preserved when persecution drove the fathers from their own green isle, to seek hospitality on foreign shores. We can but give a brief account of some of the more celebrated houses of the Order in Ireland, and name a few of the multitude who suffered there for their faith and heroic devotion to their persecuted countrymen.

The convent at Youghal claims to be the first establishment of the Order in Ireland. Some curious particulars are related as to its foundation. The Earl Maurice Fitzgerald, Lord Justice of Ireland, was building a mansion for his family in the town, about the year 1231. While the workmen were engaged in laying the foundation, they begged some money on the eve of a great feast, that they might drink to the health and prosperity of their noble employer. The earl willingly complied with their request, and desired his eldest son to be the bearer of his bounty. The young nobleman, however, less generous than his father, not only refused to give them the money, but had angry words with the workmen. It is not mentioned whether the affair came to a more serious collision; but the earl, highly incensed with the conduct of his son, ordered the workmen to erect a monastery instead of a castle, and bestowed the house upon the Franciscan fathers. The following year he took their habit, and lived in the convent until his death. This house was completely destroyed during the persecutions in the reign of Elizabeth.

The convent of Kilkenny was founded immediately after. Its benefactor was the Earl of Pembroke, who was buried in the church. Here was a remarkable spring, dedicated to St. Francis, at which many miraculous cures are said to have been wrought. The site occupied by this building was very extensive; its ruins only remain, to tell how spacious and beautiful its abbey and church must have been. It was also remarkable for the learned men who there pursued their literary toil, among whom we may mention the celebrated annalist, Clynn. He was at first guardian of the convent of Carrick-on-Suir; but about 1338 he retired to Kilkenny, where he compiled the greater part of his annals. It is probable that he died about 1350. His history commences with the Christian era, and is carried down to the year 1349. At this time the country was all but depopulated by a fearful pestilence. The good and learned brother seems to have had some forebodings of his impending fate, for his last written words run thus: "And, lest the writing should perish with the writer, and the work should fail with the workman, I leave behind me parchment for continuing it, if any man should have the good fortune to survive this calamity, or any one of the race of Adam should escape this pestilence, and live to continue what I have begun."

This abbey was also one of the great literary schools of Ireland, and had its halls of philosophy and divinity, which were well attended for many years.

In Dublin, the Franciscans were established by the munificence of their great patron, Henry III. Ralph le Porter granted a site of land in that part of the city where the street still retains the name of the founder of the Seraphic Order. In 1308, John le Decer proved a great benefactor to the friars, and erected a very beautiful chapel, dedicated to the Blessed Virgin, in which he was interred. This house was, of course, suppressed by Henry VIII. All that was valuable of material or workmanship he took to himself; the ground and the ruins he sold to a Dublin trader for a very small sum; so small, indeed, that it must have been far below the real value even of what escaped the royal rapacity. It appears that in this, as in many other instances, Henry was anxious to make the interest of those to whom he sold church property so far coincide with his own, that they might be as anxious to keep their new possessions as he had been first to obtain them. Cornelius, Bishop of Down, a Franciscan friar, and Father Thomas Fitzgerald, celebrated as a preacher, and of the noble house of the Geraldines, were both massacred here by Henry's soldiers.

But the convent of Multifarnham was the great glory of this century. It was erected in 1236 by Lord Delamere; and, from its retired situation, and the powerful protection of its noble patrons, escaped many of the calamities which befel other houses of the Order. The church and convent were built "in honor of God and St. Francis." The monastery itself was of unusual size, and had ample accommodation for a very large number of friars. Hence, in times of persecution, it was the usual refuge of the sick and infirm, who were driven from their less favored homes. The church was remarkable for its beauty and the richness of its ornaments. Here were the tombs of its noble founders and patrons, and the south-eastern window was gorgeous with their heraldic devices. The convent was situated on Lake Derreghvera, and was endowed with many acres of rich land, through which flow the Tuny and the Gain. Such a position afforded opportunity for mills and agricultural labors, of which the friars were not slow to avail themselves. The site, as we have remarked, was secluded, at some distance even from any village, and far from the more frequented roads. In process of time, the family of the Nugents became lords of the manor, but they were not less friendly to the religious. Indeed, so devoted were they to the Order, that at the time of the dissolution of monasteries, Multifarnham would have shared the common fate, had they not again and again repurchased it from those to whom it had been sold by Henry. Even during the reign of Elizabeth it was protected by the same family. But the day of suffering was even then approaching. In October of the year 1601, a detachment of English soldiers was sent from Dublin by Lord Mountjoy, to destroy the convent which had been so long spared. The friars were seized and imprisoned, the monastery pillaged, and the soldiers, disappointed in their hope of a rich booty, wreaked their vengeance by setting fire to the sacred pile.

This was on the 3d of October, the vigil of the feast of St. Francis. Some of the friars had escaped; but one novice refused to do so. He had nearly concluded the term of his novitiate; and he remained a prisoner, hoping to be sent to the castle of Loughshodie, where he knew his provincial was confined. Many bribes were offered him on the road if he would abandon his profession, and promises of wealth and advancement were pressed on him. He had already served under O'Neil and O'Donnell against Elizabeth's troops; and this too was made a plea to induce him to put off his friar's weeds, and once more to don the sword and morion. But bribes and taunts were alike unheeded. The Puritan soldiers could as little understand his motive as they did the indifference he manifested at his capture. A few hours passed, and then the gloomy prison of Loughshodie witnessed a spectacle worthy of the children of St. Francis. The novice knelt before his superior, whom (as he expected) he found here with the venerable Bishop of Kilmore, also a Franciscan, and in a brief space of time he had made his vows in the gloomy prison, and was admitted a member of the Seraphic Order.

Again and again the poor friars returned to their ruined convent. As its walls could no longer shelter them, they built for themselves some small cabins; and here they remained till fresh persecutions drove them into exile or imprisonment. Many died from the hardships they endured, or from the sufferings of their imprisonment, where often even the necessaries of life were denied to them.

The convent of Kilcrea was another sequestered spot. It was founded in the fifteenth century, by the MacCarthys, under the invocation of St. Bridget. The richness and magnificence of the church, its graceful bell tower, carved windows, and marble ornaments, showed both the generosity and the taste of the Lord Muskerry. Cormac was interred here in 1495; and many noble families, having made it their place of sepulture, protected the church for the sake of their ancestral tombs. Still it was frequently desecrated, and the friars driven again and again from their home. In the year 1614, Dermot MacCarthy apostatized; and the convent with its appurtenances was given to him, on condition that the friars should never be allowed to enter it again, and that none but Protestants should be permitted to live there.

Nor was the monastery of Timoleague less celebrated. The honor of its foundation is disputed, as well as the exact date; but as the tombs of the MacCarthys, the O'Donovans, O'Heas, and De Courcys, are in its choir, we may suppose that all had a share in the erection or adornment of this stately church. One of the De Courcy family, Edmund, Bishop of Ross, himself a Franciscan friar, rebuilt the bell tower, which rises to a height of seventy feet, as well as the dormitory, infirmary, and library. At his death in 1518, he bequeathed many valuable books, altar-plate, etc., to his brethren.

Many acts of most wanton sacrilege were committed here; and in several instances they were remarkably avenged. Once, when a body of English horse entered the church, and commenced destroying its beautiful windows and sacred images, a poor carpenter who had been employed by the friars, cried aloud to St. Francis, exclaiming, that as he was all-powerful with God, he should avenge this impiety; and declaring that, unless his prayer was heard, he would never work again in the church. Doubtless his indignation was the result of a holy zeal; for his petition was answered. Next day, when the troopers had just comfortably quartered themselves, a neighboring prince fell upon them, and only one escaped to tell the fate of his slaughtered comrades. But soldiers were not the only enemies of the poor religious. A Protestant minister, and a Protestant bishop, whose conduct has not been without its counterpart in our own days, were most forward in the work of destruction. The details are well authenticated, and too remarkable to be omitted. The minister, a Dr. Hanmer, was erecting a house for himself near Cork. Hearing of the richly carved oak wainscotings with which the piety of its founders had adorned the monastery of Timoleague, he determined the original proprietors should no longer possess what might be so serviceable to himself. To transfer the property, he chartered a small vessel at Cork, and proceeded to the monastery, where his rapacity was amply gratified. But the sacrilege was avenged. A fearful storm arose on the homeward voyage, and the vessel sank with its ill-gotten freight, until the sea shall restore her treasures at the day of Doom.

Lyons, the Protestant bishop, was not less eager to

have his share of a spoil that was so easily procured. In 1590, having occasion to erect a mill, he determined that those used by the friars should be transferred for his benefit. Accordingly, he carried off all their available machinery and hammer-stones; but no sooner was his new building erected, than a mountain torrent swept away all his work. To him it seemed only an unlucky accident; but there were many who dared affirm that the vengeance of heaven was thus exercised to punish the injustice done to the friars. His implacable hatred to the Catholics only increased. Being appointed one of queen Elizabeth's commissioners to drive the poor Irish from their homes, and to place English in possession of their houses and lands, he fulfilled his task with a degree of barbarity which called on his head the bitterest imprecations from the hapless objects of this most unjust and cruel persecution. On the Christmas Eve of 1612 he was told that immense numbers of Catholics had assembled at Timoleague for the midnight mass, which the friars, true to their faith and the special devotion of their Order, were determined to celebrate as best they could. Lyons at once set out with an armed band who usually accompanied him, and who were as reckless and cruel as he could desire. But the persecutor was stayed. Sudden illness seized Lyons almost as soon as he set out. His companions urged him to return, but he spurred on the faster, wrapping himself only in warmer cloaks. In a short time his sufferings became so acute that he was compelled to return slowly to the city. It would seem as though he recognized the Hand that smote him; for during the few remaining years of his life, his conduct was more humane.

The history of the establishment of the Order at

Donegal is amusing enough, and very characteristic of the customs of the age. In the year 1474, the Franciscans were holding a General Chapter in their convent near Tuam. In the midst of their deliberations, however, they were unexpectedly interrupted by the arrival of the Lady Nuala O'Connor, daughter of the noble O'Connor Farly, and wife of the powerful chieftain, Hugh O'Donnell. She was attended by a brilliant escort, and came for no other purpose than to present her humble petition to the assembled fathers for the establishment of their Order in the principality of Tirconnell. After some deliberation, the provincial informed her that her request could not be complied with at present, but that at a future period the friars would most willingly second her pious design. The Lady Nuala, however, had a woman's will, and a spirit of religious fervor to animate it. "What!" she exclaimed, "have I made this long and painful journey only to meet with a refusal? Beware of God's wrath! for to Him I will appeal, that He may charge you with all the souls whom your delay may cause to perish." This was unanswerable. The Lady Nuala journeyed home with a goodly band of Franciscans in her train, and soon the establishment of the monastery of Donegal, situated at the head of the bay, showed that the piety of the lady was generously seconded by her noble husband. Lady Nuala did not live to see the completion of her cherished design. Her mortal remains were interred under the high altar, and many and fervent were the prayers of the holy friars for the eternal repose of their benefactress.

The second wife of the O'Donnell was not less devoted to the Order. This lady was a daughter of Conor O'Brien, king of Thomond. Her zeal in the good work was so great that the monastery was soon completed, and the church dedicated in 1474; the ceremony was carried out with the utmost magnificence, and large benefactions bestowed on the religious. After the death of her husband—who had built a castle close to the monastery, and was buried within the sacred walls—the widowed princess retired to a small dwelling near the church, where she passed the remainder of her days in prayer and penance. Her son, Hugh Oge, followed in the steps of his good father; so judicious and upright was his rule, that it was said, in his days, the people of Tirconnell never closed their doors except to keep out the wind. In 1510, he set out on a pilgrimage to Rome. Here he spent two years, and was received everywhere as an independent prince and treated with the greatest distinction; but neither the honors conferred on him, nor his knightly fame (for it is said he was never vanquished in the field or the lists), could satisfy the desires of his heart. After a brief enjoyment of his ancestral honors, he retired to the monastery which his father had erected, and found with the poor children of St. Francis that peace and contentment which the world cannot give.

Nor was this a solitary instance of noble self-renunciation. Princes, knights and bishops, relinquished crowns, mitres and fame for the peaceful novitiate of Donegal. It was distinguished, moreover, for the literary attainments, and better still, for the sanctity of its friars. Of the saints who dwelt there, Father Bernard Grey, surnamed the *Pauper*, from his great love of poverty, demands a special notice. His parents were wealthy, and, at an early age, he was offered the hand of the heiress of a noble house, with her father's wide domains. But Bernard had another bride in view. In love with poverty, like Francis, he fled to Donegal, and was soon an inmate of its quiet novitiate, where his virtue was the admiration of all. Indeed, the chroniclers say, it even seemed as if Francis himself lived again. The first at the midnight office and in every austerity, and the poorest where all were poor, it is scarcely matter of surprise that his fame should have travelled far and wide. In 1532 the Earl of Kildare, who was then Lord Deputy, sent for him that he might personally converse with the man who had such a reputation for his sanctity and his miracles. By his desire, Bernard preached before his court at Drogheda, and so fascinated the earl by his discourse, that he not only asked him to dine at his table, but even gave him precedence of all his noble guests. After dinner he was desired to speak of the glories of Francis. In concluding a most eloquent and touching discourse, he observed, that the very honor which had been paid to himself was surely an evidence of the exalted dignity given by God in heaven to his great patron. The earl perceived at once that his own most secret thoughts had been read, and publicly declared that he had paid these honors to the friar purposely, thinking of the glory of his seraphic patron in heaven, and the place he occupied at the celestial feasts.

Among the benefactions bestowed on this community by the Prince O'Donnell was a weir, constructed at the point where the river Esk empties itself into the bay. This was an important donation to the friars, who were obliged, by their Rule, to abstain from flesh meat during a great part of the year. One day in Lent, when it came to the turn of this saintly father to serve in the refectory, the superior remarked playfully that the fish was very bad, and asked the serving brother how it was that no salmon had been taken in their weir for so long a time. Bernard replied that he did not know. The guardian answered: "Well, then, brother, I command you to bless the weir in the name of Him who filled the net of Simon at the lake of Genesareth, for I know that you are a special instrument in the hand of God." The friar obeyed, and from that day the religious never lacked an abundant supply of the most excellent fish.

Bernard died kneeling on the ground with his arms outstretched in the attitude of prayer. He had foretold the hour of his decease, and that a beloved friend of his, who was chanter in the Cathedral of Armagh, should accompany him to the kingdom of the blessed. For some time after his decease the religious enjoyed comparative quiet, but ere long the storm burst on their devoted heads. The English troops finding themselves unable to conquer the princes of Ireland while their strength was united, invented the darkest stratagems to sow discord even between brothers. Their success was but too great. Nial Garv, the brother-in-law of the noble Hugh, who then ruled Tirconnell, revolted against his kinsman, seizing the monastery and converting it into barracks for his troops. This he fortified, as also the castle of Donegal, and a neighboring monastery of the Third Order of St. Francis. O'Donnell attacked him in his stronghold. Victory had begun to declare for the rightful cause, when, on the night of the Feast of St. Michael the powder which had been stored in the monastery took fire, and exploded with a crash that was heard for miles round the country. Nial, however, still maintained his ground in the smouldering ruins, until the siege was raised by the withdrawal of the O'Donnell's troops. The work of desecration was completed by Lambert, the English Governor of Connaught. In

1602 he seized all that was moveable, profaned the chalices by using them for drinking cups, and destroyed the magnificent vestments and library, for which the convent was remarkable.

In the county Kerry, there were at least two convents of the Order—one at Ardfert, founded probably in the year 1389; the other, famous for the beauty of its ruins and its proximity to the far-famed lakes of Killarney, demands a longer notice.

The convent of Irrelagh, or as it is now called, Mucross, was founded early in the fifteenth century by a prince of the famous family of MacCarty More; known afterwards as *Tadeige Manistireach*, or Tiege of the Monastery.

According to the tradition of the county and a MS. description of Kerry written about the year 1750, and now preserved in the library of the Royal Irish Academy, the site on which the monastery was to be built was pointed out to MacCarty More in a vision, which warned him not to erect his monastery in any situation except at a place called Carrig-an-ceoil, *i. e.*, the Rock of the Music. As no such place was known to him, he despatched some of his faithful followers to ascertain in what part of his principality it was situated.

For some time they inquired in vain; but as they returned home in despair, the most exquisite music was heard to issue from a rock at Irrelagh. When the chief was made aware of this, he at once concluded it was the spot destined by Providence for his pious undertaking, which he immediately commenced. It was finished by his son Donnell in 1440. The convent was dedicated to the Blessed Trinity. It is said there was a miraculous image of the Blessed Virgin here, which brought great crowds of pilgrims. The feast of the Porziuncola was kept here long after the abbey had fallen to ruins and the friars dispersed, and was known as the Abbey-day. Until the last few years stations were held there regularly on the second of October.

The convent was not entirely abandoned until the reign of Elizabeth, but the brown habit and white cord of St. Francis is now, thank God, seen once more on the shores of Loch Lein.* The devotion of the people of Kerry to the Order can be scarcely said to have revived since it had hardly decayed; and the fervor and devotion of the Belgian friars, who are now established at Killarney, may well bear comparison with that of their saintly and persecuted predecessors.

But time would fail, were we to enumerate the glories and sufferings of the Franciscan houses in Ireland. We can but glance at them, and then pass on to tell of the cruel wrongs and sufferings inflicted on their inmates.

Clonmel monastery was founded about 1269, and probably by the Desmond family. Its benefactors were numerous. The church was one of the finest in Ireland, and remarkable for its stately marble tombs, and curiously carved figures and bas-reliefs. The monument of Butler, Baron of Cahir, was in the middle of the choir. Once, while this nobleman was attending High Mass in this church, he was told that the Earl of Ormond and the Baron of Dunboyne were pillaging his land. Undisturbed by the intelligence, the baron calmly waited the conclusion of the Holy Sacrifice, then, mounting to horse, he charged his enemies, and gained a signal victory. Here was also a miracu-

* This is the ancient and present name of the lower lake of Killarney, on the shores of which the abbey is situated; there is also a little island called Dinas, in Kenmare Bay, which anciently belonged to the friars.

lous statue of St. Francis, before which persons were often sworn, as it was usually found that they who perjured themselves were immediately overtaken by some calamity.

Both in Cork and Kilkenny were miraculous wells dedicated to St. Francis. That belonging to the former monastery was a famous pilgrimage. After the dissolution the people still flocked thither, hoping to obtain their requests through the merits of St. Francis. The convent had been sold to a Protestant, who, being annoyed by the crowd, stopped up the well, as the most effectual means of putting an end to the inconvenient devotion.

The monastery at Drogheda was founded by the Plunkets in 1240. It was a large building, and situated near the river, on the road to Armagh. The choir of the church had accommodation for two hundred friars, and the building was remarkable for the beauty of its bell tower, which was of carved stone, encased with marble. The bell towers of the Franciscan churches were, indeed, among their peculiar and characteristic features. The Darcys were great benefactors to this convent; and the tomb of John Darcy, Lord Justice of Ireland in 1323, being placed in the centre of the choir, it has been supposed by many that this family were the founders of the monastery. The friars were expelled in the reign of Elizabeth, and their convent leased to Gerald Aylmer. He afterwards sold the buildings to an English adventurer, Moses Hill, who "came to Ireland a beggar, and made himself rich on other men's purses." This man, however, did not always prosper in his undertakings. While he continued to pull down the greater part of the building, and to sell all that was available of it, misfortune followed those who had any hand in the work of destruction.

The bell tower and eastern window alone escaped his rapacity.

Such of the friars as were not imprisoned or massacred on these occasions, usually secreted themselves for a time in the neighboring woods or mountains. Then they would steal back to the ruins of their former homes, and if they could not or dared not shelter themselves under its crumbling walls, they were fain to build some rude hut, as near it as could be, there to continue their usual practices of devotion, till a fresh persecution drove them to the woods again. This experiment, however, was a dangerous one. But the friars cared little for their lives, when compared with the value of their ministrations to their afflicted countrymen. Rather would they eagerly have sought for martyrdom ; and when they fled, it was not from fear of tortures or death, but rather that, by prolonging their lives, they might longer serve the faithful people.

In 1610, a few of the friars, headed by Father Dunlevy, returned to Drogheda, and hired a house there. For a short time they remained unmolested ; but the respite was a brief one. The Lord Deputy, Sir Arthur Chichester, hearing that some of their altar-plate had escaped former sacrileges, determined that the friars should no longer possess any remnant of their property. The house was attacked by his soldiers, and all that was left of their former valuable vestments and altar-plate, seized ; the friars themselves only escaping because the armed band were too intent on plunder to pursue them.

The convent of Dundalk was one of the first suppressed. Ware says that it was remarkable for its east window, which was of most curious workmanship. The premises were sold to a family named Brandon, who were among the very few troubled with any conscientious scruples about possessing Church property. The grandson of the first lessee, to his eternal honor be it said, applied to the friars on the subject; and only retained possession of the lands and ruins by special permission of the Holy See, and on condition of renouncing his right whenever the Franciscans might be able to claim it.

CHAPTER XII.

Generosity of the Irish to English Protestants.—Martyrs.—O'Hely, Bishop of Mayo.—John Duad.—Fergal Ward, etc.—Colleges founded for the Irish.—Lisbon, Douay, Lisle, etc.—Maurice de Portu.—Martyrs at Wexford, etc.—Franciscan writers.—Fleming.—Colgan.—Hugh Ward.—The Four Masters.—Wadding.

Our readers have already been made acquainted with the sufferings inflicted on the Franciscans in England, when Henry commenced his reformation of the Church by destroying and uprooting its most ancient institutions. We will now say a few words of the principal martyrs in Ireland, and give some notice of the noble colleges founded on the continent, as a refuge for the homeless friars, and as schools to train new aspirants for the martyr's crown. Ware gives a catalogue of more than a hundred convents of the Franciscan Order, which existed in Ireland during the early part of Henry's reign. The number of friars in each must have been considerable, if we calculate it by the accommodation provided for them. What must have been the sufferings they endured when driven from their homes, and deprived at once of food and shelter? Houseless and homeless, they wandered on the mountain side, or lived in the cabins of the peasantry. Still, at that day they could exercise their sacred ministry with less fear than during the reigns of Elizabeth and

James I. Henry was rather schismatic than heretic; and if we except (a great exception, indeed) the one false opinion of his own supremacy, he scarcely differed from Catholics in belief. Indeed, he persecuted almost equally those who differed from his orthodox opinions and those who rejected his usurped supremacy. Money and permission to gratify his lawless passions were all he demanded; these once obtained, he cared little what became of the victims of his avarice.

The reign of Edward was too short to afford much opportunity for persecution; and under the rule of Mary, while the Catholics enjoyed a temporary respite, the friars again founded communities, and once more enjoyed peace and liberty. It may be remarked in passing, that the Irish displayed their characteristic generosity and hospitality during this reign by sheltering many English families, whose professions of Protestantism had made them obnoxious to the government. The Catholic corporation of Dublin alone opened no less than seventy-four houses in that city for English Protestants who sought refuge there from the unjustifiable persecutions of Mary's advisers.

On the accession of Elizabeth, new and more bitter sufferings were inflicted on the Catholics; but we do not hear that English Protestants afforded hospitality in return for what they had so lately received. The churches were desecrated, the priests driven to the wilds and fastnesses; while the prelates of the Irish Church, being foremost in their zeal, were among the first victims of unrelenting cruelty. Patrick O'Hely, Bishop of Mayo, and Cornelius O'Rourke, a secular priest, were among the earliest sufferers. Their crime was fidelity to their religion, and devotion to their afflicted countrymen. In such cases, to use the word trial, would be a mockery of truth. What was called trial was simply to pronounce a sentence of condemnation already resolved upon. They were

"Prejudged by foes determined not to spare."

The prelate and his companion expired under tortures almost too horrible to relate. They were racked; their hands and feet broken with hammers; and when their persecutors were weary, and saw life almost extinct, the martyrs were strangled. Their bodies were then hung in chains from trees for fourteen days, during which time they were used as targets by the soldiers of the Lord Deputy. Even while suffering on the rack, the holy prelate had warned Drury that before many days he would himself be judged. The prophecy was realized; before a week had passed this inhuman governor died in the greatest agony, of some unknown disease, which baffled all medical skill. Soon after, the bodies of the martyrs were conveyed to Clonmel by the Earl of Desmond, and buried there with great solemnity in the Franciscan convent. The Bishop of Kilmore, also of this Order, was imprisoned for a length of time, maimed and tortured.

Nor did the inferior clergy escape. All suffered severely, and all perhaps alike; but the Franciscans being more numerous than the other bodies of regular clergy, sent home a larger, if not a richer harvest. Wherever the faithful suffered most, there these devoted followers of their Seraphic Father were most eager to minister. Cold and nakedness, hunger and thirst, were alike unheeded. Night after night, for in the day they scarcely dared show themselves, they sought the scattered sheep of Christ, who, but for their devoted zeal, must have perished of spiritual hunger. Some, like Father John Duad, were seized while in the very act of hearing confessions; others, as Father Fergal Ward, while travelling through lonely districts to minister the sacraments to the dying. Some, like Fathers John O'Lochran, Edmund Simmons, and Donatus O'Rourke, were taken prisoners in their own convent (Down), and executed by the military after cruel tortures, because they would not reveal the treasures they were supposed to possess. Others, like Fathers Thaddeus Donald and John Hanly, of Bantry convent, were seized as they sought once more to visit their ruined monasteries; and, being tied together back to back with their own cords, were dashed down a frightful precipice which hung over the wild ocean. Even to give a mere list of the names of those who suffered under this persecution would require several pages; and if we add to the hundreds of Franciscan martyrs, the Dominicans, Carmelites, Jesuits, etc., and the secular priests, we may well shudder at the fearful amount of crime which was committed in the name of religion, and by those whose boast was freedom of conscience and an open Bible. The object of Elizabeth's government was to exterminate the Irish priesthood. This once accomplished, they hoped that the flock, being without their shepherds, would soon fall a prey to the devouring wolf. Beheading and hanging were the mildest forms of suffering inflicted on those who would neither be bribed nor intimidated. But new laborers appeared as rapidly as their predecessors were mown down.

Nor was it deemed enough that priests themselves should suffer; even they who "harbored" them were to be hanged without mercy. To complete the extermination of the faith, all Catholic education was forbidden, and it was even made punishable for any Irish family to send money abroad for the support of students on the continent, no matter how nearly related to them. It seemed, indeed, as if all was done that human forethought could devise, or force execute, to leave Ireland without a priest and without a sacrifice, and to reduce its inhabitants to the lowest state of misery and degradation.

But this barbarous intolerance evoked a spirit of indignation among the Catholic powers of Europe, and the result was a movement which effectually counteracted the exterminating policy of Elizabeth. Colleges for Irish students for the priesthood, whether secular or religious, were founded in several parts of Europe, and munificently endowed. Philip II. of Spain nobly assisted in this work. At Lisbon an Irish seminary was founded and endowed by Cardinal Henriques. The colleges of Douay, Lisle, Antwerp, Tournay, and St. Omer, were established by the exertions and principally at the expense of Christopher Cusack, a learned priest of the diocese of Meath. In Bordeaux, Toulouse and Nantes, by Anne, Queen of Austria. Others, too numerous to mention, followed rapidly, and, in the last year of this century (the sixteenth), Baron Sylveria founded the Irish college at Alcala de Henares, which he richly endowed; it became, in the next century, one of the most valuable to the Irish mission.

Among the distinguished Irish Franciscans of the sixteenth century, we must specially notice Maurice de Portu, Archbishop of Tuam, a prelate as distinguished for his piety as for his learning. He was professed at Padua, and there applied himself with great success to theological studies. He illustrated the works of Scotus with numerous notes, teaching from them with unbounded applause. His celebrity was European; his commentaries were received in all the leading schools of the continent, and led to a correspondence with their most distinguished members.

The archbishop died at the Franciscan convent in Galway, in 1516, immediately after his return from the fifth Council of Lateran.

When James I. ascended the English throne, the Irish, naturally hopeful and buoyant, were not without the most sanguine expectations. Toleration for their religion, at least, was anticipated; the few friars who had escaped martyrdom came from their caves and dens, and the priests banished to the continent returned again to their beloved Erin. Monasteries were repaired, churches rebuilt; but the calm was momentary, and presaged a more awful storm than had as yet desolated that unhappy country. In 1605 an edict was published, enforcing the sanguinary enactments of Elizabeth, and soon after a new oath was devised and required of the Catholics as a proof of their allegiance. While the faithful were in doubt what course to pursue, a brief of Paul V. declared it unlawful, which indeed had been the opinion of the great majority. In 1610 this oath was again pressed upon the nation; while Chichester, the Lord Deputy, and Knox, the Protestant Bishop of Raphoe, vied with each other in their hostility to the Catholics of Ireland. Bishops and priests were required to quit the kingdom under penalty of death; to harbor them was a crime punishable by confiscation of property, and, to complete the suppression of Popery, no Catholic was allowed to send any son or relation beyond the sea for education.

The boon of Catholic education was equally denied them at home, as no Catholic was allowed to teach. Knox and his followers now drew the sword. Elizabeth had swept away all that remained of value after the destruction of religious houses enacted by her father. The disappointed rapacity of the new persecutors was therefore fain to satiate itself with greater cruelties, and even with wanton outrages on the houses of the nobility, whose plate and furniture were torn from them under pretence that they were Popish ornaments. All was in vain. As Chichester indignantly exclaimed, Popery seemed inherent in the soil of Ireland, and the very air and climate was infected with it.

The indignation of the European powers for a time checked these persecutions, but in the reign of the fickle and unfortunate Charles, they were again renewed, while the Irish suffered, first for their faith, and then for their loyalty, and experienced treachery and ingratitude almost past belief. The Protestant body, who had hitherto so bitterly persecuted Catholics for not embracing their new opinions, were now, as is well known, equally divided as to the truth of the very "articles of faith," which by fire and sword they had striven to enforce on others. Puritanism triumphed for a time, and they who had clamored most loudly for liberty of concience for themselves, were the last to allow its free exercise to others. Who will write the chronicles of the glorious martyrs whom Cromwell's troopers and Ireton's foot soldiers sent to gain the palms of eternal victory? Who shall tell of the saintly bishops, the laborious parish priests, the patient and much enduring curates, the eloquent-tongued Dominicans, the burning-hearted Franciscans, who fled to mountain and cave, only to be captured again while attempting to discharge their holy ministry, who were martyred with a refinement of torture, by men who had the Gospel of peace ever on their lips, and the savageness of demons in their hearts and hands? To use the words of a writer on Irish ecclesiastical history, to whom we are indebted for many of these details,* "the Irish priesthood had been long since proscribed in the councils of the regicides; hence the clergy of all ranks and of every order were alike involved in the same sweeping sentence of universal extermination."

The town of Wexford, having distinguished itself for resistance to the Puritan troops, was made an object of their special vengeance. In Cromwell's letter to the Parliament on this occasion, he computes the number of the garrison who were slaughtered at two thousand, and recommends English Protestants to be sent over to occupy the places of his victims. From the body of the clergy then residing in Wexford, six Franciscan priests were selected for signal vengeance, the rest being left to indiscriminate slaughter by the soldiers. One of those victims, Father Raymond Stafford, came out of the church with a crucifix in his hand, and continued to preach to the people, and even to his murderers, until his voice was hushed in death. But we cannot wonder that special barbarities were preserved for the friars, when three hundred defenceless females, who clung for safety to the great cross in the market-place, were slaughtered without mercy by those savage men.

In Waterford, a Capuchin father remained for some time unknown, working as a gardener and coal porter for the Protestant officers, and contriving thus to minister in secret to his poor countrymen. In Drogheda and every other garrisoned town, the same scenes were enacted as at Wexford. These were what Cromwell called "crowning mercies;" "a great thing, not done by power or might, but by the Spirit of God." For these atrocities the Parliament passed a vote of

* Ecclesiastical History of Ireland, by the Reverend M. J. Brenan, O.S.F.

thanks to him, and ordered a day of general thanksgiving throughout the kingdom.

The banishment to Connaught was the consummation of misery. It was not enough that bishops, priests and friars should be driven from the kingdom or cruelly tortured; the persecuted people still clung to their faith with a tenacity which astonished and enraged their persecutors. Much had already been done in the way of exterminating the Irish race, but, in spite of famine, plague, and persecution, thousands still survived to show that the faith of their fathers would live in them to their last breath, and that prolonged tortures would only prolong their heroic constancy.

In the year 1654, on a given day, every Catholic in the kingdom, without regard to rank, age, or sex, was required to repair to Connaught, which province was now converted into a national prison. We question if ever the sun looked down on so foul an injustice, so cruel a wrong. To add to this atrocity, it was death to step beyond the limits prescribed; and any Catholic found in any other part of the kingdom could be butchered at once by the finder, without the intervention of judge or jury.* In this western Siberia, the Catholics of Ireland were imprisoned, till the death of Cromwell delivered the English from a lawless usurper, and Ireland from one of her bitterest persecutors.

* So terrible were the sufferings of the Irish at this time, that "to hell or to Connaught with you." became a national by-word. Truly, if a thoughtful mind required any argument to convince it that the Catholic faith was "the religion of the Bible," the contrast might be drawn between Ireland under Henry III., with hospitals and almshouses, and hundreds of priories and convents established, not merely for the spiritual, but even for the temporal relief of the poor, and Ireland under Henry VIII., with its poor driven from the almshouses, its sick turned out of the hospitals, its thousands of paupers whom there was none to relieve, since the monks and friars were deprived of the property which they had used only to minister to their suffering brethren.

It was at this time that the continental colleges were of such special value to the Irish nation; and with a brief mention of a few of the more distinguished Franciscans who were educated in them, we must close this chapter.

Florence Conry was born in Connaught about the year 1560. Like many an Irish youth, he was undeterred by seeing priests and friars hanged, scourged, and tortured for their faith. Eager for the same crown, he retired to Spain with three companions, and applied for admission to the Franciscan convent at Madrid, where they were received and professed. The talents of Conry, and his peculiarly sweet disposition, soon attracted the notice and affection of all; and while yet young, he was nominated to the see of Tuam. Scarcely had he settled in his native land, ere he was expelled from it again, and died an exile at the Franciscan convent of Madrid.

Nor are the Irish Franciscans without name in the republic of letters. The religious, when driven abroad, took with them all such literary treasures as had escaped the ignorant zeal of the reformers and Puritans. To these they added valuable manuscript records, which are still treasured in foreign monasteries. Patrick Fleming, a Franciscan, well skilled in antiquarian lore, had formed the design of preparing materials for the lives of the Irish saints. For this purpose he repaired to Rome in 1623, accompanied by Hugh MacCaghwell, an eminently learned ecclesiastic, who died Archbishop of Armagh. At Paris they met Father Hugh Ward, a distinguished antiquarian, who had been professed at Salamanca. A holy friendship was formed between these learned men, and an agreement entered into to compare the result of their labors. Father Fleming proceeded to Rome, where he was appointed professor of the newly-founded Irish college of St. Isidore; after a time employed in teaching, and in prosecuting his literary researches, he was appointed the first guardian of the Franciscan college at Prague, just established by the Emperor Ferdinand II. Here he obtained what may surely be called a martyr's crown. The city was besieged by the Lutheran Elector of Saxony; and Fleming, endeavoring to escape, in company with another father, was overtaken and massacred. His valuable manuscripts were not published for some years after.

Father Ward was a native of Donegal. His anxiety to rescue the history of his country from oblivion induced him to remain some years in Paris. Here the most valuable manuscripts regarding Irish history had been preserved. Green Erin had not always been the victim of persecution; and, in the sixth and subsequent centuries, was distinguished not only as an island of saints, but as an island of literary and scholastic lore. The students, who flocked to it from all parts of the Continent, had carried home the records of its earliest history, either in original manuscripts or written as they had themselves received the traditions of their learned and gifted instructors. These had been carefully preserved in the religious houses of the continent; and of these Ward determined to avail himself, in compiling a full history of his native land. Having visited the principal monastic and cathedral libraries of the continent, he retired to the convent of St. Antony at Louvain. Here he became acquainted with Brother Michael O'Clery, the principal compiler of the celebrated *Annals of the Four Masters;* and it was Ward who induced Brother Michael to return to Ireland and collect the materials for that work. Ward died before he could complete his labors. The manuscripts which he had himself compiled, with those sent to him by Fleming and O'Clery, were treasured in the archives of the Franciscan convent at Louvain, and were used by Colgan in preparing his *Acta Sanctorum.*

The history of the gifted and humble Brother Michael is truly worthy of the Order he adorned as much by his sanctity as by his learning. Though "born the heir of bardic honors," he had deliberately chosen the poverty of a mendicant friar; and, the better to practice its sublime humility, would be known only as a lay brother. O'Clery was professed at Louvain; and, as we have seen, its gifted and noble-minded guardian, Father Ward, was not slow to discover the talent so carefully concealed. Brother Michael was also a native of the County Donegal; and, after fifteen years of laborious research, he collected the most valuable memorials of the Irish saints, old penitentials, ancient martyrologies, etc. Before commencing his *Annals,* indeed, he had got into his possession almost all the ancient manuscripts and authentic records of the kingdom. Thus prepared, he retired, with five companions, to the monastery of Donegal; and there this most splendid monument of national genius was completed. The names of these pious, learned, and patriotic Irishmen deserve to be placed on record. Ferfessius and Maurice O'Conry, with Peregrine O'Duignan, were natives of Roscommon; Peregrine and Conor O'Clery of Donegal. Thus, as six were employed, the Annals might have been termed of the Six Masters. But as four took the lead, it obtained from them the name by which it is familiar to us. The fame of Brother Michael and his work extended far and wide. Antiquarians have praised, and poets have sung, of the gifted and humble lay brother.

"Other days in green Tyrconnell,
High beside its chiefs had found him
Seated at the festal table;
Now, poor brother of St, Francis,
Less than priest and more than layman,
On the threshold of the chancel
He is well content to hover."

His work, too, has been immortalized in song, as well as himself. It was—

"To save the old memorials
Of the noble and the holy,
Of the chiefs of ancient lineage,
Of the Saints of wondrous virtues,
That he might preserve the story
Of the dear ancestral island."*

We must conclude this imperfect notice of the Irish Franciscan province with Luke Wadding, a name which will be almost as familiar to our readers as those of Colgan or O'Clery. Born at Waterford in the year 1588, this gifted religious was early called to the cloister. He was professed at the convent of the Immaculate Conception near Oporto, where he soon distinguished himself as a preacher. His learning, and particularly his knowledge of languages and theology was so great, that he was appointed to attend the Bishop of Carthagena on an embassy to the Holy See, to investigate some question regarding the doctrine of the immaculate conception. After his arrival in Rome, he resided for a short time with the Cardinal Gabriel à Trejo; but a palace was neither agreeable to his humility nor suitable for his literary pursuits. His extraordinary labors in search of material for his works, and the number of volumes he compiled, have rarely been equalled. His *Annales Minorum* was his great work; but besides these volumes, which were the fruit of twenty-four years' incessant labor, he edited the works of Scotus in sixteen volumes, a *Concordantia Hebraica* in four, and more than eighteen other extensive

* *Poems*, by D. F. M'Carthy, Esq.

works on various theological subjects. At his death he left materials for further literary undertakings, which the infirmities of age alone prevented him from completing.

But the benefits conferred by this great man on his country were not merely literary. The colleges he founded still exist, as the noblest memorials of his piety and benevolence. St. Isidore's College for Franciscans, the Ludovisian College for secular priests, and the novitiate house at Capronica, were all founded by the exertions of this holy religious. As he had long acted as the representative of the Irish Church in Rome, where every matter of importance was referred to his advice, his countrymen, grateful for his invaluable services, were anxious to see him advanced to the College of Cardinals. For this purpose the Supreme Council sent a deputation to Rome with a memorial to Urban VIII. The good father heard of their intention, and contrived to possess himself of the document, which he took good care should never be presented. After his death it was discovered among his papers. Father Luke Wadding died at St. Isidore's on the 18th of November, 1657. A magnificent monument is erected to his memory in that church.

CHAPTER XIII.

Cardinal Ximenes.—His early life.—Enters the Franciscan Order.—Appointed Confessor to Queen Isabella.—Then Archbishop of Toledo.—His charities.—Expedition to Africa.—Death.—Influence in his Order.—St. Joseph of Cupertino.—His early trials.—Refused by one monastery and dismissed by another.—His ecstacies.—Devotion to the Mystery of the Nativity, and to our Blessed Lady.

If we except St. Bonaventura and St. Antony of Padua, few members of the Seraphic Order exercised on it an influence so extensive and beneficial as the great

Cardinal Ximenes. He was born in 1437, at Torriguluna, in the province of New Castile, his family poor, but of noble origin. Little is known of his early days, save that he was devout, studious, and scrupulously obedient to his parents. He was ordained priest in Rome; but on the death of his father he hastened home to assist and comfort his mother. Just as the most brilliant career of advancement, both literary and ecclesiastical, had opened before him, he turned from the attractive prospect, from fame, wealth, and advancement, to seek poverty and obscurity among the Franciscan friars of the Strict Observance. Here he not only practiced all the austerities of their rule, but, with the permission of his superiors, added considerably to their rigor. His favorite retreat was in a chestnut wood, where he had built for himself a hut; and here he frequently spent whole days in prayer and heavenly contemplation. But his extraordinary talents could not be altogether concealed. He was employed to transact the principal business of his convent, and for this purpose was frequently obliged to visit Toledo. His former diocesan was now archbishop of that city; and being desired by Queen Isabella to recommend to her a confessor, he at once proposed Ximenes, as qualified for that important charge by his piety, his learning, and his discretion. The queen was fully satisfied; and when the archbishop died shortly after, Ximenes was nominated to the vacant see. This, however, was managed with some caution; the mortified and unambitious friar was not told of his elevation until a Papal bull had been obtained, requiring him to accept the dignity under pain of canonical censure. Ximenes had no choice but to submit; and though he pined for his hut in the chestnut wood, the will of God was dearer to him than his own spiritual or temporal comfort. His life was henceforth one of heavy and anxious cares; but from the meanest domestic in his employment to the highest ecclesiastic in his diocese, none were forgotten or uncared for. He still wore his poor and patched habit, and lived in the greatest poverty and austerity.

"Matured by experience," says Hefele, in his interesting life of this great cardinal,* "and with a soul strengthened by mortification, Ximenes took possession of the archiepiscopal see of Toledo, in the fifty-ninth year of his age. Like all true reformers, he began by reforming himself, and so giving in his own life and conversation an example and a pattern to others. 'A bishop,' says St. Paul, 'is one that ruleth well his own house.'—I. Tim., iii. 4. Ximenes so faithfully followed this injunction, that we may, without the least hesitation, compare him to St. Charles Borromeo, and other heroes of the Church, who were poor in the midst of riches, hermits in the midst of the world, and models of mortification amidst pomp and luxury.

"Being a Franciscan heart and soul, Ximenes was anxious in his present new dignity, to realize in his own person the apostolic poverty and religious austerity of the founder of his Order, and thus to combine the dignity of a bishop with the simplicity of a monk. No silver, therefore, adorned his table, nor was any ornament to be seen on the walls of his apartments; nowhere could be found the least trace of luxury, nowhere the least symptom of pomp or riches. His garment was the Franciscan habit, and his food only such as the poorest monastery affords. The journeys which he was obliged to make were always performed on foot, though occasionally he made use of a mule, as most poor Spanish priests do. His palace was changed

* Translated by the Very Rev. Canon Dalton. Dolman, 1860.

into a monastery, while only ten Franciscan monks composed the staff of one who was both primate and chancellor."*

This extreme plainness of living, it is true, the archbishop afterwards modified, in obedience to a brief from Alexander VI. to that effect. But his personal mortifications he never abated. Of these, the work already quoted gives several striking details. It then continues: "He daily entertained himself with pious conversations, which he held with his religious brethren around him, and other theologians. He likewise, from time to time, renewed his fervor by making a retreat in some monastery of his Order; and there, like the humblest of the brothers, he performed with them all the religious exercises, made his confessions, and took the discipline. In a secret chamber of his palace he also frequently used the discipline with such severity on his body that Pope Leo X. was obliged to interfere. He seldom wore anything but a hair shirt next his skin."

The primate's alms were distributed with princely munificence and far-sighted wisdom. It would be impossible to recount the charitable foundations of the archbishop, or the all but unrivalled career of the statesman. Of the former, not the least useful was a house at Toledo for the reception of the clergy who might come from the country to consult him on business, and who, hitherto, were thrown on the charity of strangers or the expenses of hostelries. A home was now secured for them where they would always find a welcome, incur no expense, and be sheltered from

* Prescott relates the following anecdote from Quintanilla: "On one occasion, as Ximenes was travelling, and up, as usual, long before dawn, he urged his muleteer to dress himself quickly; at which the latter exclaimed, with an oath: 'Does your holiness think I have nothing more to do than shake myself like a wet spaniel, and tighten my cord a little?'"—*Ibid.*

commerce with the world and the dangers of a great city. Two other establishments were also founded and endowed for the education of females: one for the poor, another for persons of higher rank but decayed fortunes. Besides immense alms to various convents and churches, Ximenes founded a convent in Toledo for the benefit of those who had a vocation to the religious life, but whose poverty did not permit their being received into the cloister.*

After the death of the queen, he projected and carried out the celebrated expedition to Africa, which evidences at once his talent as a statesman, and the heavy addition to his other cares which now devolved on him. It would be out of place here to enter into details on this subject. Suffice it to say, that one among the most noted military expeditions of the world's history was organized, and the whole expense borne, by a Franciscan friar. Let it not, however, be supposed that the object of Ximenes, now a cardinal, was the mere attainment of military fame. His time, and the immense revenues of his archiepiscopal see, were not expended in idle vaunts or glittering projects. The same charity and perfection which led him so vigorously to observe his vow of poverty that he had wherewithal to found convents and endow colleges, now suggested the idea and furnished the means to deprive the Moors of their stronghold at Oran, where so many thousand Christian captives were held in im-

* May we not express regret that this most noble form of charity has found so few imitators? It is surely glorious to build material temples for the honor and worship of God; but how much more so to be the means of consecrating to Him a living soul, whose whole being would be thus dedicated to its Lord both for time and eternity! Many persons are obliged to remain in the world, who would gladly and fervently have consecrated themselves to God, did their circumstances permit; and many superiors of religious houses, particularly of enclosed Orders, who have less means of obtaining support than others, would most thankfully add to the number of their sisters, were such means provided.

prisonment and slavery; and where many, through fear of pain or love of pleasure, had apostatized from the faith.

The life of the great Cardinal closed in suffering and neglect. After the death of Ferdinand, Ximenes was appointed regent until the arrival of his grandson Charles. Evil advisers, jealous of his unusual talents and influence, induced the young king to treat him with indifference, even with contempt. But the friar had served his earthly masters only for the love of his heavenly King, and though he felt keenly what he had so little deserved, his life ended as it had began, in solitude and prayer. His last words were; "*In te, Domine, speravit: non confundar in æternum.*

Robertson, an historian unsuspected of partiality to Catholics and friars, has said of Ximenes, that he is the only prime minister mentioned in history whom his cotemporaries reverenced as a saint, and to whom the people under his government attributed the power of working miracles.*

We have spoken of Zimenes as a saint and a statesman; it remains but to say a few words of his literary fame, and the benefits he conferred on his Order. The celebrated Polyglot Bible of Alcala, generally known as the *Complutensian Polyglot*, is certainly one of the noblest works that have ever issued from the press of any country. This work was planned, carried out, and the entire expense borne by the Cardinal. It was divided into six parts, and published in four volumes. The first three contained the Hebrew, Latin and Greek, in three distinct columns. The Chaldaic paraphrase, with a Latin translation, was at the foot of the page;

* The reader is referred, for a well-drawn parallel and contrast between Ximenes and Richelieu, to the twenty-seventh chapter of Hefele's *Life* already quoted.

and in the margin, the Hebrew and Chaldaic radicals. The fourth volume contained the Greek New Testament, with a Latin translation. This great work was begun in 1502, and completed in 1522. Some of the most learned and eminent men of the age were employed in preparing these volumes for the press, the Cardinal defraying their expense and superintending the whole. The Polyglots of Paris, Antwerp and London, which were afterwards published, may have improved on this undertaking with the advance of learning, and the advantages of easier access to oriental manuscripts, but we may doubt whether they would ever have existed had not the great Polyglot of Alcala prepared the way for them, and appropriated the most laborious and expensive part of the undertaking, though probably the Bible societies of modern Europe would scarcely like to acknowledge how far they are indebted to the zeal and piety of a Franciscan friar.

The foundation of the university of Alcala was another of the princely and munificent works accomplished by Ximenes. Well might Francis I. exclaim when he beheld it, "The university of Paris was the work of many kings, but this friar has, in a few years, raised and completed its equal." Eight colleges were contained within it; among these was the college of St. Ildefonsus, one of the noblest in the world.

But Ximenes had even a more important work on hand than founding colleges or governing kingdoms, and, after the care of his diocese, to which he devoted himself with unremitting zeal, his Order claimed and received his most anxious attention. Strange to say, the piety and munificence of the Spaniards had almost proved seriously injurious to the Franciscan Order in Spain; and when Ximenes strove to effect a reform, he was not merely opposed by the superiors of such communities as had become relaxed, but by the nobles, who had in many instances founded and endowed their monasteries; but his prudence and zeal soon removed all obstacles. He was himself of the Strict Observance, and was naturally anxious that their rigid poverty should be generally observed. The Conventuals, who were permitted to possess property, had become exceedingly wealthy. The princes of the kingdom prided themselves on erecting for them magnificent churches and splendid convents, and left at their death large sums of money, that their tombs, usually of the most costly workmanship, might be repaired and guarded by the friars. The evil of this was soon manifested. The Order was enriched, and though the friars, as individuals, were poor as the poorest beggar, still the possession of large property in community brought with it the cares and the temptations which usually follow in the train of this "root of all evil." Already the strict poverty of the Observant friars had been not only sanctioned but encouraged by the Holy See. Ximenes now appealed to the same authority; he obtained a decree from Pius V. in 1466, obliging the Conventuals to embrace the strict reform, and, where this was not practicable, forbidding them to receive novices. The property which they had accumulated was employed in repairing churches and cathedrals less richly endowed, and also in establishing a permanent maintenance for the support of many convents of Poor Clares who were not endowed; experience having proved the impracticability and injurious effect of their attempting to live entirely on alms.

Lest, however, our readers should imagine that to be a Conventual, and to be relaxed, were synonymous terms, we will, in concluding this chapter, say a few words of one of the many eminent and saintly men who have perfected their sanctity, and attained their eminence, in this portion of the Order. St. Joseph of Cupertino was born in 1603, at the little town of that name. His parents were poor but pious, and his early childhood gave abundant promise of the wonderful graces which were to crown his later years; but, like many who are called to great sanctity, his life-path, even from the cradle, was marked by pain. Constant and severe illnesses, followed by miraculous cures, were his allotted portion, and his mother's natural severity and anxiety for his spiritual good, demanded of him a patience far beyond what is usual even at a more advanced age. Even in moments of the most acute pain, she required that he should utter no complaint, and if nature asserted its sway, reproofs and even severe punishments were at once inflicted. His ecstasies, which in his later years were so frequent and so marvellous, began almost in his childhood. At the age of seven, the sound of an organ, or the voices of religious, chanting the divine office, would so absorb him that he would remain motionless and unconscious of all around. The poverty of his parents required that he should learn a trade, and that of shoemaking was selected; but the young apprentice, with all his anxiety to labor, was found very incompetent for it. His heart pined for the cloister; not from a desire to lead an indolent or useless life, but rather that his time and strength might be all devoted to his God. He applied to a Franciscan convent, where an uncle was already professed, but he was rejected as apparently too dull and too ignorant to become a religious. His next attempt was with the Capuchins, but after a nine months' novitiate, he was dismissed as one who had neither a vocation for work or prayer. Indeed, it would appear as if a complete misconception of his character and abilities had been permitted, not to say appointed, by Divine Providence, either for his humiliation and perfection, or to make his vocation plainer when the haven was at last attained. Although incessantly absorbed in prayer, his outward appearance betokened nothing but stupidity, and the opinion which it suggested was confirmed by his conduct. If sent to assist in the refectory he would give the religious black bread instead of white, or break the plates and throw down the dishes, so that he was perpetually seen in penance with the fragments round his shoulders; if sent to fetch water he fared no better, for he would entirely forget the duty assigned to him, and remain by the well absorbed in prayer.

To crown his misfortunes, his health, always delicate, now gave way entirely; he was, therefore, dismissed, and of course obliged again to resume his secular clothing. The agony which this trial gave him was so great, that he declared, had his very skin been torn piece-meal from his body, he could have borne it better, and in his after life he was seen several times to swoon away even at the recollection of this terrible sorrow. It was decided by the best and holiest, that he had no vocation to religion, yet what a vocation his must have been, to persevere amid such trials! Like St. Francis, he had been born in a stable; to that great patriarch his mother had dedicated him in his earliest infancy, and a child of St. Francis he was yet to be, in spite of all opposition and difficulty. As we hope elsewhere to give a more detailed account of his most interesting life,* we now only say that he

* A series of lives of Franciscan Saints are preparing for publication.

obtained his desire, after encountering trials that would have proved insuperable to one less fervent. Miracles of the most wonderful kind, and of the most touchingly beautiful character, were of daily occurrence until the close of his earthly course. His life was indeed one long rapture of love. Like his seraphic father, the works of nature still spoke to him of nature's God, and he seemed to have inherited a like power over, and tenderness for, the animal creation. Now, he protects some leverets from the hunters; now raises some sheep to life which had been killed by hailstorms; and now brings a flock of singing birds to join their sweet notes to the chanting of the nuns of St. Clare, whose convent was close to his monastery.

Like St. Francis, too, he was specially devoted to the mystery of the Nativity, and at Christmas time was wont to receive the most especial favors. Once he built a crib in the church at Grotella; and on the vigil of the Feast, went into the country and invited the shepherds to come and assist at the midnight Mass. At ten o'clock all had assembled, and Joseph entered the church, heading the troop of peasants, who were singing and playing in their own fashion, no doubt rudely enough. But the Saint heard other music, and was ravished by sounds which are rarely permitted to fall on mortal ears. Inebriated with a joy in which the angels shared, and which perhaps they only could understand, the young friar danced round the church in ecstatic rapture. Then, with a low cry, such as a captive might utter who pined for fatherland, he gazed one moment on the tabernacle where his Beloved lay hidden, as really and as humbly as in the stable of Bethlehem. An instant more, and he had sprung aloft, and was seen kneeling on the altar and embracing the tabernacle. He remained thus for some time, and then descended again as he had risen, with a flight like that of a bird, uninjured by the blazing lights, and without having disturbed any of the ornaments on the altar. To work the most surprising miracles was so ordinary with him, that he never appeared conscious of the astonishing favors granted to his prayers.

But these wonderful graces were not without their counterbalance in suffering. After his profession, for which he had gone through so many, and such severe trials, he passed two years in a bitterness and desolation of spirit which seems, as we read of it, almost beyond endurance. Often he would go to his cell, and closing the window and the door, throw himself on the ground, passing hours in an anguish like His whose sweat on Olivet was great drops of blood. He had renounced all the innocent enjoyments of earth; and now, he was not only deprived of spiritual joys, but even plunged into the deepest gloom. This was perhaps the bitterest trial of his life. It passed away; but others succeeded, to refine and perfect his blessed soul. They came too, as trials ever come for those whom God loves most, just in the way likely to cause him most suffering.

St. Joseph died on the 18th of September, 1663. His last words were, "*Monstra te esse matrem.*" His devotion to Mary had begun in the cradle, and burned with an ever-increasing forvor through each year of his life. His particular devotion was to her immaculate conception, and even in death it seemed acceptable for her; for he was buried in a chapel dedicated to that mystery.

CHAPTER XIV.

Tartary, China and the adjacent countries.—Mission of Plano Carpino and his companions to the Grand Khan of Tartary.—Interview with Conyonk and letter of the latter to the Pope.—Embassy of religious from King Louis of France to the Grand Khan.—Discussion ordered by the Grand Khan between the Franciscans, Nestorians, Mussulmans and Buddhists. — "Society of Brother Travellers for Jesus Christ."—Friar de Monte Corvino, first Bishop and Archbishop of Khan-balik, or Pekin. — His interesting letter. — Clement V. sends seven Franciscan bishops to be the suffragans of Monte Corvino in 1307.—Blessed Oderic evangelizes nearly all Tartary, and visits his brethren in China.—Benedict III. sends Franciscans as Apostolic Nuncios to High Asia in 1338.—Missionaries sent to China in 1371.—Change of the Chinese dynasty and persecution of the Christians.—The missionaries never abandon the field. —Missions along the Glacial Sea, in the Tauro-Chrodnese, Odessa, on the Caspian Sea, in Siberia, on the Sea of Azof, and in Lithuania.

Towards the middle of the thirteenth century a new and mighty power rose up in the east which threatened to overrun the whole west, and extinguish the last vestige of civilization and Christianity. Western Europe had not forgotten the irruption of the northern barbarians, whom it took the Church so long to civilize and christianize. These formidable hordes were called Tartars, and wherever they established their power they adopted the dominant mode of worship: thus they became Buddhists in China, and Mussulmans in Persia. After having subjugated the extreme east, they advanced westward. For three years Hungary remained one vast theatre of carnage and destruction. The Christian sovereigns of Europe were called on in vain to stem this torrent. Frederick Barbarossa was then warring on the Papacy. In 1245 a council general was assembled at Lyons, and Innocent IV. mentioned, among the principal motives that had induced him to convoke it, the urgent necessity of deliberating upon the methods of defending Europe against the Tartars.

Innocent IV. requested the generals of the Franciscans and Dominicans to announce the resolution of the council, and to charge them to choose among the friars of their orders those who might be entrusted with the mission to Tartary.

Three friars of the Order of St. Francis—John of Plano Carpini, Stephen of Bohemia, and Benedict of Poland—were sent to Tartary. These embassies had the double purpose of propagating religion and civilization, and the Popes were already in the habit of choosing their missionary ambassadors to infidel nations from these two spiritual families, which, though still in their infancy (Carpini having been a companion of St. Francis), had shed such glory on the Church and rendered society immense services; and ambassadors chosen from any other class would not, perhaps, have offered, at that period, the same guarantee of skill and self-abnegation, of zeal and fidelity.

The two embassies set out in 1246—Carpini and his companion Laurence travelling through Bohemia and Silesia, and meeting at Breslau Benedict of Poland, who was to act as interpreter. Our limits will not permit us to follow them in the long and painful journeyings in these unknown regions, and among a people of which Europe knew absolutely nothing, except what had been learned by their rapid and terrible devastation.

The report of their travels was, perhaps, the most interesting and valuable that had been as yet given to Europe, and so exact, that it is still made use of by the celebrated historian Cantù; and even Abbé Huc who, a few years since, himself travelled through much of the same territory and among the same people, in his work on China, Tartary and Thibet, gives, nearly entire and with praise, the relation of the Franciscan Carpini.

At Danilou, Carpini fell dangerously ill, and had to be carried through the snow in the most severe weather. Stephen was too much exhausted to proceed further than Kieu, the metropolis of Russia, and then in the hands of the Tartars. Carpini and Benedict continued their journey, reaching the advanced posts of the Mongols, on the banks of the Dneiper, where they met the Tartar prince who held command on this frontier, and by him they were sent to the count of Baton, the grandson of Gengis-Khan. Riding at full gallop every day for five weeks, with no food but millet, and no drink but melted snow, and changing horses as often as seven times a day, they at length arrived at the encampment of Baton, on the banks of the Volga.

By Baton, they were sent to the Yellow Horde. They set out, attended by two Tartars, who had orders to make them travel very fast, though they were so weak that they could hardly keep themselves on their horses, and were obliged to use the precaution of travellers in these regions, of getting their eyes bandaged, to relieve the pain occasioned by hard galloping. Finally, on the twenty-second of July, about five months after their entrance into the Mongol territory, they arrived at the imperial residence near the Dneiper.

When they arrived at the Imperial Horde, they found that the Khan Dgotai was dead; that his widow, Tourakina, was invested with the regency until the election of his successor, and that she was making all her efforts to have her son, Conyonk, named in the kourittai, or general assembly.

The day fixed for the election arrived, and the convocation, which was to take place near a fine Take, in a district called the Seventy Hills, had set in motion all the Tartar princes of Asia, and the roads that lead from all parts of the continent to the centre of Tartary, were covered with travellers. The princes of the blood came attended by a numerous military escort; Utjukan, with his *eighty* sons; the widow of Toulom, accompanied by her children; the descendants of Dgotai, Djoutchi and Tchagatai, followed by the chiefs of their particular tribes; the military and civil governors of the Mongol possessions in China, Argoun and Massoud; the governors-general of Persia and of Imbuston and Trans-Oxiana, with the princes and lords of three countries, in their train; the sultan of Roum-Rak-Uddin; Yaroslar, the grand duke of Russia; two princes, named David, who were contending for the crown of Georgia; the brother of the sovereign of Aleppo; ambassadors from the Caliph of Bagdad and from the princes of Ismail, Mossoul, Karss and Kerman—all bringing magnificent offerings, and rivalling each other in the richness and pomp of their equipments.

In the midst of this crowd of distinguished personages, surrounded by all the splendor of Asiastic luxury, there were two persons, remarkable for the simplicity of their attire and the modesty of their behavior—the two spiritual children of St. Francis of Assisi, sent to preach the Gospel to these fierce barbarians, and teach them to seek, before all things, the "kingdom of God and His justice."

Conyonk being unanimously chosen, all the princes assembled in the palaces, and put a golden seat in the midst of them, on which he was to sit, and thus addressed him: "We will, we pray, and we command, that you have power and dominion over us all." He replied : "If you wish that I should be your king, are you resolved and disposed, each one of you, to do all that I shall command ? to come when I shall call you? to go when I shall send you ? and to kill all those whom I shall tell you to kill?" And they all answered, "We are!" Then he said to them : "Henceforward, my simple word shall serve me as a sword." Much more ceremony took place, followed by an enormous banquet, to which all the princes and princesses were invited. The repast consisted of meat, and profusion of rice and wine, from China, and of kumys, or spirits made from mare's milk. The guests drank till the middle of the night, to the sound of musical instruments and martial songs, and the feast was renewed every day for seven days.

Towards the end of August the Franciscans were admitted to an audience with Conyonk. From the Golden Horde, they proceeded to another residence, and here again they were several times admitted to the imperial court. One day they were requested to retire from the court, till further orders, which, they found out, was on account of a ceremony which they did not desire them to witness. It consisted in Conyonk's raising a great banner towards the west, and while waving it, threatening to carry fire and sword over all the countries in that direction, which should not, along with the rest of the earth, submit to his authority.

They were sent for when this ceremony was over, yet but little notice was taken of them for a whole month, and they suffered much from scarcity of food ; what was distributed to them for four days barely sufficing for one day. The grand khan at length gave a solemn audience to all the ambassadors, and the Franciscans resolved to profit by it, to fulfill, if possible, the mission with which they were charged. Having asked Conyonk why his armies conquered the world, he replied, "God has commanded me and my forefathers to exterminate criminal nations." They then stated that the Sovereign Pontiff desired to know whether the kha-khan had embraced Christianity, for such had been the report. "God knows it," he replied, "and if the Pope wishes to know too, he has but to come and see."

It is certain that Tourakina, his mother, did make some profession of Christianity, and that the emperor had in his service a great number of Christians, amongst whom were one of his ministers and a secretary.

The Franciscans had gone to Tartary, in the persuasion that the kha-khan protected the Christians, but they were not long in perceiving that this emperor, in concert with his vassals, had raised his banner against the Church and against all Christian kings and princes. The successors of Gengis-Khan acknowledged no distinct religious system, until the time of Khublai, who adopted Buddhism and compelled his subjects to follow his example; therefore, it is not surprising that Christians should have been well received by Conyonk, as he gave an equally good reception to Mussulmans and Lamas.

The ambassadors of the Pope were at length under the necessity of taking their departure, and the court began to prepare their letters.

Conyonk's answer was for a long time lost sight of, but has at length been discovered, in a manuscript of Colbert, on the Appendix to the recital of Benedict of Poland. It is as follows:

"CONYONK, BY THE POWER OF GOD, KHAN AND EMPEROR OF ALL MEN—TO THE GREAT POPE:

"You and all the Christian people who inhabit the west have

sent me a certain and authentic letter, by an ambassador, with the intention of making with us a treaty of peace. Nor has your said messenger failed to clearly express, in words, the same. Now, if this be truly so, you, therefore, O Pope, and you, all emperors and kings, and captains of cities, and governors of provinces—do not delay an instant to come before me, to define and desire this peace—that you may have our answer and will. The tenor of your letter is, in the first place: that we should be baptized and become Christians. But to this we answer, That really we do not understand why we should do the same. In the second place, you show yourself greatly surprised and moved at the death of so many men, above all, Christians, and, especially, Hungarians, Poles and Moravians. * * * This, also, I confess, I do not at all comprehend. But that we may not seem to wish to pass such argument in silence, we have thought it well to give you the following response: that is, such castigation has befallen them for not having obeyed the commandments of God and of Ghenghis-Khan, and for having, by giving ear to evil counsels, put to death our ambassadors (ambassadors of Ghenghis to the Russians had been put to death). And hence it is that God has commanded them to be annihilated, consigning them to our hands. * * * And in truth, if it were not the work of God, what could one man do against another man? But you, inhabitants of the west, say that you adore God, believing only yourselves to be Christians, whence you despise all others. But how do you know that He has really imparted such grace to you? We, also, adore God; and it is only by His power that we destroy all the nations of the east and of the west; for, without the power of God, what could man himself do?"

This letter bore the imperial seal, surrounded with the following inscription:

"God in Heaven and Cayuk-Khan on Earth! Power of God! Seal of the Emperor of all men!"

The emperor had intended to send his own envoys with this answer, but Carpini dissuaded him, by picturing the dangers of the long journey through hostile nations. His real motive was, that the envoys of Conyonk might not witness the dissension which then existed among the Christian kings of Europe.

On the 13th of November the envoys were admitted to a farewell audience with the khan, received his letter, and were afterwards conducted to the empress-mother, who gave each of them a pelisse of fox skin and a robe of other stuff.

They followed the route by which they had came, and as it was winter, they had, for the most part, to sleep upon the snow, or in a hole that they scraped in the ground. It was a bare country without any trees, and often in the morning they found themselves quite covered by the snow which the wind had drifted on them.

They reached Kien on the 9th of June, 1247, and Carpini had the joy of finding that the proposals which he had made to certain princes and bishops of Russia, for a reunion with the Church, had been accepted. After traversing Russia, Poland, Bohemia and Germany, he passed the Rhine at Cologne, continued his route by Liege and Champagne, and finally, at Lyons, placed in the hands of the Sovereign Pontiff, the letter which he had brought from the Emperor of Tartary.

John de Plano Carpini, the chief of the embassy to the Tartars, as we have said, was a companion of St. Francis and a native of Perouse, in the vicinity of Assisi. He had held responsible positions in Saxony and other parts of Germany, and, being full of zeal, had founded convents in Bohemia, Hungary, Norway, Dacia, Lorraine and Spain. He was sent by Gregory IX. to the Mohammedan chief of Tunis, and founded houses also in Barbary, and after his return from Tartary he was made archbishop of Antivari, in Dalmatia. The Pope, who had kept him for three months near his own person, then addressed him : "Be thou blessed by the Lord and by me, His Vicar ; for I see that in thee are fulfilled the sayings of the wise man, 'As the cold of snow in the time of harvest, so is a faithful messenger to them that send him, for he refresheth the soul of his master' (Prov. xxv. 3). Well done, thou good and faithful servant, since thou hast been faithful over few things I will place thee over many."

The new archbishop was sent some time afterwards on a mission to St. Louis of France, then in the east, but he did not long survive his return ; and when we consider that he was sixty-five years old when he undertook the perilous mission to Tartary, it will seem surprising that he did not sink immediately under the hardships and privations of such an expedition.

He was succeeded in the see of Antivari by his companion in Tartary, Laurence of Portugal.

In 1298 St. Louis of France had arrived at the Isle of Cyprus, on his way to the sea, for the deliverance of the Holy Sepulchre from the power of the Mussulmans, when he received an embassy from Iltechikadai, the successor of Baidjou, the commander of the Tartar forces in Persia, seeking to join the Franks against the Mussulmans. The letters of the ambassadors represented the grand khan as a zealous convert to Christianity and disposed to favor the Christians in all things.

St. Louis despatched some friars of the Order of St. Dominic, as envoys to the Emperor of Tartary, and traversing Persia, on their way to the camp of Iltechikadai, they reached the Mongol court, after a journey of nearly a year. They proceeded at the rate of ten leagues each day, finding all the districts which they traversed subject to the Tartars, and meeting in many places heaps of ruins that had been towns or cities, and piles of dead men's bones.

When they arrived at the imperial court, Conyonk was dead, but had not been replaced by a successor, and they were received by the queen-regent Ogoul. In return for the gifts which they brought, she presented the envoys with various articles, among which was, according to the Chinese custom, a piece of silk stuff. She afterwards dismissed them with honor, but without their having obtained any positive answer as to the principal object of their mission. They were even charged with a letter to King Louis, in which the khan (probably a prince temporarily associated with the Queen Ogoul in the nursery) demanded that he should send an annual tribute in gold and silver, and threatening, in case of refusal, that he should be put to the sword, as he (the khan) had served many other kings, and destroyed them and their people.

The ambassadors of Louis had found in Tartary a great number of Christians, mostly Nestorians, who offered their communion to the envoys, acknowledging that the Church of Rome was the mother of all the Churches, and that they ought to have received their patriarch from the Pope if the road to Rome had been open. The Tartars, and the khan himself, respected the name of Jesus Christ, and Maryon, who had succeeded Conyonk, showed favor to the Christians, and was even supposed to be Christian himself.

Notwithstanding the affront offered to him by the regent, Ogoul, St. Louis, who ardently desired the advancement of the faith, thought it would be desirable to raise to the Episcopal dignity, the Friars of St. Francis and St. Dominic, who were destined to preach the Gospel in Tartary. Having written to the Pope on the subject, in 1253, the latter sent to the Bishop of Tusculum, his legate at the French court, to do what he should find desirable for the good of the country, with which he was better acquainted than most others.

A new mission to Tartary was committed to the charge of two Franciscan Friars, William Rubriquis and Bartholomew of Cremona. They went from Acre to Constantinople, which was then in the hands of the Franks, and Rubriquis, preaching in St. Sophia, declared that he was going to Tartary to preach the gospel to the infidels. They embarked on the 7th of May, 1253, in a vessel which took them to Soldaya, where they organized a caravan for the long and perilous journey, consisting of eight covered carts—two of which were for beds—and five saddle-horses, for the little party, composed of the two friars, an interpreter, a guide, and a servant.

On the third day after leaving Soldaya, they met with the Tartars, and when they had seen them, and observed their manners, it seemed to them as if entering a new world.

As they went along, they preached, as well as they could by the aid of their interpreter, to these barbarous races, concerning the truths of the gospel. They suffered much from hunger and thirst, for there was nothing to be bought; and the only food they could obtain was some sour milk. The waters they came to were so fetid and muddy, with the trampling of horses, that it was impossible to drink them, so that, Rubriquis says, had it not been for the biscuit they carried with them, and the mercy of God that helped them, they would have starved. And they were better off when travelling through the desert than when they got to the Tartar's lodgings.

Thus they continued their journey, from camp to

camp, through hardships and trials of all kinds, till they reached the banks of the Don, which they were obliged to cross. Fortunately they found some small boats; and finally, at the end of a month's journey, they arrived at the encampment of Sartak, who was a Nestorian Christian. They presented him their letters from Louis; but he told them they would be obliged to have the permission of his father, Baton, to remain in the country, and said that he would send them to his court.

They were thus obliged to go to the Tartar encampment on the Volga, and were much surprised to find that it covered as much space as a great city, with its suburbs extending to the distance of three or four leagues, and containing a multitude of people.

They were conducted to the court of Baton, and thus addressed him: "My lord, we pray God, from whom all good things proceed, that as He has given you all these temporal advantages, He will, after that, be pleased to give you celestial ones also—inasmuch as the one is vain and useless without the other."

Louis had asked permission for the friars to remain in Tartary and preach the faith; but Baton said he would not assume to grant this permission—it must be obtained from the emperor, Manyon, who had been proclaimed Kha-Khan in 1250.

Again were they obliged to continue their journey, for which they were promised the means of transport, as well as provisions. For five weeks they pursued their weary way along the banks of the Volga, nearly always on foot, and often in want of food. About the middle of September, they left that river, and directed their course towards the Ural. The cold had now become intense, and the guide told them that they would have to travel four months more before reaching the court of Manyon-Khan, and that the frost in those countries was so intense that it split trees and stones. He asked them whether they could endure such a journey; and the intrepid Franciscans replied, that what other men could endure, they, by the grace of God, would be able to endure. Their food was millet, boiled in water, and kumys, with sometimes a little meat, which they were obliged to eat almost raw, for the want of fuel to cook it.

January 4th, 1254, they reached the residence of the Grand Khan, and were admitted to an audience. The felt curtain before the door was drawn up as they entered, and being Christmas season, they began to sing the hymn,

A solis ortus cardine. (Rom. Brev. Laud. Nativ.)

The khan ordered kumys, and mead, and rice wine, from China, to be brought, and seemed to take pleasure in regaling his guests, and did honor, himself, to all the liquors, which, though not very pleasant, are quite intoxicating. A long conversation followed—the khan asking Rubriquis many questions concerning the object of his journey—and the intention of the Pope and the Christian kings. But the kumys had so muddled the heads of the Tartars, that the good friar could not understand what they said. "I understood nothing from what our interpreter said, except that he was very drunk; and the emperor, in my opinion, not much better!"

During their stay at the court, they observed that Manyon-Khan and the members of his family attended equally the religious ceremonies of Armenian Christians, Mahometans, and Buddhists—and that they knew nothing of Christianity, beyond some external rites.

Towards Easter, the missionaries followed Manyon-Khan to Kara-karoum, an insignificant town, and on the approach of Easter, 1254, all the Christians of Kara-karoum earnestly besought Rubriquis to celebrate Mass—and they were of many nations—Hungarians, Alani, Russians, Georgians, and Armenians, whose confessions he heard by means of an interpreter—explaining to them, as well as he could, the commandments of God, and the dispositions necessary for worthily receiving the Sacrament of Penance. On Holy Thursday, he offered up the Sacrifice of the Mass, in the Baptistry of the Nestorians, where there was an altar. Their patriarch had sent from Bagdad a large, square parchment, consecrated with crism, which served them as a portable altar, and he used their chalice and patena of silver—two vessels of disproportionate size. He also said Mass on Easter-day, administering the holy communion to the people. On the vigil of Easter, more than sixty persons were baptized, with good order—which produced great joy among the Christians.

In Kara-karoum an opportunity soon presented itself for the friars to make a solemn profession of faith in presence of the court. The emperor, seeing around him the representatives of various religions, all claiming the truth as in their possession, determined on bringing them face to face, and making them explain their various claims in the presence of the people. He ordered that a public discussion should take place between the Christians, Mahometans, and Buddhists. It was forbidden, under pain of death, for any of the orators to say anything abusive of their adversaries, or raise any tumult.

Rubriquis disputed with the Buddhists concerning the Unity of God; and the umpires, three of the emperor's secretaries, one a Mussulman, another a Buddhist, and the third a Nestorian Christian—and even the Chinese Bonze himself—declared the Franciscan to have gained the victory. The Nestorians then resolved to enter the lists against the Mussulmans, but the latter declared that there was no ground for dispute; that they regarded the Christian law as a true one, and believed all that the gospel contained, that they acknowledged only one God, and prayed to Him every day. The conference being ended, says Rubriquis, the Nestorians and Saracens chanted together with a loud voice, but the pagans were silent; and then the whole assembly drank pretty freely.

The day after the controversy, Manyon sent for Rubriquis, and said to him: "We Mongols believe that there is one God, by whom we live and die, and towards whom our hearts are wholly turned." "May God give you His grace, that it may be so," said Rubriquis, "for, otherwise, it is impossible." The emperor then continued, "As God has given the hand several fingers, so has He prepared for men several ways by which they may go to heaven. He has given the Gospel to the Christians, but they do not obey it. He has given soothsayers to the Mongols; and the Mongols do what their soothsayers command, and they therefore live in peace."

He then terminated the interview by declaring that the missionaries had now been long enough in his empire, and that it was time they should think of returning home; and they were not afterwards allowed any more opportunity for explaining the truths of religion.

After a stay of five months at the imperial court, the missionaries prepared to depart. Manyon wished to send some ambassadors with them, but they declined this offer. He then gave them letters for Louis, of France, in reply to those they had presented. Rubriquis asked if, after having delivered these letters, he might return to watch over the spiritual welfare of the Christians in this part of Tartary. Manyon made no reply, but advising them to make the necessary provisions for their long journey, offered the usual refreshments, gave them three robes and dismissed them.

In his letter to Louis, the emperor takes the title of Son of Heaven, and Sovereign Lord; and commands him, if he wishes to merit his favor and attain his friendship, to obey, exactly, the laws of the successors of Gengis-Khan.

Rubriquis took leave of Manyon on July 8th, 1254. Bartholomew of Cremona was obliged, on account of his bad health, to remain, and he therefore set out accompanied by a single guide. On the 16th of September he reached the camp of Baton, after a march of seventy days, during which he saw but one village, and even then he could not procure so much as a little flour, so that his only food was a little kumys. For several weeks he accompanied the nomadic court of Baton, but at length quitted the Tartars, and took his way towards Caucasus; and after having traversed Armenia and Syria, arrived, August 15, 1255, at his convent of St. John d'Acre, whence he addressed his narrative to St. Louis, being immediately employed in the ministerial duties from which he had been called to undertake this mission.

It was certainly a most remarkable thing in those days to hear that, in the midst of the steppes of Tartary, and under the tent of the grandson of Gengis-Khan, a religious conference had taken place concerning the Unity of God and the Blessed Trinity, between Pagans, Christians, and Mahometans—between a Friar of St. Francis of Assisi, from the west, and a Chinese philosopher, from the remotest east. And to hear, too, of this poor Franciscan offering up the Holy Sacrifice of the Mass, according to the Latin rite—baptizing—hearing confessions, and administering communion to Christians at Karoum, the Tartar capital. No less remarkable and beautiful to hear that they sang, on entering the tent of the Tartar emperor, that beautiful hymn whose very words they were thus fulfilling, composed in the fifth century by a priest of the most western portion of the known earth:

"A solis ortûs cardine
Ad usque terræ limitem,
Christum canamus principem
Natum Maria Virgine.*

In 1252, Innocent IV. formed a body of missionaries, taken from the Franciscans, Dominicans, and other religious bodies, called the "Society of Brother Travellers for Jesus Christ;" who were to be the pioneers in opening the way for the light of the gospel among the infidel nations. It had among its members, bishops and archbishops, on whom the Holy See had conferred great powers.

Alexander IV., successor of Innocent IV., showed no less ardor for the conversion of the nations and the propagation of the faith throughout the world. In 1257, this Pope addressed a diploma to the Friars Minor, which shows how far the Order was already spread even at this early day of its career. It commences: "To our dear brothers of the Minorite Orders, in the land of the Saracens, Pagans, Greeks, Bulgarians, Cumanians, Ethiopians, Syrians, Iberians, Alans, Gazares, Goths, Zignes, Rothenes, Georgians, Nubians, Nestorians, Jacobites, Armenians, Indians, Mastelites, Tartars, Hungarians of Great Hungary, Turks, and other infidel nations of the east." Here was truly an apostolic field for the children of St. Francis.

* *Sedulius*, an Irish priest of the fifth century.—Rom. Brev. Hym. ad Lain. Nativ. D. N. J. C.

But of all the nations thus indicated, the Tartars were the most powerful, for the Emperor Manyon ruled from the most eastern parts of Asia to Constantinople, and Poland, the banks of the Danube, Bulgaria, Turkey, the principality of Antioch, in fact, the whole east, even to India, had become tributary to the Mongols.

Nicholas III. sent five Franciscan missionaries, with letters, to the "Excellent and Magnificent Prince Aboya, the illustrious king of the Oriental Tartars," and to his uncle, Kublain, "Grand-Khan, Emperor, and Moderator of all the Tartars." These friars were Gerard de Prato, Anthony of Parma, John of St. Agatha, André of Florence, and Matthew of Arezzo.

We have no details of their mission; it may be well supposed, however, that their labors bore fruit, for the Hungarian provincial of the Franciscans wrote the Sovereign Pontiff to ask a Bishop for Tartary, since, as he says, "several of our brethren who reside among the Tartars, and preach the faith of Jesus Christ to them with zeal, have, by Divine grace, converted great numbers of them."

Nicholas III. desired Philip, Bishop of Firman and Legate Apostolic, to consecrate a bishop, and assign him whatever revenues would accrue to the Holy See, in those countries. We do not know the name of this first bishop among the Tartars; but the fact shows that Christianity made great progress since the sending of the five Franciscans.

The faith could not fail to make considerable progress in High Asia, as the Friars of St. Francis were now scattered over these vast countries, preaching the gospel with zeal and perseverance. They had founded several missions, to which new apostles were continually proceeding, who counted as nothing, the fatigues and dangers of these long and toilsome journeys, if only they could make God known, and effect the salvation of souls. And we find Pope Nicholas writing to Denis, Bishop of Touris, recommending to him the Franciscan missionaries.

In 1289, important and interesting news was received at Rome, concerning the state of the Christian religion in Upper Asia, brought by missionaries who had been sent into Tartary by Bonagratia, general of the Franciscans, and who came to give a verbal account of their apostleship to the Sovereign Pontiff, after a residence of ten years in those distant regions.

These indefatigable apostles had travelled the whole of the countries subject to the Mongol power; they had seen, face to face, those Tartar Khans whose names, exploits, and atrocities, filled the world; and they had preached the gospel to those innumerable populations whom the fury of war had collected from every point of the far east, to mingle there together, and crush them in their frightful struggles. The testimony of these friars, of these priests, of these "travellers for Jesus Christ," as they were called—"*peregrinantium propter Christum*"—was in the highest degree interesting.

The chief of these Franciscan missionaries was John de Monte Corvino, a friar of singular piety, great learning, and indefatigable zeal for the propagation of the faith, who had already become famous through all the east, for his eminent abilities.

After a very short stay in the west, Corvino and his companions set out to resume their holy and laborious ministry in Upper Asia; and Nicholas IV. gave them letters to Angonn, and to Kublai, emperor of the Tartars and Chinese, who had established his court at Pekin.

John de Monte Corvino had been sent to Tartary in 1289. He crossed the Indies, and, after great fatigue, arrived at the court of the Great Khan, then fixed at Pekin, or, as it was then called, Khanbalik (royal residence). He set to work, with indefatigable ardor, at the task of converting both grandees and people ; and, after the example of the great apostle of the Gentiles, he was all things to all men, that he might gain all men to Jesus Christ.

A short time after his arrival, he succeeded in restoring to the unity of the Church, George, king of the Kéraites, who was a Nestorian, and the example of the monarch was followed by a large number of his subjects ; and he himself assumed the habit of the third order, so that he might be able to assist in the celebration of the sacred services. He also built a large and beautiful church, which was called the Roman Church, and died a fervent Christian in 1299.

Corvino erected two churches, even in the town of Pekin, where he performed the service with all the pomp of the ceremonial. He trained a large number of young Tartars to chant ; and the emperor became fond of coming to hear them, and sometimes presented the friars with marks of his esteem and veneration.

The religion of Jesus Christ thus spread rapidly among those populations formerly so plunged in gross superstition and barbarism ; and John de Monte Corvino became so thoroughly conversant with the Tartar language that he translated the Testament and Psalms into that tongue, and published an edition of it remarkable for the beauty and elegance of the characters, a performance which gained him much renown amongst a people who had already obtained some insight into the ancient civilization and literature of the Chinese.

John de Monte Corvino himself describes, with a beautiful simplicity, the difficulties he encountered, and the final success of his mission, in a letter to the Vicar-General of the Order. It is as follows:

"KHANBALIK (in the Kingdom of Cathay),
January 8, 1305.

"I, Brother John de Monte Corvino, of the Order of Minor Friars, quitted Tawns, the capital of Persia, in the year of our Lord, 1291; I penetrated into the Indies, and remained thirteen months in the Church of St. Thomas, the Apostle; there I baptized about a hundred persons, and there the companion of my journey, Brother Nicholas de Pistoria, of the Order of St. Dominic, died, and was buried. For myself, proceeding further on, I arrived at the Kingdom of Cathay, the dominion of the Emperor of Tartary, called the great Khan.

"On presenting to him the letters from the Pope, I endeavored to induce him to embrace the religion of our Lord Jesus Christ; but though he was himself too profoundly plunged in idolatry to do so, it did not prevent him from conferring many favors on the Christians. I have been at his court for two years. Certain Nestorians, who, though pretending to be Christians, conform but little to the Christian religion, have acquired much authority in this country, and will scarcely allow Christians of another creed to establish even a small oratory, in which they might preach any doctrine differing from the Nestorians. These Nestorians, either directly or by means of persons whom they have corrupted by money, raised the most determined persecutions against me, saying everywhere, that I had not been sent, in reality, by our Lord, the Pope; but that I was a dangerous spy, and seducer of the people; then they produced false witnesses who maintained that I had killed a foreign ambassador in India, who had been entrusted with a treasure to take to the emperor, which I had myself seized upon. Their persecutions lasted for nearly five years, during which time I was often in the hands of justice, and was threatened with an ignominious death; but at last, by the grace of God, the testimony of one of the criminals proved my innocence to the emperor, and at the same time showed him the malice of my enemies, who were then exiled, with their wives and children.

"I remained here alone for eleven years, at the end of which time I was joined by Brother Arnold, a German of the province of Cologne. I have built a church at Khanbalik, the principal residence of the emperor, which has been finished now for about six years, and in which there is a belfry, with three bells. In this church I have, altogether, baptized nearly 6,000 persons; and if it had not been for the calumnies of which I have spoken, the number would have been 30,000. I have purchased 150 boys, the sons of pagans, whose ages varied from seven to eleven years, who had hitherto been without any religion at all – have baptized them, and instructed them in the elements of Greek and Latin literature. I have written for their use psalters, as well as thirty-two collections of hymns, and two breviaries, so that eleven of these boys can now chant in choirs, whether I am present myself or not, as is done in our own monasteries; and several of the others are able to transcribe the psalters and other books. The emperor is very fond of hearing them sing.

"At certain hours I have the bells rung, and celebrate divine services before these children; and, not having any written service, we chant a little from memory. A prince named George, one of the illustrious race of the emperor, who was formerly a Nestorian, attached himself to me in the first year of my arrival. I converted him to the true Catholic faith; he has received minor orders, and when I celebrate divine service, he assists me, dressed in his royal robes. The Nestorians have accused him of being an apostate, and have raised persecutions against him; he has, however, restored the greater portion of his people to the true faith, and has had a church built, with true royal magnificence, in honor of the God of the Holy Trinity, and of the Pope of Rome, which he has called the Roman Church. Six years ago, in 1299, the king George died, a true Christian, having for an heir a child nine years of age.

"The brothers of the king, who adhered obstinately to their Nestorian errors, have, since his death, perverted those whom he had converted, and drew them back into their former errors. Unfortunately, I am here alone, and cannot leave the emperor;

and it is, therefore, impossible for me to visit the church, which is at a distance of twenty days' journey. If, however, I had the assistance of good missionaries I am confident I would be able to repair all this mischief, as I have still in my possession the powers conferred on me by the late king. I repeat, also, that but for the calumnies of which I have spoken, the fruit of my labors would have been very abundant, and if I could have been assisted by two or three companions, the emperor himself might, perhaps have been baptized.

"I have not, for twelve years, received any intelligence, either from the Court of Rome, or from our own Order; and I am entirely ignorant of the state of affairs in the West. I entreat the minister-general of our Order to send me an antiphonary, a list of the saints, a gradual, and a psalter, with notes, for a model; as at present I am only provided with a portable breviary, containing the short lessons, and a small missal. If I had but one copy the boys could transcribe it. I am building a second church, in order to divide these boys. But I am already old and gray—rather from toils and tribulations than age, being scarcely fifty-eight. I have learned to read and write in the Tartar language, and have translated into that tongue the whole of the New Testament and the psalter, which I have had written in very beautiful Tartar characters; and teach and preach, publicly, the law of Jesus Christ.

"I had arranged with King George to have translated, if he had lived, the whole of the Latin ritual, in order that the praises of the Lord might have been chanted every day when in his dominions. During his lifetime he was in the habit of celebrating the holy sacrifice of the Mass in his church, according to the Latin ritual. The son of the king George has been named John, in consequence of it being my name; and I sincerely hope that, with the help of God, he will follow in the footsteps of his father. According to what I have seen and heard, I do not believe that there is any other prince of the earth who can equal the Grand Khan, as to the extent of the countries where he reigns, the multitude of people whom he commands, and the amount of the treasures with which he is furnished."

But the zeal of the Holy See soon put an end to the

long and painful isolation of Corvino. In 1307 Clement V. sent seven other Franciscans to China. They were Gérard, Peregrin, André de Pérouse, Nicholas de Bantra, Peter of Castile, Andrutius d'Assisi, and William of Villeneuve. In order to give an especial authority to this mission in the extreme East, the Pope created John de Monte Corvino Archbishop of Pekin, and made the seven missionaries his suffragans. Before their departure they were consecrated, and received many privileges, to facilitate the performance of their duties in those remote regions.

Only three of these seven Franciscan Bishops reached their destination: Gérard, Peregrin, and André de Pérouse. They arrived in 1308, and consecrated John de Monte Corvino Archbispop of Pekin. Nicholas de Bantra, Peter of Castile, and Andrutius d'Assisi, died of the fatigues of the journey, soon after entering the Indies; and William of Villeneuve returned, and was appointed Bishop of Saxona, in Corsica, in 1325.

Such progress did the Chinese mission make, that in 1312, three new sees were formed, and Clement V. chose friars of the Order of St. Francis to fill them. They were Thomas, Jerome, and Peter of Florence. In the bull sent to the latter, it is stated that in consequence of the great increase of Christians throughout China and Tartary, the Sovereign Pontiff thought it advisable to create new episcopal sees, in order to facilitate the further propagation of the faith.

About this time a rich Armenian lady took up her residence in Kai-Tora, a large and beautiful town, not far from the sea, where Christianity was in a very flourishing state; and as there was no place where the faithful could meet for religious worship, this lady devoted her wealth to the building of a magnificent church, which the Archbishop Corvino made a cathedral, raising the province to a diocese, over which he placed Gérard, who, dying soon after, was succeeded by Bishop Peregrin. In 1326, this diocese was in charge of André de Pérouse.

Many other friars, through motives of piety, undertook the long and perilous journey to Central Asia, besides those despatched by the Holy See and the Christian princes. We hear of many in those remote regions, alone, without protection, food, or money—rich only in their trust in God, animated by zeal for the faith, and burning with the desire of doing good to men, and gaining souls to Christ.

One of the first and most remarkable of these voluntary apostles was the holy Franciscan, Oderic, who travelled over many parts of the world, spreading the gospel wherever he went. Inspired with the desire of devoting himself to the conversion of the infidels, he repaired, about 1314, to Constantinople, crossed the Black Sea, travelled to Trebizond, and, passing through Great Armenia to Ormuz, he there embarked for Malabar. At Tona he was informed of the glorious death of four Franciscans in Hindostan, while on their way to China. They were Thomas de Tolentino, James of Padua, Peter of Sienna, and the lay brother, Demetrius of Tiflis. He gathered their relics, and set out with them for China, visiting the islands of Ceylon, Sumatra, Java, and Borneo; and, finally reaching Han-Tcheou-Fou, he found four Franciscan friars in that celebrated city, who aided André de Pérouse in his episcopal diocese, already spoken of as possessing a magnificent cathedral, built by a pious Armenian lady. Among the neophytes there, he mentions a rich and powerful man with whom he dwelt during his residence at Han-Tcheou-Fou. Having made numerous conversions in the southern provinces of China, he proceeded towards the north, and visited several famous cities where there were neophytes or Franciscan missionaries, arriving at Khanbalik, where he found the brethren of his Order honored by the grandees and the people, and laboring with the greatest success in the conversion of the Tartars and Chinese.

After a residence of three years at Khanbalik, the zealous Oderic resolved to go still further, and seek for souls whom he might gain to Jesus Christ. Passing the great wall, he plunged into the wilds of Tartary, penetrating beyond the country of the Kéraites, the ancient kingdom of Prester John, where he found nearly all the Christians affected with the errors of the Nestorians. Here he labored with zeal and fruit in extirpating this heresy, and also baptized many infidels. Then traversing the vast province of Khan-Sou, he reached the capital of Thibet, where he found missionaries, effecting numerous conversions.

Having visited the different provinces of Thibet, Oderic crossed the Himalaya mountains, and traversed India and Persia, on his return to Europe, arriving at Pisa in 1330.

This indefatigable apostle had, in sixteen years, visited the most distant and savage regions of the globe, sowing everywhere the evangelical seed. His great humility would not allow him to speak of the success of his long apostleship ; but it is known that he converted and baptized more than twenty thousand infidels. When he returned he was so changed by the sufferings and miseries he had endured, his body was so emaciated, and his face so withered and blackened by the sun, that his relations could not recognize him.

He remained in Pisa only a few days when he set out for Avignon, to give the Sovereign Pontiff an account of the state of the missions in Upper Asia, and ask for more apostolic laborers for that field. He was already preparing to set out again for China, with a numerous band of young missionaries, when he fell dangerously ill, and had himself removed to Udine, that he might die in the convent where he had received the habit of St. Francis, and here he finished his labors in 1331; and as he had been celebrated for his eminent virtues, for the zeal of his apostleship, and the miracles he wrought during his life and after his death, the Church had him placed in the number of the Blessed.

On the death of John de Monte Corvino, Archbishop of Khanbalik, in 1330, after an apostleship of thirty-six years, the Sovereign Pontiff appointed Nicholas, of the Order of St. Francis, and professor of theology in Paris, as his successor, who set out with twenty friars and six lay brothers of the Order, for China.

In 1338, the Grand Khan of the Tartars and Chinese sent a deputation to the Sovereign Pontiff, composed of sixteen persons, the chief of whom was André, a Franciscan. The emperor wrote as follows:

"In the power of God Omnipotent, Manifesto of the Emperor of Emperors:

"We send our ambassador, André, a Frank by birth, with fifteen companions, to the Pope, the Lord of the Christians in France (the Pope was then at Avignon), beyond the seven seas, where the sun sets, in order to open a way for communications and messages from the Pope to us, and from us to the Pope.

"We pray the Pope to make mention of us in his holy prayers, and to interest himself in the Alains, his Christian children, and our servants. We beg him also to send us some horses, and other wonderful things, from the place where the sun sets.

"Written at Khanbalik, in the year of the Kat (1336), on the 3d day of the sixth moon."

The Pope, Benedict XII., received the embassy graciously, and sent an answer to the emperor, declaring the satisfaction which he experienced at learning his devotion to the Church, and exhorting him to continue his friendly conduct, and to allow the missionaries the free exercise of their functions.

In November, 1338, Benedict sent, as Apostolic Nuncio to High Asia, the four Franciscans, Nicholas Bonnet, Nicholas de Molono, John of Florence, and Gregory of Hungary. They performed the long journey by short stages, stopping in each country they traversed, visiting the most renowned princes of the East, and everywhere scattering the seeds of Christian truth.

They reached China in 1342, and had a favorable reception from the emperor. They were greatly astonished at the progress of the faith in those countries. The Christian communities were numerous and flourishing ; and the Abbe Huck says : The Franciscans, whose learning, prudence, and sanctity, had made a great impression on the people, were rapidly increasing their establishments. Those of the convent of Monte Corvino, near the imperial palace, were treated with so much attention that the emperor frequently admitted them to his table, allowed them to present themselves to him with the great people of his court, and would often ask their blessing.

This respect, and their influence, was increased by the arrival of John of Florence and his companions, invested for ten years with the dignity of Apostolic Nuncios. The emperor issued an edict, authorizing the preaching of the Christian faith throughout the empire, and commanding the other princes of the East to give the most honorable reception to the missionaries. John of Florence, the chief of the legation, traversed the provinces with indefatigable zeal ; and new churches arose for the converts, as the faith spread into all parts of the empire. At the end of twelve years he returned to Avignon, bringing with him letters from the emperor, in which, Wadding says, the good Khan pronounced a great eulogium on the Christian religion, placed all his subjects under obedience to the Sovereign Pontiff, and asked for more missionaries to finish the work of converting and civilizing his vast states. Benedict XII. was preparing to send a body of new Franciscan missionaries to China, when the revolution broke out there, which frustrated the project.

The mission of Ili-Balik, in the wilds of Tartary, bore fruits of salvation not less abundant than those of China ; and they were the Franciscans who succeeded in propagating Christianity among the populations of those great vallies on the confines of Mongolia, in the province of Ili, a dependency of Turkistan. The chief of the mission was Friar Richard, of Burgundy, Bishop of Ili-Balik, who took with him learned and zealous laborers from his own Order, among whom were Pascal of Vittoria, in Spain ; Francis of Alexandria, and Raymond of Ruffa, of the same place ; and the lay brothers, Peter Martel, of Narbonne ; and Laurence of Alexandria ; and a black named John, of India, who had been for a long time interpreter to the Archbishop of Pekin. These zealous apostles were continually traversing the vast extent of Tartary, dwelling, like the Tartars, in huts upon wheels. Having no fixed habitation, they followed the pastoral tribes, and adopted their nomadic manner of life,

But all the bright prospects of this mission were suddenly blighted by a political catastrophe. The Tartar sovereign who had been so great a friend to the missionaries, was poisoned by a prince of his family, who was a fanatical Mahometan. This usurper, enraged at the zeal shown by the Franciscans in extirpating, not only idolatry, but the Islamism which he professed, enjoined all Christians, under pain of death, to renounce Jesus Christ and become Mussulmans. The seven missionaries were chained together, and given up to the fury of the infidel mob, which stopped at no atrocity. They were beaten, stabbed, and their ears and noses cut off, and finally beheaded. This was in 1342. The Franciscan convent was pillaged and burned. The Christians were thrown into prison, loaded with chains, and cruelly treated, and the persecution did not cease until the tyrant was put to death by a Tartar chief, when the few faithful who remained were left unmolested.

In 1369 the Tartar dynasty was overthrown, and the Chinese resumed their ancient power; and as the Tartars had been more or less the protectors of the missionaries and the Christians, the latter suffered with their protectors. As the new Chinese dynasty put a stop to all communication with foreign countries, new missionaries could no longer reach Pekin. Urban V., however, sent, in 1370, several Franciscan and Dominican friars to High Asia, to replace those whom the persecution had carried away. He appointed William de Prato, a distinguished professor of the University of Paris, Archbishop of Pekin, and gave him twelve Franciscan companions; and he also organized sixty others into various embassies, which he sent to Tartary, to the emperor and to various Mongol princes.

In 1371, Urban V. appointed Francis de Podio, surnamed Catatan, Legate Apostolic, and sent him into the same country, with twelve companions, so that the Franciscan missions still continued to be kept up, even during the greatest persecutions, and amid great changes in the civil government. Some Franciscan missionaries, who escaped the massacres, struggled to keep alive the faith. In 1391 they sent Boyce of England and Ambrose of Sienna to the Sovereign Pontiff, to beg him to send missionaries to the Tartars; and they obtained permission to take back with them twenty-four Franciscans, whom we find laboring in that country ten years later; and Civezza, in his History of the Franciscan Missions, says that "from the days of Friar John de Monte Corvino to our own time, the Franciscans never entirely abandoned that country."*

History informs us that the Franciscans, after having converted all Lithuania and Lomoginzia to the faith, formed there a most flourishing province, the fathers of which, together with their brethren of Denmark, of Sweden, of Prussia, and of Saxony, advanced towards the north pole, in order to bring the light of the gospel to inhospitable Lapland; and though their efforts for this purpose were frustrated by the opposition of the Russian Government, wedded to the Greek schism, and the obstacles thrown in their way by the revolt of Luther, yet the Franciscans of Poland and Lithuania made strenuous efforts to carry the faith thither, and, at present, minister to numbers of the faithful in the territory of Archangelsk, along the glacial sea to the north, inhabited by nomad Samojedi, and are only prevented from extending their labors by the opposition of the Russian Goverment, which makes use of every means in its power for the entire destruction of the missions.

After the treaties of 1773, 1793, and 1795, when the greater part of Poland and Lithuania fell to Russia, and the remainder to Prussia, every means was made use of, especially by Russia, for the overthrow of the

* Storia Univarsale delle Missioni Franciscane. P. Marcellino da Civezza, Vol. II., chap. 19.

Catholic religion. Yet in 1842 the Franciscan province of Lithuania numbered twenty-nine convents, and six monasteries of Poor Clares—since reduced by persecution to twelve convents and four monasteries; and these are compelled to govern themselves without a provincial superior, as they are prevented from assembling in chapter for his election, according to the statutes of the Order. Still, during all this time they have preserved themselves as a province, as if by a miracle; and the present attitude of Russia towards the Holy See gives no signs of a favorable change in its course of persecution.

Notwithstanding these difficultes, the Franciscans have missions, at present, in the following places, with the designated number of Catholics in each:

Archangelsk, along the glacial sea, 1,983; Kazan, near the river Volga, 4,896; Orel, at the confluence of the rivers Oka and Orlyk, 2,395; Tomsk, on the shores of the Tom and the Obi, 1,638; Krasnojarsk, in the district of Tennisseik, 1,609; Nercynsk, in the district of Irkutsk, in the centre of Siberia, 1,200; London, in the Tauro-Chersonese, in the district of Odessa, 4,496; Iambug, 2,303, and Tagaurog, 2,500, in the district of Ekatherinowslow, on the sea of Azof; Alesandrowsk, district of Bachmutskara, 1,834; Kazickaja, district of Samare, 2,694; Astrachan, near the Caspian Sea, 757, where they have a station for the Tartars, Cossacks, Camelukes, together with colonies of Germans and Russians; Karshie-Kolodce, district of Tiflis, 2,389; Piatyhorsk, 5,477, and Vladojkankos, 2,135, district of Stanropol, in Caucasus; Kussary, in the district of Derbent, in Dgshestan, 1,192.

Besides these missions, they have, in Lithuania, the parishes of Vilna, 4,512; Creting, 3,721; Citon, 2,628;

Mohilow, number not given; Dotnow, 4,553; Valozyn, number not given.*

CHAPTER XV.

China again.—Vasco da Gama doubles the Cape of Good Hope, and enters the Indian Ocean, in 1497.—St. Francis Xavier.—Gaspard de la Croix, a Dominican, entered China, in 1555.—the Augustinians visit China in 1575.—The Franciscan Pedro Alfaro, with three others, goes there in 1579.—Martin Ignatius of Loyola, and six others, go there in 1581.—Their imprisonment and banishment.—Missionaries and martyrs in China from 1600.—Father Ricci and the Chinese rites.—Present state of Franciscan missions.

Communication between Europe and Asia was long interrupted by the sanguinary and devastating wars of Tamerlane, and when a new attempt was made to establish relations between them, the time was past for that weary and interminable land travelling which was formerly the only means of intercouse, and the ocean was beginning to be the highway uniting the most distant lands of the two hemispheres.

After a long and adventurous voyage along the coast of Africa, Diaz returned to Lisbon in 1487, and related that at the extremity of Africa he found a cape, which, on account of the violent storms he had there encountered, he had named Cape Torment; but Juan II. declared that it should rather be called Cape of Good Hope, as a happy omen of the advantages to be derived from this great discovery.

Ten years afterwards, in 1497, the good hope of King Juan began to be realized, and Vasco de Gama doubled this cape, discovering, by sea, China and the Indies, and floating the Cross and the flag of Portugal on the coast of Malabar.

Soon after this settlement at Malabar, the Por-

* Elencus Cleri Regularis Ordinis Min. S. P. Francisc. Observ. Vilna, 1842, et. 1859.

tuguese sought and established communications with China, and in 1518 an embassy, with nine vessels, commanded by Ferdinand d'Andrada, was sent thither, but, through various causes, it failed, and the ambassadors were either imprisoned or exiled.

Another attempt to open trade with China was made in 1522, but met with no better success, and it was only by bribing the Chinese officials that a contraband trade was kept up by the Portuguese, with the Isle of Sancian, and it was at this place that St. Francis Xavier died, in 1552, while on his way to China.

Three years after the death of Xavier, Gaspard de la Croix of Evora, a Dominican, succeeded in entering China, and Cardoso says that he read a narrative written by this missionary, of his adventures in China, in which it is related that many sought baptism, and that they even pulled down, with their own hands, a temple consecrated to their idols, but he was soon banished, and took refuge in the kingdom of Ormuz, whence he returned to Lisbon.

Many years elapsed before the Portuguese were able to establish any regular commercial and political relation with the jealous and suspicious Chinese, whose unfavorable disposition towards the Europeans was kept up and fomented by the Mohammedans residing at Canton. However, towards the close of the sixteenth century they gained possession of Ngao-Men, an island not far from Canton, and here rose Macao, destined to become the centre of an immense trade, and the point from which the missionaries were to go forth to evangelize China.

As early as the year 1575, Fathers Martin de Herrada, and Hinonymus Martin, of the Order of St. Augustine, the former the prior-provincial of that Order in the Philippine islands, found an opportunity of going to China with the master of a vessel which, having been sent out by the Chinese authorities against a famous pirate named Zeimahon, who was devastating the ships and maritime cities of China, had stopped at the Philippines, and there learned that the pirate had been defeated by the Spanish authorities of the islands, and had barely escaped with his life. They cherished hopes that, as bearers of this good intelligence to China, they might be favorably received in that kingdom; but after a stop of four months and sixteen days, they were required to return, and the Chinese exclusiveness gave no hope to the missionaries of being able to penetrate or remain in the celestial empire.

It is stated that the Augustinians, who were the first missionaries in the Philippine islands, finding themselves unequal to the extensive field, called on the Franciscans to come to their assistance. Philip II. of Spain and the royal council of the Indies sent thither Pedro de Alfaro, and fourteen religious of the Order of St. Francis, "as coadjutors of the Augustinians, and with instructions to enter the kingdom of China on the first opportunity, and preach the Gospel there." They set out for Spain on the festival of the Visitation of the Blessed Virgin, 1576, and after having labored in the Philippines for the space of a year, they began to make efforts to penetrate China, where their brethren of St. Francis had been the first to announce the Gospel as early as the thirteenth century, penetrating by land through Tartary, and where Friar John de Monte-Corvino had been the first bishop and archbishop. Their desire was great to visit this ancient and flourishing field of the glorious labors of their brethren; but the governor of the Philippines giving them no countenance in this undertaking, and notwithstanding the poor success of the Augustinians a little before, Friar Pedro, the custos of the Philippines, with John Baptist Pisauriensis, Sebastian of St. Francis, and Augustine de Tordessillos, with three Spaniards, set out in a small vessel, and reached China on Sunday, the 21st of June, 1579, after a miraculous voyage, having no pilot, and being entirely ignorant of the seas and coasts. They reach the city of Canton, and are visited in their vessel by one of the officers of the government, and being allowed to enter the city, they offer up the holy sacrifice of the Mass in the house of a Chinese Christian. They are then sent to the viceroy at Aucham, and finally, it is decided that they cannot remain, and they are requested to return to the Philippines, where they arrived in the month of February, 1580.

Philip II. being informed of these attempts of the Augustinians and Franciscans to announce the Gospel in China, procured a body of thirty-four friars of the Order of St. Francis, of the province of St. Joseph, in Spain, and with Michael Tolousa, as commisssary, they set out from Seville, in 1580, with authority from the apostolic nuncio, Monseñor Sega, the king, and the royal council of the Indies, to pass to New Spain, the Philippine islands, and thence to the grand kingdom of China, and endeavor to open its gates for the entrance of the Gospel. Among the Franciscans was Friar Martin Ignatius of Loyola, a relative of St. Ignatius; and the account of the expedition, as given by him, and published by Mendoza, in 1596, is the oldest and most interesting concerning the numerous countries which he visited in his voyage around the world. Leaving Seville, they touch at the Canary islands, thence to San Domingo, Vera Cruz, the city of Mexico,

Acapulco, when they embark for the Philippines, touching at the Ladrone islands on the way.

On their arrival at the Philippines, as their great desire was to go to China, the commissary of those islands made a selection of six companions, and with three Spaniards and seven Indians of the islands, they embarked for China ; and as they were ignorant of the route and country, they passed by the Bay of Canton, and approached China by the province of Chincheo. No sooner had they entered the port than they were surrounded on all sides by armed vessels, and were it not that among the Chinese soldiers there was one who had been at Luzon, and knew the strangers to be from that place, they would have been immediately put to death, for having entered China contrary to the law prohibiting all strangers from entering, except on special permission. After landing at Capsorzon, the commander of the fort ordered four of the number to be brought in his presence, and four of the religious, taking each a cross in his hand and his breviary, went, as they supposed, to meet death. After asking them whence they came, and for what purpose, and many other things, he sent them back to their vessel, with orders not to leave it without permission. Being guarded by soldiers for three days, two of the fathers were again summoned to his presence, and thence sent to a neighboring judge. They were then taken to Quisne, a distance of six leagues, before the governor of that province, where they witnessed the sentence and punishment of many Chinese, in the presence of the judge, after which they were questioned and removed to prison, where they remained several days, suffering much from hunger, thirst and the great heat. They were again called before the tribunal, and ordered to be taken to Canton, before the viceroy of the province, but a storm arising, which lasted for ten days, they were sent by land to the great city of Sanchefou. In this journey, which occupied several days, they were guarded by fifty soldiers. Here they were several times brought before the authorities and then sent to Hancheofu, a city larger than the former, making part of the journey by water, and thence they were conducted to Canton and incarcerated in the prison of Thegnesi, where were confined those sentenced to death. Here they remained for some time, being every day brought before the tribunal, together with many others condemned to death. At this time, the Tutan, or viceroy of the province, and the Chaen, or visitor-general, were in the city, as it was a time when they held a great court for clearing the prisons of the thousands, some of whom had been in them for two years. One day they witnessed the condemnation of two thousand—some to death, others to exile, and others to beatings and other manner of punishment. There happened to be in the city at that time, a Portuguese, named Arias Gonzalo de Miranda, captain-major of the city of Macao, and as soon as he understood the affair of the Franciscans, he set about procuring their liberation, and so efficacious were his efforts that he obtained the revocation of the sentence of death which had been pronounced against them, and their release from prison.

From Macao, Ignatius went to Macao, passing the Gulf of Argnas, thence to Champa and Malacca, leaving the kingdom of Camboya on the right. At that time there was a Dominican, named Sylvester, in Camboya, who, learning the language, was laboring for the conversion of the natives. He found them ready to receive the faith, and had sent to the Indies for assistance, but had never been able to procure any aid. He wrote to Friar Ignatius, at Malacca, and to other religious, beseeching them most earnestly to send some Fathers, no matter of what order, and promising that they would find a rich harvest of souls, many of whom he dared not baptize, for fear that, for want of instructions, they would return to their idolatry. But for want of religious, they were unable to send him any assistance. They learned from the bearer of this letter that the king of that place held Father Sylvester in high esteem, so that, like another Joseph, he held the second place in the kingdom, and whenever the king spoke to him he caused him to be seated. He possessed great privileges, and permission to preach the Gospel throughout the whole kingdom, and build churches, the king giving him great assistance.

After visiting several other places, of which he gives a very interesting account, Friar Ignatius returned to Spain, by way of Good Hope, in the year 1584.*

The Jesuits made the next effort to enter China, and in 1580 Father Roger went there, and was soon after joined by Father Ricci† In 1583 they were al-

* Historia de las Cosas mas Notabiles, Ritos y Costumbres, del Gran Reyno de la China par el Muy, R. P. Juan Gonzales Mendoza. Anvers: 1596.

† Father Ricci, after studying the Chinese character, had come to the conclusion that the best means for bringing them to a knowledge of the truth would be to subscribe partly to the praises lavished upon Confucius, who was regarded as a pre-eminent wise man, the master of all science, and the legislator of the empire. He imagined that the doctrines of Confucius, concerning the nature of God, bore some resemblance to those of Christianity, and that *Tien*, or heaven, as conceived, by the educated classes among the Chinese, was not the material and visible heaven, but the true God—the Lord of Heaven—the Superior Being, invisible and spiritual, of infinite perfection, the Creator and preserver of all things—the only God, in fact, whom Confucius directs his disciples to adore and worship. He adopted the same ideas with regard to the honors paid to their ancestors. He thought that the sacrifices offered to them were merely of a civil nature, and had nothing of a religious or idolatrous signification. Such was the opinion of Father Ricci and of a number of his brethren; but when Nicholas Lombard succeeded to the charge of Father Ricci, on the death of the latter, he set himself to study the works of Confucius

lowed to build a church, but were soon afterwards obliged to return to Macao. From time to time we find the missionaries of the Indies renewing their efforts to evangelize China, and by their indomitable perseverance overcoming all obstacles.

The Franciscan father, Anthony da St. Maria, di Polenza, full of zeal for the salvation of the infidels, passed to the province of St. Gregory, in the Philippine isles, where, in company with Father Gennesio da Guesada, he taught theology. Gennesio suffered martyrdom there, in 1633. Father Anthony proceeding from the Philippines to China, was constituted prefect of the missionaries of his Order in that country, which office he held for several years, from which circumstance it is evident that the Franciscans had several laborers in the missionary field of China, at that period; and that they were successful, we have the testimony of Navarette, who says: "Anthony of St. Maria and Bonaventure Ibonez converted four thousand, without Chinese rites, at Kantung." The Franciscans evidently did not coincide with Father Ricci's opinion concerning the lawfulness of the Chinese rites. Father Anthony built oratories, convents and hospices, and had the glory of suffering imprisonment and persecution and exile, for the faith which he taught—all which

and wrote a book on the subject, in which he came to the conclusion that the doctrine of the Chinese philosopher was tarnished with materialism and atheism; that the Chinese, in reality, recognized no divinity but heaven, and the general effect that it had on the beings of the universe; that the soul, in their opinion, was nothing but a subtle, aëriform substance, and that their views, as to its immortality, resembled the theory of Metempsychosis. Thus the customs of the Chinese appeared idolatrous and criminal, the sinfulness of which was to be demonstrated to those who had embraced the faith. But upon this subject there was a difference of opinion among the Jesuits themselves, which proved very injurious to the prosperity of the missions; and we meet the remark in the lives of some of the Franciscan missionaries, that they suffered on account of the question of the Chinese rites. Finally, the Church interfered to put a stop to this fatal dispute, and Clement XI., in 1715, by the bull *Ex illa die*, decided the question by their entire suppression.

he bore with patience and Christian fortitude. He wrote many works, several of which were published. Among these works was a Commentary on the Moral Philosophy of Confucius. As he was a contemporary of Gennesio who suffered martyrdom, in 1633, Anthony must have been in China several years previous to that date.

A persecution was raging at this period against the missionaries and Christians of Japan, and Brother Gabriel da Magdalena, passed from the Philippine isles to the aid of the suffering Christians in that country. Being exiled to China, he nevertheless returned to Japan, where he suffered martyrdom in 1633, together with the Franciscan Father Jerome of the Cross. Brother Gabriel was immersed in boiling water, whence he came forth unharmed, when he and Father Jerome were buried alive.

About the same time, we find Dominic of Nice, another of those travelling missionaries for Christ, evangelizing India, Tartary, Persia, China and Japan. Being miraculously endowed with the gift of tongues, he spoke the languages of those countries, without the labor of acquiring this knowledge by study, and underwent great labors, converting many and building several churches. His extraordinary acquirements were recognized by the Holy See, and by her, as well as by kings and princes, he was employed in difficult embassies, for which he was well fitted by his extensive knowledge of languages, and in which he was eminently successful. He was appointed librarian by Philip IV. of Spain, and died in 1650.

The scattered facts which have been preserved, clearly show that the Franciscan missions were flourishing in China during the last half of the seventeenth century; and during this period we find the Franciscan, Bernardine da Venezia, Bishop of Angoli, sent thither as vicar-apostolic of that country. He reached Quam-chan, the province of the metropolis of Canton, after a dangerous voyage, and perfecting himself in the language, he labored with great fruit, though he met with many difficulties from some of the missionaries themselves, who still adhered to Father Ricci's opinion with regard to the Chinese rites, which still continued to prove so injurious to the success of the missions. After a life of labor, he passed to his eternal reward, though the year of his death is unknown.

John Francis da Lionessa exercised, for fifteen years, the apostolic ministry with such zeal that he converted several thousands of the Chinese to the true faith, and was appointed vicar-apostolic for all China. Returning to Rome, on matters of the mission, he was received with marks of esteem by Innocent XII., and made bishop of Berito in 1700, and appointed archbishop of Mira, and vicar-perpetual of the Basilica of St. Peter in the Vatican, by Clement XI., in which office he continued for thirty years. He died in Rome, in 1737, at the age of eighty-two.

About this time we find the Franciscan Basilio di Gemona, a man of piety and learning, obtaining permission from the Congregation of Propaganda, to set out for China, together with four companions. Basilio having acquired the language, converted great numbers to the faith, and Innocent XI., recognizing his merits, appointed him vicar-apostolic of Xensi, in the discharge of which office, he also had many difficulties to surmount, on account of the question of the Chinese rites. Basilio died at Si-gan-foo, in 1703, aged about fifty-six; and in 1715 the Chinese rites were prohibited by Clement XI.

The Christian religion had made such progress in

China, that in 1715 there were more than three hundred churches and three hundred thousand Christians; but the Emperor Kong-hi, after having been long favorable to them, began to conceive some jealousy, and, in 1716, forbade the missionaries to build churches or make proselytes. This prince dying in 1722, his successor Yong-tching, upon complaints made by the governor of Fakien against the Christians, published most barbarous edicts against them, and they were dispersed into distant provinces, to end their days in prisons, fetters and misery. In the midst of this persecution, we find the Franciscan, Emanuel of Jesus, Bishop of Nankin, in 1729.

In 1731, the Emperor Yong-tching banished the missionaries to Macao, a small island in the province of Canton, in which the Portuguese were permitted to settle. Yong-tching died in 1736, and though his cruel persecution of the Christians was continued by his successors, yet we find the Franciscans still continuing to minister to their scattered flocks. In 1740, the Franciscan M. Concas occupied the episcopal see of Chan; in 1746, Alborneo, of the same Order, filled that of Nankin, and his successor in that see, the Franciscan Francis Destaroza de Viterbo, suffered martyrdom there on the 2d of March, 1750, at which time, notwithstanding the persecution which continued to rage against them since 1716, there were sixty thousand Christians in Nankin. The illustrious John Anthony Boker, also a Franciscan, bishop of Rosalia, and vicar-apostolic of Xensì and Xansì, was arrested and sent to Macao, where he died, in the convent of St. Francis, in 1756. The missionaries, however, still continued to find means of entering China, and Eugene da Bassano, who was laboring there as a missionary, was, on account of his merits, virtue and zeal, appointed bishop of Portuense, and made vicar-apostolic of China, where, after enduring many persecutions, he died in 1766. Atto Biagini, after passing through Syria and Egypt, where he labored for many years, and suffered much for the faith, amidst the horrors of war and pestilence, proceeded to China, and reaching Canton continued his zealous efforts for the conversion of the infidels, until he was arrested and imprisoned at Pekin, where, after horrible sufferings, he died of hunger, in 1784. About the same time, Francis Maria de Magnis da Devis, renowned for his sanctity, went as missionary-apostolic to China, and after laboring much, was appointed bishop of Millepontino. He suffered imprisonment, scourging and other torments, and also died of starvation in prison at Pekin.

Eusebius da Cittadella, a man of great piety and learning, and a profound philosopher and theologian, who had been for many years *lector* in the archiepiscopal seminary of Corfu, in 1756, set out for the Chinese mission, but on arriving at Macao, he could proceed no further, on account of the persecution which then raged in China, and the prohibition against the entrance of the missionaries, and applying himself to medicine, he practiced with such success that his renown as a physician reached the court of Pekin, whither he was invited and chosen physician to the emperor; but whilst discharging this office, he exercised the apostolic ministry with prudence and zeal, to the great profit of souls. He died at Pekin in 1785. He wrote a poem in defence of the Latin Church against the errors and schism of the Greeks.

Crescentius Cavalli, styled the Apostle of Corea, on account of the extent of his missionary labors there, was appointed bishop of Cusin in 1791, and vicar-apostolic of Xansi and Xensi, but he died in 1702, before the letters of his appointment reached China. He was universally mourned on account of his mildness and apostolic zeal. The places of the fallen missionaries continued to be filled, and in 1798 John da Triora set out from Rome for China, where he was imprisoned in 1816, and after suffering various torments, was strangled, in hatred of the faith of Christ. He was declared *Venerable* by Gregory XVI.

We have already mentioned Atto Biagini as dying in prison, at Pekin, in 1784. He had, as companion of his labors and imprisonment, Joseph Bientina, who, being liberated from prison, continued on the mission there until the close of his life in 1804.

Xansi was, from the beginning, an especial field of the Franciscans. The first vicar-apostolic, of whom we have any account, was called *Min* by the Chinese —his real name is unknown. He died a peaceful death, before the long and atrocious persecution of the Emperor Cien-lum, which commenced towards the close of the year 1784. He was succeeded by *Fan*, in Chinese—real name, unknown. He was arrested and taken to Pekin, where he died in prison, February 14, 1785. The third vicar-apostolic was Anthony d'Osimo, called *Can* by the Chinese. He was bishop of Domitianopolis. He avoided, for a short time, the persecution, but being moved with compassion for the sufferings of the Chinese Christians, who were put to the torture, in order to make them disclose the whereabouts of their pastor, he presented himself to the mandarin of the Xansi, and obtained the liberty of the Christians of his flock. He was treated humanely by the Mandarin, and in a few days sent to Pekin, where he died February, 1785. He had been probably coadjutor of Xansi, and assumed the duties of the see on the imprisonment of *Fan*. The fourth vicar-apostolic was Mariano di Narma, named by the Chinese *Crin.* He was bishop of Magedenensa, and, learning that many of the missionaries had died of want in the prisons of Pekin, went thither, moved by his ardent charity, and declaring that he also was an European, protested against the keeper of the prison, and by his great courage and management, obtained an amelioration of the condition of those still there. After his liberation from prison he returned to Xansi, where he remained concealed for a short time, when he was suffocated, April 6, 1791, by the pestiferous fumes of fires which the Chinese lighted to drive him from his concealment.

The fifth vicar-apostolic was John Baptist di Mondello—called by the Chinese *Vu*—he was bishop of Croisense, and after his liberation from the prison of Pekin remained concealed at Xansi, where he bore with constant patience calumnies which were heaped upon him. His innocence was finally recognized, though he did not seek to defend himself, and the letters of the Congregation of Propaganda, passing an encomium on his virtues, arrived only after his death.

The sixth vicar-apostolic was Louis di Signa, called by the Chinese *Tu.* He was bishop of Antedodense, appointed in 1802, and he also, after being liberated from the prison in which his predecessors had groaned, remained concealed at Xansi, where he died, after a long and painful illness.

The seventh vicar-apostolic was Gioachino Salvetti, called by the Chinese, *Gai.* He went to China in 1804; was bishop of Euriense, and succeeded to the bishopric of Xansi in 1815. He suffered the rigors of imprisonment at Canton, which brought on a paralysis of his limbs which he bore patiently until his death, September 21, 1843.

After the death of Salvetti, his coadjutor, Alfonso, was appointed first vicar-apostolic of the new vicariate of Xensi, and Gabriel da Moretta was chosen bishop of Euriense, and appointed as the immediate successor of Salvetti at Xansi, which office he still filled in 1866.

At present the Franciscans have charge of five vicariates-apostolic in China: 1. *Xen-si*, Fr. Efisio Chiais, vicar-apostolic and bishop of Irene, *in partibus*, numbering thirty thousand Catholics. 2. *Xan-si*, Fr. Gabriel Damoretta, twenty thousand Catholics. 3. *Hu-Pé*, Fr. Eustachio Zanoli — having eight missionaries, one seminary, a novitiate, ten seminarians, twenty-two churches and fifteen thousand Catholics. 4. *Hu-Nan*, Fr. Michael Navarro, bishop of Cuensi, *in partibns*, containing ten missionaries, three schools and ten thousand Catholics. 5. *Chang-Toung*, Fr. Louis da Castellazo, bishop of Zenopolis, *in partibus*, coadjutor; Hannibal Fantoni, bishop of Prienesis—having seven missionaries and ten thousand Catholics.

Besides these five vicariates, the Franciscans have missions in that of *Chang-Nan* (Nankin) which number seventy-three thousand Catholics. Louis Celestin Spelta went to China in 1845, and after laboring in the missions four years, the Franciscan Bishop Moresca, of Nankin, requested his appointment by the Holy See as his coadjutor. He was only made acquainted with the intentions of the bishop, on the arrival of the bulls, and notwithstanding his reluctance to accept the high dignity and responsibility of the episcopate, he was consecrated Bishop of Tespia, *in partibus*, and coadjutor of the bishop of Nankin, *cum jure futuræ successionis*, on the 9th of September, 1849—the Octave of the Nativity of the Blessed Virgin. The diocese of Nankin is the most extensive, the richest and the most populous in the empire. There were at that time more than thirty priests—Jesuits, Franciscans, Priests of the Holy Family, Lazarists, and Secular Priests. It also had a seminary with thirty Chinese students, and contains a Catholic population of more than seventy thousand. The great labors of the episcopacy brought on a pleurisy which reduced Bishop Spelta to the last extremity, and no hope being entertained of his recovery, he received the last sacraments; but so fervent were the prayers of the faithful of Nankin, to whom he had become endeared, that he recovered his health, as if by a miracle, though not sufficiently so to resume his labors, and by the counsel of his physicians, he sought restoration in the mild climate of the Philippine islands, where he remained for six months in the Franciscan convent of Manilla. About the middle of 1853 his health was sufficiently restored to enable him to recommence his labors, but such were the afflictions and persecutions which he now encountered, that he earnestly besought the Holy See to allow him to retire to some convent of his Order, where he might end his days in peace. The Holy See was cognizant of his afflictions, but knownig his great worth, was unwilling to dispense with the labors of such a valuable missionary, and transferred Bishop Spelta from Nankin to *Hu-Pé*, which was formed into a new vicariate from that of the Franciscan vicariate of *Hu-Nan*. He visited Rome in 1859, on matters connected with the Chinese missions, and returned Delegate Visitor Apostolic extraordinary of the Holy See, for all the Catholic missions of the Celestial empire and its adjacent kingdoms, and with powers from the Holy See, and from the minister-general, to found there a novitiate and a province of the Order of St. Francis.

But the great labors of the extensive charge of Visitor Apostolic of such a vast region, brought on an attack of the disease from which he had just recovered, and he died on the 10th of September, 1862, leaving a bright example of virtue for the imitation of his beloved fellow-missionaries.

The last martyr of the Order of St. Francis in China, was added to the list in 1861, when Father John d'Andria was put to death, on the 21st of March, by the populace of Jai-Gan-fu, where he had been stationed as missionary by the Franciscan Louis da Castellazzo, bishop of Zenopolis and vicar-apostolic of Chang-Toung.

CHAPTER XVI.

East Indies.—Bishop Vasques the first Vicar-Apostolic, and Friar John Albuquerque, the first Bishop of Goa.—The Franciscan hospitality to St. Francis Xavier.—Isle of Ceylon.—Macassar, Camboya, Java, Malacca, and other regions.—Phillipine Islands.—Labor of the Franciscans, and permanent fruits.

Emanuel the Great, who ascended the throne of Portugal in 1495, and died in 1521, named Vasco de Gama, his admiral, to find a passage to the East Indies by sea. Gama doubled the Cape of Good Hope in 1498, discovered the coast of Mozambique, and the city of Melinda, on the coast of Zanguebar, in Africa, and thence sailed to Calicut, in the East Indies. The first missionaries or chaplains who attended the Portuguese in the East Indies were Franciscans, with Bernandine, or Ferdinand Vasques, as bishop, who was apostolic vicar. De Gama made an alliance with the King of Calicut, who afterwards became a Christian. Alfonso Albuquerque, who succeeded as viceroy, in 1509, took Goa in 1510, and, fortifying it, made it the Portuguese capital in the East Indies. He procured the erection of an episcopal see there, and John d'Albuquerque, a Franciscan, was the first bishop. It was afterwards raised to the metropolitan dignity, when the bishoprics of Cochin and Malacca were erected, in 1592, and that of Méliopour in 1607.

In 1510, the Franciscans built the famous seminary college at Goa, which they conducted for twenty-eight years, until, in 1542, they donated it to St. Francis Xavier, to be applied by him, for his disciples, solely to the missions among the Indians. (Horace Turselin, Life of St. F. X.)

John Baptist Pisauriensis came to Rome from the Phillippine Islands, in 1586, and on his return received a brief from Pope Sixtus V., empowering him, together with his companions, to evangelize the Indies and China, and granting them many privileges and indulgences for their converts.

The same year, the Franciscans of Louzon, who resided at Malacca, went to announce the gospel to several of the East India islands. Their superior was Didacus à Conceptione, in the island of Tapobanertuni, or Ceylon, in the Bay of Ganges. Father Peter Manchos, with a companion, was sent to Narsiga, an opposite empire, distinct from the nine kingdoms, and which, on account of its great fruitfulness, was called by the natives a part of Paradise. They were well received by the natives, and made many converts ; but they were imprisoned by the authorities, and a large sum required for their release ; and as they were rich only in poverty, they remained in their prison, where they died the precious death of the just.

Four other men, sent to the island of Oceanica and the kingdom of Macassar, lying between the Celebes and Borneo, being invited by the king to sow the word of faith in his kingdom; but that region was so sunk in the sin of Sodom, that the corrupt inhabitants were deaf to the voice of heaven; and the missionaries having exhausted every means in their power to turn them from their crimes, were obliged to leave them to the inscrutable judgments of God.

Friar Cosimo of the Annunciation, and his companions, were entrusted with the mission in the island of Deconica de Lolor, one of the forty or more islands which lie between the Molucca Islands, the principal one of which is called Del Timor, but formerly known as Todor. Traversing these regions, and preaching the gospel everywhere, they reaped a rich harvest of souls.

This same year, the friars of the same convent of Malacca, were invited by letters from the king of Camboya, a kingdom but little inferior to the others in wealth. It is the boundary of Siam to the south. The fathers who went were Rodricus à Cruce, Gregorius à S. Francisco, Antonius de Magdalena, and Damianus de Turre. On their arrival, the king issued a decree, bearing the royal seal, empowering them to freely preach the law of Christ, and allowing every one to embrace the faith without detriment to station or property; and recognizing the same honors to be paid to the Franciscans as were given to the priests of the idols. But whilst they were gathering a rich harvest of souls, Praetus, the king of Siam, invaded the city of Camboya, and took the princes, chiefmen, and the Franciscans, prisoners, and carried them to his chief city, Odia, where they were kept in a dark prison, from which they were led forth every day, two by two, yoked like oxen, and thus compelled to draw heavy burdens through the city. One of the fathers died in this cruel slavery; and the patience and constancy of the Franciscans so astonished the inhuman king that he allowed them to return to Malacca.

Hieronymus Valente, with three companions, was sent to the island of Java, where he wrought wonders in the conversion of the pagans. Hieronymus, Emanuel Eltenses, and Paschal Conari, went to the kingdom of Bolambnan, in the eastern extremity of the same island, where they baptized the eldest son of the king and two sons of the king's brother. But the daughter of the king, in hatred of the faith, accused Father Paschal to her father, as guilty of treason. The king condemned him to death, and being pierced through the heart, he gave his soul to God. His body was buried in the church of one of the cities of that place, but afterwards translated to Malacca, where it was placed with great honor near the high altar of the Church of the Mother of God. The king being greatly enraged at this, condemned the widowed queen, who was a Christian, to death ; and cast all the missionaries and their converts into prison, where they suffered patiently all manner of abuse and want. But the innocence of the fathers being manifested, the king sent them into exile, and, reaching the city of Malacca, Hieronymus died there shortly after his arrival, full of days and of merits. Christopher of the Annunciation, with another companion, remained concealed to minister to the faithful neophytes.

Francis Almeida set out from Lisbon, on the 25th of April, 1505, with twenty-one vessels, and successively took the islands and cities of Quiloa and Mozambique, upon the eastern coast of Africa. Whilst Almeida was resting his troops at Cananor, he received, through Friar Louis, a proposition of an alliance with the king of Narzinga, and concluded a treaty with that prince.

Whilst Friar Anthony de Faurier was passing from

Sacotora to Goa, in 1510, he was shipwrecked on the coast of Camboya, and, together with his companions, held in captivity by the king. He was allowed to proceed to Goa, in order to procure their ransom, on condition that he should return, if a sufficient sum were not procured for that purpose ; and as the governor was absent when Anthony reached Goa, he returned to his captivity, according to the terms of agreement, which act of heroism so moved the king that he set all the captives at liberty. Anthony continued his apostolic labors, which were crowned with an extraordinary success.

Alfonso Albuquerque appreciated the services rendered by the Franciscans in the various parts of the Indies, where they exercised their salutary ministry. He had no more powerful aids, or faithful councillors than these humble and disinterested missionaries. He gave them the mosque of the Mussulmans at Goa, which they changed into a Christian temple. They were also assigned lands, upon which Lopez de Siguqua, the fourth governor, erected a convent, in 1518, whence, as from a centre of science and zeal, religion went forth to convert and instruct the natives—open schools for the youth—to bring corporal and spiritual assistance to the afflicted and suffering in the hospitals—to administer the sacraments—and to fulfill all the duties of their ministry, without any worldly cares or any other aim but the glory of God.

About 1552, the Franciscan Bonfer, whose apostolic zeal had led him to Goa, heard of the grandeur of the kingdom of Pégon. As he was a man of more than common learning and intelligence, according to the Jesuit Du Jarrie, and endowed with great zeal for the salvation of souls, he resolved to visit that nation and carry thither the light of the Gospel. He went from

Goa to Meliapour, where he sought an opportunity of embarking for Pégon. Through the vicar of the city, and the Jesuit, Alfonso Cyprian, he found the means of continuing his journey; and after encountering many dangers, he reached one of the ports of Pégon, where he stopped for three years, in order to learn the language, and become acquainted with the manners and customs of the people. He returned to Hindostan in 1557.

The Franciscans have had extensive and flourishing missionary posts in the Philippine Islands, from their first occupation by Spain to the present time; and they still continue in a most flourishing condition. These islands were discovered by the celebrated navigator and explorer, Magellan, who was the first to pass through the straits which still bear his name. He reached the Philippine Islands in the year 1519; but unfortunately was killed in an engagement with the inhabitants. Some years later, Philip II. of Spain, sent thither Villalaboz, to add them to his crown; and although he gave them the name which they now bear, in honor of his king, yet his expedition was a failure; and it was not until 1565, that a Spanish squadron, under the command of Lopez de Lagassi, effected a permanent settlement. In 1571, the city of Manilla was built.

The Augustinians were the first missionaries who entered this field; but not being sufficient for the labor, they invited the Franciscans to come to their assistance. The celebrated lay brother, Anthony of St. Gregory, being inspired to go to evangelize the islands of Salomone, received permission from his superior, Philip II. of Spain, and the Sovereign Pontiff, to make a selection of his brethren of the Province of St. Joseph, in Spain, for that purpose. After surmounting many difficulties, he obtained sixteen companions, who on their arrival at Seville, chose Peter Alfaro as their chief. They were about to set out for their destination, when the king, being informed by Diego Herrera, of the Order of St. Augustine, that the spiritual wants of the Philippine Islands were greater than those of Salomone, requested the Franciscans to go thither; and setting out in June, 1576, they had a prosperous voyage to New Spain, or Mexico, (which had then become the route to the Indies); but an epidemic carried off four of the number, immediately on their arrival—a fifth died in Vera Cruz, and a sixth at Jalapa; so that they were obliged to interrupt their journey. The Franciscans of Mexico offered to supply the places of those who had died; but Friar Anthony preferred to return to Spain, for new recruits, with whom, again setting out, he reached Manilla in June, 1577. They were received with great demonstrations of joy, and at first lodged in the convent of the Augustinians. Such were the auspices under which the Franciscans began their labors in the Philippine Islands, establishing, at first, the custodia of St. Philip, but a year later its name was changed to that of St. Gregory, in honor of Pope Gregory XIII.; and in 1586, it was raised to the dignity of a province by Sixtus V.

The natives are divided into various tribes, differing from each other considerably in features, shades of color, and degree of civilization. They acknowledge a Supreme Being, the Maker of the Universe, and the immortality of the soul; but have many inferior idols, to all of whom they assigned wives. They have no temples or places of public worship—all their religious rites being confined to the family. Some tribes adore the sun, and venerate the stars. They pay divine honors to the departed spirits of their ancestors—before whose images, which are kept in their houses, they offer libations of wine. They have no general political regimen whatever, each tribe being independent, and divided into families—the heads of the principal families governing. Slavery exists among them, and the children of the poor are born to serve the rich. The father's authority is unlimited. They possess but one wife, and separate at will. The penalty of adultery is death.

There are yet two hundred thousand idolators at Luzon, and eight hundred thousand at Mindanao, two of the princical islands. Such is the vast field in which the Franciscans have been laboring since 1577; and their success may be learned from the number of flourishing parishes and missionary posts which they have erected throughout the islands.

In Manilla	they	have	seven	parishes	with a	population of	33,265
" Bulacan	"	"	seven	"	"	"	52,627
" Marong	"	"	six	"	"	"	25,760
" Laguna	"	"	twenty	"	"	"	84,551
" Batangas and Nueva Ecija	"	"	five	"	"	"	34,724
" Prov. of Inf. and of Infanta and Camarines,			thirty-three,		"	"	117,546
" Tayabos	"	"	ten	"	"	"	77,714
" Albay	"	"	seven	"	"	"	96,857
" Samar	"	"	thirty	"	"	"	126,801
" Leite	"	"	twenty-six	"	"	"	112,028

In these parishes there are two hundred and seventeen friars.

The centre of these extensive operations of the Franciscans in the Philippine Islands, is the convent of Manilla, founded in 1577, and which numbered thirty-nine subjects in 1860. Twenty-six of these are preparing, either for missionary duty as pastors, for those already civilized, or as missionaries among the yet uncivilized savages. The thirteen others assist in the Royal Hospital of St. Lazarus, in Manilla, in the Infirmary of St. Anne, in the Province of Laguna, and in that of Vasa, in the Province of Camarines.

Besides these parishes, the Franciscans have seventeen missionary stations among those who are yet in the savage state. In these posts they generally have a church, residence, and school; and labor continually to draw the natives from their forests, to settle in habitations in their vicinity, and cultivate the soil.

So great has been the success of the Franciscans in civilizing and christianizing the savages of these Islands—so well known have been the immense benefits which they conferred on civil society—that in the suppression of the religious orders by the Spanish government, the Franciscan province of St. Gregory, in the Philippine Islands, was not included; but acknowledging not only its utility, but even its necessity, it permitted, in 1853, the Order to open a convent at Pastrana, to supply this province. Pastrana, in 1860, numbered thirty priests, besides the superior—twelve students in theology, eleven in philosophy, and eighteen novices—all for the mission of the province of St. Gregory. Up to the year 1865, in twelve years, the number of friars sent from Pastrana to the Philippine Islands has been one hundred and twenty.

CHAPTER XVII.

Japan.—St. Francis Xavier the first Missionary in 1549.—Taicosama expels the Jesuits about 1582.—Designs of the Japanese on the Philippine islands.—Embassy to Japan.—Taicosama sends an Embassy to the Philippines.—Japanese ask for missionaries.—Gonzales Garzia.—Second Embassy to Japan.—Bull of Gregory XIII.—Peter Baptist, missionary and ambassador to Japan.—Success of his mission—Persecution and martyrdom, by crucifixion, of Peter Baptist and twenty-five companions.—Their Canonization.—Continuation of the missions.—Louis Sotello.—New persecutions in 1613.—Missionaries and martyrs.

JAPAN is dear to the children of St. Francis, for the soil of that country is sanctified by the blood of their brethren, who were the first to suffer there the death of the Cross, for the faith, and whose names, on the 29th of May, 1862, were solemnly placed on the roll of the saints, by the present pontiff Pius IX. We shall endeavor to place the facts relating to this mission in such a light that they may be properly understood. The celebrated Franciscan, William Rubriquis, was the first to visit the vicinity of Japan, and give any information concerning that country. About the middle of the thirteenth century, still later, the illustrious traveller Marco Polo, penetrated thither; yet it was not till 1542 that Japan was opened up to European commerce by the Portuguese. In 1549 St. Francis Xavier, the Apostle of the Indies, visited that country, and meeting with a favorable reception, preached the Gospel with great fruit, though violently opposed by the Bonzes, who taking occasion of some changes in the commercial relations, which were unfavorable to the king, Saxuma, the latter prohibited the Saint from preaching, and decreed the exile of three of his Christian subjects who would not renounce the faith. However, the king was appeased, and this short persecution soon passed away. St. Francis visited Cangoxima, Firando, Meaco and Amanguchi, and passing to the Indies stopped at Goa, to procure three of his brethren to continue the Japanese mission. The kings of Nangate, Omura, Bungo and Arima, sought baptism, and there were two hundred thousand Christians in Japan when those kings sent the famous embassy to Pope Gregory XIII.

About the year 1542, Faxiba, a general of the army, afterward known as Taicosama Quatacundono, usurped the throne during the minority of the lawful prince, and though at first he tolerated the Christians, and even showed them favors, he afterwards became a most cruel persecutor.

The arrival of a Portuguese vessel, in the port of Firando, made him suspicious of the Europeans, and these suspicions being fed by the Bonze, Jacuino, an inveterate enemy of the Christians, he arrested the Jesuits, and ordered them to be sent out of the kingdom—their churches, to the number of twenty, were destroyed, and their property pillaged. Some of the Fathers, however, remained concealed in the country. Thus matters remained till 1590.

In that year, the now powerful Taicosama conceived the project of subjugating the Philippine islands, and sent an ambassador to the viceroy demanding submission to his authority. Father John Cabos, a Dominican, was sent by the Spanish authorities to treat with Taicosama, but the vessel in which he embarked to return was lost, and he was never heard from. Faranda Khiemon, however, a Japanese convert, reached the Philippine islands, as envoy of the Emperor, bearing letters in which were reiterated his former demands.*

There was at that time, in Manilla, a Franciscan, a native of the Indies, named Gonzalez Garzia, who, before he took the habit, had resided for the space of ten years in Japan, after his conversion, and being engaged in business, was well known to the Japanese Christians, who, hearing that he had became a religious, sent three letters to him by Khiemon, beseeching him to use his endeavors to have some of his brethren come to their aid, as the Jesuits had been expelled, and they were without priests. One of these letters is from the Christians of Amanguchi, number-

* Juan Francisco.—*Cronaca de la Provincia di S. Gregorio*, P. III., L. I., C. VI.

ing forty thousand, who having been for twelve years without a priest, were obliged to baptize their own children, and they write that they have heard of the manner of life of the Franciscans, from which they doubt not that many would be converted at the sight of men following the example of the apostles, as described to them by the good Father Francis Xavier. Another is from the Queen of Amacusa, Donna Grazia, who had been converted with many of her subjects, in which she says that the manner of life of the Franciscans, and especially the little value which they place on worldly goods, is well known to them; and since they live on alms, they promise to give them cheerfully, if they will come to Japan. Her subjects, number ninety districts, of from four to six hundred families each, and there are among them but two Jesuits, one only of whom is a priest. The third letter is from the faithful of Firando, Xigui, and others, who claim that Garzia should now come to their assistance, as many of them had been converted by his example while he was in Japan. From these letters it would appear that they already had some knowledge of the Franciscans; and indeed it is well attested, though we have no details, that John Poreco went to Meaco in 1582 or '83, and was there joined by some of the Order who labored in the conversion of the natives.

These letters were brought to Manilla by Khiemon, the ambassador of Taicosama, who also wrote on his arrival, to the viceroy of the Philippine islands, asking him to send some Franciscans to Japan, promising them kind reception by the emperor and people.*

Moved by these representations the viceroy determined to make choice of Franciscans for the second embassy which he was about to send to Taicosama;

* Annal. Ord. Min. Vol. XXIII., a. 1593, n. XIII.

and the universal voice designated Friar Peter Baptist, a man conspicuous for his learning, prudence and sanctity—the angel, as he was called, of the Philippines. But as Gregory XIII. had issued a bull in 1585, prohibiting any but the Jesuits from going to Japan, Peter Baptist expressed his doubts as to the lawfulness of his accepting the mission. The same question had arisen the year previous, in the case of Cabos, the Dominican ; but as his mission was purely one on matters of state, it was not deemed to contravene the prohibition of Gregory. The viceroy consulted the administrator of Manilla, and a council was held at which were present the principal men of the orders of St. Augustine, St. Dominic, St. Francis, and of the Society of Jesus. The bull of Gregory XIII. was read, and the letters of the Japanese presented ; after which Anthony Sedeno, provincial of the Jesuits, having paid a compliment to the learning, prudence and sanctity of Peter Baptist, whom he styled the firm pillar of the church of Manilla and of the Philippines, of which, he said, he was justly called the apostle, he presented a protest in the name of the Society, against the mission of the Franciscans to Japan, which went on to say, that besides the prohibition of Gregory, the Church there was now suffering more than ever before; that the missionaries were obliged to keep concealed, and that it was to be feared that if other religious went there at this time, though they might be of benefit to the suffering Christians, they would increase the persecution ; as a proof of which, it was stated that after the arrival of Cabos, Taicosama exiled the eighteen Fathers of the Society who were at Nagasaki, and burned their college and church.

The assembled Fathers, after attentively considering the subject, made the unanimous declaration that the bull of Gregory did not include the Franciscans, as there was a prior one of Paul IV., empowering them to build convents and churches, and preach the Gospel in every part of the world, which was confirmed by Sixtus V., the successor of Gregory, who, by a bull, dated November 15th, 1586, raising the custodia of the Philippines to a province, empowered them to found houses throughout the Indies and China—*except in Malacca, Siam, and Cochin-China, and those places where the Franciscans already possessed houses;* and from the fact of this exception *only* being made, it was clear that it was not the intention to include Japan.

The mission of the Franciscans being thus decided upon, the provincial of the Jesuits embraced Peter Baptist, and said that he was rejoiced that as other religious were to go to Japan, the honor had fallen upon the children of St. Francis, and that he was to be their leader, being convinced that he would show himself a brother to the persecuted and suffering religious of the Society, and that he should not take offence that he at first opposed the mission, as he had done so only in fulfilment of his office, and in order that the will of God might be made manifest.

Peter Baptist, accompanied by Bartholomew Ruiz, Francis of St. Michael, and Gonzales Garzia, set out on the 26th of May, 1593, and after a perilous voyage of thirty days, reached Firando, where they were joyfully received, and Peter Gomez, the Superior of the Jesuits, sent two of his religious to welcome them. The Emperor commissioned two of the grandees of his kingdom to conduct them to Nangoya, three leagues distant, where he held his court. Declining the pompous equipage which had been provided for them, they went thither on foot, and were received with great ceremony by Taicosama, who exclaimed, "These are true soldiers of God." Peter Baptist delivered the letters of the viceroy, and made an address to the Emperor, Brother Garzia being interpreter; and although at first he maintained his pretensions with regard to the subjugation of the Philippine islands, yet he was answered in such an explicit manner by Peter Baptist, who assured him of the independence and power of the king of Spain, and the determination of the authorities of the Philippine islands to defend themselves against any invasion, that he suddenly seemed to change his intention, and agreed to enter into a treaty of unity and commerce with the king of Spain, the conditions of which were at once drawn up. He consented that the Franciscans should remain in his kingdom as long as they pleased, and promised Peter Baptist that all their wants should be provided for, and after the interview he invited them to dine in his palace.*

They were sent by the Emperor from Nangoya to Meaco, the capital of the empire, where, by his orders, they were lodged by Tungen, a principal officer of the Court. From this place Peter Baptist wrote to his provincial a long and interesting account of his mission and its success, and already perceiving the immense field for missionaries, and the great anxiety of the Japanese Christians—many of them having flocked to the friars, both at Firando and Meaco—to procure priests, he asked for six more of the Order to be sent to Japan that year.

At this time the edict of banishment passed against the Jesuits was in force; and those of the Society who remained in Japan were obliged to keep themselves concealed. The Franciscans being now favorably received by Taicosama, took occasion, in one of their

* Benedict XIV. De Canoniz. in App.

interviews with him, to intercede for the Jesuit missionaries, and they were allowed to come forth from their retreat, and labor openly with the Franciscans.*

The friars had now been six months in Meaco, in the house of Tungen, but they had no convent or church for the accommodation of the vast numbers who flocked to them from all quarters; and they reminded the emperor of his promise to provide for their wants, telling him that they desired a place to build a church and a convent. He expressed his regret that they had not made the request before, and wrote to the governor of Meaco: "Give immediately to the fathers from Luzon a place on which to build a house and church, assigning them an income sufficient for their support; and this I desire, because they are good religious, and nowise injurious to my kingdom." They declined the income; but the location being procured, they set about the erection of a church, in which they were aided by the Christians, the governor, and Taicosoma himself sent them a considerable sum of money; so that it was completed by September, 1594.

On the receipt, in Manilla, of the news of the success of the embassy to Japan, the viceroy sent Friars Marcellus da Ribadeneira, Augustin Rodriguez, Jerome di Jésu, and Andrew of St. Anthony, as envoys to Taicosama, and aids to their brethren. Andrew died on the voyage, and the three others reached Japan, August 27, 1594. They were graciously received by the emperor, who assured them of his desire to maintain the alliance with the Philippine Islands. The church of St. Mary of the Angels, at Meaco, was dedicated with great solemnity, on the 4th of October, and the M. B.

* Barezzo Barezzi.—*Cronache* ec. v. 2, p. 1067.

S. of the Eucharist, for the first time in Japan, publicly exposed to the adoration of the faithful.

Conspicuous among those who aided the Franciscans, on their arrival, were Leo Garasuma and Michael Casaqui, both of whom took the habit of the third Order; and taking up their residence near the convent (being married), they employed their time in works of piety and devotion, their houses becoming an asylum for the poor, the sick, and the orphan. Casaqui had a son aged eleven years, who, being charmed with the friars, besought his father to permit him to live with them; and, being clothed with the habit, he dwelt in the convent. Paul Gusugui, another Japanese, whose life had been irregular, was led to follow the example of Garasuma and Casaqui, taking the habit of the third Order; and many were the conversions which followed the establishment of the convent and church at Meaco.

Thus progressed the mission in 1594, when Peter Baptist, aided by Garasuma and Casaqui, who put their wealth at his disposal, erected two grand hospitals near the convent, one for adults, and one for children, which were soon filled by the unfortunate from every part of the large city, for whom no provision had ever been heretofore made.

Among those converted to the faith, were Paul Ibarchi, a brother of Garasuma, who took the habit of the third Order, and Francis, styled the Physician, who translated several works of piety into Japanese, and wrote against the errors of their false religion; Bonaventura, whose father was a Christian, but whose mother was an idolater, though baptized, was brought up under the influence of his mother, and became a Bonze, in which capacity he acted for twenty years; but being converted by the Franciscans, he took the habit of the third Order. A youth, aged sixteen, named Gabriel, of noble family, who resided at the court of the governor of Meaco, became acquainted with the friars while at the house of Tungen, and often visited them at their convent, and finally renounced the errors of the Bonzes, and all his worldly prospects, and taking the habit of the third Order, remained in the convent.

The Franciscans were now importuned to extend their labors to Nagasaki, one of the most populous and flourishing cities of Japan ; and Peter Baptist, accompanied by Jerome of Jesus, went there towards the close of 1594. They remained with the Jesuits twenty days, and receiving permission from the governor, Terazaba, they took up their abode in a hermitage outside the city, near which was a chapel called St. Lazarus. At the end of three months, Peter Baptist determined to build a convent and church in the city, but the Bonzes incited the governor against them, and he ordered them to leave Nagasaki. However, on consultation with the governor of Meaco, who assured him of the permission given to the Franciscans by the emperor, Terazaba allowed them to return; and Jerome of Jesus and John Poreco, who had been delegated to make the visitation of the Order, set out for Nagasaki, where in a short time arose a convent, church, and hospital; and so great was the progress of the faith there, that one of the Jesuits exclaimed: "God has, indeed, reserved this afflicted church for the poor children of the Great Patriarch of the poor, Francis of Assisi; in order that, by their apostolic labors, they might aid in giving glorious testimony to the faith of Christ in the midst of these numerous idolaters." At Meaco, Thomas Idanqui, who, though a Christian, had been leading a bad life, was converted from his evil ways, and after voluntary public penance, received the habit of the third Order. Cosimo Taqui, who had been converted before the arrival of the Franciscans, also took the habit of the third Order, and his son, Maximus, aged ten years, went to reside with the friars.

As soon as the convent and church were completed at Nagasaki, John Poreco departed for Manilla, but Jerome of Jesus received as a companion a youth of ten years, named Anthony, who was given him by his pious parents.

During this time, Peter Baptist was providing for a convent at Osaca, a populous city, eight leagues from Meaco, and ninety from Jeddo ; to which he sent Marcellus da Ribadeneira and Gonzales Garzia, together with the tertian, Garasuma, and Cosimo, and here they were generously aided by Donna Grazia, who had invited the Franciscans bv letter to Gonzales Garzia. From this place they visited the neighboring city of Sacoy, but were prevented by the Bonzes from building a convent ; and, returning to Osaca, continued their labors in that city, where they also erected a hospital, as at Meaco and Nagasaki. Among the conversions here were the governor and his wife ; and Gioachino Saquiya, who became a tertian, and resided in the convent.

In 1596, two more friars were sent from the Phillippines : Martin of the Ascension, who had been in Mexico, and taught in the college at Cherubusco, and also at Manilla ; and Francis Blanco, who had also been in Mexico where he was ordained.

Peter Baptist then made the following distribution of his forces :

Nagasaki.—Guardian, Jerome of Jesus, with Bartholemew Ruiz, and Marcellus Ribadeneira, taken from Osaca.

Osaca.—Guardian, Martin of the Ascension, with Francis Parilla.

Meaco.—Peter Baptist, Augustin Rodriguez, Francis Blanco, and Gonzales Garzia, who was also to visit Osaca occasionally.

The tertians with Martin of the Ascension were the two youths Anthony and Thomas.

The others were at Meaco—Garasuma, Susuqui, Casaqui, Bonaventura, and Gabriel—where they were occupied in the hospital, which now had 230 inmates, besides children.

Among the conversions at this time, were those of John Quizaya, and the little Paul Ibarch, nephew of Garasuma and Susuqui.

Such progress had the faith made among the Japanese, that the Holy See appointed a bishop for Nagasaki, in 1596, transferring Peter Martinez, S. J., from China to that city; and his arrival was the occasion of great rejoicing to the missionaries and Christians.

But whilst the Franciscans were thus rejoicing at the arrival of a bishop, as the complement of their labors in Japan, they were suddenly astounded to hear that they were declared to have contravened the prohibition of Gregory XIII. This was but the forerunner of the terrible ordeal through which they were to pass, for having preached Jesus Christ, and him crucified. In a few months, they themselves were condemned to follow their master to the very letter, by the death of the cross.

In July, 1596, a Spanish vessel named the St. Philip, richly laden, and having on board a large supply of arms, left the Philippine Islands for the port of Acapulco, in Mexico, but was driven, by stress of weather, into the harbor of Taca, in Japan. The governor of the place, having his cupidity aroused by the sight of the rich cargo, communicated the fact to the emperor, through an officer of the court named Gibonogio, and Jacuino, a bonze, and physician to the emperor, and, having imprisoned the captain and crew, took possession of the vessel. On board the St. Philip were several religious, two Augustinians, one Dominican, and the Franciscans, Las Casas and Poreco, who were on their way to Mexico. Every effort was made use of to excite the suspicions of Taicosama against the Europeans and the missionaries. He was told that the Spaniards intended to subjugate Japan, as they had already done to Mexico, Peru, and the Phillippines; and to confirm this, they asked a pilot of the vessel if it was not the intention of the king of Spain to extend his dominion over all the world, and if, the better to accomplish this object, he did not first send missionaries, and especially Franciscans, to those nations which he intended to conquer? The pilot answered in the affirmative, and this testimony was relied on to determine Taicosama to confiscate the vessel and expel the missionaries.* And, notwithstanding the efforts of Peter Baptist and Bishop Martinez, and the good offices of Guenifoin, the governor of Meaco, the vessel was confiscated, the houses of the missionaries were surrounded by guards, except those of Nagasaki, who were ordered to be sent to the Philippines; and on the 13th December, Gibonogio announced to those in the convent of Meaco, that Taicosama had pronounced sentence of death against all except those at Nagasaki. But why this exception? There is nothing to show.

Though the sentence of death was pronounced against all the missionaries, Jesuits as well as Franciscans, in Japan, except those at Nagasaki, yet such were the representations made to Taicosama by Guen-

* Juan Francisco.—*Cronaca*, ec. l. c.

ifoin, whose two sons were with the Jesuits, and included in the sentence, that he finally excepted all the Jesuits, on condition that they should in future preach only to the Portuguese, and not propagate their doctrines among the Japanese. But the governor of Osaca, notwithstanding this exception, did not remove the guard from the house of the Jesuits at that place, and when the names of those who were to be put to death were sent to Meaco, Paul Miki, and the catechists, John de Goto and Diego Kisai, who resided with the Jesuits at Osaca, were included.

Finally, on the 30th of December, 1596, Taicosama gave orders to Gibonogio that those under arrest in their convents at Meaco and Osaca, should be transferred to the public prison of Meaco, where they were to be conducted through the most noted streets of the city to the public square, when their noses and ears were to be cut off, and then conducted through the cities of the empire to Nagasaki; where they were to be crucified. And that all might know the cause of their punishment, a soldier was to go before, showing the written announcement that they were condemned to death *for having preached the Christian religion.**

Those at Osaca being brought to Meaco, they now numbered twenty-four: Peter Baptist, Martin of the Ascension or D'Aquirre, Francis Blanco, Philip Las Casas, Gonzales Garzia, Francis de la Parilla, Michael Cosaqui, Paul Ibarchi, Thomas Idanqui, Francis the Physician, Gabriel Duizco, Bonaventura of Meaco, Thomas Cosaqui, John Quizuya, Cosimo Taquia, Anthony di Nagasaki, Louis Ibarchi, Gioacchino Sacquiye, and Matthew di Meaco, Franciscans; and Paul Miki, John de Goto, and Diego Kisai, S. J. On the

* Martinez.—*Compendio Storico, &c.*, l. III. and others.

route to Nagasaki they were followed by the tertians, Peter Suquezico and Francis Fahelante, who were bound with the others by the soldiers, so that they now numbered twenty-six.

Our limits will not permit us to follow these glorious confessors of the faith in their long and painful journey through the great cities of Japan, as well as its forests and mountains, in the severest season of the year, exposed to the brutality of the soldiery, and the opprobrium of the infidels, being made a spectacle to the whole empire, until they consummated their martyrdom of the Cross at Nagasaki, February 5, 1597.

Only three of these glorious martyrs were priests, namely, the Franciscans St. Peter Baptist, St. Martin Aguirre, and St. Francis Blanco. All but six were natives of Japan. The three priests and the lay brother, St. Francis of St. Michael, were Spaniards; St. Gonzales Garzia was a native of the East Indies, and St. Philip Las Casas, a cleric, was an American, being born in the city of Mexico. He was the last to arrive in Japan and the first to suffer martyrdom. St. Peter Baptist, the chief of the heroic band, like the mother of the Machabees, was left for the last, thus having his martyrdom and his joy multiplied by witnessing every one of his children and companions bear the palm to heaven amidst the canticles *Laudate pueri Dominum* (Praise the Lord, ye children), and *Laudate Dominum homines gentes, laudate eum omnes populi* (Praise the Lord, ye Gentiles; praise Him all ye people). Their martyrdom was one of the most remarkable in the history of the Church. All died like our Saviour on the Cross, and were transpierced by spears. They were of all ages: St. Louis being only twelve; St. Anthony, thirteen; St. Thomas, fifteen ; St. Philip, twenty-three ; and St. Peter Baptist, the chief martyr, fifty-two years old.

The sentences of their death were inscribed on their crosses, and stated that they had been condemned to that punishment for having preached the faith of Jesus Christ.

Several first-class miracles are narrated in connection with their martyrdom, but the one on which Benedict XIV. made a particular comment, was that of St. Peter Baptist, who, after his death, was seen several times during the two months which he hung on the cross, descending from it, going to his church of Nangasaki, where he would celebrate Mass, asssisted by the young martyr, St. Anthony, and then return to hang on the cross. This was authentically attested by a great number of eye-witnesses, both Christian and pagan. The words of Benedict XIV. on the subject are these: "Such a fact, thus proved and admitted, can be affirmed to have been a great miracle, as it exceeds the power of nature that a man already dead should remove from the place of martyrdom to the place of the altar, and celebrate Mass; especially that God, from the beginning, elected man to perform and administer the Sacrament, but did not elect corpses."*

Since the year 1626 the Sacred Congregation of Rites decided that the canonization might take place at any time, but God had reserved its accomplishment for the living martyr, Pius IX., who found in it a consolation in his tribulations, and gave by it, to the world, a most palpable argument of the Unity, Catholicity, and Apostolicity of the Visible, Perpetual and Infallible Church of God.

When the order for the imprisonment of the missionaries was given, Bartholomew Ruiz, Marcellus Ribade-

* Benedict XIV., App. Canoniz. Sanctorum.

neira, and Augustine Rodriguez, were at Nagasaki, and put on board a ship to be sent to the Philippines, as none of those at that city were included in the sentence of death.

John Povero had accompanied the captain of the ship St. Philip, in his journey to plead his cause before Taicosama, and was at Osaca when the friars were arrested, where he was joined by Jerome of Jesus, who was on his way from Nagasaki to Meaco, and here they remained concealed for a short time.

Jerome wrote to Peter Baptist, asking to be allowed to accompany him to martyrdom; but Peter Baptist ordered him to keep himself concealed, to minister to the Christians. He did so, visiting Meaco; but on his return to Nagasaki he was arrested and put on board a vessel to be sent to the Philippines.

John Povero returned from Osaca to Nagasaki and encountered the martyrs on their entrance into that city to consummate their sacrifice—he wished to join them—but was sent on board the vessel with those of Nagasaki, which sailed on the 30th of March, and at Meaco they found Jerome of Jesus, and the five reached Manilla together, on the 15th of April.

Jerome of Jesus had been ordered by Peter Baptist to keep himself concealed in Japan, so as to be able to minister to the Christians, and he could not rest at Manilla. Soon after, in company with Louis Gomez, he returned, but Gomez was arrested, and Jerome only escaped by his superior knowledge of the country, being obliged to keep concealed until the death of Taicosama, Sept. 16, 1598.

The conduct of Taicosama,* and his inconstancy and

* The following is from the illustrious Diego Odeardi, O.S.D., cotemporary of Peter Paptist, and afterwards Bishop of New Segovia, who died in the odor of sanctity: "The sons of the Seraphic Father St. Francis, went to Japan, which they entered in the year 1593, and

inconsistency with regard to the missionaries, remains inexplicable; at one time showing them favors and giving them full permission to build churches and preach the Gospel, and about the next instant condemning them to death for the same. His first act was the expulsion of the Jesuits and the destruction of their churches, and confiscation of their property; yet some of the fathers remained in the country, and he does not appear to have taken any measures against them. He receives the Franciscans graciously—grants them full permission to exercise their ministry—even orders his governor to furnish them a place for a church, and himself contributes towards its erection—allows them for four years to publicly teach in the cities and capital of his empire—and often bears testimony in their favor. At their instance, he withdraws the edict against the Jesuits—and all at once condemns both Jesuits and Franciscans to death, *for having preached the Christian religion against his prohibition!* Yet he makes exception of all the missionaries—Franciscan and Jesuit—in one city, Nagasaki; and finally pardons *all* the Jesuits, and allows them to remain, on condition of not teaching the Japanese, but confining themselves to their own countrymen, engaged in commerce with Japan. The only explanation of this vacillating conduct seems to be, that he feared to drive away the commerce of the Christians by open and determined prohibition of the missionaries—and that the power of the Bonzes was so great that he feared to oppose them when they demanded the sacrifice of the

Tayco, the grand emperor, having received them with great love, made them particular gifts, and gave them license to build churches; and afterwards, without any other cause than his natural inconstancy and little firmness, changing love into hatred, commanded them to be crucified as Preachers of the Gospel; having himself given them license a little before, to preach it."—*Hist. del ss. Rosario, Parte I., Libro I., Cap.* 68.

Christians. His conduct found no other explanation, even at the time, than his inconstancy and want of firmness.

The Christians were now allowed a little respite, and Jerome, coming forth from his concealment, converted many to the faith, until, gaining the favor of Daifuxoma, he was allowed to preach the Gospel of Jesus Christ in Japan. He went to Jeddo, in the kingdom of Quanto, and was the first to announce the name of Christ there, and with permission of the emperor, he built a church in that place. He traversed the whole kingdom of Quanto on foot, building many churches and converting thousands of idolators, until about the close of 1599, he was sent by Daifuxoma as envoy to the Viceroy of Manilla, to negotiate a treaty of commerce and amity with Spain. Having accomplished his mission, he returned to Meaco with three of the Order, and was graciously received by the king, who, rejoiced at his success, even embraced him, gave him permission to preach throughout the empire, and also to re-open the church and convent built by Peter Baptist, at Meaco.

This success being known by the provincial of the Philippines, he sent eight more friars to Japan—who, being protected by the emperor, and held in veneration by the people, caused religion to again flourish—founded many churches throughout the empire—numbering seven convents, as the Franciscan Province of Japan, governed by a commissary-apostolic.

Jerome of Jesus died, full of honors, at Meaco, October 6, 1601; and religion continued to flourish and spread, until 1613, when a new and terrible persecution arose, which continued for many years, and nearly extinguished Christianity in that unhappy country.

Blessed Peter of Avila, went to the Philippines, and thence to Japan. After suffering labors, injuries, affronts, and imprisonment, he consummated his martyrdom in 1622, by being burned alive. Whilst in prison, he wrote several letters, full of a vivid eloquence.

Blessed Richard of St. Anne, and Friar Vincent of St. Joseph, acquired the palm of martyrdom, with Blessed Peter of Avila, being also burnt alive. In the same year Fr. Apollinaris Franco, after having been kept in slavery for four years, in Omura, completed his course by being burnt likewise to death, and with him became martyrs for Christ, Friar Paul of St. Clare, and Friar Francis of St. Bonaventure, Japanese.

Francis Galva suffered his martyrdom in 1623. He translated from Spanish into Japanese, some lives of the saints, which he entitled Flowers of the Saints, and also some small books of the Christian doctrine.

Blessed Louis Sotelo, labored for seven years, especially in the kingdom of Voxuano, from whose king, Idate Massomanst, he obtained the privilege of preaching, and of building churches and convents, which he erected in Macao, Tusimo, Vesana, and Sacaso. He was then sent by the emperor of Japan, ambassador to Philip II., king of Spain, and by the king, Idate, now a catechumen, to Paul V., with a royal retinue, accompanied by chosen Japanese, in the year 1614. The Pope received him with distinction, nominated him Bishop of Osa, in Japan, and sent him back. Shortly after his return, a new persecution was raised against the Christians, and he, together with his companions, Louis Gassanda, and Louis, a tertian, were condemned to the flames, and died in the year 1624. There is extant a letter written by him, from his prison, to Urban VIII., on the state of the Church in Japan, which is curious and interesting.

Anthony of St. Bonaventure, after many labors, sustained for the faith of Christ, was taken at Vomura and placed in a horrid prison, and afterwards conducted to Nagasaki, where he was burned alive, Sept. 8, 1628.

Diego of St. Francis, a celebrated preacher, through the desire of co-operating in the salvation of souls, went to the Phillippine Islands, and thence to Japan, where he was made commissary of that province, in which apostolic mission he had to suffer, in Vomura, imprisonment in a horrid prison, suffering cruel treatment, from which he was afterwards released. Not long after, he again went among the Japanese, laboring much for the faith, and suffering much, and finally losing his temporal life amidst torments, gathered gloriously the palm of martyrdom, in 1633. He wrote the History of the Martyrs of Japan, of the province of St. Joseph, in the Philippines.

Alphonsus Ruiz labored for thirty years in Japan, and merited to triumph through Christ, being beheaded in the same year, 1633.

Louis Gomez, up to the 80th year of his age, labored in Japan, traversing that region, and meeting many dangers, all of which he overcame. He was arrested at Vomura, and imprisoned; thence, with others, he was taken to Jeudi, and kept in a dark prison, and there he suffered a new species of martyrdom—his feet being bound to a beam, his body was lowered in a subterranean ditch, where, losing by degrees his respiration, he completed his illustrious martyrdom for the love of Christ, 1637.

Francis of St. Mary, together with the lay brother Bartholomew Larvel, labored in the care of the infirm and the lepers, in which exercise he led many to the knowledge of the true God. The great persecution being raised against the Christians by the king of Arima, the two religious were imprisoned, and after four months of cruel imprisonment in the city of Nagasaki, they were burned alive, and went to join the other glorious martyrs.

Several other missionaries suffered martyrdom, together with the Franciscans, in these persecutions, from 1613 to 1637. Two hundred and five of these martyrs, Franciscans, Dominicans, Augustinians, Jesuits, and others, were beatified by Pius IX., on the 7th of July, of this year, 1867, and about forty of them belong to the first or third Order of St. Francis.

CHAPTER XVIII.

Discovery of America.—Columbus a Tertian.—Friar John Perez de Marchena.—Queen Isabella a Tertian.—The Franciscan *Boil* and the Benedictine Boyl.—The first Mass and the first church in America.—Garzia de Padilla the first bishop.—New missionaries with Ovando.—Francis Alexander the first victim of the American missions. John de Quevedo the first bishop in the Continent.

THE year 1492 opened up a new and vast missionary field for the children of St. Francis, by the discovery of America; and of the three personages who share among themselves the glory of that great achievement, one was a Franciscan friar, and the two others belonged to the Third Order of St. Francis. To Christopher Columbus, the Genoese navigator—the Franciscan, Father John Perez de Marchena, and Isabella, Queen of Spain—is the world indebted for the conception and accomplishment of the undertaking which gave a new continent to Europe, and a hitherto unknown people to the apostles of Jesus Christ. These three personages were eminently Catholic, and the diffusion of the light of the faith among "those who sat in darkness and the shadow of death," was the motive which actuated them in attempting the glorious but hazardous enterprise. The desire of carrying the truths of salvation to distant lands and heathen nations was, with them, paramount to all anticipation of gain, or desire of conquest, and in the accomplishment of this holy purpose, the children of St. Francis have borne a conspicuous part from the very beginning.*

Towards the close of the fifteenth century, John Perez de Marchena, a man of piety and erudition, was guardian of the small Franciscan convent of La Rabida, near the then obscure seaport town of Palos, in Andalusia, and his reputation had extended from that remote solitude, even as far as the court of Spain, whither he was called by the good and great Isabella, and where he held, for some time, the office of Confessor to the Queen. But a life at court, with its attendant distractions had no charms for the humble son of St. Francis, and he longed for the retirement and seclusion of his convent cell, where, after the duties of the sanctuary were over, he could devote his leisure hours to his favorite sciences of geography and astronomy. He sought release from the court, and his request being reluctantly granted, he returned to La Rabida.

Here nothing remarkable occurred to vary the quiet and holy routine of monastic life, until late one evening, in the summer of 1484, a way-worn traveller, apparently about forty years of age, leading a pale and tender youth by the hand, knocked at the convent gate, and, in the name of charity, asked for food and

* With Isabella, zeal for propagating the Christian faith, together with the desire of communicating the knowledge of truth, and the consolations of religion, to people destitute of spiritual light, were more than ostensible motives for encouraging Columbus to attempt his discoveries. Upon his success, she endeavored to fulfil her pious purpose. and manifested the most tender concern to secure not only religious instruction, but mild treatment, to that inoffensive race of men subject to the crown."—ROBERTSON, *History of America*, book viii.

shelter. The language of the stranger indicated that he was a foreigner, and the accent was of Italy. His countenance was so sorrowful, that the guardian, touched with compassion, inquired the cause of his dejection. In a few words, the guest related his history: He was born at Genoa; he had studied at Pavia; from his early youth he had an earnest love for the knowledge of geography and navigation; he had joined a naval expedition, under John of Anjou; had traversed the sea as a trader; had joined another naval enterprize, in the waters of Portugal, against Venice, and was, on that occasion, miraculously saved from his burning vessel; he then went to Lisbon, and there married the daughter of a celebrated navigator, whose only dowry was the nautical charts of her deceased father; the study of these charts revived his old love for the sea, and his mind was occupied with the project of discovering a western route over the Atlantic ocean to India. He had applied to his own country for assistance, to enable him to accomplish the undertading, but Genoa gave him no encouragement. He had appealed to Venice, but that republic did not appreciate his vast project. He then had recourse to Portugal, but with no better success. He made another effort to give his native Genoa the benefit of his services, but they were again rejected. Finally, he had turned his eyes towards Spain—bade adieu to his country and to his aged father, and was now in search of a sister of his departed wife, who was supposed to reside in the vicinity of Palos, and with whom he designed leaving his only child, the youth who accompanied him, whilst he pursued his journey, to lay his proposals before the court of Spain.

Friar Perez listened attentively to this recital, for his own thoughts had long been occupied with a similar project, and he prevailed on the weary and dejected traveller to rest for a time at La Rabida. After a sojourn of six months, and much interchange of thought on the great subject in which both took such a deep interest, the hospitable guardian took upon himself the care and education of the youth, and gave a letter of warm recommendation to the father, to be presented to his confrère, Ferdinand de Talavera, who had succeeded him as confessor to the Queen.

But the journey was long, and if his guest was poor by misfortuue, and without the means of defraying his expense—the Franciscan is none the less so, by choice, and the obligation of his Rule. In this extremity, the guardian has recourse to his acquaintances among the inhabitants of the neighboring town of Palos, and through his representations concerning the worthiness of his friend, and the merit of his undertaking, he readily obtains the means by which he is enabled to pursue his journey—and Christopher Columbus set out for Castile, leaving his son, Diego, at La Rabida, where he had found, in a poor Franciscan friar, that appreciation and sympathy which courts and kings had denied him.*

Spain was at that time deeply engrossed by her last and successful effort to drive the Moors from her soil, and the court was in the camp. New difficulties beset the unknown navigator. He can find no one to undertake the presentation of his proposition, and, in despair, he himself writes to the king but he does not even deign an answer; finally, through the Apostolic Nuncio, Antonio Geraldini, he obtains an audience, and Ferdinand appoints a commission to examine the matter. His hope revives. But alas! his proposals

* Cesare Cantù.—*Storia Universale.*

are rejected by the wisdom of Salamanca, as the offspring of an unsound mind—if not worse!

Columbus, still unshaken in his design, even by the six years of fruitless efforts, resolves to have recourse to France, and sets out for La Rabida, where he had met such sympathy, and where he had left his son. In April, 1492, he presents himself a second time, poor, dejected, and wayworn, at the gate of the hospitable convent, and a second time he is welcomed to the humble fare, and experiences the sincere sympathy of the poor Franciscans. For the Catholic spirit which dwells in these blessed cloisters is well known, and was often thus expressed over the door:

"Porta patens esto: nullo claudatur honesto."*

Father Perez, touched at the recital of his new disappointment, and knowing well the wisdon and goodness of Isabella, who, unfortunately had not been made acquainted with the affair, wrote to her, at once, though she was then in the midst of the camp at Santa Fè. The Queen is moved by the words of her former confessor, who portrays, in glowing language, the great glory to God and the benefit and renown to the crown of Spain, which would accrue from the proposed enterprise. She immediately puts in the hands of the messenger a letter "For John Perez de Marchena, Guardian of the Minor Observantines of St. Francis, at St. Mary's of La Rabida, near Palos." With this letter, the messenger returns after an absence of fourteen days, and a new joy fills the little community of that humble cloister. The Queen thanks Perez for his important communication; authorizes him to give hope to his friend; and requests the presence of the guardian at the camp, promising him a favorable hearing concerning the matter proposed.

* Ages of Faith.—*Digby.*

It was near midnight when the letter of Isabella reached La Rabida, and Perez resolved to set out at once for Granada; and, notwithstanding the remonstrances of Columbus, and of his brethren, the aged friar, mounted on a borrowed mule, pursues, in the stillness of the night, the lonely path which, through lofty pines, leads from the secluded convent, bearing, under his coarse habit, a heart full of hope, and his mind occupied with thoughts of a New World!*

When it is remembered that the proposal of Columbus had been rejected by so many sovereigns, as visionary, and twice condemned by the wisdom of the learned schools of Salamanca, it cannot fail to be perceived how high must have been Isabella's estimate of the talents and judgment of Friar Perez, when, at the very moment when Spain was engaged in a war, on the issue of which her existence itself depended, she found time to give the project of Columbus her most serious consideration, since it was so warmly espoused by him.

On his arrival at Granada, Perez is at once admitted to an interview with the queen, Columbus is sent for. And in the royal tent, at the camp of Santa Fè, the three great characters—Isabella, Columbus and Friar Perez—meet for the first time, and discuss the great undertaking, which has inseparably connected their names with America!

New obstacles are, however, thrown in the way by the queen's advisers, concerning the terms of agreement with regard to the powers and emoluments to be conferred on Columbus, in case he should be successful in his undertaking. But Isabella, by a resolution which adds new lustre to her name, declares that she

* Among other historical facts connected with the discovery of America, represented about the National Capitol at Washington, is the bronze representation, on one of the gates, of the Franciscan Friar on his mule.

will assume the enterprize on behalf of her own crown of Castile, and pledges even her jewels, as security for the expense of the expedition!

The little port of Palos was chosen by the queen as that from which the small fleet was to set sail; and Columbus finds himself, for the third time, a guest in the neighboring convent of La Rabida. On the 23d of May, 1492, the Royal Letters directed to the authorities of Palos requiring them to furnish all things necessary for the expedition, were read to the assembled people, in the church of St. George, in that town. The ships were to be manned by seamen chiefly of that port. But as the subject was canvassed among the people, the fears and alarms of the timorous began to take hold of the sailors and their friends. In this new emergency, the friend of Columbus, Friar Perez, again comes to his aid. He preaches to the people, and allays their fears, raising their hopes, by the prospect of the great blessing to mankind, and the honor and glory to themselves, which would not fail to be the consequence of their hearty and generous co-operation with the worthy Columbus. Thus, not only with royalty, but also with the common people and with sailors, was Friar Perez an advocate for the discoverer of America.

Finally, three ships are ready, with their armaments, the *Pinta*, furnished by John de Pennasola; the *Niña*, by young Vincent Yanez Pinzon; and the *Gallenga*, whose name is changed into that of the *Santa Maria*, by the inhabitants of Palos; the two latter vessels procured chiefly through the influence of Friar Perez. Columbus raised his admiral's flag on the *Santa Maria*, placed under the protection of Our Lady of La Rabida; and all things being now in readiness, the expedition awaited only a favorable wind from the east. As a final preparation, the whole company went in procession to the convent of La Rabida, where Father Perez offered up the Holy Sacrifice of the Mass, at which they all received holy communion. They then solemnly put themselves and their undertaking under the protection of Our Lady of La Rabida, and the good friar gave them his parting blessing.

At last, on the 3d of August, 1492, the little fleet of three vessels sailed out of the port of Palos to explore the wide expanse of unknown waters. With swelling heart, the eye of Perez followed the course of the sails, from his observatory on the convent, until they passed out of sight; and then descending to the convent chapel, he poured forth an ardent prayer before the Blessed Sacrament, for Divine protection to the heroic Columbus and his little band. Truly was every thing connected with the discovery of America eminently Catholic.

On the 6th of September, the vessels pass the most westerly of the Canary Islands; and for the first time is God adored far out on the face of the mighty deep —for the first time are the praises of Mary, "Star of the Sea," chanted on the broad expanse of the mid-Atlantic!

But new troubles are added to the perils of the voyage in unknown seas; the clouds of discontent begin to gather, and give forth ominous sounds. After weeks of voyaging, and no indications of land appearing, the companions of Columbus begin to murmur; and they even meditate casting him into the sea and returning homeward. In this trying extremity he has recourse to God, in prayer; and, as if enlightened from heaven, he predicts the appearance of land within three days, and promises that if his prediction is not fulfilled, he will then consent to return. His prediction is accomplished, and on the 12th day of October, 1492, they prostrate themselves in thanksgiving to God, before the Sign of Man's redemption, raised, for the first time, on the soil of the New World!

The months pass by, and no tidings reach the anxious relatives, in Palos, of those who, at the solicitation of Friar Perez, followed the strange navigator into those unknown seas, from which they are now never expected to return; and the guardian of La Rabida is compelled to hear the reproaches of those who already begin to look upon him as the cause of their supposed bereavement. This was a severe trial for the tender heart of the good Franciscan; but he never, for a moment, lost his confidence in the success of the enterprize, or ceased to pour forth his prayers for its divine protection.

While Friar Perez was thus praying for the absent Columbus, the latter was taking possession of the islands of the Western waters, in the name of God and his sovereign—raising the cross and unfurling the flag of Spain. The first land he approached he named San Salvador; the three next islands he calls St. Mary of the Conception, Ferdinand, and Isabella.

The Spaniards were every where kindly and graciously received and welcomed by the Indians, natives of the islands; who looked upon their new visitors with astonishment and veneration, imagining them to be beings of a superior nature, and reverencing them as children of the sun.

On the 15th of March, 1493, Columbus, returning to Spain, enters the port of Palos, in the *Niña*, and, amid the great joy and heartfelt congratulations of the whole people, relates the success of his voyage. His first visit was to La Rabida; and words would fail to convey any idea of the sentiments of gratitude to God, which filled the souls of Perez and the humble friars of that convent, which may be called the cradle of the project of the discovery of America, at the sight of their friend, and the recital of the adventures of his voyage.

As by the terms of agreement, Columbus was viceroy of the new discoveries, one of the first objects of his solicitude was to provide missionaries for the instruction of the Indians in the truths of Christianity; and for this purpose he besought Ferdinand to procure the appointment of a Vicar-Apostolic, for the government of the ecclesiastical affairs of the New World. The Sovereign Pontiff, knowing the attachment of Columbus to the Seraphic Order,* as also the conspicuous part which the Franciscans had taken in the discovery, conferred this honor on a disciple of St. Francis, and nominated Father *Bernard Boïl* Provincial of the Order in Spain, Vicar-Apostolic of the Indies, as the new discoveries were then designated. But by a sacrilegious act of treachery, which forever stains the name of Ferdinand, and tarnishes his glory, the Bulls of nomination never reached the person selected by the Pope.

There happened, at that time, to be in Castile a Benedictine monk, named Bernard Boyl, a man somewhat versed in secular affairs, and much given to diplomacy, by which means he had ingratiated himself into the good favor of Ferdinand; and, from the similarity of his name to that of the person chosen by the Holy See, the king conceived the plan of substituting *Boyl* for *Boïl*, hoping that this similarity of the names would prevent detection; or that if it were found out, it could be alleged as the cause of an error. And, under the

* Columbus had received the habit of the Third Order of St. Francis, from Friar Perez, at La Rabida, in 1492.—Roselly de Lorgues.

specious pretext that such a precious document ought not to be exposed to the dangers of the long sea voyage, a false copy of the Bull was made, with this change in the name, and delivered to *Bernard Boyl*, the diplomatist, while the king retained in his own possession the original document, appointing *Bernard Boil* the Spanish Provincial of the Franciscans. Nor can any doubt exist as to this substitution by Ferdinand. Neither could the similarity of the names have caused any mistake on the part of the king, since the Pontifical Brief, sent to Ferdinand himself, clearly expressed the *Order* to which the Vicar designated by the Pope belonged. It was directed: "To our Beloved Son, Bernard Boil, of the Order of Friars Minor, and Vicar of the said Order, in the kingdom of Spain."

But that there may be no doubt as to the deception and forgery practiced by Ferdinand, we will give the authenticated direction of the Bull, as found in the autograph register of the Apostolic Letters, issued in the first year of the Pontificate of Alexander VI. It is as follows:

"Dilecto Filio Bernardo Boil, Fratri Ordinis Minorum, Vicario dicti Ordinis in Regnis Hispaniarum."

These documents were examined, in 1851, and an authenticated copy, as above, made, under the seal of the Keeper of the Pontifical Archives, attested as follows:

"Descriptum et recognitum ex Autographo Regesto Literarum Apostolicarum Alexandri PP. VI. anno I. pag. 122, quod adservatur in tabulariis secretioribus Vaticanis. In quorum fidem hic me subscripsi et solito signo signavi.

Dabam ex tabulariis præfatis VII. Idus Febr. an. 1851.

MARINI MARINUS, Tabularior. S. R. E. Praefectus."*

This treachery of Ferdinand towards the Holy See, by which he tarnished the glory so lately acquired by

* Roselly de Lorgues, Life of Columbus.

the expulsion of the Moors from Spain, was unknown to Isabella, the pious daughter of the Church. It was never suspected by the viceroy Columbus, the ever-faithful Catholic; and though the humble Franciscan, Friar Boil, never knew of the high dignity which the Sovereign Pontiff had conferred upon him; and though he did not cross the ocean; yet was he the true, the legitimate, and the first Vicar-Apostolic of the New World.

But Divine Providence permits not the spirit of the Church to be slighted with impunity; nor can human artifice, or worldly cunning, ever thwart the divine wisdom by which she is guided. Intruded by the king into a spiritual office, contrary to the pontifical designation, the *Royal* Vicar did not receive that invisible asisstance which would have blessed his labors; hence they were without fruit; and we shall see him, in the sequel, neglecting the duties of the Apostolate, joining in the turbulent cabals of the vicious against the good and the great Columbus, and soon deserting the position into which he had been obtruded, the only record of his official action in the New World being the fulmination of censures!

We have deemed this slight digression due to the good name of Columbus, which otherwise might be supposed to be clouded by the censure pronounced against him by the Royal Vicar Apostolic Boyl.

On the 25th of September, 1493, Columbus sailed from the port of Cadiz, on his return to his colony in the Indies, with a fleet of seventeen vessels, well provided with all the necessaries for the new settlement; and among those who accompanied him were the Vicar Boyl, and a number of Franciscans and Hieronymites, for the religious instruction and conversion of the Indians.

At the earnest solicitation of the great discoverer, his first friend, steadfast patron, and ardent advocate, Friar Perez, was selected as chief of this first missionary band which set out for the New World.* He was also appointed, by royal authority, astronomer to the fleet—an office of some importance, connected with expeditions of discovery, in those days, and one for which his talents eminently fitted Friar Perez. Having obtained full powers from the General of the Order, Francis de Brescia, he made a selection of twelve Franciscans, from different parts of Spain, among whom were the Fathers Garzia da Padilla, John de Borgognon, and John Rosso. The admiral and Friar Perez went on board the largest vessel of the fleet, which was named the Graciosa Maria; and the Vicar, with the missionaries, on another vessel.

On Sunday, the 3d of November, they came to an island, but it was none of those which had been discovered in the first voyage, as they had kept a course somewhat more to the south. They named the island *Dominica*, in honor of the day on which they had discovered it; and not finding a place suitable for landing, they proceeded to another of the group not far distant, where Father John Perez de Marchena was the first to go on shore after the viceroy, and was con-

* The old historians make no allusion to any priest accompanying Columbus on his first voyage, though we have noticed such a statement in a late work; and "La Stella dell' Umbria," in its fourth number, 1864, mentions the existence of a valuable MS. of Gio. Batta: Alvi, Canon of the Cathedral of Lodi, composed from data found in the capitular archives of that city, and from data in his own possession, embracing the period between the years 1000 and 1492, the latter inclusive, in which is found the following: "1492.—In this year, Christopher Columbus, a Genoese, went to the Indies to discover a new land and new countries, and among the other men whom he took with him in his caravan, was the P. Gio: Bernard M. Costeri, da Todi, of the Order of Minors, a man of great learning, practiced in astronomy, and also likewise his confessor; whence Gabriel M. Castri, brother of the said religious, gave the name of Christopher to one of his three sons. *Ex. Lill. el Epla di Columbi olim asserval. Bened. Gabriell. et Bernard. Boccardu.*"—Cronica delle Missioni Francescane, Ottobrè, 1864.

sequently the first priest who set foot in the New World!

They next touched at an island which Columbus named St. Mary, of Guadalupe, in honor of our Lady of that title in Spain, in fulfilment of a promise made to the Franciscans of that convent, where he had been entertained the previous year. Then they named the St. Mary of the Rotunda, the Antigua, St. John the Baptist, St. Ursula, and others; and finally, on the 22d of November, they reached San Salvador, only to find, to their deep sorrow, that the fort which had been erected the previous year was entirely destroyed; and not one of their companions of the first voyage, who had been left on the island, was found to tell the tale of its destruction. They had drawn upon themselves the fury of the Indians, who had massacred them all.

No sooner had Friar Perez landed, than his first work was to erect a small chapel, which was the first ever dedicated to the service of the true God in America; and here, he who had been first of all to comprehend and appreciate the designs of Columbus—who had interceded for him at court—had consoled him in his disappointments—had aided him in fitting out his vessels—had gained for him the favor and assistance of the citizens of Palos—and had constantly prayed to God for his success—the Franciscan friar, Father Juan Perez de Marchena, guardian of the convent of Our Lady of La Rabida—here, in the small chapel built by his own hands, on the soil of the New World, he offered up, for the first time, the august sacrifice of the New Law, in the Western Hemisphere, and blessed, in the name of Jesus Christ, the land in whose discovery he had borne such a conspicuous part. Truly, America should be Catholic! It was consecrated to Catholicity from the very beginning.

This accomplished, Perez set out, at the head of his fellow-missionaries, to traverse the island, instructing the natives, as well as their slight knowledge of the language would permit; but in this work they received no assistance from the *royal* vicar, who had no taste for the laborious duties of a missionary among the heathen natives, and history testifies that whilst the pious Franciscan, John de Borgognon, and the Hieronymite, Roman Parre, applied themselves to the study of the language, the would-be superior of the mission, disgusted with the poor Indians, was himself the first to proclaim the inutility of his residence among them, and to seek his recall to Spain.*

Borgognon and Parre, after laborious application, acquired some knowledge of the Marcorix dialect, which was the one most extensively in use among the natives; and thus they were the first to speak the language of the new world. The system which they had prepared was imparted to their fellow-missionaries, and the instruction of the Indians progressed so rapidly, that the villages, on all sides, were in a short time full of neophytes, and in a few months after their arrival, they had already baptized many.

Whilst the missionaries were thus laboring for the instruction and salvation of the idolators, Columbus was laying the foundations of a city, which he named Domingo, in honor of his father, whose name was Dominico; and here, in the first city of America, Perez and his companions erected another small chapel—the second in the new world. The Most Blessed Sacrament of the Eucharist was continually kept in both these chapels, and near this last was built a residence for the missionaries. But it was poor and small; and the viceroy, at his own expense, augmented its dimen-

* Roselly de Lorgues, Life of Columbus.

sions, so that it became worthy to be called a convent, and received from Perez the name of his great patriarch, St. Francis, and he himself was the first guardian!

Thus aided and encouraged by the viceroy, the missionaries continued, with ardor, to prosecute the great work of the spiritual regeneration of the natives, and such was their success, that in a short time, the Franciscan Garzia de Padilla, the companion and fellow-missionary of Juan Perez, in America, was appointed and consecrated bishop, in Spain, of San Domingo—the first bishop of the New World—but prevented by death he never returned to America.*

When Nicholas Ovando was appointed viceroy of New Spain, instead of Bobadilla, by the advice of Cardinal Ximenes, several religious embarked with him for the New World, among whom were ten Franciscan Observantines, under the leadership of Friar Alfonsus d'Espinar. Ximenes, who preferred the interest of Jesus Christ to his own aggrandisement, wished also to employ his faithful companion, John de Trassierra, and John Robles, to whom he was warmly attached, in the conversion of the Indians. These religious, whose learning and piety had so happily disposed the Mussulmans of Granada to embrace the faith, and one of whom had already made the voyage to America, were sent out not only as missionaries to evangelize the natives, but were also empowered to pass judgment on the conduct of Bobadilla, who had

* The first project of the King and Queen of Spain had been to appoint Dr. Peter de Deza Archbishop of Xaragua, Fr. Garzia de Padilla Bishop of Larez, and Alonzo Mansa, Bishop of the Conception, but it was never carried into effect, and after the death of Queen Isabella, a new arrangement took place, and San Domingo became the first and principal see in the New World. The first metropolitan see erected in America was that of Mexico, and John Zumaraga the first archbishop, who died 1548. San Domingo was made a metropolitan see after 1548.—Torquémada, t. 3, l. 10, ch. vi. Henrion, l. 1, ch. xxxiv.

sent Columbus to Spain in chains. The Cardinal gave them bells and ornaments for the new churches, clothing for the natives, and his liberality was not less towards the idolators of America than towards the Mahometans of Spain. The flotilla left the port of San Lucar, on the 6th of February, 1502, and arrived in San Domingo on the 14th of the following April. Friar Francis Ruiz, whose health suffered much from the climate of Hayti, was compelled to return to Spain at the end of six months, and had for fellow-passenger Bobadilla, now a prisoner, who died on the voyage.

The Franciscan Fr. Alexander accompanied Columbus in his fourth voyage from Spain to America, in 1502, but when in the waters of Panama was shipwrecked and drowned. He was the first missionary who encountered death in the duties of the apostolate in the New World.

In the year 1516, some of the missionaries passed from San Salvador to the continent, which had been lately discovered, and landing on the coast of Paria, near the island of Cubagua, they there founded a convent—Juan Garces becoming vicar. They began to teach the children to read and write, and to preach to the Indians; and they baptized many, both children and adults; and so well were they received, that they passed a hundred leagues into the interior, with perfect safety.

The Franciscan Quevedo, accompanied Pedrarias to the continent, in 1513, and became bishop of Darien in 1514—the first bishop on the *continent* of America. By his interposition and exhortation, he brought about a reconciliation, in 1516, between Pedrarias and Balboa—the latter the discoverer of the territory, who had been suspended, as governor, by the former.

About the year 1522, we find Bishop Quevedo giving his advice, before the Spanish court, at Barcelona, concerning the treatment of the Indians. In a short discourse he lamented the fatal desolation of America, by the extinction of so many of its inhabitants, and acknowledged that this was to be imputed, in some degree, to the excessive rigor and inconsiderate proceedings of the Spaniards. But he declared that all the people of the New World whom he had seen, either on the continent or on the islands, appeared to him to be a race of men whom it would be impossible to instruct or improve, unless they were collected in villages and kept under continual supervision. And all the experience of the missionaries—whether in Mexico, California, Texas, Florida, Paraguay and Canada—has shown the truth of this statement, for scarcely any lasting impression could ever be made on them, so long as they roamed over the wilds without any fixed abode.

As new discoveries were made, the Franciscans were the foremost to take advantage of the fields which they opened up for the missionaries of the Gospel; and where settlements were made, there soon arose the church and convent. This was the case in Cuba, and in all the islands occupied by the Spaniards as well as on the continent.

CHAPTER XIX

Conquest of Mexico.—The Franciscans among the first missionaries.—Brother Peter of Ghent.—Friar Martin de Valencia and his twelve companions.—Establishment of missions and schools among the Indians.—Friar John de Zumarraga the first bishop and archbishop of Mexico.—College of Ilatecalco.—John Calero the first martyr.

The conquest of Mexico was only second in importance to the discovery of America, as the wealth of its mines of precious metals, especially of silver, poured an immense treasure into the lap of the mother country, and was followed by an extensive immigration to the new continent.

"The Friars Minor," says Henrion, "who went to America with the first conquerors, planted the faith in the islands of Hayti, Cuba, Cubagua, or Isle of Pearls, Porto Rico, Jamaica, St. Margaret, St. Croix, and on the coast of Cumana, in South America;" and Herrara says, that Cortes *always* had Friars Minor with him, and the letters which he wrote in 1520, asking for more friars, show how highly he appreciated their labors. Cortes sailed with his expedition from Cuba, in 1519, and the Spaniards were kindly received by the Indians of the coast where they first landed. But although they gave evidence of a nearer approach to civilization than the inhabitants of the islands, they offered immense numbers of their fellow-beings in sacrifice to their idols. But the time had arrived when the light of the Gospel was to dawn upon this benighted people who had so long sat in darkness and the shadow of Death; and so marvellous was the conquest of Cortes, that he seems to have been an instrument in the hands of Providence for the accomplishment of its great designs with respect to Mexico. History contains nothing parallel, either with respect to the boldness of the attempt, or the success of the execution; and were not the circumstances of these extraordinary transactions authenticated by the most unquestionable evidence, they would appear so wild and extravagant, as even to go beyond the bounds of fiction. But it is not our province to relate the deeds, or vindicate the character of Cortes—both have been ably done by others. The expedition set out, not with the solicitude natural to men going upon a dangerous service, but with that confidence which arises from security of success and certainty of Divine protection ; and on their standard was a large Cross, with the inscription, "Let us follow the Cross, for under this sign we shall conquer."

After establishing a post at Vera Cruz, and destroying his vessels, in order to prevent his followers from deserting him and returning to the islands, Cortes commenced his march towards the City of Mexico. Nothing remarkable occurred in his progress, until he arrived on the confines of Tlascala, when his journey was opposed by a numerous body of natives ; but they were soon routed by the Spaniards, with whom they afterwards entered into an alliance.

Many of the tribes already complained of the exactions of Montezuma, and Cortes was everywhere welcomed as one sent to deliver them from the tyranny of which they complained. In descending from the mountains of Chalcos, across which the road lay, the vast plains of Mexico opened gradually to the view of the Spaniards. "When they first beheld this prospect—one of the most striking and beautiful on the face of the earth—when they observed fertile and cultivated fields stretching further than the eye could reach—when they saw a lake, resembling the sea in extent, encompassed with large towns, and discovered the capital city rising upon an island in the middle, adorned with its temples and turrets—the scene so far exceeded their imagination, that some believed the fanciful descriptions of romance were realized, and that its enchanted palaces and gilded domes were presented to their sight—others could hardly persuade themselves that this wonderful spectacle was anything more than a dream."

Cortes soon subjected the Mexicans to the Spanish

crown, and firmly established his authority in the country; and one of the first objects of his solicitude was to procure religious instructions for the natives. Shortly after the Conquest, three Franciscan friars—John de Tecto and John de Aaora, priests, and a lay brother, called Peter of Ghent—went to Mexico, and devoted themselves to the instruction of the Indians. Brother Peter of Ghent established a school at Tetzulco—the first in Mexico.

The Franciscans, John Clapion, who had been Confessor to the Emperor, and Francis de los Angelos (Quiñones), brother of the Count de Luna, were authorized, and made preparations to set out from Spain for the Mexican mission; but the former died, and the latter was chosen minister-general of the Order, at the General Chapter of Burgos, and were thus prevented from carrying out their project. Quiñones was afterwards raised to the cardinalate of the title of Santa Cruz.

It may well be supposed, that although Friar Francis de los Angelos was prevented, by his new duties, from accomplishing, in person, his purpose of evangelizing the Mexicans, he did not cease to take every means which his position, as minister-general of the Order put in his power, to further the good work which he had so much at heart.

Looking around among the assembled friars of the Chapter, his eyes fell upon Friar Martin de Valencia,*

* The Protestant English historian, *Helps*, says of this Friar Martin de Valencia: "When he arrived in Mexico he maintained the most rigid mode of life. He went barefoot, with a poor and torn robe, bearing his wallet and his cloak on his own shoulders, without permitting even an Indian to assist in carrying them. In this fashion he used to visit the convents under his jurisdiction. Being already an old man when he arrived in Mexico, he could not learn the language with the same facility as his companions; so what he most devoted himself to was teaching the little Indian boys to read Spanish." He was accustomed to "retire to an oratory, on a mountain, where he might enjoy the most profound contemplation."

provincial of the province of San Gabriel, whom he judged to be a fit and proper person for the execution of the design which he himself had expected to carry out; and to him he gave the obedience of preparing for the mission to Mexico, and of selecting twelve companions to accompany him to preach the Gospel to the nations recently discovered by Cortes.

Friar Martin de Valencia, made choice of Friars Francis de Soto,* Martin de la Caruña, Joseph de la Caruña, John Xuares, Antonio de Ciudad Rodrigo, Toribio† de Benevento, Garcia de Cisneros, Louis de Fuensalida, John de Ribas and Francis Ximenes, and the lay brothers Andres de Cordova, and Bernardine de la Torre, the last of whom turning back, John de Palos, of the province of Andalusia, was chosen in his place, and they set sail on Tuesday, the 25th of January, 1524, from the port of San Lucar de Barrameda, they arrived at San Juan de Ulna, on the third of May, in the same year, where they were received with great joy by the Spaniards, and all their wants supplied.

Setting out barefoot, for the city of Mexico, distant sixty leagues, they passed through Tlascala, where they rested some days, during which they were astonished to behold the vast number of people who assembled in that populous city on one of the market days, and, giving thanks to God for the extensive harvest

* He afterwards refused the Archbishopric of Mexico. Whilst he was Superior in that city, he refused to sign, in the name of the Franciscans, the petition to Charles V. for the *perpetual repartiemientos*, though it was signed by the two other religious orders; and for that refusal they gained the animosity of the rapacious Europeans.

† Afterwards called *Motolinia*, who wore out his life in teaching, catechising and baptizing the Indians. He baptized no less than four hundred thousand. He was the only priest who administered the sacrament of Confirmation in Mexico, having received that power from the Pope, Leo X. He visited Guatamala and Yucatan, supplying those with missionaries. He wrote and printed the *Christian Doctrine*, in the Mexican language—the first work published in that tongue

which he had sent them to gather, though they knew not the language of the people, they began by signs to indicate to them the object of their mission.

The Indians were astonished at the appearance of the humble friars, so different in their dress and manners from the Spanish soldiers, and gave expression to their surprise, exclaiming, "*Motolinia.*" Friar Toribio de Benevento having asked one of the Spaniards the meaning of this word, he told them that it signified "*Poor.*" "This, then," said Friar Toribio, shall be my name henceforth," and ever after, he was called Friar Toribio Motolinia.

Reaching the city of Mexico, the friars were met by Cortes, accompanied by the Spanish cavaliers and the principal Indians, who showed them the greatest respect and honor; Cortes kneeling to kiss their hands, and placing his cloak under the feet of Friar Martin de Valencia.

Such had been the avidity with which the Spanish soldiers sought after gold, that they had committed many injustices against the Indians, and the poor friars of St. Francis, who lived in the most simple manner, valuing neither silver or gold, but devoting themselves to prayer, and the instruction of the people, was well calculated to disabuse their minds of the odious impression which they had received concerning everything Spanish.

The twelve friars who came with Martin de Valencia, found here five other friars of the same Order, who had come before them. Two of them, whose names are unknown, and who were buried at Tetzuco, came at the time of the Conquest. They were inhabitants of the isles which had convents at that time. The three others above mentioned, were Flammands, from the convent of St. Francis, in the city of Leute, the principal friar, John de Tecto, having been guardian of the convent. The city of Mexico being ruined by the war, and occupied by the Spaniards, they went to Tetzuco, where they were received by one of the principal Indians, who sent their children for instruction to Brother Peter of Ghent.* Here they remained, not going out of their abode, and were occupied in studying the language of the natives, when the twelve arrived. The two other friars from the Isles accompanied the Spaniards, as chaplains. All the five recognized Friar Martin de Valencia as Supreme Prelate.

The little band of friars now numbered seventeen, and as a preparation for the work they were about to commence, they gave themselves to prayer for the space of fifteen days, at the end of which a chapter was held, in which Friar Martin de Valencia gave them permission to choose a new custos, declaring that he had only been commissary until their arrival; seeing his determination they proceeded to an election, and Friar Martin was unanimously chosen.

On consultation, they proposed to divide themselves for the prosecution of their labor. Friar Martin remained in Mexico, and with him four companions. The twelve others, four each, departed for the cities of Tetzuco, Tlascala and Huxatzinco—all within twenty

* "Peter of Ghent," the Protestant writer, Helps, says, was one "who, perhaps did most service." He was a lay brother "who, in his humility, never would be anything but a lay brother." From him the Mexicans learned "to read, to write, to sing, and to play upon musical instruments. He contrived to get a large school built," in which, besides mere elementary matters, he taught them painting, carving and other arts. "Many idols and temples owed their destruction to him, and many churches their building. He spent a long life—no less than fifty years—in such labors, and was greatly beloved by the Indians, amongst whom he must have had thousands of pupils. The successor of Zumarraga one day generously exclaimed, 'I am not the Archbishop of Mexico, but Brother Peter of Ghent is!'" He composed a copious doctrinal work in the Mexican language, which was printed.

leagues of the city of Mexico. The subjects of Tetzuco numbered thirty thousand—those of Tlascala, more than two hundred thousand, and those of Huxatzinco numbered eighty thousand.

The first care of the friars was to establish schools for the instruction of the children, who in turn became the teachers of their parents, and by this means, in a short time, a large number were brought to a knowledge of the true faith, as the parents were required, by Cortes, to send their children to these schools.

Up to the year 1524, when the twelve friars entered Mexico, no church had as yet been erected. In the year 1525, the friars, aided by Cortes, and with the labor of the Indians, erected the Church of St. Francis, in the city of Mexico—the first church in New Spain—that is Mexico and Peru. It was dedicated with great pomp and ceremony, and many of the natives were baptized as the first fruits.

In the year 1526, the Franciscans were joined by the Dominicans, and Thomas Detiz, with his eleven companions, resided with the Franciscans, in their convent in the city of Mexico, until they procured a house; and henceforth the children of St. Francis and St. Dominic labored in unison for the instruction and conversion of the Indians.

The Franciscans devoted themselves assiduously to the acquirement of the language, and the first who began to preach in it were Louis de Fuensalida and Francis Ximenes, who also wrote a grammar, and translated the principles of the Christian doctrine into that tongue.

About nine months after the arrival of Father Martin and his companions, they were joined by Antonio Maldonado, Antonio Ortiz, Alonzo Herrara, Diego de Almonte, and others, of the province of San Gabriel, in Spain, and they now founded the fifth convent of Cuernavaca, whence they visited the provinces of Ocuila, Malinalco, and all the Tierra Caliente, to the Pacific—a territory of vast extent, and embracing many different tribes and tongues.

Such progress had the faith made, that in 1528, four years after the arrival of the twelve Franciscans, it was deemed necessary to appoint a bishop for Mexico, and the Seraphic Order had the honor of furnishing the first prelate of that city, John de Zumarraga, a native of Durango, in old Spain. Though he sought an obscure life, his great piety and abilities could not remain hidden, and at the instance of the emperor, Charles V., he was appointed bishop of Mexico, which dignity he only accepted in obedience to his Superior. He visited his new diocese, before his consecration, with ample powers from the Emperor, as Protector of the Indians, who suffered much from the exaction of the Europeans, and in the discharge of his duty, in which he was seconded by the friars, who were laboring for the welfare of their converts, he was much opposed by those in civil power, in Mexico; but he was unceasing in his representations of their injustice, and aided by Bartholomew Las Casas, he was finally successful in ameliorating their condition. He went to Spain in 1532, where he was consecrated, and returning the next year, he lead a most exemplary life of poverty, humility, and extreme abstinence, devoting his whole time to the instruction of the natives, confirming vast numbers. Shortly before his death, which took place in 1548, he received the bulls appointing him Archbishop of Mexico, and he was the first Archbishop in America.

In 1533, Francis de la Cruz, with six Augustinians,

entered the field of labor, with the Franciscans and Dominicans in Mexico.

At the instance of Bishop Zumarraga, Queen Isabella sent out some pious women to instruct the young girls, but as they were not bound by vows, they soon married, and these schools were discontinued in the course of a few years.

The Viceroy, Don Antonio de Mendoza, a true father to the Indians, erected and endowed a college for the instruction of their youth, in that part of Ilatelolco where the Franciscans had their convent, in order that they might have charge of it, and it soon numbered a hundred of the sons of the principal Indians.

The Church of Christ was extended by the Franciscans to the peninsula of California, the year 1596, and its first missionaries were Fr. Didacus Perdomo, Fr. Bernardine de Comudio, Fr. Nicholas de Seravia, priests, and Christopher Lopez, a lay brother.

As the Franciscans held the foremost position in connection with the planting of the faith in Mexico, it was befitting that they should also furnish the first martyr in those regions for that faith. Friar John Calero, a lay brother, was barbarously martyred by the Chichemecas, on the 10th of June, 1541. The same year, Anthony Cuellar, guardian of the convent of Ezatlan, also suffered martyrdom by the Indians. Then followed the martyrs, John Padilla, by the savages of Cibola, and John de la Cruz, who went among the Chichemecas of Zacatecas, and who was never afterwards heard of; Bernard Cousin, by the Chichemecas; and in 1555, a priest and a lay brother, by the same savages; in 1556, John de Topia, four leagues from Zacatecas, by the Quachichibes; Father Francis Lorenzo, and Friar John, by the same Indians who had put John Calero to death; John Cerrato; Paul de Azevedo; in 1560, John de Herrara, a lay brother; in 1580, John Catalano, Francis Lopez, John Closio and others; in 1582, Louis Villalupo, and five companions, suffered a most horrible martyrdom, by the idolators of Yucatan. So that up to the year 1600, a century after the arrival of Father Marchena in America, more than one hundred and fifty Franciscan missionaries had suffered martyrdom in the New World.

In 1587, the province of the Holy Gospel, of Mexico, numbered fixty-six convents, three monasteries of the Second Order and two custodias. The custodia of St. Francis of Zacatecas, numbered fourteen houses of instruction, with fifteen others called aids; and the Custodia of the Holy Redeemer, of Tampico, numbered twelve houses.

In 1564 the Council of Trent was promulgated in Spain and in all the dominions of his Catholic Majesty. In virtue of the decrees of the Council all the dioceses and curacies already established would cease to be considered as missionary, and the extraordinary faculties and privileges granted to the Regulars would be restricted only for those places where parishes had not yet been properly established. It took effect from that time in Peru, but on account of difficulties it did not in Mexico, at least entirely, until 1751, by the bull of Benedict XIV. to that purpose.

In Mexico then, as well as in other parts of Spanish America, the Regulars, in general, remained according to the common Canonical Laws, except the missionaries who were devoted to the conversion of the Indians.

The Franciscans have there, to the present, several provinces, but besides the regular provinces, they have Missionary Colleges, and an Apostolic Prefect in each college is the Superior of the missionaries and missions.

Until lately there were colleges of this kind in the city of Mexico, in Zacatecas, Pachuca, Zapapa, Orizaba, and Queretaro; but under the revolutions that are now distracting that unhappy country it is impossible to give any particulars concerning the present state of the missions and convents in Mexico.

CHAPTER XX.

Peru.—St. Francis Solano.—Chili.—The missionary colleges.—Patagonia.—Rio de la Plata.—Buenos Ayres.—Paraguay.—The Reductions.—New Granada, Guatemala, Yucatan and Nicaragua.—Modern Missionaries in South America.

The conquest of Peru, though second in time, was scarcely second in importance, to that of Mexico, both on account of the great wealth of gold which it brought to the conquerors, and the field which it opened up for the envoys of the Gospel; and here, too, the first missionary we find in the field was a Franciscan. Mark, of Nice, was with the first expedition of Pizarro, and penetrated as far as Tumbez, now Guyaquil, in the year 1527; and in 1533 the Franciscans had established a convent at Cuzco, through the influence of Father Peter of Portugal. The first death of the missionaries mentioned here is that of Brother John Callena. Captain Sebastian Benalcazar built St. Francis City over the ruins of the ancient Quito, on the equator, and Jodogue de Rürke, a Belgian Franciscan, was the first missionary here in 1534. The colleges which were erected in the neighboring cities depended on the missions of Quito. Francis of the Cross commenced a convent at Lima, in 1535, which was continued and completed by Francis Marchena and Francis d'Arragona, and the former became the first custos, in the same year. The Franciscans also built two colleges for the instruction of the natives.

"We may not stay to notice," says T. W. M. Marshall,* "one by one the men who evangelized the Peruvian races, redeeming the violence and cupidity of the soldiers of Spain, and winning the love and reverence of the native tribes in spite of the injuries which they had received from Europeans, but there is one of their number whom it is impossible not to mention, because to him was given, in a special manner, the title of Apostle of Peru. It was in 1589 that Francis de Solano sailed for America, designing to labor in the province of Tucuman, which lies between the Cordilleras and Paraguay, 'because there he might hope to find the greatest dangers, and to suffer most for the glory of God.' Father Louis Bolanos, also a Franciscan, had preceded him, and having set out from Lima, had travelled many a weary league on both banks of the Plata, but a greater than he was now to enter the same regions.

"Perfectly conversant, like most of his Order, with the dialects of the barbarous tribes whom he resolved to win, St. Francis Solano threw himself into the combat with all the ardor of an apostle. Already he had gathered thousands into the fold of Christ, when the remote eastern tribes, who wandered through the country between the Dulce and the St. Tomé, came down in vast numbers, breathing fury and slaughter against their converted brethren, and threatening the most cruel torments to all who had become Christians. The neophytes began to fly in terror, and the new

* Catholic Missions, ch. ix.

mission seemed to be menaced with swift and hopeless destruction. Then Solano went forth alone, confiding in the protection of the Mother of God, to meet the advancing multitude. He was a servant of Him who had said, 'The good shepherd giveth his life for his sheep.. The hour was come to die, and he would die as becomes an apostle. But he was only to be a martyr in desire, and having by supernatural power arrested the advance of the barbarians, he addressed to them so moving a discourse on the Passion of our Divine Lord, and exhorted them with such burning words to embrace His holy religion, that in that single day more than nine thousand were converted.

"After this he went through the land, preaching everywhere 'Jesus Christ crucified;' and everywhere he was accompanied, like the primitive missionaries, by 'signs following.' Even the wild beasts, as multitudes were able to testify, rendered him homage after their kind. And no marvel—for as one of his biographers observes, 'It is a principle of theology that the revolt of irrational creatures against man is only a consequence of man's rebellion against his Maker.' 'The pre-eminence of the Blessed Lord over inanimate matter, and much more over the animal creation,' says a living authority, is the true cause that, 'as His saints advance in holiness and in likeness to Himself, the animals obey their words, revere their sanctity and minister to their wants.'

"In 1610, St. Francis Solano died. Three hundred and four witnesses, of all ranks and classes, were exexamined on oath, and attested the prodigies which they had witnessed, and the heroicity of the virtues which had transformed a desert into a garden. Through a tract of two thousand miles he was numbered among the patrons and defenders of the faithful, and a hundred tribes burned lamps, day and night, in his honor, and called upon him to advocate their cause in heaven. Then Urban VIII., by his famous decree of 1631, peremptorily forbade all public devotion till the claims of the Saint had been further examined, and refused even to allow the process to continue until the apostolic edict was obeyed. For twenty years the grateful Indians who had loved their Father with all their hearts refused to submit, till they comprehended at length that it was not by disobeying the Vicar of Christ that they could honor one of His apostles; and so, with heavy hearts, they brought in all the lamps which they had kindled in his honor, and in 1656, his body was removed from its shrine, and carefully hidden from their sight. Nineteen years later, the decree of Beatification was pronounced, and in 1726 he was canonized.

"The faith which St. Francis Solano preached is still, in spite of many disasters, and of crimes and follies of successive rulers, the light and glory of Peru."

Martin Robleda, afterwards the first bishop of Chili, with four other Franciscans, founded the convent of St. Jago, in Chili, which became a province in 1572. The See of St. Michael, in Chili, was formed in 1570, and the Franciscan, Jerome of Villa Carilla, became the first bishop, and was succeeded by the Franciscan Jerome d'Abbrenez.

The Franciscans in Chili continued their work as in Mexico and Peru. It may not be uninteresting, therefore, to give an account of the present system of the Franciscan missions among the Indians.

In 1849, we find the two Franciscan colleges in the republic of Chili the centres of their missionary operations in that country: one that of Jesus, in the city of Castro, in the largest isle of Chiloe, founded in

1838; the other, that of St. Ildefonso, in the city of Chillan, in the province of the Conception di Penco—distant from each other eight hundred and forty miles.

In the college of Jesus, there were twenty priests, four theological students, six students in philosophy, seven in grammar, and three laics—making a total of forty. Eight of the twenty priests were born in America, and six of these eight were alumni of the college.

In that of St. Ildefonso, there were sixteen priests, and four lay brothers—making a total of twenty. The guardian and nine of the priests were born in America.

These two colleges had eighteen missions under their charge, and the Indian converts were exempt from the episcopal jurisdiction, being entirely subject to the missionaries.

The city of Valdivia is the capital of the province of the same name, in which are situated the greater part of these missions. The capital of the republic of Chili is Santiago, is nine hundred and ninety miles, by land, from Valdivia, the college of Chillon is five hundred and forty miles, and the college of Chiloe is three hundred and thirty miles. The two colleges are eight hundred and seventy miles distant from each other by land. The City of the Conception, the capital of the province of that name, is five hundred and ten miles, by land, from Valdivia.

All the missions among the infidels are situated between seventy-second and the seventy-third and one half degree of west longitude, and the thirty-sixth and forty-first latitude, south, except those of Magellan, but as the roads are miserable, and all woods and mountains, the journey from place to place cannot be judged from the distance in miles. The missions are separated from each other from twenty to thirty miles.

Each mission has one or two reductions, and many of what are designated *parzialita*, and consequently they are quite extensive, being from fifteen to thirty miles in each direction. Where the boundaries of one mission ends, those of the next begin.

Those to the north are attended from the college of Chillon, and those of the south from that of Chiloe. The missions are located in plains, surrounded by thick and impassable forests, and are placed in the narrowest portion, so that the missionaries may be as near as possible to each other. It rains continually for eight months of the year, and there are many navigable rivers which are flooded beyond measure, and close up the means of communication, so that the missionaries are often three or four months without seeing each other.

A Reduction is a people more or less numerous, and reductions are divided into *parzialita*, which is a union of several families. There is a chief at the head of every reduction, who is called Cacique; and at the head of each *parzialita*, there is another chief, subject to the cacique, and these inferior chiefs are called *Ghilmenes*. Each reduction embraces a great extension or territory of many miles, composed of plains and forests, where the scattered Indians dwell, their habitations being remote, and one or two miles from each other.

The mission consists of a small church, a dwelling for the missionary, and two other houses, one for the instruction of the men and another for the women, and a school for the Indian children—all of wood. Each mission has one or two reductions. As all the savages dwell in scattered habitations, there is an Indian salaried by the government to accompany the missionary in his visitations. This Indian sets out every fifteen days, and going through the reduction, collects the savages in numbers of from fifteen to twenty men, and as many women, and brings them to the missionary for instructions. Those who are already Christians, generally remain at the mission two weeks, and those who are not yet instructed, remain some four weeks, or even more, especially those who are preparing for the sacraments of baptism or matrimony. Those already Christians, make their confessions at the end of the two weeks, and then return to their dwellings, as do the others when they have been baptized or married. As soon as those have retired, the Indian assistant of the missionary sets out and brings in others, in the same manner, until all the men and women in the reduction have thus visited the mission, which they must do once each year.

Those already Christians, often bring their infidel relatives or friends with them, and thus the number is continually increasing. Those who reside in the vicinity of the mission, bring their children thither to be baptized on their birth, and those who dwell at a great distance, and cannot come to the mission, on account of their poverty, are visited by the missionary, both to baptize the children and instruct the adults; and when the distance is too great for the missionary to leave his post, the assistant Indian is sent to baptize the children.

Whilst the Indians remain at the mission, they are provided with food by the missionary. Their ordinary food is boiled grain, beans, corn, potatoes, and other gross food. They eat the half-raw and almost putrid flesh of dead horses, like dogs, and drink the blood of the animals which they kill.

It requires a considerable amount of provisions to supply those missions, and they are raised in each mission by the labor of the Indians, who cultivate the soil, sowing grain, beans, peas, potatoes, etc.

The women are employed in domestic duties, and they also spin and weave a coarse cloth for fifteen or twenty Indian children, who are maintained at the mission.

In each mission there is a school, with a teacher paid by the government, who teaches reading, writing, arithmetic and the catechism, to all the children of the mission, Indians and Spaniards, and some of the Indian youth show more talent than those of the Europeans.

Early every morning and every evening, after the *Angelus*, they meet together, the men and women in distinct groups, to recite prayers, under the direction of the missionary, who recites them with them, in the Auracanian language. Afterwards, by means of an interpreter, who is one of the elders of the Indians, chosen for his prudence and judgment, and good disposition, the missionary explains to them the Christian doctrine.

It is inherent in the nature of the natives (who are, in every respect, appropriately designated savages), to fly from social life, and for them, civilization, as we understand it, is of slow growth. Liberty, and the absence of every social restraint, are conditions necessary and indispensable for their existence, and they seek them at every cost; hence, they construct their dwellings in isolated places—in mountainous forests, or in small plains, in the midst of these forests—and it is a rare thing to find four or five of their huts united; so that in order to visit them it is necessary to journey one or two miles from one to the other. The missions are generally situated in the centre of their respective reductions, in secluded, desert and unpopulated places—at the foot of mountains, or in the midst of plains.

When any of the Christian Indians is sick, the missionary goes to administer the sacraments, however far they may be from the mission (there is but one missionary for each mission), and he then catechises the adult infidels, and baptizes the children, who, on account of the distance, cannot be brought to the mission.

Many efforts are made to withdraw them from their barbarous customs, with which they are deeply imbued, and it would be too long here, to describe their beastly customs. They are atheists, know no religion, and adore a principle, which they call Piglion, who is the devil to whom they offer sacrifices, and of these the number is great. Many of them cannot be converted on account of the scandal given by the Spaniards, many of whom are more brutal, ignorant, and barbarous than savages themselves, and their manners are the same, and even worse, than those of the savages; and as they dwell among them, they are the greatest obstacle to the efforts of the missionaries.

From what has been said of the Franciscan colleges of Chili it will be easy to form an idea of the other Franciscan missionary colleges in America, but especially of those of Lima, Cuzco and Ocopa, in Peru; of Tariga, Tarata, La Paz, Sucre and Potosi, in Bolivia; of San Carlos, Salta and Jujui, in the Argentine Confederation; and of the other Franciscan colleges among the Indians in America.

The Franciscan missionaries of Chili, at the request of the government, commenced a mission in Patagonia, and Fr. Domenico Pasolini, sent there in 1843, gave an interesting account of that mission in a letter written from Magellanico, port of St. Philip, June 26, 1844.

Louis de Bolanos, Alphonsus of St. Bonaventure, and Bernard de Amenta,* about the year 1537, were the first apostles along the Rio de la Plata, Buenos Ayres and Paraguay. Rio de la Plata was erected into a see in 1547, and the Franciscan, John Barrot, made its first bishop. In the year 1554, the see was elevated to a Metropolitan, and the Franciscan Peter de la Torre, successor of Fr. Barros, became its first archbishop.†

Fr. Alphonsus went several times to Spain, in order to bring new laborers for the ripen fields, and it was through him that St. Francis was induced to come to America. He succeeded in bringing twenty-five Franciscans in 1588. The mission of Paraguay had now so increased, that in 1592 it was erected into a Custodia. In the same year the said Fr. Alphonsus brought over twenty Franciscans, among whom was the renowned Fr. Martin Ignatius de Loyola, a relation of St. Ignatius, and who was afterwards elected bishop of the Assumption in 1601.

Henrion, prefacing the establishment of the celebrated Mission of the Jesuits in Paraguay, says: "In the diocess of the Assumption (Paraguay) and Buenos Ayres the Franciscans had several missions which very often were called Reductions." He goes then to show the difference between the Reductions as managed by the Franciscans and Jesuits, which was, that to Indians of the Reductions of the Franciscans it was permitted to render personal service, but not to those of the Jesuits. The Reductions of the Jesuits, in Paraguay, progressed and prospered until the year

* Friar Bernardine, with four companions, was sent to the Rio de la Plata, in 1537, and he wrote, May 1st, 1550, "that Etiguara, an Indian, had, four years before, like another precursor, announced the coming of the brothers of the Disciples of St. Thomas," and as such they were received.—Torquemada, l. 15, ch. xlviii.

† Henrion, l. 2, ch. xvi.

1641, when the royal counsel of the Indians began to interfere, ordering the banishment from Paraguay, of all the Jesuits who were not born subjects of Spain. Fr. Bernardin Cardenas, O. S. F., having been preconized bishop of the Assumption, August 18, 1640, was consecrated by the bishop of Tucuman, October, 1641. As he entered on the exercise of his functions before the reception of the bulls, the Jesuits opposed his jurisdiction on that ground. This misunderstanding was the cause of unfortunate consequences. The troubles, however, were settled in 1654. The Jesuit, P. Anthony de Roda, who, being provincial in Mexico, had shown great wisdom in the question with Bishop Palafox, was apppointed visitor, with the order to act in concert with Fr. Gabriel de Guillestigui, commissary-general of the Franciscans in Peru. Bishop Cardenas was transferred to the see of the La Sierra, and the said Fr. Gabriel de Guillestigui made bishop of Paraguay by the Holy See in December 15, 1668. Peace and prosperity was thus restored. Fifty-eight years had now happily passed away, when the ambitious Antiguera having usurped the government of Paraguay in 1724, expelled the Jesuits, and took possession of the Reductions of Parana. The bishop of the Assumption, on account of his infirmities, was absent in Spain, and the Franciscan, Joseph de Palos, a missionary of the reduction of *El Cervó de la Sol*, was made coadjutor. "This worthy prelate," says Henrion, "an angel of peace in the midst of the troubles of Paraguay, succeeded in re-establishing the Jesuits in their college in 1728." But the friends of Antiguera having heard of his death at Lima, expelled again (1728), from the Assumption, the children of St. Ignatius, to the grief of Palos, who had already become titular bishop of this city; and as if to add to his chagrin, the Franciscan, John de Arregui, whom he had consecrated bishop of Buenos Ayres, having accepted from the rebels the title of Governor of Buenos Ayres, was prevailed upon to sign a decree despoiling the Jesuits of their property. Yet the venerable prelate Palos, opened his eyes, and had the consolation of recalling the Jesuits back to the Assumption, who were even compensated for the persecution they suffered, by having a college opened for them in Buenos Ayres, and a house in the part of Montevideo, opposite it, on the east side of the Rio de la Plata. The final expulsion of the Jesuits, from Paraguay, took place in 1767, when they were suppressed also in Spain.

The Franciscans have at present, in Buenos Ayres, a college and two hospices for the civilization and conversion of the savages.

Friar Henry of Coimba, with seven of the Order, accompanied the fleet fitted out by the King of Portugal, in 1499, the command of which was given to Pedro Alvarez Cabral. The destination of the expedition was the East Indies, but in seeking to avoid the winds off the western coast of Africa, they found themselves upon the shore of an unknown country, in the tenth degree beyond the line, which was afterwards called Brazil. Having taken possession, in the name of his King, Alvarez sent one of his vessels to Lisbon, with an account of the unexpected discovery. Friar Henry and his companions planted the cross and offered up the holy sacrifice of the Mass, for the first time, in the hitherto unknown regions. The fleet of Alvarez continued on its way. No settlement was evidently made by the first discoverers, but other Franciscans soon set out for the new field, and though their success was not equal to their zealous efforts, yet they converted many of the natives, and sealed their labors with the effusion of their blood. Being thus deprived of Franciscans, the faithful Christians often sought to obtain a new supply of the Order, but various difficulties arising, this desire was not gratified until the year 1584, when George Albugurgru, the prefect of Pernambuco, besought King Philip to procure missionaries for Brazil, and the minister-general designated Melchior, of St. Catharine, custos of St. Anthony, in Brazil, appointing Francis of Bonaventure, as his companion, and successor, in case of his death, and empowering him to select eight others to accompany them. They arrived at Pernambuco, the metropolis of the province, in March, 1585, and being received with extraordinary demonstrations of joy, took up their residence for some time in the hospital near the city. In 1589, we find Melchior and his companions zealously laboring in those regions for the conversion of the infidels. By his efforts a convent was erected in the city of Parchybar, entitled St. Anthony of Padua, twenty-four leagues from Pernambuco. Two schools were erected in the custodia for the instruction of the neophytes, one at Maraconædacaca, where Bernardine de Nivibus, who died in in 1608, gained many to the faith. The other school, entitled St. Michael, was at Iguna, twenty leagues from Pernambuco.

Fr. Anthony de Campomajore made also many conversions, and in 1593, established a doctrinal house at Port of Stones, ten leagues from Iguna.

Dominic de Britto and Andrew Toledo, from Quito, in 1637, explored the Amazon river to the sea Para.

Marshall, speaking of the missions of the Jesuits in Brazil says: "For two centuries they had toiled, with results which, perhaps, none but the Franciscans had ever rivalled." He also quotes Mr. Clement Markham who says: "The Franciscans continued during a century and a half, to send devoted men into the forest, who preached fearlessly, explored vast tracts of previously unknown land, and usually ended their days by being murdered by the very savages whom they had come to humanize." Marshall then continues: "In 1701, two Franciscan fathers were martyred by the Aruans." Mr. Southly relates what befell their mutilated bodies. "They found them in a state of perfect preservation, although they had lain six months upon the ground, exposed to animals, insects and all accidents of weather, and although their habits were rotten." It was no miracle, he adds, for he did not believe in miracles, "but fraud cannot be suspected." The evidence was so conclusive, that even he could not reject it. "The whole city of Belem," he says, "saw the bodies, which were ultimately interred in the Franciscan church in that town."* The Franciscans, including the Capuchins, are working to the present in the vast fields of Brazil.

Darien, in New Granada, was the first episcopal see erected on the American Continent, and we spoke already of its first bishop the Franciscan John de Quevedo. New Granada, however, became a great missionary field, especially for the Dominicans and Franciscans. The account of the Franciscan province of New Granada, presented to the General Chapter in 1587, numbered twenty-five convents and forty-four Doctrinal Houses. Two of the missionary colleges as those already described elsewhere are at present in New Granada—one in Cali and another in Popayan.

Although the Franciscan James Testera, with four other Franciscans, in 1534, was the first to evangelize

* Page 157.

Yucatan and Guatemala;* yet in Guatemala proper the Dominicans were the first to settle in 1538. The first bishop of Guatemala, Don Francis Marroquin, in the following year, invited the Franciscans to labor in his diocess, and five friars of the province of Santiago, Spain, with Alonzo de Casasera Superior, accepted his invitation and set out for their new mission. Casasera died at Irpeaco, and the remaining five reached Guatemala, where they were received with great honor, both by the Spaniards and Indians. Some Dominicans from Mexico had entered Guatemala the previous year, and the two orders labored in conjunction, as usual, for the conversion of the Indians. The following year, at the instance of the bishop, the Franciscans sent one of their number to Spain to procure additional aid for the immense harvest, and twelve more friars set out from Santiago for Guatemala, but the greater number fell sick and died on the way.

James de Testera, returning to Mexico from the General Chapter of Mantua, was accompanied by one hundred and fifty friars, twelve of whom, under Toribio Motolinia, he sent to Guatemala.

In 1551, Francis Bustomente, the commissary-general held a chapter at Guatemala, when it was erected into a custodia of the title of the Holy Name of Jesus. In the General Chapter of Aquila, in 1559, Guatemala and Yucatan became a province, and in the General Chapter of Valladolid, in 1565, each became a separate province. About the beginning of the next century the province had twenty-eight convents, and the monastery of the Immaculate Conception at Guatemala. Among the friars who acompanied Motolinia was Peter de Batanzos, who excelled in the

* Torquemada, l. 19, ch. xiv.

knowledge of the language of the Indians, in which he wrote a grammar and vocabulary.

Among the many historical facts of the Franciscan missions, in Guatemala, we must not omit one which, unless it were well authenticated, might seem an episode of some romance, though truth is often more wonderful than fiction :*

Christoval Martinez de la Puerta, an enterprising young Andalusian, having come to America in 1600, joined at Truxillo the band of the explorers, and in his incursions among the savages he was seized with a vehement desire of effecting their conversion. To succeed in his favorite scheme, he went to Guatemala, and for want of means he offered himself as a servant to the college, that he might study and become a priest. All the hardships that the noble youth had to encounter were rendered tolerable by the hope of converting ultimately whole nations of infidels. At last the time came to make known these desires to his provincial, who being satisfied of the zeal and qualifications of Martinez, granted his request. Twice he embarked for Taguzgalpa, and twice he was driven back to Guatemala by the contrary winds. Unwilling to desist from the enterprise, he repeated his solicitations for a third trial, and the provincial yielded to the arguments which, by his direction, Martinez addressed to him in writing, (and which the curious reader may find in detail in the chronicle of Vasquez), gave him his paternal benediction and permission to depart once more for Taguzgalpa. In April, 1619, Martinez and Juan Vaena, a lay brother set out for their destination. They met with so many difficulties that it was only in the spring of 1622 they were landed at

* J. Baily, Lieut. R.M., made an English version of the History of Guatemala, by Don Domingo Juarros, which was published in London, 1823, and from it we take the narration. Part II., ch. xxxii.

the Cape of Taguzgalpa by a ship bound for Jamaica. The two missionaries found themselves on a desert shore, and not like Cortes and his brave soldiers, when they had the ships sunk at Vera Cruz, as they were able to defend themselves with arms if attacked by savages, but as they were two poor friars, with no other protection than that of Providence. Two days they passed in this solitude; on the morning of the third day, they observed a numerous body of the natives, both male and female, approaching. The last person of this company was a venerable old man with long white hair. On coming up to the missionaries he made a profound obeisance, and said in a language they could understand, that they were welcome, and asked why they had so long delayed coming, to the great risk of his dying before their arrival? He added that he had long expected them, with the greatest anxiety, to render his services; that he was not blamable for not having come before now to pay his respects, because he had understood they were to arrive by land, and had placed sentinels on the tops of the highest mountains to give him notice of their approach. Great indeed was the astonishment of Martinez and his companion at this unexpected address, and asking the old man who had given him information of their intended visit, he replied, "*Mirabile dictu.*" That being one day at work in his plantation, there appeared to him a white child, more beautiful than anything he had ever before seen or could imagine. It looked at him with great tenderness, and said, "Know that you will not die before you become a Christian; there will come here some white men, with robes of the color of this ground, reaching to their feet; when they arrive, receive them kindly, and do not permit any one to anger them, for they are ministers of God, who has granted thee this signal mark of His mercy, because thou hast done well, and hast supported those who wanted assistance." It is worthy of notice that this old man, even in his idolatry, had employed himself in acts of kindness; he cultivated maize to distribute among those who were in distress; he composed strifes, and settled all disputes among his neighbors, besides performing many other kind offices where they were wanted. Martinez was greatly rejoiced at hearing this, he comforted the old man, and promised to perform for him all the duties of a good pastor. The Indians immediately set about constructing a hut for the strangers, near a river called Xarua. On the following day they erected a very large one for a church, and crosses were raised in different places by the side of the paths, etc. The missionaries began to instruct their new friends; they baptized the old man and all his family; many of the Indians requested to have the same privilege granted to them, from the great respect they bore towards the old man, and also because they understood that these were the fathers who had so long before been announced to them by the God of the Mountain. This was the cheering prospect of affairs in Taguzgalpa, three months after the first landing of Martinez, when a boat that had been dispatched by Diego de Cañavete, curate of Truxillo, and other inhabitants of that city, anchored on the coast; it brought, as had been promised, a supply of wine and biscuit, with some altar bread. The crew of the boat landed, and soon met some Indians who conducted them to the residence of the missionaries. After mutual congratulations, the fathers gave an account of the great success that had already attended their efforts, and their visitors saw, with great astonishment, how much had been done for Christianity in so short a time. During their stay the old Indian died, and all the Spaniards assisted at the Christian rites of his funeral. When the boat was preparing to return, Martinez resolved to send Juan Vaena to Guatemala, to give the Provincial a narrative of what had occurred, and to request another priest might be sent to assist him. In September, 1622, Vaena reached the capital, and laid before the Provincial a detailed account of the expedition. The prelate was greatly rejoiced at the communication, and published an account of the fact. Brother Juan Vaena returned, and Father Benito de S. Francisco was sent with him. Martinez, in less than a year had admitted to baptism more than seven hundred adults, besides a great number of children; and in one year after, the number of the converts in the province of Taguzgalpa exceeded six thousand. In the midst of this plentiful harvest the three indefatigable laborers were cut off—they fell a sacrifice to the animosity of the unconverted Albatuinas, a neighboring nation. The bodies of the victims were carried to Truxillo, where they were buried with great pomp on the 16th of January, 1624. The precious remains were removed to Guatemala, when in 1643 the Dutch took the city, and were deposited in the church of St. Francis with the greatest solemnity.

Yucatan was for a long time attended entirely by Franciscans, and the first, second, third and fourth bishop of that diocess were all Franciscans.*

Nicaragua became a distinct Franciscan province, which, in 1587, had twenty convents. The first bishop of Nicaragua was Pedro de Zuniga, also a Franciscan, one of those who first preached Christianity to the natives, but he died before taking possession of his see.†

* Torquemada, lib. 19, ch. xxxii.
† Baily, p. 65.

The celebrated Father Antonio Margil, the great founder of the Apostolic Colleges of America, in company with Fr. Melchor Lopez, accomplished within five years the conversion of more than forty thousand souls, founded eleven villages with a church in each, in Talamanca, and three in the other nations of Costa Rica.* Fr. Margil died in 1736 at the advanced age of eighty-two years.

The city of Guatemala claims the glory of having given birth to the Franciscan, Juan Alvarez de Toledo, who, being of illustrious family, became more illustrious for his literary and religious acquirements, and was the first of her sons to obtain a mitre, having been raisod successively to the episcopal sees of Chiapa, Guatemala, and Guadalajara. He died in 1726, leaving a great numberof pious foundations established by himself. †

The Franciscans are still flourishing in Guatemala, and the Franciscan Fr. Felix Zepeda, already auxiliary bishop of Guatemala, is now bishop of Comayagua.

Mr. Marshall, in his remarks about modern missionaries in South America, among other remarkable facts concerning the Franciscans gives the following, which we willingly reproduce as an appropriate conclusion of this chapter. He says: "Before we enter the last province which remains to be visited in South America, let us notice a few additional examples, not unworthy of a moment's attention, of the language in which Protestant travellers speak of *modern* missionaries in this land. It is well to learn from such witnesses that they have not degenerated from their fathers."

A British officer, who effected a few years ago the descent of the Amazon, had for a companion, during

* Chronicles of the Colleges of Propaganda, fide lib. 5, cap. 1.
† Baily, p. 109.

a part of his voyage, a Spanish Franciscan, who, by the toils of thirty-four years had founded many new missions, without aid from any human being, and whose career included the following incident:

A little to the northeast of Sarayacu, on the river Ucayali, dwelt the Sencis, a fierce and warlike tribe, still unconverted, whose solitary virtue was dauntless courage. With a courage greater than their own, Father Plaza, the Franciscan to whom our tale refers, resolved to enter their territory. He was seized at the frontier, as he had anticipated and desired, and there was enacted the following drama:

"They asked him," says the English traveller, "whether he was brave, and subjected him to the following trial: eight or ten men, armed with bows and arrows placed themselves a few yards in front of him, with their bows drawn and their arrows directed to his breast; they then, with a shout, let go the strings, but retained the arrows in their left hands, which he at first did not perceive, but took it for granted that it was all over with him, and was astonished at finding himself unhurt." The savages had taken a captive who could give even them a lesson in fortitude; but they had another trial in store for him. "They resumed their former position, and approaching somewhat nearer, they aimed their arrows at his body, but discharged them close to his feet." The narrator adds, and perhaps no other comment could be reasonably expected from a Protestant, "that if he had shown any signs of fear, he would probably have been dispatched," but that "having, in his capacity of missionary, been a long time subjected to the caprices of the Indians, he had made up his mind for the worst, and stood quite motionless during the proof." Finally, "they surrounded him, and received him as a welcome guest." We can hardly be surprised that such a missionary—whom even Mr. Markham calls "a great and good man," whose "deeds of heroism and endurance throw the hard-earned glories of the soldier far into the shade"—should be able to found many new missions even in this nineteenth century.

But there are at this hour many such as Padre Plaza in the South American missions, as even the most prejudiced travellers attest. He himself, having recently finished his apostolic career as bishop of Cuença, was succeeded at Sarayacu by Father Cimini and three other missionaries, who ruled "about one thousand three hundred and fifty souls, consisting chiefly of Panas Indians." "The brave and indefatigable Father Girbal was a hero of the same Order, and through every Catholic province of America, English and American travellers have discovered apostles who are ready to do in the nineteenth century what their predecessors did in the seventeenth and eighteenth." He might have said what their predecessors did, in every century, from the time that America was discovered.

CHAPTER XXI.

Franciscan Missions in North America.—The United States.—Florida. John Juarez the first Missionary and Bishop, in 1526.—Second Mission in 1561.—Martyrs.—Florida becomes a Province of the Order.—Missions destroyed and the Indians reduced to slavery or driven to the everglades by the English.—New Mexico.—Mark of Nice the first Explorer and the first Missionary, in 1539.—Martyrs.—Second Mission in 1597.—Fr. Benavides and Maria de Agreda.—Texas.—Andrew Olmos the first Missionary in 1544.—Second Mission in 1685.—Their success and history.—California.—Junipero Serra.—Missions founded in 1769.—Louis Joyne the first Martyr.—Missions of San Francisco and Santa Clara.—Progress and vicissitudes of the Missions.

To FLORIDA belongs the glory of having been the first portion of the territory now within the limits of the

United States upon which dawned the light of the Gospel. The attention of the Spaniards in Mexico was turned towards Florida as early as the year 1512; but the first expeditions thither met with disaster after disaster; and from 1512 to 1542, Leon, Cordova, Ayllon, Narvaez, and Soto, successively, with most of their forces, perished in Florida, or in the valley of the Mississippi. In 1526 Pamphilus de Narvaez, in his expedition, was accompanied by some Franciscan friars, under John Juarez, one of the twelve who entered Mexico in 1524. Leaving his convent of Huextzinco, he went not only as superior of the mission, but annalists assure us that he was also Bishop of Florida. They reached the present bay of Pensacola, on the 16th of April, 1528, and advanced into the interior; but after months of toil and suffering, and finding no cities or towns, they returned to the coast, and building a few frail boats, sought to return to Mexico; but their vessels being wrecked, they escaped a watery grave, only to die by famine, or by the hands of the Indians. In company with Juarez was Brother John de Palos, also one of the original twelve.

De Soto next set out for Florida, with a splendid array, but his expedition was a total failure; and not one of the priests who accompanied him, survived to return with the small remnant which reached Tampico.

Some time after 1561, eleven Franciscan friars accompanied the expedition of Pedro Menendes, who drove the French out of Florida, where they had made a settlement, and afterwards founded St. Augustine. In 1573,* the friars received a new addition to their

* The Franciscans, Dominicans and Jesuits had made repeated attempts at planting the faith in Florida, but they had all failed. The Dominicans abandoned Florida in 1561, and the Jesuits in 1572. The Franciscans, however, were not discouraged, and their perseverance was crowned with success.—See J. G. SHEA, *Catholic Missions*, ch. I., II. and III.

number; and in 1592, twelve more arrived, under John de Silva, as superior—among whom were Francis Pareja, who drew up, in the language of the Timuquas, an abridgment of Christian Doctrine, and some other works, the first in any of our Indian languages that was issued from the press.

In 1597, at St. Augustine, Friar Corpa was obliged to reprove a son of the cacique for his scandalous life. Becoming enraged, he gathered a body of savages and coming upon the missionary, while in prayer, he was put to death by a blow of a tomahawk, and his head set on a spear. The savages, now inflamed by this bloody deed, proceeded to Topoqui, where they put Friar Rodriguez to death, after permitting him to say Mass. Passing on to the Island of Quale, they found Friars Auñon and Badajoz, who met a similar fate, as did also Velascola, at Asao. Reaching Ospa, they took Friar Avila prisoner, and sold him as a slave, in the interior. At the end of a year they were about to put him to death, when his life was claimed by an old Indian woman, whose son was then a prisoner at St. Augustine, for whom Avila was exchanged.

In 1602, the Bishop of Cuba made a visit to Florida, and several friars were sent thither. In 1603, at the general congregation of Toledo, it was erected into a custodia, with eleven convents—Pedro Ruiz being the first custos. In 1612 the custodia of St. Helena was made a province, of the same title, by the general chapter, at Rome—John de Copilla becoming the first provincial. From this time the missions progressed rapidly. Twenty-three friars were sent from Cadiz this year; and eight more came in the next year. In 1615, twelve arrived from the province of Los Angelos, in Mexico. In less than two years they were established at the principal points, and numbered twenty convents.

Nor did they confine themselves to the Spanish settlements on the coast. Among others, Alonzo Serrano penetrated the interior, and visited various localities, which long bore the names he gave them. De Courcy says of Florida: "The convent of St. Helena became the centre whence the Franciscans spread in every direction, even to the extremities of the Peninsula, and among the Apalachian clans. The faith prospered among those tribes, and the cross towered in every Indian village, till the increasing English colony of Carolina brought war into these peaceful realms. In 1703, the valley of the Apalachicola was ravaged by an armed body of covetous fanatics; the Indian towns were destroyed; the missionaries slaughtered, and their forest children—their neophytes—sharing their fate, or, still more unfortunate, being hurried away, were sold as slaves in the English West Indies. Fifty years after, the whole colony fell into the hands of England—the missions were destroyed—the Indians dispersed, and St. Helena, the convent where Christianity had radiated over the Peninsula, became a barrack—and such is that venerable monastery in our own days."*

The first explorer and missionary of New Mexico, was the Italian Franciscan, Father Mark of Nice, who also traversed Texas and Upper California. He went to Mexico in 1531; and his enthusiastic zeal being excited by the relations of the few survivors of the expedition of Pamphilus Narvaez, he resolved to penetrate the regions to the north; and accompanied by a lay brother, and a negro named Stephen, he set out from Culiacan, in 1539. Though his companion fell sick, Mark's courage did not fail, but leaving him at Petatlan, he fearlessly continued his journey through the desert which extends to the Gila, and crossing that

* Catholic Church in the United States, p. 15.

deep and wide river, he continued his route through Cibola, the Zuni of the Indians. Here, passing from tribe to tribe, and clothed in the skins of beasts, with a mantle of cotton, the courageous son of Italy imagined a glorious future for those regions, which he pictured to himself, converted to the faith and become a new missionary field of his Order; and he gave to these vast regions the name of *St. Francis!* But though the kingdom of St. Francis exists only in his narrative, yet, as if to accomplish his desire, there stands to-day a city of that name, the Carthage of the Pacific, *San Francisco;* and the Franciscans established missions there which will ever hold a place in the most glorious annals of the Church. It is true that Father Mark was not permitted to effect any missionary conquest, but he opened up the way for his successors; moreover, considering that he, alone, ventured to plant the cross upon the summits of Cibola, and returned safe by the same path which he had so courageously followed, it cannot be doubted that his undertaking was the most arduous exploration of unknown regions hitherto attempted.*

In the second expedition, to which the accounts of Mark gave rise, Father John de Padilla and Friar John of the Cross, having reached New Mexico, refused to return with the adventurer Coronado and his companions, but remained there, laboring for the conversion of the Indians. In a short time, however, they both fell victims to their zeal for the salvation of souls, and they were the first martyrs who shed their blood for the faith in those regions of North America in the United States.

No new exploration of New Mexico was undertaken

* J. G. Shea, Catholic Missions, p. 41, and De Courcy, Catholic Church, p. 13.

from this time until 1581, when, at the instance of the lay brother Augustine Rodriguez, another missionary expedition was organized, consisting of Father Francis Lopez, the learned and erudite Father John of St. Mary, and the above named brother Augustine, accompanied by ten soldiers and six Mexican Indians. But in a short time the soldiers were worn out with the fatigues of the journey, and turned back; and thus the missionaries continued on alone, sustained by the Divine Spirit, and established their mission among the Tehuas. Such was the success which crowned their labors that Father John went to Mexico to procure other missionaries to come to their aid. Full of confidence and courage, he set out alone for the nearest post, but three days after his departure, whilst he was taking a rest from his fatigues, he was surrounded by some wandering savages and put to death. Father Lopez afterwards lost his life, in an attack of savage enemies; and Friar Rodriguez, who now remained alone, also became a martyr to his great zeal in opposing vice. The same fate attended two other expeditions, God wishing to thus prepare this field for the harvest unto eternal life, by enriching it with the blood of so many laborers.

But at last, in 1597, the mission of Father Alonzo, and his seven companions, was eminently successful, and they firmly established those missions whose fruits continue to our own day, although the usual sacrifices were not wanting. Father Benavides, thirty years later, wrote to the court of Spain, that a new mission had been established at Socorro, which was the twenty-seventh in New Mexico—that at Queres, all were baptized, and many of the Indians instructed in reading and writing—that four thousand others had been baptized at Tanos; two thousand at Taos; and many more, in various other parts of that region—that convents were erected at San Antonio, Socorro, Pilabo, Sevilleta, San Francisco, Isleta, and among the Topiras, the Teoas, the Picuries, and the Zuñi; that already Santa Fè, Pecos, St. Joseph, and Queres, could boast of sumptuous churches; and that missionaries resided not only in the difficult mission of Zuñi, but also in Acoma, so often tinged with the blood of the Spaniards. In the midst of so many apostolic labors, Christian civilization made such rapid progress on the Rio Grande, that the Indians, or Puebli, as they were then called, knew how to read and write, before the Puritans had established themselves upon the coast of New England.

"Among those who contributed to bring about so happy a result, were Fathers Benavides, Lopez and Salas at Jumanas, Father Ortego, and we may add, the venerable Maria de Jesus de Agreda, whose mysterious connection with the New Mexican mission, whether now believed or not, certainly drew great attention to it, and gave it an extraordinary impulse. Benavides met a tribe which no missionary had as yet reached, and found them, to his amazement, instructed in the doctrines of Christianity. On inquiring, he learned that they had been taught by a lady, whose form and dress they described. This account he gave in his work, published in 1630. Subsequently Father Bernardino de Sena told him that the nun, Maria de Agreda, had, eight years before, related to him apparitions of a similar character. Benavides then visited her, and was at once struck with her resemblance to the lady described by the Indians, and still more so by her account of the country and the labors of the missionaries, of which she related many remarkable incidents."*

But these missions of New Mexico had to suffer, in their time, various vicissitudes, especially in the year 1660, when the priests and churches were destroyed in a general revolt, raised by the Pagan savages. The Franciscans, however, soon reëstablished themselves; and the description which Villaseñor gives of them, in 1748, is quite cheering: "The Indians," he says, "were clothed with garments woven by their women; and industry, peace, and abundance, flourished in their villages. Their edifices, built under the direction of the Franciscan Fathers, would compare favorably with those of Europe." He gives the following missions, existing in his time: Santa Cruz, Pecos, Galisteo, Paso, San Lorenzo, Socorro, Zia, Candelaras, Taos, Santa Aña, San Augustin de Isleta, Tezuque, Nambe, San Ildefonso, Santa Clara, San Juan de los Caballeros, Pecuries, Cochiti, Jemes, Laguna, Acoma, and Guadalupe, with about a hundred families in each.

All these missions continue till the present; and although they have suffered much in the continual revolutions of Mexico, the expulsion of the Spaniards, and finally, their incorporation into the United States; yet the Indians, by the grace of God, have remained Catholics, and their deputies sent to Washington, are not the least among the most civilized tribes.

Texas, like Florida and New Mexico, was early visited by the Franciscan missionaries. In the first expedition of Narvaez, some of them became victims of their zeal, in traversing Texas; and we have already seen that only four survived that undertaking. Afterwards

* J. G. SHEA, p. 81, letter of Fr. Bonavides in F. Palon Vida del P. Junipero Serra, 331, and a letter of Maria de Agreda, 337; Benavides Memorial, Madrid, 1630.

others died in the fatal expeditions of De Soto and Muscoso.* Finally, a single missionary accomplished what so many who had preceded him failed in doing. This was the Franciscan Father Andrew Olmos, who, already erudite in other Indian languages, learned easily to speak and write that of the Chichimecas; and in 1544, founded a flourishing mission in Panuco.

It was not, however, till 1685, that the mission became established in Texas, when La Salle, with some French Recollects, attempting to explore the Mississippi by way of Texas, the Spaniards, becoming jealous, considered that it was to their interest to establish missions in that region—and thus commenced the mission of St. Francis. The next year orders were sent to assign to the new field twenty-one Franciscans, fourteen priests, and seven lay brothers. Fifteen fathers set out from Monclova in May, 1692, who founded eight missions—three among the Texas Indians, four among the Cudodachos, and one along the river Guadalupe.

However, these missions did not then thrive, partly from the scarcity of provisions which occurred, and partly on account of the mutinous conduct of the Spanish soldiers under Teran de los Rios. But in October, 1715, Don Ramon was sent to Texas with a body of Franciscan missionaries, and twenty-five soldiers as an escort. The new band of apostles comprised five religious from Santa Cruz de Querétaro, with four fathers and three lay brothers from Our Lady of Guadalupe at Zacatecas, the latter having as superior the venerable Father Antonio Margil de Jesus, whose sanctity

* When De Soto first discovered the Mississippi, there was with him the Franciscan, John de Torres. The brave Ferdinand de Soto died on the banks of the great river which he discovered, and those who had survived died after, under Muscoso. Other missionaries had accompanied the expedition.

was so manifest that steps have been taken for his canonization. This holy man founded at once several missions, St. Francis among the Natchez, the Immaculate Conception among the Vidaes, St. Joseph of the Nazones, Guadalupe and Dolores, San Miguel, and Our Lady del Pilar. His labors were continued from year to year by other superiors, and the whole land, from the Rio Grande to the Sabine and Red rivers, was dotted by missions; churches were erected, books printed for the instruction of the neophytes, and before 1761 we have records of nearly seven thousand baptisms. These were all conducted by the Franciscans, chiefly from the colleges of Queretaro and Zacatecas, in Mexico; and their zeal carried them as far as the countries of the Cocos, the Osages, and the Missouris, where one of them lost his life, and another remained for some time a prisoner. Thus the missions of Texas extended as far as New Mexico, and comprehended various tribes. Among the missionaries of Texas, besides the venerable Father Margil and Father Serra the Apostle of California, conspicuous were the Fathers Joseph Guadalupe Prado and Bartholomew Garzia, and the martyred Fathers Joseph Pita, Joseph San Esteban, Alonzo Guisaldo de Ferreros, Silva and Francis Gonzabal.

These last named missions continued in a flourishing condition until the year 1812, when they were suppressed by the Spanish government, and the poor Indians remained deprived of missionaries until 1832, in which year the Franciscan Father Diaz was sent to the Nacogdoches of Monterey; but he was not destined for a long career among them, as he had scarcely labored there a year, among the scattered flock, when he fell a victim to his zeal—being put to death by some savages.

Notwithstanding this deprivation of missionaries, great numbers of the Indians remained for a long time fervent Catholics; and when Father Timon, late Bishop of Buffalo, was sent to Texas as Visitor Apostolic, he has related, himself, that he was often exhausted by the fatigues of administering the Sacrament of Confirmation to the thousands who still retained the faith.

By the zeal of Monsignor Odin, Texas was erected into the diocese of Galveston, in 1847, and he was appointed the first bishop, having been already consecrated in 1842.

From the death of Father Diaz, in 1832, the Franciscan missions were unoccupied until 1859, when Bishop Odin, knowing the immense benefits which these missionaries had conferred on the Indians, invited them to again enter their ancient field, and Father Agostino da S. Damiano d'Asti, with the Mexican tertiary, brother Trinidad de Torres, and afterwards Fathers Felice da Connobio and Pacifico d'Arlem, and the professed lay brother, Teoboldo da Novelle, entered upon the mission of Houston city and district. Fr. Augustine died March, 1866; Fr. Felix having returned to Italy, died also the same year, and for want of priests the mission was abandoned.

The soil of Texas is covered with monuments of the Franciscan missions—the many churches still existing—the aqueducts, and other public works, built by the Indians under the guidance and direction of the Franciscan Fathers—are sad memorials of what these missions once were, and of the happiness which they conferred on the savage Indians.

California, at present so renowned on account of its rich gold mines, was not less remarkable for its Franciscan missions; and the name of the great Patriarch of the Poor is inseparably joined to the Queen City of the Pacific—*San Francisco.* California is divided into upper and lower, or old California; the latter belongs to Mexico; the former has come into the possession of the United States, and of it we here speak. The missions of Upper California were founded exclusively by the Franciscans. It was in the year 1769, that the three principal posts of Upper California were founded —San Carlo di Monterey, in the north; San Diego, in the south; and San Bonaventura, in the centre. The illustrious Father Junipero Serra was chief of the undertaking. When the news of these recent foundations reached the city of Mexico, which was the headquarters of these missions, it caused such a great and universal joy, that all the bells of the city were rung. Father Serra made a request for assistance, and the superior at Mexico sent him a band of thirty companions, for the work of the new missions. The Dominicans also wished to labor in this field, and the Franciscans ceded the missions of Old California, which had been committed to them after the expulsion of the Jesuits.*

Being thus strengthened in numbers, Father Serra, after celebrating with great pomp, the Feast of Corpus Christi, set out, with Fathers Michael Pieras and Bonaventure Sitjar, to found the mission of San Antonio, on the banks of the river of that name; and there raised on high the bell which he had brought with him, he sounded it, to call the Indians to come and sit under the peaceful shadow of the cross. He also founded the mission of San Gabriele, of San Louis, and of San Juan de Capistrano, removing that of Monterey to a better site. And thus, in a short time, all

* The first missionaries in Old California were the Franciscans Didacus Perdomo, Bernardine de Comudio, Nicholas de Seravia, priests, and Christoval Lopez, lay brother.—Annales Minorum, 1596, XII. The Jesuits commenced their missions in Old California in 1642.—J. G. SHEA, Catholic Missions, p. 89.

were in good order, notwithstanding many obstacles had to be surmounted.

But in the year 1775, two Indians of the mission of San Diego, exciting more of their companions to follow them, came upon the missionary post by night, and having put Father Louis Jayme to death with cruel torments, sacked the mission and burned it to the ground. Father Vincent escaped their hands as if by a miracle. The news of this transaction caused great sadness to all, except the missionaries, who rather rejoiced at it as a heavenly benediction. "*Thanks to God!*" exclaimed the intrepid Serra, "*the seed of the Gospel is now watered with the blood of a Martyr; the mission is henceforth established!*" and more joyful than ever, he began at once to restore the mission, when the commandant, Rivera, ordered him to desist. He obeyed; but no sooner was Rivera removed from office, than he rebuilt the mission on its ruins, and then set out to found those of San Francisco and Santa Clara—the former, on the beautiful bay of San Francisco, the 27th of June, 1776, the latter on the delightful plain of San Bernardino, the 6th of June, 1777. In this manner, the indefatigable Father Serra founded nine prosperous missions in a few years, containing ten thousand Indian converts, living in harmony and peace, and progressing in civilization and religion. And in order that they might receive the graces of the Sacrament of Confirmation, he obtained the privilege, in quality of Prefect Apostolic, to administer that Sacrament.

But the hour was approaching when Father Serra was to go to receive the reward of his glorious apostleship. Worn out by so many labors, he also contracted an affection of the lungs; yet he continued to labor up to the 27th of August, 1784, when he received the Holy Viaticum from the hands of Father Palou, and was anointed. Nevertheless, he arose from his bed the next day, but was obliged to return, and sweetly breathed forth his blessed spirit, at the age of 71 years —projecting new missions up to the last moment of his life. Few of those who consecrate themselves to the conversion and civilization of the savages, merit so well of humanity and religion!*

Father Palou succeeded Father Serra, as Prefect Apostolic; and he founded the missions of Santa Barbara, of the Purissima Conception, of Santa Cruz, and of Nostra Signora della Soledad; but being called to the charge of the College of St. Ferdinand, in the city of Mexico, Father Lazven took his place, under whose administration three other missions were founded In 1798 arose the mission of San Louis, which, for the beauty of the church, and its columns, built under the direction and according to the designs of Father Peyry, excites universal admiration.

But about this period the French revolution was unfortunately shaking Europe, and the Franciscan missions of America felt its sad effects, as Spain could not send them its usual assistance. Nevertheless the missionaries, relying on themselves, continued to found new posts up to the year 1823—the last of which was St. Francis Solano, erected by Father Amoros, among the Guilucos, in the most northern part of California.

Of their prosperity, it is enough to say that they converted seventy-five thousand Indians, divided into twenty-one reductions!

But now commences the sad story of the decadence of the California missions. Mexico having thrown off the authority of Spain, and becoming an independent republic, the first governor sent to California under

*See Palou, Relacion Historica de la Vida del V. Padre Frai Junipero Serra.

the *regime*, was Echandia, who arrived there in 1824; and he became the scourge of that country, scattering and encouraging vice everywhere, and causing the destruction of all morality, and the overthrow of the missions, so that the Prefect, Father Sanchez, died of chagrin, in 1831; although a glimpse of joy enlightened his last moments, by the arrival and conduct of the new governor, Don Manuele Vittoria, who omitted no expedient to restore this ravaged vineyard of the Lord. But being soon removed from his office, the work of destruction began again; so that the celebrated Father Antonio Peyry, who for thirty-four years had admirably governed the renowned mission of San Louis Rey, founded by him, was obliged to depart, amid the sorrow and tears of his desolate Indian neophytes. The same was the case with the other missionaries; and thus the number had decreased so much that in 1833 the Mexican government had recourse to the College of Our Lady of Guadalupe, in Zacatecas, to obtain ten missionaries, who went to take charge of the most important missions in the northern part of California.

But at the same time, the secularization continuing, the extinction of the missions progressed; for, taking away from the missionaries the government of the Indians, and subjecting them to political agents, was like giving charge of the flocks to wolves. In fact, in 1834, the destruction was nearly complete, when the government solemnly decreed their extinction, already accomplished in fact. They were then composed of 30,650 Indians, who possessed 424,000 cattle; 62,500 horses; 321,500 sheep; and they harvested 122,500 bushels of grain. All which property was turned over to the government, who assigned a portion to each family. But in a short time the poor Indian neophytes were only an immense crowd of beggars; and the missionaries were deprived of their promised sustenance, so that in 1838, Father Serria, of whom a writer says it was a true happinesss to have known him, died of hunger and want, in his mission of Soledad, which he would on no consideration abandon. His death took place on a beautiful day in August, when, although broken down by suffering, he went to the church of his neophytes, to say Mass, which he had scarcely commenced, when he fell at the foot of the altar, and there died in the arms of those unhappy children among whom he had passed thirty years, occupied only in instructing and protecting them! Father Fortuni, the founder of the mission of San Raffaele, died in like manner, a short time after.

The Mexican Congress, recognizing the barbarities which had been committed, passed a decree in 1842, for the restoration of the missions. But how recover the property from the hands of the rapacious robbers to which it had committed it? It was of no avail that in that year the Franciscan Father Garzia Diego, one of the missionaries of that country, was made Bishop of California; for not even he could arrest the sacrilegious desolation. Duflot de Mofras, who visited these missions in 1842, found the mission and church of San Diego all in ruins, there remaining to Father Vincent Oliva, the missionary, only a small field, for the support of his five hundred Indians. He found the mission of San Gabriele in the same condition, where he saw the indefatigable Biscayan, Father Thomas Estenza, teaching his Indians how to make bricks! The missionaries of San Fernando, Santa Clara and Santa Ivez, saved a small portion only; but San Bonaventura, Santa Cruz, San Juan Battista, San Michele, Carmel, Conception, and San Raffaele, were in ruins and deserted! At Santa Barbara resided the gentle, generous, charitable and pious Prefect, Father Narcisco Duran. At San Louis, in extreme want, was the oldest missionary of that region, Father Raimondo Abella, whom the celebrated La Perouse had seen there in 1787, and who would, on no consideration, abandon his poor Indians. At the mission of Soledad, all was a desolate waste—without missionary, or Indian, or even an animal! the vines abandoned, the orchards growing wild, the gardens covered with weeds! At San Jose, Father Gonzales, the prefect of the missions of the north, received from the civil authority a ration of food, less than would be allotted a criminal in prison. In fine, San Francisco Solano was torn down, and the materials carried off by Don Mariano Vallejo, to build a fine and commodious house for himself!*

Such was the condition of these missions, which yet numbered thirteen Franciscan missionaries in 1842. But the desolation was not yet at an end, for then commenced the civil war, followed by the war with the United States into whose hands Upper California now came, but without any diminution of evil to the missions—the evils rather increased.†

The first bishop of this region was the Franciscan Father Diego Garzia, who died there in 1845, and the Holy See appointed as his successor, his *confrère*, Father Joseph Gonzales, but he declining, the Dominican, Father Joseph S. Alemany, was consecrated Bishop of Monterey in 1850, and who, in 1853, becoming archbishop, was translated to San Francisco. It

*Duflot de Mofras, Robinson, Bartlett, Forbes, and J. G. Shea, wrote graphic accounts of the Franciscan Missions in California, and they can be consulted for more detailed statements. ... .

†The Congress of the United States ultimately decided that all the lands and property belonging to the missionaries, come into the Union, should be considered as ecclesiastical property, and the bishops as the representatives of the Church entitled to its administration.

is said that Father Gonzales was a second time named for Monterey, but again declining, the Lazarist Father, Thaddeus Amat, was appointed.

In 1860 the Holy See erected the Vicariate Apostolic of Marysville. The Franciscans in Upper California remain still in the College of Santa Barbara, over which the venerable Fr. Gonzales presides.

CHAPTER XXII.

Franciscan Missions in North America.—The French and English Colonies.—The United States.—The French Recollects.—Champlain and Le Caron.—Mission among the Hurons.—La Salle and Hennepin.—The first Mass at Niagara Falls.—The Explorers of Lakes Erie, St. Clair, Huron, and the Mississippi River.—Tragic death of La Salle.—The Franciscans at Quebec, on Lakes Champlain, Ontario and Erie; on the Niagara and the Allegany; at Pittsburgh, Detroit, Newfoundland and Nova Scotia.—The early Franciscans in the colony of Maryland—the United States—Pennsylvania and New York.—Present Missions.

America was discovered under Catholic auspices, and by Catholics—for Europe was Catholic in 1492, and the Catholic faith was the first faith planted in the soil of the New World, by the European settlers, and the children of St. Francis were the first missionaries to announce the Gospel to the natives of the western world. This was the case not only in those portions discovered and settled by the Spaniards, but also in the more northern regions along the Atlantic coast, discovered by Cabot, under the auspices of England, after England had become Protestant; and though we often hear the United States spoken of by Protestants, as a Protestant country, as having been first sequestered by the Puritans, yet all history gives priority to the true faith, and the glory of having been its first apostles, to the Franciscans. The celebrated historian, Bancroft, says: "The unambitious

Franciscan, Le Caron, years before the Pilgrims anchored within Cape Cod, had penetrated the land of the Mohawk, had passed to the north into the hunting grounds of the Wyandots, and, bound by his vows to the life of a beggar, had, on foot, or paddling a bark canoe, gone onward and still onward, taking alms of the savages, till he reached the rivers of Lake Huron."*

Father Christian Le Clerq published the history of the Recollect missions, up to his own time, under the title, "The Establishment of the Catholic Faith in New France." We can give only a sketch:

"The pious Champlain, the founder of Quebec, desiring the conversion of the savages, more than the conquest of their lands, brought with him a band of missionaries, who labored among the several tribes bordering on the St. Lawrence, whose esteem and affection he had gained by his wise policy. And these missionaries were Franciscan Recollects of France, four of whom—three priests and one lay brother—arrived in 1615. One of these, Father John d'Olbeau, went from Jacdanssac to the mouth of the Saguenay, in order to learn the language, customs, and manner of life of the Montagnais. Another, the gentle Father Joseph Le Caron, went to evangelize the Hurons and the western tribes, after which he proposed to visit the great lakes of the west. He set out in the autumn, with twelve Frenchmen—rowing with them all the day, or carrying their little bark on their shoulders, when they met with obstacles in the stream—their only food being insipid Indian maize. After bearing great sufferings, and encountering many

* Vol. ii. p. 783. About 1611, a French Priest and two Jesuits had been as missionaries in Nova Scotia, but they did not long remain there. Mr. Bancroft mentions the Franciscans as the first missionaries ever north of the Potomac, as they had been the first south of it.

dangers, he reached the abode of the Wyandots, where he commenced his mission, offering up the Holy Sacrifice, surrounded by Champlain and his companions, and a great number of admiring natives; and whilst Champlain led his Huron allies into the heart of New York, the zealous Recollect exercised his ingenuity, studying their language, and endeavoring to reduce it to some form by written rules."

In January, Champlain returned from his expedition, and Caron accompanied him to the mountain of Tionontates, where, in announcing the Gospel, he had much to suffer from the persecution of the Ohis, or medicine men. Returning to his Huron mission, he continued indefatigable in his apostolic labors, until the flotilla prepared to return to Three Rivers, where he embarked, having gained a sufficient knowledge of the people, and composed a dictionary, which was the first in the Indian language in this part of America.

But the general government of the missions afterwards devolving on Caron, he was occupied more particularly with that of the tribes near Quebec, and the mission of the Hurons was interrupted until 1622, when Father Poulain visited it. Fathers Nicholas Viel and Gabriel Sagard, the historian, arriving in the following year, Le Caron returned with them to his old mission. They suffered much on the journey, and reached Carragouha, or St. Gabriel, on the twentieth of August, where they found their little building still standing, and commenced the community-life of the really poor of St. Francis, succoring the French, who had accompanied them, and laboring to spread the light of the Gospel among a people buried in the darkness of death.

Thus for ten years, the Franciscan Recollects of France were the only missionaries who labored in this ample territory of North America, called New France. But seeing that they were not sufficiently numerous for its wants, they invited the Fathers of the Company of Jesus, who willingly accepted the invitation, and in 1625, Fathers Charles Lalemant, Edmund Massè, and John Brebeuf, with some others, reached Quebec. The people showed themselves so discourteous towards them, that they could not find a place to live, so that the Franciscans gave them a part of their own convent and garden. In the meantime the Jesuit Brebeuf, with the Franciscan Joseph de la Roche Dallion, of the house of the Counts du Lud, were destined to labor among the Wyandots, together with Father Viel. But they found that Father Viel had been thrown into a stream by the savages, where he was drowned—and the stream is still called the Recollect's Rapid. Thus the Franciscans and Jesuits labored for five years in this field of their Master, with the same concord as if they were of the same sodality. And they would, no doubt, have continued in the same holy unity, if the English, lead by the traitor Kirk, had not launched themselves on Quebec, which they pillaged, as well as the country about—carrying off to England Champlain, and all the missionaries, both Franciscans and Jesuits.

Canada coming again into the possession of France, in 1632, the Franciscan missionaries, unsuspicious of any sinister designs, were preparing to return to their old field, when they were astonished to learn that the former missionaries of Canada—the Recollects and Jesuits—were to be excluded, and the Capuchins chosen in their stead, that they did not accept, and recommended the Jesuits, to the exclusion of the Franciscans. The Jesuits returned; the Recollects were excluded.

Le Caron, the founder of the Huron mission, one of the most illustrious servants of God, in the annals of the American missions, was so grieved at not being permitted to return to his beloved mission, that he died of a broken heart, March 29, 1632.

The Sacred Congregatien of the Propaganda, doing justice to the Recollects, desired their return; the King of France was in favor of it; and the people of Canada anxiously sought their former pastors; yet, notwithstanding this, from year to year, they always encountered some inexplicable obstacle thrown in the way by the officials of the Mercantile Company which ruled Canada.

Finally, in 1670, they were enabled to once more enter their old apostolic field, from which they had been exiled by the English, just forty years before, and they were now, moreover, appointed chaplains of the French military posts.

The provincial minister, Father Allart (afterwards bishop of Vence, in Provence), put himself at the head of the expedition, and on his return to France, left as commissary, Father Gabriel de la Ribourde, the last scion of a noble Burgundian family, and a man admirable for his singular zeal and goodness. He and Fathers Zenobius Mambré, and Louis Hennepin, became celebrated for their explorations, undertaken in company with Le Sieur de la Salle. The name of Father Hennepin is so conspicuous in the early history of North America, that he deserves more than a passing notice.

Father Louis Hennepin, although a native of Holland, belonged to the Recollects, of the province of Paris. It was the perusal, as he himself says, of the accounts of the operations and voyages of the missionaries of his Order, which awakened in him a desire to follow in their footsteps, and he was especially charmed with the relations of the missions of America, which, according to the statistics of the General Chapter of 1621, counted five hundred convents. In 1676 he was sent by his superior as a missionary to Canada.

The first place in which he began to labor, was at the source of the St. Lawrance, at the foot of Lake Ontario, where he founded a church in the vicinity of Fort Frontenac. His genius, however, was rather adapted to make grand explorations and discoveries than to be restricted to a stationary life.

Leaving Frontenac on the 5th of December, 1678, he sailed up Lake Ontario to the mouth of the Niagara River, in a bark of ten tons burden, the grandest that had heretofore navigated these waters. Here further progress was obstructed by the great Falls of Niagara, and he is supposed to have been the first European to look upon this stupendous prodigy of nature. Father Hennepin, and his sixteen companions chanted the *Te Deum* in thanksgiving, and on the eleventh of the same month, he offered up the Sacrifice of the Mass, for the first time, in sight of one of the wonders of the world—the great Falls of Niagara.

They were now obliged to construct another vessel, at some point above the cataract, in order to continue their voyage on the waters of Lake Erie, and Father Hennepin had to carry his missionary effects on his shoulders, around the Falls, for a distance of some twelve miles. They commenced constructing a new vessel at the mouth of a small stream, in the Niagara river, about five miles above the Falls; and the thousands who now yearly pass along the railroad from Buffalo to Niagara, may hear the conductor, as they near this locality, call out, "La Salle!" for the stream, and the place, still bear the name of the companion of Hennepin.

The vessel being completed, under the supervision of Signor Tonti, an Italian exile, was blessed according to the Roman Ritual, and named the *Grifon*. It was launched on the waters of Niagara, accompanied with three salutes of cannon, the chanting of the *Te Deum*, and shouts of joy.

Before proceeding on his voyage, Hennepin returned to Frontenac, and procured the assistance of Father de la Ribourde (who had been succeeded as commissary by the Provincial, Father Valentine le Roux), and Father Mambré, before mentioned, and Father Milithon accompanied them to Niagara, where he remained.

All things being now in order, on the 7th of August, 1679, the little vessel *Grifon*, having on board the three missionaries, La Salle, and twenty-eight others, entered the waters of Lake Erie and sailed to the westward. The *Te Deum* was again chanted, and the discharge of their artillery of seven cannons astonished the savages, who gave expression to their admiration by their shout "*Gannaron!*" They were then opposite the place where now rises Buffalo, the Queen City of the Lakes, and where the Franciscans have the Church of St. Patrick.

The *Grifon* was the first vessel which navigated the waters of Lake Erie, and being of sixty tons, must have appeared of surprising dimensions to the Indians, accustomed only to their small canoes. The first cape which they discovered was named St. Francis.

On the eleventh of August they entered the strait which joins lakes Erie and Huron, and as it extends itself, midway, so as to form a small lake, it was named St. Clair, which name it still retains.

On the twenty-third of August they reached Lake Huron, in the vicinity of which, the Recollects had carried the light of the Gospel, more than half a century before. Here, another *Te Deum* was sung in thanksgiving for the happy navigation of unknown waters and dangerous passages. Not being able to proceed further on Lake Superior, on account of the Falls of St. Mary, they passed to the lake of the Illinois—now Lake Michigan.

Contrary to the advice of the missionaries, La Salle now wished to send the vessel back, loaded with skins, in order to pay some debts; but it was wrecked, as is supposed, before proceeding very far. They were now compelled to continue their explorations in canoes, and passing by many incidents, we note that in the passage from the Lake to the Illinois river, they were obliged to make a journey of three leagues by land, carrying their baggage on their shoulders.

On reaching this place, they erected a fort, which they named Crevecœur, on account of the distress they suffered by the desertion of a portion of the company. Here they awaited, for some time, the return of the *Grifon*, but she never came, and La Salle resolved to return to Canada, leaving Hennepin to continue the exploration, with the condition that when he had reached the Mississippi he should turn to the north.

Father Hennepin, having as his companions, Anthony Angel and Michael Ako, set out, in a canoe, on the 29th of February, 1680, leaving at Fort Crevecœur Fathers Zenobius and Gabriel, who, in bidding him adieu, quoted these words of the Holy Scripture, to animate him: "*Viriliter age, et confortetur cor tuum.*" After eight days they entered the Mississippi, but instead of turning to the north, according to the desire of La Salle, who sought for himself the glory of exploring those regions, Hennepin was obliged, even by the threats of his companions, to first proceed to the south and then return to the north.

On the twenty-first of March, they encountered a tribe of Indians, called *Taenzas*, who treated them with great respect and kindness, and having passed the calumet of peace, with signs of joy, they commenced to pay them the same honors which they rendered their chiefs. They also kissed Father Hennepin's habit, whence it was concluded these Indians had some knowledge of the Spanish Franciscans, who, for a long time had established missions in New Mexico, in whose vicinity they now supposed themselves to be.

They halted on the twenty-third of March, which was Easter Sunday, and not being able to celebrate Mass, for the want of wine, they kept the solemnity with pious devotions. Continuing their voyage, they reached the mouth of the Mississippi and the Gulf of Mexico, where they found no inhabitants whatever. Hennepin desired to remain here for some time, in order to make observations, but his two companions, who cared little about such researches, obliged him to return. They raised a large cross of hard wood, twelve feet high, to which Hennepin attached his name and the names of his companions, together with a succinct account of this voyage, and kneeling, they sang the "*Vexilla Regis.*"

In the beginning of April they commenced to ascend the Mississippi, and for twelve days met with no mishap, being treated kindly by the different tribes of Indians along the river; but the thirteenth was an unfortunate day for Father Hennepin, being taken prisoner by a band of Sioux Indians, and marched off to a neighboring village, near where the Mississippi ceases to be navigable, on account of the falls, which he named the Falls of St. Anthony, in honor of St. Anthony of Padua, the great Thaumaturgus of his Order, under whose protection the expedition had been placed.

He was kept a prisoner for three months, during which time he suffered much from the savages, and was more than once in danger of being put to death by them. Yet he did not fail to preach Jesus Christ and the truths of the Gospel, as well as his slight knowledge of the language would permit; and was at last in some measure consoled by being able to secure the salvation of at least one soul—having baptized a dying infant, to whom he gave the name of Antoniette, in honor of St. Anthony of Padua. Finally, in the month of July, he was released from his captivity, by the exertions of Duluth, who had the previous year explored the country of the Sioux and contracted friendship with them.

On his return to Quebec, his religious brethren were greatly astonished, especially Father Hilarion Guenée, who exclaimed, "Lazarus has arisen!" They had been informed of his death, at the hands of the savages, more than two years past, and had celebrated his obsequies with a Requiem Mass.

This is a short extract from his own account of his exploration of the Mississippi, as given in his works, especially that entitled "*Nouvelle Decoverte.*"

The name of Father Hennepin, and his works, gaining favor with the public, he became the subject of attack. In the preface to the work cited, he attests, upon oath, the truth of what he relates. The following are his words: "*Je vous proteste ici devant Dieu, que ma Relation est fidèle et sincère, et que vous pouvez ajoûte foy a tout ce qui est rapparté.*" It may, indeed, be said that he was somewhat eccentric, and that he publishes facts relating both to himself and other persons, which one less truthful, and more reserved, would have either omitted or modified. In the preface mentioned, he gives his reason for dedicating his work to William III., king of England (a Protestant). It was in gratitude for a favor conferred on a monastery of Franciscan Sisters, of whom Hennepin was Confessor, and also because William was in alliance with His Catholic Majesty, of whom Hennepin was a subject. His works show that he was a pious and zealous missionary of more than ordinary talent.

As if with a prophetic spirit, he wrote of the Falls of St. Anthony of Padua, that he had given them that name, and that, in all probability, they would retain it. Not only has his prediction been verified, but a church has arisen there, dedicated to that saint; and the inhabitants have honorably perpetuated the memory of the missionary by naming the county which includes the Falls, Hennepin county.

The second exploration of the Mississippi was undertaken by La Salle, in company with Father Zenobius Membré and Signor Tonti, in 1682. When Father Hennepin separated from Fathers Gabriel and Zenobius, in 1680, the latter remained, with Tonti, among the Illinois, and began to study the language and to evangelize the Indians. But the two Fathers, together with the whole garrison of Fort Crevecœur, were obliged to abandon that post, and seek safety in flight, from the fierce Iroquois, who made an attack upon it, and on the 9th of September, 1681, after having navigated the Illinois river for the distance of five leagues, they were obliged to stop and repair their canoe, which began to leak. In the meantime the good Father Gabriel walked along the bank of the river, reciting his office, yet night approaching, and he not returning, Father Zenobius and Signor Tonti went to seek him, but in vain; for after having gone too great a distance from his companions, he fell into the hands of a wandering tribe of Indians called the Kickapoos, by whom he was impiously massacred and his head cut off. One of the savages afterwards sold his breviary to one of the Jesuit Fathers, and from him was obtained the account of his death. Father Gabriel de la Ribourde was a septuagenarian, and had spent eleven years laboring for the salvation of those savages, by whom he was put to death, whilst in the act of prayer, and the recitation of the holy office.

Father Zenobius afterwards, descending the Mississippi with La Salle, reached the Arkansas, and being pleased with their manners, he planted a Cross, and endeavored to impart to them chiefly by signs, an idea of Christianity and of the true God. The next tribe which they met was the Taenzas, a half-civilized people, scattered into eight populous villages, and here the pious Father Gabriel endeavored to give these heathens some knowledge of a faith more pure, and to elevate their minds from the sun and the fire, to Him who created things far more beautiful and powerful. They then proceeded as far as the Gulf of Mexico, when they sang a *Te Deum*, and after making the necessary observations, they ascended the river, and in the same year, both La Salle and Membré returned to France.*

The great design of La Salle was now to explore the mouth of the Mississippi from the direction of the sea, and for that end he prepared the necessary expedition. Never losing sight of the great object of propagating and establishing the true religion in the new discoveries, he procured three Sulpitians and three of our

* Membré in Shea's Discovery, &c.

Recollects to accompany him. The renowned Father Zenobius Membré was Superior, and the two others were Fathers Massimo Le Clerq and Anastasius Doway.

There was a fourth, Father Dionysius Marque, who falling grievously ill after three days of the voyage, was obliged to return. All the four were from the province of St. Anthony, in France. The Provincial, Hyacinth le Fevre, obtained the usual faculties for them from the Congregation of Propaganda, and a special brief from Innocent XI., conferring extraordinary faculties. The flotilla, consisting of four ships, one of which was named St. Francis, sailed on the 24th of July, 1684. After various vicissitudes, they entered the Gulf of Mexico the first day of the year, 1685, and Father Anastasius celebrated a solemn Mass of thanksgiving. Being uncertain as to the longitude of the mouth of the Mississippi, they coasted along until they came to the bay, where now stands Galveston, the episcopal see of Texas. Their efforts to discover the mouth of the Mississippi, by way of the sea, proving fruitless, La Salle selected twenty of the most robust of his men, and with a friendly Indian for a guide, accompanied by his brother, who was a Sulpitian, and the Recollect Anastasius Doway, they set out on the 22d of April, 1686, to make the exploration by land. After journeying on, and encountering various tribes of Indians, it happened that the nephew of La Salle, with other of the company were lost sight of for three days, and he and Father Anastasius went in search of them. At a distance of two leagues they found some of them near a river, and whilst La Salle was asking for his nephew, two traitors of the party, who were concealed among the trees, fired upon him, both shots taking effect, one in the head. Father Anastasius expected the same fate, but embracing La Salle, and bathing him with his tears, he exhorted him to pardon his murderers, and gave him absolution. The pious, generous and zealous Robert, Cavalier La Salle, died a little after, pardoning his enemies. This occurred on the feast of St. Joseph, 1687; and Anastasius, having buried the remains of La Salle, rejoined his companions, to whom he conveyed the sad intelligence. Continuing their route, they finally came to the Mississippi on the first of August, and ascending the river, in canoes, they reached Fort Crevecœur in Illinois, whence they passed down to Canada, in the beginning of 1688, and in the following August returned to France.

Fathers Membré and Le Clercq, who remained in the vicinity of the Bay of Galveston, Texas, projected a mission among the Cenis and the Assinais, but in 1687 or 1688 the fort was attacked by the Indians, and the colony massacred. Thus also did the Fathers Zenobius, Membré and Maximus Le Clercq, die martyrs to their sacred ministry. Father Le Clercq had labored for some years amongst the savage tribes of Canada, especially in the mission of the Seven Islands and of Anticosti. It was he who invented the hieroglyphics for the language of the Micmas, which still remain in use among that tribe.

The Recollects of the second period, having the charge of supplying all the French military posts with chaplains, became the first resident pastors of the principal places in North America, which were subject to France. At Fort St. Frederick, on Lake Champlain, where is now Crown Point, twelve Recollect chaplains succeeded one another, from 1732 to 1760, whose names are recorded in the register preserved in the Archives of Montreal. Another fort was erected at Orrillon, now Ticonderoga, in the State of New

York, in 1755, which was abandoned in 1759; Fort Niagara, near Buffalo, at whose erection the renowned Father Hennepin was present, and where he left the venerable Father G. Ribonde and the gentle Father Membré, was attended for some years by Father Melithon Watteau. It was abandoned for some time—rebuilt by Denonville, in 1687—and was attended by the Jesuits until 1721, in which year the French again took possession of Niagara, and the Recollects re-assumed the chaplaincy until 1759, when the defeat of the brave commandant Aubry took place.

Fort Presque Isle, where Erie, Pa., now stands; Fort Lebeuf, at Waterford, on Lake Lebeuf; Fort Machault, and Fort Venango, at the confluence of the Allegany river and French creek, now the Oil Region; and the celebrated Fort Duquesne, where Pittsburg, Pa., now stands—all had Recollects for their first chaplains, among whom was Father Emmaneul Crespel, who is well known through the account which he published of his shipwreck.

The Recollects continued at the Fort of Detroit, until 1782. Father Nicholas Benedict Constantine, the chaplain in 1706, became a victim of the savages in an encounter between the different tribes.

The French Recollects, having their headquarters at the convent of St. Mary of Angels, in Quebec, extended their operations wherever the French power went in America, even to the extreme north, in the Island of St. Pierre and Miquelon. In Newfoundland the Recollects founded a convent at Placenzia, in 1680, and the memoirs in the archives of Quebec, relate that Monsignor St. Valliar made an episcopal visitation there in 1689, accompanied by Father Georgeu and other Recollects.

Among the missions of the French Recollects are also those of Nova Scotia, the ancient Acadia. The Recollects of the province of Aquitania, in 1619, commenced a mission there, establishing their principal stations near the River St. John. Father Le Clercq makes a passing mention of this mission, in his work, referring the reader to the relation which they published of the same, but no copy of it can now be found. It is known that one of these missionaries, Father Sebastian, visited Quebec, and that he died on his way from Miscor to Port Royal; that in 1624 three other Fathers—James de la Foyer, Louis Fontinier, and James Cardon—went to join the Recollects of Quebec; and that in 1633, there were still three Fathers in the colony of La Tour, sent there by Tufet in 1630, laboring among the French and Indians. Even from this succinct notice of the Franciscan missions of the French Recollects, in North America, it may be seen, says De Courcy, that "the Recollects and the Jesuists of France traversed the territory, in every direction scattering the seed of the Gospel from the mouth of the St. Lawrence to the shores of the Pacific, and from the Gulf of Mexico to Hudson's Bay."*

The Spanish Franciscans, in the Spanish possessions; the French Recollects, in the French possessions; and the English Franciscans, in Maryland—comprise the old missions of the Friars Minor in North America. It is not generally known, even to the writers on the ecclesiastical history of the United States, that the Franciscans of the province of England established and maintained, for a long time, a mission in Maryland. The celebrated Hennepin, in his work entitled "New Discoveries," makes allusion,

* The Catholic Church, &c., p. 13.

on two occasions, to the operations of the English Franciscans in Virginia, under which designation Maryland was also included at that period; but for want of positive documents, confirming the existence of such a mission the critics looked upon the assertion of Hennepin, as having been made at random. But the evidence, proving the truth of his assertion, exists in the authentic register, in possession of the Bishop of Clifton, England. From the register, it appears that at least from the year 1671 to the year 1720, the Recollect Province of England maintained missions in Maryland, which were matters of consideration in every chapter and congregation.

Thus, on page 85, of the register, it is recorded that in the congregation celebrated on the 12th of October, 1672, in the royal residence of Somerset, the Definitorium approved the mission established in Maryland, and decreed that another priest, whom the Provincial would judge fit, should be sent thither.

Dr. Oliver, in his Collections, assures us that Father Masse Massey, of St. Barbara, was in Maryland at that time.

In the Congregation, *intermedia,* celebrated in London, on the 11th of October, 1675, it was decreed that Father Masse should be constituted Superior, and that Father Henry of St. Francis, and Basilius Hobart, should still continue in the mission of Maryland, and that Father Edward Golding should be also sent to join them.

In the Capitular Congregation, celebrated on the 6th of May, 1677, in London, in *aula Somersetana,* of the most serene Queen of England, Father Henry Carew was constituted Superior of the Maryland mission.

In the Congregation, *intermedia,* celebrated in London on the 30th of January, 1699/1700, Father James Haddock and Bruno Taylor were constiuted missionaries for Maryland.

In the congregation of the 15th of September, 1720, Father James Haddock is numbered among the names in the necrology, as having died in Terra Mariana, commonly called Maryland.

Father Polycarp Wicksted, who was destined for the Maryland mission, in the Capitular Congregation of the 10th of May, 1674, is numbered among the dead, in the Congregation of 1725, but no locality is given.

When the Very Rev. Father Pamfilo da Magliano, Custos Provincial of the United States, was going to the last General Chapter of Rome, in 1862, he visited Taunton, England, especially for the purpose of finding out something concerning the missions of the Order, and called on Monsignor Hendren—he being one of the remaining Franciscans of the old English province—by whom he was referred to Monsignor Clifford, in whose possession he found the above mentioned register, and from which he transcribed these entries.

But the particulars of the operations of the English Franciscans in Maryland, are as yet unknown, as the chronicles of the English Province have been carried off, and though search has been made, they cannot now be found.

Newfoundland was the first missionary field in North America cultivated by the Franciscans of the Green Isle. We have already mentioned the missions of the French Recollects, which extended to Newfoundland, when that island was in the possession of France. When it passed under the sway of England by the treaty of Utrecht (1713) it began to be colonized by subjects of Great Britain; and Father Louis O'Donnell, a native of Tipperary, who had been Minister-

Provincial of the Franciscans in Ireland, came to Newfoundland in 1784, the year in which the English king, George III., granted liberty of conscience to the subjects of Great Britain; and Father O'Donnell was the real father and founder of the Church now so flourishing in that island. He labored there at first as Prefect-Apostolic, but was afterwards made Vicar-Apostolic, and consecrated Bishop of Thyatire, *in partibus*, in 1796. He labored unceasingly to give stability to the Catholic colony till the advanced age of seventy, when, on account of the infirmity of old age, he obtained permission from the Holy See to return to his native country, where he died four years after. He was succeeded by his *confrère*, Father Patrick Lambert, a native of Wexford, and a religious of the same Franciscan province of Ireland, who was consecrated Bishop of Listra, *in partibus*, and was the second Vicar-Apostolic of Newfoundland. Father Thomas Scallan, a native of Wexford also, and like his predecessors, a Franciscan, was the third Vicar-Apostolic. He was consecrated Bishop of Drago, *in partibus*. Father Michael Anthony Fleming, a native of Carrick-on-Suir, and also a Franciscan of the province of Ireland, at first consecrated Bishop of Carpazia, *in partibus*, was the Vicar-Apostolic when Newfoundland was erected into a diocess, and he became its first bishop, and obtained as his coadjutor, his *confrère*, from the same Franciscan province of Ireland, Father John Thomas Mullock, who was consecrated bishop, *in partibus*, on the 27th of December, 1847, and who succeeded Bishop Fleming, on his death, in 1850. The splendid cathedral—together with the elegant episcopal palace built by him, the noble college of St. Bonaventure and other institutions that he founded—will perpetuate his name in Newfoundland. Bishop Mullock, by his vast erudition, deep knowledge, and efficacious energy, is one of the living glories of the Seraphic Order and of the Catholic Church.

The United States of America were constituted a nation in 1776, and in 1789 the Holy See founded the first diocess in the new republic, the first bishop of which was John Carroll, of the then suppressed Society of Jesus. Father Michael Egan, an Irish Franciscan, arrived in the United States about the beginning of the nineteenth century, and by his piety, learning and humility, acquired the confidence of Bishop Carroll. By an apostolic rescript of September 29th, 1804, Father Egan was authorized to found a province of the Order in the United States, but the project did not succeed at that time.

Catholicity having made great progress in the new republic of the United States, Bishop Carroll represented to the Holy See the necessity of founding four new episcopal sees—Philadelphia, New York, Boston and Bardstown. Pius VII. accorded the request, and by a brief dated the 8th of April, 1809, founded the four new sees; erected Baltimore the Metropolitan; and appointed Father Michael Egan first Bishop of Philadelphia. The bulls did not arrive until September, 1810, and on the twenty-eighth of October Bishop Egan was consecrated by Archbishop Carroll, assisted by his coadjutor Bishop Neale, and Father William Vincent Harold, a Dominican, preached on the occasion. The difficulties which he had to encounter in bringing order into the new diocess, shortened his life, and Bishop Egan died the 22d of July, 1814.

Besides Bishop Egan, another Irish Franciscan acquired great celebrity in the State of Pennsylvania, whilst it was all comprised in the Diocess of Philadelphia. Father Charles B. Maguire, who had studied at St. Isidore, in Rome, and who had also been professor there, came to the United States about the year 1812. "Father Maguire, who baptized, in Pittsburgh, the greater part of the Catholics of the present generation, was full of zeal for the glory of God. The Church of St. Patrick, even with its additions, did not seem sufficient in his eyes for the present and future wants of his people. Upon a hill in Grand street he resolved to build a cathedral, a long time before there was any talk of having a bishop in Pittsburgh; and he commenced with rare energy the construction of the Church of St. Paul, which was consecrated a year after his death, which occurred in Pittsburgh, in July, 1833."*

The first church built in the city of New York was that of St. Peter's, in Barclay street; and the first Mass was celebrated in it by the Irish Franciscan Father Nugent, on the 4th of November, 1786.†

Another Irish Franciscan, named Charles Whelan, had preceded Father Nugent, as a missionary in New York city, but both of these Fathers came in collision with the ecclesiastical authorities with regard to their faculties. The Congregation of the Propaganda had limited the Prefect-Apostolic, in granting faculties, to only those who should be sent by it, and thence arose misunderstandings, until the restriction was removed. The trustees of St. Peter's having also shown a preference for Father Nugent, because he was a better preacher, caused troubles which, finally, were terminated by the appointment, by Father Carroll, of Father William O'Brien, a Dominican, as pastor, in November, 1787. Father Whelan, retaining the confidence

* The Catholic Church in the United States. By H. De Courcy, p. 290.

† Ibid, p. 353.

of the Prefect-Apostolic, was empowered by him to found a mission in Kentucky, and Father Nugent returned to Ireland.*

Other Irish Franciscan missionaries labored in the United States, but these were the most conspicuous.

Bishop Carroll, in a letter to Rev. Richard Plowden, in 1789, mentions that in his diocess, which at that time embraced the whole United States, he had some German Recollects, with whom he was well satisfied. In the history of De Courcy, it is stated that Father Theodore Brauers, a Franciscan of Holland, had his missionary residence in Youngstown, in Westmoreland, in 1789, where he bought a lot and built a church; and that from Lake Erie to Conewagus—from the first mountains of Alleghany to the Ohio River—there was neither priest nor church, except the humble oratory of Father Brauers, where the Holy Sacrifice was offered for the salvation of men. This was the cradle of Catholicity in the diocess of Pittsburgh and Erie; and here was, in 1846, the cradle of the Order of St. Benedict in the United States. Such was the good reputation which Father Brauers had acquired among all, that the Protestant judge whose duty it was to admit his will to probate, after his death, expressed his astonishment that a man of such good sense, as Father Brauers was, should request Masses to be said for his soul!

Of the other German Franciscans alluded to in the above-mentioned letter of Bishop Carroll, we have no particulars. The German Franciscans now forming the Custodia of Cincinnati, commenced the missions in America much later, and the Franciscans of the province of Westphalia began theirs in Illinois and Missouri still later.

*The Catholic Church in the United States. By H. De Courcy, p. 352.

The Italian Franciscans came to labor in the ancient field of their brethren, in the United States, in 1855, being invited by the late bishop of Buffalo, on his visit to Rome, on occasion of the definition of the dogma of the Immaculate Conception. The first missionary expedition consisted of four, of which very Rev. Pamfilo da Magliano was chief. Others were sent from time to time, until the numbers increased so as to be constituted, formally, by Apostolic rescript of March 1st, 1861, a Custodia, or minor Province of the title of the Most Pure Conception of Mary, Virgin Immaculate, under the auspices of whom the mission was happily inaugurated.*

Fifty-seven are known to have been the martyrs who fecundated with their blood this vineyard of the Lord within the boundaries of the present United States. Thirty-six of these fifty-seven were Franciscans, sixteen Jesuits, two Dominicans, two secular priests, and one was a Sulpitian. The Franciscans and the Jesuits, in about the same relative proportion to that of their martyrs, were the principal missionaries in the territory now comprised in the United States and in the British American possessions. In Florida the Dominicans made a second attempt, after the first of the Franciscans, and the Jesuists made a third ; but it was only the new efforts of the Franciscans which were crowned with success. With this exception, the already mentioned missions of Florida, Texas, New Mexico, and Upper California, were entirely Franciscan missions.

The Franciscans, as well Spanish, as French, and

* Nicholas Devereux, of Utica, while in Rome, in 1853, had first encouraged the Franciscans to come to Allegany, in the Diocese of Buffalo, donating some land and four thousand dollars, to begin the establishment of St. Bonaventure's College.

English, and of other nationalities, whose labors have been narrated in this chapter, all belonged to the Minorite body, which includes the Observantines, the Reformed, and the Discalced (or Alcantarines). No Conventuals were found in these missions. The Capuchins were, for some time, about 1646, chaplains of the French forts on the coast of Acadia, having a convent at Penobscot, and a hospice at Kennebec. In 1722, they went to New Orleans, also as chaplains to the French forts, and they became the pastors of that city and colony, their Superior acting there as vicar-general of the Bishop of Quebec. Mention is also made of two Capuchins sent by the Congregation di Propaganda, to Maryland, about the year 1642.

The Conventual Franciscans were lately established in the United States, and the Capuchins have also at present some missions in this country.

The Sisters of the Second Order, or Poor Clares, were established about 1792, in Georgetown, and Frederick, Maryland, by some Sisters who had been driven from France, but in 1805 they left America for Europe.

In 1828 a convent of Poor Clares was established at Alleghenytown, near Pittsburg, and another at Green Bay, Wisconsin, in 1830, but they did not take root.

A house exists at present in Cincinnati of the Poor Clares, connected with the Sisters of the Poor.

As for the Third Order, there are several communities of Brothers, and a good many communities of Sisters in various dioceses, and no less flourishing is the secular Third Order.

Thus the three Orders of St. Francis, with their principal denominations, are now well represented in this great American republic, the ancient field of Franciscan missionary laborers.

CHAPTER XXIII.

The Canonized Saints—The Beatified—The Venerable—and other God's Servants of the Three Orders of St. Francis.—Pious Institutions of the Franciscans.—The Relations of the Franciscans with the Benedictines, the Dominicans, the Augustinians, the Carmelites, the Jesuits, the Minims, the Lazarists, the Redemptorists, the Passionists, the Calasanctians, the Regular Clerics Minor, the Sulpitians, and other institutes.

THE Church, in the canonization of Saints, proceeds very carefully; and none can be ever canonized or proposed for the universal honor of the Church, unless, after the most rigorous legal examination, full evidence is obtained that the Saint practiced heroic virtues while living, and wrought miracles, authenticated by eye-witnesses, after death.

Eighty-five are the canonized Saints of the Three Orders of the Seraphic St. Francis, besides the holy Patriarch himself. Forty-nine are Friars Minor, and belong to the First Order, viz.: the five Proto-martyrs, Bernard, Peter, Accoursius, Adjutus, and Otho; the seven Martyrs of Septa, Daniel, Angel, Samuel, Domnis, Leo, Hugoline, and Nicholas; the six Japanese Martyrs, Peter Baptist, Martin d'Aguirre, Francis Blanco, Philip of Jesus, Gonzalves Garcia, and Francis de Parilla; the ten Martyrs of Gorcum, Nicholas Pickius, Jerome Werdten, Julian Damos, Nicasius Stesius, Theodoric Eindem, Anthony Veerten, Godfrey Veruellanus, Francis Bruxellensian, Anthony Ornaniensian, and Peter Ascanius; the Capuchin Martyr, St. Fidelis; St. Bonaventure, Cardinal Bishop and Doctor of the Church; St. Ludovic, and St. Benvenutus, Bishops; St. Anthony of Padua, St. Bernardine, St. John de Capistrano, St. James de Marchia, St. Peter de Alcantara, St. Francis Solano, St. Peter Regalado, St. Pacificus, St. John Joseph, St. Leonard, St. Didacus, St. Paschal,

St. Benedict Nigre, St. Joseph Cupertino, St. Joseph Leonissa, St. Seraphinus, and St. Felix Cantalicio.

Five are Clarisses, and belong to the Second Order, viz.: St. Clair, St. Agnes of Assisi, St. Catharine of Bologna, St. Colette, and St. Veronica.

Thirty-one are the sons and daughters of the Regular and Secular Third Order of St. Francis, whose names are enrolled in the Litany of the Saints for the Franciscan Breviary, viz.: the seventeen Martyrs of Japan, St. Paul Sazugui, St. Gabriel de Izez, St. John Quizzuja, St. Thomas de Izas, St. Francis Japanese, St. Thomas Cosaqui, St. Joachim Saguijor, St. Bonaventure Japanese, St. Leo Garasuma, St. Mathias Japanese, St. Anthony Japanese, St. Ludovic Japanese, St. Paul Yaamigui, St. Michael Cosaqui, St. Peter Saqueixein, St. Cosmas Toquia, and St. Francis Compiten; St. Cornelius Bataudor, Martyr of Gorcum; St. Ludovic, King of France; St. Ferdinand, King of Spain; St. Ivo; St. Elzear; St. Roche; St. Conrad; St. Roso of Viterbo; St. Hyacintha; St. Angela; St. Mary Frances; St. Elizabeth, Queen of Hungary; St. Elizabeth, Queen of Portugal; and St. Margaret of Cortona.

For the beatification there is a process similar to that of the canonization. The only difference is, that for the beatification it is required that the Blessed, to receive the partial honor of the Church, has wrought, after death, four miracles, as for the canonization two more are required.

The beatified children of the Three Orders of the Seraphic Father, for whom the Church has granted Office and Mass, in the Franciscan Breviary and Missal, are over one hundred and twenty.*

* BB. Martyrs—John, Peter, Gentilis, John de Prado, Ludovic Sotelo, Peter de Avila and other Japanese Martyrs, lately beatified, and Raymond Lullo. BB. Bishops—Matthew, Benvenutus and James. BB. Confessors—Andrew of the Counts, Andrew Hibernon, Andrew

All those that are canonized must have been already beatified; and those that are beatified must first have been declared Venerable, by a decree of the Church, which is given only after having ascertained, with due process, the heroic virtues of the servant of God. There are a great many servants of God of this third kind, in the Three Orders of St. Francis, and *Venerable John Duns Scotus* is one of these.

Finally, the number of those who died martyrs, or in the odor of sanctity, and to whom the name of Blessed is attributed by custom, could hardly be counted. The author of the "*Giardino Serafico*" numbered at his time seventeen hundred blessed martyrs, and four thousand five hundred blessed confessors, virgins, and widows, whose names were in the Franciscan Martyrology and Legendary; but they are now surely more. May the holy Patriarch, St. Francis, with his many children, the Saints, the Blessed, the Venerable, and other servants of God, pray for us!

The name of "Seraphic" was given to St. Francis as well as to his Order, and history testifies that the name was not misapplied. Piety, the practical realization of the love of God and of our fellow-being, was

de Hispello, Anthony de Stronconio, Angel de Clavasio, Angel d'Acri, Archangel, Benvenutus de Gubio, Benvenutus de Recineto, Bentivolius, Bernardine de Feltre, Bernardine de Fossa, Bernard de Offida, Bernard de Corleone, Bonaventure de Potentia, Conrad de Ascoli, Conrad de Offida, Crispin, Francis de Calderola, Francis de Fabriano, Gabriel Ferretti, Giles, Guidus, Herculan, James de Bitecto, John de Parma, John de Penna, John de Duckla, Julian, Ladislas, Lawrence, Mark, Nicholas Fattore, Oderic, Pacific, Peregrinus, Peter de Molleano, Peter de Treja, Raynerius, Rizzerius, Roger, Salvator, Sanctes, Sebastian, Simon, Thomas.

BB. of the Second Order—Antonia, Cunegond, Eustockey, Hellen, Jolenta, Isabel, Louisa de Sabaudia, Mathia, Margaret Colonna, Philippa Mareri, Salome, Seraphina.

BB. Confessors, Virgins, and Widows of the Third Order—Luchesius, Peter of Siena, Gherard, John of Peace, Baptista, Delphina, Elizabeth Bona, Elizabeth de Amelia, Johanna de Signa, Lucy, Viridiana, Angela, Angelina, Humiliana, Johanna de Valois, Ludovica de Albertonibus, Michelina, Paula.

the main-spring which appears to have moved the holy Patriarch and his children, in all their operations. Hence we can easily understand how so many pious institutions owe to them their origin and propagation. It has been already mentioned that St. Francis was the first to practise the devotion to the Holy Infant Jesus in the "crib"; he obtained the "Indulgence of the Portiuncula," through his devotion to St. Mary of the Angels, and introduced into the office of the church, the commemoration of St. Peter and St. Paul. St. Bonaventure founded the first confraternity; and the given name of Gonfalone might well be taken as the standard confraternity. The beautiful devotion of the "Angelus" is attributed to him. He also composed the privileged oration "*Sacrosanctæ,*" recited at the end of the Divine Office. It is now settled that the pathetic hymn, "*Stabat Mater Dolorosa,*" was composed by the Franciscan poet, Friar Jacopone, who also composed the hymn "*Stabat Mater Gaudiosa.*" It is well known that the Franciscans were the champions of the Immaculate Conception of Mary; and the *Subtle Doctor*, John Duns Scotus, deserved the additional title of *Doctor Marianus*, for his most successful defence of this mystery. The holy exercise of the "Way of the Cross," before the fourteen stations, is acknowledged as a Franciscan Institution; and the Holy See has reserved to the Friars Minor, the faculties for their erection. The "Forty Hours Devotion" was instituted by the Franciscan Joseph da Fermo, at the Cathedral of Milan, in 1556.* The "Society for the Propagation of the Faith" was commenced by the Franciscan Friar, Hyacinth, 1632.† Hospitals for the sick; asylums for the orphan; and associations for the poor, were pro-

* Annales Min. Tom. 19. p. 54.
† Henrion.—Mission. 4 vol. IV. 10.

vided and attended by the children of him who is called the "Patriarch of the Poor," and who saw, in the sick, the orphan, and the poor, Jesus Himself.

But two institutions deserve more particular notice. The first is the Institution of the "Mont-de-piété." "Usury," says Darras, "had been the plague of the middle ages. The needy were sacrificed to the rapacity of the Jews, who lent money, at exorbitant rates, and thus succeeded in almost draining the wealth of christendom. More than once, especially in the days of the Crusades, Princes had pledged their estates in their provinces, to raise means necessary for those expeditions. But the poor men were the greatest sufferers by these exactions of the children of Israel. The first effort to deliver the world from the rapacity of these usurers was made at Perugia, in the latter half of the fifteenth century, by Barnabas of Terni, a Recollect, or Minor of the strict observance. He proposed to make a general collection throughout the city, and to apply the proceeds to the establishment of a bank for the relief of the needy. God lent a winning power to his words, for he hardly exposed his design, when all the inhabitants of Perugia brought their jewels, gems, and gold, with large sums of money, as a capital for the charitable institution, which was called the Mont-de-piété. The institution of the poor monk was soon known in all the cities of Italy. The laborer, when in want, was no longer obliged to have recourse to a Jew. By pledging some article of his poor furniture he received a certain amount of money, which he was to return at a stated time, with no other interest than a small sum to cover the indispensable expenses of the bank. Still this institution, like every truly useful invention, was subject to detraction. Some theologians thought that it possessed all the essential properties of usury, under another form. A violent discussion ensued, but without any definite result; and the question was brought before the General Council.* The Fathers to whom the matter was thus referred, were well known for their learning and charity. After a long and serious deliberation, in the course of which the numerous writings of both parties were carefully examined, the judgment was pronounced in a Papal decree. Leo, after a brief review of the whole debate, acknowledged that a sincere love of justice, an enlightened zeal for the truth, and an ardent charity, actuated both the opponents and defenders of the Mont-de-piété; but he adds that it is time for the interest of religion to put an end to the disputes which jeopard the peace of the Christian world. He to whom Christ has intrusted the care of souls, the guardian of the interest of the poor, the comforter of the suffering, forbids any one to tax with usury, the institutions founded and approved by the authority of the Apostolic See, and which require from the borrower but a trifling sum to cover the necessary expenses of their administration. He approves them as real institutions of charity, which it is well to protect and to propagate."† This institution, invented by the said Franciscan, Friar Barnabas, was established everywhere by his *confrères*. B. Bernardine de Feltra became its Apostle.

The other institution is that of the Bethlemites, of which Chateaubriand gives the following account:—"Peter de Betancourt, a friar of the order of St. Francis, being at Guatemala, a town of Spanish America, was deeply affected at the state of the slaves who had no place of refuge during illness. Having obtained by

* Council of Lateran.
† Darras.—Gen. Hist. Ch. 7th Period. c. I.

way of alms a small building which he had before used as a school for the poor, he then built himself a kind of infirmary, which he thatched with straw, for the accommodation of such slaves as had no retreat. He soon met with a negro woman, a cripple, who had been turned out by her master. The pious monk immediately took the slave on his shoulders, and, proud of his burden, carried her to the wretched hut which he called his hospital. He then went about through the whole city endeavoring to procure some relief for his patient. She did not long survive these charitable attentions ; but, shedding her last tears, she promised her attendant a celestial reward. Several wealthy people, impressed with the virtues of the friar, furnished him with money ; and Betancourt saw the hut which had sheltered the negro woman transformed into a magnificent hospital. This religious died young ; the love of humanity had exhausted his constitution. As soon as his death became publicly known, the poor and the slave thronged to the hospital, that they might for the last time behold their benefactor. They kissed his feet ; they cut off pieces of his clothes ; they would even have torn his body to obtain some relic of him, had not guards been stationed at his coffin. A stranger would have supposed that it was a corpse of a tyrant, which they were defending from the fury of the populace, and not a poor monk, whom they were preserving from its love. The order of the Friar Betancourt prospered after his death, (1667) ; America was filled with hospitals, attended by religious who assumed the name of *Bethlemites*. The form of their vow was as follows :—'I, Brother N.——, make a vow of poverty, chastity, and hospitality, and bind myself to attend poor convalescents, even though they be unbelievers and infected with contagious diseases.' If religion has fixed her stations on the tops of mountains, she has descended into the bowels of the earth, beyond the reach of the light of heaven, in quest of the unfortunate. The Bethlemite friars have hospitals at the very bottom of the mines of Peru and Mexico."*

St. Francis was so devout to St. Benedict, that he made a pilgrimage to Subiaco to visit his tomb ; and, whilst viewing the briars where the ancient Patriarch had rolled himself, naked, and meditating, enraptured on his virtues, he kissed them, they instantly blossomed into most beautiful roses.† St. Francis gave to his friars these directions in regard to the Benedictines: "You must show yourselves very grateful to the Benedictines for the good they do us. They have consecrated all our dwellings, that we shall have, in this house of God, (the Portiuncula) which is to be the model of poverty that we have to observe in all the houses of our Order, and the precious spring of sanctity, that we shall here acquire."

From the time that St. Dominic and St. Francis met for the first time, in Rome, and embraced each other, saying, "Let us be together, and no one will prevail against us," the children of both Patriarchs have followed their example. Their scholastic disputations, as Thomists and Scotists, were those of emulous brothers ; and the two Orders were, and still are, like twin brothers in the Church. As in their constitutions, the Dominicans are ordered to call the Patriarch of the Friars Minor, *Our Holy Father, St. Francis,* so the Franciscans, in theirs, are ordered to call the Patriarch of the Friars Preachers, *Our Holy Father, St. Dominic.* The offices of St. Dominic and St. Francis, are recited, with the same rite, by both Orders,

* Le Génie du Christianisme.
† Wadding, T. 2, n. 5.

on their respective festivals. On the 4th of August, each year, the General of the whole Order of St. Francis, with fourteen of his friars, goes from Araceli to Minerva, to celebrate the Solemnities of St. Dominic; and on the 4th of October, the General of the Order of St. Dominic, with fifteen of his friars, goes from Minerva to Araceli, to celebrate the Solemnities of St. Francis; and in the middle of the Refectory, on those occasions, a Dominican and Franciscan repeat, chanting, the first covenant of their Patriarchs —"*Stemus simul, et nullus praevalebit contra nos!*"

The Augustinians, after the Dominicans and Franciscans, become the Third Mendicant Order, and, as such, naturally come into relationship with them. Innocent IV., in 1253, deputed the Franciscan Friar, Simon Milanese, to settle the disputes which had arisen in their Order; and he succeeded in his trust, having brought about a reconcilation between the dissenting parties; and, by the election of Friar Lanfranco, rëestablished peace and tranquility in the Order. This fact may be sufficient to show the friendship and confidence that must have existed between these two Orders, from the very beginning. It has also been mentioned that the Augustinians having been the first missionaries in the Philippine Islands, manifested a predilection for the Franciscans, by inviting them to come to their aid in that field, in which they had been the pioneers, and where, to the present day, the Augustinians and the Franciscans, as well as the Dominicans, have most flourishing missions, having often mingled their sweat and their blood, to water that fruitful vineyard of the Lord.

The Carmelites, approved in 1226, by Honorius III., complete the number of the Four Mendicant Orders, which were compared by Pope Eugenius IV., to the four rivers of Paradise. St. Angel, Carmelite Martyr, who was in Rome in 1216, while preaching at the Lateran Basilica, suddenly announced to his audience, from the pulpit, that there were amongst them, two great pillars of the church, viz: Dominic and Francis; and immediately after his sermon he went to embrace them, and the three retired to St. Fabina, where they passed the day and night together, in prayer and holy conversation.* The part which the Franciscan, St. Peter of Alcantara, bore in the Reformation of the Carmelites, undertaken by St. Theresa, is well known.† The Chronologist of these Discalced Carmelites, exhorts his brethren to be always mindful of what this holy Father did for the Reformation, and to glory in having had him as a coadjutor of their illustrious Mother, and to call him with full voice—*Father!*

St. Ignatius, the founder of the Jesuits, having gone to Rome, in order to establish his Society, had there for his director, the Franciscan, Father Theodosius of Rome, who resided at St. Peter Montario; and it was Theodosius who induced Ignatius, even by commanding him, to accept the office of General of the Society, to which he was then elected.‡ The founder of the Jesuits was also encouraged in his undertaking by Abbess Elizabeth Rosella, a nun of St. Clare; and it is attested by several authors that he was a professed Tertian of St. Francis, before instituting the Society of Jesus.§ The Franciscan Tasseda was also a great friend of St. Ignatius, and his spiritual guide; but he did more for the Society, for he dissuaded Francis Borgia from becoming a Franciscan, and

*Wadding, T. 1. n. 26.
†Frances de St. Maria, T. 1. c. 43. n. 4.
‡Wadding, T. 14. n. 89.
§ Ferraris, Religiones. art. 5, n. 28.

induced him to enter the newly founded Society of Jesus. St. Francis Borgia always cherished an affection for the Franciscan Order, knowing that he bore the name of the glorious Patriarch, because it was through the intercession of St. Francis that his mother had safely brought him forth.* St. Francis Xavier was sincerely welcomed, on his arrival in the Indies, by the Franciscan Bishop of Goa, John Albuquerque; and it was by the Franciscans he was shown the unknown regions he had gone to evangelize.† The holy name of Jesus, for the veneration of which the Franciscan St. Bernardine of Sienna, triumphantly labored, became the sign of glory for the children of St. Ignatius.

St. Francis of Paula received in baptism the name of our St. Francis, by whose intercession his mother had obtained him; and like Anna, of old, she consecrated him from his infancy, to the Order of the Seraphic Father. But he was destined to become a Patriarch himself; and to establish an order, modeled after that of his namesake and patron. As our Friars were called *Minors*, so he called his *Minims*, that they might be the nearest to them in the rule, in the habit, and in the name.‡

St. Vincent of Paul, the founder of Lazarists, and of the Sisters of Charity, received his education from the Franciscans. "When his father had determined to educate Vincent for the Priesthood, the question arose as to the cheapest way of doing so, for his narrow means at first could furnish but little; he therefore sent him to the Franciscan Friars, at Acqs, who agreed to receive him for the small pension of sixty livres—

* Wadding, T. 18.
† Wadding, *ib.*
‡ Wadding, T. 15. n. p. 370. etc.

about six pounds a year. It was in 1588 that he began his studies with the rudiments of Latin; and in four years he had made such progress, that M. Comanet, a lawyer in the town, upon the recommendation of the father-guardian of the Convent, received him into his house as tutor to his children. This at once relieved John de Paul from the burden of his son's support, and enabled Vincent, with a quiet mind, and without misgivings on that head, to pursue his studies while he formed the character of his little pupils. For five years he continued in this position."*

One of the greatest miracles that God wrought through St. Alphonsus, the founder of the Redemptorists, was that of his bilocation, in regard to the Franciscan Pope, Clement XIV., at whose death-bed St. Alphonsus was present to assist the dying Pontiff in his last moments. His devotion towards St. Francis, and his imitation of St. Bonaventure, in his ascetic writings, are patent in all his works; and in his Moral Theology he quotes more than fifty Franciscan authors.

St. Paul Francis of the Cross, the founder of the Passionists, received his theological education from the Franciscans. Friar Dominic Maria, of Rome, the pastor of the Convent of St. Bartolomeo all' Isola, where St. Paul Francis and his brother were stopping, imparted to them the necessary knowledge of theology, and prepared them to receive holy orders. His biographers mention this fact, and also well remark that "he received the names of Paul and Francis; and truly, he well represented the sanctity of these names—a faithful follower of Paul in the zeal of a laborious apostleship—a faithful imitation of Francis, in his pov-

* H. Bedford, in the Life of the Saint.

erty—and as fervent as both, in his love for Jesus, and Him crucified."*

The Poor Clerics of the Pious Schools were instituted by St. Joseph Calasanctius, after he had, in a miraculous apparition, during the visit to the Portiuncula of Assisi, been espoused by St. Francis, with three mysterious rings which he drew from his bosom, to Poverty, Obedience, and Chastity.

St. Francis Carraciolo had received in baptism the name of Ascanio, which he changed, through devotion for his Seraphic Patron, into Francis; and having taken the name of the Patriarch, he also took the name of his Minors, calling the members of his Institute Regular Clerics *Minors*.

Chalippe, in his life of St. Francis, chapter IV., has this note: "M. Olier, who founded the Seminaries of St. Sulpice, was of the Third Order. Father Frassen says, that Olier, who was a man of most exemplary life, entered it with such fervor, that his examples drew many others into it; that he induced the ecclesiastics of his seminary and parishioners of St. Sulpice to become children of St. Francis—become, as he himself was, brother of Penance." The Sulpitian, Rev. Father Rouxel, the Spiritual Director of the Seminary in Montreal, has inherited the same spirit from M. Olier.

The Bethlemites were instituted by the Franciscan Peter de Betancourt; the Hieronymites of Fiesole, by three of the Tertians of St. Francis; and the Tertian Blessed Peter of Pisa, instituted another Congregation of Hieronymites.

Several other institutes also originated from the Franciscan Order; and the Military Order of the

* Boston Ed. and others.

Knights of the Holy Sepulchre, as well as some other Military Orders, owed their existence to the Franciscans.

CHAPTER XXIV.

The Franciscan Popes.—Nicholas IV.—Alexander V.—Sixtus IV.—Sixtus V. —Clement XIV.—Vicedominus, Pope Elect.—Julius II., a Franciscan novice.—Antipope, Nicholas V. — His abdication and penance.—Franciscan Cardinals, Patriarchs, Archbishops, Bishops, and other dignitaries.

Cardinal Ugolini, the great patron of the two orders of Preachers and Minors, having once asked Dominic and Francis if they would allow their children to accept ecclesiastical dignities, they both answered that their disciples ought to remain what they were, without being raised to any higher dignity. God, however, who exalts the humble, had so disposed that the Friars Minor, as well as the Friars Preachers, should be exalted to all the dignities of the Church—even to the Supreme Pontificate.

Nicholas IV., who, when simply Friar Jerome, of Ascoli, had been often employed as apostolic-legate in difficult missions, and had taken a prominent part in the great general council of Lyons, was created Cardinal Bishop of Palestrina, by Nicholas III., and after the death of Honorius IV., notwithstanding his humble protestations, he was elected Pope on the 22d of February, 1288. Happier in his mediation, says Darras, than Honorius, he obtained the release of Charles the Lame, whom he crowned with his own hands, in the Vatican Basilica, upon the same conditions as had been imposed upon Charles I., by Clement IV. By the treaty of Tarascon which ended this great dispute (1291), Alphonso III., renounced his claim to the Sicilian crown; Charles of Valois abandoned his pretensions to the throne of Arragon, to which he had been called by Martin IV., and Charles of Sicily gave up the duchy of Anjou, in favor of the Count of Valois. While the influence of the Pope was winning back the peace of Europe, the city of Rome was still the prey of bloody factions; but he succeeded in inducing the Ghibellines and Guelphs to agree to a compromise in 1292, although his death happening shortly after (April 4th), the two parties renewed the struggle.* Under his pontificate, Ptolemais, the only remaining stronghold of the Christians in Palestine, fell into the hands of the Mussulmans. The eighth and last crusade was terminated in 1272, and no renewal of the effort to redeem the Holy Land, seemed now possible. It was also during the pontificate of Nicholas IV. that the miraculous translation occurred, of the little house of the Blessed Virgin, from Palastine to Tersato, on the Adriatic, in Dalmatia. Friar Jerome of Ascoli, as Cardinal Prinei, and as Pope Nicholas IV., was the same wise, zealous and humble Franciscan.

Alexander V. was the next Pope chosen from among the Franciscans. The Great Western Schism was distracting the Catholic world in 1409, when the Council of Pisa turned its attention to the choice of a successor of St. Peter, whose claim should be unassailable. There were two claimants of the pontifical throne. We quote Darras: "In the preliminary meetings of the council the manner of the new election was a matter of dispute. Some were of opinion that the election should be made by the whole council; others held that the Cardinals—though they held their

*Darras' Gen. Hist. of the Church.

dignity from a somewhat doubtful source—should alone be entrusted with the choice, in order not to swerve from established usage. The latter opinion prevailed; and the Cardinals, after pledging themselves by oath, to disregard, in the holy work, all secondary personal interests, entered into conclave. Never was Heaven implored with more fervent vows for the happy issue of a Pontifical election. The council, the ambassadors, the faithful—all were in prayer. No doubt was felt that the schism was at its last gasp. On the 26th of June, A.D., 1409, all the votes centered on Cardinal Peter Philargi, of Candia, who took the name of Alexander V. Never was election more free from political intrigues and court influence. The new Pope could boast neither long lineage nor powerful relations. He had been charitably harbored, while still an infant, in the island of Candia, and knew neither father nor mother, nor kindred. His merit and intelligence supplied the want of all human recommendation. Having received the habit of the Friars Minor, he studied successively in Bologna, Oxford and Paris, and published a Commentary on the *Liber Sententiarum* of Peter Lombard, equally remarkable for depth of thought and elegance of style, and which won for its author the well-deserved admiration of the theological world. After having, for some time, held the archiepiscopal see of Milan, he was raised to the cardinalate by Innocent VII., and at length ascended the Papal throne at the age of seventy years. The election of Alexander V. gave rise to an incredible enthusiasm in the city of Pisa. The goodness of the Pontiff was as boundless as his charity; he had known misfortune, and his highest ambition was to make others happy. His bounty soon drained the Pontifical treasury, and he loved to repeat, with a true spiritual gayety, "I was once a wealthy bishop, I have since been a poor cardinal, and now I am a needy Pope."

This accession, though hailed with such joyous acclamation, only complicated, instead of extinguishing the schism. Instead of two there were now three rival claimants for the Pontifical authority. Gregory XII., in his retreat at Gaëta, was still acknowledged by the Neapolitan States, Hungary, Bavaria, Poland, and the kingdoms of the north. Castile, Arragon, Navarre, and Scotland, with the islands of Sardinia and Corsica, remained true to Bennedict XIII. The jurisdiction of Alexander V. was recognized only in France, England, Portugal and Northern Italy, though Rome soon followed their example; and Avignon, so long the dwelling of the antipopes, submitted of its own accord to the authority of the legitimate Pontiff. The envoys of the Roman people met the Pope at Bologna, whither he had proceeded after the Council of Pisa, and laid at his feet the keys of the Eternal City, entreating him to honor it by his presence. The Pope received them kindly, and promised to accede to their request. With a view to the re-establishment of unity in the Church, he convoked a General Council for the year 1412. His plan of administration also included the reform of abuses, the repression of simony, the union of the Greek and Latin Churches—now becoming daily more desirable on account of the progress of the Turks—and finally, the extinction of the Wycliffe heresy, which had left England to ravage Germany. Death, however, thwarted his plans; he expired at Bologna, on the 3d of May, A.D., 1410; his last words were addressed to the cardinals who stood about his death-bed: "Peace I leave you; my peace I give you."*

* Gen. Hist. of the Church.

Sixtus IV., called Francis Cibo, or Della Rovere da Savona, had been General of his Order four years and four months; had been made cardinal by Paul II., and after the death of that holy Pontiff was elected Pope, August 9th, 1471. His first care was to convoke a Council at Rome, for the formation of a league against the Turks; but the Christian princes having refused to send their ambassadors, he determined to carry on the work by means of his legates, in which he was partly successful. Cardinal Caraffa, with his combined fleet, took possession of Attalia and Smyrna, after a successful engagement with the Turks, and Peter d'Aubusson, Grand Master of the Knights of St. John of Jerusalem, became the successful hero of the Island of Rhodes against the hosts of Mahomet II.

He nobly maintained the rights of the Holy See against the alliance of the Florentines, France, Venice and Milan, until he gained a favorable treaty of peace in 1480. Sixtus turned their own arms against the infidels, but the death of Mahomet II. having freed Italy from the greatest danger with which it was ever threatened, he built in Rome the Church of Peace, as a lasting monument of the happy event. Sixtus IV., says Darras, inaugurated in Italy, with a firmness worthy of his character, the policy of crushing the tyranny of the petty lords.* He also issued a bull in regard to the Immaculate Conception of Mary (March 1st, 1477), and from that time the declarations of the Chair of Peter, concerning this mystery, began to be explicit, until, in our own days, it was solemnly defined a dogma of faith. He celebrated the great Jubilee Year (1475), and it was he who canonized St. Bonaventure.

Sixtus IV. restored and erected magnificent mon-

* Gen. Hist. Catholic Church.

uments in the city of Rome. The celebrated Sixtine Chapel, and the Sixtine Bridge, still retain his name. Platina, the great biographer of the Popes, was appointed by him Librarian of the Vatican Library, which he had also enriched. He died on the Feast of St. Clare, August 12th, 1484, after a pontificate of thirteen years, and was the longest lived of the Franciscan Popes.

SIXTUS V.!—Whereas his namesake, *confrère*, and predecessor, Sixtus IV., could boast of the worldly nobility of birth and family, Sixtus V. could only boast that from a swine-herd boy, he had been raised for his merits, to the Papal throne! The life of Sixtus V. was so extraordinary, that unless it was well supported by authentic history, lasting monuments, and enduring institutions, it would seem incredible. It is not surprising that romance writers have seized on the glorious name of Sixtus V., surrounded with countless anecdotes, and made him the hero of many a tale. Felix Peretti, while a boy, watching his father's swine, was discovered to be a real genius, by a Religious, Franciscan, who chanced to converse with him; and being encouraged by him to go to his convent, was afterwards received into the Order. He advanced rapidly in his career, and St. Pius V. made him cardinal. After the death of this holy Pontiff, who had consulted him on the most difficult matters, it is said that Cardinal Montalto, as he was called, "lived a secluded, quiet, frugal and industrious life, devoting his time exclusively to study and meditation;" for which reason, all the cardinals were surprised at the energy he began to display, from the very moment his election was announced in the conclave (April 24, 1585). "My time," he exclaimed, "is most precious now, and I cannot afford to waste a single moment." And he at once began to give orders, and to put them in execution, for the welfare of the State as well as of the Church. Henceforth, there was "no peace for the wicked," and security was soon restored in the Pontifical States of Italy, by the examples of stern justice he gave, even before his coronation, which took place on the first of May. On the very day he took possession of the Lateran Basilica—the first Sunday of May—he ordered a search to be made for the localities of all the old springs of water, and the city—especially the Quirinal Hill—to be supplied with the needed element. The architect, J. Fontana, after the failure of M. Costello, employing thousands of workmen, accomplished the undertaking, collecting, in one reservoir, fifty-two rivulets of excellent water, which was brought into the city, wherever it was wanted, by aqueducts, and over arches, worthy of Rome. He also caused the ancient Felician water to be introduced into the city, from a distance of thirteen miles, by costly aqueducts. He likewise caused water to be brought to Civita Vecchia, and made that port a secure harbor, and he built over the Tiber the bridge which still bears the name of *Ponte Felice.*

By his order, the largesses usually expended in honor of the new Pope, were distributed among the abodes of the poor and to the hospitals. He re-established the *Mont-de-Piété,* instituted for the relief of the necessitous poor; erected asylums, and relieved from debt existing Institutions of Mercy, introduced the industry of woollen and silk factories, and deposited in the Castle of St. Angelo some five millions of money for future contingencies.

But whilst thus attending to the care of his temporal kingdom, he was at the same time engaged in the greatest undertakings for his spiritual republic—

the Catholic Church. For the more prompt expedition of affairs, he had in operation fifteen different Congregations of Cardinals, which, "if he did not found them all, he yet gave them such a development and perfection as to make them his."* He fixed the number of cardinals at seventy, with their titles—six of bishops, fifty of priests, and fourteen of deacons—and established a high standard for the qualifications befitting that office. He regulated the visits of bishops *ad limina Apostolorum*, at every four, or five, or ten years, according to their respective distances. He encouraged and promoted missions among the heathen—to Japan, to China, to America, and to the various parts of the eastern and western continents, and stemmed the torrent of heresy in Europe.

Mary, Queen of Scots, condemned to death, in 1586, by the iniquitous commission of Elizabeth, wrote a touching letter to Pope Sixtus V., declaring her firm resolve to live and die in the Catholic faith; but the Pope had not waited for this last proof of devotion, to interest himself in behalf of the Scottish Queen. He had already appealed to Elizabeth, and urged the most pressing entreaties in her favor, and it is probable that his display of solicitude helped to delay her execution, which did not take place until February 18th, 1587. Sixtus V. issued a solemn bull of excommunication against the crowned regicide, placed England under interdict, and joined in a league with Philip II., of Spain, who fitted out the "*Invincibile Armada*," which was so disastrously scattered by the elements, before reaching the destined field of operations. He was more successful, however, with the League, or the Holy Union, "which forced upon the

* Darras' Gen. Hist. of the Church, vol. iv., Seventh Period, ch. vi., n. 10.

Calvinist, Henry of France, the conviction that he must be a Catholic prince who would wear the crown of St. Louis." Henry IV., having learned the Pope's unshaken determination, from his legates, the Dominican, Cardinal Cajetani, and the Franciscan, Bishop Panigarola, resolved "to send to Rome, as his ambassador, the Duke of Luxemburg, with the special mission of consulting the Pope on this serious matter." Olivares, the Spanish ambassador, on learning the arrival of the French commissioner, hastened to the Vatican and begged the Pope not to grant the honor of an audience to the minister of a Huguenot prince. "If your Holiness," said Olivares, "persists in admitting him, I shall be under the necessity of making a formal protest, in the name of the King, my master." "Protest!" replied the Pope; "What protest will you advance? You offend the majesty of your royal master, whose prudence I well know: you may retire!" Luxemburg was presented to Sixtus, and assured him that the hero of Arques and Ivry, was ready to kneel at the feet of his Holiness, and seek absolution and admittance into the Catholic Church. "Let him come! let him come!" exclaimed the Pope, "that I may embrace and console him!" Here, it is evident, that Sixtus V. was not acting a political part. He saw the possibility of Henry's conversion, and from that moment he could have no objection to his sitting upon the throne; and when the ambassadors of the League came to complain to Sixtus, of the favor shown to the envoy of Henry of Béarn, "So long," replied the Pope, "as we believed the League to be working for religion, we assisted it; now we are convinced that it is acting only through motives of ambition, or under a false pretense, our protection is at an end."* This is only an instance of his pure and sincere zeal for religion.

Sixtus V. was truly all to all, and all in all. With the Vatican types he issued a correct edition of the Septuagint version of the Old Testament, in both Greek and Latin; as also a revised edition of the Latin Vulgate, as had been ordered by the Council of Trent. Having, by the aid of learned men, accomplished this important work, he issued that beautiful constitution for the use of the version. He also edited the complete works of St. Bonaventure, whom he solemnly enrolled among the great doctors of the Church. His energy and his means seemed inexhaustible. While thus efficaciously engaged in so many affairs, he was also erecting or repairing the most magnificent monuments in Rome. He completed the greatest wonder of the world—the dome of St. Peter's. He established a typography in the Vatican, added the Sistine Library, and improved the interior of the palace by commodious stairs and vestibule, and decorated it with valuable paintings. In the Lateran, he repaired the Basilica, built the adjoining Apostolic Palace, and having constructed a noble edifice, he transferred, and placed there, in the *Sancta Sanctorum*, the *Scala Santa*, upon which Christ had ascended to the hall of Pilate. In the Tiberian Basilica, he completed the chapel of the Holy Crib, which he had commenced while Cardinal; translated thither, with great solemnity, the body of the Dominican Pope, St. Pius V., which he deposited in a beautiful Mausoleum, and prepared his own resting-place on the opposite side, thus cementing the friendship of the twin Orders, by adorning the same grand chapel with marble statues of St. Dominic

* Darras' Gen. Hist. Catholic Church, vol. iv.

and St. Francis. The new Temple of St. Jerome, on the Tiber, was erected, and the ancient church of St. Sabina restored, at his expense. He founded St. Bonaventure's College, in Rome, and the Picenian College, in Bologna. He adorned the capitol with the trophies of C. Marius; the Piazza of the Quirinal, with the colossal statuary of Phidia and Praxiteles; the Piazza del Popolo, the Piazza of the Esquilino, the Piazza of the Lateran, and the Piazza of the Vatican, with the prodigious Egyptian obelisks, bearing triumphantly, on high, the Holy Cross, to which he dedicated these monuments of antiquity. The admirable Trajan and Antoninian columns were raised by him, in honor of St. Peter and St. Paul—placing on the summit of the former, a metal statue of St. Peter, and on that of the latter a similar statue of St. Paul.

This enumeration of facts may be sufficient to give an idea of the greatness of Sixtus V. He died on the 27th of August, 1590; and when we remember that his Pontificate lasted only five years, the assertion of Darras will not seem too strong: "History ranks his name among those of the greatest men who have ever ruled the world."*

Clement XIV., often called Pope Ganganelli, was elected Pope, on the 19th of May, 1769, by the votes of all the cardinals, except Cardinal Orsini, "who cried out in vain that Ganganelli was a Jesuit in disguise."† Never, perhaps, in modern times, has the Pontifical See found itself in a crisis so fearful, as at the accession of Clement XIV. France and Spain, Naples, Parma and Venice, were at open war with the Holy See. Portugal, the stronghold of schism, was its determined enemy. Under Clement XIII.

* Darras' Gen. Hist. Catholic Church, vol. iv.
† Darras' Hist. cit.

those governments had already suppressed the Jesuits, and expelled them from their States; and the suppression of the Society of Jesus was now, unfortunately, the centre around which gravitated all the interests of the Church. The storm was raging—the winds were let loose upon the bark of Peter, and they threatened, unless the hand of God was stretched out to save, to bear away the Pilot in their rage. Clement XIV. held out four years in his endeavors to save the Society of Jesus, but when the last anchor of hope which he had placed in Maria Theresa of Austria gave way, then the Society, like Jonas, the Prophet, had to be sacrificed to the fury of the waves or the safety of the ship. By the Brief *Dominus ac Redemptor*, on the 31st of July, 1773, he pronounced the final sentence, and the Society of Jesus was suppressed.*

It is admitted by all historians, that Ganganelli, though seated on the Pontifical throne, made no change in the simplicity of his life and manners, and was ever gentle, kind, affable, ; always even-tempered, never hasty in his judgments, and never allowing himself to be misled by the heat of an inconsiderate zeal. He died on the 22d of September, 1774, and was miraculously assisted in his last moments by St. Alphonsus Liguori. His Pontificate was of the same duration as that of his *confrère* and predecessor, Sixtus V., and his principal Pontifical acts were the suppression of the Jesuits, and the approbation of the Passionists.

Vicedominus de Vicedominis, a nephew of Gregory X. was elected Pope in Viterbo, in the year 1276, after the death of Adrian V.; but as he died on the very day of his election, he is not found in the succession list

* Darras' Hist. cit.

of the Popes, though in his choice an honor was conferred on the Franciscan Order to which he belonged.

Julius II—Giuliano della Rovere—elected Pope in 1503, was a Franciscan novice, in the convent of Perugia, when his uncle, Sixtus IV., created him cardinal, and, therefore, he is entitled to be mentioned with the Franciscan Popes.

We may notice here that an antipope came forth from the Order, in the person of Peter Rainallucci de Corbario, who became the tool of the Emperor Louis of Bavaria, under the name of Nicholas V. But happily he repented in good time, because, "The antipope, Rainallucci of Corbière," says Darras, "hastened to Avignon, in the garb of a penitent, with a rope around his neck, and publicly threw himself at the Pontiff's feet. Touched by his sincere repentance, John kindly embraced him, offered him a lodging in his palace, and daily sent him dishes from his own table."*

Fifty-seven cardinals of the Holy Roman Church have been created from the Order of St. Francis, including the two now living—Cardinal Cyrillo de Alemeda, Primate of Spain, and Cardinal Panebianco.

The Franciscan patriarchs, archbishops and bishops, number, altogether, certainly more than two thousand five hundred. In the beginning of the past century, Pier Antonio, of Venice, published some detailed statistics of all the dignitaries of the Order, giving their names up to his time;† and the number of patriarchs, archbishops and bishops, had then reached two thousand three hundred and three—thirty patriarchs, three hundred and sixty-two archbishops, and one thousand nine hundred and eleven bishops. We could give the

* Darras' Gen. Hist. Catholic Church, Part 6, ch. v., n. 7.

† Giardino Serafico Istorico.

names of more than two hundred patriarchs, archbishops and bishops, from that time, and of them, more than fifty now living; we might even venture to say that the whole number, up to the present time, is about three thousand.

A great number of nuncios, apostolic legates, and other dignitaries of the Church, were also chosen from the Order of the Friars Minor. It was the custom of some Popes, as Eugene IV., Nicholas IV., and Calixtus III., to write to the General Chapter of the Order in these terms: "*Segregate mihi viros in obsequium Sedis Apostolicæ ab omni Ordinis officio liberos*,"—"set apart for me, men in obsequiousness of the Apostolic See, free from duties of the Order;" when so many as could be spared, would then be employed by the Holy See in honorable and important offices of the Church.*

* Van Loo, Stim. Seraph. Convers. ch. xxxvi.

BRIEF NOTICE

OF VARIOUS DISTINGUISHED MEMBERS OF THE FRANCISCAN ORDER.

Innocent III., after the prophetic vision of the poor man upholding with his shoulders the falling Basilica of the Lateran, at the sight of Francis exclaimed, "This is the man who will with his works and doctrine sustain the Church of Jesus Christ." It was, then, not only by works, but also by doctrine that the Franciscan Order was to accomplish the design of Providence. The sinister use that men often made of their learning caused the Apostle to say that knowledge puffeth up. (Cor. c. 8.) He understood undoubtedly that knowledge without charity and humility is vain or serves only to puff up. St. Francis, in the spirit of St. Paul, wisely cautioned his children to take care that knowledge might not be separated from piety. St. Anthony was appointed the first professor of the Order by St. Francis himself in these words: "To my dear brother Anthony, health in Jesus Christ, from Brother Francis. It is my wish that you should teach theology to the brethren, but in such sort that the spirit of prayer required by our Rule be not lessened either in you or in them." Those who entered the Order as lay-brothers, he did not oblige to acquire learning, but only such as were to be the dispensers of the mysteries of God, were required that they should become well learned, and in his Rule he enjoins on them "that their sermons must be examined and chaste for the utility and edification of the people announcing to them the vices and virtues, the punishment and the glory, with brevity of discourse, because brief was the word that the Lord made on earth." (Rule. Chap. 9). Hence we can well understand what was the intention of St. Francis in regard to learning. Beginning with

St. Francis himself, the Order of Friars Minor counts thousands of authors who distinguished themselves in all the branches of science, literature and art—Theology, Dogmatic, or Moral, Ascetic, Mystic; Sacred Scriptures, Jus Canonicum, Philosophy, Mathematics, History, Oratory, Poetry, Architecture, Painting, Music, Medicine, Statesmanship, and even Warfare. Wadding published a large volume of the Franciscan authors; and Sbaraglia, more recently, another large supplementary volume both of the Franciscan authors after Wadding's time, and of others that had not come to Wadding's notice.

Señor Claros well then could say lately before the Spanish Cortes: "The humble cord of St. Francis not only represents and symbolizes the excellencies of the Catholic religion, but also illustrates and enriches the sciences, the arts, and all the branches of knowledge."

We shall now proceed to mention the names of the most distinguished in each century from the foundation of the Order.

THIRTEENTH CENTURY.

(FIRST OF THE ORDER.)

St. Francis.—As an author he is accounted among the first poets who commenced to write in the Italian language.* There were several editions of the poems and other works of his, but the best are considered the editions of Antwerp 1623 in 4to.; of Salamanca 1624, and that of Paris 1641, in fol.

St. Antony of Padua—*The Thaumaturgus*, the *Ark of Testament*, the *Hammer of Heretics*—was distinguished for sanctity, and miracles, as well as for doctrine and eloquence. He was the first professor of Theology in the Order. He composed the first Concordance of the Bible called *Moral Concordance*, which was published by Wadding from a manuscript in Ara Cœli. His other works are *Commentaries* on the Holy Scriptures, and *Sermons*. Gregory IX., who styled him the Ark of the two Covenants, when he canonized him, intoned in his honor the anthem, *O Doctor optime;* and as to a Doctor, the Mass of the Doctors

* See note, page 76, in introduction to the life of St. Elizabeth by Montalembert.

is assigned to him in the missal of the Order. See his life by Fr. Servais Dirks, and chap. XX. of the first part in this book.

ALEXANDER OF HALES—*Doctor Irrefragabilis*, *Doctor Doctorum*, and *Fons Vitae*.* Darras says that "he published the first commentaries upon the *Liber Sententiarum* of Peter Lombard, and that his works on the Metaphysics of Aristotle and on the Holy Scriptures are lasting monuments of his vast learning and tireless activity."† But his greatest work was his "Summa, in which by order of Innocent IV., he methodically arranged the theological subjects. This is the first *Summa* which was compiled, and it has served as a model for all others. Pope Alexander IV. spoke in the highest terms both of the work and of its author in an appropriate Brief."‡ There is no doubt but that St. Bonaventura was his disciple, and it is asserted by good authorities that St. Thomas also was a fellow student of St. Bonaventura.|| Gerson, chancellor of the university of Paris, in speaking of Alexander's doctrine, expresses himself as follows: "It is not to be told how many excellent things it contains. I declare to having read in a treatise, that some one having asked St. Thomas what was the best method of studying theology, he replied, 'to study the works of a single theologian;' and being asked what theologian it was desirable to fix on, he named Alexander of Hales. Thus," continues Gerson, "the writings of St. Thomas, and principally the Seconda Secondae, show how familiar the works and doctrine of Alexander were to him.§

ST. BONAVENTURE—The *Seraphic Doctor*, Cardinal Bishop. We refer the reader to the VI. ch. of this book in which a biographical notice is given of this glorious Doctor of the Church. Proverbially humble as he was, he became most exalted in glory both before and after his death. His master, Alexander of Hales, called him the guileless Israelite in whom Adam seemed not to have sinned; his friend, the *Angelic Doctor*, St. Thomas, proclaimed him a Saint while yet living, and the popular saying was that "There was none more beautiful, more learned, and

* It was the custom of those times to give titles of honor to men of learning, and he was called the *Irrefragable Doctor*, *Doctor of Doctors*, and *Fountain of Life*.

† Pontificate of Alexander IV. n. 27.

‡ Chalippe, Life of St. Francis, book 4.

|| Ibid.

§ Epist. de Laudibus Bonav.

more holy than Bonaventura." As General of the Order he was its second founder after the Seraphic Patriarch, St. Francis. His influence in the Church was well felt when, through it, the long dissentient votes met in the election of the Supreme Pontiff, Gregory X. Through his influence also was held the most solemn General Council of Lyons; and in it, under the Pope, he directed all things to the successful issue of the re-union of the Greeks; which accomplished, he died on the 14th of July 1274, attended by the Pope himself, "who would officiate in person at his funeral to honor, by this glorious exception to Pontifical usage, the genius and virtues so eminently displayed by this glorious Doctor."* The celebrated Gerson was, most emphatically, an admirer of St. Bonaventura, and recommends the reading of his works as the most suitable and safe for enlightening the mind and inflaming the heart.† Trithemius in his work on Ecclesiastical Authors (CDLXIV.) lavishes likewise the highest encomiums upon his works. Such is the influence of his writings in the Church that, as Dr. Newman remarks, at the Council of Trent, they had a critical effect on some of the definitions of dogmas.‡

The published works of the Seraphic Doctor are contained in eight volumes, fol. They are the *Course of Theology* after the manner of the Book of Sentences; the ***Breviarium Theologiæ;*** *Apology of the Mendicant Orders; Commentaries on the Holy Scriptures, Sermons, Treatises of Moral and Mystic Theology, Legendaries, Religious and Devotional books, etc.* Renowned among his productions are the *Itinerarium Mentis in Deum,* and *De Reductione Artium ad Theologiam.* His works are now republished in France.

ROGER BACON—*Doctor Mirabilis.* The title of *Wonderful Doctor* was justly bestowed upon him; and the more the sciences progress, the more wonderful he appears. "He was the first to substitute experimental philosophy for the purely speculative method. He reached results that might seem incredible even with all the resources of modern science; and by his contemporaries he was more than suspected of dealings with preternatural agencies. To Roger Bacon is attributed the invention of gun-

* Darras, Pontificate of Gregory X. n. 39.

† De Liber Delect. etc.

‡ Apologia pro Vita Sua, p. 288.

powder, of the magnifying glass, the telescope, the air-pump, and of a combustible substance similar to phosphorus; at least his writings contain very exact descriptions of the manner of these discoveries."* There was no branch of literature or of science in which he did not excel. He was in early youth a brilliant poet, an eloquent orator, and became well versed in Greek, Hebrew, and the oriental languages. Of his biblical science, Andres says: "But none, to my judgment, in that century showed more fine criticism than the celebrated *Roger Bacon.* Two treatises he sent to Pope Clement in order to induce him to do what, some centuries after, his successor did, viz.: "to give a correct edition of the Scripture, and point out, etc."† The same Andres, speaking of the Gregorian correction of the Calendar says: "The anticipation of the equinoctials in the thirteenth century seemed so notable that the learned *Roger Bacon* thought himself bound in duty to give an account of it to the Pope."‡ As to his skill in mathematics, "the celebrated Roger Bacon can in some way be regarded as the honored father of the many and noble philosophers and mathematicians that England had then given the sciences."|| The subjects he treated of were indeed as various as his works were numerous. Friar Bacon entered the Order in 1234, and died at Oxford in 1292. See also what has been said of him in Chapter IV. of this work.

THOMAS DE CELANO.—This was the first writer of the Life of St. Francis, whose disciple and companion he was. The authorship of the "*Dies Iræ*" is disputed between the Dominican Frangipani and our Franciscan Thomas de Celano.§

JACOPONE DA TODI was undoubtedly the author of the hymn "*Stabat Mater Dolorosa*," and he also composed the hymn "*Stabat Mater Gaudiosa.*" He was a great Franciscan poet, and the friend and contemporary of Dante.¶ He died in 1306, and is honored with the title of Blessed.

* Darras' Pontificate of Alexander IV. n. 27.

† Della Scienza Biblica, cap. i. ‡ Della Cronologia, cap. iii.

|| Mathematiche, cap. i.

§ Montalembert, in the introduction to the Life of Elizabeth, positively asserts "it is a disciple of St. Francis—Thomas de Celano—who leaves us the *Dies Iræ*, that cry of sublime terror."

¶ Prudenzano, in his work—"S. Franc. d'Assisi e il suo secolo"—says of Dante that "the love Alighieri had of the Franciscan Rule

JOHN DE PLAN CARPINO and WILLIAM DE RUBRIQUIS were among the first missionaries who penetrated through Tartary, and their relations of those countries are to the present day the best of the kind as they are the first.

BERTHOLD DE RATISBONA—Darras, in reviewing the sixth period of his Church History, after speaking of John of Vicenza says: "Germany gave to the Church the Franciscan Friar Berthold, an equally popular preacher, whose success was wholly independent of the political controversies which John of Vicenza too often admitted into his sermons." He wrote the "Institution of a Religious Life."

FRA MINO TURRITA.—"When the Byzantines were 'lording it over Mosaics field,' Fra Mino Turrita, the Franciscan, had already gained celebrity in that art as early as the first half of the thirteenth century."* The ancient mosaics over the ceiling of the high altar of St. John Lateran, and St. Mary Major, in Rome, are works of his. As a true disciple of St. Francis he pictured the story of his Master's life in the frescoes on the left side of the lower church of Assisi, and it is said that Bartholomew of Pisa took the idea of his "Book of Conformities" from these fresco paintings.

FRA PHILIP DA CAMPELLO was a celebrated architect. The Church of St. Clare, in Assisium, was one of his works.

ARLOT DA PRATO is said to have composed the *Concordances of the Holy Scriptures*, although at present generally attributed to Hugh of St. Caro, a Dominican.

BR. HAYMO OF FEVERSHAM was commanded to revise the Breviary and Missal, by Innocent IV., and his revision again confirmed and approved by Nicholas III. was adopted for the whole Church, as is attested by Gavanto and other writers. He was General of the Order, and went as Papal Legate, with three other Franciscans, to Constantinople, to negotiate for the reunion of the Greeks (1244).

ADAM DE MARISCO, *Doctor Illustratus*, in the University of Ox-

was so much, that dying at Ravenna, in the splendor of the court of the Polentas, abjured, in those supreme hours, glory and fame, and his only aspiration was the holy poverty of the Blessed of Assisi. And to give a certain and lasting testimony of it to the generations to come, he expired with the name of Francis on his lips, and wished to descend, when dead, into the tomb shrouded in his poor habit.

* Marchesi's Painters, etc., in Preface.

ford, was an excellent geometrician at a time when mathematics were little known. He was a fellow-student and companion of St. Anthony, as has been said elsewhere.

William Ware, *Doctor Fundatus*—had Scotus among his disciples in the University of Oxford.

John de Rupella, disciple of Alexander Hales, was elected by all the votes of the University of the Sorbonne to succeed him.

John Peckham held disputations with the *Angelic Doctor.*

Matthew de Aquasparta, the Cardinal, was a great celebrity for doctrine and business.

Gabriel of Lecce was the first bishop of the Order.

John of St. Martin was the first patriarch.

Lorenzo of Portugal, sent by Innocent IV. as Apostolic Nuncio, with three other Franciscans, to the great Tartary, in 1246, converted the King of Sartaco and others to the faith.*

Br. Anselm, with two companions, sent by the same Pope to Persia, succeeded in his mission to Bajothnai, as is attested by St. Antoninus.

Jacopo of the Rosary, with his companions, sent by the same Pope to Armenia, baptized the king and converted great numbers of schismatics and heretics.

Andrew, with his companions in Georgia, reconciled to the Holy See the schismatic Patriarch of that nation, as well as Ignatius, Patriarch of the Jacobites.

Cyprian and Marino were sent by Nicholas III. as Apostolic Legates, to instruct in the faith, Stephen and Urosious, kings of Sclavonia.

FOURTEENTH CENTURY.

(second of the order.)

John Duns Scotus—*Doctor Subtilis.*—The title of Subtle Doctor was appropriately bestowed upon him on account of the acuteness of his intellect and the subtlety of his reasoning. Scholastic philosophy and theology were carried by him to their

* Sigismondo Biografia Serafica.

apex, to the *non plus ultra* of theoretical speculation; and with some meaning was it once wittingly argued that if *Tollere Thomam* was *tollere Romam*, then *Tollere Scotum* would be *tollere totum*. Wadding (1304, n. 28), on the authority of Pitts, relates that in 1300, when Scotus was professor in Oxford, the ordinary number of his scholars was three thousand, and that it kept on increasing until it reached thirty thousand, crowds being there attracted by the fame of the Subtle Doctor, and even the very professors are said to have left their chairs, and to have hung in wrapt attention on the eloquence and learning of his lectures. From Oxford, Scotus was called to the University of Paris, there to defend his thesis of the Immaculate Conception of Mary, which he did so triumphantly as to have the title of *Doctor Marianus* added to that of *Doctor Subtilis*. This champion of Mary was then directed, by his superiors, to proceed to Cologne, to defend also there, Mary's Immaculate Conception. The news of his approach having preceded him, the City of Cologne gave to him the reception of a great conqueror. There also he accomplished with equal success his task, and there he terminated the course of his earthly career at the early age of thirty-four years, on the 8th of November, 1308.

In many questions of philosophy and theology the venerable Scotus differed with St. Thomas, and gave rise to "The two most known, most powerful, and lasting sects (schools)—the *Thomists* and *Scotists*—sustained principally by the two most renowned Orders; Thomism by the Dominicans, and Scotism by the Franciscans, although the one with the other had many sectaries outside of their Orders."* "The fame of Scotus was such that his rival could not be found in any literary institution of that age, nor perhaps his equal in any national church of the Christian world for several preceding centuries."† It is said of him that "he described the divine nature, as if he had seen God; the attributes of celestial spirits, as if he had been an angel; the felicities of a future state, as if he had enjoyed them; and the ways of Providence, as if he had penetrated into all its secrets." All the works of Scotus, as published by Wadding, are contained in sixteen volumes, folio. They are generally classified

* Andres, della Filosofia, c. i.
† Brennan's Eccles. Hist., ch. iii.

thus: *Commentaria in quatuor libros Sententiarum*, or *Scriptum Oxoniense*, because written in Merton College, Oxford; *Reportata, or Reportatorum Parisiensum*, Lib. 14; *Collationes*, 23; *Phisico Theologicæ Collationes aliæ*, 4; *Quodlibeta, seu Questiones Quodlibetates*, 21; *De Primo Principio rerum*; *Theorematum*, Lib. 1; *De Cognitione Dei*, Lib. 1; *Tetragrammata quædam; Sermones de Tempore et de Sanctis; Commentaria imperfecta in Genesim, in Evangelia et in D. Pauli Epistolas; Questiones in Porphyrium et in Aristotelis Praedicamenta; Perihermenia, Priora, Elenchos de Anima*; *Metaphysica et Physica.**

So many of his disciples became distinguished Doctors that they form, with him, a most glorious galaxy in the firmament of the Franciscan Order.† The titled ones are the following: William Ockham, *Doctor Singularis;* Francis Mayron, *Doctor Illuminatus;* Anthony Andres, *Doctor Dulcissimus;* Walter Barley, *Doctor Planus et Clarus;* Landolph Caracciolo, *Doctor Collectivus;* Hugh of Castronovo, *Doctor Scholasticus;* Gerard Odon, *Doctor Moralis;* Francis of Marca, *Doctor Illustratus;* John of Ripa, *Doctor Difficilis;* Peter of Aquila, *Doctor Sufficiens*, styled also the Little Scotus; and John Bassolius, *Doctor Ornatissimus*, the Benjamin of Scotus.

WILLIAM OCKHAM, *Doctor Singularis, et Auctor Invincibils.*—Although a disciple of Scotus, he did not follow either Scotism or Thomism, but "led the Nominalist school, which had fallen into disrepute during the latter half of the thirteenth century, until, raised up again by the efforts of his powerful mind, it had, in a few years, become the preponderating system. Leibnitz gave to Nominalism a crown of glory in calling it the deepest sect of the schools. Ockham was, therefore, not only one of the most distinguished members of the Franciscan Order, but one of the brightest ornaments of Christianity."‡ He sided with the antipope, Peter de Corbario, in favor of Louis of Bavaria against John XXII., but like the antipope, his *confrère*, it is said he repented and got reconciled. His principal works were: *Treatise on the Ecclesiastical and Secular Power; In-*

* Wadding, in Vita—Wares' writings.
† Other particulars of his biography are given in chap. vi.
‡ Darras' Pontificate of John XXII., n. 3.

troduction to the Sciences; Compendium Theologiæ; and *On the Four Books of the Sentences.*

Nicholas de Lyra or Lyranus, *Doctor Utilis.*—To comprehend the truth of the title accorded him of *Useful Doctor*, it will be well to quote Andres, who, after having reviewed the method used by the commentators of the Holy Scriptures that preceded Lyra says: "The learned Franciscan, Nicholas de Lyra, in the fourteenth century, opened a new road to himself; he commenced to make use of his knowledge of the Hebrew language, and erudition, to explain certain passages of the Scriptures; he dared to abandon occcasionally the sentiment of some Father to follow his own; he knew how to find happily, at convenient places, two literal senses in the words of the Prophets; he established some rules to determine the passages where two or more senses can justly be looked for; and although he followed the used method of collecting the testimonies of other Fathers, and more theological and philosophical questions, yet he showed greater originality in his commentaries, and gave to various obscure and difficult passages opportune explanations, which even now can be consulted with utility."* The original work of Lyranus was printed at Rome, in 1472, in seven tomes, folio. It was translated from the original Latin into French, in the beginning of the sixteenth century. His work was very frequently reprinted, because it had become, as Dixon says, exceedingly popular. "The work," he continues, "was in fact considered essential to the right understanding of the Sacred Books, whence came the saying, *Si Lyra non lirasset ecclesia Dei non saltasset.*"†

Peter Aureolus, *Doctor Facundus.*—The name Aureolus (Golden,) was given him for the purity and preciousness of his doctrine, and the title *Facundus*, on account of his eloquence. Sixtus Senensis calls him a man illustrious for the perfect knowledge of the sciences, and an orator singular even to the highest admiration. Among his works is greatly esteemed his golden book condensing, with commentaries, the whole Sacred Scriptures.

William de Mara.—Being professor at Oxford, he undertook to write the *Correctorium* of the works of St. Thomas,

* Della Scienza Biblica, cap. iii.

† Dixon on S. Script., principal Commentators.

and the defence of those of St. Bonaventure; thus becoming, as it were, the precursor of Scotus and of Scotism. Besides several theological works, he wrote a treatise on the *Art of Music*.

RICHARD DE MEDIAVILLE, *Doctor Solidus et Copiosus*, was not only well versed in theology and Holy Scriptures, but in *Jus Canonicum*.

ASTESANUS was celebrated for his *Summa Astesana* of the cases of conscience, of great utility in Moral Theology.

ALVARUS PELAGIUS, Doctor in both laws, was a remarkable man. His work *De Planctu Ecclesiæ*, in which he describes and deplores the evils of the Church at his time, was of great service in remedying them, and his theological works are also of great authority.

MARCHESINO DA REGGIO LEPIDO "was the author of a work on Scripture, which had great circulation in the fifteenth and sixteenth centuries. The title of this work is *Mammotractus* (or *Mammotreptus*) *Sive Expositio in singula Bibliae Capitula*. It may be described as a grammatical exposition of the more difficult words of Scripture as they are found in the Vulgate. The work was printed at Mayence in 1470, in folio. It has been frequently reprinted."* He published also a Dictionary of Biblical Words, and another for the Breviary.

JOHN DE MONTE CORVINO, the first bishop and archbishop of China. His extraordinary missionary labors are related in Chapter XIV.

BLESSED ODERIC OF TORDINONE, was one of the most celebrated travellers of the world. His relation of the most wonderful things he had seen in his travels, are read with interest at the present day. He wrote also an abridged Chronicle from the beginning of the world to the pontificate of John XXII. More details of his missionary travels are given in Chapter XIV.

BERTHOLD SCHWARTZ, Niger, called also Constantine Auklitzen, a German, is claimed by some as the inventor of gunpowder, although more generally it is attributed to his *confrère*, Roger Bacon. The question may be settled by crediting to

*Dixon on S. Script., principal Commentators, vol. 2, dis. xviii., ch. ii.

Berthold at least the application of it to instruments of war, whereby battles have become less cruel and bloody.*

JOHN SOMMERIOUS was considered a great astronomer and mathematician in his time, and published the *Canons of the Stars*, the *Corrections of the Calendar*, and the *Metrical Faculties*.

FRA ANDREOLO FERRARI, a celebrated architect, who, with Fra Giovanni, a Dominican, had submitted to their judgment by the rival builders and engineers of the duomo of Milan, all the cases in dispute.†

FRA BARTOLOMEO DI PISA was the author of the celebrated *Liber Aureus*, (Golden Book), the Book of the Conformities of the Life of the Blessed and Seraphic Father Francis, with the Life of Jesus Christ our Lord. "This book was discredited by the heretics, and without any foundation derided by superficial savans, who may not have had the patience to read it"‡

JOHN TISSINGTON, Professor of Oxford, was one of the first doctors who wrote against Wickliffe and condemned his heresy.

WILLIAM WIDEFORD, a Doctor also of Oxford, was appointed by the Council of London to refute, with strong arguments, the principal errors of Wickliffe, which he did, as Andres says, in a work superior to his century.§

JOHN GILES OF ZAMORRA, master of Sanchez, King of Spain, was co-operator in the first translation of the Bible into the Castilian tongue; he was the author of a natural, civil and ecclesiastical *History*, in six volumes; and of a promptuary entitled *The Archive of all the Scriptures*.

JOHN OF ST. LAWRENCE wrote the Acts of the Apostles and other works, in such pure Italian, as to be taken as an authority by the Academy of the Crusca.

HUGH DA PRATO, although a missionary in Tartary, wrote several works in Italian, praised by Zeno for their elegance.

Bertrand Cardinal de la Torre, *Doctor Famosus;* Thomas Bradwardine, *Doctor Profundus;* Robert Conton, *Doctor Amenus;* Peter l'Isle, *Doctor Notabilis;* Nicholas Bonet, *Doctor Proficurus;* Gregory of Fonts, *Doctor Venerandus;* Fran-

* Fredet, Mod. Hist., p. 350. † Marchesi's Artists, ch. viii.
‡ P. Affo, Vita del B. Giovanni da Parma, App.
§ Della Teologia, cap. iv.

cis of Candia, *Doctor Fertilis;* Peter Tome, *Doctor Invincibilis;* Walter Brinkel, *Doctor Bonus; Alexander of Alexandria,* Theologian of authority; *Monald Giustinapolitanus,* Canonist and Moralist; *Durando of Campagna,* Moralist; *John English,* author of the *Evangelical Perfection; Paolino da Venezia,* historian; *John Clive,* Annalist; *William Britton,* Poet and Rhetorician; *Nicholas Montaperto,* Doctor of Sorbonne, Franciscan Poet; *William Holmes,* celebrated Navigator and Physician; *Andrew Ongaro,* and companions, Missionary Apostles of Bulgaria; *Blessed Gentile* of Mathelica, Apostle, with the gift of languages, in Persia.

FIFTEENTH CENTURY.

(THIRD OF THE ORDER.)

St. Bernardine of Sienna.—The reported triumph of the holy name of Jesus would be a sufficient glory for St. Bernardine, but he was also a particular advocate of the devotion of Mary and Joseph. The Holy See having allowed the second lessons in the office of the Most Pure Heart of Mary, and in that of the Patronage of St. Joseph, to be taken from his Sermons, we have reason to regard him, as it were, a modern Father of the Church: in fact, a petition was presented by the Fathers of the General Chapter held in Rome, in 1862, praying the Holy See to declare him a Doctor. By the observance which he perfected in his Order, and through the efforts of his apostolic labors, he begot, indeed, many children to Christ. As to his doctrine, here is a list of his works: *Sermons de Tempore, Sermons of the Saints; Sermons against the Jews; On the Apocalypse; On the Eternal Gospel; On the Christian Religion; On the Conception of the Virgin Mary; On the Passion of our Lord; On Virtues and Vices; On the Fruits of Alms; On the threefold State of the Soul; On St. Joseph, Spouse of the Blessed Virgin,* and on the *Defence of Truth.* See also Chapter VIII.

St. John of Capistrano, a disciple of St. Bernardine, and follower of his in the devotion of the Name Jesus. He was entrusted with difficult missions, as Apostolic Nuncio, by Martin V., Eugene IV,, Nicholas V., and Callixtus III. By the latter he was appointed to preach the Crusade in Germany. "The great Franciscan had already acquired a high renown by his preaching, in Bohemia, against the Hussites. He was revered by the people as a prophet, and Callixtus could have chosen no better leader for the crusaders he was sending to Hungary. . . . . St. John Capistrano, with no other weapon than a Crucifix, was ever in the breach (at the fort of Belgrade) inspiring the Christian warriors with a superhuman courage. All fell before these heroes, and the proud Sultan, seriously wounded, withdrew his shattered forces in a frenzy of rage."* His works, as an author, are principally treatises on *Jus Canonicum.*

St. James of Marca, companion of St. John Capistrano.— By Martin V., Eugene IV., Nicholas V., Callixtus III., Pius II., Paul II., and Sixtus IV., he was delegated to proceed against the heretical sects, and it is related of him that he baptized over two hundred thousand infidels, and converted in Hungary fifty thousand heretics. His works were *Commentaries on the Four Books of Sentences*, sermons and various treatises, renowned among which was that on the *Blood of Christ.*

Henry Harphius was the eminent author of the *Mystic Speculative*, and *Affective Theology; The Golden Mirror on the Ten Precepts of the Decalogue; The Mirror of Perfection; The Golden Directory of Contemplation; The Three Parts of Penance*, and various sermons.

Luca Pacioli da Borgo San Sepolcro "wrote the first work on Arithmetic that was ever printed, viz., the *Summa of Arithmetic, Geometry, Proportion, and Proportionalties*."† A certain Targiani wanted to detract from his fame by suggesting that he copied from the work of Leonard, but Andres remarks: "whatever may be about that, Luke Pacioli reduced to greater brevity the arithmetical operations of Leonard, Nemorario, Sacrobosco and other masters praised by himself, *and taught not only the rules of Arithmetic but also of Algebra.* It was then that *Algebra began to be known and to be appre-*

* Darras' Pontificate of Callixtus III.
† Andres, Matematiche, cap. ii.

ciated, which was all numerical, created, we may say, in aid of Arithmetic, and was elevated to the sublime and difficult operations to which certainly it would not have arrived before.*" The same authority, in his third chapter of Mathematics, speaking in particular of Algebra says : " Whatever may be of this public propagation of Algebra, certain it is that the first work come to light, concerning this doctrine, is the above mentioned *Summa, etc.*, of Luke Pacioli. The whole Eighth Distinction contained in six long treatises, discourses about this art, said by him, what it is in reality, *maxime necessaria* to the practice of Arithmetic and even of Geometry."

FRA GIOCONDO, OR FRA GIOVANNI GIOCONDO OF VERONA.—The question as to whether he was a Dominican or Franciscan is settled by good authorities, thus, that he had been at different periods, a Dominican, a secular priest, and a Franciscan. " This solution," says the Dominican Marchesi, " though it has some difficulties, appears to us to be reasonable, and we therefore receive it as the truest ; so much the more as it coincides with what Scaliger says, in a letter dated 1594, in which he tells us that his Father was a pupil of Giocondo, and that the latter taught him grammar and polite literature, adding that he *subsequently became a Franciscan*."† Temanza, in his life, asserts that Fra Giocondo attended the lectures of Luca Pacioli in the Franciscan Convent of Venice. Cæsar Scaliger did not hesitate to pronounce Fra Giocondo " *an old and new library of all that was good in science ;*" but as an architect he was not surpassed, as an engineer he was foremost, and as an antiquarian he had no equal. He lived to an advanced age, being born in 1430, and yet living in 1515. When and where he died is unknown. He produced the first and most copious collection of Latin inscriptions that has ever been published anterior to his time ; he erected two bridges over the Seine, in France, and succeeded Bramante as architect of St. Peter's, in Rome.

JOHN PEREZ DE MARCHENA, THE GUARDIAN OF LA RABIDA.—In the *Frank Leslie Illustrated* periodical (C. Cor.) of July 27, 1867, is a cut representing the Franciscan Convent of La Rabida where Columbus was welcomed ; and the excellent and

* Loc. Cit. † Eminent Painters, etc., ch. ix., vol. 2.

accurate little article annexed to this cut we give entire, as it shows what John Perez was: "This antique Spanish edifice was the scene of a turning point in the life of a great man, —a turning point indeed in the world's history. The little convent of Santa Maria de la Rabida stands but a short distance from the little port of Palos, in the province of Hucloa, a port now so familiar to us all. Here one night Columbus, disheartened, toil-worn and hungry, leading by the hand his son Diego, applied for a drink of water to quench their thirst. The Father Guardian of the convent, the noble-hearted Juan Perez de Marchena, was struck by the noble and venerable aspect of the man, and beauty of the boy. A few words of conversation revealed to the learned friar the greatness of his visitor, who was delighted to find, under the lowly garb of St. Francis, one who seemed to enter into his plans with a zeal and appreciation that he had hitherto failed to meet.

"Father Juan Perez opened his portals wide to receive his illustrious guest; he took up this project of Columbus, and proceeded to court, to attempt what seemed desperate—the conversion of the learned to its adoption.

"How well he succeeded we all know. He linked his own name to that of the great discoverer, and bold, in *basso rilievo*, on the bronze doors of the American Capitol, is the head of the man of science and forecast, whose ability was hidden in the designs of Providence beneath the roof of the little convent of La Rabida."

Blessed Angelus de Clavasio was the author of the celebrated *Summa Angelica*.

Blessed Pacificus de Ceredano was the author of the likewise celebrated *Summa Pacifica*.

Blessed Bernardine of Fosta, Apostolic preacher, and the author of the Life of St. Bernardine and other works.

Blessed Bernardine of Feltre, Apostle of the *Montes-de-Pieta*.

Bernardine de Busti wrote two books in defence of the *Montes-de-Pieta*, *Sermons*, *Elucidations of the Scriptures*, and composed *the Office of the Holy name of Jesus*.

Francis Viller was considered the most eloquent orator of his time, and wrote sermons and treatises.

FRANCIS XIMENES, THE PATRIARCH, wrote an excellent book on the nature of the angelic life, besides other works.

ALBERTO DA SARTIANO was interpreter for the Greeks at the Council of Florence.

PIETRO MAZZANTI corrected, revised and supplied, in several places, what was wanted in the *Commedia di Dante*, and gave a correct edition of it.

ANTHONY OF MARCA translated Dante's verses into Latin metre.

ANTHONY MEDICI of Florence made notes in all the Scriptures.

ROBERT COLMAN, Chancellor of Oxford, wrote several poems.

HENRY OF BALMA, an excellent ascetic, was the principal Director of St. Coletta.

WILLIAM OF FOLIGNO abridged the works of St. Bonaventure.

JEROME TORNIELLI, a good Canonist, was sent as Apostolic Legate to Ethiopia.

PETER PHILANTES, *Doctor Refulgidus*, became Pope Alexander V.

ALEXANDER ALEMANICUS, OF SAVOY, *Doctor Illibatus*.

JACOPO D' ASCOLI, *Doctor Profundus*.

JOHN OF RIPATRANSONE, *Doctor Difficilis*, highly honored by Sixtus IV.

SIXTEENTH CENTURY.

(FOURTH OF THE ORDER.)

FRANCIS XIMENES, " the greatest man that ever Spain produced."* If it be asserted that Cardinal Archbishop Ximenes was the greatest man that ever Spain produced, it will be scarcely hyperbolical to say that, taking all his excellencies together, it would be difficult indeed to find an equal to the true Franciscan—the wise, royal Confessor, the Reformer Primate, the noble Cardinal, the zealous Missionary, the powerful Regent, the talented Prime Minister, the able Military Commander, the constant protector of merit, virtue, and innocence ; the generous

*Fredet. Mod. Hist. p. 336.

patron of science, and the learned author of the first Polyglot. Robertson remarks that Ximenes is the only prime minister mentioned in history whom his contemporaries reverenced as a saint, and to whom the people, under his government, attributed the power of working miracles; and it may be added that, should we look for a perfect character among the eminent men of history, it would be very doubtful whether historians of all parties would settle upon any other than Ximenes. His long life of over eighty years was well spent, and he went, full of honors and merits indeed, to the enjoyment of his Lord. With truth can it be said that Francis Ximenes reflected credit and glory on his nation, his Order, his Church, and mankind. See his life, by Hufeland, and Chapter XIII. of this work.

St. Peter of Alcantara, the ghostly father of St. Teresa, renowned for his austerities and penances, composed the golden book "On Mental Prayer," "justly esteemed a masterpiece by St. Teresa, Louis of Granada, St. Francis of Sales, Pope Gregory XV., and other competent judges. This work was soon followed by another not less excellent treatise, the 'Peace of the Soul; or, Interior Life,' in which the Saint, with the pen of a proficient, lays down the rules of the contemplative life, and of the higher perfection."*

Alphonsus de Castro, one of the greatest theologians in the Council of Trent. He may be considered as the founder of that branch of theology called *Heresiology;* because although, as Andres remarks, Bernard of Luxemburgh is the first who has some right to be remembered among the heresiologists for his catalogue of all the heresies written in the sixteenth century; "more learned and more instructive is the work of Alphonsus de Castro, who, in the same century, undertook to *expose and combat, in fourteen books, all the heresies;* and notwithstanding that he savors still some of the scholastic taste, he shows, nevertheless, an erudition superior to what there had been seen in similar writings."†

Andreas de Vega was another eminent Theologian at the Council of Trent. Fr. Sigismondo asserts that he took a great part in the decrees concerning Justification, and according to

* Darras' Pontificate of Clement VII., n. 6.
† Andres, della Storia Ecclesiastica, cap. ii.

Wadding, he composed his excellent work, *De Justificatione* at the same Council.

FRANCIS ORANTES was also a prominent Theologian at the Council of Trent. During it he wrote *Locos Catholicos* and *De Justificatione*, principally against Calvin, which work was republished in Rome, in 1796. He delivered before the Council a most eloquent oration on the Feast of All Saints in 1562.

PETER CRABBE collected, with great solicitude, the Acts of the Councils from the time of the Apostles, and published them in two volumes in 1538, but having afterwards found new documents, he, in 1551, published another edition in three large volumes. Before him, there had been only a certain Merlin who attempted a similar undertaking, but his work was not so full.*

FRANCIS PANIGAROLA was the first sacred orator of renown that preached in the Italian language. "His universal celebrity," remarks the oft-quoted Andres, "induced many youths of excellent talents to take him as their model, and for a long time no manner of preaching was considered good unless it was after the fashion of Panigarola's."† "But," adds Frederic Borromeo, his contemporary, "so much beauty and grace was in him that whoever tried to imitate him, failed in his attempt."‡ When he was sent with Cardinal Cajetani, as Apostolic Legate, by Sixtus V. to Henry IV. of France, it was commonly reported that the King had more fear of the extraordinary eloquence of Panigarola than of the hosts of his enemy.

ALPHONSUS LOBO.—What was Panigarola in Italy, Lobo was in Spain. The above mentioned Cardinal Borromeo gives a glowing picture of the preaching of Lobo, whose voice, and gesture, and habit, and demeanor, and heart, and tongue, and sentiment, and affection, all helped the force and energy of his preaching.§

SIXTUS SENENSIS was a convert from Judaism to the Chrisian religion, and entered the Franciscan Order. Pius V., while still Cardinal, overcame him in the heretical convictions of which he was found to be guilty, and on account of his talents had him transferred to the Dominican Order. He com-

* Andres, Collez. Canoniche, cap. i.
† Eloquenza Sacra, cap. vii.
‡ De Sacris nostr. temp. orator.
§ Lib. ii. et al.

posed several works, of which the most famous is his *Bibliotheca Sancta.*

Didacus Stella wrote those admirable works styled the *Vanity of the World,* and *Meditations on the Love of God.*

Boniface of Ceva, among other works, wrote that on *Christian Perfection,* which he dedicated to Leo X.

Francis Arola was the author of the *Major Concordance of the Bible.*

Peter Galatinus, a converted Jew, well versed in Hebrew, Chaldaic and Greek, wrote the defence of the Vulgate edition of the Scriptures.

Urban Balsamio, a *literati,* was master of Leo X.

Seraphinus Cumivano wrote the *Conciliation* of the passages that seem to contradict each other in the Sacred Scriptures.

John Pinedar wrote the universal history of the world in thirty books, and entitled it the *Monarquia Ecclesiastica.*

Amando of Belgium composed an accurate chronicle from the beginning of the world to the year 1534, with the title, *Scrutiny of the Historical Truth.*

John Torquemada is the famous historical author of the *Monarquia Indiana.*

Alphonsus de Novo Castro merited the title of *Doctor Ingeniosissimus.*

Balthassar of Miriaca was styled the *Angelic Preacher.*

Mark de Lisbona wrote the well known Chronicles of the Friars Minor.

Louis Rodriguez and Arnold Basaccio are mentioned by Archbishop Dixon as the principal translators of several parts of the Bible into the Indian language of Mexico.*

Francis Quaresmio wrote two large volumes styled *Elucidations of the Holy Land, Historical, Theological and Moral.*

Giammaria Veimazio composed a poem on Christ and His Apostles.

Francis Mauro was praised by Aldo Manutio as a heroic poet, and composed a poem on St. Francis, in imitation of Virgil.

Jerome of Leopolis translated the Bible into the Polish

* Dixon, vol. ii., p. 250.

language, to guard the Catholics against the impositions of the Lutherans.

Simon da Carmuli is mentioned by Marchesi as an able artist in perspective.

Valentino Servanzio composed the *Diario* of the Council of Trent, of which Cardinal Pallavicini made good use.

There were so many other distinguished Franciscans in this century that it would be too long even to mention their names. It will be sufficient to add, that not less than fifty-six members of this Order assisted as Theologians at the Council of Trent.*

SEVENTEENTH CENTURY.

(FIFTH OF THE ORDER.)

Luke Wadding.—Among the distinguished Franciscans of this century, the Irish Wadding justly deserves the first place. Providence seemed to have raised up, for the Order of Minors, the right man, capable of producing and exhibiting in proper light the labors of its members for religion and society. His *Annals of the Minors*, or of the three Orders instituted by St. Francis, have immortalized his name, and are a lasting monument of glory for the institute to which he belonged. His Bibliotheque of the Franciscan Order (*Scriptores Ordinis Minorum*) may be considered as an Appendix to the Annals, and, like them, of high merit. Being a Friar Minor in heart and soul, he was a real admirer and follower of Scotus, whose works he edited in sixteen folio volumes, with erudite commentaries and the life of the Subtle Doctor, and like this same Doctor Marianus, he defended the Immaculate Conception of Mary. As he was an excellent Hebrew scholar, he published in four large volumes the *Hebrew Concordance* of his *confrère*, Fr. Mario de Calasio, with a preliminary dissertation of his on the origin, excellence and utility of the Hebrew language. He wrote and edited so many and such voluminous works as to strike with astonishment all who see them, but what must be yet more sur-

* Vanloo, Stim. Seraph. Convers. xxxvi., and others.

prising is that, considering the amount of labor they required, they have been admired by the friends of literature in every nation the world over on account of their perspicuity, the purity of their style, but above all, their accuracy.*

THE FOUR MASTERS—*Michael O'Clery, Ferfessius O'Conry, Peregrine O'Clery and Peregrine O' Dubgennan.* The *Annals of the Four Masters,* compiled by these four famed Franciscans, have been received, as Brennan remarks, with an almost sacred respect by all writers both ancient and modern. Ireland may justly feel proud of these Annals.

CLAUDIUS FRASSEN. His course of *Philosophy,* so often reprinted; his *Scotistic Theology;* and his *Biblical Disquisitions,* so highly esteemed by the students of this science; have made his name popular and revered.

BARTHOLEMEW DURANDO. His two works: *The Defence of the Scotistic Doctrine,* and *The Faith vindicated against all Heresies,* have ranked him among authoritative theologians.

BARTHOLEMEW MASTRIUS. His *Moral Theology,* according to the mind of St. Bonaventure, has placed him among the best authorities of that science.

FRANCESCO ANTONIO PAGI. This writer is acknowledged to be the best chronologist of Sacred and Profane History. His four volumes, folio, of Criticisms on the Annals of Baronius, and his *De Consulibus,* in quarto, were of the greatest service to history by correcting the mistakes made by Baronius and other annalists. He wrote also books on Oratory, Poetry, Arithmetic, History, Mathematics, and Ascetics; but these works are eclipsed by those before mentioned.

ANTHONY CORDUBA is celebrated for his *Summa of Cases of Conscience,* and other Theological and Canonical works.

FRANCIS HERRERA a celebrated professor of Theology among the Salamancists, quoted especially as a good authority in Moral Theology.

BERNARDINE A PICONIO is the author of the well-received *Triplex Expositio in Epist. S. Pauli* and *in Evangelia.*

MARCANTONIO CAPELLI OF ESTE—well versed in Greek, Hebrew, and ecclesiastical antiquities—wrote on the *Primacy of*

* Brennan's Eccl. Hist. Ireland, seventeenth century, ch. iii.

St. Peter and his Successors, and against the primacy of the King of England.

LAWRENCE, CARDINAL DE LAUREA, wrote a Compendium of the Canons of the Councils, and other works for which he gained great reputation.

JOHN DE LA HAYE edited the *Biblia Maxima*, in nineteen volumes, folio, in which he gave the comments of several authors and enriched it with Prolegomena and Cronicon.

DOMENICO DE GUBERNATIS wrote the history of the Franciscan Missions, and commenced the History of the Order on a grand scale, which he entitled *Orbis Seraphicus*, but which remains incomplete. What remains of it, however, is of great merit.

ANDREW TEBIT.—At the request of Henry II. of France, having obtained apostolical faculties, he made a tour of the world, which took him twenty-three years, travelling through every nation and taking notes of the most remarkable things. At the end of this long journey he published a *Grand Cosmography*, in several volumes.

VINCENT CANES (John Baptist,) was author of the *Reclaimed Papist; Fiat Lux; Diaphanta*, or *Exposure of Dr. Stillingfleet's Arguments against the Catholic Religion*, and other works of controversy. F. Canes was selected by the Catholic body in England to defend their cause against Dr. Stillingfleet, their most virulent antagonist, and he succeeded to the satisfaction of all.*

RICHARD MASON (Angelus à S. Maria) was the author of *Certamen Seraphicum;* the *Holy Sacrifice of the Mass*, and other Theological and Devotional works.

BENEDICT CANSFIELD (William Fitch).—His *Rule of Perfection*, written in English, was translated into Latin. He composed also the treatise *De Bene Orando*, and is said to be the author of *The Christian Knight.*

WALTER COLEMAN (Christopher à S. Clara,) who died a martyr, composed a poem called *The Duel of Death* and dedicated it to Henrietta Maria, consort of King Charles I.

JOHN CROSS, alias MORE.—Dodd attributes to him some *divine poems*, but his better-known works are *Philothea's Pil-*

* Dr. Oliver. English Franciscan Writers.

grimage to Perfection, described in a practice of Ten Days Solitude; and *An Apology for the Contemplations on the Life and Glory of Holy Mary the Mother of Jesus,* dedicated to Queen Mary, consort of King James II.

ANTOINE LE GRAND, styled by Wood "a Cartesian philosopher of great note," whose Philosophy is said to be much read in Cambridge.*

HENRY HEATH was the author of *Soliloquies and Documents of Christian Perfection,* printed at Douay in 1674, a 12mo, with his portrait. This book became rare and was priced in catalogues at three guineas and a-half. It was re-printed in London in 1844.†

GILES WILLOUGHBY translated into English the golden treatise of St. Peter of Alcantara *On Mental Prayer,* and wrote a short life of the saint.

FR. GABRIEL SAGARD was one of the first missionaries and historians of Canada.

FR. CHRISTIAN LE CLERQUE was another missionary and historian of the *Establishment of the Faith* in New France, (North America.)

FR. LOUIS HENNEPIN, the famous missionary pioneer in North America, and the author of the *Discovery; Relation of the Louisiana; Nouveau Voyage, &c.*

The following names are familiar to the readers of St. Alphonsus Liguori's Moral Theology, in which they are often quoted: *Raphael Aversa; Eligius Bassaeus; Petrus Bellochius; Joannes a Bosco; Ludovicus Caspensis; Bruno Chassarius; Franciscus a Coriolano; Cyprianus Crousers; Sebastianus Dupasquier; Thomas Hurtard; Guleilmus Herring; Petrus Marchantius; Ludovicus Miranda; Laurentius Peyrin; Basilius Pontius; Laurentius Portella,* and *Emmanuel Rodriquez.*

Distinguished in Dogmatic Theology are the following: *Joseph Vasquez; Carolus Tricassinus; Franciscus Macedo; Franciscus Porter; Nicholaus Vigerius; Franciscus Fervadentius: Hyacinthus Chever; Joannes Ximenes; Michael a Castrofranco; Zacharias Boverius; Valerianus Magnus; Bonaventura Baaon; Raymundus Caron.*

* Athenæ Oxon. ii. 620.

† Oliver, loc. cit.

In Mystic Theology: *Andreas de Soto; Salvator Vitali; Franciscus Nugent; Bartholomaeus de Sabitio; Philomenus de Cornelio; Damianus a Quinque Vulneribus.*

In Jus Canonicum: *Augustinus Matteucci; Angelus Lantusca; Christophorus Davenport; Laurentius Zambelli; Bernardinus Lockner.*

In Sacred Scriptures: *Tobias Hendshel,* who translated the Old and New Testament into German; *Martin de Castrillo; Dionysius a Bergamo.*

In Sacred Oratory: *Joannes Carthagena; Michael Vivien; Bartholomaeus de la Haye.*

In History and Biography: *Henricus Sedulius; Henricus Anville; Zacharias Boverius; Patrick Fleming; John Colgan; Illuminatus a Palermo; Benedetto Mazzara; Joseph Ximenes; Amando di Moraga; Desiderio de Cea.*

In Poetry: *Theophilus Palanzio,* Laureate Poet; *Eugene Odowhee,* author of Sacred Poetry for the people, in Irish; *Bonaventure Moroni,* Latin Poet; *Bonaventure Siabile; Ludovico Verucelio; Augustino da Vicenza; Matteo Buccilino* sang the Stigmata, and *Agostino Gallincio* sang on St. Francis, in imitation of Tasso.

In Astronomy and Mathematics: *Theophilus Bruno* and *Lorenzo Forestrani.*

In Rhetoric: *Francis de Negro* and *Ludovico Cavalci.*

In Medicine: *Francis da Sacli,* a skillful physician, published a work on Medicine which is still of great use with the people, on account of the natural remedies therein prescribed.

In Surgery: *Caesar Magatti* is said to have been the first to simplify chirurgical operations, and left a valuable work to that effect.

Pharmacy: *Felix Papera.*

EIGHTEENTH CENTURY.

(SIXTH OF THE ORDER.)

ST. LEONARD A PORTU MAURITIO, Canonized June 29th, 1867. In the eighteenth century he became renowned not only for sanctity and the abundant fruits of his apostolic missionary labors, but also for his seraphic doctrine. He was remarkable for converting obdurate sinners by his burning popular eloquence, and for propagating the devotion of the Via Crucis, or Way of the Cross, which in Rome he had erected in the Coliseum. His works are: *Quadragesimal Sermons; Sermons and Instructions for Missions; Short Discourses for Holy Communion; Catechetical Instructions; A Manual for Sisters; The Way of Paradise; The Threefold Exercise of the Via Crucis; The Excellency of the Sacrifice of the Mass, and the manner of assisting at it,* with other devotional works. These have been all lately republished in Rome.

ANÁCLETUS REIFFEUSTUEL. Before St. Alphonsus published his Moral Theology, and even after, Fr. Anaclete appears to have been one of the most discreet, most methodic and most learned authors on that subject. His *Moral Theology* went through many editions, and additions were made to it by Fr. Kressingler, and Fr. de Cimbra. He published a *Tract on Probabilism* in 2 vols. 4to, which has been often republished also, and even augmented by a supplement from the pen of the celebrated Mansi, C. M. D. His greatest work was his *Jus Canonicum Universum,* 5 vols. fol., to which he added a sixth volume to explain *Regulas Juris.* This was well received not only in Germany, but also in Rome and elsewhere. Large as the work is, yet it has passed through many editions. A compendium of it was lately published in France for the use of Seminaries.

LUCIUS FERRARIS. The *Prompta Bibliotheca,* Canonica, Juridica, Moralis, Theologica, nec non Ascetica, Polemica, Rubricistica, Historica, of Lucius Ferraris is well known to, and appreciated by ecclesiastics. In it he has arranged, in alphabetical order, all the subjects an ecclesiastic may require to know; and there is hardly any library or any ecclesiastical scholar that can do without this work, as it saves an amount of labor and of research. Benedict XIV. after examining it is reported to have said in a jocose way, that there was no more excuse for lazy people, as they could easily find out and learn ecclesiastical matters; nevertheless he himself made good use of it.

PATRITIUS SPORER is accounted among the six Casuistic

writers of large volumes in the Prolegomon of St. Liguori's Moral Theology, Part III. ch. V.

FRANCIS HENNO. His reputation for doctrine in *Dogmatic Moral* and *Scholastic Theology* is second to none of his cotemporaries. He published a large work in several volumes and one in abridgment.

FELIX POTESTAS was another eminent writer of Moral Theology, and his oft reprinted works are: *Examen Ordinandorum; Examen Ecclesiasticum; Examen Praedicatorum*, &c., &c.

FORTUNATUS A BRIXIA acquired great reputation as a philosopher by his *Course of Philosophy of the Mind and of the senses;* and as a theologian by his *System of Jansenius, Methodically exposed and Theologically refuted.*

THOMAS CHARMES' *Course of Theology* has been, and still is, used as an excellent-text book in many schools.

PHILIBERT GRUBER published a *Course of Philosophy* in eight volumes; the *Concord* of the Philosophers and Theologians in the first six centuries of the Christian era; and a *Manual of Prayer*, in German, of which ten editions were sold in a very brief time.

GIANNANTONIO BIANCHI. His work, *The Power and Polity of the Church* was, and is, a book of the time in regard to the question of the temporality of the Holy See. This illustrious writer, as Kenrick styles him,* was also a poet of some note, and wrote several dramatic works.

IDEPHONSUS BRESSANVIDO published three volumes of *Moral Instructions*, in the form of short sermons, which from the Italian were translated into French; and if translated into English would prove of much benefit to Missionaries.

FRANCIS PAGI, nephew of the great chronologist, was like him, a great chronologist and historian. He composed the *Breviary-historic chronologic-critic*, a work well executed, in which the facts of the Roman Pontiffs, and the acts of the Councils are contained.

ANTHONY VALDAGNO (alias Gaetano Rigoni) published, in four volumes, a *Compendium*, historic, civil, ecclesiastic, of the Annals of Muratori, with improvements, and the addition of

* Moral Theology, Tr. VI. C. I.

facts omitted; also a Universal History from 1749 to 1771, to serve as a continuation of the Annals.

FRANCIS AGOSTINO OSSER. So great was his fame as a mathematician that it is said he was invited by Newton to help him in some productions; and on account of his works he was enroled in England among the learned of the University.*

SERAFINO SALANDRA, celebrated as a poet in his time, composed a Drama entitled: *Adamo Caduto* (Adam Fallen.) Francesco Zigari di Paola wrote a treatise in order to show that a great part of the sentiments of *Paradise Lost*, by Milton, were taken from this Drama.

PACIFICUS BAKER. Dr. Oliver calls him an eminent spiritualist. We have from his pen *The Christian Advent; The Sundays Kept Holy; The Devout Christian's Companion for the Holy Days; The Devout Communicant; The Holy Altar and Sacrifice Explained* and the *Lenten Monitor.* He wrote also a controversial work entitled *Scripture Antiquity*, and translated from the French the *Meditations on the Lord's Prayer.*†

FRANCIS BERNARD (*a S. Francisco*) EYSTON. "We have seen his very sensible treatise on the *Creed, Decalogue, and Sacraments.* He was the author also of the *Christian's Duty.*"‡

We can give only the names of a few other distinguished writers in this century. For Theology—Dogmatic, Moral, Ascetic or Canonical: *Laurence Cozza; Sigismundus a Bononia; Bernardus a Bononia; Franciscus Jaquier; Philippus a Carboneano; Franciscus Ant. a Goritia; Hyacinthus Campion; Barnardus Santig; Sangallo; Sebastianus Dupasquier; Hayer; Valpinio; Schambogen; Unterberger; Ph. de Castellutio; B. Weston.*

Sacred Scriptures: *Setaro; Oraxio du Parma; Platner; Viviani.*

Philosophy: *L. Altieri; A. Hermann; Eduardus de Judice.*

Sacred Oratory: In Italian Oratory are still considered classical: *Pier-Maria de Pederoba*, styled by Benedict XIV. the preacher of preachers (*concionatur concionatorum;*) *Pierantonio del Borghetto; A. Terzi; F. M. Casini; Barnaba Caprile; Adeotato Turchi; G. da Bergamo; G. Platina; Casi-*

* Sigismondo, Biografia Seraf.

† English Franciscan writers. ‡ Loco cit.

miro da Firenze, (for explanations on the Gospels;) *La Selve and Fr. Gaggioli* for a promptuary of sermons.

History and Biography: *P. da Vareggio; A. da Bassano; A. da Vincenza; Pierantonio da Venezia; G. G. Sbaraglia; L. F. Chalippe; G. Tamagna; F. da Latera; A. Parkinson; Ireneo Affo'; Palou.*

Cosmography: *V. Coronelli.* Rhetoric: *A. M. Besulti.*

Belles lettres: *R. Bartoli.* Poetry: *M. Carmeli.* Music: *G. Martini.*

NINETEENTH CENTURY.

(SEVENTH OF THE ORDER.)

CYRILLO DE ALAMEDA, Cardinal Archbishop of Toledo.—A correspondent of the London *Atlas*, prefaces a series of biographies of eminent Spaniards with the following: "I commence to-day with a cardinal of high repute—Don Cyrillo de la Alameda, Archbishop of Toledo—one of the most influential men at the court of Isabella II. Don Cyrillo de la Alameda y Brea, was born in the province of La Mancha, but the date of his birth I know not. His family was noble, and intended him for the law, but the vocation of Don Cyrillo was quite different. His tender, soft, and devoted nature looked with a natural repugnance on the severe duties of a judge. To punish is no doubt the attribute of society, but to pardon is the type of Christianity.

"The vigorous mind of Don Cyrillo could not content itself with the simple calm of a secular priest's life; for an ardent imagination such as his was, it was necessary to undergo the rude discipline and cruel mortifications which are found in monasteries only. The Order of St. Francis was the poorest of all orders; its rule was the most severe, and on that account was Don Cyrillo's choice. But he had soon exhausted every sort of abnegation to be found in so limited a sphere. His heart quite yearned for further sacrifices. He set out as missionary to the River Platte, desiring to unite to the merit of a cloister abnegation the palm of a martyred saint. But God did not require so great a sacrifice. While listening to his voice, now loud and authoritative, now inspired by persuasive softness, the savages laid aside their cruel natures, their knives fell harmless before the noble breast which was boldly offered to them, their brows relaxed, the eyes became suffused with tears, and from Pagans that they were, and filled with criminal ideas, they became Christians, and retired with their blessings left upon the head which opened for them the eternal gate of heaven.

"At the River Platte Don Cyrillo played an important part in politics. At the approach of the dangers with which the colony was threatened, the *sangue ague* (blue blood) which swelled the proud veins of the *Hidalgo* prompted him to rush to its defence. As being prohibited from drawing the sword he resorted to his able pen, and founding the *Official Gazette* of Buenos Ayres, he destroyed, in the shortest space of time, the innovators and foreigners who sought to inundate the country with their pernicious pamphlets and incendiary declamations. The Viceroy, who had full confidence in Don Cyrillo, consulted him on all affairs of state, and it is to this humble Franciscan monk that is due the remarkable defence of the colony, effected by Don P. Lynan. The Emperor of Brazil, full of respect and deference for the character and intellect of Don Cyrillo, invited him to his court, and it was this humble priest of God who also carried out the negotiation for the marriage of Donna Isabel de Braganza with Ferdinand VII. of Spain, and who accompanied the Queen in her voyage to Madrid.

"The King, consulting his true interests, called Don Cyrillo to his counsels, and elevated (?) him to the dignity of General of his Order, which involves that of grandee of Spain. In the midst of this new grandeur, Father Cyrillo, by no means forgot the humble convent which had received his early vows, and he devoted to rebuild it a portion of his revenues. The other portion served only to minister to the distress of all who stood in need of help. Later, Don Cyrillo became Archbishop of Cuba, and it is perhaps due to the efforts of this pious man that Spain is the possessor of the richest colony she has. But the great moral superiority of the new Archbishop naturally served to excite both hate and envy among those by whom he was surrounded. The dean of his cathedral commenced a war of intrigue against his metropolitan, which occasioned deep disgust in the simple mind of Don Cyrillo.

"The civil war broke out. He set out for Chiavari, in Sardinia, and thence for Burgos, of which see he had been named archbishop, and after so many labors, both as priest and as diplomatist, after so many services rendered to the Crown, he reached at length the high position which he occupies at the present time—that of Cardinal Archbishop of Toledo.

"The generous heart of Don Cyrillo is proverbial. No hand stretched out to implore his aid is ever drawn back empty. His inferiors bless him, his equals seek his counsel; for this remarkable man is of that rare order which unites to intelligence of the highest rank the virtues of an apostle of the Gospel."

From this account it would appear that this Franciscan has inherited, in some measure, the greatness of his *confrère*, countryman and predecessor, Cardinal F. Ximenes. The correspondent is correct in his account, and we have only to add that he was born July 14th, 1781, and that in 1817, he was appointed General of the Franciscan Order by Pope Pius VII. Although he has now reached the advanced age of eighty-six years, yet he is in the active discharge of all his sacred and honorable duties, with a mind and intellect as vigorous as ever.

HERCULANUS OBERRAUCH. The works which he has published place him among the greatest of writers of ancient as well as modern times. We give a list of them, the first of which is his *Moral Theology* in eight large volumes; 2. *Institutions of Christian Justice*, in four volumes; 3. *Dialogues of Religion and Justice*, in four volumes;—*Six Theological Dissertations*, on the First Cause of all Things, on the *last end*, on the *concord* between grace and free will, on the sins of ignorance, on the Eternal Law of God, on *Faith, Hope, and Charity;* 5. *The Ascent*, or the Science of Perfection; 6. *Meditations* on the Passion of our Lord; 7. *Exhortations* to all the princes and people of Europe in time of war; 8. *Philosophical Dissertation* on the last end of man; 9. *Treatise* on the Election of State; 10. *Treatise* on Arts and Sciences. He died in 1808.

PHILIP NERI CHRISMANN. His *Regula Fidei Catholicæ, et*

Collectio Dogmatum Credendorum, is a golden work of Dogmatic Theology, in which he draws, in a masterly manner, the distiction between what is dogma of faith and what is not. It has been lately republished by Ph. J. Spindler.

ADALBERT WAIBL is another great theologian and writer of this century. His published works are: *Dogmatic and Mystic Theology; Moral Theology*, according to the mind of St. Liguori; *Philosophy* reduced in Compendium; *Exposition* of the Apocalypse of St. John; *History of the Church of Jesus Christ; Sacred Bible* for the use of the unlearned; *Collectanea* from the works of the Holy Fathers, and translated into German for spiritual reading of lay-people. *Novelettes* also in German for the young folks; and a *Biography of Fr. Oberrauch.*

JOSEPH AMBROSE STAPH published an *Epitome of Moral Theology*, adapted as a text-book, which was received by the public with applause, and met with general approbation. He died in 1844.

PIOUS VANDERVELDEN in 1858 finished the publication of a theoretical and practical *Moral Theology.*

ALBERT KNOLL DE BULSANO for Dogmatic-Polemic Theology is at present one of the best, if not the very best. He has published his Theology in six volumes, with a seventh for fundamental Theology; also a Compendium of the same work in two.

CHERUBINO A PALMA has also published a Dogmatic Theology, remarkable for its clear philosophical exposition of theological principles.

GAUDENZIO PATRIGNANI died in 1823 as Bishop of Ferentino. The Pope on hearing of his death exclaimed, "We have lost the best Theologian of Rome!"*

GIOVANNI TECCA DI CAPISTVANO was proclaimed General of the Order by Leo XII., and showed an extraordinary zeal during his six years government. He compiled the *General Constitutions* made by the chapters; wrote on the *Martyrdom of St. Peter on the Janiculum;* composed several ascetic works, and was generally acknowledged to be a learned theologian.

VINCENT A MASSA. We have from him several volumes of *Cases of Conscience* and a *Lyturgical Synopsis.*

ANGELO BIGONI published the *Kingdom of Jesus Christ*, in

* Sigismondo, Biografia Serafica.

eleven vols.; the confutation of Cabanis in six vols., and other ascetic works.

G. DE S. MARTIÑO was admired for his works on Natural Philosophy.

LUIGI FILIPPI, Bishop of Aquila, published a text-book of *Physics* and *Mathematics* for the students of the Order

DENIS DE S. GALLO compiled a text-book of *Logic, Metaphysics,* and *Moral Philosophy* for the students of the Order.

BENEDETTO D'ACQUISTO, Archbishop of Monreale, in Sicily, is a philosopher of great note, and has published several important works on that science.

BERNARD VANLOO is a classical Latin writer of Theological and Ascetical works.

WILLIAM PILLING "was a well-read scholar, a clear-headed theologian, and an exemplary missionary. He published *A Caveat* addressed to the Catholics of Worcester against the insinuating Letter of Mr. Wharton."*

ARTHUR O'LEARY was the great controversialist and conqueror of Dr. Blair, the Scotch Physician; of John Wesley the father of Methodism, and of Dr. Woodward, the Protestant Bishop of Cloyne. He died in 1802.

RICHARD HAYS, the Irish delegate to the Holy See in the question of Vetoism. "He published in 1823 a collection of Sermons on both natural and doctrinal subjects; they were greatly admired, but to deliver them with effect the Rev. author himself should be the preacher."† The sermons of Fr. Hayes are indeed grand and eloquent from beginning to end.

THEOBALD MATHEW has been the Apostle of Temperance, and that is sufficient to render his memory immortal.

PACIFICO DEANI is graphically described by Cardinal Wiseman as follows: "The first Sunday after arriving in Rome, our party was taken to the Church of Araceli, on the Capitol, to hear a celebrated preacher deliver a sermon of his Advent course. Hours before the time, the entire area was in possession of a compact crowd, that reached from the altar-rails to the door, and filled every aisle and all available standing room. The preacher ascended the pulpit, simply dressed in his Fran-

* Dr. Oliver, English Franciscan writers.
† Brennan. Ecclesiastical Hist. Ireland, Nineteenth Century.

ciscan habit, which left the throat bare, and by the ample folds of its sleeves added dignity to the majestic action of his arms. His figure was full, but his movements were easy and graceful. His countenance was calm, mild, unfurrowed as yet by age, but still not youthful; he seemed in the very prime of life, though he survived but a few years. To one who could not, except very imperfectly, understand the language, and who had never heard a sermon in it, the observation of outward qualities and tokens was natural, and likely to make an indelible impression. Indeed, I remember no sermon as I do this, so far as the 'faithful eyes' go. And yet the ears had their treat too. The first, and merely unintelligible accents of that voice were music of themselves. It was a ringing tenor, of metallic brilliancy, so distinct and penetrating that every word could be caught by every listener in any nook of that vast church, yet flexible and varying, ranging from the keenest tone of reproach to the tenderest wail of pathos. But the movement and gesture that accompanied its accents were as accordant with them as the graceful action of the minstrel, calling forth a varied and thrilling music from the harp. Every look, every action of head or body, every waive of the hand, and every poise of the arm was a commentary to the word that accompanied it. And all was glowing, graceful, and dignified. There was not a touch of acting about it, not an appearance of attempt to be striking.

"Then, for the first time, I felt overawed by the stillness which only the pent-up breath of a multitude can produce, while some passage of unusual beauty and overpowering force makes the hearer suspend, as far as he can, the usual functions of life, that their energies may be concentrated on a single organ. And scarcely less grand is the relief which breaks forth, in a universal murmur, a single open breath from each one swelling into a note, that conveys more applause, or at least approbation, than the clapping of twice as many hands.

"Later, it was easier to feel what the first day one could only wonder at. I remember the same preacher in the choir of St. Peter's, uttering one of those sublime passages, and lying prostrate in spirit, as the vision passed over it, scarcely daring to move, or even turn the eyes aside. He was reproving negligence in attending the celebration of the divine mysteries; and imagined the priest, rapt into Heaven, and ordered to offer the heavenly sacrifice on the altar of the Lamb there. He painted with glowing words the attitudes, the countenance, and the feelings of adoring spirits, while for only once assisting at what is, in the Church Militant, a daily privilege.

"Now, if any one will turn to the pointed sermons of Father Pacifico Deani, he may find the very sermons alluded to, and wonder that they can have been thus described. While far from pretending to make comparison between the peerless masterpiece of ancient eloquence and the humble Franciscan's devout discourses, one may be allowed to answer the objection, in the same words by which Æschines enhanced his great and successful rival's merit: 'What if you had heard him speak them?' This, no doubt, was great part of the charm, greater to one who, till then, had been accustomed to bear only the stately monotony in which the simplest lessons are often conveyed, and the unimpassioned tameness with which the most touching scenes are described, or rather narrated at home."*

FRANCIS VILLARDI is a most eloquent Latin and Italian orator and poet.

ANTONIO DA RIGNANO, now Bishop of Potenza, was renowned in Rome for Theology and Literature, and was one of the Theologians at the Definition of the Immaculate Conception.

GIULIO ARIGONI, Archbishop of Lucca, is considered the best living Italian orator.

P. DAVIDE has been the greatest organist ever known, and his compositions for that instrument have been lately published, which will supply a want much felt for church music.

FR. PERINALDI has published several interesting works on the Holy Land.

M. J. BRENNAN is the author of the popular *Ecclesiastical History of Ireland*, which has been lately republished.

MARCELLINO DA CIVEZZA has become renowned for his history of the Franciscan Missions.

JOHN STANISLAS ALBACH, who died in 1853, wrote several devotional books, which soon became so popular that of the *Sanctæ Exercitationes* there is already the seventeenth edition, and of

* Recollections of the last Four Popes, ch. ix. p. 148.

the *Horæ Devotionis*, translated into French, six editions were soon printed.

ANNIBALE DE CONTI FANTONI, a zealous Missionary, now Coadjutor Bishop of Chan-Toung, made known to Europe the wild silk worms of China, for which an honorable premium was awarded to him by the Imperial Zoological Society of France, in 1859.

SERVAIS DIRKS has proved himself to be an author of great merit by his *Life of St. Anthony of Padua*.

www.ingramcontent.com/pod-product-compliance
Lightning Source LLC
LaVergne TN
LVHW021050110826
845150LV00001B/33